W9-AWU-927

# ARIZONA
# TRAVELER'S
# HANDBOOK

# ARIZONA
# TRAVELER'S
# HANDBOOK

### Third Edition

**BILL WEIR**

## moon
PUBLICATIONS, INC.

# ARIZONA TRAVELER'S HANDBOOK

Please send all comments, corrections, additions, amendments, and critiques to:

**BILL WEIR
c/o MOON PUBLICATIONS, INC.
722 WALL STREET
CHICO, CA 95928 USA**

*Published by*
Moon Publications, Inc.
722 Wall Street
Chico, California 95928 USA
tel. (916) 345-5473

*Printed by*
Colorcraft Ltd., Hong Kong

### PRINTING HISTORY

First edition
    September 1986
Second edition
    August 1987
    March 1988
    June 1989
Third edition
    April 1990
    September 1991

© **Copyright Bill Weir 1990. All rights reserved.**

© **Copyright Moon Publications Inc. 1990. All rights reserved.**

*Library of Congress Cataloging-in-Publication Data*

Weir, Bill, 1951-
    Arizona Traveler's Handbook / Bill Weir.—3rd ed.
        p.    cm.
    Includes bibliographical references
    ISBN 0-918373-41-7 : $13.95
    1. Arizona—Description and travel—1981—Guide-books.
I. Title.
F809.3.W44 1989
917.9104'53—dc20                        89-13487
                                        CIP

**ISBN 0-918373-41-7**

Printed in Hong Kong

Cover photograph: Sunset on West Mitten in Monument Valley; photo by author.

All rights reserved. No part of this book may be translated or reproduced in any form, except brief extracts by a reviewer for the purpose of a review, without written permission of the copyright owners.

Although the author and publisher have made every effort to ensure that the information was correct at the time of going to press, the author and publisher do not assume and hereby disclaim any liability to any party for any loss or damage caused by errors, omissions, or any potential travel disruption due to labor or financial difficulty, whether such errors or omissions result from negligence, accident, or any other cause.

# ACKNOWLEDGEMENTS

Many thanks go to the hundreds of people who assisted in making the *Arizona Traveler's Handbook* as complete and accurate as it is! I am especially indebted to people of the National Park Service, U.S. Forest Service, Bureau of Land Management, U.S. Fish and Wildlife Service, Arizona Game and Fish, and Arizona State Parks, whose high standards make Arizona such a wonderful place to visit. Chambers of commerce, from the tiniest communities to the big cities, supplied valuable maps, ideas, and advice. Extra thanks go to Carol Downey of the research library in the Arizona Capitol and to staff of the Fort Verde and Jerome state historic parks for generous use of their historic photos. The friendly crew at Grand Canyon Airlines provided the author with the big picture above the Grand Canyon.

This third edition—a bigger and better book—has been a major undertaking! The dedicated crew at Moon Publications lent their talents to the massive project. Louise Foote put her pen to work to add many new drawings of Arizona wildlife to those previously drawn by Diana Lasich and Kay Stephenson. Bob Race patiently revised and re-revised nearly all the maps for this edition; he also crafted the new Mt. Elden Trails and Winslow maps. Barton Wright's excellent drawing of the Hopi Reservation, which he kindly gave permission to use in earlier editions, is now enlarged on page 119. The other top-notch maps came from the steady hands of Dave Hurst and Louise Foote at Moon Publications.

The *Arizona Traveler's Handbook* manuscript showed some dramatic improvements from the first drafts to the last, thanks to the enthusiasm and editorial skills of Deke Castleman and Mark Morris at Moon Publications, Dr. Thomas Kreider at Berea College, Kentucky, and my mother, Doris Weir. Mark also gave this edition his "eagle-eye treatment" before it went to press.

The author, not content with just writing this book, also typeset it with Ventura Publisher computer software. *Arizona Traveler's Handbook* and his *Utah Handbook* stand alone as Moon's only books typeset by the author.

Asha Johnson and Dave Hurst provided valuable advice on page layout, hyphenation tricks, and illustration sizing. Nancy Kennedy and Asha performed the task of slapping the typeset pages onto boards for the printer. Much of the credit for getting this book to you goes to Sales Manager Donna Galassi, Publicist Virginia Michaels, Promotions Coordinator Bette Wells, Administrative Assistant Lucinda Stram, Financial Wizard Cindy Fahey, Mail-room Manager Rick Johnson, and Shipper-Extraordinaire Robert Kolb. And lastly, appreciation is due my publisher, Bill Dalton, who inspired *Arizona Traveler's Handbook* and helped bring it to a successful completion.

# PHOTO CREDITS

FRONT COVER: Sunset on West Mitten in Monument Valley (Bill Weir).

BLACK AND WHITE PHOTOS: **Arizona Office of Tourism**—pages 39, 86, 106, 244, 270, 354; **Arizona State Archives**—pages 9 (right), 13, 14, 19, 34 (bottom), 97, 99, 120, 121, 229 (right), 255, 337, 350, 391, 450, 451 (top), 453, 456, 458, 462, 464, 471; **Flagstaff Chamber of Commerce**—pages 24, 29, 131, 137 (top), 146, 148, 153, 154, 183, 185, 190; **Coconino National Forest**—page 192; **Fort Verde State Historic Park**—pages 11, 181, 197 (National Archives), 198 (Mearns Collection, Library of Congress), 200 (Mearns Collection, Library of Congress), 203, 269 (Carter Collection, National Archives), 345, 369 (Carter Collection, National Archives), 370 (Carter Collection, National Archives), 371 (Carter Collection, National Archives); **Grand Canyon National Park**—pages 3 (neg. #2784), 33 (bottom; neg. #5117), 35 (neg. #826), 41 (neg. #3121), 45 (neg. #5130), 55 (neg. #2361), 62 (neg. #5563), 63 (neg. #7080); **Jerome State Historic Park**—pages 208 (left and right), 209, 210, 211, 465; **Sharlot Hall Historical Society** (Prescott)—page 212 (#ST142p); **Metropolitan Tucson Convention and Visitors Bureau, Inc.**—pages 342, 405, 406, 414, 422, 424, 425, 435, 454; **Mohave County Historical Society** (Kingman)—pages 72, 223, 227, 228, 229 (left), 230, 238, 241, 251; *Phoenix Gazette* (reprinted with permission)—page 279; **Pimeria Alta Historical Society** (Nogales)—pages 122, 442 (Rochlin Archives), 443 (Ellen Underwood Collection), 446 (bottom), 447; **Tony Rose**—pages 67, 68; **Bill Weir**—pages 6 (right), 7 (top), 9 (left), 10 (right), 21, 23, 50, 57, 69, 70, 74, 77, 78, 87, 96, 102, 104, 108, 110, 111, 112, 114, 117, 137 (bottom), 143, 145, 155, 158, 164, 166, 179, 191, 199, 217, 222, 231, 235, 236, 240, 242, 246, 247, 253, 258, 261, 264, 266, 273, 277, 278, 280, 282, 284, 285, 290, 291, 303, 304, 305, 309, 311, 319, 321, 322, 325, 327, 331, 336, 341, 356, 357, 365, 366, 367, 377, 381, 382, 383, 384, 385, 389, 390, 399, 400, 412, 420, 429, 431, 432, 436, 437, 440, 446 (top), 448, 451 (bottom), 461, 463, 466, 468, 470, 472, 474.

# ILLUSTRATION CREDITS

**Louise Foote**—pages 53, 65, 66, 89, 172, 226, 243, 265 (left and right), 314, 318, 449; **Diana Lasich**—pages 30, 32, 171, 175, 176, 177, 178; **Andy Mosier,** cartoonist—pages 5, 7 (bottom), 418; **Kay Stephenson**—title page and pages 6 (left), 31, 80, 109, 129, 152, 295, 297, 302, 360, 428.

MAJOR SOURCES OF HISTORIC ILLUSTRATIONS: *Second Annual Report of the Bureau of Ethnology 1880-81*—page 25; *Seventeenth Annual Report of the Bureau of Ethnology 1895-96* (part 2)—page 8; *Twenty-eighth Annual Report of the Bureau of Ethnology 1906-07*—page 334; *The Marvellous Country; or Three Years in Arizona and New Mexico, the Apache's Home* by Samuel Cozzens—pages 10 left, 12, 133, 267, 343, 362, 368, 393, 397, 439, 469; *The Exploration of the Colorado River and Its Canyons,* formerly titled *Canyons of the Colorado,* by John Wesley Powell; reprinted by Dover Publications—pages 1, 27, 33 (top), 47, 51, 60, 61, 73, 76, 84, 93, 95, 101, 118, 120, 127, 346; *Decorative Art of the Southwestern Indians* by Dorothy Smith Sides, Dover Publications—pages vi, 115, 174, 272, 376, 413, 430.

# CONTENTS

# MAPS AND CHARTS

# MAP SYMBOLS

FREEWAY

MAIN HIGHWAY

SECONDARY ROAD

UNPAVED ROAD

FOOT PATH

RAILROAD

BRIDGE

PASS

INTERSTATE HIGHWAY

U.S. HIGHWAY

ARIZONA HIGHWAY

POINT OF INTEREST

MOUNTAIN

WATER

— — NATIONAL BORDER

—··—··— STATE BORDER

—···—···— OTHER BORDERS

○     LARGE CITY

○     MEDIUM CITY

○     SMALL TOWN

ALL MAPS ORIENTED WITH NORTH AT
THE TOP UNLESS OTHERWISE NOTED

# IS THIS BOOK OUT OF DATE?

Nothing stays the same, it seems. Although this book has been carefully researched, Arizona will continue to grow and change. New sights and services will open while others change hands or close. Your comments and ideas to make *Arizona Traveler's Handbook* more useful to other readers will be highly valued. If you find something new or discontinued or changed, please let me know so that the information can be included in the next edition. Businesses, too, are most welcome to send a postcard or letter with updates. Corrections can often be slipped in between editions—*Arizona* is reprinted every 6 months or so.

Perhaps a map or worthwhile place to visit has been overlooked; please bring it to my attention. All contributions (letters, maps, and photos) will be carefully saved, checked, and acknowledged. If I use your photos or artwork, you will be mentioned in the credits and receive a free copy of the book. Be aware, however, that the author and publisher are not responsible for unsolicited manuscripts, photos, or artwork and, in most cases, cannot undertake to return them unless you include a self-addressed, stamped envelope. Moon Publications will have nonexclusive publication rights to all material submitted. Address your letters to:

**Bill Weir**
**c/o Moon Publications**
**722 Wall Street**
**Chico, CA 95928 USA**

---

# ABBREVIATIONS

| | | |
|---|---|---|
| AZ—Arizona | inexp.—inexpensive | res.—reservations |
| CA—California | km—kilometers | RV—recreational |
| d—double | mod.—moderate | vehicle |
| elev.—elevation | NM—New Mexico | s—single |
| exp.—expensive | NV—Nevada | tel.—telephone |
| F—Fahrenheit | ORV—off-road | UT—Utah |
| ft.—feet | vehicle | w/—with |
| jct.—junction | pop.—population | |

# INTRODUCTION

Few states have such spectacular and varied terrain as Arizona. Because most of the early travelers who crossed this land kept to the south in the hot desert valleys and plains, these regions form the popular image of Arizona even today. Yet much of the northern and eastern parts of the state have extensive coniferous forests and rushing mountain streams. Volcanic activity, uplift, faulting, and erosion have given us dozens of mountain ranges and canyons. The Grand Canyon, one of the world's greatest natural wonders, ranks at the top of most visitors' lists, but many other beautiful and intriguing places remain to be discovered. *Arizona Traveler's Handbook* will help you find them. Wilderness areas, early Spanish sites, Indian reservations, old mining towns, bright city lights— they're all covered. Practical information is given for every budget, including that of the oft-neglected low-budget traveler.

## THE LAND

Though geologically complex, the land surface of Arizona can be thought of as tilting downward to the southwest. More than 90% of the state's drainage flows into this corner via the Colorado River and its tributaries. The elevation where the Colorado River enters Mexico is only 70 feet. Mountain ranges rise in nearly every part of Arizona, but they achieve their greatest heights in the north-central and eastern areas. Humphreys Peak, part of the San Francisco Peaks near Flagstaff, crowns the state at 12,633 feet. Geographers divide Arizona into the high Colorado Plateau Province of the northeast half, and the Basin and Range Province of the rest of the state. Average elevation statewide is about 4,000 feet. Measuring 335 miles wide and 390 miles long, Arizona is the sixth largest state in the country.

## Colorado Plateau

This plateau, a giant uplifted landmass in Arizona's northeast, also extends across much of adjacent Utah, Colorado, and New Mexico. Rivers have cut into it, forming the Grand Canyon of the Colorado and other deep gorges. Volcanos have broken through the surface, leaving hundreds of cinder cones, such as multicolored Sunset Crater, and larger composite volcanos, like the San Francisco Peaks. The most recent burst of volcanic activity in Arizona took place near Sunset Crater about 700 years ago. Most elevations on the plateau range from 5,000 to 8,000 feet. Sheer cliffs of the Mogollon ("MUGGY-own") Rim drop to the desert and mark the south boundary. To the west, the plateau ends at Grand Wash Cliffs.

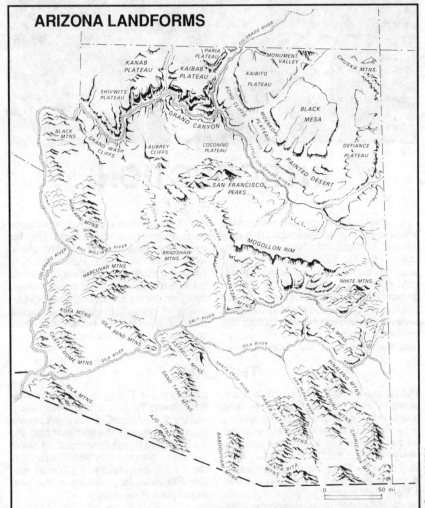

ARIZONA LANDFORMS

© MOON PUBLICATIONS

A layer of cloud has "filled" the Grand Canyon in this unusual shot.

## Basin And Range

Many ranges of fault-block mountains, formed by faulting and tilting of the earth's crust, poke through the desert plains of southern and western Arizona. Several peaks rise above 9,000 feet, creating "biological islands" inhabited by cool-climate animals and plants. Tucson-area residents can leave the Sonoran Desert and drive to the cool fir and aspen forests of Mt. Lemmon within an hour.

## CLIMATE

During any season, some part of Arizona will be enjoying near-perfect weather. Sunny skies and low humidity prevail over the entire state. Average winter temperatures run in the 50s F in the low desert and the 20s to 30s in the mountains and high plateaus. Desert dwellers endure averages in the 80s and 90s in summer, when high-country residents enjoy averages in the 70s. The highest reading ever recorded in the state hit 127° at Parker, along the Colorado River, on July 7, 1905. Even on a normal summer day in the low desert, you can expect highs in the low 100s.

### Precipitation

Rain and snowfall correspond roughly to elevation: the southwest corner receives less than 5 inches annually, while the higher mountains and the Mogollon Rim receive about 25 inches. Most precipitation falls either in winter as gentle rains and snow or in summer as widely scattered thundershowers. Winter moisture comes mostly in Dec. to March, revitalizing the desert; brilliant wildflower displays appear after a good wet season. Summer afternoon thunderclouds billow in towering formations from about mid-July to mid-September. The storms, though producing heavy rains, tend to be localized in areas less than 3 miles across. Summer thundershowers make up 60-70% of the annual precipitation in the low desert and about 45% on the Colorado Plateau.

### Storm Hazards

Rainwater runs quickly off the rocky desert surfaces and into gullies and canyons. Flash floods can form and sweep away anything in their paths, including boulders, cars, and campsites. Take care not to camp or park in potential flash-flood areas. If you come to a section of flooded roadway, a common occurrence on desert roads after storms, just wait until the water goes down, usually after only an hour or so. Summer lightning causes forest and brush fires, and it poses a danger to hikers foolish enough to climb mountains when storms threaten.

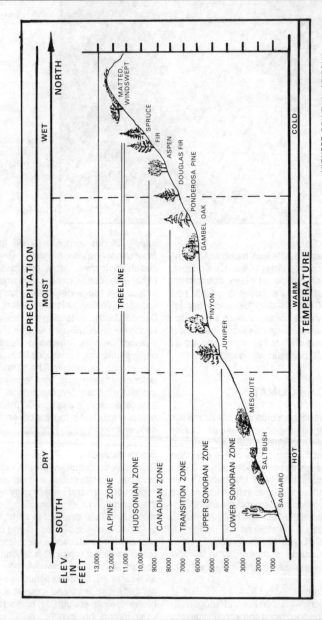

# ARIZONA LIFE ZONES

PRECIPITATION

DRY — MOIST — WET

SOUTH — NORTH

TEMPERATURE

HOT — WARM — COLD

| ELEV. IN FEET | |
|---|---|
| 13,000 | ALPINE ZONE |
| 12,000 | |
| 11,000 | HUDSONIAN ZONE |
| 10,000 | |
| 9000 | CANADIAN ZONE |
| 8000 | |
| 7000 | TRANSITION ZONE |
| 6000 | |
| 5000 | UPPER SONORAN ZONE |
| 4000 | |
| 3000 | LOWER SONORAN ZONE |
| 2000 | |
| 1000 | |

TREELINE

MATTED, WINDSWEPT
SPRUCE
FIR
ASPEN
DOUGLAS FIR
PONDEROSA PINE
GAMBEL OAK
PINYON
JUNIPER
MESQUITE
SALTBUSH
SAGUARO

HIGHEST POINT IN ARIZONA: 12,633 FEET, NEAR FLAGSTAFF.

LOWEST POINT IN ARIZONA: 70 FEET, NEAR YUMA.

# FLORA AND FAUNA

A wide variety of plants and animals find homes within Arizona's great range of elevations—more than 12,000 feet. Some plants, such as the senita cactus and elephant tree, grow only in southern Arizona and Mexico. Migratory birds often drop in. The colorful parrot-like trogon bird and more than a dozen species of hummingbirds fly up from Mexico to spend their summers in the mountains of southeastern Arizona. Canada geese and other northern waterfowl come to settle in for the winter on rivers and lakes in the low desert.

## Protected Plants

Arizona has many sensitive and endangered species. State law prohibits collecting or destroying most cacti and wildflowers without a permit from the landowner. Offenders can get a $500 fine and possible prison term. Cacti need time to grow (a saguaro takes 50 years to mature) and cannot survive large-scale collecting. Although the "jumping" cactus is a myth, at least one saguaro has struck back at its oppressor—in Feb. 1982, a man north of Phoenix shot a saguaro twice with a shotgun; a 23-foot section then broke off and crushed the gunman to death.

## LIFE ZONES

To help simplify and understand the different environments of Arizona, some scientists use the Merriam system of life zones. Because plants rely on rainfall, which is determined largely by elevation, each life zone can be expected to occur within a certain range of elevations. The elevation ranges are not exact—south-facing mountain slopes receive more sun and lose more moisture to evaporation than north-facing slopes at the same level. Canyons and unusual rainfall patterns can also play havoc with the classifications. The life zones do give us, however, a general idea of what kind of vegetation and animal life to expect while traveling through the state.

### Lower Sonoran Zone

Arizona's famed desert country of arid plains, barren mountains, and stately saguaro cacti covers about one-third of the state. The south and west sections under 4,500 feet lie within this zone. The big cities and most of the state's population are here, too. With irrigation, farmers find the land good for growing vegetables, citrus, and cotton. Cacti do well: you'll see the prickly pear, cholla, and barrel, as well as the giant saguaro whose white blossoms are the state flower. The great variety of desert shrubs and small trees includes the palo verde, ocotillo, creosote, mesquite, and ironwood. Flowering plants tend to bloom either after the winter rains (the Sonoran or Mexican type) or after the summer rains (the Mojave or Californian type).

Most desert animals retreat to a den or burrow during the heat of the day, when ground temperatures can reach 150° F! Look for wildlife in early morning, late afternoon, or

*elf owl*
*(Micrathene whitneyi)*

at night: kangaroo rats, squirrels, mice, cottontails, jack rabbits, skunks, kit fox, ringtail cat, javelina, bighorn sheep, coyote, and the extremely shy mountain lion. Common birds include the cactus wren (state bird of Arizona), Gambel's quail, Gila woodpecker, roadrunner, hawks, eagles, owls, and common raven. Sidewinder and western diamondback rattlesnakes are occasionally seen. The rare Gila monster, identified by a bead-like skin with black and yellow patterns, is the only poisonous lizard in the United States; it's slow and nonaggressive but has powerful jaws. Also watch out for poisonous invertebrates, especially the small slender scorpion, whose sting is dangerous and can be fatal for children. Spiders and centipedes can also inflict painful bites. It's a good idea to check for unwanted guests in shoes and other items left outside.

### Upper Sonoran Zone

You'll find these 4,500- to 6,500-foot elevations in central Arizona and in widely scattered areas throughout the rest of the state. Enough rain falls here to support grasslands or stunted woodlands of juniper, pinyon pine, and oak. Some chaparral-type vegetation grows here too, forming a nearly impenetrable thicket of manzanita and other bushes. Many of the same animals live here as in the Lower Sonoran Zone. You might also see black bear, desert mule deer, whitetail deer,

and the antelope-like pronghorn. Rattlesnakes and other reptiles like this zone best.

### Transition Zone

The sweet-smelling ponderosa pine trees live in this zone—at 6,500 to 8,000 feet—where much of the winter's precipitation comes as snow. Ponderosas grow in many parts of the state, but their greatest expanse (the largest in the country) lies along the southern Colorado Plateau, from Williams in northcentral Arizona eastward into New Mexico. Gambel oak, junipers, and Douglas fir are commonly found among the ponderosa. Squirrels and chipmunks rely on the pine cones for food; other animals living here include desert cottontail, black-tailed jack rabbit, spotted and striped skunks, red fox, coyote, mule deer, whitetail deer, elk, black bear, and mountain lion. Wild turkeys live in the woods, along with Steller's jays, screech owls, hummingbirds (in summer), juncos, and the common raven. Most snakes, such as the gopher, hognosed, and garter snakes, are harmless, but you could also come across a western diamondback rattler.

*desert bighorn sheep* (Ovis canadensis mexicana) *at Arizona-Sonora Desert Museum, near Tucson*

*javelina*
(Dicotyles tajacu)

**Canadian Zone**
Douglas fir dominate the cool, wet forests between 8,000 and 9,500 feet. Mixed in are Engelmann and blue spruce, white and subalpine fir, and quaking aspen. Little sunlight penetrates the closely spaced trees, which function as their own windbreak. Grasses and wildflowers grow in lush meadows amid the forests. Canadian Zone forests are found on the Kaibab Plateau of the Grand Canyon's North Rim, the San Francisco Peaks, White Mountains, and other high peaks. You'll often see or hear squirrels as they busily gather cones to last through the long winter. Deer and elk graze in this zone, but rarely higher.

**Hudsonian Zone**
Strong winds and a growing season less than 120 days long prevent trees from reaching their full size at elevations from 9,500 to 11,500 feet. Forests receive twice as much snow as the Canadian Zone just below. Often gnarled and twisted, the dominant trees are

Engelmann and blue spruce, subalpine and corkbark fir, and bristlecone pine. This zone occurs in Arizona only atop the highest mountains. On a bright summer day, the trees, grasses, and tiny flowering alpine plants are a-buzz with insects, rodents, and visiting birds, but come winter, most animals will have moved to lower and more protected areas.

**Alpine Zone**
In Arizona, this zone is found only on the San Francisco Peaks, where about 11,500 feet is the upper limit of tree growth. Freezing temperatures and snow can blast the mountain slopes even in midsummer. About 80 species of plants, many also found in the North American Arctic, manage to survive on the Peaks despite the rocky soil, wind, and cold. One species of groundsel and a buttercup grow only here. Seasonal visitors include a dwarf shrew and three species of birds: the Lincoln and white-crowned sparrows and the water pipit.

# HISTORY

## PREHISTORIC INDIANS

### Paleo-Indians
Arizona's first people discovered this land more than 15,000 years ago. They came from a hunting culture that extended across the Great Plains and into New Mexico and eastern Arizona. Spears in hand, tribesmen hunted bison, camel, horse, antelope, and mammoth. Smaller game and wild plant foods completed their diet. About 9000 B.C., when the climate became drier and grasslands turned to desert, most of the large animals died off or left. Overhunting may have hastened their extinction.

### Desert Culture Tradition
The early tribes survived these changes by relying on seeds, berries, and nuts collected from wild plants and by hunting smaller game such as pronghorn, deer, mountain sheep, and jack rabbit. Developing a precise knowledge of the land, the small bands of related families moved in seasonal migrations timed to arrive when plants of each area ripened. They traveled light, probably carrying baskets, animal skins, traps, snares, and stone tools. Most likely they sought shelter in caves or built small brush huts. Some Arizona tribes continued a similar nomadic lifestyle until the late 1800s.

### Distinct Cultures Emerge
Between 2000 and 500 B.C., cultivation skills came to the uplands of Arizona from Mexico. Indian groups, though, still kept their seasonal migrations, planting corn and squash in the spring, continuing their travels in search of wild foods, then returning to harvest their fields in autumn. Agriculture became more important about 500 B.C., when beans were introduced. The earliest pottery, to cook the beans in and to store other foods and water, was made at about the same time. The com-

bination of beans, corn, and squash gave the people a nutritious, high-protein diet.

About A.D. 200-500, as they devoted more time to farming, the tribes began building villages of partly underground pithouses near their fields. Regional farming cultures appeared: the Hohokam of the southern deserts, the Mogollon of the eastern uplands, and the Anasazi of the Colorado Plateau in the north.

### Growth And The Great Pueblos
Villages became larger and their sites more widespread as populations increased from A.D. 500 to 1100. Above-ground pueblo dwellings began to replace the old-style pithouses. Trade among the Southwest cultures and with Mexico brought new ideas for crafts, farming, and building, along with valued items such as copper bells, parrots (prized for their feathers), and seashells and turquoise for jewelry. Cotton cultivation and weaving skills were developed. Major towns appeared between A.D. 900 and 1100,

A prehistoric Hopi pottery design of a Kwataka eating an animal; the Kwataka is a legendary winged monster who troubled Hopi ancestors. This fragment was excavated at Sikyatki.

possibly acting as trade centers. Complex religious ceremonies, probably similar to those of present-day Hopi Indians, took place in kivas (ceremonial rooms) and village plazas in the uplands. Ball courts and platform mounds, most often found in the southern deserts, likely served religious and secular purposes. Desert dwellers also dug elaborate irrigation networks in the valleys of the Salt and Gila rivers.

### Decline And Consolidation

Mysteriously, people began to pack up and abandon, one by one, whole villages and regions throughout Arizona between 1100 and the arrival of the Spanish in 1540. Archaeologists try to explain their disappearance with theories of drought, soil erosion, warfare, disease, and aggression of Apache and Navajo newcomers. Refugees swelled the populations of the remaining villages during this period, then most of these too were left empty. Some Anasazi Indian groups probably survived to become the modern Hopi in northeastern Arizona. The Mogollon and Hohokam disappeared completely; the modern tribes that took their place knew nothing of the people who had built the great pueblo structures.

petroglyph at Puerco Indian Ruin,
Petrified Forest National Park

Tzoe, called "Peaches" by the soldiers because of his light complexion and rosy cheeks, was an Apache Indian scout under General Crook's command in central Arizona, 1880s.

### The Athabaskans Wander In

From westcentral Canada, small bands of Athabaskan-speaking Indians slowly migrated to the Southwest. They arrived about 1300-1500 and established territories in the east half of present-day Arizona and adjacent New Mexico. Never a unified group, they followed a nomadic life of hunting, gathering, and raiding neighboring tribes. Some of the Athabaskans, later classified as "Navajo" on the Colorado Plateau and "Apache" farther south and east, learned agriculture and weaving from their pueblo neighbors.

## SPANISH EXPLORATION AND RULE

### The Conquistadors

Estévan, a Moorish slave of the viceroy of Mexico, became the first non-Indian to enter what is now Arizona. He arrived from the south in an advance party of Fray Marcos de Niza's 1539 expedition, sent by the viceroy to search for the supposedly treasure-laden Seven Cities of Cíbola. The first of these

"cities" that the party entered was a large Zuni Indian pueblo in present-day New Mexico, where they met their deaths at the hands of the Indians. When Fray Marcos heard the news, he dared view the pueblo only from a distance. Though he returned empty-handed, his glowing accounts of this city of stone encouraged a new expedition led by Francisco Vásquez de Coronado.

Coronado departed from Mexico City in 1540 with 336 soldiers, almost 1,000 Indian allies, and 1,500 horses and mules. Instead of gold, the expedition found only houses of mud inhabited by a hostile people. Despite hardships, Coronado explored the region for 2 years, traveling as far north as Kansas. A detachment led by García López de Cárdenas visited the Hopi mesas and the Grand Canyon rim. Another officer of the expedition, Hernando de Alarcon, explored the mouth of the Colorado River in hopes of finding a water route to resupply Coronado, but he discovered the task to be impossible.

## Missions And Presidios

Nearly 100 years passed after Coronado's failed quest before the Spanish reentered Arizona. A few explorers and prospectors made brief visits, but Franciscan missionaries came to stay. They opened three missions at the Hopi villages and had some success in gaining converts, despite strong objections from traditional Hopi. When pueblo villages in neighboring New Mexico revolted against the Spanish in 1680, the traditional Hopi joined in and killed the friars and many of their followers. Missionary efforts then shifted to southern Arizona, where the tireless Jesuit priest, Eusebio Francisco Kino, explored the new land and built missions from 1691 to 1711. Harsh treatment by later missionaries and land abuses by settlers caused the Pima tribes to revolt in 1751. The Spanish then made reforms and built a presidio (military fort) at Tubac to prevent another outbreak. Similar unfair treatment by Spaniards at two missions on the lower Colorado River caused a revolt there in 1781; no attempt was made to reestablish them.

*statue of Padre Kino, Arizona Capitol*

### Arizonac

A fantastic silver strike during the Spanish era in 1736 drew thousands to an arroyo known by local Indians as "Arizonac," where sheets of native silver weighing 25-50 pounds each were said to cover the ground. The exact location is uncertain, but it was probably west of present-day Nogales. The boom soon ended, but a book published in 1850 in Spain told the amazing story. An American mine speculator picked up the tale and used it to publicize and sell mining shares. The name, shortened to Arizona, became so well known that politicians later chose it for the territory—or at least that's one theory of how Arizona got its name!

### Mexicans Take Over

This land had always been on the far fringes of civilization. Politics and the Mexican fight for independence had little effect on it, so when 3 centuries of Spanish rule came to an end with Mexican independence in 1821, almost nothing changed. In the presidios, a new flag and an oath of loyalty to Mexico marked the transition. Isolation and hostile Apache continued to discourage settlement. Mission work declined as the Mexican government forced out many of the Spanish friars.

## ARRIVAL OF THE ANGLOS

### Mountain Men

Early in the 19th century, adventurous traders and trappers left the comforts of civilization in the eastern states to seek a new life in the West. Sylvester Pattie and his son made the first known visit by Anglos to what's now Arizona in 1825. The younger Pattie later told of his adventures in *The Personal Narrative of James Ohio Pattie* (see "Booklist"). Although occasionally suffering attacks by hostile Indians, the Patties and later mountain men got along peacefully with the Mexicans and Indians already here. When U.S. Army explorers and surveyors first visited Arizona in the 1840s and 1850s, they relied on mountain men to show them the trails and waterholes.

### Americans Take Hold

Anglo traders did an increasingly large business in the Southwest after Mexican independence—their supply route from Missouri was far shorter and more profitable than the Mexicans' long haul from Mexico City. Arizona had little importance in the Mexican War of 1847-48, ignited by American desire for Texas and California, disputes over debts owed by Mexico, and Mexican indifference to seeking a political solution. The 1848 Treaty of Guadalupe Hidalgo ceded to the United States not only the two desired areas, but everything in between, including Arizona and New Mexico. Arizona remained a backwater in the early American years as part of the New Mexican Territory, created by Congress in 1850. The Gadsden Purchase added what's now southernmost Arizona in 1854.

*Al Sieber, serving as an Army scout at Camp Verde in 1877*

*a fight with the Navajo, 1870s*

### New Trails
Most of the early visitors regarded Arizona as merely a place to be crossed on the way to California. The safest routes lay within the Gadsden Purchase where Captain Philip Cooke had built a wagon road during the Mexican War. Many of the '49ers, headed for gold strikes in California, used Cooke's road, the Gila Trail. Hostile Indians and difficult mountain crossings discouraged travel farther north, even after Edward Beale opened a rough wagon road across northern Arizona in 1857. Steamboat service on the lower Colorado River, beginning in 1852, brought cheaper and safer transportation to western Arizona.

### Americans Settle In
As the California Gold Rush of 1849 died down in the mid-1850s, prospectors turned eastward to Arizona. Their first big find here was a placer gold deposit near the confluence of the Colorado River and Sacramento Wash in 1857. More discoveries followed. For the first time, large numbers of people came to Arizona to seek their fortunes in minerals. Farmers and ranchers followed to cash in on the market provided by the new mining camps and Army posts.

### Indian Troubles And The Civil War
Mountain men and government surveyors had maintained mostly good relations with the Indian tribes, but this changed only a few years after the first contacts. Conflicts between the white man and Indian over economic, religious, and political rights, as well as over land and water, led to loss of land and autonomy for the Indian. Atrocities committed by both sides resulted as each tried to drive out the other. Army forts provided a base for troops attempting to subdue the Indians and a refuge for travelers and settlers.

Most Arizonans sided with the Confederacy during the Civil War, but quickly surrendered when large numbers of federal troops arrived. The only skirmish to take place in Arizona between the North and South occurred at Picacho Pass northwest of Tucson. After a few casualties on each side, the Confederates retreated east.

## TERRITORIAL YEARS

Despite the wars and uncertainties of the early 1860s, Arizona emerged for the first time as a separate entity on Feb. 24, 1863, when President Lincoln signed the bill to make it a territory. Formerly, as part of New

Mexico, Arizona had lacked representation and law and order. In 1864, Governor John Goodwin and fellow appointed officials laid out Arizona's first capital at Prescott.

### Continuing Indian Troubles

Control of hostile Indians, especially the Apache and Navajo, proved to be the new territory's most serious problem. Although Arizona's Indians had failed to drive out the newcomers, they did succeed in holding back development. Not until the great Apache war leader Geronimo surrendered for the last time in 1886 did white residents of the territory feel safe.

### Frontier Days End

The arrival of railroads in the 1870s and 1880s and discoveries of rich copper deposits brought increasing prosperity. Ranching, farming, and logging became important too. By 1890 most of the Army forts had outlived their usefulness. Only Fort Huachuca in southeast Arizona has survived as an active military post from the Indian wars to the present.

### Mormon Settlement

Mormons in Utah, seeking new freedoms and opportunities, migrated south into Arizona. They first established Littlefield in the ex-treme northwest corner of Arizona in 1864. A flood washed out the community in 1867 but it was rebuilt in 1877. Mormons developed other parts of the Arizona Strip in the far north and operated Lees Ferry across the Colorado River, just upstream from the Grand Canyon. From Lees Ferry, settlers headed as far south as St. David (founded 1877) on the San Pedro River in Cochise County. Some settlements had to be abandoned because of land ownership problems, poor soil, or irrigation difficulties. Mormon towns prospering today include Springerville (founded 1871), Joseph City (1876), Mesa (1878), and Show Low (1890).

## STATEHOOD AND MODERN ARIZONA

It took years of political wrangling, but on Feb. 14, 1912—Valentine's Day—President William H. Taft signed the proclamation admitting Arizona as the 48th state. All of its citizens turned out for parades and wild celebrations. In Phoenix, Governor-elect George W.P. Hunt led a triumphal procession to the Capitol. Arriving in the territory as an unemployed miner in 1881, Hunt had worked his way up to become a successful merchant, banker, territorial representative, and president of Arizona's Constitutional Convention. Hunt's

*George W.P. Hunt (center) at the Constitutional Convention, 1910*

*President Taft signing the Arizona Statehood Bill*

support of labor, good roads, and other liberal causes won him seven terms in the governor's office.

Arizona lived up to its nickname, the "Copper State," riding the good times when copper prices were high, as during WW I and the Roaring '20s, and suffering during economic depressions. Water—that all-important resource for farmers and cities—also preoccupied citizens. New dams across the Gila, Salt, and Verde rivers of central Arizona ensured the state's growth. Over the Colorado River, however, Arizona officials maintained a long-running feud with California and other thirsty states. Arizona pressed for its water rights from the early 1920s until 1944, even calling out the National Guard at one point to halt construction of Parker Dam, designed to supply water for Los Angeles. Wartime priorities finally forced the Arizona Legislature to make peace and join the other river states in the Colorado River Compact.

## WW II And The Postwar Boom

World War II brought many changes and advances. The Army Air Corps, attracted by good flying weather, came to build training bases. Army officers, including General Patton, trained their soldiers on the Arizona deserts. Aeronautical and other defense industries built factories, with the result that manufacturing income jumped from $17 million in 1940 to $85 million just 5 years later. Several POW camps were built for captured Germans and Italians. Some of the unfortunate Japanese-Americans were also interned here; in fact, so many Japanese had been herded into the Poston camp (south of Parker) that for a while it ranked as Arizona's third largest city.

The war, and the air conditioning that made the low-desert summers bearable, changed the state forever. Many of the workers and servicemen who had passed through during the hectic war years came back to live. Even some of the German POWs, it's said, liked Arizona enough to return and stay. Much of the industry and many military bases remained here as well. Retired people took a new interest in the sunny skies and warm winters of the state. Whole towns, such as Sun City (developed in 1960), grew up just for the older set. Arizona has continued to grow and diversify, yet it has retained its natural beauty and Old West heritage. The boom hasn't stopped yet.

# EVENTS

Arizona has a full schedule of rodeos, parades, art festivals, historic celebrations, gem and mineral shows, and sporting events. Activities tend to shift between southern Arizona in winter and the north in summer. Stop at a chamber of commerce to see what's coming up. The office should also have a statewide *Calendar of Events,* published by the Arizona Office of Tourism.

## Major Holidays

Even though not always mentioned in the text, many museums, parks, and other tourist attractions close on such holidays as Thanksgiving, Christmas, and New Year's days; call ahead to check.

**New Year's Day:** January 1
**Martin Luther King Jr.'s Birthday:** January 15; usually observed third Mon. in January
**President's Day** (honors Washington and Lincoln): third Mon. in February
**Easter Sunday:** late March or early April
**Cinco de Mayo** (Mexican festival celebrated in many Southwest communities): May 5
**Memorial Day** (honors veterans of all wars): last Mon. in May
**Independence Day:** July 4
**Labor Day:** first Mon. in September
**Columbus Day:** second Mon. in October
**Veterans Day:** November 11
**Thanksgiving Day:** fourth Thurs. in November
**Christmas Day:** December 25

# TRANSPORT

## TOURS

See your travel agent for the latest on package tours to Arizona. Within the state, local operators offer everything from city sights to rafting trips through the Grand Canyon. Gray Line has the largest selection of bus excursions, ranging from half day to 3 days; their tours leave from Phoenix, Tucson, and Flagstaff. Smaller companies offer jeep trips to scenic spots where a car wouldn't make it; you'll find jeeps at Monument Valley, Canyon de Chelly, Sedona, Phoenix, and Tucson. You can also take flightseeing trips from many airports; the Grand Canyon is the most popular for these. The "Transport" sections in each chapter list tour operators; also ask local chambers of commerce.

## BY CAR

Public transport serves the cities and some towns but very few of the scenic, historic, and recreational areas. Unless on a tour, you really need your own transport. Most people choose cars as the most convenient and economical way to get around; they're easily rented in any sizeable town in Arizona. Phoenix and Tucson have the largest selection and also offer RV rentals. Four-wheel-drive vehicles can be very handy if you plan extensive travel on back roads. *Arizona Highways* magazine produces the best state road map; almost any chamber of commerce will have one, and it's free. The AAA *Indian Country* map has superb coverage of the Four Corners region, including the Navajo and Hopi Indian reservations; the map is free at AAA offices for members and can also be purchased in stores.

### Driveaways

These are autos to be delivered to another city. If it's a place you're headed, a driveaway can be like getting a free car rental. To do it you have to be at least 21 years old and make a refundable deposit of $75-150. There will be time and mileage limits. Ask for an economy car if you want the lowest driving costs. In a large city (Phoenix and Tucson in Arizona), look in the Yellow Pages under "Automobile Transporters & Driveaways."

### Hitchhiking

Opinions and experiences vary on hitching. It can be a great way to meet people despite the dangers and long waits. Offer to buy lunch or help with gas money to repay the driver's favor. Often rides can be arranged with fellow travelers at youth hostels. The ride boards at the University of Arizona (Tucson), Arizona State University (Tempe, near Phoenix), and Northern Arizona University (Flagstaff) list rides both available and wanted. Highway police tolerate hitchhiking as long as it doesn't create a hazard or take place on an interstate or freeway. They do routinely check IDs, however.

## BY BUS

**Greyhound Bus** offers frequent service in Arizona on their transcontinental routes across northern and southern Arizona and between Flagstaff and Phoenix. **Nava-Hopi Tours** does a Flagstaff-Sedona-Camp Verde-Phoenix-Sky Harbor Airport run and connects the Grand Canyon National Park (South Rim) with Flagstaff. **Sedona Transportation Company** serves Sedona, Cottonwood, Camp Verde, and Phoenix/Sky Harbor. **Citizen Auto Stage** will take you from Tucson or Phoenix to Nogales, just a short walk from the cheap and colorful Mexican bus lines. **Bridgewater Transport** connects Tucson with the southeastern towns of Sierra Vista, Bisbee, and Douglas. Less frequent (one or two times a day) but useful bus services include **White Mountain Passenger Line** (Phoenix to Show Low, and other eastern Arizona destinations); **Navajo Transit System** (Navajo and Hopi Indian Reservations, but doesn't connect with other bus lines in Arizona); and **LTR Stage Line** (Phoenix to Kingman and Nevada destinations). Some bus companies give a small discount for roundtrips. Greyhound often has special deals on bus passes and "one-way anywhere" tickets. Overseas residents may purchase a Greyhound Bus "Ameripass" at additional discounts outside North America.

Local bus services come in handy at the Grand Canyon National Park South Rim (summer only, free), Flagstaff, Phoenix, and Tucson. Service in other towns is usually too infrequent for the traveler. Always have exact change ready when taking local buses.

## BY TRAIN

**Amtrak** features two luxury train lines across Arizona. Both connect Los Angeles with New Orleans, Chicago, and other destinations to the east. On the northern route, the *Southwest Chief* runs daily in each direction with stops in Arizona at Kingman, Flagstaff, and Winslow. On the southern route, the *Sunset Limited* stops in Yuma, Phoenix, Tempe, Coolidge, Tucson, and Benson, but it runs only three times per week in each direction. Amtrak charges more than the buses for one-way tickets but has far roomier seating, as well as parlor cars and sleepers. Special fares and roundtrip discounts can often make train travel a good value. For information and reservations, see a travel agent or call Amtrak toll-free (800) 872-7245 anywhere in the country. A "USA Railpass" is sold by travel agents outside North America.

## BY AIR

More than a dozen major airlines fly to Phoenix and Tucson. Fares and schedules tend to change frequently—a travel agent can help find the best flights. Big-city newspapers usually have advertisements of discount fares and tours in their Sunday travel section. You'll have the best chance of getting low fares by planning a week or more ahead.

Phoenix serves as the hub for nearly all flights within the state. Destinations from Phoenix include Tucson, Sierra Vista, Yuma, Lake Havasu City, Bullhead City, Prescott, Sedona, Flagstaff, and Page. The cost per mile of these short hops is high but you'll often have excellent views!

## BY BICYCLE

Touring on a bicycle is to be fully alive to the land, skies, sounds, plants, and birds of Arizona. The experiences of gliding across the desert or topping out on a mountain pass go beyond words. Some effort, a lightweight touring or mountain bicycle, and awareness of what's going on around you are all that's needed. Start with short rides if you're new to bicycle touring, then work up to longer cross-country trips. By learning to maintain and repair your steed, you'll seldom have trouble on the road. An extra-low gear of 30 inches or less will take the strain out of long mountain grades. Arizona's sunny climate offers fine year-round cycling—just adjust your elevation for the desired temperature! Bookstores and bicycle shops have good publications on bicycle touring. As when hiking, always have rain and wind gear and carry plenty of water.

Also don't forget to wear a bicycling helmet. Cyclists with a competitive spirit can test themselves in a series of U.S. Cycling Federation-sanctioned races; local bicycle shops have schedules of races and training rides.

# ACCOMMODATIONS AND FOOD

## Motels And Hotels
The busiest seasons, when reservations come in handy, are winter in the southern desert country (Phoenix, Tucson, Yuma, etc.), and summer in the high country (Prescott, Flagstaff, Payson, Grand Canyon, etc.). Rates fluctuate dramatically with seasons at the more expensive places, where off-peak prices can even be a bargain. Economy motels either keep the same rate all year or drop only slightly in the off-season. You'll find the major hotel and motel chains well represented in Arizona. Some of Arizona's restored historic hotels retain the elegance and romance of the old days. Outstanding historic places, worth a visit to the lobby even if you're not staying there, include the Hassayampa Inn (Prescott), Copper Queen Hotel (Bisbee), El Tovar (Grand Canyon), and Gadsden Hotel (Douglas).

## Bed And Breakfasts
Following a European tradition, these private homes or small inns offer a personal touch not found in the usual accommodations. Rates range from about $20 to $100 d; always call or write ahead for reservations. You'll find B&Bs in many parts of the state—in cities, resort towns, and on ranches. Usually they're not advertised; some are listed in these pages or with local chambers of commerce. More complete statewide listings are available from **Bed and Breakfast in Arizona,** Box 8628, Scottsdale, AZ 85252; tel. 995-2831; and **Mi Casa Su Casa,** Box 950, Tempe, AZ 85280-0950; tel. 990-0682 or (800) 456-0682.

## Youth Hostels
The **American Youth Hostels (AYH)** organization offers clean and friendly accommodations for people of all ages. Hostels usually consist of dormitory rooms (separate men's and women's), kitchen, and common room. Besides being a good place for low-budget travelers, they enable you to meet visitors from many other countries. Arizona has AYH hostels in Phoenix, Flagstaff, and Tuba City; more are planned. Each visitor must bring or rent sleeping sheets and be willing to pitch in to take care of the hostel. Rates run about $10/night for members (nonmembers usually pay a few dollars more). Reservations can be made by mail with a first night's deposit.

Membership cards are sold at many of the hostels and by the national office: Box 37613, Washington, D.C. 20013-7613; tel. (202) 783-6161. One year's membership costs $10 age 17 and under, $25 age 18-54, and $15 age 55 and over. Cards are good at any hostel in the world, and foreign cards are accepted here.

**Independent hostels,** found in Flagstaff, Tucson, Holbrook (Petrified Forest National Park), and some other places, offer similar services and rates without as many rules as the AYH hostels.

## Dude Ranches
These guest ranches feature horseback riding, miles of open country, excellent food, and an informal Western atmosphere. Activities include tennis, swimming, roping and riding instruction, hayrides, cookouts, square dancing, and even the real cowboy chores of working cattle. Tucson and Wickenburg are the major guest ranch centers, but other ranches are scattered around, mainly in the southern half of the state. Rates typically run $100/person per day and include all meals and activities. Most visitors come in winter, when the desert is at its best; guest ranches often close in summer.

## Campgrounds

The best parts of Arizona lie outdoors, and you have a choice among hundreds of campgrounds: federal, state, Indian, or private. Federal government sites, the most common, are offered by the Forest Service, National Park Service, and Bureau of Land Management; sites commonly have tables, toilets, and drinking water; fees range from free to $8/night. Many state campgrounds feature showers and hookups; they're very good value at rates of $6/vehicle per night ($8 w/hookups). Some Indian reservations, most notably the White Mountain Apache and Havasupai, offer primitive campgrounds. Commercial campgrounds have the most frills—showers, laundromats, hookups, stores, gamerooms, and even swimming pools at some places; rates average about $12/night; tents may or may not be accepted. Families should be aware that many of Arizona's RV parks cater to retired people—children won't be welcome. Unless otherwise stated, all campgrounds mentioned in these pages *do* accept families.

Other types of camping can be done too. You're welcome to camp almost anywhere in the national forests. This dispersed style of camping costs nothing and for seasoned campers it gives the best outdoor experience. Since there are no facilities, the challenge is yours to leave the forest in its natural state. Be very careful with fire—try to use a campstove rather than leave a fire scar; sometimes high fire danger will close the forests in early summer. The seven national forests in Arizona cover vast expanses of mountain, plateau, and desert country from the state's far south to the far north. Stop at one of their offices for camping, hiking, and back-road suggestions and for maps ($2 each).

## FOOD

People debate whether or not Arizona has a native cuisine. Even if it doesn't, you'll find a wide selection. South-of-the-border food has a large following and a Mexican restaurant is never far away. Western-style restaurants will dish out cowboy food—beef, beans, and biscuits. Indian fry bread and the Navajo taco (beans, lettuce, tomatoes, and cheese on fry bread) can be sampled on and off the reservations. On the Hopi Reservation, a restaurant at the Cultural Center serves some unusual native fare. Tucson and Phoenix have the most cosmopolitan array of ethnic and fine-dining restaurants. Descriptions in this guide refer to price ranges for dinners (per person) as **Inexpensive** (to $8), **Moderate** ($8 to $15), and **Expensive** (over $15). Only a small sales tax is added to food; you're expected to leave a tip of about 15% for table service.

*Hopi woman preparing fry bread*

# MONEY, MEASUREMENTS, AND COMMUNICATIONS

Prices of all services mentioned in this book were current at press time. Whenever possible, taxes have been included in the stated cost. You're sure to find seasonal and long-term price changes, however, so *PLEASE* don't use what's listed here to argue with staff at a motel, campground, museum, airline, or other office!

Foreign currency can be changed in Phoenix, Tucson, and Grand Canyon Village; anywhere else in the state involves extra delay and expense at best.

## Measurements

If you ask a rancher how many kilometers to the next town, you're out of luck. Most Arizonans haven't a clue to what the metric units mean, so visitors need to know the "Olde English" system:

one inch = 2.54 centimeters
foot = 0.305 meter
mile = 1.609 kilometers
square mile = 2.590 square kilometers
acre = 0.405 hectares
ounce = 0.028 kilogram
pound (lb) = 0.454 kilograms
quart = 0.946 liter
US gallon = 3.785 liters

To figure centigrade temperatures, subtract 32 from Fahrenheit (F) and divide by 1.8.

## Time

Travelers in Arizona should remember that the state is on Mountain Standard Time all year, except for the Navajo Reservation which goes on daylight savings time (add one hour May to Oct.) to keep up with its Utah and New Mexico sections. Note that the Hopi Reservation, completely within Arizona and surrounded by the Navajo, stays on standard time year-round with the rest of the state. In summer, Arizona is on the same time as California and Nevada, but one hour behind Utah, Colorado, and New Mexico. In winter,

Arizona is one hour ahead of California and Nevada, but the same as Utah, Colorado, and New Mexico.

## Postal And Telephone Services

Normal post office hours are Mon.-Fri. 8:30 a.m.-5 p.m. and sometimes Sat. 8:30 a.m.-noon. All telephone numbers within Arizona have a **602 area code** (use when dialing 1+ or O+ numbers *inside* as well as outside Arizona). To obtain a local number from Information, dial 1-411; for a number within the state, dial 1-555-1212; and for a number in another state, dial 1, the area code, then 555-1212. Many airlines, auto rentals, and motel chains have a toll-free 800 number; if you don't have it, just dial 1-800-555-1212.

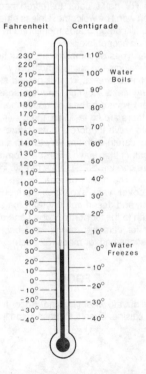

# HEALTH AND HELP

## Medical Services

In emergencies, use the emergency number listed on most telephones or dial "0" for an operator. Emergency rooms of hospitals offer the quickest help, but they cost more than a visit to a doctor's office. Hospital care is very expensive—medical insurance is recommended.

## WILDERNESS TRAVEL

### Keeping The "Wild" In Wilderness

As more people seek relief from the confusion and stress of urban life, the use of wilderness areas increases. Fortunately, Arizona has an abundance of this fragile and precious resource. The many designated wilderness areas have been closed to mechanized vehicles (including mountain bicycles) to protect both the environment and the experience of solitude. Most designated areas lie within national forest or Bureau of Land Manage-

ment lands, where you're normally free to visit anytime without a permit. Other areas, such as the national parks and national monuments and the Bureau of Land Management's Paria and Aravaipa canyons, require entry permits. Suggestions for backcountry travel and camping include these wilderness ethics:

• Before heading into the backcountry, check with a knowledgeable person about weather, water sources, fire danger, trail conditions, and regulations.

• Tell a ranger or other reliable person where you are going and when you expect to return.

• Travel in small groups for the best experience (group size may also be regulated).

• Try not to camp on meadows, as the grass is easily trampled and killed.

*on the Boulder Canyon Trail in the Superstition Mountains Wilderness*

• Avoid digging tent trenches or cutting vegetation.

• Use a campstove to avoid marring the land.

• Camp at least 300 feet away from springs, creeks, and trails. State law prohibits camping within one-quarter mile of a *sole* water source to avoid scaring away wildlife and livestock.

• Wash away from water sources.

• Don't drink water directly from streams or lakes, no matter how clean the water appears; it may contain the parasitic protozoan *Giardia lamblia,* which causes the unpleasant disease giardiasis. Boiling your water for several minutes will kill *Giardia* as well as most other bacterial or viral pathogens. Iodine chemical treatments usually work too, although they're not as reliable as boiling.

• Bring a trowel for personal sanitation; dig 4-6 inches deep.

• Bring plenty of feed for horses and mules.

• Leave dogs at home if possible; they may disturb wildlife and other hikers and foul campsites. If you do bring a dog, please keep it under physical control at all times.

• Take home all your trash so animals can't dig up and scatter it.

• Help preserve old Indian and historic ruins.

• A survival kit can make the difference if you're caught in a storm or are out longer than expected. A pocket-sized container can hold what you need for the three essentials: *fire building* (matches in waterproof container and candle), *shelter* (space blanket, knife, and rope), and *signaling* (mirror and whistle).

• If lost, *realize it,* then find shelter and stay in one place. If you're sure of a way to civilization and plan to walk out, leave a note of your departure time and planned route.

## Know Before You Go
Some of the most spectacular and memorable hiking and camping await the prepared outdoorsperson. But because Arizona's deserts and canyons are very different from most other parts of the country, even "expert" hikers get into trouble. If you're new to these outdoors, read up on the hiking conditions and talk to rangers and local hikers. Backpacking stores are good sources of information too. Start with easy trips, then work up gradually.

## Hypothermia
Your greatest danger outdoors is one that can sneak up and kill with very little warning. Hypothermia, a lowering of the body's temperature below 95° F, causes disorientation, uncontrollable shivering, slurred speech, and drowsiness. The victim may not even realize what's wrong. Unless corrective action is taken immediately, hypothermia can lead to death. This is why hikers should travel with companions and always carry wind and rain protection. (Close-fitting rain gear works better than ponchos.) Remember that temperatures can plummet rapidly in Arizona's dry climate—a drop of 40° F between day and night is common. Be especially careful at high elevations, where summer sunshine can quickly change into freezing rain or a blizzard. Simply falling into a mountain stream while fishing can also lead to hypothermia and death unless proper action is taken. If cold and tired, don't waste time! Seek shelter and build a fire; also change into dry clothes and drink warm liquids. If a victim isn't fully conscious, warm him by skin-to-skin contact with another person in a sleeping bag. Try to keep the victim awake and drinking warm liquids.

## DRIVING HAZARDS

Summer heat in the low desert puts an extra strain on both cars and drivers. It's worth double-checking to make sure the cooling system, engine oil, transmission fluid, fan belts, and tires are in top condition. Carry several gallons of water in case of breakdown or radiator trouble. Never leave children or pets in a parked car during warm weather: temperatures inside can cause fatal heat stroke in just minutes. At times the desert has *too much* water—late-summer storms frequently flood low spots in the road. Wait for the water to go down (until you can see bottom) before crossing. Dust storms also tend to be short-lived but can completely block visibility. The best thing to do in a dust storm is to pull completely off the road and stop; turn off your lights so as not to confuse other drivers.

Radio stations carry frequent weather updates when weather hazards exist. If you have a VHF radio (162.4 and 162.55 MHz), continuous weather forecasts can be received in the Phoenix, Tucson, Yuma, Flagstaff, Sedona, Glen Canyon N.R.A., and Las Vegas (NV) areas.

If stranded, whether on the desert or in mountains, stay with the vehicle unless you are *positive* of a route to help; then leave a note telling route and departure time. Airplanes can easily spot an obviously stranded car (leave hood and trunk up and tie a piece of cloth to antenna), but a person trying to walk out is difficult to see. Emergency supplies can help: blankets or sleeping bags, first-aid kit, tools and booster cables, shovel, traction mats or chains, flashlight, rain gear, water, and food (with can opener).

## FREE INFORMATION

General tourist literature and maps are available from the **Arizona Office of Tourism,** 100 W. Washington, Phoenix, AZ 85007; tel. 542-8687. The many chambers of commerce in the state will be happy to help; see "Information" under each place description in this book. Listed with them are national forest offices and other government agencies that know about outdoor recreation in their area.

## VISITING INDIAN RESERVATIONS

Meeting Arizona's Native Americans affords the chance to learn about another culture. Their lands—27% of the state—include some beautiful mountain, canyon, and desert country. Tribes in Arizona, from north to south, are Paiute, Navajo, Hopi, Havasupai, Hualapai, Yavapai, Apache, Mohave, Chemehuevi, Cocopah, Yaqui, Pima, and Papago. See descriptions in the individual travel sections of the reservations for museums, dances, crafts, recreation, and where to stay and eat. On any of the 23 reservations, keep in mind that you're a guest on private land. Most Indians are very private people; ask before taking their photos (you may need to pay a posing fee). The Hopi prohibit all photogra-

*A hole in the radiator knocks out Larry Lipchinsky's car*

*Navajo jewelry for sale*

phy, sketching, and recording in villages—don't even carry a camera there! Check to see if permits are needed before camping, hiking, or leaving the main roads. Usually a small charge applies for these activities. All fishing and hunting on Indian lands require tribal permits, though you won't need Arizona state licenses. Sometimes part of a reservation will be closed to outsiders.

Tribes you might want to visit include the Hopi for their exotic kachina dances and ancient pueblo villages, the Navajo for their remarkable land that includes Monument Valley, Canyon de Chelly, Painted Desert, and other natural wonders, the Havasupai for their "land of blue-green waters" within the Grand Canyon, and the White Mountain Apache for their forests, countless trout streams, and many fishing lakes. Indian crafts include jewelry by several tribes, Hopi kachina dolls

and pottery, Navajo rugs and sandpaintings, Apache beadwork, and Papago basketry. Two museums of Indian culture, the Heard in Phoenix and the Museum of Northern Arizona in Flagstaff, provide a good introduction to the tribes and their crafts.

## VISITING MEXICO

Arizona has always had a close relationship with Mexico. Spanish and Mexican influences show in the state's architecture, food, language, and music. About 16% of Arizona's population trace their descent back to the Spanish. Visiting Mexico is easy and simple at any of the six border crossings. Most people in the border towns understand English, and shopkeepers happily accept U.S. dollars. Nogales, close to Tucson, offers the best shopping and receives the most visitors. In all the border towns except Sonoita, you can park on the U.S. side and stroll across to the shops and restaurants in Mexico. Sonoita lies 2 miles beyond the boundary, and you'll probably want to drive there. See individual descriptions of the border towns within these pages.

## Permits

United States and Canadian citizens may visit the border towns for as long as 72 hours without any formalities; just announce your nationality when returning to the U.S. side. Identification should be carried (voter's registration, birth or naturalization certificate, passport, or affidavit of citizenship by a notary public). Travelers from other countries should ask for regulations about entering and returning *before* crossing over. Longer stays or travel to the interior require visitors to carry a tourist card, easily obtainable by U.S. and Canadian citizens at the border with proof of citizenship (a driver's license won't work), and usually good for 90 days.

Motorists may drive to the border towns and to Baja California without a permit. To go farther, vehicle permits must be obtained;

trailers and motorbikes each need one too. For the permits, easily obtained at the border, you'll need to show proof of ownership (title, bill of sale, registration, or a notarized affidavit stating that you own the vehicle or have permission to drive it in Mexico). Some car rental agencies in Arizona will allow you to drive in Mexico, but ask them first. Most U.S. insurance policies are worthless in Mexico. Unless you have Mexican insurance, the police there might throw you in jail after an accident, even if it wasn't your fault. Purchase Mexican insurance, available by the day or longer, in Arizona border towns.

## Information

Chambers of commerce on the Arizona side (Nogales, Douglas, and Yuma) know about their neighboring towns in Mexico. With luck, you might be able to find the chambers of commerce in the Mexican towns too. Sonora, the Mexican state bordering Arizona, has a tourist office in the state capital: **Secretaria de Fomento al Turismo Estado de Sonora,** Blvd. Kino No. 1000, Hermosillo, Sonora, Mexico; tel. 4-84-07 or 4-73-99.

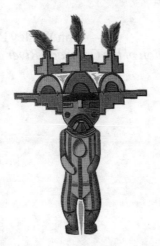

"The Grand Canyon of the Colorado is a canyon composed of many canyons. It is a composite of thousands, of tens of thousands, of gorges. In like manner, each wall of the canyon is a composite structure, a wall composed of many walls, but never a repetition. Every one of these almost innumerable gorges is a world of beauty in itself. In the Grand Canyon there are thousands of gorges like that below Niagara Falls, and there are a thousand Yosemites. Yet all these unite to form one grand canyon, the most sublime spectacle on earth...

Its colors, though many and complex at any instant, change with the ascending and declining sun; lights and shadows appear and vanish with the passing clouds, and the changing seasons mark their passage in changing colors. You cannot see the Grand Canyon in one view..."

—John Wesley Powell, from his
*The Exploration of the Colorado River and Its Canyons*

# THE GRAND CANYON AND THE ARIZONA STRIP

## INTRODUCTION

A collision of the Earth's forces—uplifting of the massive Colorado Plateau and vigorous downcutting by the Colorado River—created the awe-inspiring Grand Canyon and its many tributaries. Neither pictures nor words can fully describe them. You have to experience the Canyon by traveling along the rim, descending into the depths, and watching the continuous show of colors and patterns as the sun moves across the sky. Measurements give only a clue to the Canyon's grandeur: stretching 277 miles across northern Arizona, it averages 10 miles wide and one mile deep. Roads provide access to developed areas and viewpoints on both rims. Trails allow hikers and mule riders to descend the precipitous cliffs to the Colorado River, though most of the Park remains as remote as ever, rarely visited by humans.

Northward, between the Colorado River and the Utah border, lies the isolated Arizona Strip. This land of forests, desert grasslands, mountains, and canyons covers 14,000 square miles, yet it supports only 3,200 people. The Grand Canyon presents a formidable barrier between them and the rest of the state; all highway traffic has to follow a circuitous route around the mighty chasm. Residents of Moccasin in the Arizona Strip must drive 357 miles to their Mohave County seat at Kingman, detouring through Utah and Nevada before reentering Arizona at Hoover Dam, in order to cover 140 miles as the crow flies. Historically, the Strip has far more in common with Utah, whose Mormon pioneers first settled this region. Today, it appeals to those who love wilderness and solitude. Travelers can wander the canyons, back roads, and trails here without meeting another soul. Its other attractions include fishing and boating on Lake Powell, historic Lees Ferry (15 river miles below Lake Powell), and Pipe Spring National Monument, an early Mormon ranch.

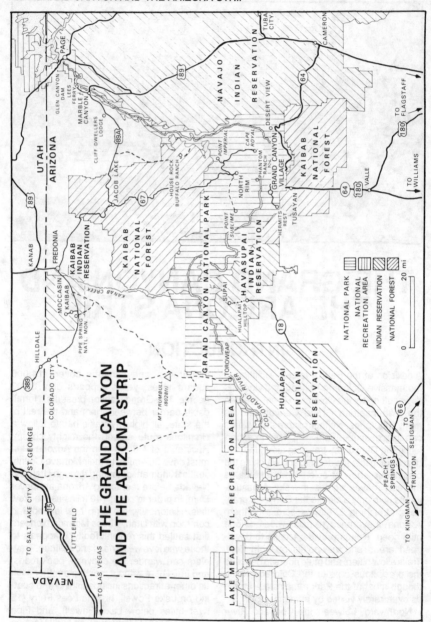

THE GRAND CANYON
AND THE ARIZONA STRIP

## THE LAND

This is a land of time. Tracing down the Grand Canyon's massive cliffs with your eyes, or walking below the rim, you see limestones composed of animals who lived in long-departed seas, sandstones formed of ancient desert sand dunes, and shales made of silt from now-vanished rivers and shores. Volcanic eruptions have left their record as layers of ash, cinders, and lava. Still farther into the Canyon lie the roots of mountain ranges, whose peaks towered over a primitive land 2 billion years ago. Time continues to flow in the Canyon with the cycles of the plants and animals that live here, and with the erosive forces of water and wind ever widening and deepening the chasm.

Geologists have a hard time telling the age of the Grand Canyon itself, though it is far younger than even the most recent rock layers—those on the rim, which are about 250 million years old. They lay at sea level 65 million years ago when the earth's crust began a slow uplift. Somewhere between 5 and 20 million years ago, the ancestral Colorado River took its present course and began to carve the Canyon. Gradual uplift continued, giving the waters even greater power. Today, the South Rim reaches elevations of 7,000-7,500 feet, while the North Rim towers about 1,000 feet higher. Still young, the Colorado River drops through the Canyon at an average gradient of 7.8 feet per mile, 25 times the gradient of the lower Mississippi.

### Climate

The Grand Canyon has been compared with an inverted mountain. Temperatures change with elevation as on a mountainside, but with added canyon peculiarities. In winter, the sun's low angle allows only a few hours of sunlight a day to reach the Inner Gorge, creating a cooling effect. The situation reverses during the summer, when the sun's high angle turns the canyon into an oven. At night, temperatures often drop lower than you'd expect; that's because cold, dense air on the rims pours over the edge into the depths.

*Vista Encantadora on the North Rim*

In one day, a hiker can travel from the cold fir and aspen forests of the North Rim to the hot cactus country of the Canyon bottom—a climate change equal to that between Canada and Mexico. In the Inner Gorge (elev. 2,570 feet at Phantom Ranch), summer temperatures soar, with average highs over 100° F; early July commonly sees the thermometer top 115°. Spring and autumn offer pleasantly warm weather—the best times to visit. Winter down by the river can be fine too; even in Jan., days warm up to the 50s or low 60s and it rarely freezes. Only about 7 inches of precipitation make it to the bottom in an average year; snow and rain often evaporate completely while falling through the mile of warm Canyon air.

The South Rim has pleasant weather most of the year. Summer highs reach the mid-80s, cooling to highs in the upper 30s and lower 40s during winter. Winter campers will need warm sleeping bags to combat frosty nights when temperatures go down to the teens. Yearly precipitation at the South Rim's Grand Canyon Village (elev. 6,950 feet) is about 14.5 inches with snow accumulations seldom exceeding 2 feet.

Although averaging only 1,000 feet higher, the North Rim really gets socked in by winter storms. Snow piles up to depths of 6-10 feet in an average season, and the National Park Service doesn't even try to keep the roads open from early Nov. to mid-May. Summers can be a joy in the cool fresh air; highs then run in the 60s and 70s. Bright Angel Ranger Station (elev. 8,400 feet) on the North Rim receives about 23 inches of annual precipitation.

Most moisture falls in the winter and during late summer (mid-July to mid-Sept.). Summer rains often arrive in spectacular afternoon thunderstorms, soaking one spot in the Canyon and leaving another a short distance away bone dry. The storms put on a great show from the rim viewpoints, but you should take cover away from the edge if the hair on your head stands on end or if you smell ozone. As in mountain areas, the Grand Canyon's weather can change rapidly. Always carry rain gear if heading down a trail.

## FLORA AND FAUNA

The seemingly endless variations of elevation, exposure, and moisture allow for an astonishing range of plant and animal communities. The Canyon also acts as a barrier to many nonflying creatures, who live on just one side of the Colorado River or only in the Inner Gorge. Some mammals, such as mountain lion, spotted skunk, cliff chipmunk, and common pocket gopher, evolved into separate subspecies on each rim.

### Spruce-Fir Forest
You'll find dense forests of spruce and fir and groves of quaking aspen on the Kaibab Plateau of the North Rim, mostly above 8,200 feet. Common trees include Engelmann and blue spruce, Douglas, white, and subalpine fir, aspen, and mountain ash. Lush meadows, dotted with wildflowers in late summer, spread out in shallow valleys at the higher elevations. Animals of the spruce-fir forest include mule deer, mountain lion, porcupine, red and Kaibab squirrel, Uinta chipmunk, long-tailed vole, and northern pocket gopher. The shy Kaibab squirrel, easily identified by his all-white tail and tufted ears, lives only on the North Rim. He probably evolved from

*Kaibab squirrel* (Sciurus kaibabensis)

some Abert squirrels who crossed the Colorado River long ago, perhaps during Pleistocene time. Birds you might see are turkey, great horned owl, saw-whet owl, broad-tailed hummingbird, hairy woodpecker, hermit thrush, Clark's nutcracker, Steller's jay, and mountain bluebird.

## Ponderosa Pine Forest
Stands of tall ponderosas grow between elevations of 7,000 and 8,000 feet on both rims. Mature forests tend to be open, allowing in sunlight for Gambel oak, New Mexican locust, mountain mahogany, greenleaf manzanita, cliffrose, wildflowers, and grasses. Animals and birds found here include most of those of the spruce-fir forests. The Abert squirrel, though common in the Southwest, lives only on the South Rim within the Park. He has tufted ears and a body and tail that are mostly gray with white undersides.

## Pinyon-Juniper Woodland
These smaller trees take over in drier and more exposed places between elevations of 4,000 and 7,500 feet. Commonly found with them are broadleaf yucca, cliffrose, rabbitbrush, Mormon tea, sagebrush, fernbrush, serviceberry, and Apache plume. Mule deer, mountain lion, coyote, gray fox, desert cottontail, Stephen's wood rat, pinyon mouse, rock squirrel, cliff chipmunk, lizards, and snakes (including rattlesnakes) make their homes here. Birds include pinyon and scrub jays, mourning dove, plain titmouse, Bewick's wren, and black-throated gray warbler.

## Desert Scrub
Except near permanent water, the low-desert country below 4,500 feet cannot support trees. You'll find such hardy plants as blackbrush, Utah agave, narrowleaf yucca, various cacti, desert thorn, Mormon tea, fourwing saltbush, and snakeweed. Animals include bighorn sheep, black-tailed jackrabbit, spotted skunk, desert woodrat, antelope ground squirrel, and canyon mouse. Most reptiles hole up during the day, though lizards

*Abert squirrel* (Sciurus aberti)

seem to tolerate higher temperatures than snakes. Chuckwalla, spiny and collared lizard, common kingsnake, whipsnake, and Grand Canyon rattlesnake live in this part of the Canyon. The shy Grand Canyon or pink rattlesnake, a subspecies of the prairie rattler, lives nowhere else. Birds of the desert scrub have to either look elsewhere for nesting trees or choose a spot in cliffs or on the ground. Species you might see include the common raven, turkey vulture, golden eagle, red-tailed hawk, rock and canyon wrens, and black-throated sparrow.

## Riparian Woodlands
Until 1963, seasonal floods of the Colorado River ripped away most vegetation below the high-water mark. Then, when the upstream Glen Canyon Dam was completed, tamarisk (an exotic species originally from the Arabian deserts) began to take over formerly barren beaches. Native cattail, coyote willow, and arrowweed now thrive too. Seeps and springs in side canyons support luxuriant plant growth and supply a drink for desert wildlife. Beaver, river otter, ringtail cat, raccoon, Woodhouse's toad, white-footed deermouse, tree lizard, spotted sandpiper, blue grosbeak, and Lucy's warbler make their homes near the streams. Fremont cottonwood trees in the tributaries provide welcome shade for overheated hikers. The cold, clear waters that flow from Glen Canyon Dam have upset breeding patterns of the seven native fish species, who now spawn in warmer waters at the mouths of the Little Colorado River and Havasu Creek. Rainbow trout and 10 other species have been introduced.

# HISTORY

## The First Peoples
Indians knew of this land and its canyons centuries before the white man came. At least 4,000 years ago, a hunting and gathering society stalked the plateaus and canyons of northern Arizona, leaving behind stone spear points and some small split-twig figures resembling deer or sheep. Preserved in caves of the Grand Canyon, these figurines have a carbon-14 date of 2000 B.C. This culture apparently departed about 1000 B.C., leaving the Canyon unoccupied for the next 1,500 years.

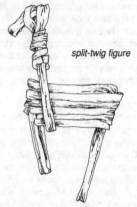
split-twig figure

## The Anasazi Arrive
Prehistoric Anasazi came to the Grand Canyon area about A.D. 500. Like their predecessors, they hunted deer, bighorn sheep, rabbit, and other animals, while gathering such wild plant foods as pinyon nuts and agave. The Anasazi also made fine baskets and sandals. At their peak between 1050 and 1150, they grew crops, crafted pottery, and lived in above-ground masonry villages. At about the end of this period, drought hit the region and may have caused its abandonment. By 1150 nearly all the Anasazi had departed from the Grand Canyon, leaving more than 2,000 sites behind. Most likely they migrated east to the Hopi mesas.

## Other Indians Come To The Canyon
While the Anasazi kept mostly to the east half of the Grand Canyon (east of today's Grand Canyon Village), another group of hunter-gatherers and farmers, the Cohonina, lived downstream between A.D. 600 and 1150. They adopted many of the agricultural and building techniques and crafts of their Anasazi neighbors. In 1300 the Cerbat, probable ancestors of the modern Havasupai and Hualapai Indians, migrated onto the Grand Canyon's South Rim from the west. They lived in caves or brush shelters and ranged as far upstream as the Little Colorado River in search of game and wild plant foods. The Cerbat also planted crops in areas of fertile soil or permanent springs. It's possible that the Cerbat had cultural ties with the earlier Cohonina. Nomadic Paiute Indians living north of the Grand Canyon made seasonal trips to the North Rim, occasionally clashing with the Cerbat when one group raided the other. The Paiute lived in brush shelters and relied almost entirely on hunting and gathering. They spent summers on the Kaibab Plateau and other high country, then moved to lower elevations for the winter. Hopi Indians knew of the Grand Canyon too; they came for religious pilgrimages and to collect salt.

## The Modern Tribes
Today the Havasupai live 35 air miles northwest of Grand Canyon Village in Havasu Canyon, a tributary of the Grand Canyon, and on lands atop the South Rim. The waterfalls, travertine pools, and greenery of their remote canyon have earned it fame as a "Shangri-la." To the west of the Havasupai, the large Hualapai Reservation spreads across much of the Grand Canyon's South Rim. The only road access to the Colorado River within the Canyon goes through their lands. A small band of Paiute Indians lives on the Kaibab Reservation, just west of Fredonia in far northern Arizona.

## Spanish And American Explorers
In 1540, when Francisco Vásquez de Coronado led an expedition in search of the Seven Cities of Cibola, Hopi Indians told a

detachment of soldiers about a great canyon to the west. Hopi guides later took a party of Coronado's men, led by García López de Cárdenas, to the South Rim but kept secret the routes into the depths. The Spaniards failed to find a way to the river and left discouraged. Franciscan priest Francisco Tomás Garcés, looking for souls to save, visited the Havasupai and Hualapai in 1776 and was well received by the Indians. Historians credit Garcés with naming the Rio Colorado ("Red River").

James Ohio Pattie and other American fur trappers probably came across the Grand Canyon in the late 1820s, but they gave only sketchy accounts of their visits. Lieutenant Joseph Ives led the first real exploration of the Colorado River. He chugged 350 miles by steamboat upstream from the river's mouth in 1857-58 before crashing into a rock in Black Canyon. The party continued overland to the Diamond Creek area in the western Grand Canyon. Most of the Canyon remained a dark and forbidding unknown until Major John Wesley Powell bravely led a boat expedition through it in 1869. On this trip and a second one in 1871-72, Powell and his men made detailed drawings and took notes on

*Major John Wesley Powell*

the geology, flora and fauna, and Indian ruins. Powell recorded his experiences in *Canyons of the Colorado* (now published as *The Exploration of the Colorado River and its Canyons*).

*Havasupai woman with child in burden basket, late 1800s*

John Hance and
his burros

## Ranching On The Arizona Strip

Not many pioneers took an interest in the prairie here—the ground proved nearly impossible to plow and lacked water for irrigation. Determined Mormons began ranching in the 1860s despite the isolation and Navajo raids. They built "Winsor Castle," a fortified ranch, in 1870 as a base for a large church-owned cattle herd. Mormons also founded the towns of Fredonia, Short Creek (now Colorado City), and Littlefield. Some of these settlers had fled Utah to escape federal laws prohibiting polygamy. About 3,000 members of a polygamous, excommunicated Mormon sect still live in Colorado City and neighboring Hilldale, Utah. Federal and state officials raided Colorado City several times, most recently in 1953, when 27 arrests were made (all received one-year probations). Now government policy seems to be "live and let live."

## Miners And Tourists

After about 1880, prospectors entered the Grand Canyon to search for copper, asbestos, silver, and lead deposits, despite the remoteness and difficult terrain. Their trails, many following old Indian routes, are still used by modern hikers. In 1883 stagecoaches began bringing tourists to see the Canyon at Diamond Creek, where J.H. Farlee opened a four-room hotel the following year. Prospectors Peter Berry and Ralph and Niles Cameron built the Grandview Hotel in 1895 at Grandview Point and led tourists down their trail to Horseshoe Mesa. Other prospectors, such as John Hance and William Bass, also found guiding visitors to be more profitable than mining. Tourism began on a large scale soon after the railroad reached the South Rim in 1901. The Fred Harvey Company purchased the Bright Angel Lodge, built the deluxe El Tovar Hotel, and took over from the small operators. As the Canyon became better known, President Theodore Roosevelt and others pushed for greater federal protection. First a forest reserve in 1893, the Grand Canyon became a national monument in 1908, then a national park in 1919. The Park's size doubled in 1975 when legislation extended the boundaries west to Grand Wash and northeast to Lees Ferry. Grand Canyon National Park now includes 1,892 square miles and receives more than 4 million visitors annually.

# VISITING GRAND CANYON NATIONAL PARK

Most people head first to the South Rim, entering at either the South Entrance Station near Grand Canyon Village or the East Entrance Station near Desert View. A 26-mile scenic drive along the rim connects these entrances. The South Rim features great views, a full range of accommodations and restaurants, and easy access—just 58 miles north of I-40 from Williams. Roads and most facilities stay open all year. Attractions include the Visitor Center, Yavapai Geology Museum, Tusayan Pueblo ruin, West Rim Drive to Hermit's Rest (8 miles), and East Rim Drive to Desert View (25 miles). The South Rim also has most of the Canyon's easily accessible viewpoints and trails. It's not surprising, then, that large crowds of visitors, especially in summer, are the main drawback of this part of the Canyon. The Park collects an admission fee of $10/motor vehicle ($4/bus passenger or bicyclist) that's good for 7 days at the south and east entrances of the South Rim and at the main entrance of the North Rim. Except as noted, the Visitor Cen-

ter, museums, programs, and trails have free admission once you're in the Park. Budget travelers can save money by stocking up on groceries and camping supplies at Flagstaff, Williams, or other towns away from the Canyon; prices within the Park run up to 25% higher.

Only about one in 10 visitors makes it to the North Rim, but that visitor receives a reward of pristine forests, rolling meadows, splendid wildflower displays, and superb panoramas. Viewpoints here provide a perspective of the Canyon dramatically different from the lower South Rim. The North Rim's Bright Angel Point area offers lodging, dining, and camping facilities similar to the South Rim's, though on a smaller scale (no McDonald's here). Unless you want to ski in (backcountry permit required), the North Rim is open only from mid-May to Oct. or Nov., depending on the timing of the first big winter storm. Although the rims stand just 10 miles apart, motorists on the south side must drive 215 miles to get here.

*tourists at Grandview Hotel (first on rim), 1899*

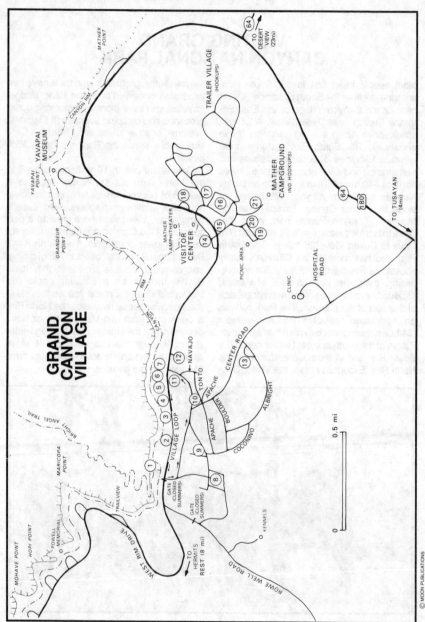

GRAND CANYON VILLAGE

© MOON PUBLICATIONS

Adventurous travelers on the North Rim willing to tackle 61 miles (one way) of dirt road can head over to **Toroweap Overlook,** a 3½-hour drive from the Bright Angel Point area. You'll be perched a dizzying 3,000 feet directly above the Colorado River at one of the Canyon's most spectacular viewpoints. Don't expect any facilities other than the road to get you here (passable by cars in good weather) and an outhouse or two. Obtain a backcountry camping permit beforehand and bring all supplies, including water. Low elevations (4,500-5,000 feet) allow access most of the year; check road conditions first with a ranger; tel. 638-7888. Toroweap lies 91 river miles downstream from the developed areas of the Park; see pp. 54-56 for directions to drive here.

## SOUTH RIM SIGHTS

**Mather Point**
The first overlook you'll reach when coming from the south, Mather Point is located where

the south entrance road curves west to Grand Canyon Village. Stephen Mather served as the National Park Service's first director and was in office when the Grand Canyon joined the park system on Feb. 26, 1919. Below Mather Point (elev. 7,120 feet) lie Pipe Creek Canyon, the Inner Gorge of the Colorado River, and countless buttes, temples, and points eroded from the rims.

**Visitor Center**
Dioramas and other exhibits introduce you to the Park's early Indian residents, miners, explorers, early tourists, and natural history. A riverboat display in the courtyard shows the variety of craft that have run the Colorado. Oldest is a 1909 cataract boat used by the Stone Expedition, which put in at Green River, Wyoming, on Sept. 12, 1909, and came out 37 days and 1,300 miles later at Needles, California. Short movies and slide presentations illustrate the Park and suggest ways to see it. A bulletin board in the lobby lists ranger-guided rim walks, Canyon talks, and evening presentations. A ranger at the desk will answer your questions and give out maps and brochures. A bookstore offers a good selection of Canyon-related books, posters, topo maps, slides, videos, and postcards. The Visitor Center is open daily 8:00 a.m.- 5 p.m., extended in summer; tel. 638-7888 (automated switchboard with recording of scheduled programs and other park information), 638-7772/7804 (TDD information for hearing-impaired people). It's located on the east side of Grand Canyon Village, 3 miles in from the South Entrance Station.

**Yavapai Museum**
Set on the brink of the Canyon, this geologic museum illustrates the long history of the rock layers revealed below. Panels identify the many buttes, temples, points, and tributary canyons seen through the windows. Rock samples let you compare formations from the ancient Vishnu Schist of the Inner Gorge to the youngest rocks on the rim. Fossils show life as ancient as the one-billion-year-old algae in Bass Limestone. A "geologic clock" graphically ticks off the time

## GRAND CANYON VILLAGE

1. Bright Angel Trailhead; Kolb Studio
2. Bright Angel Lodge and Restaurant
3. Thunderbird Lodge
4. Kachina Lodge
5. El Tovar Hotel and Restaurant
6. Hopi House (souvenirs)
7. Verkamp's (souvenirs)
8. Maswik Lodge and Cafeteria
9. Community Building
   (Over the Edge Theatres)
10. ranger office
11. historic railroad station
12. public garage
13. Albright Training Center
14. Shrine of the Ages
15. RV dump station
16. Mather Center (store, post office, bank)
17. Yavapai Lodge and Cafeteria
18. service station
19. Backcountry Reservations Office (BRO)
20. Camper Services (showers, laundromat)
21. Sage Loop Campfire Circle

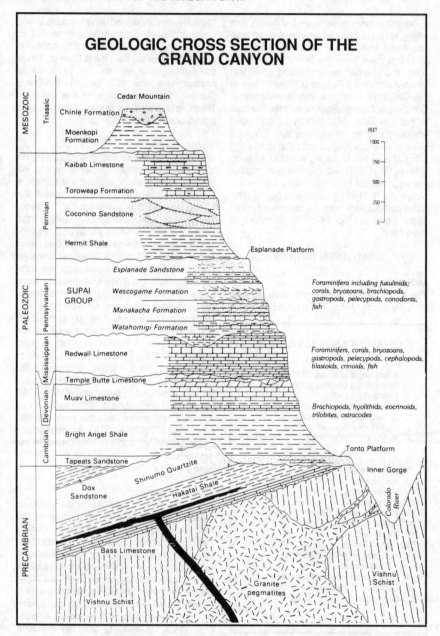

# GEOLOGIC CROSS SECTION OF THE GRAND CANYON

| | | |
|---|---|---|
| MESOZOIC | Triassic | Cedar Mountain |
| | | Chinle Formation |
| | | Moenkopi Formation |
| | Permian | Kaibab Limestone |
| | | Toroweap Formation |
| | | Coconino Sandstone |
| | | Hermit Shale |
| PALEOZOIC | Pennsylvanian | SUPAI GROUP: Esplanade Sandstone, Wescogame Formation, Manakacha Formation, Watahomigi Formation |
| | Mississippian | Redwall Limestone |
| | Devonian | Temple Butte Limestone |
| | Cambrian | Muav Limestone |
| | | Bright Angel Shale |
| | | Tapeats Sandstone |
| PRECAMBRIAN | | Dox Sandstone, Shinumo Quartzite, Hakatai Shale, Bass Limestone, Vishnu Schist, Granite pegmatites |

FEET
1000
750
500
250
0

Esplanade Platform

*Foraminifera including fusulinids; corals, bryozoans, brachiopods, gastropods, pelecypods, conodonts, fish*

*Foraminifers, corals, bryozoans, gastropods, pelecypods, cephalopods, blastoids, crinoids, fish*

*Brachiopods, hyolithids, eocrinoids, trilobites, ostracodes*

Tonto Platform

Inner Gorge

Colorado River

Vishnu Schist

Edwin D. McKee, U.S. Geological Survey Professional Paper 1173; G.P.O. 1982

*view from
South Rim*

required to form the rock layers revealed by the Colorado River. The clock takes 3 minutes to complete a cycle, with each "tick" representing 11 million years. Exhibits present both Indian legends and scientific versions of the Canyon's formation. Educational video programs entertain the kids. Open daily 9 a.m.-5 p.m., extended in summer. Books, maps, slides, videos, and postcards can be purchased. Yavapai Museum is located 0.8 mile northeast of the Visitor Center by road or one mile by foot trail.

## South Rim Nature Trail
People of all ages can enjoy a walk along this easy trail. The 3.5-mile section between the Yavapai Museum past the El Tovar Hotel to Maricopa Point is paved and nearly level. Pick up biology and geology brochures (\$.25 each) for the self-guiding trail at the Visitor Center, Yavapai Museum, or outside Verkamp's Curios (next to El Tovar Hotel). Start anywhere along the way as there are no keyed trail numbers. You'll enjoy views from many different vantage points. The South Rim Trail continues west 5 miles as a dirt path to Hermit's Rest, at the end of West Rim Drive. Another unpaved segment heads east

0.5 mile from Yavapai Museum to Mather Point. The free Canyon shuttle bus (operates in summer, about every 15 min.) stops at eight places near the South Rim Trail.

## West Rim Drive
The Fred Harvey Company built this 8-mile-long road from Grand Canyon Village to Hermit's Rest in 1912. Pullouts along the way allow stopping to enjoy the views. Your map will help to pick out Canyon features: the Bright Angel Trail switchbacking down to the grove of trees at Indian Gardens; Plateau Point at the end of a short trail from Indian Gardens; the long, straight Bright Angel Canyon on the far side of the river; the many majestic temples rising to the north and east; and rapids of the Colorado River. Hermit's Rest (restrooms, gift shop, and drinking water) marks the westernmost viewpoint and end of the drive. During summer a free shuttle bus runs the length of the drive; other times you can take your own vehicle. Bicyclists enjoy this drive too, and they aren't affected by the summer ban on cars.

If you've walked to Hermit's Rest on the South Rim Trail, you'll probably want to rest too. Louis Boucher, the Hermit, came to the

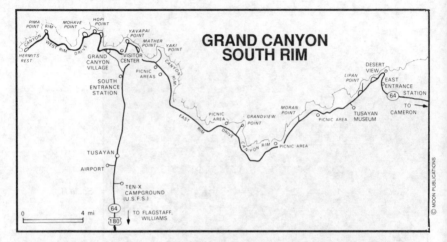

© MOON PUBLICATIONS

Canyon in 1891 and stayed 21 years; he lived at Dripping Springs and built the Boucher Trail to his mining claims in Boucher Canyon. Hermit Trail, built by the Fred Harvey Company after Louis Boucher had departed, begins just beyond Hermit's Rest at the end of a gravel road. The trail descends to the Tonto Trail and on to the river at Hermit Rapids. Visitors taking this trail between 1912 and 1930 could stay at a tourist camp located partway down on the Tonto Platform; only foundations remain today. A branch in the upper trail goes to Dripping Springs and Boucher Canyon.

### East Rim Drive

Outstanding overlooks line this 26-mile drive between Grand Canyon Village and Desert View. Each has its own character and is worth a stop, but many people consider the aptly named Grandview Point one of the best. It's 12 miles east of Grand Canyon Village (14 miles before Desert View), then 0.8 mile north. Sweeping panoramas take in much of the Grand Canyon from this commanding site above Horseshoe Mesa. The vastness and intricacies of the Canyon show themselves especially well here. Other major viewpoints on the East Rim Drive include Yaki Point, Moran Point, Lipan Point, and Desert View. At Lipan, by looking both up- and down-

canyon, you can see the entire geologic sequence that makes up the Canyon. Hiking trails into the Canyon leave from or near each of these overlooks too (see "Inner Canyon Hiking," p. 56).

### Tusayan Ruin

Prehistoric Anasazi Indians built this pueblo about A.D. 1185. Archaeologists who excavated the site in 1930 named it "Tusayan," a Spanish term used for Hopi Indian territory. A small museum introduces the Anasazi culture with artifacts and models of dwellings; exhibits describe modern tribes of the region too. Outside, a short, self-guided trail leads to the plaza and ruins of living quarters, storage rooms, and two kivas. A leaflet (pick up at museum, $.25) describes how the Anasazi farmed and obtained some of their wild foods. Perhaps 30 people lived here, contending with poor soil, low rainfall, and scarce drinking water. After staying 15-20 years they moved on. The museum is open daily 8 a.m.-6 p.m. in summer (8 a.m.-5 p.m. in winter). It's on the East Rim Drive, 23 miles east of Grand Canyon Village and 3 miles west of Desert View.

### Desert View

This overlook offers a stunning view at the end of the East Rim Drive. Although the surrounding pinyon pines and junipers suggest a lower elevation, this is the highest viewpoint on the South Rim (elev. 7,500 feet). To the east lies the multihued Painted Desert that gave the viewpoint its name. Below, to the north, the Colorado River flows out of Marble Canyon, then curves west. The strange-looking Desert View Watchtower incorporates design elements from both prehistoric and modern Indian tribes of the region. The Fred Harvey Company built the 70-foot structure in 1932, using stone around a steel frame. The interior ($.25 admission) contains reproductions of a Hopi altar, wall paintings, and petroglyphs; stairs lead to windows at the top. Desert View has a snack bar, general store, service station, and campground; the campground and some services close in winter. A short nature trail loops around the point. Energetic hikers can head cross-country to Zuni and Papago points off the East Rim Drive, or take the long 12-mile roundtrip route to Comanche Point north of Desert View; ask a ranger at Desert View for directions. Eastward from Desert View, Highway AZ 64 continues for 17 miles to an overlook of the Little

Colorado River Gorge on the Navajo Indian Reservation, then another 15 miles to Cameron on US 89.

## Cape Solitude

Adventurous drivers with *high-clearance 4WD vehicles ONLY* can bump their way north from Desert View about 15 miles to Cape Solitude, a memorable overlook high above the confluence of the Colorado and Little Colorado rivers. The road is very rough and steep in places, but you'll be far from the crowds. Experienced mountain bicyclists can do this trip too. Anyone going to Cape Solitude should be self-sufficient and have water and emergency supplies, because rangers seldom patrol this road; check with a ranger before heading out. You can camp near Cape Solitude with a permit from the Backcountry Reservations Office in Grand Canyon Village. Topographic maps show the back roads to the Cape and other destinations, such as Cedar Mountain. From Desert View, turn north on the road signed "District Ranger Office" between the campground turnoff and the East Entrance Station.

*Tusayan Ruin*

## SOUTH RIM ACCOMMODATIONS

There's too much at the Grand Canyon to see in one day! In Grand Canyon Village you can stay right on the rim at Bright Angel Lodge, Thunderbird Lodge, Kachina Lodge, or El Tovar Hotel. Other lodges lie back in the woods. The town of Tusayan, just outside the Park (9 miles south of Grand Canyon Village), has additional places to stay. Reservations are essential in the busy summer season and a good idea the rest of the year.

### Youth Hostel
The **Grand Canyon International Youth Hostel** has CLOSED, unfortunately. Check with other hostels for news about a possible new one here.

### Grand Canyon Village
**Grand Canyon National Park Lodges** operates all the lodges here, and Moqui Lodge just outside the South Entrance Station. Make reservations at Box 699, Grand Canyon, AZ 86023; tel. 638-2401 (advance reservations) or 638-2631 (same-day reservations).

One of the grand old hotels of the West, **El Tovar** has offered the finest accommodations and food at the Canyon since 1905. This national historic landmark offers 14 styles of rooms with all the modern conveniences, yet it keeps an old-fashioned ambience. Many rooms have canyon views; rates run $101.28-233.16 s or d. **Kachina** and **Thunderbird** lodges, also on the rim, offer deluxe modern rooms; $85.46 or $91.79 s or d. The historic **Bright Angel Lodge** sits on the rim a short distance from the Bright Angel trailhead. The lobby, patio, restaurant, and lounge make popular gathering spots for hikers and other visitors. Rates for cabins are $53.81-190.96 s or d; rooms in the lodge cost $33.76-39.04 s or d (shower down hall) and $46.42 (with bath). The Bright Angel History Room displays memorabilia from early tourist days and a "geological fireplace" in which Canyon rocks have been laid, floor to ceiling,

in their proper stratigraphic sequence. The Transportation Desk in the lobby organizes scheduled bus service, bus and air tours, mule trips, and accommodations at Phantom Ranch (bottom of Canyon). **Maswik Lodge,** 2 blocks south of Bright Angel Lodge, has economy sections ($41.15 or $47.48 s or d), deluxe units ($55.92 or $89.68 s or d), and a cafeteria. **Yavapai Lodge's** modern rooms cost $67.52 or $78.07 s or d; there's also a cafeteria; closed Nov.-Feb., except open holidays; located near the Visitor Center, one mile east of Bright Angel Lodge.

### Tusayan
**Moqui Lodge,** just outside the South Entrance Station and one mile north of Tusayan, offers rooms at $65.41 s or d from March 16 to Oct. 31, then reduced rates off-season; closed Jan. and Feb.; tel. 638-2401 (advance reservations), 638-2424 (same-day reservations). The lodge has a restaurant, an information desk from which tours and horseback riding can be arranged, a gift shop, and a service station. **Quality Inn-Grand Canyon,** 9 miles south from Grand Canyon Village in Tusayan, is open all year with a restaurant, swimming pool, jacuzzi, and gift shop; $77-87.57 s or d from April 7 to Oct. 31; $51.70-65.41 s or d in winter; tel. 638-2673. **Seven Mile Lodge** has rooms at $61.19 s, $65.41 d in summer and $33.76 s, $40.09 d in winter; tel. 638-2291. The nearby **Grand Canyon Squire Inn** (Best Western) features deluxe rooms at $89.68 s or d from May 1 to Oct. 31 and during Christmas holidays, then $58-73.85 s or d the rest of the year; amenities include a restaurant, swimming pool, jacuzzi, sauna, exercise room, tennis courts, bowling, and gift shop; tel. 638-2681.

### Valle
Highways US 180 from Flagstaff and AZ 64 from Williams meet at this road junction 24 miles south of Grand Canyon Village. Stay at **Grand Canyon Inn,** $46.80-68.25 in summer and reduced rates off-season; closed Jan. and Feb.; tel. 635-9203. The Inn's restaurant serves breakfast, lunch, and dinner daily.

## SOUTH RIM CAMPGROUNDS

Campgrounds also tend to be crowded in summer. If you don't have a reservation, it's recommended that you arrive before noon to look for a site. Rangers enforce the "no camping outside designated sites" policy with a stiff fine. Backpackers inside the Canyon need free permits from the Backcountry Reservations Office (see "Inner Canyon Hiking," p. 56). Dispersed camping in the Kaibab National Forest just south of the Park is another possibility; just don't camp along the highways. The Forest Service office (across from Moqui Lodge) near Tusayan can make suggestions; the Kaibab Forest map shows the back roads.

### Inside The Park
**Mather Campground** is conveniently located south of the Visitor Center in Grand Canyon Village; tel. 638-7888. Open early April to end of Nov., though one loop stays open in winter; sites have drinking water but no hookups; $10/night ($5 w/Golden Age pass). Backpackers can camp at a walk-in area for $1/person; no reservations needed. Showers, laundromat, and ice are available for a small charge at **Camper Services,** adjacent to the campground. Reservations can be made in advance up to 8 weeks (56 days) for family sites and 12 weeks (84 days) for group sites from March to Nov. through Ticketron (Box 62429, Virginia Beach, VA 23462) or at any Ticketron outlet. Allow at least 2 weeks to make reservations by mail. The Ticketron Automated Information Center can be reached at tel. (212) 399-4444. **Trailer Village,** just east of Mather Campground, offers RV sites for $16.88 w/hookups all year; make reservations with Grand Canyon National Park Lodges (Box 699, Grand Canyon, AZ 86023); tel. 638-2401 (advance reservations), 638-2631 (same-day reserva-

tions). **Desert View Campground,** near the East Entrance Station (26 miles east of Grand Canyon Village), has sites with drinking water but no hookups; open mid-May to end of Sept.; $6; no reservations taken.

### Outside The Park
**Grand Canyon Camper Village** in Tusayan (9 miles south of Grand Canyon Village) has sites for tents and RVs, $11.55 ($16.80 w/hookups) and tipi tent accommodation (warmer months only; $14.70); has coin showers; stores and restaurants are nearby; Box 490, Grand Canyon, AZ 86023; tel. 638-2887. **Ten X Campground** has drinking water but no hookups; open May 1 to Oct. 31; $7; a half-mile nature trail provides an introduction to the natural history of the area; from Tusayan go south 3 miles to the turnoff (between Mileposts 233 and 234), then east 0.25 mile; tel. 638-2443. **Flintstone Bedrock City** campsites in Valle cost $10.50 for tents or RVs ($14.17 w/hookups); has coin showers, store, snack bar, and theme park; open mid-April to end of Oct.; self-contained vehicles can park in winter; tel. 635-2600.

## SOUTH RIM FOOD

### Grand Canyon Village Area
**El Tovar Hotel** offers elegant dining daily for breakfast, lunch, and dinner (mod. to exp.); tel. 638-2631 (dinner reservations recommended). **Bright Angel Lodge** has two places at which to eat: an informal restaurant serving breakfast, lunch, and dinner daily (mod.) and the **Arizona Steakhouse,** which serves steaks, fish, chicken, and ribs for dinner daily (mod.); tel. 638-2631. **Maswik Lodge,** 2 blocks south of Bright Angel Lodge, has a large cafeteria open daily for breakfast, lunch, and dinner. **Yavapai Lodge,** near the Visitor Center, has a smaller cafeteria open daily for breakfast, lunch, and dinner from March to Oct. and winter holidays. **Babbitt's**

Store (near the Visitor Center) has a deli counter and tables. **Yavapai Fast Food** in Yavapai Lodge is open April to October. **Bright Angel Fountain** serves ice cream and other snacks on the Canyon rim behind Bright Angel Lodge; open about May to September. Buy groceries at **Babbitt's Stores,** located in Grand Canyon Village, Desert View, and Tusayan.

## Tusayan

**Moqui Lodge** has a Mexican-American restaurant; open daily for breakfast and dinner only; closed Jan. and Feb.; tel. 638-2424. You'll also find restaurants at the **Quality Inn-Grand Canyon** (tel. 638-2673) and **Grand Canyon Squire Inn** (tel. 638-2681). The **Steak House** features mesquite-grilled steaks and other fare; open daily for dinner. **We Cook Pizza, Etc.** offers Italian sandwiches and dinners as well as pizza; open daily for lunch and dinner; tel. 638-2278. There's a **McDonald's** in town too, but don't expect it to have the same prices as at home; the staff will happily give you a handout explaining why their costs are so high.

## SOUTH RIM SERVICES

### Entertainment

The **Grand Canyon IMAX Theatre** in Tusayan shows an impressive movie, *The Grand Canyon—The Hidden Secrets* on a giant screen with six-track stereo sound. The 34-minute presentation briefly covers history, wildlife, river-running, flying, and scenic viewpoints of the Canyon. Showings take place hourly 8:30 a.m.-8:30 p.m. every day (reduced hours in winter); $6 adult, $4 children 3-11; tel. 638-2468/2203.

**Over the Edge Theatres** presents a dazzling multimedia show about the Canyon's history and beauty; the half-hour show takes place in the Community Building in Grand Canyon Village (see map); open daily 9 a.m.-9 p.m. in summer, then 10 a.m.-3 p.m. and 5-8 p.m. in winter; $4 adult, $2 children age 8-15; tel. 638-2224/2229. For **night life** in Grand Canyon Village, try the El Tovar's

cocktail lounge (often has piano music), Bright Angel Lodge's cocktail lounge (varied live music many evenings), Maswik Lodge's main lounge (varied live music many evenings) or sports lounge (has big-screen TV), and Yavapai Lodge's lounge (dancing with live bands or DJ; open March to Oct.). Rangers present evening programs year-round; check the bulletin board at the Visitor Center to find out what's on and where.

### Shopping

The **Visitor Center** has a good bookstore that sells topo maps. **Babbitt's** stores—at Mather Center (south of the Visitor Center), Desert View, and Tusayan—have groceries, camping and hiking supplies, clothing, books, maps, and souvenirs. **Grand Canyon Trail Guides,** located just west of Mather Campground, offers camping and hiking gear for sale and rent and does repairs; closed in winter. **Lookout Studio,** on the rim near Bright Angel Lodge, sells beautiful rock, mineral, and fossil specimens. Indian crafts, postcards, and other souvenirs can be purchased at **El Tovar Hotel, Bright Angel Lodge, Hopi House, Verkamp's Curio, Hermit's Rest, Desert View Lookout Tower,** and **Gallery at the Grand Canyon** (Tusayan).

### Other Services

**Bank** and **post office** are south across the road from the Visitor Center; the bank has an ATM and can cash traveler's checks, exchange foreign currency, do wire transfers, and give cash advances on Visa and MasterCard, but it cannot cash out-of-town checks. **Grand Canyon Medical Clinic** offers medical and dental services; tel. 638-2551; if there's an emergency after hours, call 638-2477. A **pharmacy** is here too; tel. 638-2460 (see map for location). For an ambulance, call 638-2477 or 638-7888. National Park Service staff provide the handicapped with wheelchairs, an access information booklet, Braille literature, sign-language interpreter, and other help; ask at the Visitor Center or write ahead to the Park.

**Theft** has become a problem at the Canyon—be sure to keep valuables hidden or take them with you. Park rangers patrol the Park, serving as law enforcement officers and firemen; see them if you have difficulties. **Pets** won't be welcomed in the lodges or permitted on the inner-canyon trails, but they can stay in the kennels at Grand Canyon Village (see map). **Camper Services,** next to Mather Campground, has a laundromat and showers—a welcome sight to any traveler who's been a long time on the road or trail.

## SOUTH RIM INFORMATION

The **Visitor Center** has exhibits, slide shows, movies, bookshop, bulletin board of scheduled events, and an information desk; open daily 8 a.m.-5 p.m., extended in summer; tel. 638-7888 (automated switchboard with recordings of activities and programs); located on the east side of Grand Canyon Village, 3 miles north of the South Entrance Station. Stop at the **Backcountry Reservations Office,** south of the Visitor Center, for hiking information and backcountry camping permits (dayhikers don't need a permit); open daily 7 a.m.-noon and 3-5 p.m. in summer, then 8 a.m.-noon and 3-5 p.m. the rest of the year; tel. 638-7888 (call after 11 a.m. to speak with someone in person). For a **weather forecast** and winter road conditions, call 638-7888. **Hearing-impaired** people can use the TDD number for park information, 638-7772/7804. Pick up a copy of *The Guide* newspaper for the latest visitor information. Park address is Box 129, Grand Canyon, AZ 86023. You can reach many information recordings and all of the park offices through the **automated switchboard;** tel. 638-7888.

The **Kaibab National Forest,** though little known in the shadow of Grand Canyon National Park, offers both developed and primitive camping. Stop at the **Tusayan Ranger Station** for a map and information. Staff can also give directions for hiking the Red Butte Trail, a 2.5-mile roundtrip climb up the prominent butte 12 miles south of Tusayan, and the 10-mile (one-way) Coconino Rim Trail, a section of the Arizona Trail just south of the Park. The office is in the

Tusayan Administrative Site, across from Moqui Lodge just outside the South Entrance Station; Box 3088, Grand Canyon, AZ 86023; open Mon.-Fri. 8 a.m.-noon and 12:30-4:30 p.m.; tel. 638-2443.

## SOUTH RIM TOURS

### Mule Rides
Sure-footed mules have carried prospectors and tourists in and out of the Canyon for more than a century. The large animals, a crossbreed of female horses and male donkeys, depart daily all year for day and overnight trips. Although easier than hiking, a mule ride should still be considered strenuous—you need to be able to sit in the saddle for long hours and control your mount. Day trips go down the Bright Angel Trail to Indian Gardens

*visitors at head of Bright Angel Trail in early 1900s; Teddy Roosevelt is in foreground*

and out to Plateau Point, a spectacular overlook directly above the river; the 12-mile, 7-hour roundtrip costs $64. On the overnight trip you follow the Bright Angel Trail all the way to the river, cross a suspension bridge to Phantom Ranch, spend the night in a cabin, then come out the next day via the South Kaibab Trail; $206 ($359/two, $163 each additional person) including meals and cabin. Three-day/two-night trips offered Dec.-Feb. cost $267 ($468/two, $217 each additional person).

All of these trips are definitely not for those afraid of heights; if you're in doubt, Fred Harvey Movies (Box 709, Grand Canyon, AZ 86023) will send a color Super-8 movie or videotape ($16 postpaid) showing what it's like in the saddle. Requirements for riders (enforced!) include good health, weight under 200 lbs. (91 kg), fluency in English, height over 4 feet 7 inches (140 cm), and ability to mount and dismount without assistance. No pregnant women are allowed. A hat (tied under chin), long pants and a long-sleeved shirt, and sturdy shoes (no open-toed footwear) should be worn. Don't bring bags, purses, or backpacks, but you can carry a canteen and a camera or binoculars. Reservations should be made 9-12 months in advance for summer and holidays. Also be sure to claim your reservation at least one hour before departure. Without a reservation, there's a chance of getting on by signing up for the waiting list, especially off-season; register by 10 a.m. the day before you want to go. Mules will also carry hikers' overnight gear to Phantom Ranch, $35 in, $25 out (30 lb. limit). For information, reservations, and standbys see the Bright Angel Transportation Desk (tel. 638-2631) or contact Grand Canyon National Park Lodges, Reservations Dept., Box 699, Grand Canyon, AZ 86023; tel. 638-2401 (advance reservations).

## Horse Rides

**Apache Stables** offers short rides through the Kaibab National Forest ($15/one hour, $22.50/2 hours), 4-hour trips to the South Rim ($40), a cowboy breakfast ride, and other excursions. Season lasts April to mid-Nov., depending on weather. Make reservations at Moqui Lodge (one mile north of Tusayan); tel. 638-2424.

## Bus Tours

The **Fred Harvey Transportation Co.** will show you the sights of the South Rim with narration about the Canyon's history, geology, and wildlife. Hermit's Rest Tour visits viewpoints of the West Rim Drive (2 hours; $10). Desert View Tour travels along the East Rim Drive (3¼ hours; $16, or $18 including Hermits Rest Tour). Sunset Tour goes over to Yaki Point (1½ hours; $6.50; summer only). Ancient Ones Tour takes in the lands of prehistoric Indians on East Rim Drive, Little Colorado River Canyon, Wupatki, Sunset Crater, Walnut Canyon, and Museum of Northern Arizona (11 hours; $60). Monument Valley Expedition visits the striking landscape of buttes and sand dunes on the Navajo Indian Reservation (11-13 hours; $65). A River Raft Excursion runs the smooth-flowing Colorado River in Marble Canyon, near Lees Ferry; stops on the drive there take in highlights of the East Rim Drive and Navajo Indian Reservation (12 hours; $65; late May to early Nov.). Tours in the Park leave daily (twice a day in summer for the Hermit's Rest and Desert View tours); check departure days for tours

*Vishnu Temple, from North Rim*

outside the Park. Get tickets at Bright Angel, Maswik, or Yavapai Lodge transportation desks; children under 16 (under 12 for tours out of Park) go at half price. No reservations needed, though you could make them for the Ancient Ones, Monument Valley, and River Raft tours; Box 699, Grand Canyon, AZ 86023; tel. 638-2401.

**Air Tours**
Flights over the Canyon provide breathtaking views and offer a look at some of the Park's remote corners. About 40 scenic-flight companies operate helicopters or fixed-wing aircraft here. The 50,000-plus flights a year sometimes detract from the wilderness experience of backcountry users—Tusayan's airport is the third busiest in the state. However, restrictions on flight routes and elevations help minimize the noise. Scenic flights depart all year from Tusayan Airport, while Grand Canyon Helicopters and Kenai Helicopters leave right from the village of

Tusayan. Transport from hotels to terminals is available. Rates listed are per adult; children under 12 usually fly at a discount.

**Grand Canyon Airlines** started flying here in 1927 with Ford Trimotors. Today they use high-wing, twin-engine planes on 45- to 50-minute flights over both rims of the Canyon ($50); tel. 638-2407 or (800) 528-2413 out of state. **Air Grand Canyon's** high-wing Cessnas offer three loops: a 30- to 40-minute flight over the Canyon ($45), a 50- to 60-minute trip over the eastern Canyon ($60), and a 90- to 100-minute grand tour of both Havasu and Grand canyons ($115); tel. 638-2686 or (800) 247-4726. **Windrock Air Tours** flies high-wing Cessnas to many destinations; Grand Canyon trips range from 35 minutes ($45) over the main gorge to 90 minutes ($110) over both east and west sections of the Canyon; other flights go to Monument Valley, Bryce Canyon, Zion, Lake Powell, Sedona, Prescott, Bullhead City, and Phoenix; tel. 638-9591/9570.

**Grand Canyon Helicopters** flies across the Canyon (30 minutes; $75); over the eastern Grand Canyon (50 minutes; $150); and to Havasu and Grand canyons (60 minutes; $150); you can also land at Supai village in Havasu Canyon and visit the waterfalls ($387), or spend the night ($412); tel. 638-2419, 252-1706 in Phoenix, or (800) 528-2418 out of state. **Kenai Helicopters** heads across the Canyon (25-30 minutes; $75) and over the eastern Grand Canyon (55-60 minutes; $150); closed Dec. 1-Feb. 15; tel. 638-2412. **AirStar Helicopters** will take you across the Canyon (25-30 minutes; $75), around the eastern Grand Canyon (50-60 minutes; $147), and on sunrise and sunset flights (35-40 minutes; $98) from the airport; tel. 638-2622.

## SOUTH RIM TRANSPORT

### Shuttle Services

The Park Service runs two free shuttle services from late spring to early autumn to reduce traffic congestion. The **Village Loop Shuttle** connects the Visitor Center, Yavapai Museum, campgrounds, lodges, shops, and offices of Grand Canyon Village; service operates daily every 15-20 minutes from early morning to late at night. The **West Rim Drive Shuttle** leaves from the road junction in front of Bright Angel Lodge and goes to Hermit's Rest, with stops at eight overlooks; operates daily every 15 minutes from about 7:30 a.m. to 6:45 p.m. Two "Hiker's Specials" leave in the morning from the Backcountry Reservations Office for the South Kaibab trailhead. (In the off-season, Fred Harvey Co. runs a shuttle to the South Kaibab trailhead for a charge.) **Tusayan-Grand Canyon Shuttle** connects Bright Angel Lodge and other places in Grand Canyon Village with Tusayan and the airport all year (small charge); tel. 638-2475. **Trans Canyon** offers daily roundtrip van service to the North Rim May 21-Oct. 23; Box 348, Grand Canyon, AZ 86023; tel. 638-2820.

### Auto Rentals And Taxi

Rent cars from **Budget** (tel. 638-9360) or **Dollar Rent A Car** (tel. 638-2625), both at Grand Canyon Airport. For a taxi, call **Fred Harvey Transportation Dispatch** at 638-2822.

### Bus

**Nava-Hopi** buses go to Flagstaff (three times daily in summer and twice daily the rest of the year); fares are $11.75 one way, $22.30 roundtrip, or $10.70 roundtrip w/bus pass. See the Bright Angel Lodge Transportation Desk for schedules and tickets; no reservations needed.

### Train

Passenger trains rolled into the railroad station at the Grand Canyon from 1901 to 1968. Twenty-one years later, in 1989, the **Grand Canyon Railway's** steam trains again began to provide service from downtown Williams to the historic log depot in Grand Canyon Village. Trains are scheduled once or twice daily except in winter, when they run on some holiday weekends only. Roundtrip fares are $41.96 adult ($2 less if you have a park pass), $22.68 children; tel. (800) THE-TRAIN.

### Air

Scheduled services of **America West** connect the Grand Canyon Airport twice daily with Flagstaff ($29-47 one way), Phoenix ($65-79 one way or $98 roundtrip), and Las Vegas ($29-99 one way); tel. 638-9544 or (800) 247-5692. **Scenic Airlines** and **Air Nevada** also fly to Las Vegas. Scenic Airlines offers 5-14 flights out daily, $109 one way, $169 roundtrip; a "K-class" fare of $59 one way is offered on the first flights out and the last in; make reservations at least 2 weeks ahead in summer and 2 days in winter; tel. 638-2436 or 800-634-6801. Air Nevada has a similar service with 2-6 flights daily, $109 one way, $149 roundtrip, and $49 K-class; tel. 638-2441 or (800) 634-6377. Flights between Las Vegas and the Grand Canyon often go over the Canyon—an added bonus.

## NORTH RIM SIGHTS

"Two rims, two worlds"—the North Rim offers an experience very different from that of the South Rim. Elevations 1,000-1,500 feet higher result in lower temperatures and nearly 60% more precipitation. Rain and snowmelt over time have cut deeply into the North Rim: it is now about twice as far removed from the Colorado River as the South Rim. Dramatic vistas from the north inspired early explorers to chose names like Point Sublime, Cape Royal, Angel's Window, and Point Imperial. Even away from the viewpoints, the North Rim has great beauty. Spruce, fir, pine, and aspen forests thrive in the cool air. Wildflowers bloom in blazes of color in the meadows and along the roadsides.

Visitor facilities and major trailheads are located near Bright Angel Point, a 45-mile drive south from Jacob Lake in the far north of Arizona. The road to Bright Angel Point opens in mid-May, then closes after the first big winter storm, any time from early Oct. to the end of November.

### Bright Angel Point

Park at the end of the highway, near Grand Canyon Lodge, and follow the paved foot trail to the tip of Bright Angel Point, an easy half-mile roundtrip walk. Roaring Springs Canyon on the left and Transept Canyon on the right join the long Bright Angel Canyon below. John Wesley Powell's expedition camped at the bottom of this canyon and gave the name Bright Angel Creek to its crystal-clear waters. Listen for Roaring Springs far below on the left, and look to see where the springs shoot out of the cliff. A pumping station at their base generates electricity and supplies drinking water to both North and South rims. Roaring Springs makes a good dayhike or muleback-ride destination via the North Kaibab Trail (see "Inner Canyon Hiking," pp. 60-61). Transept Canyon, which usually has only a small flow, can be entered from the North Kaibab Trail; it's best done on an overnight trip. Up on top, Transept Trail (1.5 miles one way) winds along the canyon rim between Grand Canyon Lodge and the campground.

### Cape Royal Scenic Drive

Paved roads lead to some of the North Rim's

*Mt. Hayden, from Point Imperial*

most spectacular viewpoints. **Point Imperial** (elev. 8,803 feet) offers the highest vantage point from either rim. Views encompass impressive geology in the Park's eastern end. You can see Nankoweap Creek below, Vermilion Cliffs on the horizon to the north, rounded Navajo Mountain on the horizon in Utah to the northeast, Painted Desert to the east, and the Little Colorado River Canyon across to the southeast. Hikers can descend to Nankoweap Creek and the Colorado River on the difficult Nankoweap Trail (see "Inner Canyon Hiking," p. 56); the trailhead is northeast of here near Saddle Mountain. Point Imperial is 11 miles from Grand Canyon Lodge; go north 3 miles from the lodge, turn right 5.3 miles on Cape Royal Drive, then left 2.7 miles to the parking area.

Cape Royal Drive continues beyond the Point Imperial turnoff past **Vista Encantadora, Walhalla Overlook,** and other viewpoints to a parking area just before **Cape Royal.** Total driving distance from Grand Canyon Lodge is 23 miles one way. A trail continues south 0.6 mile from the parking lot to Cape Royal. On the way you'll see **Angel's Window,** a massive natural arch. A short side trail actually goes on top of the arch. **Cape Royal** is the southernmost viewpoint of the North Rim in this part of the Grand Canyon: Freya Castle lies to the southeast, nearby Vishnu Temple and Creek and distant San Francisco Peaks are to the south, and a branch of Clear Creek Canyon and flat-topped Wotans Throne lie to the southwest.

A short hike on **Cliff Spring Trail** leads through some pretty scenery. The one-mile roundtrip trail descends into a forested ravine, passes a small Indian ruin, and goes under an overhang to the spring. The canyon walls open up impressively as you near the spring. It's possible to continue on a rougher trail another half mile for more canyon views. Cliff Spring Trail begins from Angel's Window Overlook, a small pullout on a curve of Cape Royal Drive, 0.9 mile past Walhalla Overlook and 0.5 mile before road's end.

**Point Sublime**

A 17-mile dirt road, negotiable only by high-clearance vehicles, goes to this overlook and picnic area west of Bright Angel Point. The way is bumpy and not always passable; check at the North Rim Entrance Station or the Information Desk at Grand Canyon Lodge. Views take in an impressive amount of Canyon, truly sublime. Tiyo Point provides another perspective between Bright Angel Point and Point Sublime; the Tiyo Point road turns south from the Point Sublime road. You can camp with a permit from the North Rim Backcountry Reservations Office, located in the ranger station. The drive to Point Sublime or Tiyo Point begins 2.7 miles north of Grand Canyon Lodge; turn west onto the road signed "Widforss Point trailhead."

**East Rim View**

Expansive vistas across the Marble Canyon area greet visitors at this overlook on the east edge of the Kaibab Plateau. The site (elev. 8,800 feet) is on Kaibab National Forest land several miles north of Grand Canyon National Park. From the AZ 67 turnoff in De

Motte Park, 0.8 mile south of the North Rim Country Store, turn east 5 miles on Forest Route 611 and follow signs. Cars can easily travel the gravel roads. East Rim View is a great spot to watch sunrises and the colors reflected off the distant Vermilion Cliffs and Painted Desert at sunset. Good places for primitive camping can be found in the conifer and aspen forests nearby; the Forest Service has a pair of outhouses but no other facilities. No permit or fee is needed to camp. Hikers can do some of the Arizona Trail from here or descend into North Canyon in the Saddle Mountain Wilderness.

Many other viewpoints, scenic drives, and trails can be visited in the Kaibab National Forest; visit the offices in Jacob Lake or Fredonia. Either office or the Information Desk in the Grand Canyon Lodge should have the forest map and *Recreation Opportunity Guide* for the North Kaibab Ranger District.

### Widforss Trail
Gently rolling terrain, fine canyon views, and a variety of forest types attract hikers. From the edge of a meadow, the trail climbs a bit, skirts the head of Transept Canyon, then runs across a plateau covered by ponderosas to an overlook near Widforss Point. The trail and point honor Swedish artist Gunnar Widforss, who painted the national parks of the West between 1921 and 1934. Haunted Canyon lies below at trail's end, flanked by The Colonade on the right and Manu Temple, Buddha Temple, and Schellbach Butte on the left; beyond lie countless more temples, towers, canyons, and the cliffs of the South Rim. Widforss Trail is 10 miles roundtrip (allow 5 hours). Many people enjoy going just partway. Mule deer can often be seen along the trail. From Grand Canyon Lodge, go 2.7 miles north on the highway, then turn left one mile on a dirt road; turnoff is 0.3 mile south of the Cape Royal turnoff.

### Ken Patrick Trail
The 9.9-mile trail offers forest scenery and views across the headwaters of Nankoweap Creek. From Point Imperial, the Ken Patrick

winds about 3 miles along the rim to Cape Royal Road, then continues 7 miles through forest to the North Kaibab trailhead; you'll drop 560 feet in elevation. A section of switchbacks about halfway may be overgrown. Allow 6 hours for the entire hike (one way). Trailheads are near the south end of Point Imperial parking area, on Cape Royal Road one mile east of the Point Imperial junction, and the upper end of the North Kaibab trailhead parking area (2 miles north of Grand Canyon Lodge). Ken Patrick worked as a ranger on the North Rim for several seasons in the early 1970s. He was shot and killed while on duty at Pt. Reyes National Seashore by escaped convicts in 1973.

### Uncle Jim Trail
The first mile follows the Ken Patrick Trail (from the North Kaibab trailhead), then the trail turns southeast to Uncle Jim Point. Allow 3 hours for the 5-mile round trip. Mules take only 2 hours—ask at the Mule Rides Desk in the Grand Canyon Lodge lobby. Views from the point take in Roaring Springs Canyon and

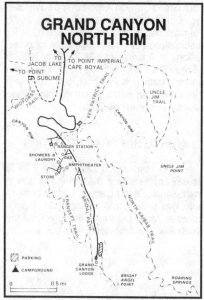

GRAND CANYON NORTH RIM

© MOON PUBLICATIONS

North Kaibab Trail. James "Uncle Jim" Owens served as the Grand Canyon Game Reserve's first warden from 1906 until establishment of the national park.

### Winter Activities

In winter, a deep blanket of snow covers the Kaibab Plateau's rolling meadow and forest country. Cross-country skiers and snowshoers find the conditions ideal. The **Canyoneers** operate cross-country ski facilities and offer tours, accommodations, and food in the Kaibab National Forest north of the Park. The **North Rim Nordic Center at Kaibab Lodge** provides rentals, instruction from beginner to advanced, tours, set track, groomed trails, and unlimited backcountry skiing; the season runs about mid-Dec. to mid-April; located 26 miles south of Jacob Lake off AZ 67. **Kaibab Lodge** offers rustic accommodations and a restaurant year-round; winter visitors can use the hot tub. You have a choice of bunks in yurts ($15.83/person) or private cabins ($63.30 s or d). Canyoneers provides SnowVan transportation to Kaibab Lodge or you can ski in. Air service from Grand Canyon Airport may be available too. Contact the Canyoneers at Box 2997, Flagstaff, AZ 86003; tel. (800) 525-0924 for reservations out of state, 526-0924 for reservations in Arizona, or 638-2389 for Kaibab Lodge. The Park itself has no facilities open on the North Rim in winter; you can camp here, however, with a permit from the Backcountry Reservations Office.

## NORTH RIM PRACTICALITIES

The road from Jacob Lake to the Rim is usually open earlier in the spring and later in the fall than Grand Canyon Lodge, restaurants, gas station, and campground. A signboard at Jacob Lake near the turnoff for the North Rim lists what services are available.

### Accommodations And Campgrounds Inside The Park

**Grand Canyon Lodge,** overlooking Transept Canyon near Bright Angel Point, has the North Rim's only accommodations within the Park. Four types of lodging are offered: "Frontier Cabins" ($47.84 s or d); "Western Cabins" ($62.61 s or d); "Pioneer Cabins" ($54.17 four or five persons only); and modern motel rooms ($56.28 s or d); charge for each additional person is $5.28 in cabins and rooms. Open mid-May to late Oct.; reservations (w/deposit) are recommended. Contact TWA Services, Box 400, Cedar City, Utah 84721; tel. (801) 586-7686.

**North Rim Campground,** 1.5 miles north and west of Grand Canyon Lodge, has drinking water but no hookups; open mid-May to mid-Oct.; $10/night ($5 w/Golden Age pass). Backpackers can camp at a walk-in area for $1/person; no reservations needed. Coin-operated showers, laundromat, store, and ice are available next to the campground. Reservations can be made in advance up to 8 weeks (56 days) for family sites and 12 weeks (84 days) for groups through Ticketron (Box 62429, Virginia Beach, VA 23462) or at any Ticketron outlet. The Ticketron Information Center can be reached at (212) 399-4444. Allow at least 3 weeks to make reservations by mail. The campground may be open early and late in the season on a first-come, first-served basis; check with the Park.

### Accommodations And Campgrounds Outside The Park

**Kaibab Lodge,** 18.5 miles north of Bright Angel Point, offers cabins and a restaurant; see "Winter Activities" above. Across the highway, **North Rim Country Store** sells groceries, camping and auto supplies, and gas and diesel; open mid-May to mid-November. **Jacob Lake Inn,** open all year, is 45 miles north of the North Rim at Jacob Lake on US 89A; it has an Indian crafts shop,

*mountain lion*
(Felis concolor)

groceries, gas, restaurant, basic motel rooms ($52.50-63), and cabins ($42-52.50 April-Nov. only); tel. 643-7232.

**De Motte Forest Camp,** 18.5 miles north of Bright Angel Point, is open early June to late Sept. with drinking water but no showers or hookups; $6/night. **Jacob Lake Forest Camp,** at Jacob Lake, has drinking water but no showers or hookups; open mid-May to late Oct.; $7/night. **Jacob Lake RV Park,** located one-half mile off AZ 67 just south of Jacob Lake, is open May 1 to Oct. 31 with tent spaces ($7) and RV sites ($14-16 w/hookups); reservations can be made at Jacob Lake, AZ 86022.

**Food And Services**
**Grand Canyon Lodge** serves breakfast, lunch, and dinner (mod.) in a huge rustic dining room with Canyon views; open daily mid-May to late Oct.; reservations requested for breakfast and dinner; tel. 638-2611. A **cafeteria,** also part of the lodge, offers faster service and lower prices but no atmosphere; open in season for breakfast, lunch, and dinner. The **Western Saloon** is in the lodge.

**Post office** and **gift shop** are in Grand Canyon Lodge. **North Rim Pub and Game Room,** located next to the campground, has indoor diversions and snacks. A small **general store** and a **service station** are also near the campground. In **emergencies,** see

a ranger or call 911. Recorded **weather forecasts,** tel. 638-7888.

**Information, Mule Rides, Tours, And Transport**
Rangers staff the **Information Desk** in the Grand Canyon Lodge's lobby daily 8 a.m.-6 p.m. (may be extended); tel. 638-7864. They'll give you times of nature walks and Canyon lectures. Obtain backpacking permits and information from the **Backcountry Reservations Office** (Box 129, Grand Canyon, AZ 86023) on the South Rim or at the ranger station on the North Rim (turnoff from the highway is 0.25 mile north of the campground turnoff). The North Rim "BRO" is open daily in season 7-11 a.m. and 4-5 p.m. mountain standard time. The park's **automated switchboard** has recorded information and will connect you to any office; tel. 638-7888.

**Mule rides** take you along the rim and into the Canyon. One-hour rim rides cost $10, 2-hour rim rides to Uncle Jim's Point are $20, half-day trips down the North Kaibab Trail to the tunnel are $25 (minimum age 8); and the full-day rides to Roaring Springs are $52 including lunch (minimum age 12); see the Mule Rides Desk in the lodge lobby. Requirements for riders are similar to those of South Rim trips. Reservations for the mules are a good idea; tel. 638-2292 at the lodge, or tel. (801) 679-8665 before June 1st.

Narrated **bus tours** visit Cape Royal, Point Imperial, and other highlights of the North Rim (3 hours; $12 adult, $7 children age 4-12); make reservations at the Mule Rides Desk in the lodge.

**North Rim Hikes and Tours** offers a variety of guided hikes in and near the Grand Canyon; operated by the Canyoneers at Kaibab Lodge (18.5 miles north of Bright Angel Point and 26 miles south of Jacob Lake). In winter, the **North Rim Nordic Center at Kaibab Lodge** offers cross-country ski trails and tours and accommodations; see "Winter Activities" above. Make reservations with the Canyoneers at Box 2997, Flagstaff, AZ 86003; tel. (800) 525-0924 out of state, 526-0924 in Arizona, or 638-2389 for Kaibab Lodge.

**Trans Canyon** offers daily roundtrip van service to the North Rim May 21-Oct. 23; Box 348, Grand Canyon, AZ 86023; tel. 638-2820.

## TOROWEAP

This seldom-visited area of the North Rim lies between Kanab Canyon to the east and the Pine Mountains (Uinkaret Mtns.) to the west. An overlook (elev. 4,552 feet) provides awesome Canyon views from sheer cliffs that drop nearly 3,000 feet to the river below. Toroweap, also known as "Tuweap" or "Tuweep," is 145 road miles west from the developed North Rim area at Bright Angel Point. The views, many hiking possibilities, and solitude reward those visitors who make it here.

**Sinyala Butte,** 25 miles east from the overlook (upriver), marks the mouth of Havasu Canyon. Most of the Havasupai Indians who live on their reservation are in Supai Village, 11 miles up Havasu Canyon. The **Hualapai Indian Reservation** lies directly across the Colorado River from the overlook; use binoculars to look for old hogans and a trail leading down to a spring. **Lava Pinnacle,** also known as Vulcan's Forge or Thor's Hammer, sits in the middle of the river directly

below. This 50-foot-high lava neck is all that remains of an extinct volcano. **Lava Falls,** visible downstream, roars with a vengeance. Debris from Prospect Canyon of the South Rim forms the rapids, perhaps the roughest water in the Grand Canyon. Water flowing between 12,000 and 20,000 cubic feet per second drops abruptly, then explodes into foam and spray. On a scale of one to 10, river runners commonly rate this rapids a "10-plus." The steep Lava Falls Trail leads down to the rapids from a nearby trailhead (see "Inner Canyon Hiking," pp. 63-64).

**Vulcan's Throne,** the 600-foot-high rounded hill just west of the overlook, is one of the youngest volcanos of the area. Between 30,000 and 1,200,000 years ago, eruptions of red-hot lava built about 60 volcanic cones in the area and even formed dams across the Colorado River. One of the dams towered nearly 500 feet, but the river washed it away long ago.

Forests cover **Mount Trumbull** (elev. 8,028 feet) to the north. Mormons logged trees here to build their temple in St. George, Utah. John Wesley Powell named the rounded peak for a Connecticut senator. The summit is a 3-mile-roundtrip hike via Nixon Springs; elevation gain is 1,600 feet.

Pinyon pine, juniper, cactus, and small flowering plants cover the plateau. Watch for rattlesnakes. Hikers can find many easy rambles across the plateau near the overlook or scramble up Vulcan's Throne. More adventurous hikes in the area include Lava Falls or Tuckup trails (see "Inner Canyon Hiking," pp. 63-64).

**Practicalities**

A camping area sits close to the overlook at the end of the road; sleepwalking isn't recommended here! More sheltered camping spots can be found farther back from the rim. There's no camping charge, but you need a permit from the Backcountry Reservations Office (Box 129, Grand Canyon, AZ 86023) on the South Rim, from the North Rim BRO, or from the Tuweep Ranger Station. Bring water, extra food, and camping gear.

*view upstream from Toroweap Overlook*

From AZ 389, 9 miles west of Fredonia, turn south at the sign "Mt. Trumbull 53 miles." The road to Toroweap (65 dirt miles one way) is in mostly good condition when dry. Watch for livestock and take it slow through the washes. The last few miles are a bit rocky, but cautiously driven cars can make it OK. The Tuweep Ranger Station is on the left about 5.5 miles before the overlook. Beyond the ranger station, Toroweap Point (summit elev. 6,393 feet) towers on the left and dumpy Vulcan's Throne (summit elev. 5,102 feet) sits on the right. You can also drive to Toroweap on a 90-mile (one way) dirt road from St. George or a 55-mile (one way) primitive road from Colorado City. Avoid driving these roads after heavy rain or snow. Snows usually block the road from St. George between Oct. and May. No water, food, or gas is available in this backcountry. Bring a map as signs may be missing at some junctions. Check on road conditions before coming out; tel. 638-7888. Obtain hiking information and emergency help at the Tuweep Ranger Station (open all year).

## INNER CANYON HIKING

Hiking in the Canyon, even a short way, provides a better look and appreciation for the wonders within. Always keep in mind, however, that the Inner Canyon is a wilderness area, subject to temperature extremes, flash floods, rockslides, and other natural hazards. Careless hikers have ruined their Canyon trips by hiking without water and doing other foolish things. Always carry (and drink!) water. All too often people will walk merrily down a trail without a canteen, then suffer terribly on the climb out. Only the Bright Angel and North Kaibab trails have sources of treated water. In summer, carry one quart (liter) of water for each hour of hiking; half a quart per hour should be enough in the cooler months. Hikers have had good experience with electrolyte-replacement drinks such as the Gookinaid E.R.G. brand.

Canyon trails have little shade—you'll probably want a hat, sunglasses, and sunscreen. Footgear should have good traction for the steep trails; lightweight boots work well. Instep crampons (metal plates with small spikes) can be helpful on icy trails in winter and early spring at the higher elevations. Well-fitting raingear will keep you dry during rainstorms; ponchos, on the other hand, provide less protection against wind-driven rain. Be careful if rockscrambling—soft and fractured rocks predominate in the Canyon. Don't swim in the Colorado River; its cold waters and swift currents are too dangerous.

### Permits
You'll need a free permit for all overnight camping trips, but you don't need one if you dayhike or have reservations to stay at Phantom Ranch. Obtain permits from rangers at the Backcountry Reservations Office (BRO) on the South Rim (next to Camper Services), North Rim BRO at the Ranger Station (turnoff from the highway is 0.25 mile north of the campground), and Tuweep Ranger Station (Toroweap area of North Rim). Ask for the *Trip Planning Packet,* which has regulations, a map, and reservation request form. The Park Service limits the number of campers in each section of the Canyon to provide visitors a wilderness experience and to protect the land from overuse. Try to make reservations as early as possible, especially for holidays and the popular months of March to May. Reservations, which can be made only by mail or in person, are accepted for the remainder of the current year and, after Oct. 1, for the following calendar year as well. An important requirement to remember is that reserved permits *must* be picked up by 9 a.m. on the first day of the trip or the *entire* reservation will be canceled; call 638-7888 beforehand if you think you'll be late. Permits may be picked up at either rim, but normally not earlier than one day before. Experienced hikers who plan to hike in an area far from the Backcountry Reservations offices, such as Kanab or Nankoweap Canyons, may request the permits to be mailed; contact the BRO for the application procedure.

Don't despair if you arrive without a reservation; sign up on the waiting list as soon as the office opens on the day before you want to hike. Return by 9 a.m. the next day to find out what's available. All this must be done in person.

## Hiking Information

Several guidebooks have trail descriptions of the Canyon (see "Booklist"), but the best source of information is the **Backcountry Reservations Office (BRO)** on the South Rim; open in summer 7 a.m.-noon and 3-5 p.m., then 8 a.m.-noon and 3-5 p.m. the rest of the year. Visit them or write Box 129, Grand Canyon, AZ 86023. The **Backcountry Information Line** is open Mon.-Fri. 11 a.m.-5 p.m.; tel. 638-7888. Rangers staff the Backcountry Reservations Office in the North Rim Ranger Station daily 7-11 a.m. and 4-5 p.m. from late May to mid- or late October. Topo maps and hiking guides are sold at the Visitor Center's bookstore and other shops in Grand Canyon Village and Tusayan.

## MAINTAINED TRAILS OF THE INNER CANYON

*Inner Gorge near Phantom Ranch*

Three kinds of hikes can be taken in the Inner Canyon. You can follow maintained trails, unmaintained trails, or routes. Park Service rangers usually recommend that first-time visitors try one of the maintained trails to get the feel of Canyon hiking. These trails are wide and well signed. Rangers and other hikers will be close at hand in case of problems. Camping along maintained trails is restricted to established sites at Indian Gardens, Bright Angel, and Cottonwood. Mice and other varmints at these campgrounds have a voracious appetite for campers' food—keep yours hung out of reach or risk losing it!

**Phantom Ranch,** on Bright Angel Creek at the bottom of the Canyon, offers dormitory beds ($19), cabins ($53 s or d, $10 each extra person), meals (breakfast $8.50, box lunch $6.50, stew dinner $14, steak dinner $23.50), drinks, and snacks. You must make advance reservations for meals and accommodation with the Bright Angel Lodge Transportation Desk or with Grand Canyon Lodges, Box 699, Grand Canyon, AZ 86023; tel. 638-2401. If you'd rather have your gear carried, mules will do it for $35 in and $25 out (30-lb. limit). Mules will carry you too (see "South Rim Tours," pp. 45-46).

## Bright Angel Trail

Havasupai Indians used this route from the South Rim to reach fields and a spring at Indian Gardens. Prospectors widened the trail in 1890 and later extended it to the Colorado River. Now it's the easiest and most-used trail into the Canyon. Trailhead is just west of Bright Angel Lodge in Grand Canyon Village. Resthouses 1.5 and 3 miles below the rim have emergency telephones and usually offer water from May 1 to September 30. One-way distances from the top are 4.6 miles to Indian Gardens (campground, water, and ranger station), 7.8 miles to Colorado River, and 9.3 miles to Bright Angel Creek (campground, water, ranger station, and Phantom Ranch). Allow 4-5 hours on the descent to the river and 8-10 hours

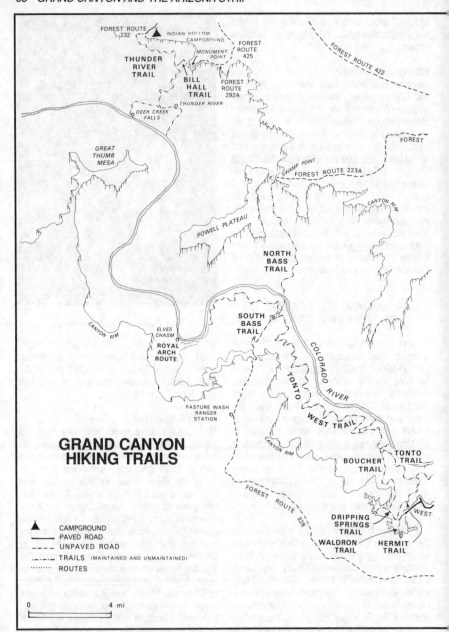

FOREST ROUTE 232

INDIAN HOLLOW CAMPGROUND

FOREST ROUTE 425

MONUMENT POINT

THUNDER RIVER TRAIL

BILL HALL TRAIL

FOREST ROUTE 292A

FOREST ROUTE 422

DEER CREEK FALLS

THUNDER RIVER

GREAT THUMB MESA

FOREST

SWAMP POINT

FOREST ROUTE 223A

CANYON RIM

POWELL PLATEAU

NORTH BASS TRAIL

ELVES CHASM

SOUTH BASS TRAIL

COLORADO RIVER

ROYAL ARCH ROUTE

CANYON RIM

TONTO

PASTURE WASH RANGER STATION

WEST TRAIL

**GRAND CANYON HIKING TRAILS**

TONTO TRAIL

BOUCHER TRAIL

CANYON RIM

FOREST ROUTE 328

WEST

DRIPPING SPRINGS TRAIL

WALDRON TRAIL

HERMIT TRAIL

▲ CAMPGROUND
PAVED ROAD
UNPAVED ROAD
TRAILS (MAINTAINED AND UNMAINTAINED)
ROUTES

0      4 mi

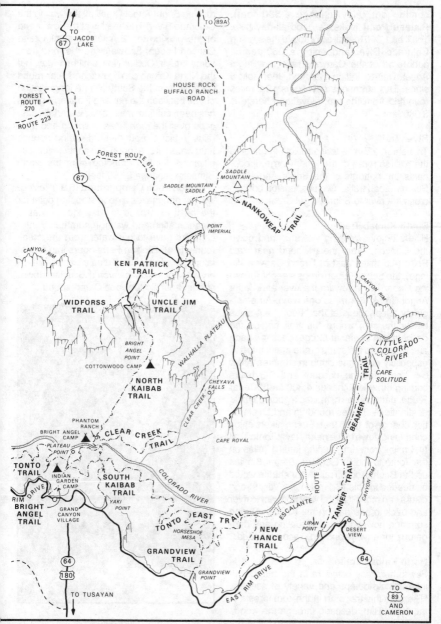

TO (67)
TO JACOB LAKE

TO (89A)

FOREST ROUTE 270
ROUTE 223

HOUSE ROCK BUFFALO RANCH ROAD

FOREST ROUTE 610

(67)

SADDLE MOUNTAIN

SADDLE MOUNTAIN SADDLE

NANKOWEAP TRAIL

POINT IMPERIAL

CANYON RIM

KEN PATRICK TRAIL

CANYON RIM

WIDFORSS TRAIL

UNCLE JIM TRAIL

WALHALLA PLATEAU

LITTLE COLORADO RIVER

BRIGHT ANGEL POINT

COTTONWOOD CAMP

NORTH KAIBAB TRAIL

CHEYAVA FALLS

CAPE SOLITUDE

CLEAR CREEK

BEAMER TRAIL

PHANTOM RANCH

CLEAR CREEK TRAIL

CAPE ROYAL

BRIGHT ANGEL CAMP

PLATEAU POINT

TONTO TRAIL

COLORADO RIVER

CANYON RIM

INDIAN GARDEN CAMP

SOUTH KAIBAB TRAIL

RIM DRIVE

BRIGHT ANGEL TRAIL

YAKI POINT

GRAND CANYON VILLAGE

TONTO

EAST TRAIL

ESCALANTE ROUTE

TANNER TRAIL

LIPAN POINT

DESERT VIEW

CANYON RIM

HORSESHOE MESA

NEW HANCE TRAIL

GRANDVIEW TRAIL

(64)

(64)
(180)

TO TUSAYAN

GRANDVIEW POINT

EAST RIM DRIVE

TO (89) AND CAMERON

© MOON PUBLICATIONS

coming out (elev. change 4,500 feet). **Plateau Point** makes a good all-day hike. You'll be 1,300 feet directly above the swirling Colorado River and enjoy a 360-degree panorama of the Canyon. Take the Bright Angel Trail to Indian Gardens, then follow signs. This strenuous dayhike is 12.2 miles roundtrip from the rim; elevation change is 3,080 feet.

### River Trail
This short, 1.7-mile trail parallels the river in the twisted rocks of the Inner Gorge. It connects the bottoms of the Bright Angel and South Kaibab trails. Two suspension bridges cross the river to Bright Angel Creek.

### South Kaibab Trail
Hikers enjoy sweeping views up and down the Canyon. From the trailhead near Yaki Point (4.5 miles east of Grand Canyon Village), the South Kaibab drops steeply, following Cedar Ridge toward the river and Bright Angel Creek (6.4 miles one way). An emergency telephone is at the "Tipoff," 4.4 miles below the rim, where the trail begins the descent into the Inner Gorge. Lack of shade and water and the steep grade make this trail especially difficult to climb in summer. Allow 3-5 hours for the descent and 6-8 hours coming out (elev. change 4,800 feet). Cedar Ridge, partway down, makes a good dayhike destination—3 miles roundtrip and an elevation change of 1,160 feet. Strong hikers enjoy continuing down to the nearly level Tonto Trail (4.4 miles from rim), turning left 4.1 miles on the Tonto to Indian Gardens, then 4.6 miles up the Bright Angel Trail. A car shuttle would be needed for this 13.1-mile hike. Very strong hikers can make it all the way from rim to river and back in one day on the Kaibab. During summer, however, this is grueling and dangerous for *anyone* and isn't recommended.

### North Kaibab Trail
Few other trails compare in the number of interesting sidetrips and variety of scenery. Hikers on this trail start in the cool forests of the North Rim, descend through the woods into Roaring Springs Canyon, then follow the rushing Bright Angel Creek all the way to the Colorado River. Trailhead is at the lower end of the parking lot, 2 miles north of Grand Canyon Lodge. Snows close the road from some time in Oct. or Nov. until mid-May, but the North Kaibab can be reached year-round via trails from the South Rim. A long section of trail between the rim and Roaring Springs has been cut into sheer cliffs; waterfalls cascade over the rock faces in spring and after rains. A picnic ground near Roaring Springs has water; it's a good destination for day hikers (9.4 miles roundtrip from the North Rim; elev. change 3,160 feet).

**Cottonwood Campground** (6.9 miles below the rim) makes a good stopping point for the night or a base for day trips. It has a ranger station and water in summer. Winter campers have to get water from the creek (purify first). **Ribbon Falls** pours into a miniature paradise of travertine and lush greenery; it's in a side canyon 1.5 miles downstream from Cottonwood Campground.

*Inner Gorge*

The North Kaibab Trail continues downstream along Bright Angel Creek and enters the dark contorted schists and other rocks of the ancient Vishnu Group. Near the bottom you'll walk through Phantom Ranch, then Bright Angel Campground. Most people can go down the 14.2-mile North Kaibab in 8-9 hours of steady hiking (elev. change 5,700 feet). Climbing out can take 10-12 hours, best done over 2 days. Fishermen often have good luck catching rainbow trout in Bright Angel Creek, especially in winter.

## UNMAINTAINED TRAILS OF THE INNER CANYON (SOUTH RIM)

These trails lead to some beautiful corners of the Park. You'll find solitude and get new perspectives of the Canyon. Hikers need to be self-reliant on the unmaintained trails—they must know where water sources are, be able to use map and compass, and handle emergencies. Most trails follow prehistoric Indian routes or game trails that miners improved to pack out ore in the late 1800s. Trail conditions vary widely; some remain in excellent condition, while others have dangerous spots or require careful map reading. Although the Park Service calls the trails "unmaintained," trail work may be done if a section becomes impassable. Hermit Trail and parts of the Tonto Trail have designated camping areas that you're required to use. The following trails are listed from west to east on the South Rim, then west to east on the North Rim.

### Tonto Trail
Hikers in a hurry will find the Tonto frustrating as they wind in and out of countless canyons. This 92-mile trail contours along the Tonto Plateau, connecting most of the South Rim trails between the mouth of Red Canyon at Hance Rapids and Garnet Canyon far downstream. The Canyon panorama continually changes as you walk along, sometimes taking in spectacular views from the edge of

*Pinnacles of the Kaibab Formation*

the Inner Gorge. Most of the way is gently rolling (average elev. 3,000 feet). You might lose the trail occasionally, but with attention to rock cairns and the map, you'll soon find it again. The sun bears down relentlessly in summer, when it's best to hike elsewhere.

### South Bass Trail
William Bass learned about this route from the Havasupai Indians in the 1880s, then started a small tourist operation. Bass also built a trail up to the North Rim, crossing the river by boat and later by a cage suspended from a cable. No crossing exists today. The South Bass Trail is generally good and easy to follow. It drops to the Esplanade, a broad terrace, then down to the river. You'll need a high-clearance vehicle to reach the trailhead, 4 miles north of Pasture Wash Ranger Station; ask at the Backcountry Reservations Office for directions. Hiking the 9-mile trail to the river takes about 5 hours down and 9 hours up (elev. change 4,400 feet). No reliable water is available before the river.

**Boucher Trail**

Louis Boucher, the "Hermit," came to the Canyon in 1891 and mined copper along Boucher Creek until 1912. Steep terrain and rockslides in a couple of sections can make the trail difficult—it's best for experienced hikers with light packs. Take Hermit and Dripping Springs trails (see below) to Boucher Trail. The Boucher contours along the base of the Hermit Shale high above the west side of Hermit Canyon and affords excellent panoramas. You'll reach the Tonto Trail just before Boucher Creek. The route down the creek to Boucher Rapids on the Colorado River is an easy 1.5 miles. From the Hermit trailhead on the West Rim Drive, it's 11 miles to Boucher Creek; allow 7-8 hours down and 9-10 hours coming up (elev. change 3,800 feet). The Boucher, Tonto, and Hermit trails make a fine 3- or 4-day loop hike. Boucher and Hermit creeks have year-round water.

**Hermit Trail**

Although named for Boucher, the trail was actually built by the Fred Harvey Company for tourists about 1912. Visitors took this route to Hermit Camp, which operated until 1930. Most of Hermit Trail is in good condition; the few places covered by rockslides can be easily crossed. The trail begins just beyond Hermit's Rest, at the end of the 8-mile West Rim Drive. Water is available at Santa Maria Spring (2 miles one way) and Hermit Creek (7 miles one way). Hermit Rapids on the Colorado River is an easy 1.5-mile walk down the bed of Hermit Creek; a sign on the Tonto Trail points the way down to Hermit Creek. Elevation change from rim to river is 4,300 feet: allow 5-6 hours going down and 8-10 hours climbing out.

Hermit Trail also connects with Waldron, Dripping Springs, and Tonto trails. Day hikers can head to Dripping Springs, a 6-mile round-trip hike taking 4-6 hours (elev. change 800 feet). Descend the Hermit Trail 1.5 miles, then turn left 1.5 miles on Dripping Springs Trail. Water should be carried for the entire trip as the springs have only a tiny flow. Hikers with high-clearance vehicles can also reach the upper ends of Waldron and Dripping Springs trails; see a topo map. The 22.5-mile Hermit Loop hike which follows the Hermit,

*Louis Boucher (far left) at his mine*

*Hermit Camp*

Tonto, and Bright Angel trails has become popular. Water is found on this loop year-round at Monument Creek and Indian Gardens and seasonally at Salt and Horn Creeks. Hikers can easily descend the bed of Monument Creek to Granite Rapids (1.5 miles one way).

## Grandview Trail
Day hikers frequently use this steep but scenic trail to Horseshoe Mesa. Trailhead is at Grandview Point on the East Rim Drive. Miners improved an old Indian route in 1892 so they could bring out high-grade copper ore from Horseshoe Mesa. Mining ceased in 1907, but mine shafts, machinery, and ruins of buildings remain. **Cave of the Domes,** a limestone cavern on the west side of the mesa, has some good passages; look for a trail fork west of the butte atop the mesa. Three trails descend Horseshoe Mesa to the Tonto Trail. Bring water, as the springs shown on the map are either unreliable or difficult to reach. Allow 6 hours for the 6-mile round-trip hike to Horseshoe Mesa (elev. change 2,600 feet).

## New Hance Trail
John Hance, one of the first prospectors to get into the tourist business, built this trail down Red Canyon in 1895. The unsigned trailhead is about one mile southwest of Moran Point turnoff on the East Rim Drive; get directions from a ranger. Suited for more experienced hikers, the trail descends steeply (poor footing in places) to the river at Hance Rapids. Most of the way is easy to follow, especially if you're descending. No reliable water is available before the river. The 8-mile trail takes about 6 hours to descend and 8-10 hours to climb out (elev. change 4,400 feet).

## Tanner Trail
Seth Tanner improved this Indian trail in the 1880s to reach his copper and silver mines along the Colorado River. Although in good condition and easy to follow, the Tanner Trail is long (10 miles one way) and dry. It's best hiked in the cooler months. Hikers often cache water partway down for the return trip. Trailhead is about 100 yards back down the road from Lipan Point parking lot, off the East Rim Drive. Allow 6-8 hours for the descent and 8-10 hours coming out (elev. change 4,700 feet.

## Beamer Trail
This slim path begins at Tanner Canyon Rapids (lower end of Tanner Trail) and follows the river 4 miles upstream to Palisades Creek, then climbs to a high terrace for the remaining 5 miles to the Little Colorado River confluence. No camping is allowed within one-half mile of the confluence.

## UNMAINTAINED TRAILS OF THE INNER CANYON (NORTH RIM)

### Lava Falls Trail
The Colorado River explodes in a fury of foam and waves at Lava Falls, reached by this short but steep trail from the Toroweap area of the North Rim. Cairns mark the way down a lunarlike landscape of volcanic lava. Barrel cactus thrive on the dark, twisted rock.

Although the trail (actually more of a route) is only 2 miles long one way, it should be considered difficult because of the steep grades and poor footing in places. Summer temperatures get *extremely* high (elevation at the river is only 1,700 feet). Carry plenty of water. From Toroweap Overlook (see "Toroweap" above), backtrack on the road 2.5 miles and look for a dirt track on the left (3.5 miles south of Tuweep Ranger Station); follow it 2.5 miles across Toroweap Lake (normally dry) and around the west side of Vulcan's Throne. The way is too rough for cars and impassable for any vehicle if the lake has water in it. At road's end, the trail descends to a hill of red cinders about two-thirds of the way down; the last part of the descent follows a steep gully. Lava Falls lies 0.3 mile downstream. Camping is possible along the river with a permit. Allow 2 hours going down and 4 hours coming out (elev. change 2,500 feet).

## Tuckup (Tuweep) Trail

Experienced canyon hikers looking for solitude and expansive vistas can try this faint trail. It follows the Esplanade of the North Rim for more than 70 miles between the Toroweap Point area and Hundred and Fifty Mile Canyon. Back roads lead to trailheads near these two areas and to upper Tuckup Canyon, about the halfway point on the trail. A variety of trips can be done in this remote area; hikers have followed the Tuckup Trail from Toroweap Point to Cottonwood Canyon, descended Cottonwood and Tuckup canyons to the Colorado River (rope needed), hiked the shore downstream to Lava Falls Trail, and ascended back to Toroweap in a week or so of travel. Springs of varying reliability provide water along the Tuckup Trail. Talk with rangers knowledgeable about the area for trailhead, spring, and hiking conditions.

## Thunder River Trails

Thunder River blasts out of a cave in the Muav Limestone, cascades one-half mile, then enters Tapeats Creek. It's not only the world's shortest river but suffers the humiliation of being a tributary to a creek! Deer Creek Falls,

another attraction in the area, plummets more than 100 feet onto the banks of the Colorado River. Cottonwood trees, willows, and other cool greenery grace the banks of Thunder River and both creeks. Trails are generally good and easy to follow, though spring runoff and rains can make Tapeats Creek too high to cross safely.

Two trails descend from the North Rim, the **Thunder River Trail** from Indian Hollow Campground at the end of Forest Route 232, and the **Bill Hall Trail** from the east side of Monument Point at the end of Forest Route 292A. The Bill Hall Trail saves 5 miles of walking but the steep grade can be hard on the knees. Trailheads are reached by turning west on Forest Route 422 from AZ 67 in De Motte Park (one mile south of Kaibab Lodge and 17.5 miles north of Bright Angel Point); see the Kaibab National Forest map (North Kaibab Ranger District). It's about 35 miles of dirt road from the highway to either trailhead. Cars can negotiate the roads in good weather, but winter snows bury this high country from about mid-Nov. to mid-May. Thunder River and Bill Hall trails both drop steeply to the Esplanade, where they meet. Thunder River Trail then switchbacks down to Surprise Valley, a giant piece of the rim that long ago slumped thousands of feet to its present position. Surprise Valley turns into an oven in summer and lacks water.

**Deer Creek Trail,** marked by a large cairn in Surprise Valley, splits off to the west for Deer Creek, 3.5 miles away. A short walk down Deer Creek leads to the falls and a trail to the river just west of the falls.

**Thunder River Trail** goes east across Surprise Valley, drops to Thunder River, and follows it to Tapeats Creek. Except at high water, Tapeats Creek can be followed 2.5 miles upstream to its source in a cave. The Colorado River is a 2.5-mile hike downstream from the junction of Thunder River and Tapeats Creek. Camp at the designated sites near this junction, downstream on the Colorado River, or along upper Deer Creek. Good fishing attracts anglers to Tapeats Creek and may have in the past as well—prehistoric Cohonina Indians left ruins along the creek.

*The ringtail cat (Bassariscus astutus) prowls the Grand Canyon and its tributaries. He likes campers' food, so hang yours well out of reach!*

The trek from Bill Hall trailhead at Monument Point to Tapeats Rapids is 12 miles one way (elev. change 5,250 feet); allow 7 hours to the upper campsite on Tapeats Creek and 9 hours all the way to Tapeats Rapids. Thunder River, 9 miles from the Bill Hall trailhead, is the first source of water.

### North Bass Trail

This difficult trail drops from Swamp Point on the North Rim into Muav Canyon, which winds down to Shinumo Creek and the Colorado River. The trail reaches the Colorado about 0.3 mile below where the South Bass Trail comes down on the other side. No crossing exists today, though people have hitched rides to the other shore with rafting groups. Only experienced hikers should tackle this long and faint trail. Muav Saddle Spring, White Creek (above the Redwall cliffs), and Shinumo Creek have water. Shinumo Creek has trout as well. Shinumo can be difficult to cross in spring. Allow 3-4 days for the 28-mile roundtrip to the river (elev. change 5,300 feet). The trailhead at Swamp Point can be reached by a high-clearance vehicle via Forest Routes 422, 270, 223, and 223A.

### Clear Creek Trail

This trail, in very good condition and easy to follow, is the North Rim's version of the Tonto Trail. Clear Creek Trail begins 0.3 mile north of Phantom Ranch and climbs 1,500 feet to the Tonto Plateau. It then winds in and out of canyons until dropping at the last possible place into Clear Creek, 9 miles from Phantom Ranch. Carry water (there's no source before Clear Creek) and be prepared for very hot weather in summer. The best camping sites lie scattered among the cottonwood trees where the trail meets the creek. Day hikers enjoy the first mile or so of Clear Creek Trail for scenic views of the river and Inner Gorge. Strong hikers can go all the way to Clear Creek and back in a long day. Better still would be to come for several days. **Cheyava Falls,** highest in the Canyon, is a 6- to 8-hour roundtrip up the long northeast fork of Clear Creek. The falls put on an impressive show only in spring and after heavy rains. Other arms of the creek offer good hiking too; the one branching east about 0.5 mile downstream from the end of Clear Creek Trail flows through a narrow canyon in quartzite. You can also go down Clear Creek to the Colorado River, a 5- to 7-hour roundtrip hike through dark and contorted schist and granite. A 10-foot-high waterfall 0.5 mile from the river can be bypassed by clambering around to the right.

### Nankoweap Trail

Dangerous ledges on the Nankoweap Trail discourage those hikers afraid of heights. If you don't mind tiptoeing on the brink of sheer cliffs, this trail will open up a large section of the Park for your exploration. Trailhead is at Saddle Mountain Saddle, 2.4 crow-flying miles northeast of Point Imperial. You can't drive to the trailhead, however; it must be approached on foot: either 3 miles one way from the end of House Rock Buffalo Ranch

Road (south from US 89A), or 3 miles one way from the end of Forest Route 610 (east off AZ 67). Both access roads are dirt, passable by cars, but the House Rock Buffalo Ranch Road lies at a lower elevation and is less likely to be snowed in. The Nankoweap Trail drops several hundred feet, then contours along a ledge all the way to Tilted Mesa before descending to Nankoweap Creek. Some care in route-finding will be needed between Tilted Mesa and the creek. Nankoweap Creek, 10 miles from the trailhead, is the first source of water; you may want to cache water partway down to use on the return. The remaining 4 miles to the river are easy. Allow 3-4 days for the roundtrip (elev. change 4,800 feet).

## ROUTES OF THE INNER CANYON

The Canyon has thousands of possible routes for the experienced hiker. Harvey Butchart, who has done more off-trail hiking than anyone else, describes many routes in his three books (see "Booklist"). The Backcountry Reservations Office can suggest interesting routes too, and give you an idea of current conditions. Also you'll probably get ideas of your own from hiking in the Canyon and studying maps. Keep in mind that much of the Canyon's exposed rock is soft or fractured—a handhold or foothold can easily break off. The Colorado River presents a major barrier, as the water is too cold, wide, and full of treacherous currents to cross easily.

### Royal Arch Loop
This rugged trip to Royal Arch and Elves Chasm has been described as "fantastic" by experienced hikers. The route follows parts of the South Bass and west Tonto trails to make a long loop with the Esplanade Route and Royal Arch Canyon. Allow a minimum of 5 days for this one and be prepared for plenty of rough spots. Note that fewer than half the people who attempt this loop actually make it! Sections of the route are *very* difficult to follow. The Royal Arch-Colorado River section is very exposed and requires a 50-foot rope. An easier hike takes the Tonto Trail to its end at Garnet Canyon, descends to the Colorado, and follows the river to Elves Chasm; return is the same way. Royal Arch is just 0.5 mile upstream from Elves Chasm, but you'll need to backtrack one mile up the Colorado River to the well-trodden route used for reaching the arch. A 15-foot section of travertine takes some skill to climb, but there's often a piece of rope to help (carry your own 50-foot rope though).

### Escalante Route
The Tonto Trail gives out at Hance Rapids, but you can continue upstream to Tanner Rapids and the Tanner Trail. Cairns mark the 15-mile Escalante Route. Expect rough terrain and difficult route-finding in some sections. The Colorado River, easily accessible only at the ends of the route, provides the only reliable source of water. The route is somewhat easier to hike in the downstream direction (Tanner to Hance).

*spotted skunk* (Spilogale putorius)

*rafting through Marble Canyon*

## RUNNING THE COLORADO RIVER

A great adventure, running the Colorado River through the Grand Canyon provides excitement of roaring rapids and tranquillity of watching Canyon walls glide by. Although explorers of 100 years ago feared this section of river and portrayed it in dark and gloomy drawings, boating the entire Grand Canyon is an enjoyable and safe experience today. Running the Colorado opens up some of the most beautiful and remote corners of the Canyon. River parties make frequent stops to explore the twisting side canyons, old mining camps, and Indian ruins along the way. Within the Grand Canyon, the Colorado River flows 277 miles, drops 2,200 feet, and thunders through 70 major rapids.

### River Tours
Twenty companies offer a wide variety of trips through the Canyon, ranging from one-day introductions to adventurous 20-day expeditions. Write the Grand Canyon National Park for a list of companies (Grand Canyon, AZ 86023) or ask at the Visitor Center. If possible, make reservations (w/deposit) 6 months in advance with the tour operator to assure your choice of trip. All but one of the tour companies use rafts of varied sizes; the exception is Grand Canyon Dories, which uses sturdy wooden boats. Both oar-powered and motorized craft run the river. The oar- or paddle-powered trips give a more natural and quieter experience but take half again as much time. Motor-powered rafts can zip through the entire Canyon in 6 days or go from Lees Ferry to Phantom Ranch in as few as 2 days. River-running season normally lasts from April to Oct., though only oar-powered craft depart after mid-September. Most trips put in at Lees Ferry, just upstream from the Park, and take out downstream at Diamond Creek or Lake Mead. Shorter trips can be taken by using hiking trails or helicopters. If you'd like just a taste of river

*lower Marble Canyon*

running, take a one-day trip from Glen Canyon Dam to Lees Ferry with Wilderness River Adventures based in Page (see Page "Tours"), or raft the lower Grand Canyon with Hualapai Tribal River Runners based in Peach Springs (see "Visiting the Hualapai Indian Reservation" below).

Typical trips and approximate costs on commercial *oar* trips are: 12 days from Lees Ferry to Diamond Creek (226 miles; $1,150); 5 or 6 days from Lees Ferry to Phantom Ranch (87.5 miles; $525); and 8 or 9 days from Phantom Ranch to Diamond Creek (138.5 miles; $850). Equivalent *motorized* trips are 8 days from Lees Ferry to Diamond Creek ($800); 3 or 4 days from Lees Ferry to Phantom Ranch ($400); and 5 days from Phantom Ranch to Diamond Creek ($500). Many other combinations are available too. Discounts may be given for groups, children under 14, early booking, and early or late in the season.

If you've children in tow, check to see if there's a minimum age; sometimes this is left up to you, other times operators require minimum ages of between 8 and 16 years. Trips usually include land transportation; most depart from Flagstaff, Page, St. George, or Las Vegas. Meals, camping gear, and waterproof bags are usually included in the price. Experienced kayakers can tag along with many of the tours and get a lower rate. You can also organize your own Canyon expedition, but you must plan far in advance and meet all the Park Service requirements; contact the **River Permits** office; tel. 638-7843.

**Canoeing The Lower Grand Canyon**
Canoes in the Grand Canyon? Yes, in the last 40 miles within the Park. A power boat is needed to carry the canoes from Lake Mead to Separation Canyon (Mile 240 on the river). Most of the southern shore on this trip belongs to the Hualapai Indians; obtain permits from them if you plan to camp or hike on their land. David Lavender wrote an article in the Sept. 1985 *Arizona Highways* about his 5-day canoe trip from Separation Canyon to Pearce Ferry.

# HAVASUPAI AND HUALAPAI INDIAN RESERVATIONS

## VISITING HAVASU CANYON

Havasu Canyon encloses a land of towering cliffs, blue-green waters, breathtaking waterfalls, and lush vegetation. Havasu Creek rushes through the canyon past the Indian village of Supai before beginning its wild cascade down to meet the Colorado River. The canyon and its creek, located about 35 air miles northwest of Grand Canyon Village, belong to the Havasupai Indians (*havasu* means "blue" and *pai* means "people").

Havasupai had lived here long before the first white men arrived. The tribe farmed the fertile canyon floor during the summer, then moved up to the plateau after harvest. They wintered atop the plateau, gathering the abundant wild foods and firewood. Spanish missionary Francisco Garcés visited the Havasupai in 1776, reporting them to be a happy and industrious people. Though a peaceful tribe, they still suffered the usual fate of American Indians: they were confined in 1882 to a tiny canyon reservation while ranchers grabbed their plateau lands. The Havasupai protested but had to wait until 1975 for their winter homelands to be returned. The Havasupai Reservation now spans 188,077 acres; most of the 500-600 tribal members on the reservation live in Supai village.

### Getting There

The tribe wisely decided against allowing a road to invade their canyon home, so most residents and tourists arrive by mule, horse, or on foot. Helicopters provide another option, though the noisy machines seem out of place here. The 8-mile trail from Hualapai Hilltop to Supai is the usual way in. From Seligman on I-40, take AZ 66 northwest for 28 miles, then turn right 63 miles on a signed road, paved all the way to Hualapai Hilltop. If coming from the west, take AZ 66 northeast out of Kingman for 60 miles, then left 63 miles. *Fill up with gas before leaving AZ 66; no water, supplies, or stores are available after turning off.* The road to Hualapai Hilltop climbs into forests of ponderosa pine that give way to pinyon and juniper, then desert grasslands close to the rim. Hualapai Hilltop has parking areas and stables. Various shortcuts on dirt roads can be taken to Hualapai Hilltop, but they have poor signing and rough surfaces.

*trail to Supai*

## Hiking In

You *must* obtain advance reservations to camp or to stay in the lodge. From Hualapai Hilltop (elev. 5,200 feet), the trail descends at a moderate grade into Hualapai Canyon for the first 1.5 miles, and then levels off slightly for the remaining 6.5 miles to Supai village (elev. 3,200 feet). About 1.5 miles before the village, the trail joins the sparkling waters of Havasu Canyon. Avoid the heat of day in summer when highs can go over 100° F. Always carry drinking water. All visitors must pay a $12 entrance fee ($8 in winter) on arrival at Supai. The tribe asks you to leave pets, booze, and firearms at home. To preserve the canyon floor, no fires or charcoal may be used; campers need to bring a stove if they plan to cook.

## Sights

The famous sights of the canyon begin 1.5 miles downstream from Supai. Three waterfalls plunge over cliffs of Redwall Limestone in a space of just 2 miles. You'll first come to 75-foot-high **Navajo Falls,** which has several widely spaced branches. It's named after a 19th-century Havasupai tribal chief who was kidnapped by Navajo Indians as an infant and raised as a Navajo. Not until he had grown to manhood did he learn of his true origin and return to the Havasupai. Spectacular **Havasu Falls** drops 100 feet into a beautiful turquoise-colored pool rimmed by travertine deposits. Clear inviting waters make the spot perfect for a swim or picnic.

**Mooney Falls,** most awe-inspiring of all, plummets 196 feet into another colorful pool. The Havasupai named this most sacred of the waterfalls "Mother of the Waters." The falls take their present name from a prospector who died here in 1880. Assistants were lowering Daniel Mooney down the cliffs next to the falls when the rope jammed. Mooney hung helpless as the rope frayed and broke. He fell to his death on the rocks below, but 10 months passed before his companions could build a wooden ladder down the falls and bury the travertine-encrusted body. A rough trail descends beside the falls along the same route hacked through the travertine by miners a year after Mooney's death. You'll pass through two tunnels and then ease down with the aid of chains and iron stakes. At the bottom (as soon as your knees stop shaking!), you can enjoy a picnic or swim in the large pool. You'll see holes high on the canyon walls from which miners once took silver, lead, zinc, and vanadium.

**Beaver Falls,** 2 miles downstream from Mooney, makes a good dayhike from the campgrounds or Supai village. You'll pass countless inviting travertine pools and small cascades, of which Beaver Falls is the largest. The trail, rough in places, crosses the creek three times, climbs high up a cliff, then descends and crosses a fourth time below Beaver Falls. The trail continues downstream along Havasu Creek 4 more miles to the Colorado River. Travel fast and light if going to the river, as camping is prohibited below Mooney Falls. Photographing any of the falls can be a challenge; best chances for getting them in full sunlight are in May, June, and July.

*descending to the base of Mooney Falls*

## Havasu Campground

Most visitors prefer to camp, listening to the sounds of the canyon and enjoying the brilliant display of stars in the nighttime sky. Havasu Campground begins 0.25 mile below Havasu Falls. It has spring water, picnic tables, litter barrels, and pit toilets. What most campers don't know is that the campground extends 0.75 mile along Havasu Creek to the brink of Mooney Falls. You'll enjoy more solitude by walking to the far end. Theft is a serious problem in the campground; don't leave valuables in tents or lying around. You must obtain advance reservations and pay $9/night per person ($7 in winter) to camp. Camping outside the established campground is prohibited. Call 448-2121 or write Havasupai Tourist Enterprise, Supai, AZ 86435. Pay on arrival at Supai. Try to make reservations far ahead, especially for holidays, weekends, and all of May, June, and July.

## Accommodations And Food

The village of Supai offers the modern **Havasupai Lodge;** rooms have a/c, two double beds, and private bath; $45 s, $50 d, $8 each additional person (in winter, Nov. 1-March 31, rates drop to $30 s, $35 d, $8 each additional person). Obtain the required reservations from Havasupai Lodges, Supai, AZ 86435; tel. 448-2111. A cafe nearby serves breakfast, lunch, and dinner; open daily about 7 a.m.-6:30 p.m. Try their Indian taco. Ice cream costs a bundle—$1 for a cone or $2.75 for a large milkshake, but other prices aren't so bad. A store across the street sells meats, groceries, and cold drinks; open daily 7 a.m.-6 p.m.

## Services

Send your postcard home via the only pack train mail in the country, with a postmark to prove it! The **post office** is open weekdays 9 a.m.-4 p.m., next to the store. If you'd rather ride than walk, local families will take you and your gear on **horses or mules** from the parking lot at Hualapai Hilltop to Supai ($70 roundtrip) or to the campgrounds ($90 roundtrip). Try to get an early start from Hualapai Hilltop, especially in the warmer months; a small surcharge is added for departures after 9 a.m. A sightseeing trip from Supai to the falls and back costs $35. You'll get a horse or a mule, depending on what's available. Advance reservations (at least 3 weeks) and a 50% deposit must be made with Havasupai Tourist Enterprise, Supai, AZ 86435; tel. 448-2121. Always call one day before coming to check that your animal is available. Visitors may also bring their own horses if they take along feed and pay a $15 trail fee. A **health clinic** in Supai can provide emergency medical care.

# VISITING THE HUALAPAI INDIAN RESERVATION

The Hualapai ("Pine-tree People") Indians once occupied a large area of northwestern Arizona. In language and culture, they have close ties with the Havasupai and Yavapai tribes. Early white visitors enjoyed friendly relations with the Hualapai, but land seizures and murders by the newcomers led to warfare. Army troops defeated the Indians and herded them south onto the Colorado River Reservation, where many died. Surviving Hualapai fled back to their traditional lands, part of which later became the Hualapai Indian Reservation. About half of the 1,400 tribal members live on their 993,000-acre reservation. Much of the lower Grand Canyon's South Rim belongs to the tribe.

## Peach Springs

This small town, 54 miles northeast of Kingman on AZ 66, is the only town on the reservation. Peach Springs has neither charm nor anything to see, but it's the place to obtain permits for recreation and back-road use on the reservation. A river trips office organizes one- and 2-day rafting trips through the lower Grand Canyon. There's no place to stay, but nearby Truxton (9 miles southwest) has two motels. Peach Springs does have a cafe serving basic American and Mexican food along with Indian fry bread. There's also a grocery store.

*Farlee Hotel near Diamond Creek; built in 1894, and in ruins when this picture was taken, about 1914*

## Diamond Creek Road

This scenic 21-mile gravel road goes north from Peach Springs to the Colorado River at Diamond Creek, providing the only road access to the river within the Grand Canyon. You'll enjoy fine canyon views, though not as spectacular as the developed areas of the Grand Canyon National Park. Except for river-runners, who use the road to take out or put in their boats, few people visit this out-of-the-way spot. Yet the very first organized groups of tourists to the Canyon bounced down the road to Diamond Creek in 1883. A hotel built here and used 1884-89 was the first at the Grand Canyon.

During dry weather, cars with good ground clearance can make it in. Summer rains (July and Aug.) necessitate use of a truck. Except for some picnic tables and an outhouse or two, the area remains undeveloped. Hikers can explore Diamond Creek and other canyons; see Stewart Aitchison's *A Naturalist's Guide to Hiking the Grand Canyon.* First step before attempting to travel Diamond Creek Road is a short stop at the Hualapai River Runners office to obtain permits and information on road conditions. Sightseeing permits cost $3/day per person (age 12 and over). Camping costs $7/day per person (includes sightseeing fee). Fishermen age 12 and over need a $8/day tribal license (only $1/day if you also purchase a camping permit). Diamond Creek Road turns off AZ 66 beside the River Runners office in town.

## River Running

**Hualapai Tribal River Runners** offers one- and 2-day motorized-raft trips down the lower Grand Canyon between Diamond Creek and Pearce Ferry on Lake Mead. The 2-day trip allows a more leisurely pace and time for hiking. Rates include food, accommodations (including a room the nights before and after the trip), and transportation from Peach Springs. Season lasts from May to Oct.; write for the schedule well in advance so reservations can be made with Hualapai Tribal River Trips, Box 246, Peach Springs, AZ 86434; tel. 769-2219, 769-2210, or (800) 622-4409 (out of state). The office is open daily in summer (May to Oct.) and Mon.-Fri. 8 a.m.-4:30 p.m. the rest of the year. Look for the office at the corner of AZ 66 and Diamond Creek Road in town next to the Cash and Carry Market.

# THE ARIZONA STRIP

Lonely and vast, the "Strip" lies north and west of the Colorado River. Phoenix and the rest of the state seem a world away, cut off by the Grand Canyon. The Arizona Strip's history and geography actually tie it more closely to Utah. Some beautiful canyon and mountain country await the adventurous traveler. In addition to Grand Canyon National Park and Glen Canyon National Recreation Area, nine designated wilderness areas totaling nearly 400,000 acres protect some of the most scenic sections. Several tiny communities in the Arizona Strip offer food and accommodations for travelers. More extensive facilities lie just outside the region: Page across the river to the east and Kanab and St. George across the Utah border to the north. Navajo Bridge, near Lees Ferry historic site, serves as the gateway to the Arizona Strip for most visitors.

## LEES FERRY

The deeply entrenched Colorado River cuts one gorge after another as it crosses the high plateaus of southern Utah and northern Arizona. Settlers and travelers found the river a dangerous and difficult barrier until well into this century. A break in the cliffs above Marble Canyon provided one of the few places to build a road to the water's edge. Until 1929, when Navajo Bridge first spanned the canyon, vehicles and passengers had to cross by ferry. Zane Grey expressed his thoughts about this crossing, known as Lees Ferry, in *The Last of the Plainsmen* (1908): "I saw the constricted rapids, where the Colorado took its plunge into the box-like head of the Grand Canyon of Arizona; and the deep, reverberating boom of the river, at flood height, was a fearful thing to hear. I could not repress a shudder at the thought of crossing above that rapid."

The Dominguez-Escalante Expedition tried to cross at what's now known as Lees Ferry in 1776, but without success. The river proved too cold and wide to swim safely, and winds frustrated the attempts to raft across. The Spaniards had to go 40 miles upriver into present-day Utah before finding a safe ford. About 100 years later, Mormon leaders began eyeing the Lees Ferry crossing as the most convenient route for expanding Mormon settlements from Utah into Arizona. After

*Marble Canyon*

Jacob Hamblin led a failed attempt at rafting in 1860, he returned 4 years later and made it across safely. Although Hamblin was the first to recognize the value of this crossing, it now bears the name of John D. Lee. This colorful character gained notoriety in the 1857 Mountain Meadows Massacre. One account of this unfortunate chain of events relates that Paiute Indians, allied to the Mormons, attacked an unfriendly wagon train of gentiles; Mormons then joined in the fighting until all but the small children of the wagon train, too young to tell the story, lay dead.

To get Lee out of sight, the Mormon Church leaders asked him to start a regular ferry service on the Colorado River, which he began in 1872. One of Lee's wives remarked on seeing the isolated spot, "Oh, what a lonely dell!" which became the name of their place. Lee managed to establish the ferry service despite boat accidents and sometimes hostile Navajo, but his past caught up with

him. In 1877, authorities took Lee back to Mountain Meadows where a firing squad and casket awaited.

Miners and farmers came to try their luck along the Colorado River and its tributaries. The ferry service continued too, though it suffered fatal accidents from time to time. The last run took place in June 1928, while the bridge was being constructed 6 miles downstream. The ferry operator on that trip lost control in strong currents and the boat capsized; all three persons aboard and a Model-T Ford were lost. Fifty-five years of ferryboating had come to an end. Navajo Bridge opened in Jan. 1929, an event hailed by the Flagstaff *Coconino Sun* as the "Biggest News in Southwest History."

The Lees Ferry area and the canyon upstream are in the Glen Canyon National Recreation Area. Grand Canyon National Park begins just downstream. *Rangers of the National Park Service administer both areas.

*hull and boiler of the* Charles H. Spencer

### Lonely Dell Ranch And Lees Ferry
Old buildings, trails, mining machinery, and a wrecked steamboat can be toured in these historic districts. A self-guided tour booklet, available at the sites, identifies historic features and gives their backgrounds. A log cabin thought to have been built by Lee, root cellar, blacksmith shop, ranch house, orchards, and cemetery are at Lonely Dell Ranch, a short distance up the Paria River. Historic buildings near the ferry crossings include Lees Ferry Fort (built in 1874 to protect settlers from possible Indian attack, but used as a trading post and residence), a small stone post office (in use 1913-1923), and structures occupied by the American Placer Company and the U.S. Geological Survey.

Charles Spencer, manager of the goldmining company, brought in machinery for a sluicing operation, an amalgamator, and drilling equipment. His company first tried using mule trains in 1910 to pack coal for the operation from Warm Creek Canyon, 15 miles upstream. When this didn't work, company financiers shipped a 92-foot-long steamboat, the *Charles H. Spencer,* in sections from San

Francisco the following year. The boat performed poorly too, burning almost its entire load of coal to make just one roundtrip. It was used only five times. The boiler, decking, and hull of the old steamboat can still be seen at low water on the shore. Although Spencer's efforts to extract fine gold particles proved futile, he continued to prospect in the area as late as 1965 and made an unsuccessful attempt to develop a rhenium mine. A paved road to Lees Ferry turns north from US 89A just west of Navajo Bridge. Follow the road in 5.1 miles and turn left 0.2 mile for Lonely Dell Ranch Historic District or continue 0.7 mile on the main road to its end for Lees Ferry Historic District.

## Spencer Trail
Energetic hikers climb this unmaintained trail for fine views of Marble Canyon from the rim, 1,500 feet above the river. The ingeniously planned route switchbacks up sheer ledges above Lees Ferry. It's a moderately difficult hike to the top, 3 miles roundtrip; carry water. From Lees Ferry parking lot at the end of the road, follow the path through the historic district to the steamboat wreck, then take the trail leading to the cliffs.

## Boating And Fishing
A fish-cleaning station and parking area are on the left just before the launch areas. At road's end, a paved upriver launch area is used by boaters headed toward Glen Canyon Dam; Grand Canyon river-running groups use the unpaved downriver launch area. Powerboats can go 14.5 miles up Glen Canyon almost to the dam. The Park Service recommends that you have a boat at least 16 feet long and a minimum 25-h.p. motor to cope with the swift currents. Boating below Lees Ferry is prohibited without a permit from Grand Canyon National Park because rapids and currents are extremely hazardous. Rainbow trout flourish in the cold, clear waters released from Lake Powell through Glen Canyon Dam. Fishermen should be able to identify and must return to the river any of the endangered native fish—the Colorado squawfish, bonytail chub, humpback chub, and razorback sucker.

## Campground
Sites at **Lees Ferry Campground** have drinking water but no showers or hookups; $6/night. From US 89A, take the Lees Ferry Road in 4.4 miles and turn left at the sign. The ranger station is just past the campground turnoff; obtain boating, fishing, and hiking information here (open irregular hours) or look for a ranger; tel. 355-2234. The National Park Service allows boat camping on the Colorado River above Lees Ferry only at one of the several developed campsites. These sites lack piped water but are free. (Purify river water before drinking.)

# MARBLE CANYON TO FREDONIA ON US 89A

## Marble Canyon Lodge
John Wesley Powell named the nearby section of Colorado River canyon for its smooth, marblelike appearance. The lodge, on US 89A at the turnoff for Lees Ferry, offers motel rooms and kitchenettes ($36.93 s, $50.64 d and up; less in winter), restaurant (American food for breakfast, lunch, and dinner daily), store (groceries, camping supplies, and Indian crafts), post office, gas station, and paved airstrip; tel. 355-2225.

## Lee's Ferry Lodge
The lodge has motel rooms ($29 s, $38 d), restaurant (American food for breakfast, lunch, and dinner daily), gift shop, and sporting goods store. Located on US 89A, 3 miles west of Marble Canyon and 38 miles east of Jacob Lake; tel. 355-2223.

## Cliff Dweller's Lodge
About 1890, Anglo traders built an unusual trading post underneath a giant boulder. The old buildings can still be seen along the highway beside the modern motel. Cliff Dweller's Lodge offers rooms ($37.98 s, $47.48 d; less in winter), restaurant (American food for breakfast, lunch, and dinner), small store, and gas station. On US 89A, 8 miles west of Marble Canyon and 33 miles east of Jacob Lake; tel. 355-2228.

*view of Marble Canyon from Vermilion Cliffs*

### San Bartolome Historic Site
Markers tell the story of the Dominguez–Escalante Expedition, which camped near here in 1776. Led by two Spanish priests, the group struggled to find a route through this rugged terrain so that they could return to Santa Fe. The priests made some promising contacts with Indian groups in present-day Utah, but failed in their quest to cross overland to California. The signposted site is on the north side of US 89A about midway between Marble Canyon and Jacob Lake.

### Vermilion Cliffs
These sheer cliffs have a striking red color and appear to burst into flame during sunsets. The cliffs dominate the northern horizon for many miles along this section of highway; a hilltop pullout 11 miles east of Jacob Lake on US 89A has the best panorama.

### Jacob Lake
High in the pine forests (elev. 7,925 feet), this tiny village is conveniently located on US 89A at the AZ 67 turnoff for the Grand Canyon

North Rim. The nearby lake honors Mormon missionary and explorer Jacob Hamblin. **Jacob Lake Inn** offers basic motel rooms ($52.50-63), cabins (April-Nov. only; $42-52.50), restaurant (American food for breakfast, lunch, and dinner), grocery store, Indian crafts shop, and service station; open all year; tel. 643-7232. **Jacob Lake Forest Camp** has sites with drinking water but no hookups; open mid-May to late Oct.; $7/night. **Jacob Lake RV Park,** located one-half mile off AZ 67 just south of Jacob Lake, is open May 1 to Oct. 31 with tent spaces ($7) and RV sites ($14-16 w/hookups); Jacob Lake, AZ 86022. For advice on hiking, camping, scenic drives, and other recreation in the surrounding Kaibab National Forest, stop in at the **North Kaibab Visitor Center,** next to Jacob Lake Inn; open daily mid-May to mid-Oct.; tel. 643- 7298.

The **Canyoneers** operate cross-country ski facilities and offer tours, accommodations, and food in the Kaibab National Forest near Jacob Lake. The **North Rim Nordic Center** has over 25 km of set track and trails, rentals, instruction from beginner to advanced, and tours; the season runs Dec. 1-March 15, sometimes longer; located one-half mile southwest of Jacob Lake on Forest Route 579. **North Rim Winter Camp,** at the North Rim Country Store (26 miles south of Jacob Lake at Milepost 605), features mostly backcountry skiing, though some track is set; services include heated yurts, food, tours, and instruction; open the same Dec.1-March 15 season. **Kaibab Lodge** offers more deluxe accommodations and food across a meadow from the North Rim Winter Camp. You can drive to the North Rim Nordic Center in winter, but *not* to the Kaibab Lodge and North Rim Winter Camp. Canyoneers provides SnowVan transportation to these last two places or you can ski in. Air service from Grand Canyon Airport may be available too. Contact the Canyoneers at Box 2997, Flagstaff, AZ 86003; tel. (800) 525-0924 for reservations out of state, 526-0924 for reservations in Arizona, 638-2383 for North Rim Winter Camp, or 638-2389 for Kaibab Lodge.

## Fredonia

Though just a tiny town (pop. 1,220), Fredonia is the largest community on the Arizona Strip. Nearby forests supply a lumber mill operated by Kaibab Industries. Mormon polygamists, seeking refuge from federal agents, settled here in 1885. They first called their place Hardscrabble but later chose "Fredonia," perhaps a contraction of the words "freedom" and *"dona"* (Spanish for wife).

Two modest motels lie along Main St. (US 89A): **Blue Sage Motel and RV** is at 330 S. Main St.; $7.50 RV w/hookups, $21.50 s, $32.25 d; closed in winter; tel. 643-7125. **Ship Rock Motel** is across the highway at 337 S. Main St.; $23.65 s or d; closed in winter; tel. 643-7355. For Mexican and American food, dine at **Nedra's Cafe,** 165 N. Main St.; open Mon.-Sat. for breakfast, lunch, and dinner (and Sun. for lunch and dinner in summer); tel. 643-7591. **Traveler's Inn Res-**taurant serves steak, seafood, and other fare 3 miles north of town; open weekdays for lunch and dinner, Sat. for dinner only; tel. 643-7402. The **city park** offers picnic tables, playground, and outdoor pool; turn 2 blocks east at the sign on Hortt from N. Main. **Post office** is at 85 N. Main Street. The **North Kaibab Ranger District** office can tell you about hiking, Grand Canyon viewpoints, and back roads of the national forest north of the Grand Canyon; a North Kaibab Forest map costs $2; open daily 7 a.m.-7 p.m. from mid-May to mid-Oct. and Mon.-Fri. 7:30 a.m.-4 p.m. in winter; 430 S. Main St. (Box 248, Fredonia, AZ 86022); tel. 643-7395.

## PIPE SPRING NATIONAL MONUMENT

Step back to the days when cowboys and pioneers first settled this land. Excellent exhibits in Winsor Castle, an early Mormon ranch southwest of Fredonia, provide a look into frontier life. Abundant spring water attracted prehistoric basketmaker and pueblo Indians, who settled nearby more than 1,000 years ago, then departed. Nomadic Paiute Indians came more recently and now live on the surrounding Kaibab-Paiute Indian Reservation. Mormons discovered the springs in 1858 and began ranching 5 years later, but swift Navajo raiding parties stole some stock and killed two men who pursued the Indians. A treaty signed in 1870 between the Mormons and Navajo ended the raids and opened the land to development.

Brigham Young, the Mormon president, then decided to locate the church's southern Utah tithing herd at Pipe Spring. A pair of two-story stone houses went up with walls connecting the ends to form a protected courtyard. Workmen added gun ports "just in case," but the settlement was never attacked. The structure became known as Winsor Castle because the ranch's superintendent, Anson P. Winsor, possessed a regal bearing and was thought to be related to the English royal family. Winsor built up a sizable herd of cattle and horses and oversaw dairying and

*Winsor Castle*

farming at the ranch. A telegraph office (Arizona's first) that opened in 1871 brought Utah and the rest of the world closer. Travelers frequently stopped by. In fact, so many newlyweds passed through after having been married in the St. George Temple that their route became known as the Honeymoon Trail. In the 1880s, the Mormon Church entered a period of turmoil and feared that the federal government would seize church property in the dispute over polygamous marriages. Winsor Castle, whose importance to the church had been declining, was sold to a non-Mormon.

President Harding proclaimed Pipe Spring a national monument in 1923 "as a memorial of Western pioneer life." National Park Service staff keep the frontier spirit alive by maintaining the ranch as it was in the 1870s. Activities such as cattle branding, gardening, weaving, spinning, quilt-making, and baking still take place on a small scale. You can take a short tour of Winsor Castle or explore the restored rooms and outbuildings on your own. A half-mile loop trail climbs the small ridge behind the ranch to a viewpoint; signs tell of the history and geology of the area.

### Visitor Center

Historic exhibits are open daily 8 a.m.-4 p.m. year-round; $1/person admission; tel. 643-7105. A short video introduces the monument. Blacksmithing, branding, and other cowboy chores sometimes take place in the summer months. Produce from the garden and goodies from the kitchen may be sold or given away. A gift shop offers regional books and Southwestern Indian arts and crafts. The snack bar's menu includes such items as cowboy beans and beef similar to those eaten here 100 years ago. The Paiute tribe operates **Heart Canyon Campground** 0.5 mile northeast of the monument; sites have showers and stay open all year: $5, $10 w/hookups. Nearest grocery stores, restaurants, and motels are in Fredonia. Pipe Spring National Monument is just off AZ 389, 14 miles southwest of Fredonia.

## PARIA CANYON

The wild and twisting canyons of the Paria River and its tributaries offer a memorable experience for experienced hikers. Silt-laden waters have sculptured the colorful canyon walls, revealing 200 million years of geologic history. Paria means "Muddy Water" in the Paiute language. You enter the 2,000-foot-deep gorge of the Paria in southern Utah, then hike 37 miles downstream to Lees Ferry in Arizona, where the Paria empties into the Colorado River.

Ancient petroglyphs and campsites show that pueblo Indians traveled the Paria more than 700 years ago. They hunted mule deer and bighorn sheep while using the broad, lower end of the canyon to grow corn, beans, and squash. The Dominguez-Escalante Expedition stopped at the mouth of the Paria in 1776 and were the first white men to see the Paria River. After John D. Lee began the Colorado River ferry service in 1872, he and others farmed the lower Paria Canyon. Pros-

*Paria Canyon*

pectors came here to search for gold, uranium, and other minerals, but much of the Paria Canyon remained unexplored. In the late 1960s, the Bureau of Land Management (BLM) organized a small expedition whose research led to protection of the canyon as a primitive area. The Arizona Wilderness Act in 1984 designated Paria Canyon a wilderness, along with parts of the Paria Plateau and Vermilion Cliffs.

Allow 4-6 days to hike the Paria Canyon because of the many river crossings and because you'll want to make sidetrips up some of the tributary canyons. The hike is considered moderately difficult. Hikers should have enough backpacking experience to be self-sufficient, as help may be days away. Flash floods can race through the canyon, especially from July to September. Rangers close the Paria if they think a danger exists. Because the upper end has the narrowest passages (between Miles 4.2 and 9.0), rangers require that all hikers start here in order to have up-to-date weather information. You must have a permit, which is issued free (no more than 24 hours in advance) by the BLM rangers at the Paria Canyon Ranger Station near the trailhead (open Thurs.-Mon. 8-11 a.m. from mid-March to mid-Nov.) or at the Kanab Area Office, 318 N. 100 East in Kanab, Utah 84741 (open Mon.-Fri. 7:45 a.m.-4:30 p.m. year-round); tel. (801) 644-2672. Both offices provide weather forecasts and brochures with map and hiking information.

All visitors need to take special care to minimize impact on this beautiful canyon. Check the BLM "Visitor Use Regulations" for the Paria before you go. They include no campfires in the Paria and its tributaries, a pack-in/pack-out policy (including TP!), and that latrines be made at least 100 feet away from the river and campsite locations.

Best times to travel along the Paria are from about mid-March to June and Oct. and November. Winter hikers often complain of painfully cold feet. Wear shoes suitable for frequent wading; canvas shoes work better than heavy leather hiking boots. You can get good drinking water from springs along the way (see the BLM hiking brochure for locations); it's best not to use the river water because of possible chemical pollution from farms and ranches upstream. Normally the river is only ankle deep, but it can be waist deep in a few spots in the spring or after rainy spells. During thunderstorms, it can be over 20 feet deep in the Paria Narrows, so heed weather warnings! Quicksand, most prevalent after flooding, is more of a nuisance than a danger—usually it's just knee deep. Many hikers carry a walking stick to probe the opaque waters for good crossing places.

**Wrather Canyon Arch**
One of Arizona's largest natural arches lies about one mile up this side canyon. The massive structure has a 200-foot span. Turn right (southwest) at Mile 20.6 on the Paria hike. The mouth of Wrather Canyon and other points along the Paria are unsigned; you need to follow your map.

**Trailheads**
The BLM Paria Canyon Ranger Station is in Utah, 30 miles northwest of Page on US 89 near Milepost 21. It's on the south side of the highway, just east of the Paria River. Actual trailhead is 2 miles south on a dirt road near an old homestead site called White House Ruins. Exit trailhead is at Lonely Dell Ranch near Lees Ferry historic site, 44 miles southwest of Page via US 89 and 89A.

**Shuttle Services**
You'll need to do a 150-mile roundtrip car shuttle for this hike or make arrangements for someone else to do it for you, using either your car (about $55), or theirs ($125-150). Contact: Marble Canyon Lodge (tel. 355-2225), Ken Berlin (tel. 355-2286), Richard Clark (tel. 355-2281), or Steve Knisely (602-355-2295); all can be reached at Marble Canyon, AZ 86036.

**Buckskin Gulch**
This amazing tributary of the Paria has convoluted walls hundreds of feet high, yet it narrows to as little as 4 feet in width. In places the walls block out so much light that it's like

walking in a cave. Be *very* careful to avoid times of flash-flood danger. Hiking can be strenuous with rough terrain, deep pools of water, and log and rock jams that may require the use of ropes. Conditions vary considerably from one year to the next. You can descend into Buckskin from two trailheads, Buckskin and Wire Pass, both reached by a dirt road. The hike from Buckskin trailhead to the Paria River is 16.3 miles one way and takes 12 or more hours. From Wire Pass trailhead it's 1.7 miles to Buckskin Gulch, then 11.8 miles to the Paria. You can climb out on a trail to a safe camping place about halfway down Buckskin Gulch. Carry water to last until the mouth of Buckskin Gulch.

# PAGE

Before 1957, only sand and desert vegetation lay atop Manson Mesa where Page now sits, 130 miles north of Flagstaff, Arizona, and 72 miles east of Kanab, Utah. In that year the U.S. Bureau of Reclamation decided to build a giant reservoir in Glen Canyon on the Colorado River. Glen Canyon Dam was to become one of the largest construction projects ever undertaken. The 710-foot-high structure would create a lake covering 250 square miles with a shoreline of nearly 2,000 miles. Workmen hastily set up prefabricated metal buildings for barracks, dining hall, and offices. Trailers rolled in, one serving as Page's first bank. The Bureau of Reclamation named the construction camp for John C. Page, who served as the Bureau's first commissioner from 1937 to 1943.

The remote desert spot gradually turned into a modern town as schools, businesses, and churches appeared. Streets were named and grass and trees planted, and Page took on the appearance of American suburbia. The town still has a new and clean look. Though small (pop. 7,100), it's the largest community in Arizona's far north, and offers travelers a good selection of places to stay and eat. Wedged between the Arizona Strip to the west, Glen Canyon National Recreation Area to the north, and the Navajo Reservation to the east and south, Page makes a useful base for visiting all these areas. The townsite (elev. 4,300 feet) overlooks Lake Powell and Glen Canyon Dam; the large Wahweap Resort and Marina are just 6 miles away. Unless you take a commercial flight in you'll need your own transport to get here.

## Powell Museum

This collection honors scientist and explorer John Wesley Powell. In 1869 he led the first expedition down the Green and Colorado river gorges, then ran the rivers a second time in 1871-72. It was Powell who named the most splendid section the "Grand Canyon." Old drawings and photographs illustrate his life and voyages. Fossil and mineral displays interpret the thick geologic section revealed by canyons of the Colorado River system. Other exhibits contain pottery, baskets, weapons, tools of Southwestern Indian tribes, and memorabilia of early pioneers and the founding of Page. Travel info, Lake Powell boat tours, one-day river trips, flightseeing tours, and regional books are available. Summer hours (June to Sept.) are Sun. 10 a.m.-6 p.m. and Mon.-Sat. 8 a.m.-6 p.m.; May and Oct. hours are Mon.-Sat. 8 a.m.-5 p.m.; March, April, and Nov. hours are Mon.-Fri. 9 a.m.-5 p.m.; closed in winter; tel. 645-9496. The museum is in downtown Page at the corner of Lake Powell Blvd. and N. Navajo Drive.

*canyon wren*
(Catherpes mexicanus)

## Diné Bí Keyah Museum
### (Big Lake Trading Post)
This small collection of modern and prehistoric Indian artifacts is on the second floor; open daily 6 a.m.-9 p.m.; free admission; tel. 645-2404. Big Lake Trading Post is 1.3 miles southeast of town on AZ 98. Indian crafts, groceries, and fishing supplies are sold.

## Accommodations
All of Page's motels lie on or near Lake Powell Blvd., a 3.25-mile loop designated US 89L that branches off the main highway. The summer rates listed here drop substantially in winter. **Desert Lake Motel** is at 121 S. Lake Powell Blvd; $43.40-54.25 s, $48.83-59.68 d; tel. 645-2488. **Empire House Motel** has a coffee shop and swimming pool at 100 S. Lake Powell Blvd.; $45.57 s, $48.83; tel. 645-2406. **Page Boy Motel** has a swimming pool at 150 N. Lake Powell Blvd.; $30.38 s, $36.89 d; tel. 645-2416. The **Weston Lamplighter Motel** (Best Western) also offers a swimming pool at 201 N. Lake Powell Blvd.; $60.76 s, $66.19 d; tel. 645-2451. **Holiday Inn** features a swimming pool, restaurant, and views over Lake Powell from 287 N. Lake Powell Blvd.; $85.72 s, $92.23 d; tel. 645-8851 or (800) HOLIDAY. The **Inn at Lake Powell** has fine views, swimming pool, and an adjacent restaurant; $60.76-73.78 s, $67.27-81.38 d at 716 Rim View Dr. and Lake Powell Blvd. (across from Holiday Inn); tel. 645-2466 or (800) 826-2718.

## Campgrounds
**Page-Lake Powell Campground** offers sites for tents and RVs, $14.11 no hookups, ($17.36 w/hookups); has showers; located 0.7 mile southeast of town on AZ 98; tel. 645-3374. Other campgrounds, an RV park, and motels are in the Wahweap area (see "Lake Powell" below).

## Food And Entertainment
**Glen Canyon Steak House** serves American food daily for breakfast, lunch, and dinner; specialties include steaks, seafood, ribs, and chicken; live country-rock bands perform evenings Tues.-Sun.; 201 N. Lake Powell Blvd.; tel. 645-3363. **Ken's Old West Restaurant** has steak, prime rib, and seafood; open daily for dinner; country-western bands provide music Tues.-Sat.; 718 Vista Ave. (across from Glen Canyon Steak House); tel. 645-5160. **Family Tree Restaurant** in the Holiday Inn offers a varied menu and is open daily for breakfast, lunch, and dinner; 287 N. Lake Powell Blvd.; tel. 645-8851.

Stop for Chinese food at **Yen Jing** (open Mon.-Fri. for lunch and daily for dinner; 125 S. Lake Powell Blvd.; tel. 645-3244); **Starlight** (open daily except Sun. for breakfast, lunch, and dinner; 46 S. Lake Powell Blvd.; tel. 645-3620); and **Dynasty** (open daily for breakfast, lunch, and dinner; 716 Rim View Dr. next to Inn at Lake Powell; tel. 645-8113). **Zapata's Mexican Restaurant** is open daily except Sun. for lunch and dinner; 615 N. Navajo Dr.; tel. 645-9006. Pizza, spaghetti, and other Italian fare are served by **Strombolli's Pizza** (open daily for breakfast, lunch, and dinner; 711 N. Navajo Dr.; tel. 645-2605) and **Bella Napoli** (open Mon.-Sat. for dinner in spring, then daily for dinner until mid-autumn; closed in winter; 810 N. Navajo Dr.; tel. 645-2706). Buy **groceries** at Safeway (Page Plaza at corner of Lake Powell Blvd. and Elm St.), Bashas' (644 N. Navajo Dr.), or at Mrs. C's Health Food Center (32 S. Lake Powell Boulevard). Catch movies at **Mesa Theatre,** 42 S. Lake Powell Blvd.; tel. 645-9565.

## Events
For more information about Lake Powell's events, contact Lake Powell Resorts and Marinas; tel. (800) 528-6154 (278-8888 in greater Phoenix). To learn about other events, contact Page/Lake Powell Chamber of Commerce; tel. 645-2741.

**January:** Hole-in-Rock Commemoration on Lake Powell celebrates the 1880 crossing of the Colorado River by Mormon pioneers; historic programs and tours take place at Wahweap and Bullfrog marinas. Striper Derby continues at Lake Powell (see November, below). **February:** Striper Derby continues at Lake Powell. **March:** Hot Air Balloon Regatta flies over the Page area. Bullfrog Open

awards prizes to biggest largemouth bass.
**May:** Four-H Horse Show. Page Open Rodeo. **June:** Big Lake Trading Post sponsors an Indian Market with crafts and dancing on the last weekend. **July:** Fourth of July celebration with food, games, and fireworks at Page Memorial Park. Pioneer Day Parade on third weekend. **August:** Halls Crossing-Bull-frog Swim is an early morning swimming race between the two marinas. **September:** Northern Arizona Fall Roundup Rodeo. Rod Run (show of custom and antique cars). Lake Powell Triathlon takes place at Bullfrog Marina. **November:** Fishermen compete for the biggest striped bass in the Striper Derby, lasting through Feb. at Lake Powell. Bull-

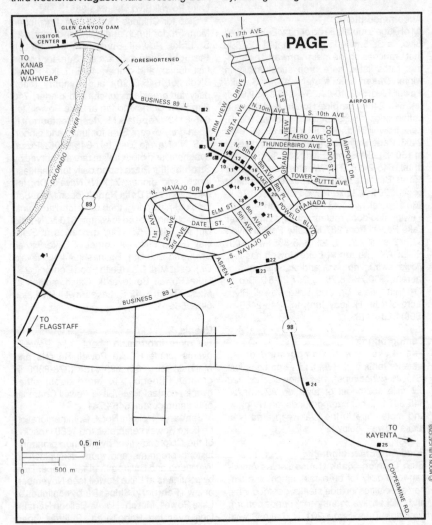

frog's Festival of Lights Parade. **December:** Here Comes Santa Parade in Page and Wahweap Festival of Lights Parade on Lake Powell. Striper Derby continues at Lake Powell.

## Services And Recreation

**Post office** is at 615 Elm St.; tel. 645-2571. **Page Hospital** is at the corner of Vista Ave. and N. Navajo Dr.; tel. 645-2424. In **emergencies** (police, fire, medical), dial 911.

Page High School has an indoor **swimming pool** (open all year) near the corner of S. Lake Powell Blvd. and AZ 98; tel. 645-8801. Play **tennis** at the courts on S. Lake Powell Blvd. (Church Row). **Glen Canyon Golf and Country Club** has a 9-hole golf course west of town on US 89; tel. 645-2715.

### PAGE

1. Glen Canyon Golf & Country Club
2. McDonald's
3. Holiday Inn
4. Inn at Lake Powell; Page/Lake Powell Chamber of Commerce
5. Weston Lamplighter Motel
6. Glen Canyon Steakhouse
7. Ken's Old West Restaurant
8. Page Hospital
9. Page Boy Motel
10. public library
11. Blue Water Adventures
12. Powell Museum
13. Bella Napoli
14. Zapata's Mexican Restaurant
15. Lakeview Shopping Center
16. Strombolis's Pizza
17. Starlite Restaurant; Pleasure Bound Bookstore; Wilderness River Adventures; Mesa Theatre
18. post office
19. Page Plaza
20. Empire House Motel; Desert Lake Motel; Yen Jing Restaurant
21. Page Memorial Park
22. Page High School
23. tennis courts
24. Page-Lake Powell Campground
25. Big Lake Trading Post

## Information

**Page/Lake Powell Chamber of Commerce** has information about the sights and services of the area; staff also book lake and river tours and scenic flights; open Mon.-Fri. 8 a.m.-6 p.m. in summer and 8 a.m.-5 p.m. the rest of the year; located at the Inn at Lake Powell, 716 Rim View Dr. (Box 727, Page, AZ 86040); tel. 645-2741. The **public library** is open daily except Sun.; corner of 697 Vista Ave. and N. Lake Powell Blvd.; tel. 645-2231. **Pleasure Bound Bookstore** has regional titles and general reading at 48 S. Lake Powell Blvd. in Adkinson Mall; tel. 645-5333.

## Tours

**Lake Powell Overland Adventures** (tel. 645-5501/3155) and **Duck Tours** (tel. 645-2741/2955) offer back-road drives to Corkscrew (Antelope) Canyon and other destinations in the area. **Wilderness River Adventures** offers half-day raft trips down the Colorado River from just below Glen Canyon Dam to Lees Ferry, 15 miles of smooth-flowing water; $31.75 adult, $21.15 children under 12; the trips leave daily May to Sept. and can be arranged (6 person minimum) the rest of the year, weather permitting; Grand Canyon raft trips of 3-12 days are offered too; 50 S. Lake Powell Blvd. in Lakeview Shopping Center; (Box 717, Page, AZ 86040); tel. 645-3279 (800-528-6154 outside Arizona). **Blue Water Adventures** runs a scuba dive shop and leads snorkeling and scuba trips on Lake Powell; 697 N. Navajo Dr.; tel. 645-3087. **Lake Powell Air Service's** long list of "flight-seeing" trips includes Lake Powell and Rainbow Bridge (one-half hour, $47), Grand Canyon (1½ hours, $110), Monument Valley (1½ hours, $105; $135 w/ground tour), and Bryce Canyon (1½ hours, $105); a 2-person minimum applies to most tours; children 12 and under get 30% off; scenic flights to Phoenix, Las Vegas, Salt Lake City, and Grand Junction can also be arranged; tel. 645-2494. Boat tours to Rainbow Bridge and other destinations leave from the nearby Wahweap Marina; see "Lake Powell" below.

**Transport**
No bus service at press time. Wahweap Lodge and most area motels will provide transportation for guests to and from the airport. Rent cars at the airport from **Avis** (tel. 645-2494) or **Budget** (tel. 645-3977). From Page's airport on the east edge of town, **Sky West Airlines** flies once or twice daily (one-way fares) to Flagstaff ($68), Phoenix ($106), St. George ($66), Salt Lake City ($111), Las Vegas ($103), and other destinations; tel. 645-9200 or (800) 453-9417.

# GLEN CANYON NATIONAL RECREATION AREA

This vast recreation area covers 1.25 million acres, most of which spreads northeast into Utah. Lake Powell stands out as the centerpiece, surrounded by beautiful canyon country. Just a handful of roads approach the lake, so you'll need to do some boating or hiking to explore this unique land of water and rock. The recreation area also includes a beautiful remnant of Glen Canyon in a 15-mile section of the Colorado River from Glen Canyon Dam to Lees Ferry (see pp. 73-75).

*island monument in Glen Canyon*

## LAKE POWELL

Conservationists deplored the loss of remote and beautiful Glen Canyon of the Colorado River beneath Lake Powell. Today, we have only words, pictures, and memories to remind us of its wonders. On the other hand, the 186-mile-long lake now provides easy access for many people to an area most had not even known existed. Lake Powell is the second largest man-made lake within the United States. Only Lake Mead, farther downstream, has a greater water-storage capacity. Lake Powell, however, has three times more shoreline—1,960 miles—and holds enough water to cover the state of Pennsylvania a foot deep! Bays and coves offer nearly limitless opportunities for exploration by boaters. Only the lower part—Glen Canyon Dam, Wahweap Resort and Marina, Antelope and Navajo canyons, and the lower parts of Labyrinth, Face, and West canyons—extends into Arizona. The elevation of the surface fluctuates from 3,640 to 3,700 feet. The Carl Hayden Visitor Center, perched beside the dam, has tours of the dam, related exhibits, and an information desk for all the Glen Canyon National Recreation Area.

### Climate

Summer, when temperatures rise into the 90s and 100s F, is the busiest season for swimming, boating, and water-skiing. Visits during the rest of the year can be enjoyable too, though activities shift more to sightseeing, fishing, and hiking. Spring and autumn are the best times to enjoy the backcountry. Winter temperatures drop to highs in the 40s and 50s, with freezing nights and the possibility of snow. Lake surface temperatures range from a comfortable 80˚ in Aug. to a chilly 45˚ in January. Chinook winds can blow day and night for periods from Feb. to May. Thunderstorms in late summer bring strong, gusting winds with widely scattered rain showers. Annual precipitation averages about 7 inches.

## Geology, Flora, And Fauna

The colorful rock formations rising above the lake's surface tell a story of ancient deserts, oceans, and rivers. Uplift of the Colorado Plateau beginning about 60 million years ago started a cycle of erosion that has carved canyons and created delicately balanced rocks and graceful natural arches and bridges.

The desert comes right to the edge of the water, because fluctuating lake levels prevent plant growth along the shore. Common plants of this high-desert country are prickly pear and hedgehog cacti, rabbitbrush, sand sagebrush, blackbrush, cliffrose, mariposa and sego lilies, globemallow, Indian paintbrush, evening primrose, penstemon, and Indian rice grass. Pinyon pine and juniper trees grow on the high plateaus. Springs and permanent streams support sandbar willow, tamarisk, cattail, willow, and cottonwood. Look for hanging gardens of maidenhair fern, columbine, and other water-loving plants in small alcoves high on the sandstone walls.

Most animals are secretive and nocturnal; you're most likely to see them in early morning or in the evening. Local mammals include pronghorn, mule deer, mountain lion, coyote, red and gray foxes, ringtail cat, spotted and striped skunks, bobcat, badger, river otter, beaver, prairie dog, Ord kangaroo rat, blacktailed jack rabbit, several species of squirrels and chipmunks, and many species of mice and bats. Some lizards you might see sunning on a rock are collared, side-blotched, desert horned, and chuckwalla. Snake species include common kingsnake, gopher, striped whipsnake, western rattlesnake, and western diamondback rattlesnake. Birds stopping by on their migrations include American avocet, Canada goose, and teal. Others, such as blue heron, snowy egret, and bald eagle, come for the winter. Birds you might spot any time of the year are American merganser, mallard, canyon wren, pinyon jay, common raven, redtailed and Swainson's hawks, great horned and long-eared owls, peregrine and prairie falcons, and golden eagle.

## Recreation At Lake Powell

If you don't have your own craft, Wahweap and other marinas will rent a boat for fishing, skiing, or houseboating. Boat tours visit Rainbow Bridge (the world's largest natural bridge) and other destinations from Wahweap, Bullfrog, and Halls Crossing marinas. Sailboats find the steadiest breezes in Wahweap, Padre, Halls, and Bullfrog bays, where spring winds average 15-20 knots. Kayaks and canoes can be used in the more protected areas. All boaters need to be alert for approaching storms that can bring wind gusts up to 60 mph. Waves on open expanses of the lake are sometimes steeper than ocean waves and can exceed 6 feet from trough to crest. Marinas and book stores sell navigation maps of Lake Powell. You'll need an Arizona fishing license for the southern 5 miles of lake and a Utah license for the rest of Lake Powell. Licenses and information can be obtained from marinas on the water or sporting goods stores in Page. Fishermen catch largemouth, smallmouth, and striped bass, northern and walleye pike, catfish, crappie, and carp. Smaller fish include bluegill, perch, and sunfish. Wahweap has a swimming beach (no lifeguards), and boaters can find their own remote spots. Scuba divers step underwater to swim with the sizable bass. Hikers have a choice of easy daytrips or long wilderness backpack treks. The canyons of the Escalante in Utah rate among America's premier hiking areas (see the *Utah Handbook*). Other good hiking areas within or adjacent to Glen Canyon N.R.A. include Rainbow Bridge National Monument (see pp. 103-104), Paria Canyon (see pp. 78-80), Dark Canyon, and Grand Gulch. National Park Service staff at the Carl Hayden Visitor Center can suggest trips and supply trail descriptions. Several guidebooks to Lake Powell have detailed hiking, camping, and boating information. Most of the canyon country near Lake Powell remains wild and little explored—hiking possibilities are limitless! Be sure to carry plenty of water.

## GLEN CANYON DAM

Construction workers labored from 1956 to 1964 to build this giant concrete structure. It stands 710 feet high above bedrock, and its top measures 1,560 feet across. Thickness ranges from 300 feet at the base to just 25 feet at the top. As part of the Upper Colorado River Storage Project, the dam provides water storage (its main purpose), hydroelectricity, flood control, and recreation on Lake Powell. Eight giant turbine generators churn out a total of 1,150,000 kilowatts. at 13,800 volts. Vertigo sufferers shouldn't look down when driving across Glen Canyon Bridge, just downstream of the dam; cold, green waters of the Colorado River glide 700 feet below.

### Carl Hayden Visitor Center
Photos, paintings, movies, and slide presentations in the Visitor Center show features of Glen Canyon National Recreation Area, including Lake Powell and construction of the dam. A giant relief map helps to visualize the rugged terrain surrounding the lake; look closely and you'll spot Rainbow Bridge. Guided tours inside the dam and generating room depart daily every hour 8 a.m.-4 p.m. in summer. You can take a self-guided tour daily 8 a.m.-4 p.m. in summer and 8:30 a.m.-4 p.m. the rest of the year. National Park Service staff operate an information desk where you can find out about boating, fishing, camping, and hiking in the immense Glen Canyon National Recreation Area (or write Box 1507, Page, AZ 86040); tel. 645-2511 or 645-2471. The Glen Canyon Natural History Association has a variety of books about the recreation area and its environs for sale next to the information desk. A Navajo rug exhibit illustrates the many different patterns used. Souvenirs, snacks, and postcards can be purchased at a gift shop in the Visitor Center building. The Carl Hayden Visitor Center is open daily 8 a.m.-6 p.m. in summer and 8:30 a.m.-5 p.m. the rest of the year. Tours, exhibits, and movies are free. In summer, you can attend a campfire program several nights a week at nearby Wahweap Campground amphitheater.

*skimming the waters of Lake Powell*

**1.** the San Francisco Peaks from atop Sunset Crater (climbing Sunset Crater is no longer permitted); **2.** Lockett Meadow and the Inner Basin of the San Francisco Peaks; **3.** Inner Basin of the San Francisco Peaks; **4.** Hart Prairie and the San Francisco Peaks; **5.** inside Tonto Natural Bridge, near Payson (all photos by B. Weir)

1. Mary Lou Gulley, owner and guide at Mystery Castle near Phoenix; 2. shopping on the Navajo Indian Reservation; 3. DeGrazia Studio, Tucson; 4. Tony Rose on the Beamer Trail, Grand Canyon National Park; 5. Melanie Bertram showing off Onyx Bridge in Petrified Forest National Park; 6. Carlos Villanueva coming down the lower Paria Canyon (all photos by B. Weir)

*Wahweap Marina*

## MARINAS

The **National Park Service** provides public boat ramps, campgrounds, and ranger offices at most of the marinas. Rangers know current boating and back-road conditions, primitive camping areas, and good places to explore. **Lake Powell Resorts & Marinas** operate marina services, boat rentals, boat tours, accommodations, RV parks, and restaurants; contact them for information and reservations (strongly recommended in summer) at 2916 N. 35th Ave., Suite 8, Phoenix, AZ 85017-5261; tel. (800) 528-6154 (278-8888 in greater Phoenix). To make reservations 7 days or less in advance, contact each marina or resort directly. All the marinas stay open year-round; you can avoid crowds and peak prices by coming in autumn, winter, or spring. Private or chartered aircraft can fly to Page Airport and airstrips near Bullfrog and Halls Crossing marinas.

### Wahweap

The name means "Bitter Water" in the Ute Indian language. Wahweap Lodge and Marina, Lake Powell's biggest, offers complete boaters' services and rentals, guided fishing trips, deluxe accommodations, an RV park, and fine dining. Wahweap is 7 miles northwest of Page, 5 miles beyond the Visitor Center. **Wahweap Lodge** offers several types of rooms starting at $68.84 s, $77.54 d in summer (May 15 to Oct. 15); $51.70 s, $58.29 d in spring and autumn; and $41.41 s, $46.68 d in winter (Nov. 1 to March 31). Guests enjoy lake views, restaurants, and, in summer, live entertainment and dancing. Contact Lake Powell Resorts & Marinas for reservations at 2916 N. 35th Ave., Suite 8, Phoenix, AZ 85017-5261; tel. (800) 528-6154 (278-8888 in greater Phoenix). Wahweap Lodge & Marina can also be reached at Box 1597, Page, AZ 86040; tel. 645-2433. **Lake Powell Motel** has less expensive rooms nearby at Wahweap Junction (4 miles northwest of Glen Canyon Dam on US 89); $47.48 s, $53 d in summer; $35.61 s, $39.83 d in spring and autumn; and $28.49 s, $31.91 d in winter; call 645-2477 or contact Lake Powell Resorts & Marinas for reservations.

An **RV park** with coin showers and laundry costs $15.82 w/hookups ($11.87 in winter). **Wahweap Campground** is operated first-come, first-served by the National Park Service; sites have drinking water but no showers or hookups; $6; campers may use the showers and laundry facilities at the RV park. Primitive camping (no water or fee) is available at **Lone Rock** in Utah, 6 miles northwest of Wahweap off US 89. Boaters may also camp along the lakeshore, but not within one mile of developed areas. A free picnic area and fish-cleaning station are located just west of Wahweap Lodge. Public boat ramps are located adjacent to the lodge and at State Line, one mile northwest of the lodge. During summer (June 1 to Sept. 30), you can obtain recreation information from the **Wahweap Ranger Station** near the picnic area; at other times see the staff at Carl Hayden Visitor Center.

The marina offers six **lake tours,** ranging from an hour-long paddle-wheel cruise around Wahweap Bay ($7.50 adult, $5 children) to an all-day trip to Rainbow Bridge, 50 miles away ($50.95 adult, $25.50 children). Half-day trips to Rainbow Bridge cost $39.75 adult, $19.95 children. **Boat rentals** include a 16-foot skiff with 25-h.p. motor ($52.75/day), an 18-foot powerboat with 120-h.p. motor ($155.61/day), and several sizes of houseboats starting at $648.53 for three nights. Fishing gear and water-skis can be rented too. Rental and some tour rates drop as much as 40% off-season.

### Dangling Rope

This floating marina lies 42 miles uplake from Glen Canyon Dam. The only access is by boat. Services include a ranger station, store, minor boat repairs, gas dock, and sanitary pump-out station. A dangling rope left behind in a nearby canyon, perhaps by uranium prospectors, prompted the name. The dock for Rainbow Bridge is 10 miles farther uplake in Bridge Canyon, a tributary of Forbidding Canyon.

### San Juan

A marina is planned for the south side of the lake's San Juan Arm. Ask at the Carl Hayden Visitor Center for current information.

Boats can be hand launched at **Clay Hills Crossing** at the upper end of the San Juan Arm. An unpaved road branches 11 miles southwest from UT 276 (road to Halls Crossing) to the lake; don't attempt the dead road after rains. River runners on the San Juan often take out here; no facilities are provided.

### Halls Crossing-Bullfrog Ferry

The *John Atlantic Burr* ferry can accommodate vehicles of all sizes and passengers for the short 20-minute crossing between these marinas. Halls Crossing and Bullfrog marinas lie on opposite sides of Lake Powell about 95 lake miles from Glen Canyon Dam, about midway up the length of the lake. Sections of paved Highway UT 276 connect each marina with UT 95. The ferry's daily schedule has six roundtrips from May 15 to Oct. 15, then four roundtrips the rest of the year; no reservations needed. You can pick up a schedule from the marinas. Service is suspended for a brief time annually, usually in Nov., for maintenance; signs at the UT 276 turnoffs will warn you when the ferry is closed.

### Halls Crossing

In 1880, Charles Hall built the ferry used by the Hole-in-the-Rock pioneers, who crossed the river to begin settlement in southeast Utah. The approach roads were so bad, however, that he moved the ferry 35 miles upstream to present-day Halls Crossing in the following year. Business continued to be slow, and Hall quit running the ferry in 1884.

Arriving at Halls Crossing by road, you'll first reach a small store offering **housekeeping units** (trailers: $74.18 d in summer, $55.63 d in spring and autumn, and $44.61 d in winter), an **RV park** ($16.13 w/hookups in summer, $9.68 w/hookups in winter), and gas pumps; the store may close in winter, but services are still available (ask at the trailer office next door). Coin-operated showers and laundry at the RV park are also open to the public. The separate National Park Service **campground,** just beyond and to the left, has sites with a good view of the lake, drinking water, and restrooms; $6. Continue 0.5 mile on the main road to the boat ramp and **Halls Crossing Marina.** The marina has a larger store (groceries and fishing and boating supplies), tours to Rainbow Bridge, a boat rental office (fishing, ski, and houseboat), gas dock, slips, and storage. The **ranger station** is nearby, though rangers are usually out on patrol; look for their vehicle in the area if the office is closed. Contact Lake Powell Resorts & Marinas for accommodation, boat rental, and tour reservations at 2916 N. 35th Ave., Suite 8, Phoenix, AZ 85017-5261; tel. (800)

528-6154 (278-8888 in greater Phoenix); the marina can also be reached at Hwy. 276, Lake Powell, UT 84533; tel. (801) 684-2261.

Stabilized Anasazi ruins at **Defiance House** in Forgotten Canyon make a good boating destination 12 miles uplake; a sign marks the beginning of the trail to the ruins. You can also take 2½-hour boat tours to Defiance House from Bullfrog Marina.

## Bullfrog

Before the days of Lake Powell, Bullfrog Rapids gave boaters a fast and bumpy ride. Bullfrog Marina now rivals Wahweap in its extensive visitor facilities. If driving in from either the ferry or the highway, you'll first see a large campground on the left; sites have drinking water and restrooms; $6. Continue on the main road to a junction; a service station here offers repairs and supplies. Continue straight at the junction for a picnic area, a ranger station/visitor center, Bullfrog Clinic, and the boat ramp; turn right at the service station for Defiance House Lodge and Restaurant, Trailer Village, Bullfrog Painted Hills RV Park, and Bullfrog Marina. The **ranger station/visitor center** is open daily 8 a.m.-4:30 p.m. in summer and intermittently the rest of the year; tel. (801) 684-2243. The **clinic** is open mid-May to mid-Oct. and can be reached at tel. (801) 684-2288.

**Defiance House Lodge** offers luxury accommodations (rates are similar to Wahweap's) and the **Anasazi Restaurant** (open daily for breakfast, lunch, and dinner). The front desk at the lodge also handles **housekeeping units** (trailers) and an **RV park** (both located nearby with rates similar to those at Halls Crossing) and **tours** to Rainbow Bridge and Defiance House. Showers, laundry, convenience store, and post office are at **Trailer Village.** The RV park also has showers. Ask rangers for directions to primitive camping areas with vehicle access elsewhere along Bullfrog Bay.

All-day **Rainbow Bridge tours** usually leave daily from April 15 to Oct. 1 and stop on request to pick up passengers at Halls Crossing Marina; (may have a passenger minimum; $50.95 adult, $25.50 children). **Defi-**

*Ord kangaroo rat*
*(Dipodomys ordi)*

**ance House tours** leave on request during the same season (may have a passenger minimum; $16.25 adult, $11.25 children). **Bullfrog Marina** has a store, rentals (fishing, ski, and houseboat), gas dock, slips, and storage. Contact Lake Powell Resorts & Marinas for accommodation, boat rental, and tour reservations at 2916 N. 35th Ave., Suite 8, Phoenix, AZ 85017-5261; tel. (800) 528-6154 (278-8888 in greater Phoenix); Bullfrog Resort & Marina can also be reached at Box 4055-Bullfrog, Lake Powell, UT 84533; tel. (801) 684-2233.

## Hite

In 1883, Cass Hite came to Glen Canyon in search of gold. He found some at a place later named "Hite City" and set off a small gold rush. Cass and a few of his relatives operated a small store and post office, the only services for many miles. Travelers wishing to cross the Colorado River here had the difficult task of swimming their animals across. Arthur Chaffin, a later resident, put through the first road and opened a ferry service in 1946. The Chaffin Ferry served uranium prospectors and adventurous motorists until the lake backed up to the spot in 1964. A steel bridge now spans the Colorado River far upstream. Cass Hite's store and the ferry site are underwater about 5 miles downlake from Hite Marina.

The uppermost marina on Lake Powell, Hite lies 141 lake miles from Glen Canyon Dam. From here boats can continue uplake to the mouth of Dark Canyon in Cataract Canyon at low water or into Canyonlands National Park at high water. Hite tends to be quieter than the other marinas and is favored by some fishermen and families. Turnoff for the marina is from UT 95 between Hanksville and Blanding. On the way in, you'll find a small **store** with gas pumps, **housekeeping units** (trailers; same rates as at Halls Crossing), and a primitive **campground** (no drinking water; free). Primitive camping is also available nearby off UT 95 at Dirty Devil, Farley Canyon, White Canyon, Blue Notch, and other locations. **Hite Marina,** at the end of the access road, has a small store, gas dock, boat rentals (fishing, ski, and houseboat), slips, and storage. Hikers can make arrangements with the marina to be dropped off or picked up at Dark Canyon. A **ranger station** is occasionally open; look for the ranger's vehicle at other times. Contact Lake Powell Resorts & Marinas for accommodation and boat rental reservations at 2916 N. 35th Ave., Suite 8, Phoenix, AZ 85017- 5261; tel. (800) 528-6154 (278-8888 in greater Phoenix). Hite Marina can also be contacted at Box 501, Lake Powell, UT 84533; tel. (801) 684-2278.

## ARIZONA STRIP WILDERNESS AREAS

All nine of these were designated as wilderness areas under the 1984 Arizona Wilderness Act. For hiking and access information in all but the Paria Canyon-Vermilion Cliffs and Saddle Mountain wildernesses, contact the Bureau of Land Management's **Arizona Strip District** office, 390 N. 3050 East, St. George, UT 84770; open Mon.-Fri. 8 a.m.-4:30 p.m.; tel. (801) 673-3545. **Kanab Resource Area** office takes care of the Paria Canyon-Vermilion Cliffs Wilderness at 318 N. 100 East, Kanab, UT 84741; open Mon.-Fri. 7:45 a.m.-4:30 p.m.; tel. (801) 644-2672. The U.S. Forest Service manages Saddle Mountain and part of Kanab Creek Wilderness areas; its **North Kaibab Ranger District** office is at 430 S. Main St. in Fredonia (Box 248, Fredonia, AZ 86022); open Mon.-Fri. 7:30 a.m.-4:30 p.m.; tel. 643-7395.

### Beaver Dam Mountains Wilderness
This 19,600-acre wilderness includes alluvial plains and rugged mountains of extreme northwestern Arizona and part of adjacent

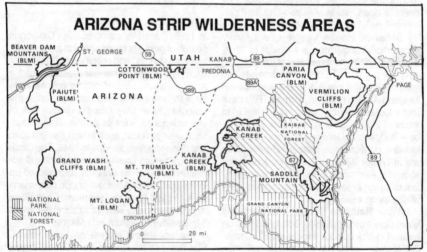

ARIZONA STRIP WILDERNESS AREAS

Utah (north of I-15 and the Virgin River). Desert bighorn sheep, desert tortoise, raptors, the endangered woundfin minnow, Joshua trees, and several rare plant species live here. No trails, but hikers enjoy going cross-country through the beautiful Joshua tree forest at the lower elevations. Cedar Pocket Rest Stop on I-15, 20 miles southwest of St. George, is a good starting point.

## Paiute Wilderness

This 84,700-acre wilderness is located in the extreme northwest corner of Arizona (south of I-15 and the Virgin River). The jagged Virgin Mountains contain a wide variety of plant and animal life from desert country at 2,400 feet to pine and fir forests at 8,012 feet atop Mt. Bangs. Several hiking trails wind through the rugged terrain. Sullivan Trail, a rough route, begins 1.5 miles downstream and across the Virgin River from Virgin River Campground (near I-15, 20 miles southwest of St. George); the trail climbs through Sullivan Canyon to Atkin Spring and on to the summit of Mt. Banks, a strenuous 12-mile hike one way.

## Grand Wash Cliffs Wilderness

Grand Wash Cliffs mark the southwest edge of the Colorado Plateau and form a major landmark of the western Grand Canyon. The wilderness protects 36,300 acres along a 12-mile section of the cliffs in an extremely remote part of Arizona. Desert bighorn sheep and raptors live in the high country, while desert tortoises forage lower down. Hikers can use an abandoned mining road, now closed to vehicles, along the base of the cliffs and explore rarely visited side canyons.

## Mount Logan Wilderness

Scenic features of this 14,600-acre volcanic region include Mt. Logan (7,866 feet), parts of the Uinkaret Mountains, and a large natural amphitheater on the west side known as "Hell's Hole." Oak, pinyon pine, and juniper woodlands cover the lower slopes. Higher and more protected areas support ponderosa pine and aspen. Kaibab squirrels, intro-duced in the early 1970s, now flourish in the forests. A road approaches the east side of Mount Logan; hikers can climb to the summit via some abandoned roads and a cross-country route; the hike is about 1.5 miles one way. Mt. Logan and nearby Mt. Trumbull wildernesses lie north of the Toroweap area of the Grand Canyon. John Wesley Powell named both peaks after U.S. senators.

## Mount Trumbull Wilderness

Located a short distance northeast of Mount Logan, this 7,900-acre wilderness protects the wooded slopes of Mt. Trumbull (8,028 feet). Geology, forests, and wildlife are similar to Mt. Logan's. A trail runs up the southwest side of Mt. Logan's summit via Nixon Spring; the hike is about 1.5 miles one way. Mormon pioneers built a steam-powered sawmill at the spring in 1870 to supply support timbers for the St. George Temple.

## Cottonwood Point Wilderness

The 6,500-acre wilderness contains multi-colored 1,000-foot cliffs, jagged pinnacles, and wooded canyons. Springs and seeps in the main canyon east of Cottonwood Point support a world of greenery, an oasis surrounded by desert. It's on the Utah border near Colorado City, west of Fredonia. Dirt roads from AZ 389 provide access.

## Kanab Creek Wilderness

This is the largest canyon system on the Grand Canyon's North Rim. Headwaters lie 100 miles north on the Paunsaugunt Plateau in Utah. The wilderness area protects 77,100 acres along the Kanab and its tributaries. Springs in Kanab Canyon nourish large cottonwood trees and lush growths of desert willow, tamarisk, maidenhair fern, and grass. From Hack Canyon, a popular entry point, hikers can descend 21 miles down Kanab Creek to the Colorado River; allow three days for the one-way trip. You'll need a Grand Canyon backcountry permit to camp below the junction with Jumpup Canyon. See Stewart Aitchison's *A Naturalist's Guide to Hiking the Grand Canyon* for a trail description.

**Saddle Mountain Wilderness**
Much of the 40,600-acre wilderness covers the densely forested Kaibab Plateau. Mountain lion, bear, and mule deer roam the area. North Canyon Wash is noted for its pure strain of native Apache trout. Saddle Mountain (8,424 feet) is northeast of the Bright Angel Point area on the Grand Canyon's North Rim.; you can see Saddle Mountain from Point Imperial viewpoint. A network of trails provide access to hikers and horseback riders.

**Paria Canyon-Vermilion Cliffs Wilderness**
The Paria Canyon, colorful cliffs, giant natural amphitheaters, sandstone arches, and parts of the Paria Plateau are protected by this 110,000-acre wilderness. Wonderful swirling patterns in sandstone hills enthrall visitors on top of the plateau. Hikers also enjoy following the 37-mile Paria Canyon, described earlier in this chapter, to its end at Lees Ferry. The 1,000-foot-high, rose-hued Vermilion Cliffs meet the Paria Canyon mouth at Lees Ferry.

*Kanab Creek, near the junction with the Colorado River*

*a passage in Walpi, 1890*

# NORTHEASTERN ARIZONA

## INTRODUCTION

This is Indian country, a place made special by ancient cultural traditions of Native Americans—traditions that have survived to the present. The hard-working Hopi have been here longest. Ruins, occupied by their ancestors as long ago as 1,500 years, lie scattered over much of northeastern Arizona and adjacent states. The once warlike and greatly feared Navajo came relatively late, perhaps 500 years ago. Today, Indians welcome visitors who respect tribal customs and laws. You'll have an opportunity here to glimpse a unique way of life in a land of rare beauty.

### THE LAND

Multihued desert hills, broad mesas, soaring buttes, vast treeless plains, and massive mountains give an impression of boundless space. Northeastern Arizona sits atop the Colorado Plateau, whose elevations range mostly between 4,500 and 7,000 feet. Several pine-forested ranges rise above the desert near Arizona's borders with Utah and New Mexico. Navajo Mountain, just across in Utah, ranks as the highest peak in the area at 10,388 feet. And nearby you'll find Rainbow Bridge, the world's highest natural stone span over water. The bridge can be reached by boat on Lake Powell or by a spectacular 26- to 28-mile roundtrip hike. The beautiful canyons in Navajo and Canyon de Chelly national monuments also offer excellent scenery and hiking.

### Climate
Expect warm to hot summers and moderate to cold winters. From spring to autumn is the ideal time to visit, though winds in March and April can kick up dust and sand. The rainy

# NORTHEASTERN ARIZONA

© MOON PUBLICATIONS

months are July through September. Storms usually pass quickly, but flash floods pose a danger in low-lying areas.

## HISTORY

### The Hopi

Legends and long-abandoned pueblos indicate that Indian groups have lived here for many hundreds of years. Old Oraibi, a Hopi village dating from at least A.D. 1150, is thought to be the oldest continuously inhabited settlement in the United States, and some Hopi identify even older village sites as homes of their ancestors. Indians of today recognize northeast Arizona's great beauty—and probably the Ancient Ones did too—but it was of minor interest to early Europeans. Spanish explorers began to arrive in the 1500s, looking for gold and treasure, but left empty-handed. Desiring to save Hopi souls, Spanish friars arrived about 1630 and had some success. But traditional Hopi leaders, fearing the loss of their own culture, joined with the New Mexico pueblos in a revolt against the Spanish in 1680. Hopi killed any foreigner unable to escape, massacred many of their Christian followers, and tore down the mission buildings. During the 1800s, American frontiersmen arrived seeking mineral wealth and fertile lands, but they too usually met with disappointment. So the Hopi continued to farm in relative peace, raising their crops of corn, squash, and beans.

### The Navajo

The semi-nomadic Navajo, relatives of the Athabascans of western Canada, wandered into the area between A.D. 1300 and 1600. This adaptable tribe learned agriculture, weaving, pottery, and other skills from their pueblo neighbors and became skilled horsemen and sheepherders with livestock obtained from the Spanish. But the Navajo's old habits of raiding neighboring tribes and white men later almost caused their downfall. In 1863-64 the U.S. Army rounded up all the Navajo they could find, and they forced the survivors to make "The Long Walk" from Fort Defiance in eastern Arizona to a bleak camp at Fort Sumner in eastern New Mexico. This attempt at forced domestication failed dismally, and the Navajo were released 4 years later to return to their homeland.

### Indian Reservations

In 1878 the federal government "awarded" land to the Navajo that has grown to become a giant reservation spreading from northeast Arizona into adjacent New Mexico and Utah. The Navajo Nation, with 172,020 members (1986), now ranks as the largest Indian tribe in the country. About 76,000 live on the reservation in Arizona. In 1882 the federal government also recognized the Hopi's age-old land rights by setting aside land for them. The approximately 7,000 Hopi today live on a reservation completely surrounded by Navajo land. Government officials have redrawn the reservation boundaries of the Navajo and Hopi many times, but never to the satisfaction of all parties. In 1978, congressional and court decisions settled a major land dispute between the two tribes in favor of the Hopi. The victorious Hopi regained part of the territory previously designated as joint-use but largely settled by Navajo. To the Hopi this was long-overdue justice, while the Navajo called it "The Second Long Walk." The Navajo and Hopi Indian Relocation Commissioners have estimated that it may take until 1995 and cost $339 million to resettle families in their respective reservations.

## INDIAN CULTURES

The white man has always had difficulty understanding Arizona's Indians, perhaps

*Navajo Fire Dance*

because the Native American cultures emphasize very different spiritual values. The Hopi and Navajo exist in accord with nature, not against it, in adapting to the climate, plants, and animals of their land. Yet when visiting Indian villages, outsiders often see only the material side of the culture—the houses, livestock, dress, pottery, and other crafts. One has to slow down and look much deeper to get even a small insight into Indian ways. The Hopi and Navajo differ greatly in their backgrounds, too. You'll notice right away that the Hopi usually live in compact villages, even if this means a long commute to fields or jobs, while the Navajo spread their

*wolf kachina*

houses and hogans across the countryside, often far from their nearest neighbor.

## Ceremonies

Religion forms a vital part of both Navajo and Hopi cultures. Most Navajo ceremonies deal with healing. If someone is sick, the family calls in a medicine man who uses sand paintings, chants, and dancing to effect a cure. These events, often held late at night, aren't publicized. If you're driving at night and see large bonfires outside a house, it's likely there's a healing ceremony going on. You shouldn't intrude on any ceremony unless you've been invited.

The Hopi have an elaborate, almost year-round schedule of dances in their village plazas and kivas (ceremonial rooms). Some, such as those in the kivas, are closed to outsiders, but the others can be witnessed by the public. Nearly all Hopi dances are prayers for rain and fertile crops. The elaborate, brilliant masks, the ankle bells, the drums and chanting—all invite the attention of the supernatural spirits (kachinas) who bring rain. Men perform these dances, and while they are dancing, they too are kachinas. At the end of the line of dancers, you might see boys who are learning; dance steps must be performed precisely. Remember while you're watching that this is a religious service. Dress respectfully, keep clear of the performers, be quiet, and don't ask questions. Hopi ceremonies generally take place on the weekends; call or ask at the Hopi Cultural Center or the Hopi Tribe's office of Public Relations (phones and addresses listed under "Information" below).

## Arts And Crafts

The strength of Navajo and Hopi cultures is evident in their excellent art and crafts. The best work commands high prices but can be a fine memento of a visit to the Indian lands. Trading posts and Indian crafts shops on and off the reservations have large selections. To learn what to look for in Indian art before a trip to the reservations, drop in at the Heard Museum in Phoenix or the Museum of Northern Arizona in Flagstaff. The Navajo have

*a Hopi family, early 1900s*

earned fame for their silver jewelry and woven rugs. Colorful velveteen blouses and long flowing skirts worn by the Navajo women can sometimes be purchased at trading posts. (The style was adopted during the Navajo's stay at Fort Sumner in the 1860s. It was what Army wives were then wearing!) The Hopi make basketry, silverwork, pottery, and the exotic kachina dolls carved from cottonwood. Artists of both tribes create attractive paintings and prints with Indian motifs. Be careful when shopping; wherever there are tourists, there may be tourist junk. Indians know what their crafts are worth so bargaining is not normally done, but there's no law against it either. Prices often come down at the end of the tourist season in Sept. and October.

**Visiting The Indians**

Seeing and learning about Indian cultures on the reservations reward visitors with new insights. It's easy to visit the Indian lands; the tribes ask guests to follow only a few rules. Hordes of eager photographers besieged Hopi villages from the late 1800s until early in this century, when the Hopi cried "No more!" And that's the way it is now—photography is generally forbidden in all Hopi villages. Even the sight of a camera will upset some tribal members. The Navajo are more easygoing about having their photos taken, but you should always ask first. Expect to pay them a posing fee unless it's a public performance. Indian lands, though held in trust by the government, are private property; get permission before leaving the roadways or designated recreational areas. Don't remove anything. For example, a few feathers tied to a bush may appear to be a harmless souvenir, but they are of great religious importance to the Indian who put them there. Normal good manners, respect, and observance of posted regulations will make your visit pleasurable for both you and your hosts.

## PRACTICALITIES

### Accommodations And Food

Because of the distances involved, visitors usually want to stay overnight on or near the reservations. Most towns have a motel or two that can easily be full in the tourist season—advance bookings are a good idea. The few trailer parks tend to fill with construction workers if a project is going on; again it's best to call or write ahead instead of counting on space. Most campgrounds have few or no facilities; only some have water. Accommodations in towns outside the reservations (Flagstaff, Winslow, Holbrook, Page, etc.) are another possibility.

Indians enjoy American and Mexican dishes as well as the ever-present fast foods. Try the Navajo taco, a giant tortilla smothered with lettuce, ground beef, beans, tomatoes, chiles, and cheese. The Hopi Cultural Center restaurant on Second Mesa has many Indian specialties, but chances are the Hopi family at the next table will be munching on hamburgers. No alcohol is sold or permitted on the Navajo and Hopi reservations; you won't find much nightlife either.

### Information

Not always easy to get! Motels and trading posts can be helpful; tribal police located in the towns know regulations and road conditions. Visit museums run by the Navajo at Window Rock and Tsaile and by the Hopi on Second Mesa. Local newspapers (in English) report the latest politics, sports, and social events, but not religious ceremonies. The **Navajoland Tourism** office has literature and information for visitors to the Navajo Indian Reservation; open Mon.-Fri. 8 a.m.-5 p.m. in the Economic Development Bldg., 2.6 miles west of Window Rock on AZ 264; Box 663, Window Rock, AZ 86515; tel. 871-6659. Fishing and hunting on the Navajo reservation require tribal permits from **Navajo Fish & Wildlife**, Box 1480, Window Rock, AZ

86515; tel. 871-6451/6452. Arizona Game and Fish has no jurisdiction over the reservation; you only need the tribal permits. For hiking and camping information and permits on Navajo lands, contact the **Navajo Parks and Recreation Dept.** at Box 308, Window Rock, AZ 86515; tel. 871-6645.

The **Hopi Tribe's Office of Public Relations** provides information for visitors to the Hopi Indian Reservation; office is in Kykotsmovi, one mile south of AZ 264 in the Tribal Headquarters building; Box 123, Kykotsmovi, AZ 86039; tel. 734-2441, ext. 341 or 360. The **Hopi Cultural Center** on Second Mesa has a museum, motel, campground, and restaurant; Box 67, Second Mesa, AZ 86043; tel. 734-2401. Either place can tell you about upcoming dances open to the public. The Hopi generally won't allow hiking, fishing, or hunting by outsiders.

### What Time Is It?

This must be the question most frequently asked by visitors! While most of the United States goes on daylight saving time from late April to late Oct., most of Arizona stays on mountain standard time. The big exception is the Navajo Reservation, which goes on daylight saving time in order to keep in step with its New Mexico and Utah portions. Keep in mind the time difference on Navajoland during daylight saving time or you will always be one hour late! The Hopi Indians, who rarely agree with the Navajo anyway, choose to stay on standard time with the rest of Arizona. And then there is Indian Time, a slightly looser concept than most Americans have.

### Getting Around

Your own transport is by far the most convenient, but tours to the highlights of Indian country leave from major centers (see the "Transport" sections under the Grand Canyon, Flagstaff, Phoenix, and Tucson headings). **Navajo Transit System** (based in Fort Defiance, tel. 729-5449) offers bus service across the Navajo and Hopi reservations from Fort Defiance and Window Rock in the east to Tuba City in the west, daily Mon.-Fri.

in each direction, $13.05 one way for the whole distance. Stops on this route (east to west on AZ 264) are Fort Defiance (PHS Hospital and 7-11 Store), Window Rock (Fed-Mart parking lot), St. Michaels, Cross Canyon Trading Post, Ganado Post Office, Burnside Thriftway Store (near junction of US 191), Standing Rock, Steamboat Trading Post, Toyei School, AZ 77 junction, Keams Canyon Trading Post, Polacca Circle-M store, Second Mesa Trading Post, Hopi Cultural Center, Kykotsmovi turnoff, Hotevilla turnoff, Coal Mine Mesa, and Tuba City (Shopping Center, Community Center, and PHS Hospital). Navajo Transit System also heads north from

Window Rock and Fort Defiance to Kayenta, Mon.-Fri., $12.35 one way, with stops at Fort Defiance 7-11 Store, Navajo (in New Mexico), Navajo Community College at Tsaile, Chinle (Baldwin's Market, Shopping Center, PHS Hospital), Many Farms, Rough Rock junction, Chilchinbito junction, and Kayenta (7-11 store and police station). Navajo Transit also leaves Fort Defiance and Window Rock Mon.-Fri. for the New Mexico towns of Crown Point and Gallup. You'll often see Indians hitchhiking, and you can too. Be prepared for long waits (traffic is light) and rides in the back of pickups.

# WESTERN NAVAJO COUNTRY

## CAMERON

The **Cameron Trading Post,** built in 1916 beside the Little Colorado River, commemorates Ralph Cameron, Arizona's last territorial delegate before statehood. The trading post's strategic location near the Grand Canyon makes it a popular stopping point. Facilities include a motel ($29.13 s, $40.68 d and up), RV park ($12.60 w/hookups; no tents), restaurant (open daily for breakfast,

lunch, and dinner), grocery store, Indian crafts shop, post office, and service station. For information and reservations, contact Cameron Trading Post, Box 339, Cameron, AZ 86020; tel. 679-2231. Cameron is on US 89, one mile north of the junction with AZ 64 to the Grand Canyon and 54 miles north of Flagstaff.

**Vicinity Of Cameron**
Colorful hills of the **Painted Desert** lie to the north and east. To the west, the high, sheer walls of the **Little Colorado River Canyon**

*a Navajo camp,
early this century*

make an impressive sight even with the Grand Canyon so near. The best viewpoint is 15 miles west on AZ 64, about halfway to Desert View of the Grand Canyon National Park. Besides the view, you'll also have a chance to look at Navajo jewelry here.

Drop in at the **Cameron Visitor Center,** at the US 89-AZ 64 junction, for information about the Navajo Indian Reservation; open about Mon.-Fri. and summer weekends 8 a.m.-5 p.m. **Navajo Arts & Craft Enterprise** sits next door with a good selection of Indian crafts. **Grand Canyon Junction RV Park,** across US 89, is open all year with sites for tents ($7.50) and RVs ($13 w/hookups); showers cost extra; tel. 679-2281.

**Gray Mountain Trading Post,** 10 miles south of Cameron on US 89, has the Gray Mountain Motel, Gray Mountain Restaurant (open daily for breakfast, lunch, and dinner), Indian crafts shop, and grocery store. The motel has a pool and playground; rates run $20-50 s or d depending on season; Box 29100, Gray Mountain, AZ 86016; tel. 679-2214.

## TUBA CITY

This administrative and trade center for the western Navajo has nothing to do with tubas and is not much of a city. The town (pop. about 5,000) commemorates Chief Tuba of the Hopi tribe. An oasis of green lawns and shade trees, Tuba City contrasts with the surrounding desert. The springs nearby attracted Mormons, who founded a settlement in 1877. They could not get clear title to the land, however, and the U.S. Indian Agency took it over in 1903. Besides the U.S. government offices, the town has a hospital, schools, and a bank. Tuba City is near the junction of AZ 264 to the Hopi mesas and US 160 to Monument Valley.

### Practicalities
The **Tuba City Youth Hostel** provides the only inexpensive place to stay on the reservation; $10/person; no kitchen. Open weekdays 8 a.m.-midnight and weekends 4 p.m.-midnight. Write or call first to the Hotel Management Program, Gray Hills High School, Box 160, Tuba City, AZ 86045; tel. 283-6271. From the junction of US 160 and AZ 264, go northeast 0.5 mile on US 160 to just past the pedestrian overpass, then turn left to the high school. **Tuba City Motel** sits in the center of town, one mile north of the highway junction. Rooms cost $42 s or d; tel. 283-4545. **Pancho's Family Restaurant,** next to the Tuba City Motel, serves Mexican-American food at moderate prices; open daily for breakfast, lunch, and dinner.

The unusual octagonal **Tuba City Trading Post** next door sells groceries and Indian crafts. **Peking Garden Restaurant,** one-half block east of the trading post, serves American and Chinese food; open Mon.-Sat. for lunch and dinner. Several fast-food places and some grocery stores line the road into town. **The Truck Stop Restaurant** is on the highway at the turnoff for Tuba City. **Toh Nanees Dizi Shopping Center,** one-half mile northeast on US 160, has Mikey's Pizza, a supermarket, movie theater, and other shops. The motel and trading post may know of Indian dances or events, both Navajo and Hopi. The **Western Navajo Fair,** held in Oct., features a rodeo, arts and crafts, dance performances, and other entertainment.

## VICINITY OF TUBA CITY

### Dinosaur Tracks
Distinct footprints can be seen 5.5 miles west of Tuba City on US 160, about midway between Tuba City Junction and US 89. Look for a small sign on the north side of the highway between Mileposts 316 and 317. Some Navajo jewelry stalls will probably be here too. Scientists think carnivorous biped reptiles about 10 feet tall made these tracks, now preserved in sandstone.

### Elephant's Feet
This pair of distinctive sandstone buttes stands near Red Lake, 21 miles northeast of Tuba City on US 160.

*Betatakin Point Overlook*

# NORTHERN NAVAJO COUNTRY

## NAVAJO NATIONAL MONUMENT

The monument preserves three spectacular prehistoric Indian cliff dwellings, last occupied about 700 years ago. The now-vanished Anasazi (a Navajo word for "Ancient Ones") who once lived here probably are ancestors of the present-day Hopi. Of the three sites, Betatakin is the most accessible and can be seen from a viewpoint near the Visitor Center. Rangers lead groups into Betatakin during spring, summer, and autumn; contact the monument for tour times. Keet Seel, to the northeast, is the largest cliff dwelling in Arizona. You get there by a 16-mile roundtrip hike or horseback ride. Inscription House, to the west, is the smallest of the three ruins; it's currently closed to the public. Inscription House Trading Post should not be confused with the ruins, which lie some distance away.

The monument's headquarters and Visitor Center can reached by following US 160 northeast from Tuba City for 52 miles (or southwest 22 miles from Kayenta), then turning north 9 miles on AZ 564 at Black Mesa Junction.

## Visitor Center

The Anasazi left many questions behind when they abandoned this area. You can learn what is known about these people, as well as some of the mysteries, at the Visitor Center. Exhibits, which show fine examples of prehistoric pottery wares and other artifacts, attempt to piece together what life was like for the Indians. An excellent 25-minute movie about the Anasazi is shown every other hour, and a 5-minute slide show can be seen on request. You can peek into an old-style Navajo forked-stick hogan and a sweathouse behind the Visitor Center. Rangers will answer questions and have books and maps for sale. A gift shop offers Indian jewelry (Hopi, Navajo, and Zuni) and Navajo rugs; open mid-April to mid-November. The Visitor Center is open daily 8 a.m.-5 p.m. except Thanksgiving, Christmas, and New Year. Contact the monument at HC 71, Box 3, Tonalea, AZ 86044-9704; tel. 672-2366.

## Sandal Trail

This easy trail begins behind the Visitor Center and winds through a pinyon pine and juniper forest to Betatakin Point Overlook.

The paved trail is one-mile roundtrip and drops 160 feet to the overlook. Labels along the way identify native plants and describe how Indians used them. Bring binoculars or use the free telescope to see details of the ruins.

### Visiting Betatakin

Betatakin (Navajo for "Ledge House") ruins lie tucked in a natural alcove on the far side of a canyon. The alcove measures 452 feet high, 370 feet across, and 135 feet deep. It contains 135 rooms and one kiva. Inhabitants built and abandoned the entire village within two generations, between A.D. 1250 and 1300. The ruins may be visited only with park rangers, who lead one or two trips a day from May to September. Starting from the Visitor Center, the 5-mile roundtrip trail is well graded but drops 700 feet, which you'll have to climb on the way back. After passing through an aspen grove on the canyon floor, the trail climbs a short distance to the ruin. Allow 5-6 hours for the trip and a look around the ancient dwellings. Trailhead elevation is 7,200 feet. Thin air can make the hike very tiring—people with heart or respiratory problems shouldn't go.

### Visiting Keet Seel

This isolated cliff dwelling is one of the best preserved in the Southwest. Keet Seel (Navajo for "broken pottery") has 160 rooms and four or five kivas. The site, 8 miles away by trail from the Visitor Center, may be visited from the end of May to early September. A permit is required, and there's a limit of 20 people per day. Reservations must be made at least one day in advance (but not more than 2 months) with Navajo National Monument, H.C. 71, Box 3, Tonalea, AZ 86044-9704; tel. 672-2366. Pick up your permit before 9 a.m. (daylight saving time) on the day of your hike or you lose your space. The

Betatakin

hike's first 1.5 miles runs along the rim on a dirt road to Tsegi Point. There the trail descends 1,000 feet to the canyon bottom, goes downstream a short distance, then heads upstream into Keet Seel Canyon. You may have to do some wading. Carry water—the streams are polluted by livestock. The ruins look as though they were abandoned just a few years ago, not 7 centuries! Visitors may not enter the site without a ranger, who is stationed nearby. Backpackers can stay in a primitive campground (free) near Keet Seel. You can rent horses for the trip from a local Navajo family for about $40/person. Some riding experience is advised, and riders must be at least 12 years old. Write to the Austins, c/o Horseback Reservation, Navajo National Monument, H.C. 71, Box 3, Tonalea, AZ 86044-9704.

### Accommodations And Food

A free **campground** with water and restrooms near the Visitor Center is open mid-May to mid-October. Rangers present campfire programs in summer. **Tsegi Canyon Inn** ($36.75-47.25 s, $40.95-51.45 d) and cafe (open daily for breakfast, lunch, and dinner) are 20 miles away on the road to Kayenta; tel. 697-3793. Kayenta, another 9 miles, has two motels and several restaurants. **Black Mesa Shopping Center,** 9 miles south of the monument at the junction of AZ 564 and US 160, has the closest cafe, grocery store, and service station. The road south from here goes to coal mines of the Peabody Coal Company, a major place of employment for the Navajo.

### Shonto

This Navajo settlement sits in a small canyon southwest of the monument. A trading post offers groceries and Navajo crafts. The shaded park in front is a good spot for a picnic. A chapter house and BIA (Bureau of Indian Affairs) boarding school are nearby. Shonto is 10 miles from the monument by a rough and sandy road not recommended for cars or 33 miles via US 160 on paved roads.

## RAINBOW BRIDGE NATIONAL MONUMENT

The bridge forms a graceful span 290 feet high and 275 feet wide; the Capitol building in Washington, D.C., would fit neatly underneath. Easiest way to Rainbow Bridge is by boat tour on Lake Powell from Wahweap, Bullfrog, or Halls Crossing marinas.

The more adventurous can hike to the bridge from near Navajo Mountain Trading Post (just north across the Arizona-Utah border on the east side of Navajo Mountain) or from the Rainbow Lodge ruins (just south of the Utah-Arizona border on the west side of Navajo Mountain). Rugged trails from each of these points wind through highly scenic canyons, meet in Bridge Canyon, then continue 2 miles to the bridge. The hike on either trail or a loop with both (car shuttle needed) is 26-28 miles roundtrip. Hikers must be experienced and self-sufficient on these trails, which cross a wilderness. Because the trails are unmaintained and poorly marked, bring a Navajo Mountain (Utah) 15-minute topo map.

No camping is allowed at Rainbow Bridge and no supplies are available; Dangling Rope Marina and National Park Service ranger station are 10 miles away *by water only.* Best times to go are April to early June, Sept., and October. Winter cold and snow discourage visits, and summer is hot and brings hazardous flash floods. The National Park Service has "Hiking to Rainbow Bridge" trail notes; Glen Canyon N.R.A., Box 1507, Page, AZ 86040; tel. 645-2511/2471. Obtain the required tribal hiking permit ($5 one person, $10 group of 2-10, $20 group of 11 or more) and camping permit ($1/person per night) by mail (allow 2 weeks) from Navajo Parks Dept., Box 308, Window Rock, AZ 86515; tel. (602) 871-6645. You can also get these permits in person from the tribal office building in Window Rock or the Cameron Visitor Center (junction of US 89 and AZ 64 near the Grand Canyon); both offices are open Mon. to Fri. about 8 a.m.-5 p.m.; the Cameron office is also open weekends from April to September.

*Rainbow Bridge*

The only road access to the Navajo Mountain area is Indian Route 16 from AZ 98, between Page and Kayenta in Arizona. To reach the east trailhead, drive north 32 miles on Indian Route 16 past Inscription House Trading Post to a road fork, then turn right 6 miles to Navajo Mountain Trading Post (tours, gas, supplies, and info usually available). Continue on the main road 6.5 miles (go straight at the four-way junction) to an earthen dam. Keep straight across the dam, take the left fork after 0.5 mile, then go 1.6 miles to Cha Canyon Trailhead at the end of the road. The west trailhead is reached by driving north 32 miles on Indian Route 16 and turning left about 6 miles at the road fork to the Rainbow Lodge ruins. Always lock vehicles and remove valuables at trailheads. Because Navajo Mountain is sacred to the Navajo, permission to climb it is needed from Navajo Parks Department. Guided hikes and horseback rides to Rainbow Bridge and Navajo Mountain can be arranged through **Navajo Mountain Trading Post**, Tonalea, AZ 86044.

## KAYENTA

The "Gateway to Monument Valley" is a town of 3,400 in a bleak, windswept valley. Its name is loosely derived from the Navajo word Teehindeeh, meaning "boghole," as there were once shallow lakes here. Kayenta, a handy stop for travelers, has two good motels and several restaurants.

### Accommodations
**Wetherill Inn** is in the center of town on US 163, one mile north of US 160. Its name honors John Wetherill, an early trader and rancher of the region who discovered Betatakin, Mesa Verde, and other major Anasazi sites; rooms cost $62 s, $68 d in summer; tel. 697-3231. The **Holiday Inn**, on US 160 at the turnoff for Kayenta, has rooms ($89 s, $98 d in summer), restaurant, and pool; tel. 697-3221 or (800) HOLIDAY. The **Coin-Op Laundry** in town has tent and RV spaces at $8.75 w/hookups; showers are also available for noncampers; tel. 697-8282/3400.

### Food

The **Holiday Inn's** restaurant has good Navajo tacos and standard American fare; open daily for breakfast, lunch, and dinner. **El Capitan Cafe** is nearby on the other side of the highway; open daily for breakfast, lunch, and dinner. **La Fiesta Cafe** serves Mexican and American food; open Mon.-Fri. and sometimes Sat. for lunch and dinner; located on US 163 between the Kayenta turnoff and town. **Golden Sands Cafe,** near the Wetherill Inn, offers American food daily for breakfast, lunch, and dinner. **Mikey's Pizza** next to the Teehindeeh Shopping Center serves pizza. Buy groceries at the supermarket in the shopping center or at the **Kayenta Trading Post** (behind the Wetherill Inn).

### Shopping And Services

Look for Indian crafts at both motels, Kayenta Trading Post, and Burch's Trading Company (near Wetherill Inn). Tours in 4WD vehicles to Monument Valley and surrounding country can be arranged from both motels; costs start at about $24/half day or $40/full day with a minimum of four or six persons.

## MONUMENT VALLEY

Towering buttes, jagged pinnacles, and rippled sand dunes make this an otherworldly landscape. Changing colors and shifting shadows during the day add to the enchantment. Most of the natural monuments are remnants of sandstone eroded by wind and water. Agathla Peak and some lesser summits are roots of ancient volcanos, whose dark rock contrasts with the pale yellow sandstone of the other formations. The valley lies at an elevation of 5,564 feet in the Upper Sonoran Life Zone; annual rainfall averages about 8.5 inches.

In 1863-64, when Kit Carson was ravaging Canyon de Chelly in Arizona to round up the Navajo, Chief Hoskinini led his people to the safety and freedom of Monument Valley. Merrick Butte and Mitchell Mesa commemorate two miners who discovered rich silver deposits on their first trip to the valley in 1880.

On their second trip both were killed, reportedly shot by Paiute Indians. Hollywood movies made the splendor of Monument Valley known to the outside world. *Stagecoach,* filmed here in 1938 and directed by John Ford, became the first in a series of westerns that has continued to the present. John Wayne and many other movie greats rode across these sands.

The Navajo have preserved the valley as a tribal park with a scenic drive, visitor center, and campground. From Kayenta, go 24 miles north on US 163 and turn right 3.5 miles.

### Visitor Center

Information desk, exhibits, and Indian crafts shop are open daily about 7 a.m.-7 p.m. from May to Sept., then daily 8 a.m.-5 p.m. the rest of the year; tel. (801) 727-3287. Visitors pay a $2.50 ($1 age 60 and over; under 12 free) collected on the entrance road.

### Monument Valley Drive

A 17-mile, self-guided scenic drive begins at the Visitor Center and loops through the heart of the valley. Overlooks provide sweeping views from different vantage points. The dirt road is normally OK for cautiously driven cars. Avoid stopping and becoming stuck in the loose sand that sometimes blows across the road. Allow 1½ hours for the drive, open the same hours as the Visitor Center. No hiking or driving off the signposted route is allowed. Water and restrooms are available only at the Visitor Center.

### Valley Tours

Take one of the guided tours leaving daily year-round from the Visitor Center to visit a hogan, cliff dwelling, and petroglyphs in areas beyond the self-guided drive. The trips last 2½-3 hours and cost $15/person. Shorter trips of 1½ hours cost $12/person. Guided horseback rides cost $15 for 1½ hours; longer day and overnight trips can be arranged too; March to Nov. from the Visitor Center. If you'd like to hike in Monument Valley, you must hire a guide; hiking tours of 2 hours to a day or more can be arranged at the Visitor Center.

## Accommodations

Sites at **Mitten View Campground** near the Visitor Center cost $10; hot showers are available at an extra charge. Season is early April to mid-October. Tenters should be prepared for winds in this exposed location. Goulding's Lodge (see below) has the nearest motel, restaurant, and store. Motels are also found at Kayenta in Arizona and at Mexican Hat and Bluff in Utah.

## Goulding's Lodge And Trading Post

Harry Goulding and his wife Mike opened the trading post in 1924. It's located 2 miles west of the US 163 Monument Valley turnoff, just north of the Utah-Arizona border. **Goulding's Museum,** in the old trading post building, displays prehistoric and modern Indian artifacts, movie photos, and memorabilia of the Goulding family; open daily, except closed in winter; there's a small entrance fee. Motel rooms start at $83.85 s or d in summer, less off-season; guests can use a small indoor pool. A gift shop sells souvenirs, books, and high-quality Indian crafts. The nearby store has groceries and gas pumps. Monument Valley tours operate year-round; $23/half

day, $43/full day with a six-person minimum; children under 12 go at half price. The lodge and store stay open all year, though the museum, restaurant, and gift shop close in winter. For accommodation and tour info, write Box 1, Monument Valley, UT 84536; tel. (801) 727-3231.

**Monument Valley KOA Campground** offers tent and RV sites a short drive west; rates are $12.84 no hookups, $18.19 w/hookups; open April 1 to Nov. 1; tel. (801) 727-3280. The Seventh-day Adventist Church runs a hospital and mission nearby.

## FOUR CORNERS MONUMENT

An inlaid concrete slab marks the point where Utah, Colorado, New Mexico, and Arizona meet. It's the only spot in the United States where you can put your finger on four states at once. Ute and Navajo Indians set up dozens of craft booths in summer. Over 2,000 people a day are said to stop at the marker in the summer season. Average stay? Seven to 10 minutes. On the other hand, five national parks and 18 national monuments are within a radius of 150 miles from this point!

*Monument Valley*

# EASTERN NAVAJO COUNTRY

## CANYON DE CHELLY NATIONAL MONUMENT

Within the monument, you'll find prehistoric Anasazi cliff dwellings and traditional Navajo ways preserved in spectacular canyons. The main canyons are 26-mile-long Canyon de Chelly (pronounced "d'SHAY") and adjoining 35-mile-long Canyon del Muerto. Sheer sandstone walls rise up to 1,000 feet, giving the canyons a fortress-like appearance. Allow at least a full day to see some of the monument's 83,840 acres. Rim elevations range from 5,500 feet at the Visitor Center to 7,000 feet at the end of the scenic drives. April to Oct. is the best time to visit. Winter brings cold weather and a chance of snow. Afternoon thunderstorms arrive almost daily in late summer. Thousands of waterfalls cascade over the rims when it's raining but stop when the skies clear.

### The First Peoples

Nomadic tribes roamed the canyons over 2,000 years ago, collecting wild foods and hunting game. Little remains of these early visitors, but they must have found welcome shelter from the elements in the natural rock overhangs of the canyons. The Anasazi ("Ancient Ones" in the Navajo language), from their first appearance about A.D. 1, lived in caves during the winter and brush shelters in summer. By A.D. 500 they were cultivating permanent fields of corn, squash, and beans and were making pottery. They lived at that time in year-round pithouses, structures partly underground and roofed with sticks and mud.

Around A.D. 700 the population began to move into cliff houses of stone masonry constructed above ground. These pueblos (Spanish for "villages") also contained underground ceremonial rooms, known as kivas, used for social as well as religious purposes. Most of the cliff houses that you now see in Canyon de Chelly date from the Anasazi golden age, A.D. 1100-1300, when an estimated 1,000 people occupied the many small villages. At the end of this period the Anasazi mysteriously vanished from these canyons and from their other large population centers as well. Archaeologists aren't sure why, but causes may include drought, overpopulation, soil erosion, and warfare. It's likely that some of the Anasazi moved to the Hopi mesas. Hopi religion, traditions, and farming practices have much in common with those of the Ancient Ones. During the next 400 years, Hopi farmers sometimes used the canyons during the growing season, but they returned home to the mesas after each harvest.

### The Navajo Arrive

First entering Canyon de Chelly about A.D. 1700, the Navajo found it an ideal base for raiding nearby Indian and Spanish settlements. In 1805 the Spanish launched a punitive expedition during which soldiers reported killing 115 Navajo, including 90 warriors. The Navajo version of the battle claimed the dead were mostly women, children, and old men. The overhang where the killing took place became known as Massacre Cave. During periods of the Mexican era, raids took place in both directions; the Navajo raided for food and livestock while Mexicans came to steal women and children for slaves. Contact with Americans went badly too—settlers encroached on Navajo lands and soldiers proved deceitful. Navajo raids finally came to an end after the winter of 1863-64, when Colonel Kit Carson led detachments of the U.S. Cavalry into the canyons. The Army destroyed livestock, fruit trees, and food while skirmishing with the Indians. The starving Navajo then had no choice but to surrender and leave for a desolate reservation in eastern New Mexico. In 1868, after 4 miserable years there, they were permitted to return to their beloved canyons. Today, some of the same families continue to farm the canyon floors and graze sheep. You can see their distinctive round hogans (houses) next to the fields. More than 50 families live in the canyons, but most find it more convenient to spend winters on the canyon rims and to return to their fields after the spring floods have subsided.

### Visitor Center

Exhibits show the spread of Indian history from the Archaic Period (before A.D. 1) to the present, with many displays of artifacts. You can take a close look at a Navajo hogan outside next to the Visitor Center. Rangers know about scheduled hikes, programs, and tours, and they'll answer your questions. Books related to the region are sold. Open daily 8 a.m.-6 p.m. from May 1 to Sept. 30, and daily 8 a.m.-5 p.m. the rest of the year; Box 588, Chinle, AZ 86503; tel. 674-5436.

### Sights

Canyons de Chelly and del Muerto each have a paved scenic rim drive with viewpoints along the edges. Or you can travel inside the

*lower White House ruin*

canyons by 4WD vehicle, horseback, or on foot. With the exception of White House Ruin Trail, *visitors must have an authorized Navajo guide or be with a monument ranger to enter any canyon.* This rule is enforced! It protects the ruins and the privacy of families living in the canyons. All of the land belongs to the Navajo people; the National Park Service only administers policies within the monument boundaries.

### Hiking

**White House Ruin Trail** is the only hike that can be done without a guide; see description under "South Rim Drive of Canyon de Chelly" below. Rangers lead free half-day hikes in the lower canyon daily from late May to the end of September. The hiking pace is easy, but comfortable walking shoes, water, insect repellent, and hat are needed. Some wading is usually necessary—in fact, you may insist on it; under a hot summer sun, with red rocks all around you, the cool water and shade of the trees are irresistible! Meet the ranger at the Visitor Center; check departure time the day before—hikes leave promptly. Also, it's a good idea to make reservations the day before as group size is limited.

By hiring a guide you can hike almost anywhere. The ranger at the Visitor Center can help make arrangements and issue the necessary permit. Guides charge $7.50/hour for up to 10 people. Overnight trips are possible with additional charges (per group) of $10/night for the guide and $20/night for the land owner.

### Horseback Riding

**Justin's Horse Rentals** is near the entrance to the South Rim Drive; look for the stables on the north side of the drive just past the Thunderbird Lodge/Cottonwood Campground turnoff. Rides, available all year, cost $7/hour for each rider and $7/hour for the guide (one per group); you can arrange trips of 2 hours to several days; Box 881, Chinle, AZ 86503; tel. 674-5678. **Twin Trail Tours,** on the north rim of Canyon del Muerto, has two rides, each 12 miles roundtrip. Both descend into the canyon; one goes upstream to Big

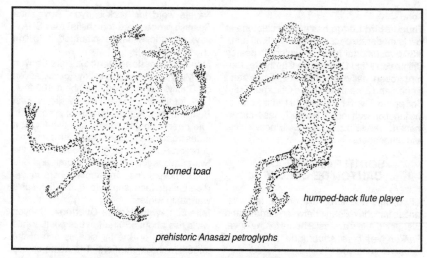

*horned toad*

*humped-back flute player*

*prehistoric Anasazi petroglyphs*

Cave and Mummy Cave, and the other downstream to Standing Cow Ruin and Antelope House Ruin. Riders have to walk during the 700-foot descent. The starting point is 7.6 miles from the Visitor Center on the North Rim Drive. Tours depart Mon.-Sat. at 9 a.m. from May 15 to Oct. 15; cost is $45/person; group and overnight trips can be arranged too; Box 1706, Window Rock, AZ 86515; tel. 674-5985 (local) or 729-5906 (Window Rock area). You can also ride your own horse by arranging board and feed (best to bring) at one of the stables near the park and by hiring an authorized Navajo guide, preferably from one of the horse concessions.

**Canyon Driving Tours**
Jeep tours of both canyons leave the Thunderbird Lodge daily at 9 a.m. and 2 p.m. during the main season. From mid-Nov. to early March, you should call ahead to make sure there will be a trip, since there's a minimum of eight passengers. The trips, very popular with visitors, go half day ($25.20 adult, $18.90 children 12 and under) and full day ($43.05/person including lunch; summer only). You'll enjoy unobstructed views from the back of open trucks, which stop frequently for photography and viewing ruins. You can also take your own vehicle (must be 4WD) if

you hire a guide ($7/hour) and obtain a permit at the Visitor Center.

**Accommodations And Campground**
**Thunderbird Lodge,** within the monument one-half mile south of the Visitor Center, has attractive landscaping with lawns and shade trees. A cafeteria and large gift shop are here too. The lodge began as a trading post for the Navajo in 1902; tourists later began showing up in sizable numbers and the facilities were expanded to accommodate them. Summer rates (April 1-Oct. 31) start at $63 s, $67.20 d (less in winter); Box 548, Chinle, AZ 86503; tel. 674-5841/5842. **Cottonwood Campground,** between the Visitor Center and the Thunderbird Lodge, offers pleasant sites with many large cottonwood trees. Open all year, but water is on only April to Oct.; no showers or hookups; free. Only group sites can be reserved. Rangers present campfire programs from late May to the end of September. A **picnic area,** near the campground, is shaded by cottonwoods; has water except in winter.

   **Canyon de Chelly Motel** is in Chinle on Indian Route 7, about 2 miles west of the Visitor Center; summer rates (April 1-Oct. 31) are $67.52 s, $71.74 d (less in winter); Box 295, Chinle, AZ 86503; tel. 674-5875/5288.

### Food

**Thunderbird Lodge** has a good cafeteria at low to moderate prices, open daily 6:30 a.m.- 8:30 p.m. (shorter hours in winter). In nearby Chinle you'll find **Canyon de Chelly Restaurant** (open daily for breakfast, lunch, and dinner) and a Kentucky Fried Chicken. **Tseyi Shopping Center,** on US 191 just north of the junction with Indian Route 7, has a supermarket, Val's Pizza, Taco Bell, post office, and other shops.

## SOUTH RIM DRIVE OF CANYON DE CHELLY

All pullouts and turns are on the left. Distances include mileage between turnoffs and overlooks. Allow at least 2 hours for the drive. *Parked vehicles should be locked and valuables removed.*

**Mile 0: Visitor Center.** The nearby canyon walls stand only about 30 feet high where the Rio de Chelly enters Chinle Wash.
**Mile 2.0: Tunnel Canyon Overlook.** The canyon is about 275 feet deep here. Rangers often lead short hikes down the trail in this side canyon. Don't go hiking without a ranger or Navajo guide!
**Mile 2.3: Tsegi Overlook.** A Navajo hogan and farm can be seen below. Tsegi is the

Navajo word for "rock canyon," which the Spanish pronounced "de chelle" (day SHAY-yay). American usage changed it to "de chelly" (d'SHAY).
**Mile 3.7: Junction Overlook.** Here Canyon del Muerto, across the valley, joins Canyon de Chelly. Canyon depth is about 400 feet. Look for the two Anasazi cliff dwellings. First Ruin is in the cliff at the far side of the canyon. The pueblo has 10 rooms and two kivas; it dates from the late 11th to late 13th centuries. Junction Ruin lies straight across, where the two canyons join. It has 15 rooms and one kiva. These ruins, and most others in the monument, face south to catch the sun's warmth in winter.
**Mile 5.9: White House Overlook.** Canyon walls rise about 550 feet at this point. White House Ruin, on the far side, is one of the largest in the monument. The name comes from original white plaster on walls in the upper section. Portions of 60 rooms and four kivas remain in the two sections, but it's estimated there may have been 80 rooms before flood waters carried away some of the lower ruin. As many as 12 Anasazi families may have lived in this village about A.D. 1060-1275. The trail to White House Ruin begins about 500 feet to the right along the rim from the overlook. Many trails connect the rim with the canyon bottom, but few are as

*mouth of Canyon de Chelly*

*jeep tours in
Canyon de Chelly*

easy as this one. It's known to the Navajo as Women's Trail, because women often used it to move sheep in and out. Allow 2 hours for the 2.5-mile roundtrip and bring some water. This is the only hike in the canyon permitted without a guide; you're asked to stay on the trail. A pamphlet describing the trail can be purchased at the Visitor Center.

**Mile 12.0: Sliding House Overlook.** The ruins across the canyon on a narrow ledge are well named. Indians who constructed the village on this sloping ledge tried to brace rooms with retaining walls. Natural depressions at the overlook collect water, still sometimes used by the Navajo.

**Mile 14.4: Wild Cherry Overlook.** A scenic viewpoint above upper Wild Cherry Canyon.

**Mile 19.6: Face Rock Overlook.** Small cliff dwellings sit high on the rock face opposite the viewpoint. They look impossible to reach, but the Anasazi cleverly chipped foot and hand holes into the rock.

**Mile 20.6: Spider Rock Overlook.** The South Rim Drive ends here. Rock walls plummet 1,000 feet from the rim to the canyon floor. Spider Rock, the highest of the twin spires, rises 800 feet from the bottom of Canyon de Chelly. Spider Woman, a benevolent Navajo deity, makes her home here. A darker side of her character, according to one legend, is her taste for naughty children.

When Speaking Rock, the lower pinnacle, reports misbehaving children to Spider Woman, she catches and eats them. Look for the sun-bleached "bones" on top of her spire! You can see tiny cliff dwellings in the canyon walls if you look hard enough. Monument Canyon comes in around to the right. Black Rock Butte (7,618 feet high), on the horizon, is either the weathered heart of an extinct volcano or a volcanic intrusion.

## NORTH RIM DRIVE OF CANYON DEL MUERTO

All turnoffs are on the right. Distances include mileage between turnoffs and overlooks. Allow at least 2 hours for the drive. *Parked vehicles should be locked and valuables removed.*

**Mile 0: Visitor Center.** Cross the nearby Rio de Chelly bridge and continue northeast on Indian Route 64.

**Mile 5.9: Ledge Ruin Overlook.** The ruin, set in an opening 100 feet above the canyon floor, has 29 rooms, including two kivas and a two-story structure. It dates from A.D. 1050-1275. Walk south a short way to another overlook; a solitary kiva is seen high in the cliff face. A hand- and toe-hold trail connects it with other rooms in a separate alcove to the west.

*Canyon del Muerto from Mummy Cave Overlook*

**Mile 10.0: Antelope House Overlook.** This large site had 91 rooms and a four-story building. The village layout is clearly seen—you look almost straight down on it from the overlook. Round outlines are kivas. The square rooms were for either living or storage. Floods have damaged some of them, perhaps while the Anasazi still lived here, and the site was abandoned about 1260. The site's name comes from paintings of antelope, some thought to have been done by a Navajo artist in the 1830s. The Tomb of the Weaver sits across from Antelope House in a small alcove 50 feet above the canyon floor. Here, in the 1920s, archaeologists found an elaborate burial of an old man. The well-preserved body had been wrapped in a blanket made from what appeared to be golden eagle feathers. A cotton blanket was enclosed and the whole burial covered with cotton yarn topped with a spindle whorl. Look for Navajo Fortress, the sandstone butte across the canyon, from a viewpoint a short walk east from Antelope House Overlook. When danger threatened, the Navajo climbed up the east side using log poles as ladders. They pulled in the uppermost logs and any attackers received a hail of rocks. Navajo used the natural fortress from the Spanish years until Kit Carson's campaign.

**Mile 18.7: Mummy Cave Overlook.** Archae-ologists in the late 1800s named the large cliff dwelling for two mummies found in the talus slope below. Canyon del Muerto (Spanish for "Canyon of the Dead"), reportedly also took its name from this find. Mummy Cave Ruin sits within two separate overhangs several hundred feet above the canyon floor. The largest section is on the east (to the left) and has 50 rooms and three kivas, while the western cave has 20 rooms. Between these sections is a ledge with seven rooms, including a three-story tower of unknown purpose. The tower dates from about A.D. 1284 and is thought to have been built by Anasazi from Mesa Verde in Colorado.

**Mile 20.6: Massacre Cave Overlook.** North Rim Drive ends here. In 1805, hoping to end the Navajo menace, Antonio de Narbona led an expedition of Spanish soldiers and allied Indians to these canyons. A group of fleeing Navajo managed to scale the nearly 1,000 feet to this overhang on the only route to it. Narbona's troops, however, reached the rim overlooking the cave and fired down. Narbona's account listed 115 Navajo killed and 33 taken captive. From Yucca Cave Overlook nearby, you can see a cave with at least four rooms and a kiva. A small cave to the left was used for food storage; a hand- and toe-hold trail connected the two alcoves.

## VICINITY OF CANYON DE CHELLY NATIONAL MONUMENT

### Chinle

This small spread-out town lies just west of Canyon de Chelly National Monument. The name Chinle is a Navajo word meaning "Water Outlet"—the Rio de Chelly emerges from its canyon here. A trading post opened in 1882, the first school in 1910, and the nearby monument headquarters in 1931. Chinle has a motel, several restaurants, a supermarket, shops, laundromat, and service stations. The post office is in Tseyi Shopping Center.

### Navajo Community College (Tsaile Campus)

Recognizing the need for college education, the Navajo Tribe in 1957 established a scholarship fund, financed by their royalties from oil. Most students had to leave the reservation for their college education, but the cultural gap between the Navajo and outside world proved too great, and many students dropped out. To solve this dilemma, the tribe created Navajo Community College in 1969. Students used temporary facilities at Many Farms, Arizona, until 1973, when campuses were completed here at Tsaile and at Shiprock, New Mexico. Now a 2-year program helps students prepare for university life off the reservation. They can also choose from

many Navajo and Indian studies courses—crafts, language, politics, music, dance, herbology, holistic healing, and others. The colleges offer vocational training and adult education too.

The unusual campus layout resulted from Navajo elders and medicine men getting together with the architects. Because all important Navajo activities take place within a circle, the grounds were laid out in that shape. If you know your way around inside a hogan, you'll find it easy getting around the campus: the library is tucked in where the medicine bundle would be kept during a ceremony, the cooking area (dining hall) is in the center, sleeping (dormitories) in the west, teaching area (classrooms) in the south, and recreation area (student union and gym) in the north. The central campus entrance, marked by the glass-walled Ned A. Hatathli Center, faces east to the rising sun.

The **Hatathli Museum** claims to be the "first *true* Indian museum." Managed entirely by Indians, the collection takes up two floors of the hogan-shaped Hatathli Center. Exhibits interpret the cultures of prehistoric Indians as well as Navajo and other modern tribes. The museum and adjacent sales gallery are open Mon.-Fri. 8:30 a.m.-noon and 1-4:30 p.m.; donation; tel. 724-3311. **Navajo Community College Press** sells books on the Navajo and related topics on the first floor of the Hatathli Center; open Mon.-Thurs. 8 a.m.-5 p.m. and Fri. 8 a.m.-noon. The college's library and dining hall are also open to

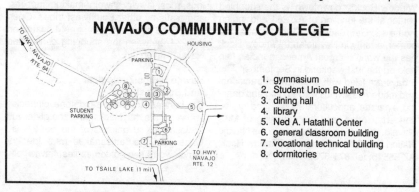

## NAVAJO COMMUNITY COLLEGE

TO HWY NAVAJO RTE. 64
HOUSING
PARKING
STUDENT PARKING
TO TSAILE LAKE (1 mi)
PARKING
TO HWY NAVAJO RTE. 12

1. gymnasium
2. Student Union Building
3. dining hall
4. library
5. Ned A. Hatathli Center
6. general classroom building
7. vocational technical building
8. dormitories

visitors. The Tsaile campus is 23 miles east of the Canyon de Chelly Visitor Center and 54 miles north of Window Rock.

**Wheatfields Lake**
This large mountain lake lies in a ponderosa and pinyon pine forest east of Canyon de Chelly National Monument. Visitors enjoy camping and trout fishing at this pretty spot. You'll need Navajo fishing and boat permits, as on all tribal waters. Campground costs $1/person age 6 and over. Lakeside Store sells groceries, fishing supplies, and permits. Wheatfields Lake is 10 miles south of Tsaile and 44 miles north of Window Rock on Indian Route 12.

# WINDOW ROCK

In the early 1930s, "The Rock With a Hole in It" so impressed the Commissioner of Indian Affairs, John Collier, that he chose the site for a Navajo administration center. An octagonal Navajo Council House went up, and Window Rock became the Navajo Nation capital. The structure represents a great ceremonial hogan; murals on interior walls depict Navajo history. Tribal Council delegates meet to decide on policies and regulations for the reservation. Window Rock is a small (pop. about 3,000) but growing town at an elevation of 6,750 feet. Besides the Council Chambers and offices, there are a museum, small zoo, two parks, a motel, and a shopping center. Window Rock's "downtown" is the shopping center at the junction of AZ 264 and Indian Route 12. Get ready for a traffic light at the corner, a rarity in Navajoland. Window Rock has the world's largest American Indian fair, held on the first weekend in September. The 5 days are filled with a mixture of traditional and modern festivities with singing and dancing, a parade, agricultural shows, food, crafts, concerts, rodeo, and the crowning of Miss Navajo. Write for a brochure from the Navajo Nation Fair Office, Drawer U, Window Rock, AZ 86515; tel. 871-6702/6703.

Window Rock

**Navajo Tribal Museum**
Exhibits introduce you to the land and early cultures of the region, then summarize the history of the Navajo people. Examples of Navajo weaving and silversmithing show the development of varied, distinctive styles. The museum has a good selection of Navajo and regional books for sale. A large arts and crafts shop in the same building sells Navajo paintings, rugs, jewelry, jewelry-making supplies, and crafts by other Southwest tribes. Open Mon.-Fri. 8 a.m.-4:45 p.m.; free. Located on AZ 264, between the shopping center and Navajo Nation Inn.

**Navajo Nation Zoological And Botanical Park**
Set beneath towering sandstone pinnacles known as the "haystacks," the zoo gives you a close look at animals of the Southwest. Once past the rattlesnakes near the entrance, you'll see golden eagles, hawks, elk,

wolves, bobcats, mountain lions, coyotes, black bears, and other creatures. Domestic breeds include the Navajo Churro sheep, introduced to the Southwest by the Spanish; the sheep has a double fleece and often has four horns. Prairie dogs, free of restricting cages, run almost everywhere. Native crops grow near the forked-stick and crib-log hogans in summer. Visit daily 8 a.m.-5 p.m.; free. Located north of AZ 264 one-half mile east of Window Rock Shopping Center.

### Tse Bonito Tribal Park

This open area between the the zoo and highway has a couple of shaded picnic tables, but no water. A spring, now dry, gave the place its Navajo name meaning "Water Between the Rocks." The Navajo camped here in 1864 on their "Long Walk" to eastern New Mexico.

### Window Rock Tribal Park

A beautiful spot shaded by juniper trees at the foot of the Window Rock. The "window" is a great hole, averaging 47 feet across, in a sandstone ridge. Loose stones just below the hole mark the site of a prehistoric Indian pueblo. You're not allowed to climb up to it, but a trail around to the left passes through wonderfully sculptured hills. The park has picnic tables, water, and restrooms. Turn east off Indian Route 12 about one-half mile north of AZ 264, then head one-half mile in, passing the Council Chambers on your left just before the park.

### Accommodations And Campgrounds

**Navajo Nation Inn** has a dining room and swimming pool. Rooms cost $50 s, $55 d; Box 1687, Window Rock, AZ 86515; tel. 871-4108. Located on AZ 264, just east of the shopping center. Window Rock lacks trailer parks or developed campgrounds, but there's plenty of room in **Tse Bonito Tribal Park,** mentioned above; a $1/person camping fee might be charged.

### Food

The **Navajo Nation Inn's** dining room is open daily for breakfast, lunch, and dinner. **Window Rock Shopping Center,** at the highway intersection, has a supermarket and a fast-food restaurant. **Basha's,** just west on AZ 264, has a supermarket and deli. **Kentucky Fried Chicken** is east one mile across into New Mexico. **Tuller Cafe** is 2 miles west near St. Michaels.

### Services

Visit the **Window Rock Shopping Center** for the post office, bank, auto repairs, movie theater, and other stores.

### Information

The **Navajoland Tourism** office has literature and information for visitors to the Navajo Indian Reservation; open Mon.-Fri. 8 a.m.-5 p.m. in the Economic Development Bldg., 2.6 miles west of Window Rock on AZ 264; Box 663, Window Rock, AZ 86515; tel. 871-6659. Fishing and hunting on the Navajo Indian Reservation require tribal permits from **Navajo Fish & Wildlife,** located behind the Motor Pool; Box 1480, Window Rock, AZ 86515; tel. 871-6451/6452. Arizona Game and Fish has no jurisdiction over the reservation; you need only the tribal permits. For hiking and camping information and permits on Navajo lands, contact the **Navajo Parks and Recreation Dept.,** next door to the Zoological and Botanical Park; Box 308, Window Rock, AZ 86515; tel. 871-6645.

*detail from a Navajo blanket*

**Transport**
**Navajo Transit System** connects Window Rock with many communities on the Navajo and Hopi reservations; see "Getting Around," pp. 98-99.

## VICINITY OF WINDOW ROCK

### Fort Defiance
Permanent springs in a nearby canyon attracted the Navajo, who named the area Tsehotsoi, "Meadow Between the Rocks." Colonel Edwin Vose Sumner had another name in mind in Sept. 1851, when in defiance of the Navajo, he established a fort on an overlooking hillside. Though the Navajo nearly overran Fort Defiance in 1860, the Army successfully repelled the attacks until the fort was abandoned during the Civil War. In 1863-64, Colonel Kit Carson headquartered at the fort while rounding up and moving out the Navajo. After they returned, destitute, in 1868, the first Navajo Agency offices issued them sheep and supplies here. The first school on the reservation opened in 1869, and the first regular medical service in 1880. The old fort is gone now, but the town remains an administrative center with a hospital, schools, and Bureau of Indian Affairs offices.

### Navajo, New Mexico
Trees from the extensive woodlands that surround the town of Navajo supply the town's large sawmill. **Navajo Pine Shopping Center** has a supermarket, cafe, and post office. Nearby **Red Lake,** named for the color of its aquatic vegetation, has fishing and primitive camping. Navajo is 17 miles north of Window Rock on Route 12, on the way to Wheatfields Lake, Tsaile, and Canyon de Chelly. This scenic, high-country road crosses pastures and forests in the foothills of the Chuska Mountains.

### St. Michael's Mission
In 1898, Franciscan friars opened a mission to serve the Navajo. The large stone church dates from 1937, when it replaced an earlier adobe structure. St. Michael's School, opened by Sisters of the Blessed Sacrament

in 1902, is a short distance away. A small historical museum now occupies the original mission building. Step inside to see displays of Indian culture and life of the early missionaries. Regional books, cards, and posters are sold. Open Mon.-Sat. 9 a.m.-5 p.m. and Sun. 10 a.m.-6 p.m. from Memorial Day to Labor Day; other times by appointment; free; tel. 871-4171. St. Michael's Mission is 2.5 miles west of Window Rock on AZ 264, then 0.2 mile south at the sign.

### Summit Campground
Escape the summer heat by picnicking or camping among the cool ponderosa pines. Head 9 miles west of Window Rock on AZ 264 (19 miles east of Ganado) to where the road climbs over a 7,750-foot pass. The turnoffs (on both sides of highway) are signed "Rest Area." Picnic tables are provided but no water; a camping charge of $1/person age 6 and over may be collected.

## GANADO

The Spanish called this place Pueblo Colorado ("Red House") after a nearby Anasazi ruin. The name later changed to Ganado, honoring one of the great Navajo chiefs, Ganado Mucho, or "Big Water Clansman," a signer of the treaty of June 1868 that returned the Navajo lands. A Presbyterian mission founded here in 1901 provided the Navajo with a school and hospital. The school grew into the 2-year College of Ganado, where students learned forestry, business administration, and general subjects, but the school recently closed.

Visit the nearby Hubbell Trading Post, Arizona's most famous, to experience a genuine part of the Old West (see below). Ganado is on AZ 264, 30 miles west of Window Rock, 38 miles north of Chambers and I-40, 44 miles east of Keams Canyon, and 36 miles south of Chinle. No accommodations in the area, but you can find American and Mexican food at **Ramon's Restaurant,** open daily except Sun. for breakfast, lunch, and dinner; turn north on the street opposite the junction of AZ 264 and US 191 (from Chambers).

**Ganado Lake**
Fishermen try their luck at Ganado Lake, which also offers picnicking and primitive camping. From town, head east 1.5 miles on AZ 264, then north about one mile on Indian Route 27. Watch for sandy spots on the road to the lake.

## HUBBELL TRADING POST NATIONAL HISTORIC SITE

John Lorenzo Hubbell began trading in 1876, a difficult time for the Navajo, who were still recovering from their traumatic internment at Fort Sumner. Born in New Mexico, Hubbell had already learned some Navajo ways and language by the time he set up business. Money rarely exchanged hands during a transaction; the Indian would bring in blankets or jewelry and receive credit. He would then point out desired items: coffee, flour, sugar, cloth, harnesses, or other manufactured items. If there was still credit left, he usually preferred silver or turquoise to money. Tribesmen bringing wool or sheep to the trading post usually received cash, however.

*Navajo weaving at Hubbell Trading Post*

Hubbell distinguished himself by his honesty and closeness to the Navajo. His insistence on excellence in weaving and silverwork led to better prices for Indian crafts-people. Also, the trading post helped bridge the Anglo and Indian cultures: Navajo often called upon Hubbell to explain government programs and to write letters to officials explaining their concerns.

**Visitor Center, Hubbell's House, And Trading Post**
National Park Service exhibits and programs explain not only Hubbell's work, but how trading posts once linked the Navajo with the outside world. Weavers (usually women) and silversmiths (usually men) often demonstrate their skills in the Visitor Center. Books about Indian art and culture are sold. You can take a scheduled guided tour of Hubbell's house or a self-guided tour of the grounds; free. The house contains superb rugs, paintings, baskets, and other crafts collected by Hubbell until his death in 1930, then by the Hubbell family until 1967. The trading post still operates much as it always has. You can buy high-quality crafts or 'most anything else. Shelves are jammed with canned and yard goods; glass cases display pocket knives and other small items; horse collars and harnesses still hang from the ceiling; and Navajo still drop in with items for trade. A tree-shaded picnic area is next to the Visitor Center. Open daily 8 a.m.-6 p.m. from June to Sept., and 8 a.m.-5 p.m. the rest of the year; closed Thanksgiving, Christmas, and New Year's Day. Located one mile west of Ganado.

# HOPI COUNTRY

For centuries the Hopi people have made their homes in villages atop three mesas, finger-like extensions of Black Mesa to the north. Early European visitors dubbed these extensions First Mesa, Second Mesa, and Third Mesa, counting from east to west. Arizona 264 skirts First Mesa and crosses over Second and Third mesas on the way from Window Rock to Tuba City. The mesas have provided the Hopi with water from reliable springs as well as protection from enemies— the 600-foot cliffs discouraged assailants. Hard-working farmers, the Hopi are usually peaceable and independent. They keep in close touch with nature and have developed a rich ceremonial life to maintain balance and harmony with their surroundings and one another. Villages remain largely autonomous even today. The Hopi Tribal Council, which the federal government had the Hopi organize, serves mainly as a liaison between villages and agencies of the federal and state governments.

### Visiting Hopi Villages
The Hopi tend to be very private people, yet they do welcome visitors to their lands. Policies, which vary from village to village, will often be posted. All villages prohibit disturbing activities such as photography, sketching, and recording. Keep cameras hidden away in your car! Try to visit only between 8 a.m. and 5 p.m. to give residents their privacy. Walpi, and possibly other villages, may ask that visitors enter only with an authorized Hopi guide.

The best time to visit a village is when a ceremony takes place that is open to the public. The inhabitants will be expecting visitors and you'll be able to see more of the Hopi culture. Dances take place in plazas in one or more villages on many weekends; good sources to find what's coming up are the Hopi Tribe's Office of Public Relations (tel. 734-2441, ext. 341 or 360) and Second Mesa Cultural Center (tel. 734-2401).

## KEAMS CANYON

Not a Hopi village, but an administrative town with a hospital and various U.S. government agencies. It's the easternmost community on the Hopi Reservation. The settlement lies at the mouth of a scenic wooded canyon named after Thomas Keam, who built a trading post here in 1875. From the town, the canyon winds northeast for about 8 miles; the first 3 miles contains a road. Kit Carson engraved his name on Inscription Rock, about 2 miles beyond town. You'll pass some pleasant picnic spots on the way.

### Practicalities
**Keams Canyon Motel** has basic rooms ($30 s, $35 d, $45 kitchenettes) at the turnoff for Keams Canyon; tel. 738-2297. A **picnic area**

*Hopi man spinning*

**1.** a Navajo and his sheep (Arizona Office of Tourism); **2.** trekking through Paria Canyon (B. Weir);
**3.** Pine Country Rodeo, Flagstaff (B. Weir); **4.** rafting in the Grand Canyon (Arizona Office of
Tourism); **5.** the Narrows of Paria Canyon (B. Weir)

1. Keet Seel Ruin, Navajo National Monument; 2. prehistoric pottery fragments; 3. Box Canyon Ruin, Wupatki National Monument; 4. Wupatki Ruin, Wupatki National Monument; 5. Betatakin Ruin, Navajo National Monument (all photos by B. Weir)

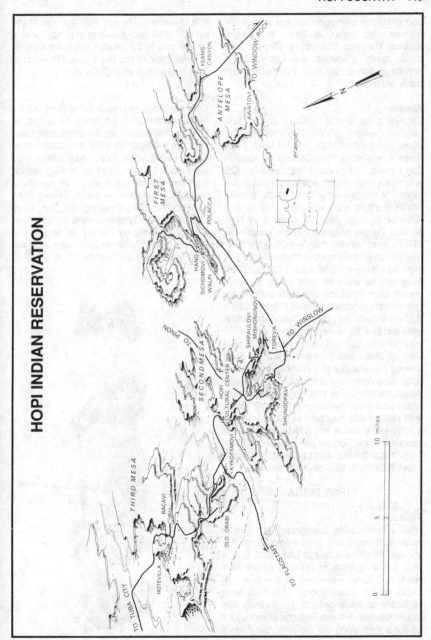

HOPI INDIAN RESERVATION

and **primitive campground** are across the highway; no water, facilities, or charge. **Keams Canyon Shopping Center** has Indian crafts, groceries, and fast foods. A service station is next door. **Post office** and **bank** are in town.

### Awatovi

Beginning as a small village in the 12th century, Awatovi (ah-WAHT-o-vee) had become an important Hopi town by 1540, when Spanish explorers from Coronado's expedition arrived. Franciscan friars came in 1629 and built a large church and friary using Indian labor. The mission lasted for 51 years. In 1680, fearful that their ways would be destroyed by Christianity, Hopi villagers joined their New Mexico Pueblo neighbors in the successful overthrow of Spanish rule, wrecking the Awatovi church and killing most of the priests. The mission was re-established in 1700, but other Hopi villages were so angered by this continued alien influence that they banded together and promptly destroyed Awatovi. Of the 800 inhabitants, they massacred almost all the men and took the women and children to other Hopi villages. Spanish troops retaliated a year later with little effect. Further missionary efforts among the Hopi by the Franciscans proved futile. Only ghosts live at Awatovi today—it was never resettled. The ruin sprawls across 23 acres on the southwest tip of Antelope Mesa, with piles of rubble as high as 30 feet. To visit you'll need a permit and a Hopi guide; ask in advance at the Cultural Preservations Office, Hopi Tribal Headquarters, Box 123, Kykotsmovi, AZ 86039; tel. 734-2441, ext. 209.

## FIRST MESA

### Polacca

With an increasing population, some Hopi have built houses in settlements below the mesas, as at Polacca (po-LAH-kah). Still, if you ask a resident of Polacca where he's from, he'll likely name one of the three villages on the mesa above. Christians tend to locate on lower ground; you'll rarely see churches atop a mesa. Polacca stretches for about a mile along the highway, but there's little of interest. The big thrill is a visit to the top of First Mesa. A paved road climbs steeply for one mile to the crest. If you have a trailer or large vehicle, you must park it in Polacca or at a parking area halfway up.

### Hano

The first village you reach *looks* Hopi, but it's really a settlement of the Tewa, a Pueblo tribe from the Rio Grande region to the east. Fleeing from the Spanish after an unsuccessful revolt in 1696, some Tewa had sought refuge with Hopi living here. Hopi leaders agreed, on the condition that the Tewa act as guardians of the access path to the mesa. Despite living close to the Hopi for so long, the Tewa have kept their own language and ceremonies. Hano's fascinating history is detailed in *A Tewa Indian Community in Arizona* by Edward P. Dozier (see "Booklist").

*Hopi woman, 1890*

## Sichomovi

To the visitor, Hano and the Hopi village of Sichomovi (see-CHO-mo-vee) appear as one, but residents know exactly where the line is. Sichomovi is considered a branch of Walpi, the village at the tip of the mesa.

## Walpi

One of the most inspiring places in Arizona, Walpi (WAHL-pee) stands surrounded by sky and distant horizons. Ancient houses of yellow stone appear to grow from the mesa itself. Coming from Sichomovi, you'll see that the mesa narrows to just 15 feet before widening again at Walpi. Visitors may enter this traditional village only with an authorized Hopi guide; Walpi is small (pop. about 30), and its occupants are sensitive. Free tours to Walpi leave either from Ponsi Hall, in Sichomovi, or from the tourist booth at Walpi Parking Lot farther on. The 40-minute walking tours leave daily 9:30 a.m.-4:20 p.m.; tel. 737-2262 (Ponsi Hall) or 737-2670 (Community Development office; also a good source of information about dances on First Mesa).

Unlike other Hopi villages, Walpi lacks electricity or running water. Residents have to walk back toward Sichomovi to obtain water or to wash. Look for bowl-shaped depressions used to collect rainwater on the far side of Walpi. Precipitous foot trails and ruins of old defenses and buildings cling to the mesa slopes far below. Walpi, inhabited for more than 300 years, is well known for its ceremonial dances and crafts. Kachina dolls carved by the men and pottery made by the women are sold in the village; signs indicate which houses sell crafts. With sweeping panoramas at every turn and a determined hold on traditions, Walpi is probably the most rewarding of all the Hopi villages.

## SECOND MESA

### Second Mesa (Junction)

Highways AZ 264 and AZ 87 meet at the foot of Second Mesa, 7 miles west of Polacca and 60 miles north of Winslow. Here you'll find **Secakuku Trading Post** (supermarket, open daily), **Second Mesa Restaurant and Curio,**

*Walpi, "Sky Village"*

*Hopi Snake Dance*

and a **post office. Honani Crafts Gallery** and a service station are one-half mile west at the turnoff for Shipaulovi and Mishongnovi villages.

### Shipaulovi And Mishongnovi
These two traditional villages are close neighbors on a projection of Second Mesa. Dances often take place; ask at the Cultural Center for dates. You reach Shipaulovi (shih-PAW-lo-vee) and Mishongnovi (mih-SHONG-no-vee) by a short paved road which climbs steeply from AZ 264, one-half mile west of the intersection with AZ 87, or by a mesa-top road (also paved) 0.2 mile east of the Cultural Center. Mishongnovi is the easternmost village, at the end of the mesa.

### Shungopavi
Shungopavi (shong-O-po-vee or shih-MO-pah-vee) is the largest (pop. 742) of the three

Second Mesa villages. Dances performed include the Butterfly Dance (a social dance), and the Snake Dance (late Aug. in even-numbered years). Buy crafts from the villagers or at **Dawa's Art and Crafts** on the road into the village. Shungopavi is 0.8 mile south off AZ 264, midway between the junction with AZ 87 and the Cultural Center.

## HOPI CULTURAL CENTER

Proclaiming itself "At the Center of the Universe," this excellent pueblo-style museum-motel-restaurant-gift shop complex is popular with both visitors and local Hopi. The motel desk is a good source for finding out about dances on the reservation. The Hopi Cultural Center is on the west side of Second Mesa just before the road plunges down on the way to Third Mesa. For a shortcut to Chinle and Canyon de Chelly, turn north off AZ 264 beside the Cultural Center to Pinon Trading Post, 26 miles (partly paved), then east 42 miles on paved roads.

The museum has good exhibits of Hopi customs, ceremonies, crafts, and history; open all year about Mon.-Fri. 8 a.m.-5 p.m. and Sat.-Sun 9 a.m.-4 p.m. (in winter, Sat. hours change to 9 a.m.-3 p.m. and closed Sun.); $3 adult, $1 children 13 and under; tel. 734-6650. The Hopi consider some ceremonial objects of their religion to be secret and they won't be displayed. To learn more of Hopi mythology and customs, dig into off-reservation sources such as the NAU Special Collections or Museum of Northern Arizona libraries, both in Flagstaff.

The modern motel has rooms at $50 s, $55 d, $5 each additional person. Reservations are recommended; Box 67, Second Mesa, AZ 86043; tel. 734-2401. Camping and picnic grounds are next door, between the Cultural Center and Hopi Arts and Crafts shop. No water or hookups, but you can use the restrooms in the Cultural Center; free. Showers may be available in mornings for a small fee; ask at the motel.

The restaurant serves good American and Hopi dishes. This is your big chance to try ba-duf-su-ki (pinto bean and hominy soup), or maybe some nok-qui-vi (traditional stew of Hopi corn and lamb), or breakfast of blue pancakes made of the unusual Hopi corn! Open daily for breakfast, lunch, and dinner.

Three small shops display a good stock of Hopi silverwork, kachina dolls, pottery, paintings, baskets, and weavings. **Hopi Arts and Crafts** (Silvercrafts Cooperative Guild), a short walk across the camping area, houses an even bigger selection. You can often see Hopi silversmiths at work here.

# THIRD MESA

## Kykotsmovi

The name means "Mound of Ruined Houses." Hopi from Old Oraibi (o-RYE-bee) founded this settlement near a spring at the base of Third Mesa. Peach trees add greenery to the town. Kykotsmovi (kee-KEUTS-mo-vee), also known as New Oraibi, is headquarters for the Hopi Tribal Council. The **Office of Public Relations** provides information for visitors; located near the Tribal Council building one mile south of AZ 264; Box 123, Kykotsmovi, AZ 86039; tel. 734-2441, ext. 341 or 360. **Picnicking** and

**primitive camping** are at Oraibi Wash, 0.8 mile east of the Kykotsmovi turnoff, and at a rest area overlook 1.2 miles west on the climb to Oraibi. **Kykotsmovi Village Store** has groceries and Indian crafts. **Hopikiva Arts & Crafts** shop is on the highway just east of the turnoff. Indian Route 2 leading south to Leupp (pronounced "LOOP"), is paved and the shortest way to Flagstaff.

## Old Oraibi

This dusty pueblo perched on the edge of Third Mesa dates back to A.D. 1150, and is probably the oldest continuously inhabited community in the United States. The 20th century has been difficult for this ancient village. In 1900 it ranked as one of the largest Hopi settlements, with a population of over 800, but dissension caused many to leave. The first major dispute occurred in 1906 between two chiefs, You-ke-oma and Tawa-quap-tewa. Instead of letting fly with bullets and arrows, the leaders staged a strange "push-of-war" contest. A line was cut into the mesa and the two groups stood on either side. They pushed against each other as hard as they could until one group lost, You-ke-oma's. He and his faction then left to establish

continued on page 126

Matilde Coxe Stevenson, anthropologist, backed up by her husband, won't take "no" for an answer when Hopi object to her prying into ceremonial secrets. (from an engraving published in the Illustrated Police News, March 6, 1886)

# HOPI KACHINAS

Kachinas appear to the Hopi from about the winter solstice (Dec. 21) until mid-July. They dance and sing in unison, symbolizing harmony of good thought and action. This harmony is needed for rain to fall and life to be balanced. For the rest of the year the kachinas stay in their home in the San Francisco Peaks. A kachina can take three forms: it may be the powerful unseen spirit, it may be the dancer who is filled with the spirit, or it may be the wooden figure that represents the spirit. Dancers are always men, even when representing the female kachinas, as the Hopi believe that men have closer contact with the supernatural. This is balanced by gifts of kachina figures presented by dancers to the girls and women during ceremonies. Each village has its own style and choice of ceremonies and dances. The following is a general outline.

# HOPI CALENDAR

### Wuwuchim And Soyala (November-December)

These months symbolize the time of creation of the world. The villages tend to be quiet as Hopi spend time in silence, prayer, and meditation. Wuwuchim, a tribal initiation ceremony, marks the start of the ceremonial calendar year. Young men are initiated into adulthood when they join one of four ceremonial societies. The society a man joins depends on his sponsor. After joining, the initiate receives instruction in Hopi creation beliefs. A new name is given him and his childhood name will not be used again. Only Shungopavi village does the entire Wuwuchim ceremony and then not every year; other villages do part of the Wuwuchim.

The Soyala Kachina staggers in from the west in the winter solstice ceremony. He has been away and idle the past 6 months and so has lost much of his strength. As the days are getting longer now, the Hopi begin planning for the upcoming planting season—thus fertility is a major concern in the ceremony.

### Buffalo Dances (January)

Men, women, and children perform this social dance in the plazas. The dances also deal with fertility, especially the need for winter moisture in the form of snow.

### Powamuya, The "Bean Dance" (February)

Bean sprouts have been grown in a kiva as part of a 16-day ceremony. On the final day, kachina dancers form in a long parade through the villages. Children of about 13-14 years are initiated into kachina societies during the Powamuya. The ogre kachinas appear on First and Second mesas.

### Kiva Dances (March)

A second set of nighttime kiva dances consists of Anktioni or "repeat dances."

### Plaza Dances (April, May, And June)

The kachina dancers perform in all-day ceremonies lasting from sunrise to sunset, with breaks between dances. The group, and the people watching, concentrate their thoughts in a community prayer for the spirits to bring rain for the growing crops.

### Niman, The "Home Dance" (July)

At the summer solstice (June 21), the plaza dances end and preparations begin for the Going Home Ceremony. In a 16-day rite, their last of the season, kachina dancers present the first green corn ears, then dance for rain to hasten growth of the remaining crops. Their spiritual work done, the kachinas return to their mountain home.

**Snake, Flute, And Butterfly Dances (August)**

The Snake and Flute ceremonies, held in alternate years, represent the clan groups, who perform them for a good harvest and prosperity. The Snake Dance, usually closed to non-Indians, takes place in even-numbered years at Shungopavi and in odd-numbered years at Mishongnovi. The snakes, often poisonous rattlers, act as messengers to the spirits. The Flute Ceremony takes place in odd-numbered years at Shungopavi and Walpi. The Butterfly Dance, a social dance performed mainly by children, takes place in all villages. It also celebrates the harvest; dances continue into September.

**Women's Society Dances (September And October)**

Held in the plazas, these ceremonies celebrate the harvest with wishes for health and prosperity. Chaos reigns during the Basket Dances; women dancers throw out baskets and other valuables to the audience, which engages in a mad free-for-all to grab the prizes. End of the ceremonial year.

continued from page 123

Hotevilla about 4 miles away. This event was recorded 0.25 mile north of Oraibi with the line and inscription: "Well, it have [sic] to be done this way now, that when you pass this LINE it will be DONE, Sept. 8, 1906." A bear paw cut in the rock is the symbol of Tawa-quap-tewa and his Bear Clan, while a skull represents You-ke-oma and his Skeleton Clan. Other residents split off to join New Oraibi at the foot of the mesa. A ruin near Old Oraibi on the south end of the mesa is all that remains of a church built in 1901 by the Mennonite minister, H.R. Voth. Most villagers disliked having this "thing" so close to their homes, and they must have been elated when lightning destroyed the church in 1942. Old Oraibi is 2 miles west of Kykotsmovi. Avoid driving through the village and stirring up dust; park outside (or next to Old Oraibi Crafts shop) and walk. **Monongya Gallery,** near the turnoff for Old Oraibi, and **Old Oraibi Crafts,** in the village, have Hopi art and crafts. **Hopi Gallery of Art** is on the highway 2 miles toward Hotevilla.

## Hotevilla

The name Hotevilla (HOAT-vih-lah) means "Skinned Back." When villagers obtained spring water from a cave, they often scraped their backs on the low ceiling. Hotevilla is a traditional village known for its dances, basketry, and other crafts. Founded in 1906 after the split from Old Oraibi, Hotevilla got a shaky start. Federal authorities demanded that the group return to Old Oraibi so that children could be enrolled in school there. Twenty-five men agreed to take their families and move back despite the continued bad feelings. But 53 others refused to leave Hotevilla. The recalcitrant men then wound up in jail for 90 days or more while their school-age children were forcibly taken to the boarding school in Keams Canyon. Women and infants of these men fended for themselves at Hotevilla that first winter, with little food and inadequate shelter. In the following year the men returned to build better houses

and plant crops. Exasperated authorities continued to haul You-ke-oma off to jail for his lack of cooperation and refusal to send village children to school. Trying another tack in 1912, government officials invited the chief to Washington for a meeting with President Taft, but the meeting didn't soften You-ke-oma's stance. The turnoff for Hotevilla is 3.7 miles northwest of Old Oraibi and 46 miles southeast of Tuba City.

## Bacavi

The losing side of the 1906 split that returned to Old Oraibi was accepted back only under federal government pressure. Resentment continued to smolder between the two groups. At one point, when two of the returning women died in quick succession, cries of witchcraft went up. Finally, in Nov. 1909, tensions became unbearable. The unwelcome group packed their bags once more and settled at a new site called Bacavi (BAH-kah-vee) Spring. The name means "Jointed Reed," after a plant found at the spring. Bacavi lies on the opposite side of the highway from Hotevilla.

## Coal Mine Canyon

A scenic little canyon 31 miles northwest of Bacavi (15 miles southeast of Tuba City) on AZ 264. Look for a windmill and Coal Mine Mesa Rodeo Ground on the north side of the highway (no signs), and turn in across the cattle guard. Indians have long obtained coal from the seam just below the rim.

## Moenkopi ("The Place Of Running Water")

This Hopi village lies 2 miles southeast of Tuba City. Prehistoric Pueblo Indians built villages in the area but had abandoned them by A.D. 1300. Chief Tuba of Oraibi (48 miles southeast) founded Moenkopi in the 1870s. Mormons constructed a woolen mill in 1879 with plans to use Indian labor, but the Indians apparently disliked working with machinery and the project failed. Water from springs irrigates fields, an advantage not enjoyed by other Hopi villages.

# NORTHCENTRAL ARIZONA

## INTRODUCTION

The high country of northcentral Arizona offers dramatic and varied scenery. Cool forests, which cover much of the region, provide a delightful respite from the desert in the warmer months. The remarkably diverse landscapes of the region entice many visitors, whatever their style of travel. Highways wind through many scenic and historic areas, yet backcountry travelers can explore all day on trails or forest roads without crossing a paved road. Fishermen can choose among many lakes on the Colorado Plateau and streams below it. In winter, skiers come to enjoy the downhill runs on the San Francisco Peaks near Flagstaff and the shorter runs on Bill Williams Mountain near Williams. Cross-country skiers can strike out on their own or glide along groomed trails near the San Francisco Peaks or at Mormon Lake.

### THE LAND

Most of northern Arizona lies atop the Colorado Plateau—a giant uplifted landmass extending into adjacent Utah, Colorado, and New Mexico. As the land rose, vigorous rivers cut deeply through the rock layers, revealing beautiful forms and colors of countless canyons. While the rivers cut down, volcanos shot up. For millions of years, large and small volcanos have been sprouting in the San Francisco Volcanic Field around Flagstaff. The most striking include the San Francisco Peaks, whose highest point—Humphrey's Peak—at 12,633 feet is Arizona's tallest. Sunset Crater, the state's most beautiful, is the youngster of the field. It last erupted about 700 years ago—just yesterday, geologically speaking. A crater of a different sort lies east of Flagstaff: Meteor Crater formed sometime between 30,000 and 50,000 years ago when a speeding mass of rock smashed into the earth, displacing an estimated 300 million tons of material. Northcentral Arizona's elevations drop more than 9,000 feet from the heights of Humphrey's Peak to the lower Verde and Agua Fria river valleys to the south. Most of the region lies between 4,000 and 8,000 feet. Sheer cliffs of the Mogollon (pronounced "MUGGY-own") Rim mark the southern edge of the Colorado Plateau.

## Climate

Expect a cool, invigorating mountain climate over most of northcentral Arizona. Outdoorsmen find spring, summer, and fall temperatures ideal in the higher country, where temperatures peak in the 70s and 80s F. Lower valleys often bake in the heat then, but you can always reach the mountains in less than an hour. From early July into September, thunderstorm clouds billow into the air, dropping scattered downpours. Winter brings a battle between snow and sun. Cold-season temperatures vary greatly from the bitter cold of storms to the warmth of bright Arizona sunshine. In Flagstaff (elev. 7,000 feet), average winter lows run in the teens, warming to highs in the lower 40s F, although almost anything's possible. Be prepared for anything from subzero to spring-like temperatures! Skiers enjoy the snow, though not many people brave the higher elevations for camping or backpacking. Lower country experiences milder winters with only occasional snowfalls. Annual precipitation, which arrives mostly in summer and winter, varies between 10 and 30 inches, depending on elevation and rain shadows.

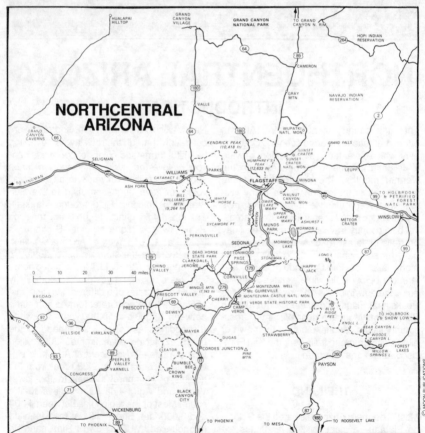

## Flora And Fauna

The great range in elevation, together with a varied topography, provide many different habitats for wildlife. Tiny alpine plants hug the ground against strong winds and extreme cold on the highest slopes of the San Francisco Peaks, where no trees can survive. At lower elevations, dense groves of aspen, firs, and pines thrive on the mountainsides and in protected canyons. Squirrels busy themselves storing away food for the long winters here, while larger animals just visit for the summer.

Vast forests of ponderosa pine and Gambel oak cover much of the Colorado Plateau. Elk, mule deer, a few black bear, coyote, and smaller animals make these forests their home. Some of the many birds you'll likely see include the ubiquitous common raven, noisy Steller's jay, and feisty hummingbird. Drier parts of northcentral Arizona support forests of juniper, pinyon pine, oak, and Arizona cypress. In other semi-arid zones, dense shrubs and stunted trees of the chaparral separate the ponderosa forests above from the desert below. Common plants of the chaparral include manzanita, silk-tassel-bush, shrub live oak, catclaw acacia, and buckbrush. Streams flowing from the Mogollon Rim attract animals from both the plateau and the desert, and often support beaver.

black-tailed jack rabbit
(Lepus californicus)

Arizona Game and Fish Department stocks nonnative rainbow trout in lakes and permanent streams.

In drier country grow the grasses, yuccas, agave, cacti, catclaw acacia, and other plants of the desert. Wildlife at home here include the coyote, gray fox, spotted skunk, black-tailed jack rabbit, desert cottontail, deer mice, side-blotched lizard, gopher snake, and western rattlesnake. Herds of pronghorn, a graceful antelope-like creature, roam the arid grasslands north of the San Francisco Volcanic Field. Birds such as the golden eagle, red-tailed hawk, and common raven find good scavenging in the desert, but usually nest elsewhere. Gambel's quail, roadrunner, horned lark, and black-throated sparrow make use of bushes for cover and nesting sites.

Canyons create strange variations in climate: a north-facing slope may have dense growths of firs and pines while only yuccas, grasses, and sparse stunted trees can grow on the opposite slope. Or you could see juniper trees growing near the top of a canyon and Douglas firs below, a reversal of the normal order of climate zones.

## HISTORY

### Native Americans

Archaeologists have dated prehistoric Indian sites along the Little Colorado River back as far as 15,000 B.C., when now-extinct species of bison, camels, antelope, and horses roamed the land. Although some Indian groups acquired agriculture between 2,000 and 500 B.C., they maintained a seasonal migration pattern of hunting and gathering. These nomadic groups planted corn, squash, and beans in the spring, continued their travels, and then returned to harvest their fields in the autumn.

From about A.D. 200 to 500, as the Indians devoted more time to farming, they built clusters of pithouses (partly underground rooms) near their fields. Regional cultures then began to form: the Anasazi of the Colorado Plateau, the Mogollon of the eastern Arizona uplands, and the Hohokam of the desert to the south. A fourth culture evolved near present-day Flagstaff between A.D. 900 and 1000 as a blend of the three earlier cultures. These people are known as Sinagua (Spanish for "Without Water") because the area's porous volcanic soil quickly absorbs rains and snowmelt.

As the societies developed further, they started to build pueblos above ground. Villages, usually located on hilltops or in cliff overhangs with an eye to defense, became widely scattered over northcentral Arizona. By about A.D. 1100 the population had reached its peak. Inhabitants then mysteriously began to abandon villages and even whole areas. Archaeologists explain these departures by theories of drought, soil erosion, disease, and raids by the newly arrived Apache. By the 1500s, when Spanish explorers came to northern Arizona, the pueblo Indians had retreated to northeast Arizona and adjacent New Mexico. Thousands of empty villages remain in northcentral Arizona, some protected in the four national monuments of Wupatki (north of Flagstaff), Walnut Canyon (east of Flagstaff), Tuzigoot (southwest of Flagstaff), and Montezuma Castle-Montezuma Well (south of Flagstaff). You might also discover ruins while hiking in the backcountry. Sometime after about A.D. 1400, bands of Yavapai and Apache moved into the Verde Valley and Mogollon Rim areas. They did some farming, but obtained most of their food by hunting and collecting wild plants.

### White Men Search For Gold And Silver
Antonio de Espejo, the first of several Spanish explorers, visited northcentral Arizona in 1583 seeking precious metals. Later expeditions located claims near present-day Prescott, but the Spaniards never developed them. When American prospectors rediscovered the deposits in the early 1860s, they had to work their mines in the face of attacks from Apache Indians. Fort Whipple, built by the Army in 1863, provided some protection.

### Americans Settle In
In 1864, surveyors marked out a town along Granite Creek near Fort Whipple. Carved out of the wilderness, the carefully planned community was to become Arizona's territorial capital. Arizona had just been separated from New Mexico, and President Lincoln wanted the capital a comfortable distance from the southern settlements of Tucson and Tubac, where too many Texans and other Confederate sympathizers lived. But the town's settlers didn't forget Arizona's Spanish-American heritage; they christened their settlement "Prescott" after William Hickling Prescott, author of *The History of the Conquest of Mexico*.

Development farther north took longer. Captain Lorenzo Sitgreaves had brought a surveying expedition across northern Arizona in 1851, leading to the building of rough wagon roads by Beale and others, but hostile Indians and poor farming land discouraged settlement. The coming of the railroad in 1882, thriving lumber mills, and success in sheep and cattle ranching opened up the region and led to the growth of railroad towns such as Flagstaff and Williams.

## TRANSPORT

You really need your own vehicle to visit the national monuments and most of the scenic and recreation areas. Tours make brief stops at highlights of the region but tend to be rushed; see "Transport" in the Flagstaff section. Greyhound provides frequent bus service across northern Arizona via Flagstaff and between Flagstaff and Phoenix. Other bus lines connect Flagstaff with the Grand Canyon to the north and with Sedona, Prescott, and Camp Verde to the south. Amtrak runs daily trains across northern Arizona in each direction between Los Angeles (CA) and Albuquerque (NM) and beyond. Regional airlines serve Flagstaff, Sedona, Prescott, and the Grand Canyon.

# FLAGSTAFF

Surrounded by pine forests in the center of northern Arizona, Flagstaff (pop. 45,000) has long been an important stop for ranchers, Indians, and travelers. The older, downtown part of Flagstaff still has a bit of frontier feeling, expressed by its many historic buildings. But what most visitors first see of the small city is the seemingly endless line of flashing signs advertising a profusion of motels, restaurants, bars, and service stations. However, there's far more to see here than Flagstaff's "auto row." To visit the distant past when the land was being uplifted, volcanos were erupting, and the early Indians were arriving, just head over to the Museum of Northern Arizona. To learn what the pioneers were doing here 100 years ago, drop in at the local Pioneer Historical Museum. See work by local artists in the Art Barn, Coconino Center for the Arts, and the University Art Gallery. For an outer-worldly trip, go to Lowell Observatory where astronomers discovered Pluto or to the U.S. Geological Survey where astrogeologists are busy mapping celestial bodies. To be outdoors, just head for the hills—Arizona's highest mountains begin at the northern outskirts of town. In summer, the mountains, hills, and meadows offer pleasant forest walks and challenging climbs. Winter snows turn the countryside into some of the state's best downhill and cross-country skiing areas. As a local guidebook, *Coconino County, the Wonderland of America,* put it back in 1916, Flagstaff "offers you the advantages of any city of twice its size; it has, free for the taking, the healthiest and most invigorating of climates; its surrounding scenic beauties will fill one season, from May to November, full to overflowing with enjoyment the life of any tourist, vacationist, camper or out doors man or woman who will but come to commune with nature."

## History

Indian groups had settled near the site of present-day Flagstaff, but their villages were long abandoned when the first white men arrived. Many ruins of old pueblos lie near town. Walnut Canyon National Monument, just east of Flagstaff, contains well-preserved cliff dwellings of the Sinagua people. Spanish explorers and missionaries knew of the Flagstaff area, but they had little interest in a place that offered no valuable minerals to mine or souls to save. Beginning in the 1820s, mountain men such as Antoine Leroux became expert trappers and guides in this little-known region between Santa Fe and California. Early travelers sent out glowing reports of the climate, water, and scenery of the region, but hostile Apache, Navajo, Yavapai, and Paiute Indians nearby discouraged settlement. Despite the dangers, people in the East began to take a new interest in moving west to improve their lives.

In 1873, Samuel Cozzens, after a term as judge in Tucson and travels in the Southwest, went back east and stirred up the enthusiasm

*Flagstaff and the San Francisco Peaks; Northern Arizona University is in the foreground*

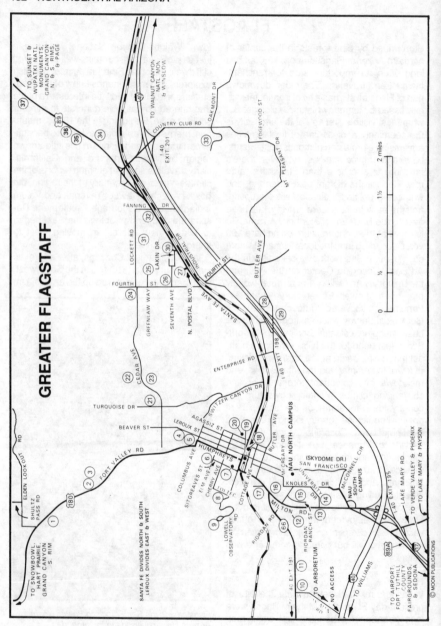

# GREATER FLAGSTAFF

TO SUNSET &
WUPATKI NATL.
MONUMENTS,
GRAND CANYON
N, & S. RIMS,
& PAGE

TO WALNUT CANYON
NATL. MON.
& WINSLOW

COUNTRY CLUB RD

OAKMONT DR

EDGEWOOD ST

I-40 EXIT 201

MT PLEASANT DR

FANNING DR

LOCKETT RD

LAKIN DR

INDUSTRIAL DR

BUTLER AVE

FOURTH ST

GREENLAW WAY

SEVENTH AVE

N. POSTAL BLVD

FOURTH ST

SANTA FE AVE

CEDAR AVE

ENTERPRISE RD

I-40 EXIT 198

TURQUOISE DR

SWITZER CANYON DR

AGASSIZ ST

BEAVER ST

LEROUX ST

BUTLER AVE

NAU NORTH CAMPUS

FORT VALLEY RD

COLUMBUS AVE

SITGREAVES ST

ELM AVE

CHERRY AVE

HUMPHREYS

McCREARY DR

(SKYDOME DR.)
SAN FRANCISCO

ELDEN LOOKOUT RD

SANTA FE DIVIDES NORTH & SOUTH
LEROUX DIVIDES EAST & WEST

SHULTZ
PASS RD

TO SNOWBOWL,
HART PRAIRIE,
GRAND CANYON
S. RIM

TOLTEC

COTTAGE AVE

KNOLES DR

UNIVERSITY DR

McCONNELL CIR

NAU SOUTH
CAMPUS

LOWELL
OBSERVATORY

RIORDAN RD

MILTON

RIORDAN RANCH ST

I-40 EXIT 195

I-40 EXIT 191

TO ARBORETUM

NO ACCESS

TO WILLIAMS

LAKE MARY RD

TO VERDE VALLEY & PHOENIX

TO LAKE MARY & PAYSON

TO AIRPORT,
FORT TUTHILL
COUNTY
FAIRGROUNDS,
& SEDONA

0   ½   1   1½   2 miles

© MOON PUBLICATIONS

of prospective settlers with a large, well-illustrated book entitled *The Marvellous Country; or Three Years in Arizona and New Mexico, the Apache's Home*. The subtitle went on to explain: "Comprising a Description of this Wonderful Country, Its Immense

---

## GREATER FLAGSTAFF

1. Museum of Northern Arizona
2. Pioneer Historical Museum
3. Coconino Center for the Arts; Art Barn
4. Flagstaff Medical Center (both sides of Beaver St.)
5. Fort Valley Shopping Center
6. Flagstaff High School
7. public library
8. Thorpe Park; Adult Center
9. Lowell Observatory
10. Woody Mountain Campground
11. Kit Carson RV Park
12. University Plaza Shopping Center
13. Sherwood Forest Shopping Center
14. Green Tree Village Shopping Center
15. Riordan State Historic Park
16. Northern Arizona University Campus
17. Greyhound Bus; Nava-Hopi Tours
18. Amtrak
19. chamber of commerce
20. post office (downtown branch)
21. Flagstaff Ice Rink
22. Buffalo Park
23. U.S. Geological Survey (Flagstaff Field Center)
24. East Flagstaff Jr. High School
25. U.S. Forest Service (supervisor's office)
26. K Mart Shopping Center
27. post office (main)
28. Black Bart's Steak House & RV Park
29. Little America
30. Kachina Square Shopping Center
31. Bushmaster Park
32. Park Santa Fe Shopping Center
33. Fairfield Continental Golf Course; Ashley Restaurant
34. Flagstaff Mall (enclosed)
35. U.S. Forest Service (Peaks Ranger Station)
36. Elden Trailhead
37. KOA Campground

---

Mineral Wealth, Its Magnificent Mountain Scenery, the Ruins of Ancient Towns and Cities Found Therein, With a Complete History of the Apache Tribe, and a Description of the Author's Guide Cochise, the Great Apache War Chief, the Whole Interspersed with Strange Events and Adventures." Cozzens's book sold well in New England and soon he was busy giving talks to eager audiences. With each retelling of Arizona's wonders, his descriptions made the climate, forests, water, and mineral wealth sound better and better. By 1875, the Arizona Colonization Company, with Cozzens as president, was established in Boston. In Feb. 1876, a group of about 50 men, each with 300 pounds of tools and clothing, set off for Arizona under the auspices of the Company. In May a second group set off for the "marvelous country." All this was done without any prior visit to the proposed site along the Little Colorado River!

After 90 days of arduous travel, the first group arrived only to find the land already taken by Mormons, whom they distrusted. The group continued west to the San Francisco Peaks and started to build a settlement, naming it Agassiz. But finding no land suitable for farming or mining, they gave up and left for Prescott and California, even before the second group arrived. The second group gave up too, but not before erecting a flagpole to celebrate the Fourth of July. Thomas Forsythe McMillan, who arrived from California with a herd of sheep in 1876, became Flagstaff's first permanent settler. Other ranchers then moved into the area; the total population in the 1880 census was 67. On Aug. 1, 1882, the rails reached Flagstaff. Construction of the railroad brought new opportunities, new stores, restaurants, saloons, banks, and Flagstaff's first physician.

## Flagstaff's Flagpoles

It's obvious that Flagstaff was named for a flagpole, but the question is, *which* flagpole. The first Boston group claimed that they had put up a flagpole in April or May of 1876, *before* the Fourth of July celebration of the second group. Both groups later claimed that their pole was the town's namesake. Some early settlers regarded a tall tree, trimmed of all branches, at the foot of McMillan Mesa as *the* flagstaff. But others disputed the origin, some claiming that Lt. Beale had delimbed the tree in the 1850s, and others saying it was a relic from a railroad-surveying party later on. In addition, no record exists that a flag ever flew from the tree. Another flagpole, said to have stood near Antelope Spring, did fly a flag. At any rate, citizens got together in the spring of 1881 and chose the name "Flagstaff" for their settlement.

# SIGHTS

## Pioneer Historical Museum

This venerable stone building was put up in 1907-08 as the Coconino County Hospital for the Indigent. Townspeople also knew it as the "poor farm," because stronger patients grew vegetables in the yard. Occupants received tobacco but no alchohol. Today the building serves as a museum and headquarters for the Northern Division of the Arizona Historical Society. Old photos, branding irons, saddles, logging tools, and other artifacts show life in Flagstaff's pioneering days. A giant stuffed bear greets you on reaching the second floor; slip by him to see more exhibits. One room displays camera gear and photos of Emery Kolb, who came to the Grand Canyon in 1902, set up a photo studio there with his brother Ellsworth, and continued taking movies and stills until 1976. Another room has memorabilia of Percival Lowell and his observatory, including a mechanical computer used from 1912 to the 1930s. More exhibits can be seen, when staffing permits, outside on the grounds. The restored Ben Doney Cabin (1880s) has been moved here from a site east of town. Antique cars, buggies, and other large items are in the annex behind the museum. A lineup of old farm machinery sits on the lawn nearby. The Pioneer Historical Museum is open Mon.-Sat. 9 a.m.-5 p.m. and Sun. 1:30-5 p.m.; donation; tel. 774-6272. From downtown, the museum is on the right about 2 miles northwest on US 180.

## Coconino Center For The Arts

The center celebrates art in northern Arizona through exhibitions and musical performances, along with some theater and dance. Special workshops and demonstrations often accompany the exhibitions. The large gallery hosts some fine shows, including four annual exhibits of *Trappings of the American West* (a tribute to the American cowboy) in early summer, *Festival of Native American Arts* (art and crafts by Indians of the Four Corners region) in midsummer, *Wood, Fiber & Clay* (a show by northern Arizona's artisans) in autumn-winter, and *Youth Arts Month* (by "artists of tomorrow") in spring. Musicians present traditional and modern Indian music during the *Festival of Native American Arts*. At other times you can enjoy folk, ethnic, jazz, or classical concerts. The gift shop offers a fine selection of artworks, Indian jewelry and other crafts, ceramics, posters, and books. The center is open daily 9 a.m.-5 p.m. from April to December, then Tues.-Sat. 9 a.m.-5 p.m. and Sun. 11 a.m.-5 p.m. the rest of the year; modest admission fees apply to concerts and exhibits; tel. 779-6921. Drive 2 miles northwest on US 180, turn in at the sign beside the Pioneer Historical Museum, and go one block.

## The Art Barn

Regional artists and art patrons have banded together to operate this large sales gallery. You'll find a good selection of works by both Indian and Anglo artisans. Items include paintings, prints, sketches, photography, ceramics, Indian jewelry, kachina dolls, and Navajo rugs. Prices can be very good too, since there's no middleman or big advertising budget. The Art Barn is open Tues.-Sat. 10 a.m.-5 p.m. year-round; tel. 774-0822. It's conveniently located next to the Coconino Center for the Arts, above.

## Museum Of Northern Arizona

This active museum has excellent displays of regional natural history, archaeology, and Native American art. Contemporary Indian exhibits illustrate cultures of northern Arizona tribes and their basketry, pottery, weaving, kachina dolls, and ceremonies. A full-size kiva model has wall paintings from ruins of Awatovi. An art gallery features outstanding Indian and Western art. The popular museum-sponsored Zuni, Hopi, and Navajo shows take place in midsummer, exhibiting the best art and crafts produced by each tribe. The museum's shop sells Indian crafts, including Navajo blankets, Navajo and Hopi jewelry, Hopi kachina dolls, and pottery by Hopi and New Mexico pueblo tribes. A bookshop offers a large selection of books and posters related to the region. You may use the library, one of the most extensive in the Southwest, located across the highway in the Research Center; open Mon.-Fri. 9 a.m.-5 p.m. A visit to the Museum of Northern Arizona is highly recommended for anyone planning to purchase Indian crafts or to visit the Indian reservations of northern Arizona. Set beside a little canyon in a pine forest, the museum is open daily 9 a.m.-5 p.m.; $3 adult, $1.50 children 5-21; tel. 774-5211. From downtown Flagstaff head 3 miles northwest on US 180; the museum is on the left.

## Lowell Observatory

Flagstaff's clean, dust-free air and usually cloudless skies attracted Dr. Percival Lowell, a rich astronomer from New England. He founded Lowell Observatory in 1894 atop Mars Hill, just west of downtown, for studying the solar system. His enthusiasm and dedication led to some controversy as well as important discoveries. For example, during long hours of observing Mars on cold Flagstaff nights, Lowell began seeing lines on the planet's surface. He thought of them as "canals" and cited them as proof of life on Mars. The more Lowell peered through his telescope, the more lines he saw! Not every astronomer of the time could see these markings, and today we know from spacecraft photos that the canals were only imaginary. Through studies of the orbits of Uranus and Neptune, the outermost known planets at the time, Lowell predicted in 1902 the existence of another planet farther out. Using Lowell's calculations, a worker at the observatory discovered the planet Pluto in 1930. After Lowell died in 1916, the observatory continued under his endowment and remains a prominent planetary-research center.

You're welcome to see the exhibits in the dome-topped visitor center, take tours of the 1896 Clark refractor telescope, and attend star-gazing sessions; donation; tel. 774-3358. It's a good idea to call ahead for the current schedule; tel. 774-2096 (recording). The visitor center is open Mon.-Sat. 9:30 a.m.-5 p.m., Sun. 12-5 p.m. in summer, then reduced hours and days the rest of the year. In summer, daily one-hour tours begin at 10 a.m. (except Sun.) and 1:30 p.m. Tours start with a slide show to illustrate the history and work of the observatory, then visit the 1896 24-inch Clark refractor telescope. On the first of every month, and Wed., Fri., and Sat. nights during the summer (weather permitting), the observatory presents a planetary slide show and lets visitors gaze through a telescope; open 8-10 p.m. The observatory is one mile from downtown; walk or drive west on Santa Fe Ave. (don't turn with highway) to the signed road up Mars Hill.

## Astrogeology

Many of the scientists at the Flagstaff Field Center of the U.S. Geological Survey study and map the Moon, planets, and other bodies of our solar śystem. At the same time they investigate landforms on Earth such as volcanos and sand dunes, which are thought to be formed by the same processes as the extraterrestrial features. The Apollo astronauts learned their lunar geology here, and were later guided on the Moon by scientists from the Center. There's no visitor center or regular tours, but you're welcome to see exhibits in the hallways. Giant maps and spectacular color photos taken by spacecraft cover the walls. Photos include Jupiter and Saturn and their moons, remote-sensing products showing the Earth's features, and views sent back by landers on Mars and Venus. The geology of the Moon and of most solid-surfaced planets and their satellites has been mapped in surprising detail. Even cloud-covered Venus is being mapped using radar images with computer-generated color. Building 1 (Astrogeology) has most of the exhibits and a specialized library that you may use. More maps and photos can be seen in the hallways of Buildings 3 and 4. You may visit Mon.-Fri. 8 a.m.-4:30 p.m. Remember that the people working here are normally too busy to show visitors around. Also, don't enter offices or labs unless invited. Tours for scientific or educational groups can be arranged; call or write in advance to the Planetary Data Facility, 2255 N. Gemini Dr., Flagstaff, AZ 86001; tel. 527-7262. The U.S. Geological Survey is atop McMillan Mesa off Cedar Ave., 1.5 miles northeast of downtown.

## Riordan State Historic Park

The Riordan brothers, Timothy and Michael, arrived in Flagstaff during the mid-1880s and later took over the Arizona Lumber & Timber Company's large operation. Both became involved with the social, business, and political life of early Flagstaff. In 1904, they built a grand mansion just south of downtown. A "Rendezvous Room" (or billiard room) connected the wing occupied by each brother's family. The architect Charles Whittlesey, who

also designed El Tovar Hotel on the rim of the Grand Canyon, used a similar "rustic" style of logs and stonework for the exterior. The brothers christened their joint home Kinlichi, Navajo for "Red House." Tours inside give a good idea of how well-to-do people lived in Flagstaff during the early 1900s. Tour guides explain history and architectural features. Open daily 8 a.m.-5 p.m. from mid-May to mid-Sept. and daily 12:30-5 p.m. the rest of the year; $2 adult, free for children 17 and under. It's best to phone in advance to make a reservation because you may enter only in a tour group and the times may change; tel. 779-4395. This bit of historic Flagstaff is at 1300 Riordan Ranch St. (behind Wendy's) between S. Milton Rd. and Northern Arizona University, about one-half mile south of downtown.

## Northern Arizona University (NAU)

Flagstaff's character and population owe much to this school located south of downtown. The University got its start in 1899 as Northern Arizona Normal School, using a vacant reformatory building. Four young women received their diplomas and teaching certificates two years later. In 1925 the school began to offer a four-year Bachelor of Education degree and took the name Northern Arizona State Teachers College. The program broadened over the years to include other degrees, a program in forestry, and graduate studies. In 1966 the institution become a university. Its sprawling campus now covers 686 acres, supplemented by the School of Forestry's 4,000-acre laboratory forest. Be ready for almost anything in the **NAU Art Gallery,** Room 231 Creative Arts Bldg. (#4 on NAU map);call 523-3471 to find what's going on and when.

Visitors are welcome in the university's art gallery, food services, theater and sporting events, indoor swimming pool, and libraries. To learn about NAU and its services and events, call or visit the University Union Information Desk (#5 on NAU map; tel. 523-2391) or call the switchboard (tel. 523-9011). A free shuttle bus makes a loop around the northern and southern parts of the main campus. The

24-inch Clark refractor telescope at Lowell Observatory

Jay Inge working on a map of Ganymede (a moon of Jupiter) at the U.S. Geological Survey

# DOWNTOWN FLAGSTAFF

## DOWNTOWN FLAGSTAFF

1. Flagstaff Medical Center
2. Fort Valley Shopping Center
3. Expeditions (river-running gear)
4. Humphrey Summit Ski (downhill and cross-country)
5. Clark House Restaurant
6. Flagstaff High School
7. Thorpe Park; Adult Center
8. public library
9. Andy's Sporting Goods (fishing and hunting)
10. Four Winds Traders (Indian crafts)
11. chamber of commerce
12. Orpheum Theatre
13. Peace Surplus (camping gear)
14. Alpine Pizza
15. Weatherford Hotel (youth hostel)
16. Choi's Luncheonette
17. Hong Kong Cafe
18. Amtrak
19. Kathy's Cafe
20. Cafe 19
21. Monte Vista Hotel
22. McGaugh's Newsstand
23. Café Espress; Martan's Burrito Palace
24. Grand Canyon Cafe
25. post office (downtown branch)
26. Greyhound Bus; Nava-Hopi
27. Cottage Place Restaurant
28. NiMarco's Pizza
29. Macy's Coffee House & Bakery; La Bellavia Sandwich Shoppe
30. Du Beau Motel (youth hostel)
31. Downtowner (youth hostel)
32. Milushka's; Morning Glory Cafe; Cosmic Cycles; The Inner Basin
33. El Charro Cafe
34. The Lost Norwegian Restaurant

© MOON PUBLICATIONS

route follows Dupont Ave., Knowles Dr., McConnell Circle, and Skydome Dr.; ask someone the location of the stop nearest you. The service runs about every 15 minutes Mon.-Thurs. 7:35 a.m.-10 p.m. and Fri. 7:35 a.m.-4 p.m. during the main school terms. To park on campus, pick up a free visitors permit from the Parking Office at Lumberjack Stadium (#7 on NAU map).

## The Arboretum

Plant enthusiasts at the Arboretum perform research with native and nonnative flora that do well in the cool climate of the Flagstaff area. A wide variety of plants and trees grows on the 200-acre grounds, despite the short 75-day growing season at an elevation of 7,150 feet. Tours of 45-60 minutes introduce the projects done here and take you through the solar greenhouse and the outdoor plots. You'll see some endangered species that staff work to propagate. Exhibits include gardens of wildflowers, herbs, vegetables, and traditional Indian plants. A visit to the Arboretum is enjoyable just to see and learn about flora of the region. Anyone landscaping or gardening in northern Arizona can gain a wealth of information about what plants do best here and which require the least amount of water. Annual events are the National Garden Week Celebration in early May to kick off the gardening season, then a big plant sale in late June. The Arboretum is open all year Mon.-Fri. (and Sat. in summer) 10 a.m.-3 p.m.; guided tours begin at 11 a.m. and 1 p.m.; free admission; tel. 774-1441. Summer (June-Sept.) is the best time to visit. From S. Milton Road in Flagstaff, head west 1.9 miles on Old Hwy. 66, then turn south 3.8 miles on Woody Mountain Road; push the button to open the entrance gate.

NORTHERN ARIZONA UNIVERSITY

© MOON PUBLICATIONS

0        ¼ mile

## NORTHERN ARIZONA UNIVERSITY

1. North Union
2. Administration Building
3. main library (Cline)
4. Creative Arts Building
5. University Union
6. Natatorium
7. Lumberjack Stadium (also parking permits)
8. bookstore and post office
9. University Dining Hall
10. Skydome (Walkup)
11. special collections library
12. South Campus Student Union
13. South Campus Dining Hall

# FLAGSTAFF ACCOMMODATIONS

(summer-weekend rates for basic room)

## DOWNTOWN

| MOTEL/HOTEL | ADDRESS | RATES | TEL. # | FEATURES |
|---|---|---|---|---|
| Birch Tree Inn Bed & Breakfast | 824 W. Birch Ave. | $59.40 s, $64.80 d | 774-1042 | 1917 home |
| Dierker House Bed & Breakfast | 423 W. Cherry Ave. | $26 s, $40 d | 774-3249 | historic home w/antiques |
| Du Beau Motel | 19 W. Phoenix Ave. | $22 s, $27 d | 774-6731 | free breakfast; youth hostel |
| Weatherford Hotel | 23 N. Leroux St. | $22 s, $24 d | 774-2731 | youth hostel |
| Monte Vista Hotel | 100 N. San Francisco St. | $25.92 s, $34.56 d | 779-6971 | 1927 hotel |
| Sierra Vista Motel | 9 E. Phoenix Ave. | $22 s, $27 d | 774-6371 | free breakfast |
| Townhouse Motel | 122 W. Santa Fe. Ave. | $32.40 s or d | 774-5081 | |

## NORTH OF DOWNTOWN

| MOTEL/HOTEL | ADDRESS | RATES | TEL. # | FEATURES |
|---|---|---|---|---|
| Ski Lift Lodge | US 180 & Snow Bowl Rd. | $46.42 s or d | 774-0729 | close to skiing |
| Walking L Ranch Bed & Breakfast | Elden Lookout Rd. | $47.48 s, $52.75 d | 779-2219 | in forest closed in winter |

## SOUTH OF DOWNTOWN

| MOTEL/HOTEL | ADDRESS | RATES | TEL. # | FEATURES |
|---|---|---|---|---|
| Flamingo Motor Hotel | 560 W. Old Hwy. 66 | $26.85 s or d | 779-2251 | some kitchenettes |
| Saga Motel | 820 W. Old Hwy. 66 | $43.40 s, $47.74 d | 779-3631 | pool |
| Hidden Village | 822 W. Old Hwy. 66 | $54.25 s or d | 774-1443 | pool |
| Days Inn | 1000 W. Old Hwy. 66 | $67.27 s, $73.78 d | 774-5221 or (800) 325-2525 | pool |
| Highland Country Inn | 223 S. Sitgreaves St. | $43.20-66.96 | 774-5041 | pool, kitchenettes |
| Spur Motel | 224 S. Mikes Pike St. | $36.89 s, $49.91 d | 774-8888 | |
| Starlight Motel | 500 S. Milton Rd. | $37.98 s, $45.57 d | 774-7301 | |
| University Inn | 602 S. Mikes Pike St. | $43.20 s, $54 d | 774-4581 | pool |

| Quality Suites Hotel | 706 S. Milton Rd. | $93.91 s, $104.16 d | 774-4333 or (800) 228-5151 | free breakfast |
| Arizonan Motel | 910 S. Milton Rd. | $56.42-81.38 | 774-7171 | kitchenettes |
| Rodeway Inn West | 913 S. Milton Rd. | $58.59 s, $62.93 d | 774-5038 or (800) 228-2000 | pool |
| Comfort Inn | 914 S. Milton Rd. | $62.93 s, $68.36 d | 774-7326 or (800) 221-2222 | pool |
| Autolodge | 1313 S. Milton Rd. | $45.78 s or d | 774-6621 | |
| Quality Inn | 2000 S. Milton Rd. | $67.27 s, $74.87 d | 774-8771 or (800) 228-5151 | pool |
| Travelodge Suites | 2755 Woodlands Village Blvd. | $64 s, $74.87 d | 773-1111 | breakfast, pool, exercise room |
| Arizona Mountain Inn | 685 Lake Mary Rd. | $64.80-151.20 | 774-8959 | cottages, free breakfast |

## EAST OF DOWNTOWN

| MOTEL/HOTEL | ADDRESS | RATES | TEL. # | FEATURES |
| --- | --- | --- | --- | --- |
| Snowbowl Motel | 618 E. Santa Fe. Ave. | $48.83 s or d | 774-4877 | kitchenettes |
| Whispering Winds Motor Hotel | 922 E. Santa Fe. Ave. | $43.40 s or d | 774-7391 | pool |
| Evergreen Inn | 1008 E. Santa Fe. Ave. | $42.32 s, $53.17 d | 774-7356 | pool, kitchenettes |
| West Wind Motel | 1416 E. Santa Fe. Ave. | $37.98-92.23 | 774-5123 | pool |
| Red Carpet Motel | 1500 E. Santa Fe. Ave. | $37.98-92.23 | 779-4469 | kitchenettes |
| Red Roof Inn Motel | 1526 E. Santa Fe. Ave. | $35.81 s or d | 774-2791 | |
| King's House Motel (Best Western) | 1560 E. Santa Fe. Ave. | $58.59-69.44 | 774-7186 or (800) 528-1234 | pool, continental breakfast |
| Western Hills | 1612 E. Santa Fe. Ave. | $38 s or d | 774-6633 | pool, kitchenettes |
| Frontier Motel | 1700 E. Santa Fe. Ave. | $54.25 s or d | 774-8993 | |
| Chalet Lodge | 1990 E. Santa Fe. Ave. | $48.83 s or d | 774-2779 | |
| Wonderland Motel | 2000 E. Santa Fe Ave. | $48.83 s or d | 779-6119 | |
| Twilite Motel | 2010 E. Santa Fe. Ave. | $37.98-48.83 | 774-3364 | kitchenettes |
| Timberline Motel | 2040 E. Santa Fe. Ave. | $37.98-48.83 | 774-7481 | |
| 66 Motel | 2100 E. Santa Fe. Ave. | $26.04 s, $28.21 d | 774-6403 | |
| Whiting Bros. Motel | 2138 E. Santa Fe. Ave. | $34.72 s, $41.23 d | 774-7308 | kitchenettes |
| Flagstaff Motel | 2204 E. Santa Fe Ave. | $32.55 s, $34.72 d | 774-0280 | |
| Alpine Motel | 2226 E. Santa Fe. Ave. | $34.56 s or d | 779-3136 | |

| Hi-Land Motel | 2326 E. Santa Fe. Ave. | $41.23 s or d | 774-5434 | |
| Five Flags Inn | 2610 E. Santa Fe. Ave. | $57.51 s, $66.19 d | 526-1399 | pool |
| Americana Motor Hotel | 2650 E. Santa Fe. Ave. | $39.06 s, $41.23 d | 526-2200 | pool |
| Pine Crest Motel | 2818 E. Santa Fe. Ave. | $32.70-59.95 | 526-1950 | kitchenettes |
| Carousel Inn Motel | 2918 E. Santa Fe. Ave. | $42.32-74.87 | 526-3595 | |
| Pony Soldier Motel (Best Western) | 3030 E. Santa Fe. Ave. | $59.68 s or d | 526-2388 or (800) 528-1234 | pool |
| Geronimo Motel | 3100 E. Santa Fe. Ave. | $42.32 s or d | 526-2091 | |
| Crown Motel | 3300 E. Santa Fe. Ave. | $43.40-73.78 | 526-1826 | 24-hr. restaurant |
| Super 8 Motel | 3725 N. Kaspar Ave. | $41.87-61.71 | 526-0818 | jacuzzi, sauna |
| Fairfield Flagstaff Resort | 2580 N. Oakmont Dr. | $86.40-183.60 | 526-3232 or (800) 352-3524 | townhouses |

## BUTLER AVENUE AREA

| MOTEL/HOTEL | ADDRESS | RATES | TEL. # | FEATURES |
|---|---|---|---|---|
| Motel 6 | 2010 E. Butler Ave. | $27.07 s, $33.58 d | 774-1801 | pool |
| Howard Johnson Hotel | 2200 E. Butler Ave. | $74.87 s, $80.29 d | 779-6944 or (800) 654-2000 | suites, pool |
| Flagstaff Inn | 2285 E. Butler Ave. | $52.08 s, $61.85 d | 774-1821 or (800) 533-8992 | pool |
| Little America | 2515 E. Butler Ave. | $74.87 s, $92.23 d | 779-2741 or (800) 352-4386 | suites, pool |
| Ramada Inn | 2320 E. Lucky Ln. | $67.27 s, $73.78 d | 526-1150 or (800) 228-2828 | suites, pool |
| Rodeway Inn East | 2350 E. Lucky Ln. | $59.68 s, $65.10 d | 779-3614 or (800) 228-2000 | pool |
| Regal Inn | 2440 E. Lucky Ln. | $36.76 s, $42.18 d | 774-8756 or (800) 851-8888 | pool |
| Allstar Inns | 2500 E. Lucky Ln. | $27.13 s, $32.55 d | 779-6184 | pool |
| Travelodge | 2520 E. Lucky Ln. | $56.42 s, $60.76 d | 779-5121 (800) 255-3050 | pool, kitchenettes |

## Motels

Accommodation costs fluctuate with the seasons and day of the week, summer weekends being the most expensive. The rates listed above apply on summer weekends and include tax. Off-season, prices can drop substantially, especially at the more expensive places. Rates may rise a bit during the ski season, depending on demand. Light sleepers should be aware that many motels sit near the railroad tracks!

## Youth Hostels

The historic **Weatherford Hotel** in downtown Flagstaff offers bunkbeds in shared rooms for $9 to members year-round. It's centrally located at the corner of 23 N. Leroux St. and Aspen Ave.; tel. 774-2731. Nonmembers can buy a 3-day temporary membership for $3 or a one-year card for $20. Sheets cost an extra $1. A 3-day stay limit sometimes applies. Regular hotel rooms are available too, $22 s and $24 d. Hostelers have use of a kitchen or can dine downstairs in Charly's, the hotel's restaurant and pub. Musicians often perform foot-tapping bluegrass, country, or folk in the evenings here. Car rental discounts can be arranged at the hostel; four people can rent a car (24 hours) to visit the Grand Canyon at a cost of about $10/person, cheaper than taking the bus. J.W. Weatherford came to Flagstaff in 1887 from Texas and stayed 47 years. He built the hotel, quite elegant in its day, in 1897. Weatherford's other projects included an opera house (now the Orpheum

Theatre) and the Weatherford Road (now a hiking trail up the Peaks).

**Downtowner Independent Youth Hostel** offers a choice of dorm beds at $8 and beds in double rooms at $10; open from about May 15th to Aug. 20th; no hostel card needed. Guests have use of a kitchen and receive discounts at local businesses, including car rentals. Located downtown at 19 S. San Francisco and Phoenix Ave.; tel. 774-8461.

The **Du Beau Motel** also runs an independent hostel, no hostel card needed, for $11. Motel rooms cost $22 s, $27 d. Breakfast is included for both hostel and motel guests. Downtown at 19 W. Phoenix Ave.; tel. 774-6731.

Although the youth hostels are the cheapest places for solo travelers, a party of two or more can often do better in a motel. Drive along East Santa Fe Ave. to look for the bargain places; the "strip" extends 3 miles. Most motels signpost their prices so just turn in where they're lowest if you want to save money.

## Campgrounds

None of the campgrounds have locations close to downtown, where the bus and train connections are; you really need your own vehicle to camp. For developed campgrounds, all with showers except as noted, try: **Fort Tuthill County Campground,** open early May to late Sept., $7 for tent or RV; water and electric hookups cost an extra $1; 5 miles south of downtown off I-17 Exit 337; tel. 774-3464. **Black Barts RV Park** is open all year, $6.48 tent and $17.28 RV w/hookups; 2 miles east of downtown near I-40 Butler Ave. Exit 198; tel. 774-1912. **Flagstaff KOA** is open all year, $17.36 tent or RV w/water and electric ($18.45 full hookups); 5 miles northeast of downtown on Santa Fe Ave./US 89 (one mile north from I-40 Exit 201); tel. 526-9926. **Big Tree Campground,** also open all year, is 0.5 mile farther north on US 89 than the KOA, $13.25 tent or RV w/hookups; tel. 526-2583. **Greer's Camp Townsend** is an adult RV park for self-contained rigs (no restrooms or showers), located across the highway from Big Tree

Campground; open mid-April to mid-Oct.; $13.65 w/hookups; tel. 526-4977. **J&H RV Park** has sites for RVs only at 7901 N. Hwy. 89 (3 miles north of I-40 Exit 201); open March-Dec.; $7.56 RVs no hookups, $12.80 RVs w/hookups; tel. 526-1829. **Kit Carson RV Park** is open year-round, $10 tents, $15 RVs w/hookups; located 2 miles west of downtown on W. Old Hwy. 66 (I-40 Exits 191 or 195); tel. 774-6993. **Woody Mountain Campground** is 0.5 mile farther west than Kit Carson; open early May to end of Oct.; $13.02 tents or RVs without hookups, $17.36 w/hookups; tel. 774-7727.

Established campgrounds on U.S. Forest Service land lie 14 or more miles outside of Flagstaff: southeast off the Lake Mary Road (see p. 176), south in Oak Creek Canyon (see p. 187), and north near Sunset Crater National Monument (see p. 157). If you would rather get away from civilization, consider dispersed camping on Forest Service lands surrounding town; the ponderosa pine forests have lots of room but no facilities—just be sure you're not on private or state land. The Coconino National Forest map comes in handy to show which is Forest Service land and where the back roads go. Carry water and be *very* careful with fire in the forests; in dry weather the Forest Service often prohibits all fires in the woods and may even close some areas.

## FOOD

Flagstaff, for its size, has an amazing number of places at which to eat. But then, it has many hungry tourists and students. Most restaurants cater to the eat-and-run crowd. You'll find the well-known chains and fast-food places on the main highways, but with a little effort you can discover some unique restaurants and cafes.

### Downtown
Come here for local atmosphere—old-fashioned "home-style" eateries abound. **Charley's Pub and Restaurant,** in the old Weatherford Hotel, serves good American food; open weekends for breakfast and daily for lunch and dinner at 23 N. Leroux St.; tel.

779-1919. **Choi's Luncheonette** dishes out bargain-priced breakfasts and lunches daily except Sun., but don't expect much decor; 7 E. Aspen Ave.; tel. 774-3492. **Cafe 19** has a breakfast and lunch menu with omelettes, soups, salads, and an "international sandwich" list; open Tues.-Sat. at 19 E. Aspen Ave.; tel. 774-7434. The historic Monte Vista Hotel offers a **coffee shop** (open daily for breakfast, lunch, and dinner) and **Cookies** (open daily for dinner from Oct. to March) at 100 N. San Francisco St.; tel. 779-6971. **Café Espress** serves homemade natural foods, including many vegetarian items; fancy coffees from the espresso bar and baked goodies from the oven are other attractions; open daily for breakfast, lunch, and dinner at 16 N. San Francisco St.; tel. 774-0541. **Kathy's** is a cozy little cafe with the American standbys and a few exotic items like Aussie burgers and Navajo tacos; open daily for breakfast and lunch at 7 N. San Francisco St.; tel. 774-1951.

If you're looking for inexpensive Chinese-American food and don't care about the decor, try the **Grand Canyon Cafe** (110 E. Santa Fe Ave.; tel. 774-2252) or the **Hong Kong Cafe** (6 E. Santa Fe Ave.; tel. 774-9801); both are open Mon. to Sat. for breakfast, lunch, and dinner. Good Mexican food, again without the decor, is served at **Martan's Burrito Palace** (10 N. San Francisco St.; 779-5409) and **El Charro** (409 S. San Francisco St.; 779-0552); both closed on Sunday. **Kachina Downtown** serves Mexican food in a fancier setting; open Mon.-Sat. for lunch and dinner at 522 E. Santa Fe Ave.; tel. 779-1944. **Ernesto's Restaurant** has inexpensive Mexican, Italian, and American items; open daily for breakfast, lunch, and dinner at 21 S. Sitgreaves; tel. 774-8604.

**Milushka's Deli and Coffee House** prepares great lunches of sandwiches, soups, salads, and desserts from Czech, Italian, American, and other recipes; open Mon.-Sat. at 121 S. San Francisco St.; tel. 774-8272. **Delhi Palace** will treat you to fine Indian vegetarian and nonvegetarian cuisine; open daily for lunch (buffet or a la carte) and dinner at 2700 S. Woodland Village Blvd., next to

Walmart; tel. 556-0019. **Hassib's** serves tasty Middle Eastern, Greek, and Indian specialties (deli and takeout too); open Mon.-Sat. for lunch and dinner at 211 S. San Francisco St.; tel. 774-1037. **Macy's European Coffee House and Bakery** offers a big selection of fresh-roasted coffee and a menu of pasta dishes, sandwiches, soups, salads, quiches, and home-baked goodies; open daily for breakfast, lunch, and dinner at 14 S. Beaver St.; tel. 774-2243. **La Bellavia Sandwich Shoppe** is a cozy little cafe for breakfast and lunch; open daily at 18 S. Beaver St.; tel. 774-8301. Places for pizza and Italian sandwiches include **NiMarco's Pizza** (open daily; 101 S. Beaver St.; tel. 779-2691) and **Alpine Pizza** (open daily; 7 N. Leroux St.; tel. 779-4109).

For elegant and romantic dining, make a reservation at one of the following three restaurants: The **Cottage Place** serves American and continental specialties; open Tues.-Sun. for dinner at 126 W. Cottage Ave.; tel. 774-8431. The **Clark House** offers fine French and Italian cuisine amidst many antiques in a historic 1911 residence; open daily for lunch and dinner at 503 N. Humphreys St.; tel. 774-1343. The **Lost Norwegian** features daily specials from Greece, Germany, Italy, Norway, or India; open Tues.-Sat. for lunch and dinner in Bailey's General Store, 304 S. Elden St. and Butler Ave.; tel. 774-8530.

## Northern Arizona University

**North Union** (#1 on NAU map) has a cafeteria and the Timber Inn (barbecued beef). In the **University Union** (#5 on NAU map) you'll find the Atrium (restaurant with a garden atmosphere serving lunches of specialty sandwiches, salads, and soups), Pizzano's (pizza and pasta); Mt. Jacks (fast food), The Eatery (deli sandwiches, soups, salads, bakery, and fast food), and Scoops (ice cream). In the center of campus, the **University Dining Hall** (#9 on NAU map) has a large cafeteria. **South Campus Dining Hall** (#13 on NAU map) has a cafeteria, and **South Campus Student Union** (#12 on NAU map) offers El Rancho Rojo (tacos, enchiladas, and burritos).

## Other Areas

The large Mexican-American population of Flagstaff provides the town with some tasty food. In addition to those listed under "Downtown," cafes include the **Kachina** (closed Mon.-Tues.; 2220 E. Santa Fe Ave.; tel. 779-5790) and **La Villa Bonita** (closed Sun.; 4217 N. US 89, at I-40 Exit 201; tel. 526-8406). If you'd like Mexican food in a more elegant setting, try **Ramona's Cantina** (University Plaza, off S. Milton Road; tel. 774-3397) or **El Chilito** (1551 S. Milton Road; tel. 774-4666). **Mama Luisa's** has excellent Italian cuisine (lunches are the best value) at Kachina

*Santa Fe Avenue in downtown Flagstaff*

Square, corner of E. Santa Fe Ave. and Steves Blvd.; tel. 526-6809 (reservations advised). **The Pasta Works** dishes out generous servings of Italian food in an informal atmosphere; 2700 S. Woodlands Village Blvd. (in the Walmart Center off S. Milton Road); tel. 774-6775. Dine Chinese at **Szechuan** (1451 S. Milton Road; tel. 774-8039); **Hunan West** (closed Mon.; University Plaza off S. Milton Road; tel. 779-2229); **Hunan East** (2028 N. 4th St.; tel. 526-1009); **Afton House** (very pleasant decor; 3050 E. Santa Fe Ave. next to the Pony Soldier Motel; tel. 526-2545); and **Mandarin Garden** (Park Santa Fe Shopping Center, 3518 E. Santa Fe Ave.; tel. 526-5033).

Some popular American places include the two **Sizzlers** (2080 S. Milton Road; tel. 779-3267 and 3540 E. Santa Fe Ave.; tel. 526-3391); **Buster's** (1800 S. Milton Road in Green Tree Village; tel. 774-5155); **Furrs Cafeteria** (1200 S. Milton Road; tel. 779-4104); **The Adobe Grill** (good Mexican food too; 914 E. Santa Fe Ave.; tel. 774-4802); **Cattleman's Club** (1612 E. Santa Fe Ave. in Western Hills Motel; tel. 774-6633); **Little America** dining room and coffee shop (2515 E. Butler Ave.; tel. 779-2741; for a splurge, take in their all-you-can-eat Sunday brunch from 9 a.m.-2 p.m.; $13 adult, $9.49 children 7-12); **Ashley's** (Fairfield Flagstaff Resort, 2580 N. Oakmont Dr.; tel. 526-9324); and **Christmas Tree Restaurant** (5200 E. Cortland Blvd. (Continental); tel. 779-5888).

**Black Bart's Steak House** serves up steaks, seafood, and other American fare; open daily for dinner; singing waiters and waitresses entertain you, and during summer there's a dinner theater; 2760 E. Butler Ave. (near I-40 Exit 198); tel. 779-3142. Many locals say the best steaks in town are served at **Bob Lupo's Horsemen Lodge,** which has trout and other specialties too; open for dinner daily except Sun.; located on US 89, 8.5 miles northeast of downtown (3.5 miles north from I-40 Exit 201); tel. 526-2655.

## Food Stores
**New Frontiers** has natural foods at 801 S. Milton Road; tel. 774-5747. You'll find supermarkets in most of the shopping centers (see Greater Flagstaff map).

*Cowboys aim for the paydirt in rodeos throughout Arizona*

# ENTERTAINMENT

## Movies

Catch movies downtown in the **Orpheum Theatre**, 15 W. Aspen Ave.; tel. 774-7823. To find out what's being shown on the NAU campus, call 523-2391. The **University Plaza Theatres** (University Plaza, off S. Milton Road; tel. 774-4433) and **Green Tree Village Theatre** (1800 S. Milton Road; tel. 779-3202) are both south of downtown. East of downtown, see movies at **Flag-East Theatre** (2009 N. 4th St.; tel. 774-6992) and at **Flagstaff Mall Cinema** (4650 N. US 89; tel. 526-4555).

## Dinner Theater

During summer, actors ham it up with melodrama, song and dance, and other vaudeville acts at **Black Bart's Steak House Saloon & Old West Dinner Theatre**, 2760 E. Butler Ave. near I-40 Exit 198; tel. 779-3142.

## Nightlife

For varied entertainment downtown—could be rock, country, folk, blues, or poetry reading—try **Charly's** (23 N. Leroux St.; tel. 779-1919) or **The Monsoons** (22 E. Santa Fe Ave.; tel. 774-7929). East of downtown, the **Museum Club** presents country, rock, blues, and reggae bands at 3404 E. Santa Fe Ave.; tel. 526-9434. The **Lounge at Little America** offers a dance floor and mostly Top 40 music, 2515 E. Butler Ave.; tel. 779-2741.

## Culture And Sports At NAU

Northern Arizona University presents theater, opera, dance, concerts, and a variety of sports events. For information and tickets, contact NAU Central Ticket Office in the University Union (#5 on NAU map); tel. 523-2000 (recorded Hotline) and tel. 523-5661 or 523-5662 (for tickets).

## Events

Flagstaff-area people put on a variety of festivals, fairs, shows, and concerts during the year. The Flagstaff Visitor Center will tell you what's happening; tel. 779-3733 (recording)

or 774-9541. Major annual events include— **May:** Cinco de Mayo (parade, coronation, dance, and barbecue by the Mexican-American community). **June:** Horse Show, Pine Country Rodeo and Parade, Festival of Native American Arts (Indian art and craft exhibitions, demonstrations, and dance performances), and Gem & Mineral Show. **July:** Festival of the Arts (concerts, musicals, and plays), Festival of Native American Arts continues, Fourth of July Fireworks, and horse racing. **August:** Festival of the Arts continues, Festival of Native American Arts continues, Festival in the Pines (arts and crafts with musical performances), and Coconino County Fair.

# RECREATION

Impress your friends by saying you went skiing and swimming on the same day in Flagstaff! Try the **indoor pools** at the university's Natatorium (#6 on NAU map; tel. 523-4508) or East Flagstaff Junior High School (corner of N. 4th St. and Cedar Ave.; tel. 779-7690). The **indoor pool** at **Flagstaff High School** is open in summer at 400 W. Elm Ave.; tel. 779-7690. Play **tennis** at the courts in Thorpe Park (off Toltec St. in west Flagstaff) or Bushmaster Park (off Lockett Road in east Flagstaff); both parks also offer picnic tables and playgrounds. Joggers and strollers alike enjoy **Buffalo Park,** off Cedar Avenue. **Ice skate** from mid-Oct. to mid-March at Flagstaff Ice Rink, 1850 N. Turquoise Dr.; tel. 774-1051. Play **golf** at Fairfield Continental Country Club's 18-hole course, 2580 N. Oakmont Dr. (take I-40 Exit 201, go south 0.8 mile on Country Club Road, then turn right on Oakmont Dr.); closed in winter; tel. 526-3211.

## Horseback Riding

The Flagstaff area has some great horse country. If you don't have your own steed, local riding stables can provide one. Advance reservations should be made. In winter, stables usually close; their horses often head south to join the snowbirds on the desert. **Don Donnelly Stables** at the Flying Heart

Barn has rides on and near the San Francisco Peaks; hourly ($10/first hour), all-day, and overnight trips can be arranged, hayrides and cookouts too; head 3.5 miles north on US 89 from I-40 Exit 201; tel. 526-2788. **Ski Lift Lodge Stables** leads rides near the San Francisco Peaks; $15/hour; go 7 miles northwest of town on US 180; tel. 774-0729. **Hitchin' Post Stables** offers rides in the woods from the stables at Fairfield Flagstaff Resort; $15/hour or $24/2 hours; barbecue hayrides are scheduled too; tel. 526-3232, ext. 5205.

## Downhill Skiing

**Fairfield Snowbowl,** on the San Francisco Peaks, has some of Arizona's best downhill action. Four chairlifts service about 32 trails ranging from novice to expert. You'll drop 2,300 feet from the top of Agassiz Chair Lift. Some runs exceed 2 miles. With sufficient snow, the season begins Thanksgiving Day and lasts through Easter; tel. 779-4577 for snow and road conditions. Be sure to call before coming out, because Flagstaff weather is notoriously unpredictable. Open for skiing weekends 8 a.m.-4 p.m. and weekdays 9 a.m.-4 p.m. Lift tickets cost $25 ($20 half day) for adults and $12 ($10 half day) for ages 8-12. Skiers age 7 and under or 65 and over go for free, and everyone skis free after 3 p.m. The Snowbowl has a beginner package and a ski school (all levels). Rentals (skis, boots, and poles) are available on the mountain at the Hart Prairie Day Lodge. To reach the Snowbowl, drive northwest 7 miles from downtown on US 180 to the turnoff, then either take the shuttle bus ($3 roundtrip) or drive the remaining 7 miles (paved). Call 779-1951 for info about lifts, rentals, and instruction. **Ski Lift Lodge** provides the closest place to stay and a restaurant; open all year, it's at the junction of US 180 and the Snowbowl Road; tel. 774-0729. **Fairfield Flagstaff Resort** offers package deals with accommodations, dinner, skiing, and transportation; tel. 526-3232, ext. 5225 (local), (800) 352-3524 (in state), or (800) 526-1004 (out of state).

## Cross-country Skiing

**Flagstaff Nordic Center** offers 40 km of groomed trails ranging from beginner to advanced near Hart Prairie and the San Francisco Peaks. A 5-km marked trail leads to the Hochderffer Hills, a popular area for telemark skiing. The center features a ski school, rentals, and snack bar. A busy schedule of races, clinics, and full-moon tours fills the calendar. Open daily from about mid-Nov. to mid-April; trail fee is $4.50-8 adult, $3-4 children age 5-12; tel. 774-6216 (recorded ski report). Take US 180 northwest 15 miles to near Milepost 232. Cross-country skiers also head

*downhill at the Snowbowl*

to Hart Prairie and Wing Mountain, two undeveloped skiing areas near the San Francisco Peaks. The rolling meadow and forest country is ideal for ski touring. Hart Prairie can be reached by driving 9.5 miles northwest of town on US 180, then turning right on the south end of Forest Route 151 as far as the road is clear. Parking on US 180 is prohibited. For Wing Mountain, continue on US 180 just past the Hart Prairie Road and turn left onto Forest Route 222B (228B on some maps). For road and skiing conditions near the Peaks, call the Forest Service (Peaks Ranger Station) at tel. 526-0866.

The groomed trails and good snow of Mormon Lake also attract cross-country skiers. Drive 20 miles southeast on Lake Mary Road and turn right 8 miles on Mormon Lake Loop Road. Two ski areas, open daily, offer maintained trails ($2 weekdays, $4 weekends), rental waxless ski sets ($10 complete w/trail fee), and instruction (starts at $8 for 2 hours in a small group). Trails range from easy to challenging in both places. **Mormon Lake Ski Center,** in the village of Mormon Lake, has 38 km of trails running along the lake shore and on Navajo Ridge. This is probably the best place for beginners; tel. 1-354-2240 (toll call from Flagstaff). **Mormon Lake Lodge** has four motel rooms and some cabins; tel. 774-0462 (Flagstaff) or 354-2227 (local). **Montezuma Nordic Ski Center,** 4 miles north of Mormon Lake village, offers 21 km of trails through the Dairy Spring Canyon area; tel. 1-354-2221 (during season). For the Mormon Lake area road and ski conditions, call the Forest Service (Mormon Lake Ranger Station) at tel. 527-7474.

# SHOPPING

## Art Galleries And Indian Crafts

Shops in downtown Flagstaff display a wealth of regional art and crafts. Indian artists produce especially distinctive work; you'll see paintings, jewelry, Navajo rugs, Hopi kachina dolls, pottery, and baskets. **Four Winds Traders,** at 118 W. Santa Fe Ave., is one of the largest and best Indian galleries; Indians

themselves also shop here for stones and jewelry-making supplies; closed Sun. and Monday. Look for other shops and galleries nearby on Santa Fe Ave., N. Leroux St., N. San Francisco St., and Aspen Avenue. The **Silversmith,** south of downtown at 1431A S. Milton Road, features Hopi, Navajo, and Zuni jewelry; Indian craftsmen often give demonstrations; sandpaintings and Kaibab sandstone photographs (photos printed on rock slabs) are sold too; closed Sunday. The gift shops at the **Museum of Northern Arizona, Coconino Center for the Arts,** and the **Art Barn,** all northeast of town on US 180, have excellent selections of Indian art and crafts.

## Camping Supplies

Outdoors supplies, books, maps, and information are available from **The Edge** (also rentals of camping gear; Flagstaff Mall; tel. 526-5795); **Mountain Sports** (1800 S. Milton Road; tel. 779-5156); **The Inner Basin** (also rentals of mountain bicycles; 111-B S. San Francisco St.; tel. 779-0259); **Peace Surplus** (14 W. Santa Fe Ave.; tel. 779-4521); and **Popular Surplus** (901 S. Milton Road; tel. 774-0598). Rock climbers can get gear and info at The Inner Basin and The Edge. **Andy's Sporting Goods** specializes in hunting and fishing gear at 107 W. Aspen; tel. 774-4401. **Expeditions, inc.** carries river-running equipment, including kayaks, rafts, wet and dry suits, and river books; they also organize Grand Canyon raft trips; 625 N. Beaver St.; tel. 779-3769.

## Ski Rentals And Supplies

You can get both cross-country and downhill rentals in town at **Humphrey Summit Ski** (505 N. Beaver St.; tel. 779-1308; and at the Snowbowl turnoff; tel. 774-7852) and **Mountain Sports** (1800 S. Milton Road; tel. 779-5156). Cross-country ski equipment is also available at **The Edge** (Flagstaff Mall; tel. 526-5795) and **The Inner Basin** (111-B S. San Francisco St.; tel. 779-0259), as well as **Flagstaff Nordic Center** and the two **Mormon Lake ski centers.**

## SERVICES

The main **post office** is at 2400 N. Postal Blvd., just north of E. Santa Fe Ave.; tel. 527-2440; branches are downtown at 104 N. Agassiz St. and at the university in the basement of the bookstore (#8 on NAU map). If you need to see a doctor it's cheaper to go directly to a doctor's office than to the hospital. You'll find many offices along N. Beaver Street. **Flagstaff Medical Center,** the local hospital, is at 1200 N. Beaver St.; tel. 779-3366. In **emergencies** (police, fire, and medical) dial 911. Summer jobs can often be found in Flagstaff but pay tends to be rock bottom; for **job information** contact the Dept. of Economic Security, 397 Malpais Lane; tel. 779-4513.

The **Adult Center** hosts several clubs and offers classes in yoga, martial arts, dancing, and a wide variety of other subjects. You're sure to find something of interest if staying in town awhile. Organizations meeting here include the Flagstaff Hiking Club, Northern Arizona Paddlers Club, and Street Masters Car Club. The Adult Center is on the west edge of downtown next to Thorpe Park at 245 N. Thorpe Road; tel. 774-1068.

## INFORMATION

The very helpful **Flagstaff Chamber of Commerce/Visitor Center** staff can answer your questions and tell you what's going on. The office is downtown at 101 W. Santa Fe Ave. (Flagstaff, AZ 86001); open daily 8 a.m.-9 p.m. (until 5 p.m. on Sun.); tel. 774-9541 or (800) 842-7293. A Current Events Hotline recording has upcoming events; tel. 779-3733.

The **U.S. Forest Service** has information and maps about camping, hiking, and road conditions in the Coconino National Forest surrounding Flagstaff. The **Supervisor's office** is at 2323 E. Greenlaw Ln. (Flagstaff, AZ 86004) behind Knoles Village Shopping Center (see map); open Mon.-Fri. 7:30 a.m.-4:30 p.m.; tel. 527-7400. You can purchase any of the National Forest maps for Arizona here ($2 each). The Coconino Forest map is also available at the chamber of commerce and sporting goods stores. For more detailed information on the Mt. Elden, Humphrey's Peak, and O'Leary Peak areas, contact the **Peaks Ranger Station** at 5075 N. Hwy 89 (Flagstaff, AZ 86004); open Mon.-Fri. 7:30 a.m.-4:30 p.m. (sometimes Sat. in summer); tel. 526-0866. For the lake and forest country south of Flagstaff, contact the **Mormon Lake Ranger District Office** at 4825 Lake Mary Road (Flagstaff, AZ 86001); open Mon.-Fri. 7:30 a.m.-4:30 p.m.; tel. 527-7474.

**Arizona Game & Fish Department** has fishing and hunting licenses and information at 310 Lake Mary Road (Flagstaff, AZ 86001); tel. 774-5045.

### Libraries
A good place for a rainy day, a long bus wait, or learning more about Arizona. The **Flagstaff City Library's** attractive ski-lodge architecture makes it an especially enjoyable place; downtown at the corner of 300 W. Aspen Ave. and Sitgreaves St.; open Mon.-Thurs. 10 a.m.-9 p.m., Fri. and Sat. 10 a.m.-6 p.m., and Sun. 1-4 p.m.; tel. 774-4000 (recorded information), 779-7670 (reference desk); you'll find many good regional books in the Arizona Collection. NAU's **Cline Library** (#3 on NAU map) has not only many books and periodicals, but a large map collection; hikers can plan trips and copy maps here; open Mon.-Thurs. 7:30 a.m.-11 p.m., Fri. 7:30 a.m.-6 p.m., Sat. 8 a.m.-6 p.m., and Sun. 1-11 p.m.; tel. 523-2171. The university's **Special Collections Library** (#11 on NAU map) contains an outstanding array of Arizona-related publications and photos; open Mon.-Fri. 8 a.m.-5 p.m.; tel. 523-5551. The **Museum of Northern Arizona** has an excellent regional library in the Research Center across the highway from the museum; open Mon.-Fri. 9 a.m.-5 p.m.; tel. 774-5211.

### Bookstores
**McGaugh's Newsstand** downtown features a good selection of newspapers, magazines, Arizona books, and general reading at 24 N. San Francisco Street. The **NAU Bookstore** (#8 on NAU map) also has many regional and

general reading publications. The **Museum of Northern Arizona** sells excellent books on regional Indian cultures, archaeology, and natural history; 3 miles northwest on US 180. For new and used books, including many regional titles, drop into **Bookman's Used Books** at 1520 S. Riordan Ranch Street. Both **B. Dalton Bookseller** (University Plaza) and **Waldenbooks** (Flagstaff Mall) have good regional and general reading selections.

## TRANSPORT

### Tours

**Nava-Hopi Tours** (The Gray Line) operates regional bus tours and scheduled Grand Canyon bus service. The tours tend to show a lot in a short time. Nava-Hopi offers day trips to Flagstaff area (Museum of Northern Arizona, Walnut Canyon, Sunset Crater, and Wupatki; $28), Grand Canyon ($30), Oak Creek Canyon-Sedona-Montezuma Castle-Jerome ($28), Hopi Indian Reservation ($62), Petrified Forest-Painted Desert-Meteor Crater ($54.50), and Monument Valley ($70). Except for the Grand Canyon tour, Nava-Hopi requires at least 24 hours' advance notice; children under 12 go at half price; some tours don't operate in winter. Buses leave from the Greyhound station (399 S. Malpais Lane, off Sitgreaves St., 0.5 mile south of Santa Fe Ave.) and other points in Flagstaff; tel. 774-5003 or (800) 892-8687. **Northern Arizona Wilderness Tours** offers a similar selection of trips; the tours use smaller vehicles and tend to be less formal; staff will help plan custom tours too; make reservations two weeks in advance, if possible; tel. 525-1028. **Seven Wonders Scenic Tours** has van excursions to scenic and cultural areas of northern Arizona; tel. 526-2501. For an aerial perspective, fly with **Alpine Air Service** from the Flagstaff airport to Meteor Crater, Sunset Crater, Oak Creek Canyon, Sedona, and other scenic spots; tel. 779-5178.

### Car Rental And Taxi

A car rental allows more extensive sightseeing than public transport and costs less if several people get together. Rates fluctuate with supply and demand, competition, and the mood of the operators; call around for the best deals. See the Yellow Pages for agencies; they're located both in town and at the airport. For a taxi, call **Alpine Taxi Cab** (tel. 527-2400), **Dream V.I.P. Taxi** (tel. 774-2934), **Flagstaff Taxi** (tel. 774-1374), or **Fleet Taxi** (tel. 774-9102).

### Local Bus

**Pine Country Transit** serves most of the city with two routes Mon.-Fri. and one route on Sat.; no service Sun.; tel. 779-6624 or 779-6635; pick up a schedule at the chamber of commerce. A free **trolley service** operates in summer among the major motels and shopping areas; schedules are at local businesses and the chamber office.

### Long-distance Bus

**Greyhound Bus** offers daily departures (with sample one-way fares and destinations) to: Phoenix (5X daily, $21), Prescott (1X, $14), Holbrook (4X, $18), Gallup (5X, $38), Kingman (4X, $26), Los Angeles (3X, $65), Las Vegas (3X, $51), and San Francisco (3X, $139). A small discount is given for roundtrips. The station is 0.5 mile south of central downtown at 399 S. Malpais Ln.; open 24 hours; tel. 774-4573. **Nava-Hopi** buses head north to the Grand Canyon (three times daily in summer and twice daily in winter; $11.75 one way, $22.30 roundtrip, $10.70 roundtrip with bus pass) and south to Sedona (twice daily; $5 one way, $9.50 roundtrip) and Glendale/Phoenix/Sky Harbor Airport (twice daily; $22.50 one way, $42.50 roundtrip); tel. 774-5003 or (800) 892-8687. Buses leave from the Greyhound station.

### Train

**Amtrak** trains leave daily in the evening for Los Angeles ($79 one way), and daily in the morning for Albuquerque ($61 one way) and on to New Orleans or Chicago. Amtrak often gives substantial discounts on roundtrip tickets. The station is downtown at 1 Santa Fe Ave; open 5:15 a.m.-10:30 p.m.; tel. (800) 872-7245 for reservations or tel. 774-8679 for the station.

## Air

**America West** flies six times daily to Phoenix ($39-73 one way), at least once daily to the Grand Canyon ($29-47 one way), and five times daily to Las Vegas ($69-89 one way); tel. (800) 247-5692 (reservations) or 525-1346 (airport). **Skywest Airlines** flies four times daily south to Phoenix ($73 one way) and twice daily north to Page ($68 one way);

onward connections go to Yuma, St. George, and other destinations. Discounts apply to roundtrip tickets purchased 7 days and 14 days or more in advance (must have a Sat. night stopover); tel. (800) 453-9417 for reservations or tel. 774-4830 for the airport. Pulliam Field, Flagstaff's airport, is 5 miles south of town; take I-17 Exit 337.

# EAST OF FLAGSTAFF

## WALNUT CANYON NATIONAL MONUMENT

Sinagua Indians chose this pretty canyon in which to build their pueblo homes more than 800 years ago. Ledges eroded out of the limestone cliffs provided shelter from rain and snow—the Sinagua merely had to build walls under their ready-made roofs. Good farmlands, wild plant foods, and forests filled with game lay close at hand. The clear waters of Walnut Creek flowed in the canyon bottom. Sinagua occupied this site from A.D. 1120 to 1250, then decided for unknown reasons to leave. Perhaps some of their descendants now live among the modern Pueblo tribes. More than 300 Sinagua cliff dwellings remain here, and some can be seen and entered along a loop trail constructed by the National Park Service.

*Arizona rose*
(Rosa arizonica)

## Visitor Center

A small museum displays pottery and other artifacts of the Sinagua. Exhibits also show how the Indians farmed and how they used wild plants for baskets, sandals, mats, soap, food, and medicine. A map illustrates trading routes to neighbors of other cultures. Video programs can be seen on request. Rangers will answer your questions about the archaeology and natural history of Walnut Canyon. During the summer, they give talks several times a day. A good selection of books, maps, and videos related to the monument and region may be purchased.

The self-guided one-mile **Island Trail** begins behind the Visitor Center and winds past 25 cliff dwellings. Take some time and get a feeling of what it was like to live here as a Sinagua. The paved path descends 185 feet, which you'll have to climb on the way out. Allow 45 minutes to an hour for the Island Trail. Because of the high elevation (6,690 feet), the trail isn't recommended for people with walking, breathing, or heart difficulties. The easier **Rim Trail** visits two scenic viewpoints and two stabilized surface dwellings; signs describe the varied plant and wildlife found here; allow 20-30 minutes for the half-mile loop. Vegetation changes dramatically from the pinyon and juniper forests near the rim to the tall Douglas firs clinging to the canyon ledges. Black walnut and several other kinds of deciduous trees grow at the bottom. Walnut Canyon National Monument remains open all year (except Thanksgiving and Christmas), though snows can close the trails for short periods. The Visitor Center is

*Grand Falls of the Little Colorado River*

open in summer daily 7 a.m.-6 p.m., and the rest of the year daily 8 a.m.-5 p.m.; Island Trail closes one hour before the Visitor Center; $1/person (age 17 and over) or $3/family entrance fee; tel. 526-3367. You'll find picnic areas near the Visitor Center and on the drive in. From Flagstaff, head east 7 miles on I-40 to Walnut Canyon Exit 204, then go south 3 miles on a paved road.

## GRAND FALLS OF THE LITTLE COLORADO RIVER

In the spring, this thundering torrent of muddy, brown water plunges 185 feet into the canyon of the Little Colorado River about 30 miles northeast of Flagstaff. Best time to see the spectacle is during runoff in March and April; in other months the river may dry up to an unimpressive trickle. A lava flow from Merriam Crater, the large cinder cone 10 miles southwest, created the falls about 100,000 years ago. The tongue of lava filled the canyon, forcing the river out of its gorge, around the dam, then back over the rim into the original channel. Grand Falls is on the southwest corner of the Navajo Indian Reservation. From Flagstaff, take US 89 north 1.8 miles past Flagstaff Mall and turn right 8 miles on the Camp Townsend-Winona Road, then turn left onto the Leupp (pronounced "LOOP") Road; follow it northeast 13 miles to the sign "Grand Falls 10 miles" and turn left. The Grand Falls road is dirt but OK for cars. You'll see hues of the Painted Desert as the road descends to the river. Other approaches: I-40 Winona Exit 211 (7 miles east of Flagstaff), drive 2 miles on the Townsend-Winona Road, then right on Leupp Road to the Grand Falls turnoff; I-40 Exit 245 (46 miles east of Flagstaff), take AZ 99 to Leupp then Leupp Road to Grand Falls turnoff. From Kykotsmovi, on the Hopi Indian Reservation, take paved Indian Route 2 southwest 49 miles to Leupp, then Leupp Road to Grand

Falls turnoff. Free admission, though the Navajo Tribe asks that you help keep the area clean and leash your dogs so they won't disturb livestock.

## METEOR CRATER

A speeding mass of meteoric iron smashed into the earth's crust here about 49,000 years ago. Though larger impact craters have been discovered on our planet, none have been so well preserved. The giant pit measures 570 feet deep and 4,100 feet across—enough room for 20 football fields! White men first discovered the crater in 1871, though scientists didn't agree on its meteoric origin until 1929. Apollo astronauts learned about crater geology here and practiced traveling on lunarlike surfaces. A Visitor Center perched on the edge of Meteor Crater has exhibits on meteorites and the Apollo program. You can get a close look at a hefty 1,406-pound meteorite found nearby and hear a recorded lecture about the crater's origin and history. Apollo exhibits include a test capsule, space suit, an Astronaut Hall of Fame, and short films. Staff at the privately owned Meteor Crater won't let you descend the hazardous trail into the crater, but you may walk the 3.5-mile rim trail around it. Avoid this hike if thunderstorms threaten. Lapidary, gift, and coffee shops are in the Visitor Center. Meteor Crater is open daily 6 a.m.-6 p.m. in summer (mid-May to mid-Sept.), 8 a.m.-5 p.m. in winter (mid-Nov. to mid-March), and 7 a.m.-5 p.m. the rest of the year; tel. 526-5259. Admission is $6 adult, $5 age 60 and over, $2 children 13-17, and $1 children 6-12. Meteor Crater is located 40 miles east of Flagstaff and 20 miles west of Winslow; take I-40 Meteor Crater Exit 233, then head south 6 miles on a paved road.

**Meteor Crater RV Park** offers year-round camping for RVs ($15.75; no tents) and a store near the I-40 exit for Meteor Crater; tel. 289-4002.

*Meteor Crater*

# NORTH OF FLAGSTAFF:
# THE SAN FRANCISCO VOLCANIC FIELD

Volcanic peaks, cinder cones, and lava flows cover about 3,000 square miles around Flagstaff. The majestic San Francisco Peaks, highest of all in Arizona, soar 5,000 feet above the surrounding plateau. Eruptions beginning about 10 million years ago formed this giant volcano. Glaciers then carved deep valleys on its slopes during Pleistocene ice ages. Hundreds of small cinder cones, of which Sunset Crater is the youngest, surround the "Peaks." There's no reason to assume that the San Francisco Volcanic Field is finished, either! The area has experienced volcanic activity, with periods of calm, all during its long history. Past eruptions have varied greatly—sometimes quiet and some-times violent. Peaceful today, the volcanic field presents some impressive landscapes and geology. Many of the peaks and hills make good day-hike destinations. Foresters at the **Peaks Ranger Station** have maps and hiking information for this region; 5075 N. Hwy. 89, Flagstaff, AZ 86004; tel. 526-0866.

Indians of northern Arizona look to the San Francisco Peaks as a sacred place. The Hopi believe the Peaks to be the winter home of their kachina spirits and the source of clouds that bring rain for crops. The Peaks also have a prominent place in Navajo legends and ceremonies as one of the cardinal directions. In 1984 the federal government set aside 18,200 acres of this venerable volcano for the Kachina Peaks Wilderness.

## SUNSET CRATER VOLCANO NATIONAL MONUMENT

Sunset Crater Volcano, a beautiful black cinder cone tinged with yellows and oranges, rises 1,000 feet above jagged lava flows about 15 miles northeast of Flagstaff. Although more than 700 years have passed since the last eruptions, the landscape still has a lunarlike appearance. Trees and plants struggle for a foothold. Visitor Center exhibits illustrate the forces deep within the earth and their fury during volcanic eruptions. A seismograph keeps track of the earth's movements. Film clips of Hawaiian volcanic eruptions show how Sunset Crater may have looked during its periods of activity. Rangers give varied programs, mainly during the summer, on geology, seismology, birds, and other topics. Check the bulletin board at the Visitor Center for what's on.

The self-guided **Lava Flow Trail,** which begins 1.5 miles east of the Visitor Center, loops across a lava flow at the base of Sunset Crater; allow one-half to one hour for the one-mile walk. A trail leaflet, available at the start and at the Visitor Center, explains

*San Francisco Peaks
from the rim of Sunset Crater*

# THE SAN FRANCISCO VOLCANIC FIELD

TO LEUPP & GRAND FALLS

MERRIAM CRATER

WINONA

HANKS TRADING POST

WUKOKI RUIN

DONEY PICNIC AREA

WUPATKI VISITOR CENTER

WUPATKI NATIONAL MONUMENT

LOMAKI RUIN

CITADEL RUIN

545

BLACK BOTTOM CRATER

MOON CRATER

DOUBLE CRATER

510

LAVA

DEADMAN MESA

STRAWBERRY CRATER

PAINTED DESERT VISTA

SUNSET CRATER NATL. MON.

779

O'LEARY PEAK (8,916 ft)

BONITO LAVA FLOW

SUNSET CRATER (8,029 ft)

LAVA

89

SUNSET CRATER VISITOR CENTER

LENOX CRATER

546

WALNUT CANYON NATL. MONUMENT

40

DONEY PARK

PEAKS RANGER STATION

EAST FLAGSTAFF

BLACK BILL PARK

LAVA

S P CRATER

S P CRATER HIKE

COLTON CRATER (7,368 ft)

COLTON CRATER HIKE

ELDEN (9,299 ft)

MT. ELDEN TRAILS

DRY LAKE HILLS

SHULTZ PASS

420

557

556

INNER BASIN TRAILS

HUMPHREY'S PEAK (12,633 ft)

ABINEAU & BEAR JAW TRAIL LOOP

WHITE HORSE HILLS

522

WEATHERFORD TRAIL

SNOW BOWL SKI LIFT

FLAGSTAFF

RED MOUNTAIN TRAIL

RED MOUNTAIN

KENDRICK PARK

418

KENDRICK MTN.

HOCKDERFER HILL

516

FLAGSTAFF NORDIC CENTER

LAKE MARY ROAD

17

SLATE MOUNTAIN

SLATE MOUNTAIN TRAIL

180

191

CRATER LAKE

BULL BASIN

KENDRICK TRAILS

90

90A

171

245

WING MTN.

WING MTN. CROSS COUNTRY SKI AREA

628

DEPOT

ARMY

RED HILL

PUMPKIN CENTER

90

KENDRICK MTN.

194

786

GOVERNMENT CAVE

GOVERNMENT MTN.

GOVERNMENT PRAIRIE

171

141

BELLEMONT FLAT

NAVAJO

BELLEMONT

PRAIRIE

GARLAND

LITTLE SQUAW MTN.

144

SITGREAVES PEAK (9,388 ft)

SITGREAVES MTN.

SPRING VALLEY CROSS COUNTRY SKI AREA

141

PARKS

146

40

SPRING VALLEY

422

74

PITTMAN VALLEY

10 miles

8

6

4

2

0

© MOON PUBLICATIONS

geologic features and ecology. You'll see fumaroles (gas vents), lava bubbles, squeeze-ups, and lava tubes that appear to have cooled only yesterday. The adventurous can step inside the ice cave; bring a flashlight (and a spare) and expect to crawl in some sections. Rangers have forbidden hiking on Sunset Crater itself, because earlier climbers wore a deep gash in the soft cinder slopes. The damage has been repaired, but you'll have to hike elsewhere. **Lenox Crater** (elev. 7,240 feet), one mile east of the Visitor Center, provides a firsthand look at a cinder cone with a crater. It's an easy climb, taking 30-45 minutes to the rim and back; elevation change is 280 feet.

Sunset Crater's first eruptions in A.D. 1064 or 1065 sent local Indian groups running for safety. Activity had subsided enough by 1110 for Sinagua and Anasazi to settle in the Wupatki Basin, 20 miles northeast of Sunset Crater. Some of their ruins and a museum can be seen in Wupatki National Monument (see below); take the Sunset Crater-Wupatki Loop Road. Lava flows and smaller ash eruptions continued in the Sunset Crater area until about A.D. 1250. Back in the late 1920s some Hollywood film-makers thought Sunset Crater would make a great movie set. They planned to use dynamite to get the needed special effects of an avalanche, but local citizens put a stop to that. Sunset Crater became a national monument in 1930.

**Bonito Campground,** across the road from the Visitor Center, is open from early May to mid-Oct.; $7. The campground has drinking water and restrooms but no showers. Rangers hold campfire programs on summer evenings. Picnic areas are near the Visitor Center, at the Lava Flow Trail, and at Painted Desert Vista (between Sunset Crater and Wupatki national monuments). The Visitor Center is open all year (except Christmas and New Year's Day) 8 a.m.-5 p.m. with extended hours in summer; road and trails stay open all day; tel. 527-7042. The admission fee of $3/vehicle ($1 bus passenger or bicyclist) also includes entry to Wupatki National Monument. You can reach the Visitor Center by driving north 12 miles from the Flagstaff Mall on US 89, then turning east 2 miles on a signed road.

### O'Leary Peak

Weather permitting, the summit of this 8,965-foot lava-dome volcano provides outstanding views into Sunset Crater and of other features in the area. Forest Route 545A begins about 0.2 mile west of Sunset Crater Visitor Center and climbs 5 miles to the fire lookout tower at the top. The road is unpaved and has some steep grades. A gate partway up may block vehicular traffic. You can park at the second switchback and walk the last mile. Rangers from Sunset Crater provide bus trips up O'Leary in summer. At the summit, you'll have the best views of the colors of Sunset Crater and the Painted Desert beyond in the late afternoon; best views of the San Francisco Peaks are in the morning.

## WUPATKI NATIONAL MONUMENT

The Sinagua, prehistoric Indian farmers, settled in small groups near the San Francisco Peaks in about A.D. 600. They lived in partly underground pithouses and tilled the soil in the few areas having sufficient moisture for their corn and other crops. The eruption of Sunset Crater in A.D. 1064 or 1065 forced many to flee, but it also improved the marginal soils. Volcanic ash, blown by the wind over a large area, added minerals to the ground and enabled it to retain more of the rainfall. After about 1110, the Sinagua, joined by Anasazi from northeastern Arizona, settled in Wupatki Basin. This valley, about 20 miles northeast of Sunset Crater, became the center of a group of cosmopolitan villages. Mogollon, Hohokam, and Cohonino tribes influenced the mix of Sinagua and Anasazi cultures. Trade, good crop yields, and exchange of ideas gave the people a new life. Large, multistoried pueblos replaced the brush shelters and pit houses of former times. By about 1150, some villages had consolidated and built walls, which possibly indicated the strain of population pressure. No evidence of conflict has been found,

*Wukoki Ruin*

though. During the 1200s, people began to leave the area, perhaps because of drier conditions and declining soil fertility. By 1300 only ruins remained. Archaeologists think that the inhabitants retreated southward to the Verde Valley and northeastward to the Hopi mesas. Hopi legends trace their modern Parrot Clan to Wupatki and their Snake Clan to nearby Wukoki. An estimated 2,000 archaeological sites lie scattered within the monument. Some of the best have road and trail access, but most of the monument remains closed to visitors. You'll need a permit to hike beyond the open sites. Overnight camping is not allowed, with the exception of the Crack-in-Rock hikes led by rangers in April and October.

### Wupatki Visitor Center

Pottery, tools, jewelry, and other artifacts of the early cultures are on exhibit. A Wupatki room reconstruction shows how the interior of a typical living chamber might have looked. You'll also learn a little about the present-day Navajo and Hopi tribes who live near the monument. Insect and flowering-plant collections illustrate the life of this high-desert country. You can purchase books, posters, maps, and videos related to the region. Rangers give archaeology talks (15 minutes) and lead tours (30-45 minutes) of adjacent Wupatki Ruin; most programs take place in

summer, but groups can arrange them at other times. Wupatki Visitor Center is open 7 a.m.-7 p.m. in summer (Memorial to Labor Day weekends) and 8 a.m.-5 p.m. the rest of the year; closed Christmas and New Year's Day; tel. 527-7040. The Visitor Center is 14 miles east of US 89 between Flagstaff and Cameron, 20 miles north of Sunset Crater National Monument. Doney Mountain Picnic Area and scenic overlook sit between cinder cones about 3 miles northwest on the loop road. The nearest accommodations and supplies are in Flagstaff and Gray Mountain. Closest camping is at Sunset Crater and Flagstaff.

### Wupatki Ruin

At its peak, Wupatki (Hopi for "Tall House") contained over 100 rooms and towered as high as four stories. A self-guided trail, beginning behind the Visitor Center, explains many of the features of Wupatki; pick up a trail brochure at the start. The "ball court" at one end of the village resembles those used in Mexico for games, which likely had a religious function. The court is one of several found in northern Arizona, probably introduced by the Hohokam of the southern deserts. Archaeologists reconstructed it from a wall remnant; the rest of Wupatki Ruin is only stabilized. An open-air amphitheater lies to one side of Wupatki; perhaps village meetings and ceremonies took place here. A blowhole, 100 feet east of the ball court, must have had religious importance for the people. A system of underground cracks may connect this natural feature with other blowholes in the area; air will blow out, rush in, or do nothing at all, depending on weather conditions. Cavers once tried to enter the system but couldn't get through the narrow passageways.

### Wukoki Ruin

(Hopi for "Big and Wide House.") Indians lived in this small pueblo for three generations. You can step inside the rooms for a closer look. From the Wupatki Visitor Center, drive 0.25 mile toward Sunset Crater, then turn left 2.6 miles on a paved road.

### Citadel Ruin

This fortress-like pueblo, perched atop a small volcanic butte, stood one or two stories high and contained about 50 rooms. From the top, look for some of the more than 10 other ruins nearby. On the path to the Citadel, you'll pass the pueblo of **Nalakihu** (Hopi for "House Standing Outside the Village"). Nalakihu had two stories with 13 or 14 rooms. Both sites can be visited on a short, self-guided trail. From Wupatki Visitor Center, drive 9 miles northwest on the loop road.

### Lomaki Ruin

Lomaki (Hopi for "Beautiful House") is one of the best preserved ruins in the monument. Tree-ring dating of its roof timbers indicates that the occupants lived here from about A.D. 1190 to 1240. The small, two-story pueblo had at least nine rooms. A quarter-mile trail from the parking area also passes small ruins beside Box Canyon. The turnoff for Lomaki is 9 miles northwest of Wupatki Visitor Center, 0.25 mile beyond Citadel Ruin on the opposite side of the road.

### Crack-in-Rock Ruin

Rangers lead overnight backpack trips to this dramatic ruin during April and October. Crack-in-Rock sits atop an easily defended

mesa with sweeping views of the Little Colorado River and distant hills. A wealth of petroglyphs has been carved around the base of the mesa and on two nearby mesas. You'll also see many other pueblo sites on the way in and out. The 14-mile roundtrip ranger-guided hike is of moderate difficulty. There's a $10 charge. Call or write for information at least 2 months in advance from Wupatki National Monument, HC 33, Box 444A, Flagstaff, AZ 86001; tel. 527-7040.

## STRAWBERRY CRATER WILDERNESS

Eruptions of slow-moving basaltic andesite formed the crater 50,000-100,000 years ago, then breached the east side. A lava field spreads out northeast of the crater. Strawberry Crater's jagged features contrast with the surrounding cinder cones of much younger age. Because the San Francisco Peaks form a rain shadow over this area, it receives only about 7 inches of annual precipitation. Sparse vegetation of juniper, pinyon pine, cliffrose, and a few ponderosa pines cover the gently rolling terrain of cinders and lava. The 10,140-acre wilderness offers good cross-country hiking and the challenge of a climb to the crater summit. Indian ruins can be discovered too.

Strawberry Crater lies northeast of Flagstaff between Sunset Crater and Wupatki national monuments. The wilderness boundary is just north of the Painted Desert Vista area on the road between the monuments, but a long hike is required to reach the crater from here. Best way to the crater is by driving about 16 miles north from the Flagstaff Mall on US 89 to the bottom of a long grade, turning east 3.4 miles on Forest Route 546, then continuing 1.1 miles east on Forest Route 779 to the power lines. An unmarked trail contours around the crater to the left to the inner basin; this is the best route to the summit. Help preserve Strawberry Crater by not hiking on the steeper slopes, as they are fragile and easily damaged.

## MOUNT ELDEN TRAIL SYSTEM

To reach the summit of Mt. Elden, the 9,299-foot peak on the north edge of Flagstaff, you can hike any of several good trails or drive up a rough road. Many different loop and traverse trips can be made. Wildflowers, various types of forests, and panoramic views reward those making the trip even partway up. A fire-lookout tower marks the summit. Climb the tower, if it's open, for the best views. On a clear day you'll see much of northcentral Arizona: Oak Creek Canyon and Mormon Lake to the south; the Painted Desert to the east; Humphrey's Peak, Sunset Crater, and other volcanos to the north; and Bill Williams Mtn. to the west. Flagstaff lies directly below, spread out like a map. The hiking season runs from about May to Oct., longer for the drier eastern slope. Carry water. To avoid the hair-raising experience of an afternoon thun-

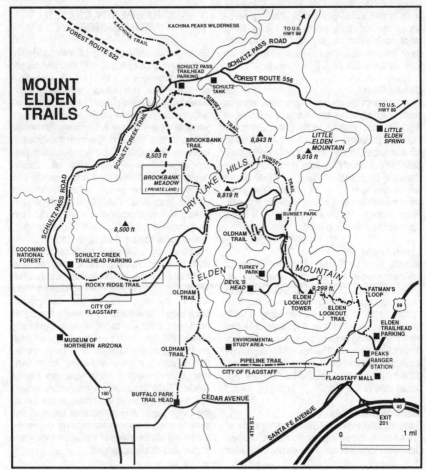

Courtesy of Coconino National Forest

derstorm, set out early during July and Aug. when they are likely. Allow at least half a day for a hike to the summit and back; trail mileages given below are one-way distances. Elevations on Mt. Elden range from 6,900 to 9,300 feet. Hikers, horseback riders, and mountain bicyclists all use this trail system, so keep an eye out for other users. Contact the Peaks Ranger Station for current trail information; tel. 526-0866.

## Elden Lookout Trail

This 3-mile trail seems easy at first, but then it begins a steep climb up the rocky east slope of Mt. Elden to the lookout tower. Elevation gain is 2,400 feet. Begin from the Elden Trailhead (elev. 6,900 feet) on US 89, just past the Peaks Ranger Station on US 89. From Flagstaff, head east through town on Santa Fe Ave. or take I-40 Exit 201 toward Page. The grades and loose surface of this trail make it too hazardous for horse travel, nor is it recommended for mountain bikes.

## Fatman's Loop Trail

An easy one-mile walk, except for a few short steep sections, past volcanic rock formations and diverse plant life. Views take in parts of east Flagstaff and beyond; elevation gain is 1,600 feet. The loop begins from the lower part of Elden Lookout Trail. It's also not suitable for horses or mountain bikes.

## Sunset Trail

Alpine meadows and forests on the north side offer some of Mt. Elden's most pleasant hiking. The 4-mile trail climbs gradually through pines, firs, and aspen to Sunset Park and on to the summit. The Radio Fire of 1977 caused the scars visible on the east slope below. Panoramas take in the Peaks, Sunset Crater, and countless other features. Elevation gain is 1,300 feet. Begin from the Schultz Pass Trailhead (elev. 8,000 feet), located just west of Schultz Tank. To reach the trailhead, follow US 180 northwest 3 miles from downtown Flagstaff to Schultz Pass Road and turn right 4 miles. This and the following Mt. Elden trails can be traveled on horseback or mountain bike.

## Schultz Creek Trail

The gentle 3.5-mile trail parallels an intermittent creek between the lower ends of Sunset and Rocky Ridge trails. Elevation change is 800 feet. Schultz Creek Trailhead (elev. 7,200 feet) is a short way off Schultz Pass Road, about 2 miles in from US 180. Motor bikes sometimes use Schultz Creek Trail.

## Rocky Ridge Trail

Black-jack ponderosa pine, Gambel oak, alligator juniper, cliffrose, and yucca line this western approach to Mt. Elden. The easy 2.2-mile trail begins from Schultz Creek Trailhead (see previous trail description) and connects with the Oldham Trail. Elevation gain is minimal.

## Brookbank Trail

The easy 2.5-mile trail climbs through a forested drainage to the edge of Brookbank Meadow, owned by the Navajo Tribe, and continues to meet Sunset Trail at a low saddle. Elevation gain is 1,000 feet. The trailhead (elev. 7,800 feet) can be reached by hiking the Oldham Trail or by driving 0.5 mile in on Schultz Pass Road from US 180, then going 2.5 miles up the Mt. Elden Road.

## Oldham Trail

At 5.5 miles, this is Mt. Elden's longest trail. The trail begins at the north end of Buffalo Park (elev. 7,000 feet) in Flagstaff and climbs gradually past boulder fields and cliffs on the west side of Mt. Elden. You'll cross the Mt. Elden Road several times as the trail winds higher through the forest and meadows to the summit ridge. Elevation change is 2,000 feet.

## Pipeline Trail

The easy 2.8-mile trail follows a gas pipeline right-of-way between Oldham and Elden Lookout trails. You'll see old lava flows on the south side of Mt. Elden and cross the Elden Environmental Study Area. The Forest Service set aside the study area in the mid-1970s for school and environmental groups. Ponderosa pines and Gambel oaks dominate the forest at the trail's 7,100- to 7,200-foot elevations.

## SAN FRANCISCO PEAKS

**Kachina Peaks Wilderness** protects about 18,200 acres of the Peaks. The name was chosen because of the religious importance of the area to the Hopi Tribe. The Forest Service has a network of trails in the wilderness, some of which are described below. For current hiking conditions, maps, and other trails, contact the Peaks Ranger Station; tel. 526-0866.

### Lamar Haines Memorial Wildlife Area
A small pond fed by two springs attracts birds and other wildlife. Ludwig Veit, for whom the springs are named, homesteaded here in 1892. Petroglyphs can be found nearby on the volcanic rocks. From the parking area, near Milepost 4.5 on the paved Snowbowl Road, walk through the gate and turn right 0.7 mile on an abandoned road. Lamar Haines (1927-86) was active in education and conservation in the Flagstaff area.

### Agassiz Skyride
Hop on this chairlift for the most leisurely way to the heights. You'll be swept from 9,500 to 11,600 feet with some fantastic views. The Skyride operates daily 10 a.m.-4 p.m. from Memorial Day weekend to Labor Day and weekends into Oct. (weather permitting); $7 adult, $5 for seniors 65 or over, and $3.50 for children 12 or under; tel. 779-6127. From Flagstaff, drive 7 miles northwest on US 180, then turn right 7 miles up the Snowbowl Road to its end. You can't hike from the upper chairlift station, though. The Forest Service closed Agassiz Peak to protect the fragile alpine vegetation, including *Senecio franciscanus,* found only on the San Francisco Peaks. Hikers headed for Humphrey's Peak must take the Humphrey's Peak or Weatherford trails, described below.

### Humphrey's Peak Trail
The alpine world on the rooftop of Arizona makes a challenging dayhike destination. Get an early start, as it usually takes about 8 hours to the summit and back on the 9-mile-roundtrip trail. To protect fragile alpine tundra, the Forest Service asks that you stay on the designated trails above 11,400 feet. Also, don't build campfires or set up camps here. Snow blocks the way much of the year, so the hiking season is usually only from late June to September. Be prepared for bad weather by taking good rain and wind gear; getting caught in a storm near the top with just a T-shirt and shorts could be deadly. Lightning frequently zaps the Peaks, especially during July and Aug.; you'll want to stay off if storms threaten. In winter, winds and subzero cold can be extremely dangerous— only the most experienced groups should attempt a climb then. Carry plenty of water, because you'll use more when hiking at these high elevations. A climb to the summit is strenuous, but many hikers enjoy shorter walks on the trail. The trail begins from the Snowbowl area (elev. 9,300 feet), contours under the Hart Prairie chairlift, then switchbacks up the mountain. You'll be in dense forests of Engelmann spruce, corkbark fir, and quaking aspen. Near 11,400 feet, stunted Engelmann spruce and bristlecone pine trees cling to the precarious slopes. Higher still, only tiny alpine plants survive the fierce winds and long winters. At the saddle (elev. 11,800 feet), turn left for Humphrey's Peak and follow the trail along the ridge. On a clear day you'll see a lot of northern Arizona and some of southern Utah from the 12,633-foot summit.

### Weatherford Trail
J.W. Weatherford completed this toll road into the Peaks in 1926, using only hand labor and animals. Cars could then sputter their way up to Doyle and Fremont saddles. The road later fell into disrepair. Today the Weatherford Road is just for hikers and horseback riders; mechanized vehicles (including mountain bicycles) are prohibited. Although it's possible to reach the summit of Humphrey's Peak on the Weatherford Trail, the long 20-mile roundtrip discourages most climbers. Leisurely dayhikes just partway up might be the best bet. The Weatherford Trail's gentle grade and excellent views make it a good

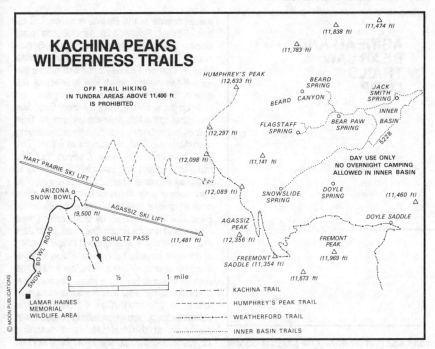

# KACHINA PEAKS WILDERNESS TRAILS

(11,838 ft)
(11,474 ft)
(11,783 ft)

HUMPHREY'S PEAK
(12,633 ft)

BEARD SPRING

JACK SMITH SPRING

BEARD CANYON

OFF TRAIL HIKING
IN TUNDRA AREAS ABOVE 11,400 ft
IS PROHIBITED

INNER BASIN

BEAR PAW SPRING

FLAGSTAFF SPRING

(12,297 ft)

552B

(12,098 ft)
(11,141 ft)

DAY USE ONLY
NO OVERNIGHT CAMPING
ALLOWED IN INNER BASIN

HART PRAIRIE SKI LIFT

ARIZONA SNOW BOWL

(12,089 ft)

SNOWSLIDE SPRING

DOYLE SPRING

(11,460 ft)

(9,500 ft)

AGASSIZ SKI LIFT

DOYLE SADDLE

TO SCHULTZ PASS

(11,481 ft)

AGASSIZ PEAK
(12,356 ft)

FREMONT PEAK
(11,969 ft)

SNOW BOWL ROAD

FREEMONT SADDLE (11,354 ft)

(11,673 ft)

0     ½     1 mile

LAMAR HAINES
MEMORIAL
WILDLIFE AREA

© MOON PUBLICATIONS

— · · — · · —   KACHINA TRAIL
— — — — —   HUMPHREY'S PEAK TRAIL
— · — · — · —   WEATHERFORD TRAIL
· · · · · · · · · · · ·   INNER BASIN TRAILS

choice for a family outing. Energetic hikers can head up the Weatherford Trail to Humphrey's Peak and then descend the shorter Humphrey's Peak Trail, if they can arrange a car shuttle. Carry water. Easiest approach to the Weatherford Trail is to drive 2.5 miles up the Snow Bowl Road from US 180, turn right on Forest Route 522 until it gets too rough for cars (after about 3 miles), and continue on foot for about one mile. Another way is to drive to Schultz Pass Trailhead (see directions for Sunset Trail, p. 161) and walk across the road to the Weatherford Trail.

### Kachina Trail

This new trail on the southern slopes of Humphrey's Peak is 6.3-miles long (one way). From the upper trailhead, on the east end of the lower Snowbowl parking lot (elev. 9,300 feet), the Kachina winds east through spruce, fir, aspen, and ponderosa pine forests to the Sunset Trailhead at Schultz Pass (elev. 8,000 feet). Carry water.

### Inner Basin Hiking

The San Francisco Peaks form a giant U-shaped valley known as the Inner Basin. Aspen, fir, and spruce thrive here. Lockett Meadow, at the Inner Basin entrance, can be reached by car from the northeast. You have to park here and continue on foot. Other roads and trails extend as far as 3.5 miles up the Inner Basin, all offering wonderful hiking. Elevations range from 8,600 feet at Lockett Meadow to about 11,000 feet at Snowslide Spring. The many springs in the Inner Basin supply some of Flagstaff's water, but most have been covered and locked; it's safest to carry your own water. Aspen trees put on a magnificent golden show in late Sept. and early October. You can camp near Lockett Meadow, but not in the Inner Basin just beyond. From Flagstaff drive north on US 89 about 13 miles beyond the Flagstaff Mall and turn left on Forest Route 552. The turnoff lacks signing; look for a dirt road beside a large black-cinder pit between Mileposts 431

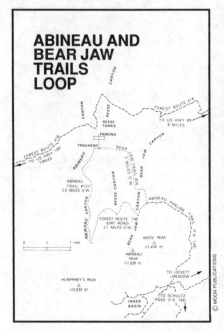

## ABINEAU AND BEAR JAW TRAILS LOOP

and 432 (turnoff is 0.7 mile past the Sunset Crater jct.). Follow Forest Route 552 past the cinder pit for 1.3 miles, then turn right just before a gravel pit; Lockett Meadow is 3.5 miles farther. Low-slung cars and large vehicles shouldn't attempt this road.

### Abineau And Bear Jaw Trails

These two trails climb about halfway up the north side of the San Francisco Peaks. On either path you'll enjoy cool forests of pine, fir, and aspen. Wildflowers grow in rocky alpine meadows near the top of Abineau Trail. Both trails start near Reese Tanks. Abineau Pipeline Trail, a dirt road closed to vehicles, connects the upper ends. With this road, Abineau and Bear Jaw make a good 6.5-mile hiking loop. Abineau is probably the prettier of the two, a good choice if you don't want to do the whole loop. The trailhead is on the opposite side of the Peaks from Flagstaff. Either take US 180, Forest Route 151 (second turnoff), and Forest Route 418 around

the west side of the Peaks, or follow US 89 and Forest Route 418 around the east slopes; see the Coconino Forest map. Beginning at Flagstaff, each route is about 26 miles long. A sign on Forest Route 418 marks the turnoff for the trailhead, which is about 0.5 mile in. Drive in as far as you can, park, and walk up the road to a T-intersection: Bear Jaw Trail goes to the left, Abineau to the right. Tree blazes mark both trails. Shortly after turning onto Abineau Trail, keep right at a fork. The trail soon enters Abineau Canyon (actually more of a valley) and stays in it all the way to Abineau Pipeline Trail, 2.5 miles away. You can retrace your steps or turn left 2.1 miles on the pipeline trail to the upper trailhead for Bear Jaw Trail, marked by stone cairns, tree blazes and a wide spot in the road. Bear Jaw Trail, 2 miles one way, doesn't follow a valley at all—you have to be *very* careful to look for the tree blazes. Take special care near the bottom when following a road, because the trail later turns left away from the road; this turn is easy to miss! Allow 4-5 hours for the complete loop. You'll be starting at 8,400 feet elevation at the trailhead and reaching 10,400 feet at the upper end of Abineau Trail. Carry water and raingear.

*view of SP Crater from Colton Crater*

## SP CRATER AND COLTON CRATER

These two volcanic craters, about 14 miles due north of the San Francisco Peaks, offer interesting geology and good hiking. You'll get some insight into the powerful forces that created them and that still lie underfoot. SP Crater's graceful shape and the black tongue of lava flowing from its base resemble the better known Sunset Crater. SP even has some reddish lava on its rim. Although Sunset Crater has been closed to climbing, you're still free to hike up SP Crater. The near-perfect symmetry of this cinder cone has earned it a photo in many geology textbooks. Actually "SP" isn't the real name of this little volcano. Most likely prudish map makers got red faces on hearing what the local cowboys called it. They saw the black "spatter" on the rim of the bowl-shaped crater and the "leaking" lava flow below, and said "It looks just like a shit pot." Anyway, the name stuck.

### Climbing SP Crater

The climb is moderately difficult; you'll be ascending 800 feet to the rim. Any time of the year is OK if the weather is good. The Coconino Forest map or the 15-minute SP MTN topo map help in navigating the dirt roads, none of which have signs. From Flagstaff, drive 27 miles north on US 89 to Hank's Trading Post (Milepost 446). Or, from the Wupatki National Monument turnoff, go north 1.2 miles to the trading post. Turn left (west) on the unsigned dirt road just south of the trading post. You'll be able to pick out SP, straight ahead, among the other volcanoes by its height and symmetry. Keep left where the road forks after 0.5 mile. When SP Crater is on your right, 6 miles in from the highway, you'll pass a large, black water tank on the left and then come to another road fork. Keep right at the fork, then look for a vehicle track on the right 100 yards farther. Take this track for 0.5 mile and park. (People four-wheeling beyond this point have made deep ruts on the slope.) Follow the track on foot to the grassy ridgetop (SP Crater adjoins it on the right),

then start up the black-cinder slope of SP itself; there's no real trail—it's one step up and two steps sliding back on the loose cinders. Perseverance will get you onto the rim for a close look at the lava formations and a panoramic view of the San Francisco Volcanic Field. Walking around the rim is rewarding, but descending into the 360-foot-deep crater is hazardous. The thick, blocky lava flow from SP's base extends 4.3 miles north. It's about 70,000 years old.

### Climbing Colton Crater

If you'd like to see another volcano or want an easier hike, visit nearby Colton Crater. Colton is 2 miles due south of SP; take the other fork near the black water tank and go south 2 miles to an intersection with a road from the right. Park near here and head up the gentle slope to the rim, ascending about 300 feet. A gigantic explosion blew out the center of this volcano when hot basaltic magma met water-saturated rocks. Rock layers can be seen clearly. A baby red cinder cone, only 500 feet across, sits at the bottom of Colton Crater. It's an easy walk to the crater floor, actually 260 feet lower than the land outside the crater. Or you can walk around the rim through juniper and pinyon trees, climbing about 600 higher than the lowest part of the rim.

## SLATE MOUNTAIN

A well-graded trail provides good views in all directions as you wind your way up. Kendrick Peak is to the south, the San Francisco Peaks to the southeast, and Red Mountain—with its distinctive red gash—just to the north. Trail markers label many of the trees and plants. Flowers line the way from spring through fall. Early settlers mistook the fine-grained, light-gray rock of the mountain for slate, but geologists say it's rhyolite, a volcanic rock. Hiking time is about 3 hours for the 5-mile roundtrip on which you'll climb 900 feet. The 8,215-foot summit makes a pleasant spot for a picnic. Hiking season runs about May to Oct.; carry water. To reach the trailhead, drive northwest 27 miles from

Flagstaff on US 180, then turn west 2 miles on Forest Route 191 (between Mileposts 242 and 243 on US 180). A sign marks the trailhead.

## RED MOUNTAIN

Ever wanted to walk into the heart of a volcano? Then try Red Mountain, 33 miles northwest of Flagstaff. Unusual erosion has dissected the cinder cone from the summit straight down to its base. Walk through a little canyon between towers of black cinders to enter the volcano. A 6-foot-high stone wall here is the only real climb! Ranchers built the wall to make a stock pond, but cinders have filled it in. Either clamber over this former dam or take the trail up the cinder slope to the right. Beyond the dam you'll enter a magical land of towering pinnacles and narrow canyons. It's a great place to explore; kids will love it. Trees offer shade for a picnic. Most of Red Mountain is soft volcanic tuff. Look for the rocks and minerals that weather out of it: blocks and bombs of lava; small crystals

of plagioclase feldspar (transparent, with striations); black, glassy pyroxene and hornblende; and volcanic dust, cinders, and lapilli (large cinders). A lava flow covers part of Red Mountain's southwest side about 100 feet below the summit. To reach the top (elev. 7,965 feet), take the trail back out of the crater and climb the more gentle cinder slopes on the southeast side. You'll be ascending about 1,000 feet. Red Mountain is easily reached by driving 33 miles northwest from Flagstaff on US 180 (or 42 miles southeast from Grand Canyon National Park) to Milepost 247, then turning west on the dirt road here. Red Mountain lies 1.5 miles in, but vehicles can go only 0.5 mile. You can't miss seeing the red cinders of the volcano. A less used road forks off to the left and climbs most of the way to the summit.

## KENDRICK PEAK WILDERNESS

Although the San Francisco Peaks have higher elevations, Kendrick Peak might well

*inside Red Mountain*

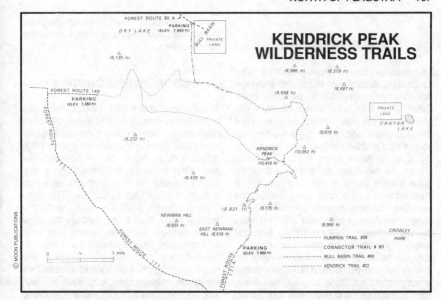

KENDRICK PEAK
WILDERNESS TRAILS

have the better view—you'll get not only a splendid panorama of northern Arizona from Kendrick, but a view of the Peaks themselves. The Painted Desert, Hopi mesas, and far-distant Navajo Mountain lie to the northeast; the north rim of the Grand Canyon juts up to the north; Sitgreaves and Bill Williams mountains poke up to the west; Oak Creek Canyon and the Mazatzals are to the south; and the magnificent San Francisco Peaks, surrounded by many smaller volcanos, rise directly to the east. Three trails, ranging in length from 7 to 11 miles roundtrip, lead to Kendrick's 10,418-foot summit and fire-lookout tower. Hiking season lasts from about late June to Sept.; longer on the southern Kendrick Trail. Carry water.

### Kendrick Trail #22
This shortest trail (7 miles roundtrip) is the one most used. Because it climbs the sunny southern slopes, it's the best choice early or late in the season. The trail follows an old fire road the first 1.5 miles before narrowing, but it remains well graded and easy to follow to the top. A lookout cabin, equipped with a wood stove and three bare bunk beds, sits on the ridge 0.25 mile below the summit. Hikers may use this little cabin, which has withstood the elements since 1912. To reach the trailhead, take I-40 Bellmont Exit 185 (10 miles west of Flagstaff), follow the frontage road one mile west, drive 12 miles north on Forest Route 171, then turn right one mile on a road signed "Kendrick Trail."

### Pumpkin Trail #39
The longest approach (11 miles roundtrip) starts west of Kendrick Peak. Pumpkin Trail has the added feature of enabling you to use the one-mile Connector Trail and part of Bull Basin Trail to make a loop. Allow a full day. To reach the trailhead, follow directions for Kendrick Trail #22, but continue on Forest Route 171 another 4.5 miles, then turn right one mile at the sign for Pumpkin Trail.

### Bull Basin Trail #40
This 9-mile-roundtrip route from the north may be a little difficult to follow at first. To reach the trailhead, continue 2.5 miles on Forest Route 171 past the Pumpkin Trail turnoff, turn right 1.5 miles on Forest Route 144, then turn right 6 miles on Forest Route 90.

## GOVERNMENT CAVE

This neat little cave is located about 4 miles south of Kendrick Peak. Maps also show the natural underground tunnel as "Lava River Cave." Red-hot lava broke through the ground near the San Francisco Peaks about 100,000 years ago, then moved westward across Hart and Government prairies, reaching a thickness of more than 100 feet in places. As the outer layers of the smoking mass cooled, some of the fiery-hot interior burst through a weak spot, partly draining the lava flow. This underground river of fire eventually cooled too. A collapsed ceiling reveals the passageway. No one knows the total length of this lava-tube cave, but about 0.7 mile can be easily explored. The interior remains cool year-round, so a jacket or sweater is recommended. Bring at least two flashlights to explore the cave; it would be *no fun* to have to feel your way out because your one and only light died!

The walls and ceiling form an amazingly symmetrical tunnel. The former lava river on the floor still has all the ripple marks, cracks, and squeeze-ups of its last days. There's only one main passageway, though a small loop branches off to the right about one-third of the way through and then rejoins the main channel. The main channel is large with plenty of headroom, except for a section about two-thirds of the way through where you'll have to do some stooping. To reach Government Cave, follow directions to Kendrick Peak above, but go only 7.5 miles north on Forest Route 171. Turn right 0.5 mile on the road signed "171B." The cave and turnoff are shown on the Coconino and Kaibab (Williams, Chalender, and Tusayan districts) forest maps. A large ring of stones marks the cave entrance.

## SITGREAVES MOUNTAIN

Great views and pretty forests make the 9,388-foot summit of Sitgreaves an attractive destination. Reddish cinder cones, forested mountains, and vast grasslands stretch to the distant horizon. Allow about 4 hours to hike the 4 miles to the top and back. Carry water. Hiking season for this northern approach lasts from about May to October. The route follows a valley from the trailhead to the summit ridge, then turns right up the ridge to the highest point. No established trails or signs exist on Sitgreaves but none are needed—just stay in the valley until you reach the ridge. But be sure to descend via the same valley, unless you want a much longer hike! Walking is a bit easier if you keep to the right when going up (not so many fallen trees). Beautiful groves of aspen find this cool, moist, sheltered area to their liking. Sitgreaves Mountain lies about 7 miles north of I-40, about two-thirds of the way from Flagstaff to Williams. To find the trailhead you'll need either the Coconino or Kaibab (Williams, Chalender, and Tusayan districts) forest map. Take I-40 Pittman Valley Exit 171, go north 7 miles on Forest Route 74 to its end, turn right 3 miles on Forest Route 141 (Spring Valley Road), then look *real hard* on the right for a small road. The turnoff is very easy to miss and probably won't be signed. Map designations for the turnoff are T.23N., R.3E., sec. 13. Cars can be driven in about one mile. When the road gives out, continue walking in the same direction up the valley.

# WEST OF FLAGSTAFF

## WILLIAMS

Small and friendly, Williams proclaims itself "Gateway to the Grand Canyon." The town (pop. 2,700) nestles among pine-forested hills and expansive meadows at an elevation of 6,780 feet. Downtown Williams may lack charm, but it does offer less expensive accommodation and food than often-crowded Grand Canyon Village to the north. Arizona 64, on the west edge of town, is the shortest route (58 miles) between I-40 and the famous park. Most travelers, in a hurry to get someplace else, miss the pretty country surrounding Williams—splendid Sycamore Canyon, small fishing lakes, high volcanos, forest drives, and hiking trails.

## History

Charles Rodgers, the first white settler here, set up a cattle operation in 1878. The railroad and lumber town founded several years later took its name from Bill Williams Mountain just to the south. The mountain in turn commemorated Ol' Bill Williams, who roamed the West as a mountain man from 1825 until his death at the hands of Ute Indians in 1849. He earned a reputation as a skilled marksman, trapper, trader, and guide—a colorful and controversial figure to the end. Today the Bill Williams Mountain Men carry on his adventurous spirit. The group dresses in buckskin clothing and fur hats, stages an annual 180-mile horseback ride from Williams to Phoenix, and works to keep the history of the mountain man alive. The Buckskinners, a family-oriented group, puts on frontier-era garb and holds black-powder shoots.

A more recent period of Western history came to an end at Williams in Oct., 1984, when I-40 bypassed the last section of old US Route 66. A sentimental ceremony, complete with songwriter Bobby Troup of "Route 66" fame, marked the transition. The famous highway from Chicago to Los Angeles had carried many families to a new life in Arizona and California. Its replacement, I-40, now lies in an unbroken 2,400-mile path from Durham, N.C., to Barstow, California.

## The Train

In 1901, passenger trains first steamed out of Williams to the Grand Canyon's scenic splendors. The railroad service ended in 1968, but recently started up again after a 21-year hiatus. **Grand Canyon Railway's** steam trains now provide service from downtown Williams to the historic log depot in Grand Canyon Village. Trains are scheduled once or twice daily except in winter, when they run on some holiday weekends only. Roundtrip fares are $41.96 adult ($2 less if you have a park pass), $22.68 children; tel. (800) THE-TRAIN.

## Accommodations And Campgrounds

Business Route I-40 divides downtown to become Bill Williams Ave. (eastbound) and Railroad Ave. (westbound). Most of Williams' 24 motels lie along Bill Williams Avenue. **Kaibab Trailer and RV Park** offers sites for $12.25 w/hookups (no tents); open all year and has showers; from AZ 64 on the east edge of town, take Rodeo Dr. (beside Canyon Motel), then right on Homestead Road; tel. 635-2413. Two KOA campgrounds lie a short distance from Williams: **Circle Pines KOA** is 3 miles east at I-40 Exit 167; $14.18 tents, $17.33 RV w/hookups; has tennis, badminton and basketball courts, game room, indoor pool, and summer horseback riding; open year-round; tel. 635-4545. **Grand Canyon KOA** is 5 miles north of Williams on AZ 64 (I-40 Exit 165) on the way to the Grand Canyon; $14.65 tents, $17.80 RV w/hookups; offers an indoor pool, showers, and other amenities; open March 1 to Nov. 1; tel. 635-2307. **Red Lake Campground,** 10 miles north on AZ 64 from I-40 Exit 165, is open all year and has coin-operated showers; $9.45 tents, $14.70 RV w/hookups; tel. 635-4753.

The Forest Service has four campgrounds, all on small fishing lakes, with drinking water but no showers, from early May to about mid-Oct.; $6-7 night. Elevations range from 6,600 to 7,100 feet. Kaibab, Dogtown, and White Horse Lake campgrounds remain open in winter, though snow occasionally closes roads; no fee or water. Boaters can use motors up to 8 h.p. on Cataract and Kaibab lakes but only electric motors on the other lakes. **Cataract Campground** is 2 miles northwest of town; head west on Railroad Ave. across I-40 to Country Club Dr. (or take I-40 Exit 161 and go north), then turn right one mile immediately after going under railroad tracks; entrance is on the left; closed mid-Oct. to early May. **Kaibab Campground** is 4 miles northeast of town; drive east on Bill Williams Ave. across I-40 (or turn north from I-40 Exit 165), go north 2 miles on AZ 64, then left one mile at the sign. **Dogtown Campground** and several trails lie 7.5 miles southeast of town (see "Vicinity of Williams"); drive 3.5 miles south on Fourth St. (Perkinsville Road), turn left 3 miles on Forest Route 140, then left one mile at the sign. **White Horse Lake Campground** is 19 miles southeast, near Sycamore Canyon; go 8 miles south on Fourth St., turn left on Forest Route 110, and follow signs. **White Horse Lake Resort** offers similar camping, cabins with cooking facilities, and a small store with groceries, fishing supplies, and rental boats. Fishermen catch trout and catfish in White Horse Lake. Winter visitors enjoy ice fishing, cross-country skiing, and snowmobiling.

## Food
**Rod's Steak House** is a Western-style restaurant with good steaks, seafood, and sandwiches; open daily for lunch and dinner at 301 E. Bill Williams Ave.; tel. 635-2671. **Old Smoky's Restaurant** is a good place to head for breakfast; it also serves sandwiches and burgers for lunch; open daily at 624 W. Bill Williams Ave.; tel. 635-2091. The **Coffee Pot Restaurant** is open daily for breakfast and lunch and Fri.-Sun. for dinner, at 117 E. Bill Williams Ave.; tel. 635-9339. **Parker**

**House Restaurant** (525 W. Bill Williams Ave.; tel. 635-4590) and the nearby **Hoffman House** (425 W. Bill Williams Ave.; tel. 635-9955) serve breakfast, lunch, and dinner daily. **Tracker's Restaurant** specializes in barbecued ribs at 137 W. Railroad Ave.; open Tues.-Sun. for lunch and dinner; tel. 635-4101. **El Sombrero Cafe** serves Mexican food at 126 W. Railroad Ave.; open Mon.-Wed. and Fri. for lunch and dinner, Sat. for dinner; closed Sun. and Thurs.; tel. 635-2759. **Tiffany's Italian Shop,** a popular local hangout, dispenses beer and pizza daily at 233 W. Bill Williams Ave.; tel. 635-2445. Other eateries include the **Hot Dog Corral** for fast food and ice cream at 401 W. Bill Williams Ave., and **Denny's** for standard American meals at 2550 W. Bill Williams Avenue.

## Events
The Buckskinners and Mountain Men ride into town for the **Bill Williams Rendezvous** on Memorial Day weekend. Powder shoots, canoeing, roping, and cow-chip-throwing contests are held along with an arts and crafts show and barbecue. Townsfolk celebrate the **Fourth of July** with fireworks, roping events, an ice cream social, and a barbecue. **Arizona Cowpuncher's Reunion and Old Timer's Rodeo** brings in working cowboys for competitions, a parade, and barn dances on the first weekend of August.

## Services And Recreation
**Post office** is on First St., just south of Bill Williams Avenue. **Williams Emergency Center** provides medical treatment at 301 S. Seventh St.; tel. 635-4441. **Buckskinner Park** (on Sixth St. one mile south of Bill Williams Ave.) is a pleasant spot for a picnic. Williams' **swimming pool** (open in summer) is at 603 N. Second St.; tel. 635-9958. Two **tennis courts** are near the high school; take Ninth St. (opposite the chamber of commerce) south to Oak St. and turn right one block. Play golf at the nine-hole **Williams Municipal Golf Course**; go west on Railroad Ave. across I-40 (or take I-40 Exit 171 and head north) and go one mile; tel. 635-2084.

Downhill ski in winter at the small **Williams Ski Area**. It's 4 miles south of town on Bill Williams Mountain. Facilities include a 2,000-foot poma lift (600 vertical feet), 700-foot rope tow for the beginners' slope, snack bar, rental shop, and ski shop. Cross-country skiers can also rent gear and ski on some marked trails. Season lasts from about mid-Dec. to end of March; turn south 2.2 miles on Fourth St., then right at the sign; tel. 635-9330.

The Forest Service has **cross-country ski trail loops** near Spring Valley; go 14.5 miles east on I-40 to Parks Exit 178, then head north 6 miles on Forest Route 141; pick up a ski trail map at the Forest Service office, 501 W. Bill Williams Avenue. Undeveloped cross-country ski areas include the White Horse Lake area and Sevier Flat and Barney Flat on the way there. **Benham Snow Play Area** is on the right, 4 miles south of town on Fourth Street.

### Information

**Williams-Grand Canyon Chamber of Commerce** gets so many travelers headed for the Grand Canyon that they carry maps and brochures for that area too. The helpful office is open in summer Mon.-Sat. 8 a.m.-5 p.m. and Sun. 9 a.m.-1 p.m.; the rest of the year is Mon.-Fri. 8 a.m.-5 p.m. and Sat. 9 a.m.-1 p.m.; located on the west edge of town at 820 W. Bill Williams Ave. (Box 235, Williams, AZ 86046); tel. 635-4061.

To find out about hiking, camping, fishing, and road conditions in the Kaibab National Forest, visit the **Chalender Ranger District** office downtown at 501 W. Bill Williams Ave. (Williams, AZ 86046); open Mon.-Fri. 7:30 a.m.-4 p.m.; tel. 635-2676. The **Williams Ranger District** office of the Kaibab National Forest is 1.5 miles west of downtown on the I-40 frontage Road (Rt. 1, Box 142, Williams, AZ 86046); tel. 635-2633. You can visit either office for recreation information and forest maps, though the Chalender office specializes in areas east of town, while the Williams office concentrates on the Bill Williams Mountain area.

The **public library** is at 113 S. First St., just south of Bill Williams Ave.; tel. 635-2263.

### Transport

**Greyhound** offers several east- and westbound departures daily; no station in town—buses stop at the corner of Bill Williams Ave. and Third Street.

## VICINITY OF WILLIAMS

### Grand Canyon Deer Farm

A well-run petting zoo for children, where they can get up close to hand-feed deer, llamas, miniature donkeys, and other tame animals. The Deer Farm is open daily in summer 8 a.m.-dusk, daily in spring and autumn 9 a.m.-dusk, daily in Nov. and Dec. 10 a.m.-dusk; call for days and hours in Jan. and Feb.; $4 adult, $2 children 3-13; tel. 635-4073. It's located 8 miles east of Williams, just off I-40 at the Pittman Valley/Deer Farm Exit 171.

### Bill Williams Mountain

The summit of this 9,255-foot peak can be reached by either of two hiking trails or by road. Pine, oak, and juniper trees cover the lower mountain slopes, and dense forests of aspen, fir, and spruce grow in protected valleys and at the higher elevations. On a clear day, after climbing more than 2,000 feet to the top, you'll have views of the Grand Canyon to the north, San Francisco Peaks and many smaller volcanos to the east, Sycamore Can-

*black bear*
(Ursus americanus)

*raccoon* (Procyon lotor)

yon and parts of the Verde Valley to the south, and vast rangelands to the west. Climb up the Forest Service lookout tower at the top for the best views, if it's open. Hiking season lasts from about June to September. Carry water on either trail. By doing a car shuttle, both trails can be linked together, or a trail can be hiked just one way. The 7-mile roundtrip **Bill Williams Mountain Trail** climbs the north face of Bill Williams Mountain. You'll reach the road about 0.5 mile from the summit; either continue on the trail across the road or turn up the road itself. Bill Williams Mountain Trailhead (elev. 7,000 feet) is near the Williams Ranger Station, 1.5 miles west of town; from I-40, take Exit 171 toward Williams, then turn right (west) 0.7 mile on the frontage road. The 6-mile roundtrip **Benham Trail** climbs the south and east slopes, crossing the road to the lookout tower several times. To reach the Benham Trailhead (elev. 7,265 feet) from Williams, go south 3.5 miles on Fourth St., then turn right about 0.3 mile on Benham Ranch Road. The gentler grade of this trail makes it good for horseback riders as well as hikers. You can also drive up (high-clearance vehicles recommended); from Williams head 4.7 miles south on Fourth St., then turn right 7 miles on Forest Route 111. The road closes in winter.

## Dogtown Trails

Dogtown Lake has a campground and some good hiking in the area. **Dogtown Nature Trail** is an easy, level, 0.75-mile loop in Dogtown Wash; interpretive signs tell of the forest environment; trailhead (elev. 7,100 feet) is at the east end of the lake. **Dogtown Lake Trail** offers a pleasant 1.8-mile stroll around the lake. **Davenport Hill Trail** begins at the east end of Dogtown Nature Trail, follows Dogtown Wash 0.3 mile, climbs to a flat, follows an old logging road, then turns north to the 7,805-foot summit. You'll pass through ponderosa pine, Douglas fir, white fir, and aspen. The trail is 5 miles roundtrip and has an elevation gain of 700 feet.

## Sycamore Canyon Point

Though similar in beauty and size to Oak Creek Canyon to the east, Sycamore Canyon remains much as it always has, without any roads or "facilities." Elk, deer, black bear, and other animals find food and shelter on the canyon's rim and within its depths. Hikers and horseback riders may visit by using a network of trails (see "Sycamore Canyon Wilderness," p. 196). Sycamore Canyon Point, 23 miles southeast of Williams, offers a breathtaking panorama. From town, drive 8 miles south on Fourth St./Perkinsville Road, then turn left on Forest Route 110 to its end, 15 miles farther. The last 5 miles is single lane and may be signed "not for low-clearance vehicles," but it may be OK for cautiously driven cars. No trails enter the canyon from this side, although you can spot one of the paths coming down the opposite side.

## Sycamore Trail

This 11-mile loop overlooks parts of upper Sycamore Canyon and goes past seasonal waterfalls, lumbermill and railroad sites, lily ponds (good swimming), and pretty forest country. Stone cairns mark the trail, shown on both the Kaibab and Coconino forest maps. Trailheads are southeast of Williams near the junction of Forest Routes 13 and 56, at the end of Forest Route 56, at Pomeroy Tanks off Forest Route 109, and at Sycamore Falls off Forest Route 109; see the Kaibab or Coconino forest maps for the many ways to get here. If you're in the mood for just a short hike, walk 0.3 mile south from the end of Forest Route 56 to an overlook of Sycamore Canyon. The Forest Service office in downtown Williams has a map and trail description for Sycamore Trail.

## Sycamore Falls

Two waterfalls can easily be reached near White Horse Lake. The spectacle, however, takes place only during the spring runoff and after heavy rains. (These are the same waterfalls seen along Sycamore Trail mentioned above.) From the store at White Horse Lake (see "Williams Campgrounds," p. 170), cross the cattle guard in front and turn right 2 miles (north) on Forest Route 109 to the Sycamore Falls Trailhead (about 2 miles south of the junction with Forest Route 13). A small waterfall is in a canyon just to the right, but walk ahead and a bit to the left to see a larger fall, 80-100 feet high.

## Perkinsville Road

Beginning as Fourth St. in downtown Williams, Perkinsville Road heads south through the pine forests of the Mogollon Rim, drops down to the high-desert lands of the Verde Valley, crosses the Verde River at historic Perkinsville Ranch, then climbs rugged hills to the old mining town of Jerome. The first 25 miles is paved, followed by 27 miles of dirt. Though dusty and bumpy in spots, the route is usually OK in dry weather for cars. No vehicle should attempt the unpaved section after winter snowstorms or heavy summer rains. Allow 3 hours to enjoy a one-way drive, more if you'd like to stop to admire the views, drive up Bill Williams Mountain, visit White Horse Lake, go out to Sycamore Canyon Vista, or do other exploring. Stock up on gas and water before heading down this lonely road. The Prescott National Forest map covers the entire route.

## ASH FORK

Declaring itself the "Flagstone Capital of USA," Ash Fork is in high-desert grasslands, 19 miles west of Williams and 50 miles north of Prescott. The location at the junction of I-40 and US 89 makes the small community a handy stopping place for travelers. The town grew up around a railroad siding built near Ash Creek in 1882; passengers and freight transferred to stagecoaches or wagons for Prescott and Phoenix. After a long history as a railroad town, Ash Fork (pop. 650) now serves as a highway stop and a center for livestock raising and sandstone quarrying.

## Accommodations And Campgrounds

As in Williams, most of the motels and other businesses lie along two parallel one-way streets; take I-40 Exits 144 or 146. Places to stay include **Stagecoach Motel** (823 Park Ave.; tel. 637-2278); **Copper State Motel** (101 E. Lewis Ave.; tel. 637-2335); and **Ashfork Inn** (west of downtown near I-40 Exit 144; tel. 637-2501).

**Ash Fork KOA** has a swimming pool and showers; $12.08 tents or RVs without hookups, $15.49 w/hookups; turn in on Eighth St. beside Stagecoach Motel; tel. 637-2521. **Cauthen's Hillside RV Park** on the south frontage road near I-40 Exit 144; $5.25 tents or RVs without hookups, $12.60 w/hookups; showers cost an extra $1; tel. 637-2300. Both campgrounds stay open all year. They're also close to the noise of I-40.

## Food

**Bull Pen Restaurant,** on the east side of town, stays open 24 hours; it has the standard cafe menu and a "broil your own steak," which you select from a display case. The **Ranch Cafe,** Lewis St., serves American breakfasts and lunches. **Pattie's Place** is a 24-hour cafe serving American food at the west edge of town near the Ashfork Inn.

## SELIGMAN

Another railroad town, Seligman (pop. 510) also now relies more on ranching and tourist business. The first residents arrived in 1886 and called their place "Prescott Junction," because a rail line branched south to Prescott. The Prescott line was later abandoned, but the town survived. Its present name of "Seligman" honors the brothers who had connections with the railroad and owned the Hash Knife Cattle Company. Modern travelers on I-40 can take Exits 121 or 123 for the motels and restaurants in town or head off on old Route 66. This former transcontinental highway is 19 miles longer to Kingman than I-40, but it offers a change of scenery and pace and a bit of nostalgia for America's motoring past. Also take the old highway to reach the Havasupai and Hualapai Indian reservations (see the "Grand Canyon and Arizona Strip" chapter). Two motels are in Truxton, and one is at the Pearce Ferry turnoff (6 miles west of Hackberry). If approaching Seligman from the east, you can take a shortcut (saves 4 miles) on the old Route 66; turn off I-40 at Crookton Road, Exit 139.

**Accommodations And Campgrounds**
Nearly all businesses lie along Chino Avenue. Places to stay include **Motel Deluxe** (203 E. Chino Ave.; tel. 422-3244); **Canyon Shadows Motel** (114 E. Chino; tel. 422-3255); **Romney Motel** (122 W. Chino; tel. 422-3294); **Supai Motel** (134 W. Chino; tel. 422-3663); and **Navajo Motel** (west edge of town; tel. 422-3204).

**Seligman KOA,** just east of town, has a swimming pool and showers; $11.60 tent, $13.72 RV w/hookups; tel. 422-3358. **Northern Arizona Campground,** on the west end of town, charges $8.40 for tents or RVs without hookups and $11.55 w/hookups; tel. 422-3549.

**Food**
**Country Inn Restaurant** is an American cafe open daily for breakfast, lunch, and dinner on the east edge of town. **Aztec Cafe** in downtown serves Mexican and American food; open daily for breakfast, lunch, and dinner. The **Copper Cart Restaurant,** also downtown, offers a varied American menu; open daily for breakfast, lunch, and dinner. Get your malts, sodas, and fast food at **Delgadillo's Snow Cap** (take out). **Seligman Sundries** features an old-fashioned ice cream parlor. **Mr. J's Coffee Shop** is a cafe offering American breakfasts, lunches, and dinners on the west edge of town.

## GRAND CANYON CAVERNS

Large underground chambers and pretty formations of this limestone cave attract travelers on old Route 66. The caverns are 25 miles northwest of Seligman, then one mile off the highway. A giant dinosaur model stands guard in front. On the 45-minute guided tours, you descend 21 stories by elevator to the caverns and walk about 0.75 mile (some steps). Tours operate daily 6 a.m.-6 p.m. in summer and 10 a.m.-5 p.m. in winter (closed Dec. 24 and 25 and possibly the last 3 weeks in Jan.); $5.75 adult, $3.75 children 6-14. A gift shop at the entrance has a small museum of mining and ranching artifacts (free). **Grand Canyon Caverns Inn** offers year-round accommodations ($33.76 s, $40.09 d). A nearby campground has drinking water but no showers or hookups; $5. The restaurant at the caverns is open about the same hours as the tours. For information on cave tours or motel reservations, call 422-3223.

# SOUTH OF FLAGSTAFF:
# LAKE AND RIM COUNTRY

More than a dozen mountain lakes lie across the pine-forested plateau country southeast of Flagstaff. Fishermen, picnickers, hikers, and campers enjoy the quiet waters, rolling hills, and scenic canyons of this region. Animal life flourishes—you might spot elk, deer, turkey, maybe even a bear. Abert squirrels with long, tufted ears are often seen. Best times to see wildlife are early and late in the day. Rim-country temperatures remain comfortably cool even in midsummer, and showers fall almost daily in the afternoons of July and August. Campgrounds, well known to hot desert dwellers, often fill up during the peak summer months. You'll find less crowded conditions early and late in the season, or anytime away from the developed sites. Nearly all the campgrounds have been established by the U.S. Forest Service; most have drinking water, though none have showers or hookups. Campgrounds usually stay open from about May to September. Do-it-yourself dispersed camping may be done almost anywhere in any season within the national for-

ests, though you're asked to avoid camping where prohibited by signs, on meadows, and within ¼ mile of springs, streams, stock tanks, or lakes. Only fee campgrounds have trash collection; elsewhere you need to pack yours out. Boats are limited to electric motors at the smaller lakes and 8-h.p. gas motors at some of the larger ones; no restrictions apply on Upper Lake Mary.

## MORMON LAKE
## RANGER DISTRICT

For information about recreation and road conditions in this area, stop at the **Mormon Lake Ranger District Office** at 4825 Lake Mary Road (Flagstaff, AZ 86001); the office is about one mile from US 89A; open Mon.-Fri. 7:30 a.m.-4:30 p.m.; tel. 527-7474.

### Lower And Upper Lake Mary
Beginning just 8 miles from Flagstaff, these long, narrow reservoirs offer fishing, boating, and birdwatching. Walnut Creek, which was

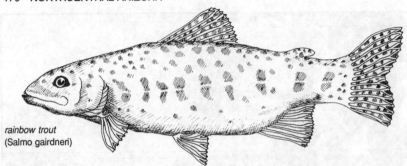

*rainbow trout*
(Salmo gairdneri)

dammed to form these lakes, once continued downstream through Walnut Canyon past the many Sinagua Indian ruins there. The Riordan brothers, who built the first reservoir early in this century to supply water for their sawmill, named the lake for one of their daughters.

Lower Lake Mary, the first built, now varies greatly in size depending on rainfall and water needs. Lower Lake Mary Boating and Picnicking Area, near the dam, offers tables, grills, ramadas, and a place to hand-launch boats. Fishing is mostly for northern pike.

Water-skiers zip across Upper Lake Mary in summer; it's one of the few lakes in this part of Arizona long and deep enough for the sport. Anglers pull catfish, northern pike, walleye, sunfish, and bluegill from the waters. Upper Lake Mary Picnic Area has tables, grills, ramadas, and two paved boat ramps; on Lake Mary Road 0.8 mile upstream from the dam. The Narrows Picnic Area, on Lake Mary Road 1.5 miles farther uplake, features a fishing area with wheelchair access, tables, grills, ramadas, and a paved boat ramp.

**Lakeview Campground** provides the closest camping to the lakes, but sites are too small for trailers. The campground is across the road from the Narrows of Upper Lake Mary (14 miles southeast of Flagstaff); has drinking water and $5/night charge. Lake Mary Road parallels the shores of both lakes; from downtown Flagstaff, head south on Milton Road, turn right on Forest Meadows Ave. just before the I-40 junction, and follow signs for Lake Mary Road. I-40 travelers should take Exit 195B for Flagstaff, then turn left on Forest Meadows Ave. and follow signs. If driving north on I-17, take Exit 339 just before the I-40 junction.

**Marshall Lake**
This small trout lake lies north of Upper Lake Mary. There's a primitive boat ramp. Take the signed Marshall Lake turnoff from Lake Mary Road between Upper and Lower Lake Mary and go 3 miles to Marshall Lake.

**Ashurst Lake**
Fishermen pursue rainbow trout in this small lake. Windsurfers also find it good for their sport. Two campgrounds, both with water and $5/night fee, sit beside the lake: **Ashurst Campground** on the west shore and **Forked Pine** on the east side. There's a boat ramp near the entrance to Ashurst Campground. From Flagstaff, go 18 miles southeast on Lake Mary Road, then turn left 4 miles on paved Forest Route 82E. **Coconino Reservoir,** one mile south on a dirt road, also has a good reputation for rainbow trout.

**Pine Grove Campground**
Entrance to this large campground is opposite the turnoff for Ashurst Lake, 18 miles southeast of Flagstaff; turn west 0.8 mile on Forest Route 651 from Lake Mary Road. Camping area has drinking water, paved roads, and a $7/night charge. Although not on a lake, Pine Grove is within a few miles of Upper Lake Mary, Ashurst, and Mormon lakes.

## Mormon Lake

Mormon settlers arrived on the shores of this lake in 1878 and started a dairy farm. Although it's the largest natural lake in Arizona, average depth is only 10 feet. Water level fluctuates; when it's low there's not much more than a marsh. Anglers, though, have reeled in some sizable bullhead catfish and northern pike. Boats need to be hand-carried to the water. Lake Mary Road parallels the east shore and Mormon Lake Loop Road (Forest Route 90) circles around the west side. **Dairy Springs** and **Double Springs campgrounds** on this loop road both have drinking water and a $5/night fee. From Flagstaff, head 20 miles southeast on Lake Mary Road, then turn right 4 miles on Mormon Lake Loop Road to Dairy Springs, or go 2 miles farther to Double Springs.

**Lakeview Trail** (2 miles roundtrip) climbs a small hill from Double Springs Campground. For an even better view, hike 1,500 feet above Mormon Lake on the 6-mile-roundtrip **Mormon Mountain Trail**; start near Dairy Springs Campground. Learn more about the plants and animals of the area on a self-guided **nature trail,** also beginning near Dairy Springs Campground. **Ledge Trail,** an easy 1.5-mile-roundtrip hike from Dairy Springs Campground, runs out to a ledge overlooking the lake.

**Montezuma Lodge,** tucked in the woods 0.25 mile beyond Dairy Springs Campground, has cabins from early May to the end of Oct., $45 s or d; tel. 354-2220. **Mormon Lake Lodge,** on the loop road at the south end of the lake, serves as a recreational center for many visitors. The lodge offers a variety of rooms and cabins ($26.25-78.75 s or d), a cafe serving breakfast and lunch, a Western-style steak house, saloon, grocery store with fishing and hunting supplies, and a gas station; tel. 774-0462 (Flagstaff) or 354-2227 (local). **Mormon Lake Ski Touring Center,** located across the road, offers trails, rentals, and lessons for cross-country skiers (see "Recreation" in the Flagstaff section). **Munds Park,** 11 miles west of the Mormon Lake Loop Road via unpaved Forest Route 240, has a motel, an RV campground, restaurants, and a service station. Munds Park is at I-17 Exit 322 (18 miles south of Flagstaff).

## Kinnikinick Lake

A good fishing lake for rainbow and brown trout with an occasional catfish. Because the lake lies off the paved roads, you're more likely to find solitude here. Kinnikinick Lake has a free campground and boat ramp but there's no drinking water. From Flagstaff, go southeast 25 miles on Lake Mary Road to just past Mormon Lake, turn left 4 miles on Forest Route 125, then right 4 miles on Forest Route 82.

## LONG VALLEY RANGER DISTRICT

The **Happy Jack Ranger Station,** 13 miles south of Mormon Lake on Lake Mary Road, can advise on camping, hiking, and backroad conditions in the Long Valley Ranger District; open Mon.-Fri. (daily mid-May to late Oct.) 7:30 a.m.-4 p.m.; HC 31, Box 68, Happy Jack, AZ 86024; tel. 527-7371.

## Stoneman Lake

An unusual lake set in a circular depression. Geologists have not decided whether this is an old volcanic crater or a sinkhole. Fishermen do agree that its waters are a hot spot

*turkey* (Meleagris gallopavo)

for yellow perch; some state records have been landed here. Pike and sunfish are also caught. There's a boat ramp but no campground on the lake. To get here, either take the I-17 Stoneman Lake Exit 306 (34 miles south of Flagstaff) and go east 9 miles on mostly paved Forest Route 213, or head south on Lake Mary Road 8 miles past Mormon Lake and turn west 6 miles on Forest Route 213.

### West Clear Creek Wilderness
The transparent waters of this year-round creek wind below pretty canyon walls on their way to the Verde River. Of the many canyons in the Mogollon Rim, west Clear Creek has the greatest length—40 miles. Cross-bedded patterns of ancient sand dunes in the Coconino Sandstone show up clearly on the sheer cliffs. The creek offers excellent hiking, swimming, and fishing, though it may be difficult to entice the trout onto a hook.

Several trails into the canyon provide a choice of dayhikes and overnight trips. Adventurous hikers could spend a week making their way downstream to Bull Pen Ranch or Clear Creek Campground. Or, you can do easy dayhikes in the upper reaches of West Clear Creek and in the tributaries of Willow and Clover creeks; Maxwell Trail provides the easiest access to this area. The warmer months are best for a visit to the canyon. There isn't much of a trail, so you'll be wading and swimming much of the time. In spring, snow melt can raise the stream level too high for hiking, as can very heavy rains anytime. Water is always available from the creek

(purify first). Hikers should keep in mind that trails *out* can be difficult to spot. Exceptions include the Tramway Trail (marked by a steel cable across the creek) and a trail near the powerlines (two sets of high-tension lines shown on Coconino Forest map).

A hike between these points makes a good overnight backpack, but you'll have to cross a deep pool about 150 feet long hemmed in by cliffs (best done in a small inflatable boat). The pool is about 0.7 mile upstream of the powerlines. Many more deep pools, including one 0.25 mile long, have to be crossed if you're going downstream from the powerlines.

To reach the Tramway trailhead (Forest Trail 32), go 8 miles south of Happy Jack on the Lake Mary Road, then 8 miles in on dirt Forest Routes 81 and 81E; keep straight past the turnoff for Maxwell Trail, go about 1.5 miles, then turn left at the fork. Tramway descends steeply less than a mile into the canyon. At the powerlines downstream, a rough trail connects the creek with Forest Route 142A on the south rim. This trailhead is about 18 miles southwest of Clints Well via AZ 87 and Forest Routes 142 and 142A. Roads to the trailheads may be too rough for cars after heavy rains.

### Clints Well
Natural springs here, a rarity in the region, have long been a stopping place for travelers. They were named for Clint Wingfield, an early pioneer. Lake Mary Road (Forest Hwy. 3) meets AZ 87 at Clints Well; turn left for Winslow, right for Payson and Mesa. A small

*beaver* (Castor canadensis)

*view from the Mogollon Rim*

Forest Service campground near the end of Lake Mary Road is free but lacks water. **Long Valley Cafe,** grocery store, and service station are 0.5 mile south on AZ 87.

### Kehl Springs

A small campground near the Mogollon Rim; no drinking water or charge. Aspen and oak trees put on a colorful display in autumn. The Mogollon Rim and great views lie just a short walk away. From Clints Well, go southwest 3.3 miles on AZ 87, then left on Forest Route 147 to the Rim Road (see Coconino Forest Map). These roads tend to be rough and dusty, but should be OK for carefully driven cars in good weather.

### Cinch Hook Snow Recreation Area

Winter storms on the Mogollon Rim transform a large gravel pit into a snowy playground. Families bring their sleds, toboggans, inner tubes, and saucers to slide the slopes of this three-sided bowl. The grades, relatively smooth and free of trees and large rocks, range from very gentle for the toddler set to steep for thrill seekers. The Forest Service clears an area in the center for parking and provides outhouses; foresters may limit the number of visitors on weekends if the slopes get too crowded. The recreation area is just east of the junction of AZ 87 and Forest Highway 9 (General Crook Trail), both paved

highways. Chains or snow tires are strongly recommended for both the highway grades and the snow area.

## BLUE RIDGE RANGER DISTRICT

For camping, fishing, hiking, and back-road information in the Blue Ridge Reservoir area, contact the **Blue Ridge Ranger Station.** The office is open Mon.-Fri. 7:30-noon and 1-4 p.m., and sometimes Sat. in summer; H.C., Box 300, Happy Jack, AZ 86024; tel. 477-2255. From Clints Well, go northeast 10 miles on AZ 87 to the office on the right.

### Blue Ridge Reservoir

Hemmed in by the canyon walls of East Clear Creek, this skinny lake offers good trout fishing (best in spring and autumn) and great scenery. Steep terrain makes road access difficult; small boats can be launched. Trails lead to the water's edge, but fishing is easier from a boat. **Rock Crossing Campground** nearby has good views and ranks as one of the most popular camping spots on the Mogollon Rim. Season runs Memorial Day to Labor Day; drinking water is supplied and there's a $5/night fee. From Clints Well, go northeast 5 miles on AZ 87 and turn right 3 miles on Forest Route 751 to the campground, then another 3 miles to the dam. The smaller **Blue Ridge Campground** has the same season and charge; trailers are limited to 16 feet. From Clints Well, go northeast 9 miles on AZ 87 and turn right one mile on Forest Route 138. Fishermen use Blue Ridge Campground as a base for Blue Ridge Reservoir, East Clear Creek, and Long Lake. You can also camp at Long Lake (no facilities). Catfish and northern pike are the most sought after in Long Lake, but the waters have trout, bass, walleye, and panfish as well.

**East Clear Creek Hiking**

This canyon may not be as spectacular as some other places on the Rim, but the trailheads are easily reached. Deep, clear pools invite swimming or solitary fishing. Rock formations, birds, flowers, and forests make for pleasant hiking. Beavers live and work along the stream, though you'd be lucky to see one of these shy, nocturnal animals. Watch out for snakes; most are harmless, but rattlesnakes live here too. A rough trail follows the canyon, crossing the creek at many places. Crossings shouldn't be more than knee deep, though spring snow melt or heavy rains anytime can make the creek too high for hiking. Long pants will protect your legs from the bramble patches. Water is always available (purify first). This creek has no relation to West Clear Creek. East Clear Creek flows northeast, in the opposite direction, and joins the Little Colorado River near Winslow.

Of all the trailheads, Macks Crossing, only 2 miles from AZ 87, is the easiest to get to. From Clints Well, go 15 miles northeast (4.5 miles past Blue Ridge Ranger Station) and turn right on Enchanted Lane (shown as Forest Route 137 on the Coconino Forest map). After a short distance, turn right on Green Ridge Road and go 0.7 mile. Then turn right again on Juniper which leads to Forest Route 137. The narrow, rocky road descends one mile across a cliff face (no guard rails!) to the creek. Park at the top or at several places on the way down. Near the creek and on the other side, the road is too rough for cars. From Macks Crossing, a good overnight loop hike (15 miles) can be made by going upstream on East Clear Creek to Kinder Cross-

ing Trail, taking this trail to Forest Route 137, and following the forest road back to Macks Crossing. The section of road takes only 2-3 hours of easy walking—at least three times as fast as hiking in the creek! Kinder Crossing Trail also has a west trailhead on Forest Route 95, about 4.5 miles south of Blue Ridge Ranger Station. The trail (#19) is marked by tree blazes down to the creek, then by stone cairns and tree blazes for 0.5 mile downstream along the creek before climbing the other side of the canyon to Forest Route 137. (Note that both the topo and Coconino Forest maps may incorrectly show the trail as simply crossing the creek and climbing the opposite side, instead of following the creek 0.5 mile.) Horse Crossing Trail #20 (see Coconino Forest map) also descends into the canyon from both sides. Kinder Crossing and Horse Crossing trailheads should be distinct and signed. Horse Crossing Trail can be very difficult to spot while walking along the creek; careful attention to a topo map and tree blazes is necessary.

**Knoll Lake**

A rocky island in the middle gives the lake its name. Knoll Lake is located in Leonard Canyon, several miles north of the Mogollon Rim. A campground on a hill overlooks the lake. Camping season lasts from Memorial Day to Labor Day; drinking water and $5/night charge. A road and a hiking trail lead down to the boat ramp. Fishermen come mostly to seek out rainbow trout. Getting here involves about 28 miles of dirt road from either AZ 87 or Woods Canyon Lake off AZ 260.

# CHEVELON RANGER DISTRICT

Foresters at the Chevelon Ranger District of the Apache-Sitgreaves National Forest have information and maps about recreation in the Mogollon Rim country south of Winslow; open daily in summer 8 a.m.-4:30 p.m., then Mon.-Fri. 7:30 a.m.-4 p.m. the rest of the year; the office is 42 miles south of Winslow on AZ 99 (HC 62, Box 600, Winslow, AZ 86047); tel. 289-2471.

*summer camp at Fern Springs on the Mogollon Rim, 1887. The
woman, Mrs. Ella Mearns, was the wife of Fort Verde's surgeon.*

### Chevelon Crossing
This small campground overlooks Chevelon
Creek many miles downstream from Woods
Canyon Lake. The sites remain open most of
the year (elev. 6,200 feet); no water or fee.
Parking is tight; small vehicles will have an
easier time. Best fishing is in the large pools
upstream that harbor rainbow trout. There
are three routes to this out-of-the-way campground: Forest Route 504 is the usual way in;
turn off AZ 260 one mile west of Heber. Or
take AZ 99 south from Winslow and turn left
on Forest Route 504. Or you can take Forest
Route 169 by turning north from Forest Route
300 (the Rim Road) west of Woods Canyon
Lake.

### Chevelon Canyon Lake
This long, skinny reservoir is 12 miles upstream from Chevelon Crossing via Forest

Routes 169 and 169B. See the Apache-Sitgreaves Forest map for other ways of getting
here. The lake offers trophy fishing for rainbow and brown trout; fishermen must use
artificial lures and observe size and catch
limits. With 208 surface acres, it's one of the
larger lakes on the Mogollon Rim. A primitive
campground (elev. 6,400 ft.; no water or fee)
is near the north shore.

### Bear Canyon Lake
Fishermen may use only artificial lures at
this trout lake. The shore is steep and tree-
covered, so it's easier to use boats for fishing.
But you'll have to hand-carry them to the
water. A campground (no water or fee) is near
the north end. From Woods Canyon Lake, go
west 10 miles on Forest Route 300 (the Rim
Road), then turn north 2.5 miles on Forest
Route 89.

## Woods Canyon Lake

This popular lake was one of the first of seven lakes made on the Rim. Camp at either **Aspen Campground** ($8/night) or **Spillway Campground** ($10/night) nearer the lakeshore; both have drinking water. Season runs May to September. A store, which stays open into the fall, has groceries, boat rentals, and motors (only electrics permitted here). **Rocky Point Picnic Area** is on the south side of the lake; free but day-use only. From AZ 260, near the edge of the Mogollon Rim, turn northwest 4 miles on paved Forest Route 300.

## HEBER RANGER DISTRICT

See foresters at the **Heber Ranger Station** for recreation information in the Rim Country southwest of Heber. The office is open Mon.-Sat. 8 a.m.-4:30 p.m. (and Sun. 8 a.m.-4:30 p.m. in summer and the Christmas season). Contact the office at Box 968, Overgaard, AZ 85933; tel. 535-4481. An **information trailer** is often open in summer; it's a short way in on Forest Route 300 (Rim Road) toward Woods Canyon Lake from AZ 260.

## Willow Springs Lake

Fishermen catch mostly rainbow trout in this U-shaped lake. There's a boat ramp but no campground. You may camp in designated dispersed areas nearby or at **Sinkhole Campground**; no water, though a small fee applies in the mid-May to late Sept. season; turn in 0.5 mile on Forest Route 149 from AZ 260. Willow Springs Lake is 3.5 miles farther in. **Rim Campground** has similar facilities and season; it's on Forest Route 300 about one mile west from AZ 260. Forest Route 149 turns off AZ 260 about one mile east of the Rim Road junction and 4 miles west of Canyon Point Campground.

## Canyon Point Campground

This large, easily accessible campground has drinking water and is open mid-May to late September. Sites cost $6/night ($8/night for larger pull-through spaces). **Sinkhole Trail** begins from Loop "B" and leads to a sinkhole (one mile roundtrip). Canyon Point Campground lies just off AZ 260, 5 miles east of the Woods Canyon Lake turnoff.

## Forest Lakes Touring Center

In winter, cross-country skiers come here to use the approximately 35 km of marked and groomed trails and skating lanes atop the Mogollon Rim. The Center also offers rentals, lessons, and tours. Summer visitors can rent canoes for use on the nearby Rim lakes; rentals ($15/day) include paddles and life jackets. For ski or canoe information and winter road conditions, call 535-4047. Stay in cabins year-round at the **Forest Lakes Touring Center**; $36.75-63 d Fri.-Sun. and holidays, $26.25-42 d Mon.-Thurs.; tel. 535-4047. **Forest Lakes Lodge** has motel rooms open all year at $51.70 s, $56.97 d Fri.-Sat. and holidays; $36.93 s, $47.48 d Sun.-Thurs.; tel. 535-4727. Forest Lakes Touring Center is in the village of Forest Lakes on AZ 260 (6.5 miles east of the Woods Canyon Lake turnoff or 36 miles east of Payson).

## Black Canyon Lake

This small trout lake doesn't have a campground, but **Black Canyon Rim** and **Gentry** campgrounds are within a few miles. They stay open all year (when not blocked by snow); no water or fee. From Canyon Point Campground, go east 4.5 miles on AZ 260, turn right 2.5 miles on Forest Route 300, then left 3 miles on Forest Route 86 to Black Canyon Lake; see the Apache-Sitgreaves Forest map.

# SEDONA AND THE RED ROCK COUNTRY

Drifting clouds, towering pinnacles, and sheer canyon walls create a magical setting for the Red Rock Country of Sedona. Monoliths of vivid red sandstone appear as if cast adrift from the Mogollon Rim. Oak Creek, which carved this landscape, glides gracefully through Sedona. A ribbon of green along the creek contrasts sharply with the surrounding desert.

### Early History
The prehistoric Hohokam and Sinagua Indians tilled the soil along Oak Creek for their corn, beans, and squash long before the white men came. American settlers first arrived in the late 1800s to farm and run cattle in the valley. The town dates from 1902, when Theodore Schnebly opened a post office and named it "Sedona" after his wife. Schnebly also built a wagon road up the rim in the same year to haul vegetables and fruit to Flagstaff and lumber back to Sedona; his trips took about 11 hours each way.

### Modern Times
From a tiny agricultural community just 20 years ago, Sedona has developed into a major art center, resort, and spiritual focus. The present population of more than 11,000 includes many retired people, artists, and nature lovers. Sunny skies and pleasant temperatures prevail here. At an elevation of 4,300 feet, Sedona avoids the extremes found in the low desert and high mountains. The community lies 28 miles south of Flagstaff and sprawls haphazardly around the junction of US 89A and AZ 179. You'll hear residents refer to this junction as the "Y" when giving directions.

**Vortexes**

New Age people believe that strong spiritual energies concentrate here in vortexes (psychic-energy points). In the early 1980s, Page Bryant and her otherworldly guide, Albion, identified seven vortexes in the Sedona area. Prominent among these are Bell Rock and Airport Mesa, with their "electric energy" that energizes and inspires visitors, and Cathedral Rock with its calming "magnetic energy." You'll often see altars or medicine wheels made of rocks at the sites. If you'd like to learn more about these energy fields, drop into **The Center in Sedona...All for the New**

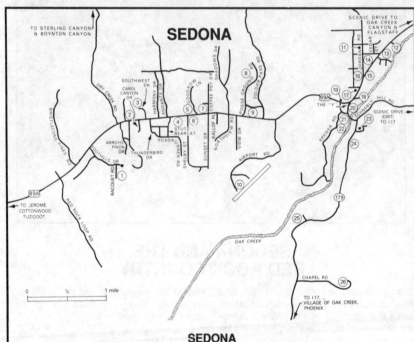

## SEDONA

1. Sedona Racquet Club
2. Fourno's Restaurant; White House Inn; Crystal Magic
3. Hunan Restaurant
4. Food Among the Flowers; The Center in Sedona for the New Age
5. Shugrue's Restaurant
6. Plaza West Mall
7. Coffee Pot Restaurant
8. Sedona Community Park
9. Flicker Shack
10. Sedona Airport
11. public library
12. Sedona Arts Center ("The Barn")
13. Arroyo Roble Hotel
14. Oaxaca Restaurant
15. Orchard Inn and Grill
16. Novaki Restaurant
17. chamber of commerce
18. L'Auberge de Sedona
19. post office
20. Doll Museum; Book Loft; Artesania Plaza; Cedars Resort; The Hideaway
21. Tlaquepaque; Los Abrigados
22. U.S. Forest Service (Sedona Ranger District office)
23. Hozho Center
24. Oak Creek Owl Restaurant
25. Poco Diablo Resort
26. Chapel of the Holy Cross

© MOON PUBLICATIONS

**Age** or at one of the spiritual bookstores; see "Information" below. Sedona tour operators offer Vortex Tours to the sacred sites. Ask the operators about them—each company offers a different perspective; see "Tours" below.

## SIGHTS

In addition to the surrounding scenery, attractions include outstanding art galleries, elegant restaurants, and luxurious resorts. The showiest place in town is **Tlaquepaque** (t'lah-kay-PAH-kay), a recreated village reminiscent of a suburb of Guadalajara, Mexico. Among the tiled courtyards and fountains you'll find restaurants and a great variety of art galleries and crafts shops—no two alike.

South of town, the **Chapel of the Holy Cross** presents a striking sight atop a sandstone ridge; you're welcome to visit 9 a.m.-6 p.m. daily; drive 3 miles south on AZ 179 to Chapel Road and turn left one mile. Meet trout at the **Page Springs Hatchery**, open daily 8 a.m.-4 p.m.; tel. 634-4805. From the "Y," head southeast 10 miles on US 89A, then turn left 2.5 miles on Page Springs Road.

Probably the prettiest sights belong to nature herself. **Oak Creek Canyon**, just up-stream from Sedona, is the best known and easily reached. A 16-mile drive north on US 89A toward Flagstaff takes you through this canyon, past dramatic rock formations and dense forests. In autumn (mid-Oct. to mid-Nov.), turning leaves add to the rich hues of the sculptured canyon walls.

Some of the best panoramas of the Sedona area are seen from **Schnebly Hill Road**; take the signed turnoff from AZ 179 (0.5 mile south of the US 89A jct.); you'll soon leave the pavement and wind high up the cliffs of the Mogollon Rim, reaching Exit 320 of I-17 11.5 miles farther (20 miles south of Flagstaff). Cautiously driven cars can usually make this trip in good weather (call the National Forest office in Sedona for road conditions; tel. 282-4119). Hikers can head into wilderness to explore the West Fork of Oak Creek, Wilson Mountain, Munds Mountain, Pumphouse Wash, and hundreds of other areas.

## ACCOMMODATIONS

Be sure to have reservations if you're coming for the weekend—the popular places fill up fast during the April to Nov. peak season. Prices in Sedona tend to run on the high side

Chapel of the
Holy Cross

then, but drop 10% or so in winter. (Rates listed below apply in peak season, though they can go higher during holidays.) Campers headed for Oak Creek Canyon on a summer weekend should plan to arrive Fri. morning. Most campsites here stay open only in summer, and all close in winter. The Camp Verde and Cottonwood areas to the south offer less expensive motels and year-round camping.

## Bed And Breakfasts

**Cathedral Rock Lodge Bed and Breakfast** is a country house outside town on the Red Rock Loop Road; $68.25-94.50 s or d; tel. 282-7608. **Bed & Breakfast in Red Rock Country** has a music box museum in addition to the usual amenities; 3085 W. Hwy. 89A; $44-55 s or d; tel. 282-3419. **Sipapu Lodge** offers a Southwestern atmosphere in West Sedona; $60.50-88 s or d; tel. 282-2833. **Graham's Bed and Breakfast** is in the Village of Oak Creek, 6 miles south on Hwy. 179; has a pool and spa; $94.50-131.25 s or d (closed in Jan.); tel. 284-1425. **Pumpkinshell Ranch Bed and Breakfast** lies out in the country near Cornville, about 15 miles from Sedona; $50 s or d; tel. 634-4797.

## Motels

From the "Y" in town, head south for **Sedona Motel** (on Hwy. 179 one block south of Hwy. 89A; $59.67-76.25 s or d; tel. 282-7187) and **Quality Inn/King's Ransom** (0.5 mile south on Hwy. 179; $55.25-92.82 s, $77.35-92.82 d; tel. 282-7151 or 800-228-5151).

Head north from the "Y" for **Star Motel** (295 Jordan Road off N. Hwy. 89A; $38.68 s, $44.20 d; tel. 282-3641); **Cedars Resort** (20 N. Hwy. 89A; $44.20-75.14 s or d; tel. 282-7010); **Canyon Portal Motel** (210 N. Hwy. 89A; $44-64 s or d; tel. 282-7125); **Matterhorn Motor Lodge** (301 N. Hwy. 89A; $59.67-66.30 s or d; tel. 282-7176); **Best Western Arroyo Roble Hotel** (400 N. Hwy. 89A; $77.35 s, $88.40 d; tel. 282-4001); and **La Vista Motel** (500 N. Hwy. 89A; $43.10-65.20 s or d; tel. 282-7301).

Head west from the "Y" for **Sky Ranch Lodge** (on Airport Road; $49.73 s, $55.25 d; tel. 282-6400); **Black Forest House** (50 Willow Way, off W. Hwy. 89A; $55.25-68.51 s or d; tel. 282-2835/9416); **Sugar Loaf Lodge** (1870 W. Hwy. 89A; $42-66.30 s or d; tel. 282-9451); **Las Casitas Apartments** (665 Sunset Dr.; $66.30/night s or d, $387/week s or d; tel. 282-2644. **Sunset Inn Sedona** (2545 W. Hwy. 89A; $43.10 s, $49.73 d; tel. 282-1533); and **White House Inn** (2986 W. Hwy. 89A; $44.20-55.25 s or d; tel. 282-6680).

The Village of Oak Creek, 6 miles south on Hwy. 179, has the **Bell Rock Inn** (6246 Hwy. 179; $44.31-94.95 s or d; tel. 282-4161) and **Quail Ridge Resort Apartments** (120 Canyon Circle Dr.; $46.42-86.51 s or d (a 2- or 3-day minimum applies on weekends); tel. 284-9327).

## Sedona Resorts

**Poco Diablo** ("Little Devil") **Resort** features all the amenities: fireplaces, a fine restaurant, swimming pools, jacuzzis, tennis and racquetball courts, 9-hole golf course, etc.; rates run $105-260 d. Poco Diablo is 2 miles south on Hwy. 179 from Hwy. 89A; tel. 282-7333 (local), (800) 352-5710 in Arizona, or tel. (800) 528-4275 out of state. **L'Auberge de Sedona** offers luxurious cottages in a French country inn atmosphere; rates of $276-470 include breakfast and six-course French dinners; rooms in the Lodge at L'Auberge run $132.60-154.70 s or d; rooms at Orchards at L'Auberge cost $99.45-149.18; located beside Oak Creek at 301 Little Lane (off N. Hwy. 89A one block north of Hwy. 179); tel. 282-7131 or (800) 272-6777. The Spanish-style **Los Abrigados** resort, next to Tlaquepaque, features an excellent restaurant, Sedona Health Spa, pool, tennis courts, and spacious accommodations; $160-238 s or d; 160 Portal Lane; tel. 282-1777, (800) 822-2525 in Arizona, (800) 521-3131 nationally, or (800) 521-1182 Canada. **Enchantment** has 12 tennis courts, a spa and fitness center, swimming pools, and a variety of luxury accommodations at 525 Boynton Canyon Road; $180-460 d European plan or $240-580 d modified American plan; tel. 282-2900, (800) 843-1691 in Arizona, or (800) 826-4180 out of state.

**Oak Creek Canyon Resorts**
You'll find rustic cabins and plush lodges tucked back in the woods within Oak Creek Canyon. These resorts, listed in the order you'll find them on a drive north from Sedona, stay open all year except as noted. **Lomacasi Cottages** (open Feb. 1 to Dec. 1; $60.78-105 s or d; tel. 282-7912) and **Red Rock Lodge** ($44.20-138.13 s or d; tel. 282-3591) lie just north of Sedona on N. Hwy. 89A. **Briar Patch Inn** has rooms ($100.23 s or d) and a variety of cottages ($125.55-136.10 s or d) 3 miles north on Hwy. 89A; tel. 282-2342. **Oak Creek Terrace Resort,** 4.5 miles north of Sedona on Hwy. 89A, has motel rooms ($63.30-79.13 s or d) and cabins ($93.90-162.47 s or d); tel. 282-3562. **Slide Rock Lodge** is 6 miles north of Sedona on Hwy. 89A, just south of the famous Slide Rock swimming area; rooms cost $52.75-79.13 s or d, cabins are $110.78-121.33 s or d; tel. 282-3531. **Garland's Oak Creek Lodge** is 8 miles north of town on Hwy. 89A; open April 1 to mid-Nov.; rates include family-style meals (breakfast and dinner): $111.60 s, $153.60 d for a small cabin, $135.60 s or $177.60 d for a large cabin; tel. 282-3343. **Junipine Resort** features modern and spacious accommodations and a restaurant 8.3 miles north of Sedona on Hwy. 89A; $134-158 s or d, $204-236 up to four people; tel. 282-3375, (800) 842-2121 in Arizona, or (800) 542-8484 out of state. **Forest Houses Resort** has large housekeeping units 9.4 miles north of Sedona on Hwy. 89A; $79.13-94.95 s or d (a 5-day minimum stay applies in summer); closed Jan. 1-March 15; tel. 282-2999. **Don Hoel's Cabins** are 9.5 miles north of town on Hwy. 89A; the rustic cabins start at $40.10 s or d; closed Jan.; tel. 282-3560.

**Campgrounds**
Some of the prettiest places lie in Oak Creek Canyon. The U.S. Forest Service maintains five campgrounds here, all on Hwy 89A (mileages are north of Sedona): **Manzanita** (6 miles), **Banjo Bill** (8 miles), **Bootlegger** (8.8 miles), **Cave Spring** (11.5 miles), and **Pine Flat** (12.5 miles). All except Bootlegger have drinking water, but none have hookups or

showers. Trailers and large RVs (up to 28 feet) have adequate room only in Cave Spring and Pine Flat campgrounds. The campgrounds, all $8/night, begin to open mid-March and start to close early Sept.; some may stay open later, call to check. Dispersed camping is forbidden in Oak Creek Canyon, but you can find a spot in the national forests elsewhere. The Sedona Ranger Station can tell you about camping and hiking in the area; tel. 282-4119.

**Rancho Sedona RV Park** offers shaded sites along Oak Creek all year for tents ($12.10) and RVs ($15.13 no hookups, $20.08 w/hookups); has showers and laundry; centrally located 0.5 mile south on Hwy. 179 from Hwy. 89A, then left 3 blocks on Schnebly Hill Road; tel. 282-7255. **Hawkeye Red Rock RV Park** also has shaded sites year-round along Oak Creek for tents ($11.10) and RVs ($11.10 no hookups, $18.87 w/hookups); has showers and laundry; on the north edge of uptown Sedona at 40 Art Barn Road; tel. 282-2222. **Oak Creek Mobilodge** is one mile south on Hwy. 179 from Hwy. 89A; $15 RV w/hookups (no tents); tel. 282-7701.

# FOOD

**American And Continental**
You can enjoy some of Arizona's finest dining in Sedona. Reservations are advised at the more expensive places. The **Oak Creek Owl** features American and continental cuisine in an elegant atmosphere with excellent service; the foyer is a small art gallery; open daily for lunch and dinner (mod. to exp.); 0.5 mile south on Hwy. 179 from Hwy. 89A; tel. 282-3532. **Rene at Tlaquepaque** serves outstanding American and continental cuisine in a French Provincial atmosphere; open for lunch and dinner daily except Tues. and the month of Jan. (mod.); in Tlaquepaque, 0.3 mile south on Hwy. 179 from Hwy. 89A; tel. 282-9225. **L'Auberge de Sedona** is an elegant French restaurant; open daily for breakfast, lunch, dinner, and a Sunday brunch (very exp.); 301 Little Lane (off N. Hwy. 89A one block north of Hwy. 179); tel. 282-1667.

The **Gourmet Club of Sedona** specializes in German-French food; open Tues.-Sat. for dinner at 50 Willow Way in West Sedona; tel. 282-2835/9416. **Los Abrigados** resort's Canyon Rose dining room serves American and continental cuisine daily for breakfast, lunch, and dinner (mod.-exp.); the Grand Brunch is claimed to be "the finest Sunday brunch presentation in all of Arizona" (open 10 a.m.-2 p.m.; $20.28 adult); 160 Portal Lane (0.2 mile south on Hwy. 179 from Hwy. 89A); tel. 282-1777. The Willows dining room in **Poco Diablo Resort** offers an extensive menu of American and Continental dishes daily for breakfast, lunch, and dinner (mod.-exp.); there's a daily buffet, but the Sunday brunch buffet offers overwhelming choices (open 10:30 a.m.-2:30 p.m.; $16 adult); located 2 miles south on Hwy. 179 from Hwy. 89A. The **Enchantment** resort serves fine Continental cuisine and has beautiful canyon views; open daily for breakfast, lunch, and dinner (very exp.); 525 Boynton Canyon, off Dry Creek Road; tel. 282-2900. **Humphrey's** has earned fame for its excellent seafood and steaks; open daily for lunch and dinner (mod.-exp.); 1405 W. Hwy. 89A; tel. 282-7745. **Eat Your Heart Out** is a favorite place for lunch and good for dinner too; open daily for lunch and dinner (inexp.-mod.); 350 Jordan Road off N. Hwy. 89A; tel. 282-1471. **Shugrue's** features steak and seafood among their other specialties; open daily for breakfast (except Mon.), lunch, and dinner (mod.); 2250 W. Hwy. 89A; tel. 282-2943. **Fournos** offers a varied continental and seafood menu (some Greek dishes); usually open Sun. for brunch, Fri. for lunch, and Thurs.-Sat. for dinner (mod.); 3000 W. Hwy. 89A; tel. 282-3331. The **Orchards American Grill at L'Auberge** specializes in unusual regional American fare; open daily for breakfast, lunch, and dinner (mod.); 254 N. Hwy. 89A; tel. 282-7131.

**American Cafes**
If you're looking for a good inexpensive meal, try the **Prickly Pear of Sedona** for a varied selection of meat, pasta, and vegetarian dishes; open daily except Mon. for lunch and dinner at 2611 W. Hwy. 89A; tel. 282-3378.

**Coffee Pot Restaurant** has 101 omelets on the menu and serves breakfasts all day; open daily for breakfast, lunch, and dinner at 2050 W. Hwy. 89A; tel. 282-6626. **Food Among the Flowers** serves tasty vegetarian natural foods; open daily except Tues. for breakfast, lunch, and dinner; 2445 W. Hwy. 89A; tel. 282-2334. **The Sedona Airport Restaurant** offers hearty eating as well as good views atop Airport Mesa; open daily for breakfast, lunch, and dinner; take Airport Road off Hwy. 89A; tel. 282-3576. The **Novaki**, despite its Hopi Indian name, serves American breakfasts and lunches daily (inexp.); N. Hwy. 89A at Jordan Road; tel. 282-1666. The **Hitching Post Restaurant** is open daily for breakfast, lunch, and dinner in the Uptown Mall, 269 N. Hwy. 89A; tel. 282-7761. **White House Inn** has a small restaurant open 24 hours at 2986 W. Hwy. 89A; tel. 282-6680. **Rainbow's End Restaurant** is a small cafe with generous servings; open Mon.-Sat. for lunch and dinner at 3635 W. Hwy. 89A; tel. 282-1593.

**Mexican**
**El Rincon Restaurante Mexicano,** in Tlaquepaque, serves excellent Mexican/Navajo-inspired food; open Tues-Sat. for lunch and dinner, and Sun. for lunch (inexp.-mod.); tel. 282-4648. The **Oaxaca Restaurante** offers Mexican and American dining; open daily for breakfast, lunch, and dinner (inexp.-mod.); 231 N. Hwy. 89A; tel. 282-4179. At both restaurants, you can enjoy the Mexican atmosphere inside or dine in the patio.

**Italian**
**The Hideaway,** overlooking Oak Creek, has good Italian food—spaghetti, fettuccini, manicotti, pizza, etc.; open daily for lunch and dinner (inexp.) in Country Square shopping center (on Hwy. 179, 0.2 mile south of Hwy. 89A); tel. 282-4204. **Spices Italian Cafe** offers tasty cuisine from Italy too; open Mon.-Fri. for lunch and daily for dinner (inexp.); 2321 W. Hwy. 89A; tel. 282-5219. **D.J.'s Pizza Hop** makes tasty pizza in a 1950s setting; open daily except Thurs. for lunch and dinner in Artesania Plaza, 251 Hwy. 179; tel. 282-4229.

**Chinese**

The **Hunan** is open for lunch and dinner daily except Mon. (inexp.-mod.); 55 Sinagua Dr. (go 3 miles west on Hwy. 89A from the "Y" and follow signs); tel. 282-3118.

**Out-of-town Dining**

Some of the resorts in Oak Creek Canyon offer fine dining to the public; be sure to make reservations for dinner before coming out. **Garland's Oak Creek Lodge** serves memorable meals for breakfast and dinner during their April to mid-Nov. season (exp.); 8 miles north of Sedona on Hwy. 89A; tel. 282-3343. The **Junipine Resort** serves Southwestern and continental fare Mon.-Sat. for breakfast, lunch, and dinner, and Sun. for breakfast and lunch (mod.-exp.); 8.3 miles north of Sedona on Hwy. 89A; tel. 282-3375.

The Village of Oak Creek, on Hwy. 179 about midway between Sedona and I-17, has several good places to eat: **Bell Rock Inn** serves American food daily for breakfast, lunch, and dinner (inexp.-mod.); 6246 Hwy. 179; tel. 282-4161. **Wild Turkey Inn** is an informal American restaurant open daily for lunch and dinner (inexp.-mod.); 6375 Hwy. 179; tel. 284-1604. **The Happy Cooker** cafe is open daily for breakfast and lunch and Mon.-Sat. for dinner (inexp.); the Cooker features home-style food and it claims to have the best hamburger in Sedona; Castle Rock Plaza, 6446 Hwy. 179; tel. 284-2240. **La Paloma Mexican Restaurant,** also in Castle Rock Plaza, is open Mon.-Sat. for lunch and dinner; tel. 284-2151. Buy breakfast, sandwiches, and baked goodies at **Sedona Bakery** (closed Sun.) in Castle Rock Plaza. **Mandarin House II** serves good Chinese food; open daily for lunch and dinner at 6486 Hwy. 179; tel. 284-9088.

The Western-style **Page Springs Restaurant** overlooks Oak Creek downstream from Sedona; steak, seafood, and chicken dominate the menu (inexp.-mod.); open daily for lunch and dinner; go southwest 10 miles on Hwy. 89A (from the "Y"), then turn left 2.5 miles on Page Springs Road; tel. 634-9954. During the day (8 a.m.-4 p.m.) you may visit the trout at **Page Springs Hatchery** across the road. **Vince's Little Star** is a cozy Italian restaurant in downtown Cornville; open Tues.-Sat. for dinner (inexp.-mod.); from the Page Springs Restaurant, continue 4 miles to the end of the road, then turn right one mile (or take the I-17 Cornville exit and go northwest 9 miles); tel. 634-4063 (reservations recommended).

## OTHER PRACTICALITIES

**Entertainment**

See the latest flicks at the **Flicker Shack,** located in a shopping center on W. Hwy. 89A (1.5 miles west of the "Y"); tel. 282-3777. You might catch a concert or play at the **Sedona Arts Center** ("The Barn") at N. Hwy. 89A and Art Barn Road on the north edge of town; tel. 282-3809. To get the latest on Sedona's music, events, and nightlife, check the weekly *Sedona Times* or *Red Rock News* newspapers.

**Events**

Sedona goes Irish every March for a **St. Patrick's Day Parade,** said to be the largest in the West. Clowns, bands, and floats march through town in a noisy celebration. A Queen of the Green receives her crown in a gala coronation ball prior to the big day. **Hopi Days,** in April, brings Hopi Indians to town for dances, food, arts, and crafts. Fireworks light the sky on **July Fourth.** Other annual Sedona events celebrate music and the arts: **Chamber Music Festival** in June; **Pops Concert in the Park** in Sept.; **Jazz on the Rocks** festival in Sept.; **Fiesta del Tlaquepaque** (mariachi bands, Native American dances, food, art, and crafts) on the first weekend in Oct.; and the **Apple Festival** (entertainment, arts and crafts, and food at Slide Rock State Park) in October. More than 5,000 candle-lit luminarias brighten Tlaquepaque during the **Festival of Lights** in Dec.; usually held on the second Sat. before Christmas. **Christmas caroling** takes place at Tlaquepaque on the following day.

### Recreation

**Slide Rock State Park,** 6.5 miles north of Sedona in Oak Creek Canyon, attracts many swimmers; the fun is in sliding through a natural chute (wear jeans, as this is hard on the seat!). Try to avoid summer weekends when the spot becomes crowded. Other attractions of the park's 55 acres include a half-mile trail along the creek, picnicking, and the apple orchard; a snack bar sells apple juice and sandwiches (may close in winter). Slide Rock State Park is open all year for day-use only; tel. 282-3034. **Grasshopper Point** is another natural swimming hole, 2 miles north of town. **Lions Park Picnic Area/ Sedona Community Park** has picnic tables, playground, and ballfields on Posse Ground Road, 0.3 mile north of Hwy. 89A. The **Sedona Racquet Club** has tennis and racquetball courts, year-round pool, jacuzzi, weight room, and snack bar on Racquet Road (3.8 miles west on Hwy. 89A from the "Y," south on Foothills Dr., then right on Racquet Road;); tel. 282-5783/4197. **Poco Diablo Resort** offers tennis courts (call and ask for the tennis shop to make reservations) and a 9-hole golf course; the resort is 2 miles south of town on Hwy. 179; tel. 282-7333. **Village of Oak Creek Country Club** has an 18-hole course; go 6.5 miles south of the "Y" on Hwy. 179, then right on Bell Rock Road; tel. 284-1660. **Sedona Golf Resort** also has an 18-hole course open to the public in Village of Oak Creek; 7256 Hwy. 179; tel. 284-9355 (258-1443 in Phoenix). **Canyon Mesa Country Club** offers a 9-hole course at 500 Jacks Canyon Road in Village of Oak Creek; tel. 284-2176.

Fishermen can pull rainbow trout from Oak Creek. **Rainbow Trout Farm** offers easier fishing but has a charge; equipment is supplied and no license is needed; located 3 miles north of Sedona in Oak Creek Canyon; open daily 7:30 a.m.-5:30 p.m. all year; tel. 282-3379. **Kachina Riding Stables** offers trail rides year-round in the Red Rock Country around Sedona; the stables are 6 miles southwest of town off lower Red Rock Loop Road; $15/1 hour, $25/2 hours, $75-80/all day; breakfast, steak, and pack trips can be arranged too; call 282-7252 for directions and reservations.

### Services

The **post office** is conveniently located on Hwy. 89A just west of the "Y." Nearest hospital is the **Marcus Lawrence Hospital** at 202 S. Willard in Cottonwood, 19 miles southwest of Sedona; tel. 282-1831 or 634-2251. For **emergencies** (fire, police, ambulance) call 911.

*Slide Rock in Oak Creek Canyon*

 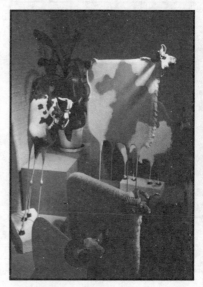

art in Tlaquepaque galleries

## Shopping

What Sedona lacks in size as an art center, compared with Santa Fe or Scottsdale, it strives to make up for in higher quality. Its 25 or so art galleries display an impressive range of original art. Southwestern themes run through much of the work—in colors, forms, Indian motifs, and cowboy legends. Most of the art galleries lie along the first half-mile of Hwy. 179 south of the "Y," and in "Old Town," the first half-mile of Hwy. 89A north of the "Y." Tlaquepaque (0.3 mile south on Hwy. 179 from Hwy. 89A) makes a good starting point for a trip into Sedona's art world. Fountains, sycamore-shaded courtyards, and the Spanish-Colonial architecture create a delightful atmosphere. Even nonshoppers will enjoy exploring the many shops and galleries here, no two alike.

Many of Sedona's cultural activities center on the **Sedona Arts Center,** on the north edge of town at N. Hwy. 89A and Art Barn Road. Changing art exhibits can be seen Tues.-Sat. 10:30 a.m.-4:30 p.m. and Sun. 1:30-4:30 p.m. (closed last week of Dec. and first week of Jan.); free. A gift shop offers work by local artists. Sedona Arts Center often schedules concerts, plays, and other evening events; tel. 282-3809.

## Information

**Sedona-Oak Creek Canyon Chamber of Commerce** has a good supply of literature and information on sights, services, and coming events; open Mon.-Sat. 9 a.m.-5 p.m. and Sun. 10 a.m.-4 p.m.; located at the corner of N. Hwy. 89A and Forest Road, just north of the "Y" (Box 478, Sedona, AZ 86336); tel. 282-7722 or (800) 288-7336. The **Sedona Ranger District** office of the U.S. Forest Service can tell you of Indian ruins, camping, hiking, and road conditions in the National Forests surrounding Sedona; trail descriptions, forest maps, and books are available; open Mon.-Fri. 7:30 a.m.-4:30 p.m.; located at 250 Brewer Road (take the street opposite the post office on W. Hwy. 89A); Box 300, Sedona, AZ 86336; tel. 282-4119.

*Oak Creek near Sedona*

**Sedona Public Library** is open Mon.-Sat. (call for hours); located on Jordan Road off N. Hwy. 89A; tel. 282-7714. **Sedona Lodging Information** provides accommodation information and reservations for many of the places in the Sedona area; tel. 282-1117. The latest on dining, nightlife, art exhibits, events, and local news is listed in the weekly *Sedona Times* and *Red Rock News*.

**The Worm Books & Music** has an excellent selection of regional, New Age, general reading, and audio tapes at 207 N. Hwy. 89A; tel. 282-3471. **The Book Loft** features both new and used books at 175 Hwy. 179; tel. 282-5173. New Age bookstores include **The Eye of the Vortex** (1405 W. Hwy. 89A; tel. 282-5614); **Crystal Magic** (2978 W. Hwy. 89A; tel. 282-1622); and **Golden Word Book Centre** (3150 W. Hwy. 89A; tel. 282-2688). **The Center in Sedona...All for the New Age** serves residents and visitors interested in metaphysics with information of events and services; open daily at 2445 Hwy. 89A; tel. 282-1949.

**Tours**

Four companies offer jeep trips into the rugged backcountry. The first two listed offer relatively gentle rides and the other pair has some serious four-wheeling on very difficult roads. **Time Expeditions** specializes in trips to prehistoric Indian ruins; its vortex tours approach the subject from a scientific background; a 2½-hour tour to a well-preserved cliff dwelling costs $35/person (other trips can be arranged too); tel. 282-2137. **Sedona Adventures** offers "Jeepster" touring with a mix of backcountry rides and hiking ($24-29 for 2-hour trips); vortex "self-discovery" tours and "pampered camping" overnight trips are offered too; tel. 282-4114. **Pink Jeep Tours** (tel. 282-5000), and **Sedona Red Rock Jeep Tours** (tel. 282-2026) offer a variety of scenic, historic, and vortex trips at similar prices.

For the best views, take a flight with **Air Sedona**; short local tours cost $10-20/person (minimum 2); longer flights take in the Grand Canyon and Havasupai at $70/person (minimum 3), or the Grand Canyon and Havasupai, Meteor Crater, Canyon de Chelly, Monument Valley, and Lake Powell at $150/person (minimum 3); other destinations can be arranged too; tel. 282-7935. **Arizona Helicopter Adventures** offers five tours of the Sedona area lasting 10-60 minutes at rates of $28.50-225 depending on flight time and number of passengers; Sedona Airport; tel. 282-0904. Fly high in a balloon with **The Inflated Ego** (tel. 284-9483) or **Northern Light Balloon Expeditions** (tel. 282-2274).

**Transport**

**Susie's Trolley** provides a narrated tour through town past the shopping areas, motels, and RV parks, taking about an hour for a roundtrip; closed in winter; all-day-ticket fares are $4 adult, $1 children; tel. 284-0549; pick up a schedule from the chamber of commerce.

For a taxi, call **Bob's Taxi Service**; tel. 282-1234/8777. **Cars** can be rented at the airport or in town; see the Yellow Pages.

**Nava-Hopi** provides bus service twice daily north to Flagstaff and south to Phoenix and Sky Harbor Airport; from the Texaco Service Station at the "Y,"; tel. 282-4162 or (800) 892-8687. **Sedona Shuttle** goes three times daily south to Camp Verde, Cottonwood, Phoenix, and Sky Harbor Airport ($30 one way, $50 roundtrip) and twice daily north to Flagstaff ($10 one way); the shuttle leaves from the Sedona Texaco Station at the "Y" and from Bell Rock Inn in Village of Oak Creek; tel. 282-2066.

**Air Sedona** flies four times daily to Phoenix ($40 one way); tel. 282-7935 or (800) 228-7654 in Arizona. Sedona's airport sits atop a mesa southwest of town; take Airport Road from W. Hwy. 89A.

## HIKING IN THE SEDONA AREA

Rugged canyons, delicate natural arches, and solitude await those who venture into the backcountry. Much of this land remains unchanged from prehistoric times. Hiking possibilities have almost no limit—you can venture on easy dayhikes or chart a week-long trek across the wilderness. Spring and autumn have the most pleasant temperatures, but hiking is possible all year. Summer visitors can avoid the 100°-plus temperatures in the desert by getting an early start and heading for the higher country; winter hikers keep to the desert and canyon areas when snow blocks trails in the ponderosa pine forests above.

Best source of information for backcountry travel is the U.S Forest Service office in Sedona (250 Brewer Road; tel. 282-4119). Their Coconino Forest map ($2) shows back roads and many of the trails. Look in libraries for the out-of-print *Oak Creek Canyon and the Red Rock Country of Arizona* by Stewart Aitchison; this handy-sized guide has a good introduction and descriptions of hiking trails and back roads. The following six hikes will acquaint you with this colorful land. The first five lie within the **Red Rock/Secret Mountain Wilderness** area; no mechanized vehicles allowed.

### Devil's Bridge Trail #120
From the trailhead (elev. 4,600 feet), a well-graded path climbs steadily through juniper, pinyon pine, Arizona cypress, and manzanita to the base of a long natural arch. You can't see the bridge until you're almost there, but when you arrive, the majestic sweep of the arch and fine views of distant canyons and mountains reward your effort. The 1.8-mile-roundtrip hike has an elevation gain of 400 feet. A smaller trail forks off to the right about 330 feet before the bridge and climbs steeply to the top of the arch. Devil's Bridge lies northwest of Sedona on the other side of a ridge. From the "Y" in Sedona, head west 3.1 miles on US 89A, turn right 2.1 miles on paved Dry Creek Road (Forest Route 152), then turn right 1.2 miles on dirt Sterling Canyon Road (Forest Route 152C). Sterling Canyon Road is not recommended during wet weather and may be too rough for cars at any time; check with the Forest Service. The trailhead should be signed. The first part of the trail follows a badly eroded jeep road.

### Vultee Arch Trail #22
This hike follows Sterling Canyon upstream to a small natural bridge visible in the sandstone to the north. Though the canyon is dry most of the time, Arizona cypress, sycamore, ponderosa pine, and other trees and plants find it to their liking. Trailhead elevation is 4,800 feet, and you'll be climbing 400 feet higher on the 3.4-mile-roundtrip trail. Carry some water, especially if it's a hot day. The arch and a bronze plaque at the end of the trail commemorate aircraft designer Gerard Vultee and his wife Sylvia, who died when their plane hit East Pocket Mesa to the north during a snowstorm on Jan. 29, 1938. Trailhead for Vultee Arch is at the end of Sterling Canyon Road; follow directions for Devil's Bridge Trail, but continue 3 miles past that turnoff to road's end.

### Sterling Pass Trail #46
A hike over Sterling Pass (elev. 5,960 feet) from Oak Creek Canyon will also take you to Vultee Arch. Begin from the west side of US

89A, 6 miles north of Sedona; the trailhead (elev. 4,840 feet) is a short way south of Slide Rock Lodge and 300 feet north of Manzanita Campground. The trail ascends through a small canyon to the pass, then drops into Sterling Canyon and joins Vultee Arch Trail; 2.4 miles one way. This approach to Vultee Arch avoids the rough drive on Sterling Canyon Road to reach the Vultee Arch Trailhead.

VICINITY OF SEDONA

## Wilson Mountain Trail #10

Energetic hikers will enjoy this trail from the bottom of Oak Creek Canyon to the top of Wilson Mountain. A stiff 2,300-foot climb is followed by a long, level stretch extending to the north edge of the flat-topped mountain. Total trail length is 9 miles roundtrip, or 6 miles roundtrip if you turn around where the trail levels off on the summit plateau. Two very different trails, South Wilson and North Wilson, start from the bottom (elev. 4,600 feet), meet partway up on First Bench, then continue as one trail to the top. South Wilson Trail begins at the north end of Midgley Bridge (1.9 miles north of the "Y" on US 89A) and switchbacks through Arizona cypress, juniper, pinyon pine, agave, yucca, and other sun-loving plants. Higher up, manzanita, shrub live oak, and other chaparral-zone plants become more common. North Wilson Trail, on the other hand, climbs steeply through a cool canyon filled with tall ponderosa pine and Douglas fir; trailhead is on US 89A just north of Encinoso picnic area (5.3 miles north of the "Y"). A stone cairn marks the junction of the trails at First Bench.

This large, level area dates from long ago, when a piece of Wilson Mountain's summit broke off and slid partway down. More climbing takes you to the rim of Wilson Mountain; keep right where the trail forks and follow the path north to some spectacular viewpoints. From the northernmost overlook, tiny Vultee Arch can be seen far below across Sterling Canyon. Beyond, on the horizon, stand the San Francisco Peaks. Small meadows and forests of ponderosa pine and Gambel oak cover the large expanse of Wilson's summit. Carry 2-3 quarts of water. Ignore old trail descriptions of South Wilson Trail heading up Wilson Canyon; the new route leaves the canyon directly from the trailhead near Midgley Bridge.

Wilson Canyon and Mountain get their name from Richard Wilson, a bear hunter who lost to a grizzly in June 1885. Wilson's bear gun was being repaired on the day he spotted grizzly tracks in Oak Creek Canyon, but he set out after the bear anyway with a smaller rifle. Nine days later, horsemen found Wilson's badly mauled body up what's now Wilson Canyon.

## East Pocket (A.B. Young) Trail #100

This well-graded trail climbs out of Oak Creek Canyon to East Pocket Mesa, located north of Wilson Mountain. The trail makes more than 30 switchbacks to reach the ponderosa pine-forested rim, a 1,600-foot climb and 3.2 miles roundtrip. From the rim, the trail climbs gently to East Pocket Knob Lookout Tower, another 0.8 mile and 400 feet higher. You can enjoy the good views of Oak Creek Canyon on the way up, from the rim, and atop the lookout tower (open during the fire season in summer). The trailhead (elev. 5,200 feet) is across Oak Creek from Bootlegger Campground (just north of Milepost 383 on US 89A, 8.8 miles north of Sedona). Wade or hop stones across the creek (don't cross if flooded) to a dirt road paralleling the bank, and look for a well-used trail climbing the slope. After leaving the woodlands along Oak Creek, the trail ascends through chaparral vegetation. Allow 3-4 hours and carry 1-2 quarts of water. Cattlemen built the trail in the 1880s to bring their herds to pasture. The Civilian Conservation Corps under A.B. Young improved it in the 1930s.

## West Fork Trail #108

An easy, almost level trail extends about 2.5 miles upstream through the narrow canyon of West Fork, a major tributary of Oak Creek. Sheer canyon walls rising hundreds of feet, luxuriant vegetation, and the clear stream make this an idyllic spot. Because of the numbers and diversity of plant and animal species here, the lower 6 miles of the canyon has a "Research Natural Area" designation. The stream, which you'll be crossing many times, is usually only ankle deep for several miles. Carry water and plenty of film. Don't camp or build fires in the Natural Area. Finding the trailhead takes some effort, but it's there. Look for two large wood posts with a heavy chain between them on the west side of US 89A midway between Mileposts 384 and 385 (10 miles north of Sedona). A day-use parking area is 0.15 mile north of the entrance. An old asphalt-paved trail descends to Oak Creek, then a dirt trail continues past the ruins of Mayhew's Lodge and into West Fork Canyon.

Although most visitors come for a leisurely dayhike, strong hikers can travel the entire 14-mile length of West Fork canyon in one day if they have an early start and a car shuttle. If making the 14-mile trip, start at the upstream trailhead, where Forest Route 231 (Woody Mountain Road) crosses West Fork. (Woody Mountain Road begins as a turnoff from Business I-40, about 2 miles west of Flagstaff.) Only the lower end of the canyon has a trail; in other parts you'll be walking in the streambed or clambering over boulders. The first 6 miles from the upper trailhead is usually dry, but this stretch is followed by a series of deep pools that may require swimming. You should avoid any hiking in the canyon after heavy rains because of possible flooding. The rough terrain and deep pools make backpacking difficult, so most people make the trip as a long dayhike.

### Lower Pumphouse Wash
Some boulder-hopping and wading here will take you through a beautiful pristine canyon. Though millions of motorists have crossed the Pumphouse Wash Bridge on their drive through Oak Creek Canyon, hardly any have ventured into this little tributary canyon. The 3.5-mile (one way) hike is best done from May to Oct., after the spring snow melt is over. You'll want to choose a warm, sunny day to enjoy the nifty swimming holes on the way. There's no trail in the canyon; the route involves walking over boulders, wading, and possibly some swimming. Allow 4 hours for the trip—more if you'll be playing in the water a lot. The lower trailhead is Pumphouse Wash Bridge at the bottom of the switchbacks on US 89A (13.5 miles north of Sedona); upper trailhead is an unsigned pulloff on the east side of US 89A about 300 feet south of Milepost 391 (16.5 miles north of Sedona). From the upper trailhead, go east 0.5 mile away from the highway (no trail; climb over the fence) and descend the moderate slope into Pumphouse Wash. Be alert for rattlesnakes on the rim, though they're rarely seen in the canyon. At the bottom, turn right (downstream) until you come to the highway bridge, a total descent of 800 feet. Look for signs of beaver houses dug into the streambanks. You'll recognize the Coconino Sandstone that forms the canyon's cliffs by its long, graceful crossbeds; this rock was once sand dunes in a long-ago desert.

## SYCAMORE CANYON WILDERNESS

Imagine Oak Creek Canyon without the highway, resorts, campgrounds, and town of Sedona. That's what Sycamore Canyon is, a twisting slash in the earth 21 miles long and up to 7 miles wide. As the crow flies, Sycamore Canyon is about 15 miles west of Oak Creek Canyon. A wilderness designation protects the canyon; only hikers and horseback riders may descend into its depths. Several trails wind down to Sycamore Creek, mostly from the east side, but not a single road! Motorists may enjoy the sweeping view from Sycamore Point on the west rim, approached from Williams (see p. 172). Sycamore Canyon Wilderness is under the confusing jurisdiction of three different national forests: Coconino, Kaibab, and Prescott. The ranger station in Sedona (Coconino National Forest) is your best source of information for trail conditions, trailhead access, and water sources; 250 Brewer Road.; tel. 282-4119. The May 1985 issue of *Arizona Highways* magazine has a story of a Sycamore Canyon hike and beautiful photos.

# ALONG THE VERDE RIVER

Below the cream- and red-colored cliffs of the Mogollon Rim, the Verde (Spanish for "green") River brings life to its broad desert valley. The waters come from narrow canyons of Oak Creek, Wet and Dry Beaver creeks, West Clear Creek, Sycamore Creek, and other streams. Prehistoric Indians made camps in the area, finding a great variety of wild plant foods and game between the 3,000-foot elevation of the lower valley and the Rim country 4,000 feet higher. From about A.D. 600 to 700, Indian groups began cultivating the Verde Valley, taking advantage of the good climate, fertile lands, and abundant water. Trade and contacts with the Hohokam culture to the south also aided development of the region. Hohokam people probably migrated into the Verde Valley too, though archaeologists have difficulty determining whether the early farming communities were actually Hohokam or just influenced by their culture. The Verde's inhabitants learned to grow cotton, weave cloth, make pottery, and build ball courts. Sinagua from the Flagstaff area arrived between A.D. 1125 and 1200 and gradually absorbed the cultures already here. Villages then started to consolidate. Large, multistoried pueblos replaced the small pit houses of earlier times.

Two of these pueblos, Montezuma Castle and Tuzigoot, are now national monuments and easily visited. Archaeologists don't know why, but the Verde Valley's population had departed from the area by 1425. The elaborate Hohokam culture, based in the Gila and Salt river valleys to the south, also disappeared about this time. Perhaps some of the Sinagua migrated northeast, eventually arriving at the Hopi and Zuni pueblos.

Early Spanish explorers, arriving a century and a half later, found small bands of nomadic Tonto Apache and Yavapai Indians roaming the valley. In language and culture, the Tonto Apache had ties with Apache and Navajo tribes to the east, while the Yavapai shared cultural traits with the Hualapai and Havasupai to the northwest. Anglos and Mexicans poured into the valley during a gold rush at the Hassayampa River and Lynx Creek in 1863. Farmers and ranchers followed, taking for themselves the best agricultural lands along the Verde. The displaced Indians attacked the settlements but failed to drive off the newcomers. Soon the Army came in to make patrols and build Camp Lincoln (later Camp Verde). General George Crook subdued the tribes by clever campaigning and by enlisting scouts from other Apache groups.

*posed photo of Apache Indian scouts, late 1800s*

*mule litter of the U.S. Army Medical Corps, Fort Verde in 1880s*

The Tonto Apache and Yavapai Indians received the Rio Verde Reservation in 1873, but the federal government took it away 2 years later and ordered them to leave for San Carlos Reservation, 150 miles away. In the cold Feb. of 1875, the Indians started the 2-week journey on foot; of the 1,451 who started, at least 90 died from exposure, were killed by infighting, or escaped. Early in this century some Apache and Yavapai received permission to return to their Verde River homelands. What were once thousands of Indians occupying millions of acres now number less than 1,000 people on a few remnants of their former lands on the Camp Verde, Prescott, and Fort McDowell reservations.

Anglo farmers in the Verde Valley prospered after the Indian wars ended. Cottonwood, founded in 1879, became the valley's main trading center. Copper mining succeeded on a large scale at Jerome, which sprang to life in 1882 high on a mountainside. Mine company officials built a giant smelter below Jerome in 1910 and laid out the town of Clarkdale. Ore bodies become depleted in the early 1950s, however, forcing many residents of Jerome and Clarkdale to seek jobs elsewhere. Today the Verde Valley prospers from some industry, farming, and popularity with tourists and retirees.

## CAMP VERDE

Early in 1865, 19 men set out from Prescott to start a farming settlement in the Verde Valley. They knew the mining camps around Arizona's new capital would pay well for fresh food. The eager farmers chose lands where West Clear Creek joins the Verde, about 5 miles downstream from the modern town of Camp Verde. After planting fields, digging an irrigation system, and building a fort, they saw their hopes nearly come to an end when Indian raids destroyed much of the crops and livestock. Army troops then marched in and built Camp Lincoln, one mile north of the present townsite. As too many place names commemorated the former president, the Army later had to change the post's name to "Camp Verde." Untamed Indians kept the cavalry and infantry busy during the late 1860s and early 1870s. Infantry also built a road, later known as the General Crook Trail, west to Fort Whipple (near Prescott) and east along the Mogollon Rim to Fort Apache. In 1871 the post moved one mile south to its current location, where more than 20 buildings were neatly laid out around a parade field. The name changed to "Fort Verde" in 1879, but the Indian wars were almost over.

A battle in 1882 at Big Dry Wash marked the last large engagement between soldiers and Indians in Arizona. Having served its purpose, Fort Verde closed in 1891. Civilians then took over the land and buildings. Today exhibits and the four surviving fort buildings at Fort Verde State Historic Park give a feeling of what life was like for the enlisted men, officers, and wives who lived here. Other attractions near town include the multistoried cliff dwelling of Montezuma Castle, the unusual springs at Montezuma Well, camping, hiking, and rafting the Verde River.

## SIGHTS

### Fort Verde State Historic Park

Like most posts of the period, Fort Verde never had a protective wall around it, nor did Indians ever attack. Army patrols used Fort Verde as a supply post and staging area. The 10-acre park preserves the administration building, commanding officer's house, bachelors' quarters, the doctor's quarters, and part of the old parade field. Begin your visit at the adobe administration building, used by General George Crook during his winter campaign of 1872-73 that largely ended Indian raids in this region. Exhibits illustrate life of the soldiers and their families, Apache Army scouts, settlers, and prospectors who came through here more than 100 years ago. You'll see old photos, maps, letters, rifles, uniforms, pack saddles, a map of the Army's heliograph communications network, and Indian crafts. The three adobe buildings of "Officers' Row" have been restored and furnished as they were in the 1880s. Fort Verde State Historic Park is open daily 8 a.m.-5 p.m.; $1 adult, children under 18 free; tel. 567-3275. From Main St. in Camp Verde (2 miles east of I-17 Exit 285), turn north one block on Lane Street.

### Montezuma Castle National Monument

This towering cliff dwelling so impressed early visitors that they thought the famous Aztec ruler of Mexico had built it. Actually, this pueblo was neither a castle nor part of Montezuma's empire. Sinagua Indians built it in the 12th and 13th centuries, toward the end of their stay in the Verde Valley. The five-story stone and mortar structure contains 20 rooms tucked back under a cliff 100 feet above Beaver Creek. The overhang shielded the village from rain, snow, and the hot summer sun but allowed the low winter sun's rays to warm the dwellings. The well-preserved ruins, once occupied by about 50 people, are too fragile to enter; you have to view them from below. An even larger pueblo once stood against the base of the cliff; "Castle A" had six stories and about 45 rooms, but little remains today. A level, one-third-mile trail loops below Montezuma Castle to foundations of this ruin.

The Visitor Center displays artifacts of the Sinagua and has exhibits depicting their everyday life. Other exhibits describe plants, animals, and geology of the Verde Valley. Related books, videos, and maps are sold. Giant Arizona sycamore trees shade a picnic area beside the river. Montezuma Castle National Monument is open daily 8 a.m.-5 p.m. in winter, extended to 8 a.m.-6 p.m. in

*Montezuma Castle*

*Dr. Edgar A. Mearns, post surgeon at Fort Verde 1884-88, spent much of his spare time excavating prehistoric Indian sites in the Verde Valley.*

spring and autumn and 8 a.m.-7 p.m. in summer (Memorial Day to Labor Day); $1/person or $3/family; tel. 567-3322. Take I-17 Exit 289 and follow signs 2 miles; from Camp Verde, drive north 3 miles on Montezuma Castle Road, then turn right 2 miles at the sign.

### Montezuma Well

This natural sinkhole and small lake, 11 miles northeast of Montezuma Castle, is worth visiting both for its scenic beauty as a desert oasis and for the Indian ruins here. A one-third-mile, self-guiding loop trail climbs to the rim. Other trails wind down to the lake and to the outlet where water enters an ancient irrigation ditch. The sinkhole measures 470 feet across and is only partly filled by a 55-foot-deep lake. Cool, clear waters of the lake attract ducks, coots, and other birds. The Sinagua built pueblos here between A.D. 1125 and 1400 and used the water to irrigate their crops. Parts of their villages and irrigation canals can still

be seen. Modern farmers continue to use the water, which flows at 1,100 gallons/minute. Look for the Hohokam pithouse exhibit beside the road on the left 0.25 mile before Montezuma Well. Timbers that once held up the walls and roof have long since rotted away, but distinct outlines remain of the supporting poles, walls, entrance, and fire pit. A tree-shaded picnic area is located 0.5 mile before Montezuma Well. Montezuma Well is part of Montezuma Castle National Monument and is open during the same hours. No visitor center or admission charge. From Camp Verde or Montezuma Castle, take I-17 north to Exit 293 and follow signs 5 miles; another approach is to take I-17 Sedona Exit 298 and head south 4.5 miles on a gravel road.

## PRACTICALITIES

### Accommodations

In Camp Verde, stay at the **Fort Verde Motel** ($30.10 s, $32.25 d; tel. 567-3486) or **Chaparral Motel** ($26-36 s or d; tel. 567-3451), both downtown on opposite sides of Main Street. **Cliff Castle Lodge (Best Western)** offers luxury accommodations, restaurant, pool, and spa; $68.36 s, $77.04 d; 3 miles outside town on Middle Verde Road near the turnoff for Montezuma Castle, or take I-17 Exit 289; tel. 567-6611 or (800) 528-1234. **Beaver Creek Inn** is north in the planned community of Lake Montezuma, near Montezuma Well; $41.15 s, $50.64 d; take I-17 Exit 293 and follow signs 3 miles; tel. 567-4475.

### Campgrounds

**Yavapai-Apache RV Park** is 3 miles north of town at the junction of I-17 Exit 289 and Middle Verde Road (Montezuma Castle Exit); $5 tent, $8 RVs w/hookups; open all year and has showers; check in at the Short Stop Grocery; tel. 567-3109. **Verde River Resort** offers year-round sites for tents ($12) and RVs ($14-18 w/hookups) near the river; amenities include showers, pool, jacuzzi, tennis, miniature golf, fishing, scheduled activities, and a store; take Finnie Flats Road (AZ

260) or I-17 Exit 285, go northwest 2 miles past I-17, then turn right 1.1 miles on Horseshoe Bend Dr.; tel. 567-5262. The Forest Service has **Clear Creek Campground** (6 miles southeast on Main St./General Crook Hwy.) and **Beaver Creek Campground** (take I-17 north to Sedona Exit 298 and turn south 2 miles on Forest Route 618). Sites have drinking water all year and a $5 fee.

### Food
At **Valley View Restaurant,** you can choose from seafood, steak, chicken, veal, and pork dishes, as well as a long list of sandwiches, while enjoying views of the Verde Valley; open daily for breakfast, lunch, and dinner; located on the north edge of downtown; tel. 567-3592. An old-style atmosphere graces the turn-of-the-century **Montezuma Inn Cafe and Deli**; open daily except Sun. for breakfast and lunch on Main St.; tel. 567-6209. The **Steakhouse** is a cafe serving standard American fare on Main St.; open daily for breakfast, lunch, and dinner (except closed Wed. afternoon) on Main St.; tel. 567-3497. The **Branding Iron Restaurant** (Ft. Verde Shopping Center; tel. 567-3136) and **JJ's Family Restaurant** (Main St.; tel. 567-6521) are two other cafes downtown; both are open daily for breakfast and lunch, weekends for dinner. **Custard's Last Stand** is a bakery with a fast-food cafe; open daily for breakfast and lunch on Main St.; tel. 567-9900. **Cliff Castle Lodge** offers fine dining daily for breakfast, lunch, and dinner; 3 miles north of town on Montezuma Castle Hwy.; tel. 567-6611. **Vivianos Mexican Restaurant** is open daily except Mon. for lunch and dinner on the south edge of town (South Access Road); tel. 567-9966. **La Fonda Mexican Restaurant** is about 4 miles outside town on Finnie Flats Road (AZ 260) toward Cottonwood; go 2 miles past I-17, then turn right 0.1 mile on Horseshoe Bend Dr.; open Tues.-Thurs. for dinner and Fri.-Sun. for lunch and dinner; tel. 567-3500. Stop for pizza at **Babe's Round Up** on Montezuma Castle Road at the north edge of town; tel. 567-6969; or **Crusty's Pizza** in the Outpost Mall on Finnie Flats Road; tel. 567-6444. **Beaver Creek Restaurant,** beside Beaver Creek Golf Course at Lake Montezuma (near Montezuma Well), offers a wide range of food; dinner specialties include steaks, prime rib, and seafood; open daily except Mon. for breakfast, lunch, and dinner; tel. 567-4492. Buy groceries at **Basha's** in the Outpost Mall on Finnie Flats Road or **Fairway** in Fort Verde Shopping Center, off N. Main Street.

### Events, Services, And Shopping
Fishermen try their luck in the **Catfish Contest** on Memorial Day weekend. During **Fort Verde Days** on the second weekend in Oct., the community brings back the old days with cavalry parades and drills, a barbecue, mule race, roping events, art shows, games, and a dance. The **post office** is just west of downtown on Finnie Flats Road. Play golf at **Beaver Creek's** 18-hole course at Lake Montezuma (near Montezuma Well); tel. 567-4487. **San Dominique Winery** welcomes visitors daily 10 a.m.-5 p.m. all year; the winery specializes in production of high-quality varietal wines; located 9 miles south of Camp Verde off the I-17 Cherry Road East Exit; tel. 945-8583 (Scottsdale office). **White Hills Indian Arts** on Main St. offers a good selection of jewelry and other work by Indians of Arizona and New Mexico; tel. 567-3490.

### Information
The **Yavapai-Apache Visitor Center** is just off I-17 at Middle Verde Road Exit 289 for Camp Verde and Montezuma Castle. Stop here for slide programs and exhibits on nearby sights, regional information, and Indian crafts. The building itself, designed by Hopi architect Dennis Numkena, is worth a visit. Elements of Hopi legends fit into the design: the ladder-shaped tower in the center represents a rise into the Fourth World—the most perfect one; the whirlwind or eternity symbol appears at many places inside and out; and a well-like structure inside symbolizes the Sipapu, where the Hopi emerged into the world. Open daily 8 a.m.-5 p.m. (8 a.m.-6 p.m. in summer); free; tel. 567-5276. The **Camp Verde Chamber of Commerce** will also help you with area sights and services; open

Mon.-Fri. 9 a.m.-4 p.m. and sometimes on Sat. in summer; downtown at Main and First (Box 1665, Camp Verde, AZ 86322); tel. 567-9294.

The **Verde Ranger District** office of the Prescott National Forest has information on running the Verde River and on camping, hiking, and road conditions for the lands south and west of town; books and maps can be purchased; open weekdays 8 a.m.-4:30 p.m.; head southeast one mile from downtown on Main St./General Crook Hwy. (Box 670, Camp Verde, AZ 86322); tel. 567-4121.

**Beaver Creek Ranger District** office of the Coconino National Forest will help you explore the Mogollon Rim country north and east of Camp Verde; open Mon.-Fri. 7:30 a.m.-noon and 1-4:30 p.m., also Sat. from April to Nov. (call for hours); located north of Camp Verde near Beaver Creek Campground—take I-17 north to Sedona Exit 298, then turn south 2 miles on Forest Route 618 (HC 64, Box 240, Rimrock, AZ 86335); tel. 567-4501.

## VICINITY OF CAMP VERDE (BEAVER CREEK RANGER DISTRICT)

### Wet Beaver Creek Wilderness

Sycamore, cottonwood, ash, alder, Arizona walnut, and wildflowers grow along this pretty creek. Yet, a short way from the water, the prickly pear cactus, agave, Utah juniper, and pinyon pine of the high desert take over. You might see mule or whitetail deer, ringtail cat, coyote, javelina, Gambel's quail, red-tailed hawk, bald eagle (winter), and great blue heron. Keep an eye out for rattlesnakes and poison ivy. Verde trout, some brown and rainbow, and suckers live in the creek, though most people find fishing conditions poor. Hikers enjoy trails along the lower creek, climbs to the Mogollon Rim, and difficult routes through the upper canyons. The many swimming holes in Wet Beaver Creek are at their best in summer, though the lower canyon offers pleasant hiking year-round. To reach this 6,700 acres of rugged wilderness, take

I-17 Sedona Exit 298, turn southeast 2 miles on Forest Route 618, then left 0.25 mile at the sign to the **Bell Trail #13** (elev. 3,820 feet). **Beaver Creek Ranger District** office, a short drive beyond the trailhead turnoff, has maps and trail descriptions; see Camp Verde "Information" above. The first 2 miles of trail follows an old jeep road into the canyon, where the way narrows to a footpath. **Apache Maid Trail #15** begins at this point and climbs steeply out of the canyon to the north, then continues at a moderate grade to Forest Route 620 near Apache Maid Mountain; 9.5 miles one way and a 2,380-foot elevation gain. The Bell Trail continues upstream another mile past pretty pools to Bell Crossing, where it crosses the creek and climbs out to the west (good views) to Forest Route 214 near Five Mile Pass; 10.8 miles one way and a 2,450-foot elevation gain. The "Crack," a deep pool 150 feet upstream from Bell Crossing, makes a good turnaround point for a leisurely dayhike. (Please don't camp here, as the area gets heavy use.)

Adventurous hikers can continue upstream if they're willing to swim through many deep pools of cold, clear water; bring some flotation, especially if toting a camera or pack. Experienced hikers can also enter the upper canyon via Waldroup, Jacks, or Brady canyons. These routes involve some brush and descents on small cliff faces. Contact foresters at the Beaver Creek Ranger Station for advice on exploring this area. Beaver Creek (treat before drinking) and unpalatable stock tanks are the only sources of water, so it's best to bring your own. Topo maps should be carried for travel off-trail or to follow the sometimes-faint trails on the Rim.

### West Clear Creek Wilderness (Western End)

The 13,600-acre wilderness holds some of the most awe-inspiring canyon country of the Mogollon Rim; see "West Clear Creek Wilderness," p. 178. Deep pools in the middle section and few access points anywhere make most of the wilderness difficult to visit. The lower end of the canyon, however, can easily be explored on **West Clear Creek Trail #17.**

From I-17, take any of the Camp Verde exits and drive through town, continue east 5 miles on the General Crook Trail (Forest Highway 9), turn left (north) 2 miles on Forest Route 618, then right (east) 4 miles to the east end of Bull Pen dispersed camping area (elev. 3,700 feet). The first 6 miles of trail is an easy walk along the creek past fishing spots and swimming holes. You'll have to cross the creek several times, which can be difficult or impossible during high water. After 6 miles, the trail turns northwest and climbs steeply 2 miles to Forest Route 214A (elev. 5,780 feet).

**Blodgett Basin Trail #31** can be combined with the Clear Creek Trail and 2.5 miles of forest roads (214A and 214) to make a 12.7-mile loop. The trailhead is a bit easier to reach than the one for Clear Creek Trail. From the General Crook Trail, turn north 4 miles on Forest Route 618, then east 4.3 miles on Forest Route 214 to the trailhead (elev. 5,280 feet). Blodgett Basin Trail drops steadily in 2.5 miles to West Clear Creek Trail, about 0.5 mile in from Bull Pen. To make the loop, turn up West Clear Creek Trail to its end at Forest Route 214A, follow the road 1.2 miles to Forest Route 214, then turn left 1.3 miles to the Blodgett Basin Trailhead.

**Fossil Springs Wilderness**
Springs gush forth millions of gallons of heavily mineralized water per hour northwest of Strawberry. The water, a constant 72° where it emerges, supports a lush riparian environment. The 11,550-acre wilderness protects the scenic beauty and abundant wildlife of Fossil Creek and some of its tributaries. Few trails enter the canyons, so much hiking is cross-country. Several trails provide access to the wilderness from the north and south sides. The Flume Road, between the springs and Irving Power Plant, is open for hikers and bicyclists but closed to motor vehicles. The power plant has been producing electricity at this remote location since 1916. Contact the Beaver Creek Ranger District office (see Camp Verde "Information" above) for trailhead locations and hiking conditions.

**General Crook National Recreation Trail**
This historic trail dates back to 1871, when the Army needed a trail to supply their forts and secure the region from hostile Apache. In that year, General George Crook led a small group of cavalry to survey the route from Fort Apache in eastern Arizona to the territorial capital in Prescott. Work began in

*General George Crook on his mule "Apache"; Indian scout Chief Alchesay stands on right, late 1870s*

1872, and 2 years later the first wagon trains covered the 200-mile distance. The route had long been abandoned when groups of Boy Scouts and others cleared and marked the old path for a bicentennial project. About 138 miles are now open to hikers and horseback riders. From Camp Verde, the western section stretches 21 miles through Copper Canyon to Cherry Road. The long eastern section of trail climbs from Camp Verde to the pine-forested Mogollon Rim and follows it 114 miles to a point west of Show Low. Much of the way appears as the old Army cavalry knew it. Some mileposts, carved on boulders or trees, can still be seen. Spring and autumn are the best times to hike; cross-country skiers can tour the higher elevations in winter. For trail information, obtain *A Guide to the General Crook Trail* by Eldon Bowman, published by the Museum of Northern Arizona and the Boy Scouts of America in 1978, or contact the U.S. Forest Service. The July 1982 issue of *Arizona Highways* has good photos and historical articles on the General Crook Trail.

## VICINITY OF CAMP VERDE (VERDE RANGER DISTRICT)

### River Running On The Verde
Experienced boaters in kayaks or rafts can venture downriver from Camp Verde to Sheep Bridge (near Horseshoe Reservoir), 59 miles away. People are just beginning to discover this wild and scenic stretch of river. You're likely to see well-preserved Indian ruins and wildlife along the way. An area of shoreline is closed Dec.-April to protect a bald eagle nesting site. The main river-running season lasts from Jan. to early April during spring runoff, but inflatable kayaks can sometimes negotiate the shallow waters off-season. The ice-cold water in winter and spring necessitates use of full or partial wet suits. With time for rest stops and scouting rapids, rafts typically average 2 miles per hour. The stretch between Beasley Flats and Childs has the wildest water. Canoeists often have trouble negotiating the rapids here and

wind up with a smashed boat. Unless you really know what you're doing in white water, it's best to avoid the potentially dangerous conditions below Beasley Flats. The Forest Service has a *River Runners Guide to the Verde River;* contact the Verde or Beaver Creek ranger districts (see Camp Verde "Information") or the Tonto National Forest office at 2324 E. McDowell Road in Phoenix; tel. 225-5200. From about Feb. to May, you can join commercial trips down the Verde led by **World Wide Explorations** (Box 686, Flagstaff, AZ 86002; tel. 774-6462); **Desert Voyagers** (Box 9053, Scottsdale, AZ 85252; tel. 998-RAFT); or **Arizona Whitewater Expeditions** (Box 26028, Tempe, AZ 85282; tel. 831-0977).

Another possibility is canoeing or tubing the leisurely section of river between Cottonwood and Camp Verde. **Adventures Unlimited** (HC, Box 518, Camp Verde, AZ 86322; tel. 567-9222) rents canoes with paddles and life jackets; in summer they also rent tubes.

### Pine Mountain Wilderness
Pine Mountain (6,814 feet) crowns the Verde Rim south of Camp Verde. The wilderness is small, about 20,000 acres, but offers solitude and natural beauty far from towns and highways. Chaparral, juniper and pinyon woodlands, and majestic ponderosa pine forests cover the rough terrain. You might see mule or whitetail deer, javelina, bear, or mountain lion. To reach the trailhead, take I-17 Exit 268 (Dugas Road) located 18 miles south of Camp Verde and 6 miles north of Cordes Junction; then head east 22 miles on dirt Forest Route 68 to the Salt Grounds (0.25 mile before Nelson Place). This road is best driven by cars only in good weather. From the parking area there's a one-mile walk to the wilderness boundary. An 8-mile roundtrip loop can be done to the top of Pine Mountain using Forest Trails 159, 14, 161, and 12. Allow 6 hours for this trip and carry water. Elevation gain is about 1,600 feet. See the Prescott, Tonto, or Coconino forest maps and the Tule Mesa (7.5 minute) topo map. The Verde Ranger District office in Camp Verde can tell you the road and trail conditions.

## COTTONWOOD

Named for the trees along the Verde River, Cottonwood provides a handy base for visiting the old mining town of Jerome, the prehistoric Tuzigoot ruins, and other attractions of the Verde Valley. The town is located 16 miles northwest of Camp Verde, 19 miles southwest of Sedona, and 41 miles northeast across Mingus Mountain from Prescott. Cottonwood has two downtowns—a new section along US 89A and the original "Old Town," now bypassed by the highway. Clarkdale, just 2 miles northwest of Cottonwood, has many old houses and businesses dating from its years as a smelter town. Although a lot of residents lost their jobs when the smelter shut down in 1952, others were glad to be rid of its heavy black smoke. A newer industry, the Phoenix Cement Company, supplied the cement used in building Glen Canyon Dam on the Colorado River near Page.

### Tuzigoot National Monument

Sinagua Indians built and lived in this hilltop pueblo from A.D. 1125 to 1425. Tuzigoot ("TOO-zee-goot") stood two stories high in places and contained about 92 rooms. At its peak, the pueblo housed 250 people. The large size of the ruin is thought to be the result of a drought in the 1200s, which forced many dry-land farmers to resettle at Tuzigoot and other villages near the Verde River. Most rooms lacked doorways—a ladder through a hatchway in the roof permitted entry. The original roofs, now gone, were pine and sycamore beams covered by willow branches and sealed with mud. While excavating the site in

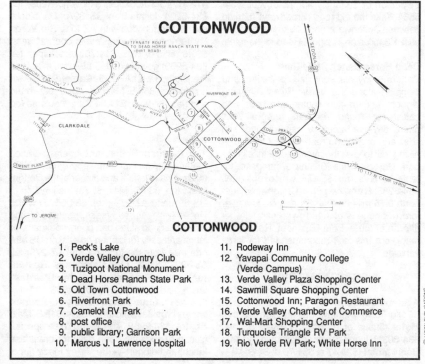

## COTTONWOOD

1. Peck's Lake
2. Verde Valley Country Club
3. Tuzigoot National Monument
4. Dead Horse Ranch State Park
5. Old Town Cottonwood
6. Riverfront Park
7. Camelot RV Park
8. post office
9. public library; Garrison Park
10. Marcus J. Lawrence Hospital
11. Rodeway Inn
12. Yavapai Community College (Verde Campus)
13. Verde Valley Plaza Shopping Center
14. Sawmill Square Shopping Center
15. Cottonwood Inn; Paragon Restaurant
16. Verde Valley Chamber of Commerce
17. Wal-Mart Shopping Center
18. Turquoise Triangle RV Park
19. Rio Verde RV Park; White Horse Inn

© MOON PUBLICATIONS

1933-34, University of Arizona researchers found a wide variety of artifacts, including the grave offerings contained in 450 burials. A Visitor Center next to the ruins displays some of the finds, including stone axes and tools, projectile points, pottery, turquoise and shell jewelry, and religious objects. Other exhibits illustrate what's known about the Sinagua's agriculture, weaving, building techniques, and burials. A reconstruction shows how one of Tuzigoot's rooms might have looked when the Sinagua lived here. Outside, a quarter-mile trail loops through the maze of ruins. You can climb up to a second-story lookout at the summit. The Apache name "Tuzigoot" was chosen for this site because the word has a nice ring to it; originally the name referred to nearby Peck's Lake and meant "crooked water." Tuzigoot National Monument is open daily 8 a.m.-5 p.m., extended to 8 a.m.-7 p.m. in summer (Memorial Day to Labor Day); $1/person or $3/family admission; tel. 634-5564. Take the old road (Broadway) running between Cottonwood and Clarkdale, then turn east 1.3 miles on Tuzigoot Road to the ruins.

### Dead Horse Ranch State Park
Visitors enjoy pleasant fishing, hiking, and camping along the Verde River. A fishing lagoon has trout in winter and bass and catfish year-round. The park, open all year, offers day-use areas, a campground with showers, and group reservation facilities. A hiking trail follows the river for one mile in the park. Day use costs $3/vehicle, campsites for tents or RVs run $6 ($8 w/hookups); tel. 634-5283. From Main St. in Cottonwood, turn north 0.75 mile on Fifth St. and cross a river ford (a bridge is planned); you can take an alternate route from Tuzigoot Road (see map), but this isn't recommended for large vehicles.

## PRACTICALITIES

### Accommodations
In Old Town Cottonwood, stay at **Sundial Motel** ($28 s or d; 1034 N. Main St.; tel. 634-8031). In the newer part of town try **Little Daisy Motel** ($28.47 s, $31.76 d; 34 S. Main

St.; tel. 634-7865); **View Motel** with swimming pool and spa ($32.85 s, $35.04 d, $43.80 d kitchenettes; 818 S. Main/US 89A; tel. 634-7581); **Rodeway Inn** with restaurant, year-round pool, and spa ($41.61-45.57 s, $45.57-50.37 d; 302 S. US 89A; tel. 634-4207 or 800-228-8000); **Willow Tree Inn** ($41.61 s, $43.80 d; 1089 AZ 279 near junction with US 89A; tel. 634-3678), or the Best Western **Cottonwood Inn** with swimming pool, spa, and restaurant ($56.94 s, $65.70 d on summer weekends, reduced rates other times; 993 S. Main St. at corner of US 89A and AZ 279; tel. 634-5575 or tel. 800-528-1234).

### Campgrounds
Besides Dead Horse Ranch State Park, described above, you can stay at any of the following: **Turquoise Triangle RV Park** has showers and is open all year; $9-12 tents, $12 RVs no hookups, $16 w/hookups; tel. 634-5294; located on US 89A, 1½ blocks east of the junction with AZ 279. **Rio Verde RV Park** has showers and is open all year; $9.45 tents or RVs ($14.70 w/hookups); tel. 634-5990; go east on US 89A one mile from the junction with AZ 279. **Camelot RV Park** is in town at 858 E. Main St.; open year-round and has showers; $14.04 RV w/hookups (no tents); tel. 634-3011.

### Food
The **Paragon Restaurant** offers a varied menu and pleasant atmosphere; open daily for breakfast, lunch, and dinner at the Cottonwood Inn, 933 S. Main St. (at the junction of US 89A and AZ 279); tel. 634-5575. **White Horse Inn** features steaks, seafood, prime rib, and a good salad bar; open weekdays for lunch and daily for dinner; go east on US 89A one mile from the junction with AZ 279; tel. 634-2271/8652. **Las Campanas Restaurant** in the Rodeway Inn serves breakfast, lunch, and dinner daily.; 302 S. US 89A; tel. 634-4207. **Little Acorn Family Restaurant** serves breakfast and lunch daily; 315 S. Main St.; tel. 634-9952. The **Menu Tree** specializes in breakfasts; open daily for breakfast, lunch, and dinner; Verde Valley Plaza (junc-

tion of US 89A and Cottonwood St.); tel. 634-7920. For Cantonese dining, stop at **House of Chin**; open daily except Mon. for breakfast, lunch, and dinner at E. Main and 12th Streets.; tel. 634-8702. **Golden Dragon** features Mandarin and Szechuan cuisine in the Sawmill Square Shopping Center; open daily except Mon. for lunch and dinner; tel. 634-0588. **Guero's,** also in the Sawmill Square Shopping Center, serves Mexican and American food; open Mon.-Sat. for lunch and dinner; tel. 634-6470. **Tacos y Mas** is another south-of-the-border cafe, open Mon.-Sat. for lunch and dinner; in Clarkdale at 1000 S. Main St.; tel. 634-2771. Pick up pizza and Italian sandwiches at **The Pizza Station** (open daily) at 140 S. Main St.; tel. 634-5000. **JR's Black Hills Restaurant** has steaks, seafood, barbecued ribs, and other items; open Tues.-Sat. for lunch and dinner; 910 Main St. in Clarkdale; tel. 634-9792. Buy groceries at **Smith's** in the Wal-Mart Shopping Center, at **Safeway** in the Sawmill Shopping Center, or at **Basha's** in Verde Valley Plaza. **Mount Hope Natural Foods** is on the west edge of Old Town Cottonwood at 104 Main Street.

### Entertainment And Events
Catch movies at the **Old Town Palace,** 914 N. Main St. in Old Town Cottonwood; tel. 634-7167. Major annual events include the **Verde Valley Fair** in April, **Verde Valley Gem and Mineral Show** in March, **Peck's Lake Barbecue and Fireworks** on July Fourth, and a **Christmas Parade** in December.

### Services
**Post office** is at 700 E. Mingus Avenue. Medical services are provided by the **Marcus J. Lawrence Hospital,** 202 S. Willard St.; tel. 634-2251. A **swimming pool** (open in summer; tel. 634-7468) and **tennis courts** are at Garrison Park, near the corner of E. Mingus Ave. and Sixth Street. Play golf at **Verde Valley Country Club's** 9-hole course; turn east on Tuzigoot Road from Broadway (between Cottonwood and Clarkdale), cross the Verde River, then turn left on Sycamore Canyon Road; tel. 634-5491.

### Information
The **Verde Valley Chamber of Commerce** will tell you about the sights, events, and facilities in the area; open daily (except holidays) 9 a.m.-5 p.m.; tel. 634-7593. The office is in an adobe-style building conveniently located at the intersection of US 89A and AZ 279 (1010 S. Main St., Cottonwood, AZ 86326). Cottonwood's **public library** is at 401 E. Mingus Ave.; tel. 634-7559. **Jesse's Books-Music-Video** sells regional books and topo maps among their many other offerings; in the Wal-Mart Shopping Center.

### Tours And Transport
Ride the rails through the Verde River Canyon with **Arizona Central Railroad**. Trips begin in Clarkdale and head upcanyon. You have a choice of a basic excursion, one with a box lunch, or with a Western barbecue and live entertainment. Make reservations at Box 103, Clarkdale, AZ 86324; tel. 639-0010.

**Sedona Transportation Company** operates twice daily between Sedona and Phoenix with a stop at Cottonwood; area tours can be arranged too; tel. 282-2066.

# JEROME

Jerome, clinging to the slopes of Cleopatra Hill above the Verde Valley, might be Arizona's most unusual town—in both its layout and its history. For more than 70 years its booming mines produced copper, gold, and silver. Most residents departed after 1953 when the mines closed, but Jerome survived. Museums, art galleries, antique shops, and restaurants have brought the hillside town back to life. Old-fashioned buildings—some restored, others abandoned but still standing—add to the atmosphere. Walking Jerome's winding streets is like touring a museum of early 20th C. American architecture. From almost any point in town, you can enjoy expansive views across the Verde Valley to the Sedona Red Rock Country, Sycamore Canyon, the Mogollon Rim, and the pointed San Francisco Peaks. Three very different museums will introduce you to the people and mining history of the area .

*William A. Clark (1839-1925) was the owner of United Verde Mine in Jerome and the founder of Clarkdale.*

*James S. "Rawhide Jimmy" Douglas (1867-1949); he purchased the Little Daisy Mine in 1912, then built the mansion now used as Jerome State Historic Park.*

## History

Prehistoric Indians came long ago to dig the brilliant blue azurite and other copper minerals for use as paint and jewelry. Spanish explorers, shown the diggings by Indian guides, failed to see any worth in the place. In 1876, several American prospectors staked claims to the rich copper deposits, but they lacked the resources to develop them. Eugene Jerome, a wealthy lawyer and financier, saw a profit to be made and offered backing to mine the ore. A surveyor laying out the townsite named it in honor of the Jerome family, though Eugene himself never visited the area. From the time the United Verde Copper Company began operating in 1882, the town's economy went on a wild roller-coaster ride dependent on copper prices. Mines closed for brief periods, then rebounded. So many saloons, gambling dens, and brothels thrived in Jerome that a New York newspaper called it the "wickedest town in the West." Fires roared through the frame houses and businesses three times between 1897 and 1899, yet Jerome rose to become Arizona's fifth largest city. Floods and underground blasting shook the earth so much that buildings keeled over; the town's famous sliding jail took off across the street and down the hillside, where it can be seen today. Banks refused to take the average Jerome house or business as collateral. The community experienced its greatest prosperity during the roaring twenties, when its population hit 15,000. The stock market crash and ensuing depression spelled disaster for the copper industry; mines and smelter shut down and the population plummeted to less than 5,000. World War II brought Jerome's last period of prosperity before the mines shut down for good in 1953. Many people thought Jerome would become a ghost town when the population shrank to only 50 souls. But, beginning in the late 1960s, artists, shop owners, tourists, retirees, and others rediscovered Jerome's unique character and setting.

## SIGHTS

### Jerome State Historic Park

The Douglas Mansion, built in 1917 by James "Rawhide Jimmy" Douglas, tops a hill overlooking the Little Daisy Mine. Today, the old mansion abounds with Jerome's mining lore. Outside you can see a giant stamp mill and the more primitive *arrastre* and Chilean wheels once used to pulverize ore. Signs at viewpoints identify some of Jerome's historic buildings. Indoors, a video presentation illustrates the many changes Jerome has seen. An assay office, the Douglas library, old photos, mining tools, smelter models, and mineral displays show different aspects of the effort expended to gain metals from the earth.

Upstairs, a neat three-dimensional model shows Jerome's mine shafts, underground work areas, and geologic features. Jerome State Historic Park is open daily 8 a.m.-5 p.m.; $1 adult, children under 18 free; tel. 634-5381. A small picnic area beside the mansion has expansive views of the Verde Valley. Turn off US 89A at Milepost 345 at the lower end of Jerome (8 miles west of Cottonwood), then follow the paved road one mile.

### Jerome Historical Society Mine Museum

Look for the two large half-wheels at the corner of Main St. (US 89A) and Jerome Avenue. Paintings, photos, stock certificates, mining tools, and ore samples illustrate Jerome's development. Open daily 9 a.m.-4:30 p.m.; $.50 adult, children under 12 free; tel. 634-5477.

*Jerome's smelter about 1890; main stack towered 160 feet and measured 22 feet in diameter. Miners' houses cling to hillside in background.*

### Gold King Mine Museum

If you're fascinated by old machinery, or if you've ever wanted to poke around a ghost town, this collection just might satisfy your curiosity. Among the hoists, pumps, engines, and ore cars, look for a short replica of a mine shaft, which may be entered, and an assay office complete with a stuffed miner. A small petting zoo attracts the kids. On most days you can watch the antique sawmill in operation. Enter through the gift shop, which sells mining memorabilia and other souvenirs. Open daily 9 a.m.-5 p.m.; $2 adult, $1 children 6-17; tel. 634-0053. From the upper switchback on US 89A in Jerome, turn northwest one mile on the Perkinsville Road; on the way you'll pass a large open-pit mine on the left, where Jerome's smelter was located at the turn of the century.

## PRACTICALITIES

### Accommodations

Modern motels have yet to hit town; if that's what you're looking for, stay in Cottonwood, 8 miles below. Jerome does offer two hotels,

old-fashioned by today's standards but well kept. Reservations should be made for weekends. The **Connor Hotel** at 168 Main St. has rooms ranging from $27.25 s or d (bath down the hall) to $32.70-49.05 s or d (larger rooms with shower); light sleepers should choose rooms away from the downstairs bar; tel. 634-5792. The **Miner's Roost Hotel,** 311 Main St., features Victorian-style rooms, some with private bath, at $31.50-47.25 s or d including breakfast; tel. 634-5094. **Nancy Russell's Bed and Breakfast** is in a turn-of-the-century miner's house, $60 s or d; Box 791, Jerome, AZ 86331; tel. 634-3270.

### Campgrounds

Stay at **Dead Horse Ranch State Park** or RV parks in Cottonwood below town, or at the cool **Mingus Mountain Campground** in the hills above. Mingus Mountain Campground is open about early May to early Nov.; no water or fee; head 8 miles southwest on US 89A, then left 3 miles on Forest Route 104.

### Food And Entertainment

The **House of Joy** certainly has a reputation. In the old days, its painted ladies operated a

*the blast furnace of Jerome's first smelter, 1880s*

*power room of the United Verde Mine, 1911*

lively business in the house. Present owners have kept the red lights and other brothel decor while offering excellent continental cuisine at moderate prices. This popular dining spot is open only for dinner on Sat. and Sun.; make reservations well in advance by calling after 9 a.m. on Sat. or Sun.; tel. 634-5339. House of Joy is on the right on Hull St., just after the beginning of the uphill one-way section of US 89A. **Macy's European Coffeehouse and Bakery** serves sandwiches, baked goodies, fancy coffees, and other refreshments; open daily in morning and afternoon at the fork in the road in Flat Iron District; tel. 634-2733 (this Macy's is an offshoot of the one in Flagstaff). **Betty's Ore House,** 309 Main St., serves breakfast, lunch, and dinner daily; tel. 634-5094. **Maude's Downstairs Cafe,** at 115 Jerome Ave., prepares homemade breakfasts, lunches, and baked goods. **English Kitchen,** 119 Jerome Ave., is an old-style cafe serving breakfast and lunch; closed Monday.

For entertainment, locals hang out in the Spirit Room of the **Connor Hotel** and at **Paul & Jerry's Saloon,** both on upper Main Street.

**Events**
The **Jerome Home Tour** visits historic houses and buildings not normally open to the public (third weekend of May). A varied program of folk, Western, and rhythm and blues comes to town in the **Music Festival,** held in autumn.

**Shopping, Services, And Information**
Shops up and down Main St. display a wide variety of artwork, crafts, antiques, jewelry, and clothing. The **post office** is at 134 Main Street. Obtain free maps and brochures at the **chamber of commerce** in the foyer of the New State Motor Company on Main St. (next to the post office); Box K, Jerome, AZ 86331; tel. 634-2900. **Jerome Public Library** at 109 Jerome Ave. is open only a few days a week.

*bicycle race on Cortez Street, ca. 1900*

# PRESCOTT AND VICINITY

That's "Prescutt," pardner. Unlike most Western towns that boomed haphazardly into existence, Prescott was carefully laid out. The mile-high town rests in a mountain basin ringed by the pine-forested Bradshaws, towering Thumb Butte, jumbled mass of Granite Mountain, boulder-strewn Granite Dells, and vast grasslands of Chino and Lonesome valleys. Downtown, the Doric-columned courthouse sits in a spacious, grassy plaza surrounded by tall elm trees. The equestrian statue in front commemorates the spirit of William "Bucky" O'Neill, a newspaperman, sheriff, mayor, adventurer, and Spanish-American War hero. He led a company of Theodore Roosevelt's Rough Riders to Cuba, where an enemy bullet cut him down. The Palace Bar, on Montezuma St. opposite the courthouse, carries on the tradition of "Whiskey Row," where more than 20 saloons went full-blast day and night at the turn of the century. The Sharlot Hall Museum, 2 blocks west, preserves Prescott's past with early buildings and excellent historical collections. On the other side of town, the Smoki

(SMOKE-eye) Museum has a wealth of artifacts from American Indian cultures. About 100 Yavapai Indians live in the Prescott area, mostly on their 1,400-acre reservation just north of town. Though Prescott is small (pop. 25,000), it has several art galleries, an active artists' community, two colleges, and an aeronautical university. Just outside town you'll discover the area's beautiful forests, fishing lakes, mountains, and remote ghost towns.

## History

Soon after Congress carved the territory of Arizona from New Mexico in 1863, Governor John Goodwin and a party of appointed officials set off from Washington. Their arduous 3-month journey took them to the rich mineral districts in central Arizona, a promising new land that was relatively free from Confederate sympathizers, who lived mostly in the southern towns of Tucson and Tubac. The party first set up a temporary capital at Fort Whipple in Chino Valley. Then, to be closer to mining activities and timbered land, both the government and fort moved 17 miles south to a site along Granite Creek. Fort Whipple then served as a center for campaigns against hostile Tonto Apache and Yavapai Indians during the 1860s and 1870s. Sentries had to be constantly alert against Indian attacks as workmen felled trees to build the Capitol and Governor's Mansion. Early citizens named their settlement after William Hickling Prescott, a historian noted for his writings about Mexico. Unlike towns to the south that had adobe buildings and a strong Spanish-Mexican flavor, Prescott took its character from settlers of New England and the Midwest. Vast forests provided timber for log cabins and later frame buildings.

In 1867 the Legislature had a change of heart and moved down to Tucson. Prescott's future looked bleak, as Apache attacks and high transportation costs threatened further mining or agricultural development. Then improved mining techniques and new gold strikes in the 1870s brought the region back to life. The Legislature even returned in 1877 before going to Phoenix for good in 1889. By then Prescott had become a thriving city and no longer needed the politicians' business. Mining, ranching, and trade prospered. Even a disastrous fire in 1900, which wiped out Prescott's entire business district including Whiskey Row, couldn't destroy community spirit. Undaunted, the saloon keepers moved their salvaged stock across the street and continued serving libations as the fires blazed. Within days townsfolk began rebuilding, creating the downtown you see today. Agriculture and a bit of mining continue in the Prescott area, but it's the ambience of the place that draws most people. Part of its charm lies in the many historic buildings lining Prescott's tree-shaded streets, the clean, pine-scented air, and the agreeable four-season climate.

## SIGHTS

### Sharlot Hall Museum

Not one but a dozen buildings make up this excellent historical museum. Start anywhere you like. Open Tues.- Sat. 10 a.m.-5 p.m. (to 4 p.m. in winter) and Sun. 1-5 p.m., closed Mon. (unless a national holiday). All exhibits have free admission (donations accepted). The complex is at 415 W. Gurley St., 2 blocks west from the Plaza. Offices, research library, conservation laboratory, and rotating exhibits are in the modern, solar-heated **Museum Center**; tel. 445-3122. Sharlot Hall founded the museum in 1928 by displaying her own collection in the Governor's Mansion. Herself a pioneer, she arrived in Arizona in 1882 by wagon train at the age of 12. She developed an interest in the land and people of Arizona and then shared her thoughts in writings and poems. From 1909 to 1911 she served as the territory's first historian, traveling Arizona's primitive roads to collect information and stories firsthand.

The two-story **Governor's Mansion,** built from logs on this site in 1864, looks too primitive for a "mansion" by our standards, but in those days most people lived in tents or lean-tos. Governor John Goodwin and Territorial Secretary Richard McCormick occupied opposite ends. The territorial Legislature met here for their first session while waiting for the Capitol to be finished. One room pays tribute to Sharlot Hall by displaying many of her personal belongings. The rest of the mansion has been restored and furnished as it was during the early years.

**Sharlot Hall Building,** built in 1934, houses most of the Indian and pioneer displays. Well-done exhibits show military life at Fort Whipple, ranching, saloons, stores, recreation, and Prescott heroes. An Indian room displays many fine examples of Indian pottery, basketry, jewelry, and other crafts from both prehistoric and modern tribes of the Southwest.

The **Fremont House** was built in 1875 and moved to this site in 1972. It contains furnishings typical of a well-to-do family in the late 1870s. John C. Fremont, Arizona's fifth territorial governor, rented the house from 1878 to 1881. He had earned fame as an explorer of the West during the 1840s, but he failed miserably in Arizona politics. Fremont didn't care for Prescott's climate and spent long periods back East or in Tucson. Public pres-

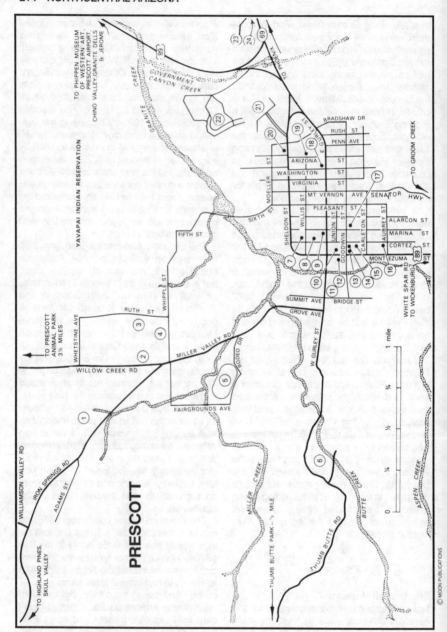

PRESCOTT

© MOON PUBLICATIONS

sure forced his resignation after 3 years in office. The **Bashford House** (built in 1877 and moved here in 1974) contains a gift shop. Books on Arizona history, Papago Indian baskets, other crafts, and souvenirs can be purchased. William Bashford bought the house and remodeled it during the 1880s in an ornate late-Victorian style.

The museum complex also includes smaller buildings. The **Ranch House** is a little log cabin with branding irons, saddles, harnesses, and other cowboy gear. **Fort Misery,** one of Prescott's earliest buildings, dates from 1864 when it was a general store. Later, according to one story, Judge John Howard took it over and dispensed "misery" to lawbreakers; the cabin appears as when he lived in it. The **School House** is a replica of the territory's first public school, built near Granite Creek in 1864. A **blacksmith shop** sees use in restoration projects, such as the mu-

seum's 1887 Porter locomotive. Each of the more than 350 flowers in the **rose garden** commemorates an outstanding Arizona woman.

**Smoki Museum**

From a split-twig figure 3,000-4,000 years old to baskets and pottery of modern tribes, this collection preserves a wide variety of Southwest Indian artifacts. A kiva floor plan duplicates one at Oraibi on the Hopi Reservation. A Zuni Shalako (spirit of the rain clouds) towers 10 feet high. Some of the pottery and stone tools come from prehistoric pithouses excavated in nearby Chino Valley. Open Tues.-Sat. 10 a.m.-4 p.m. and Sun. noon-4 p.m. from June 1 to Aug. 31; other times groups can visit by appointment (contact the chamber of commerce; tel. 445-2000). Admission is $1 adult, children under 12 free. The pueblo-style museum building is at 100 N. Arizona St., one block north off E. Gurley Street.

White members of the community organized the Smoki "tribe" in 1921. Their original purpose was to entertain visitors with Indian dances at the annual Frontier Days celebration. Later the group took a more serious interest in collecting rituals, dances, and artifacts. Members of the semisecret organization can be identified by a four-dot tattoo on the side of their left hands. The Smoki have come under heavy fire from Hopi and other Indian tribes who find the dances offensive and who object to "secret" religious items in the museum. But the Smoki continue their spectacular annual performance, which always includes the Smoki Snake Dance with live bull snakes. The Smoki ceremonials take place on the first or second Sat. evening in August.

**The Bead Museum**

A *bead* museum? Yes, this collection contains beads and personal adornments from the far corners of the world and from many times. Open Mon.-Sat. 9:30 a.m.-4:30 p.m.; free. Beads are also for sale. Enter through Liese Interiors and Artifacts on Whiskey Row, 140 S. Montezuma St.; tel. 445-2431.

---

## PRESCOTT

1. Ponderosa Shopping Center
2. Yavapai Regional Medical Center
3. Prescott High School
4. YMCA
5. Yavapai County Fairgrounds
6. Plaza Shopping Center
7. Murphy's Restaurant
8. Head Hotel
9. Hassayampa Inn
10. courthouse and plaza
11. Sharlot Hall Museum
12. Whiskey Row; Bead Museum
13. Prescott Chamber of Commerce
14. post office
15. Hotel Vendome
16. Prescott National Forest (supervisor's office)
17. public library
18. Ken Lindley Field
19. Smoki Museum
20. Greyhound Bus
21. Yavapai Community College
22. Fort Whipple (now a VA Hospital)
23. Sheraton Resort
24. Prescott National Forest (Bradshaw District office)

## Phippen Museum Of Western Art

Paintings, sketches, and bronzes by outstanding artists celebrate Western heritage and art. Promising new artists receive attention too. The museum honors George Phippen, a well-known Western artist who founded Cowboy Artists of America and served as their first president. A gift shop sells cards, jewelry, crafts, and artworks. Open daily except Tues. 1-4 p.m. from Jan. 2 to May 14, then Mon. and Wed.-Sat. 10 a.m.-4 p.m. and Sun. 1-4 p.m. from May 15 to Dec. 31.; $2 adult, $1.50 senior 60 and over, $1 children and student (free for ages under 12); tel. 778-1385. The museum is in a ranch-style building 6 miles north of Prescott at 4701 N. Hwy. 89 (one mile north of the US 89A turnoff).

## Prescott Animal Park

Meet denizens of the Southwest, exotic creatures, and farm animals at this small but growing zoo. A reptile house holds scaled friends. Open daily (closed Mon. in winter) 10 a.m.-5 p.m.; $2 adult, $1 children under 15; tel. 778-4242. Located about 6 miles north of town on Heritage Park Road, just off Willow Creek Road.

## Fort Whipple

This historic Army fort dates from 1863. It honors Brig. General Amiel Weeks Whipple, who served with the Army's Corps of Topographical Engineers until he was killed in the Civil War. The post played a major role during the Indian wars and was maintained until 1912. Ten years later it became a Veterans Administration hospital. Many of the military buildings dating from the turn of the century remain, including barracks and officers' quarters. You're welcome to visit the hospital grounds, though there's no museum or visitor center. Fort Whipple is on the northeast edge of town off US 89.

# ACCOMMODATIONS

Prescott has a good selection of places to stay. Try to have a reservation for weekends during the warmer months, as lots of desert refugees come up then. Rates tend to go up on summer weekends and drop a bit in winter (regular summer rates shown below). Book way in advance for Frontier Days, held around July Fourth, and expect to pay more.

## Historic

Prescott's old hotels, dating from the early 1900s, offer a real experience. The **Hassayampa Inn** stood as the town's grand hotel in 1927 and still does today, thanks to a recent renovation. The plush lobby has a painted ceiling, old piano, and other antiques. All rooms now have private baths and a/c; $56.94-105.12 s, $67.89-105.12 d. The hotel's Peacock Room offers elegant dining. Located at 122 E. Gurley St.; tel. 778-9434 (or Phoenix tel. 257-8884). **Hotel Vendome** (built 1917) also offers attractively restored rooms with private baths, $38.33-65.70 d, ($49.28-76.65 d Fri. and Sat.); 230 S. Cortez St.; tel. 776-0900. The **A.J. Head Hotel** (built 1898-1903) has been restored on a more modest scale; rooms, some with private bath, cost $21.40-39 s, $24.40-42 d; weekly rates run $75.60-128 s, $86.40-138.80 d; a restaurant serves dinner Wed.-Sun.; 129 N. Cortez St.; tel. 778-1776. **Highland Hotel** (built 1903) used to be a brothel where the girls scouted potential customers from the bay windows. The hotel has not been much restored, but then neither have the prices; rooms (bath down hall) cost $15.88 s or d; also weekly and monthly rates; located on Whiskey Row at 154 S. Montezuma St.; tel. 445-9059. **Hotel St. Michael** began life in 1900 as the Hotel Burke; rooms, all with private bath, start at $27.38 s, $31.21 d; a San Francisco-style coffeehouse serves refreshments; at the corner of 205 W. Gurley and Montezuma sts.; tel. 776-1999.

## Bed And Breakfast

**Prescott Pines Bed and Breakfast** has rooms for $46-71 s or d on the south edge of town at 901 S. White Spar Road (S. US 89); tel. 445-7270. Nearby **Prescott Country Inn Bed and Breakfast** offers cottage suites at $53.66-108.41 s or d; 503 S. Montezuma; tel. 445-7991. The **Marks House Inn Bed and Breakfast** is an 1894 Victorian house;

$81.75-120 s or d; 203 E. Union; tel. 778-4632. **Lynx Creek Farm Bed and Breakfast** features an organic orchard and garden and farm animals, 5 miles east on AZ 69; $89-100 s or d; tel. 778-9573.

## Motels

Places to stay include: **Wheel Inn Motel** ($28.47-39.42 s, $32.85-43.80 d; close to downtown at 333 S. Montezuma St.; tel. 778-7346); **Sierra Inn** ($43.80 s, $49.28 d; 809 White Spar Road; tel. 445-1250); **Comfort Inn** ($43.55 s, $48.63 d; 1290 White Spar Road; tel. 778-5770); **Motel 6** ($27.32 s, $33.89 d; 1111 E. Sheldon St.; tel. 776-0160); **Apache Lodge Motel** ($30.66 s or d; 1130 E. Gurley St.; tel. 445-1422); **Colony Inn** ($36.72 s, $45.36 d; 1225 E. Gurley St.; tel. 445-7057); **Best Western Prescottonian Motel** ($49.27-65.70 s, $60.23-82.13 d; 1317 E. Gurley St.; tel. 445-3096 or 800-528-1234); and **Sheraton Resort** ($91.38-107.50 s, $102.13-118.25 d; 1500 Hwy. 69, then up the hill; tel. 776-1666 or 800-325-3535). **Airport Centre Inn** is near the airport and Antelope Hills Golf Course at the junction of US 89 and Willow Creek Road; $32.85 s, $41.61 d; tel. 778-6000.

## Campgrounds

**White Spar Campground,** 2.5 miles south of downtown on US 89, has drinking water year-round but no showers or hookups; $6; one loop stays open in winter (obtain water then from a faucet near the campground entrance). **Indian Creek Campground** is 4 miles south on US 89, then left 0.7 mile on Forest Route 97; open mid-May to the end of Sept. (no water or fee). **Lynx Lake** and nearby **Hilltop campgrounds** sit above a pretty lake containing trout and catfish. Sites are open mid-May to the end of Sept. with drinking water but no showers or hookups, $6. Picnickers may use tables near the boat ramp free of charge. You can reserve sites at Lynx Lake Campground through MISTIX; tel. (800) 283-CAMP. To reach Lynx Lake, head east 3 miles on AZ 69 (from N. US 89), then turn south 2.5 miles on Walker Road; Hilltop campground is one mile farther. A cafe, store,

*Granite Basin Lake*

and boat rentals are at the north end of Lynx Lake. **Granite Basin Campground** lies near a small lake at the base of Granite Mountain, northwest of town; open all year; it may have water and fee; from W. Gurley St., turn northwest 4.3 miles on Grove Ave./Miller Valley Road/Iron Springs Road, then turn north 3.5 miles on Forest Route 374. **Lower Wolf Creek Campground** (south of town) is open mid-May to mid-Nov.; no drinking water or fee; take Senator Hwy. (Forest Route 52) south 7.5 miles, then turn west one mile on Forest Route 97; or from US 89, 4 miles south of Prescott, turn east 5 miles on Forest Route 97. Groups can reserve **Upper Wolf Creek Campground** with the Forest Service. You and your horse can stay at **Groom Creek Horsecamp's** individual ($6) and group reservation sites; open year-round with water; located near the start of Forest Trail 307; go 6.5 miles south on the Senator Hwy. from town.

**Watson Lake Park,** beside Granite Dells, is open all year and has showers; $6.45 tents, $8.60 RV w/electric hookups, no charge for day use; tel. 778-4338; 4 miles north of town on US 89. **Point of Rocks RV Campground,** just north of Watson Lake Park, is open all year with RV sites at $13.13 w/hookups (no tents); tel. 445-9018. **Willow Lake RV and Camping Resort** features a swimming pool, fishing, store, and showers; $10.17 tent or RV no hookups, $13.38 RV w/hookups; tel. 445-6311; located 5 miles north of town off Willow Creek Road.

**Powell Springs Campground,** near the village of Cherry between I-17 and Prescott, stays open all year and has spring water (no charge); from the turnoff on AZ 169 (5 miles west of I-17 and 25 miles east of Prescott) turn north 4 miles on Forest Route 372.

# FOOD

**American And Continental Cuisine**
**Murphy's** serves sandwiches, steak, prime rib, seafood, and other dishes in an old mercantile building dating from 1890; dim lighting, antiques, and greenery add to the romantic setting; open daily for lunch and dinner (mod. prices) at 201 N. Cortez St.; tel. 445-4044. The **Peacock Room** of the Hassayampa Inn has an old-fashioned atmosphere for its varied menu of American and continental specialties; open for Sunday brunch and daily for breakfast, lunch, and dinner (mod.); 122 E. Gurley St.; tel. 778-9434. **Prescott Mining Company** features steak, prime rib, seafood, chicken, and veal in a rustic atmosphere; open daily for lunch and dinner, Sat. and Sun. for brunch (inexp. to mod.); 155 Plaza Dr. (behind Plaza Shopping Center); tel. 445-1991. The **Pine Cone Inn's** menu lists steaks, seafood, and other American cuisine; open daily for breakfast, lunch, and dinner (mod.); live dinner music is featured many nights; 1245 White Spar

Road; tel. 445-2970. The **Thumb Butte Room** at the Sheraton Resort offers fine dining for Sunday brunch and daily for breakfast, lunch, and dinner (mod.); you have a choice of indoor or patio seating at the resort's hilltop location; 1500 Hwy. 69; tel. 776-1666.

**Mario's** serves Italian dinners, pizza, and sandwiches at two locations (inexp.): east of downtown at 1505 E. Gurley/AZ 69 (open daily for lunch and dinner; tel. 445-1122) and downtown at 107 S. Cortez St. (open Mon.-Sat. for lunch and Fri. and Sat. for dinner; tel. 445-1301). **Roman Deli Italian Restaurant** features pasta dishes, veal, and seafood; open daily except Sun. for lunch and dinner (inexp. to mod.); 623 Miller Valley Road; tel. 778-0740.

**Inexpensive American**
**Greens & Things** offers omelets, Belgian waffles, bagels, sandwiches, and fruit drinks; open daily except Sun. for breakfast and lunch at 106 W. Gurley St.; tel. 445-3234. **Maude's** serves breakfast and lunch Mon.-Sat. at 146 S. Montezuma St. (Whiskey Row); tel. 778-3080. **Berry's Pie Pantry & Restaurant,** open daily for lunch and dinner, has two locations: in an old Victorian house at 111 Grove Ave. (just off W. Gurley St.); tel. 778-3038; and at 1106 E. Gurley St.; tel. 778-6330. **K-Bob's Steak House** cooks up mesquite-broiled steaks, fried chicken, kabobs, and sandwiches; open daily for lunch and dinner at 1355 Iron Springs Road; tel. 778-0866. Enter the **Dog House** for a choice of many different hot dogs (other sandwiches too); open daily except Sun. for lunch at 126 S. Montezuma St.; tel. 445-7962. One of Prescott's many American cafes, the **Prospector's Skillet** is open daily for breakfast, lunch, and dinner (24 hours on weekends) at 1317 E. Gurley St. (N. US 89); tel. 776-1500. **Juniper House** is a family restaurant open daily for breakfast, lunch, and dinner at 810 White Spar Road (S. US 89); tel. 445-3250. **Super Carrot Natural Foods** offers health foods and a lunch counter; open Mon.-Sat. at 236 S. Montezuma St.; tel. 776-0365.

### Other Cuisines

**Los Amigos Casita** serves Mexican food Tues.-Sat. for lunch and dinner (inexp.) on Whiskey Row at 150 S. Montezuma St.; tel. 445-3683. **El Charro,** another inexpensive Mexican cafe, is open Mon.-Sat. for lunch and dinner at 120 N. Montezuma St.; tel. 445-7130. Dine Chinese at the **Canton Cafe,** open daily for lunch and dinner (inexp. to mod.) at 1102 Willow Creek Road; tel. 445-0070. The **China Jade Restaurant** specializes in Mandarin-style cuisine; open Sun. for dinner and Mon.-Sat. for lunch and dinner (inexp. to mod.) at 1459 W. Gurley St. (Fry's Shopping Center); tel. 445-4072.

## OTHER PRACTICALITIES

### Entertainment

There's something happening every summer night on the **Courthouse Plaza**—could be a concert, dance, or speech. **Yavapai College** sponsors a variety of performances and other events; call the switchboard at 776-2220. Catch movies at the **Marina Theatres** (205 N. Marina and Willis sts.; tel. 445-1010) or **Plaza West Cinemas** (Fry's Shopping Center at 1509 W. Gurley St.; tel. 778-0207). The bars along Whiskey Row (Montezuma St.) sometimes have live bands. The **Pine Cone Inn** offers more sedate live dinner music (usually from the '40s) at 1245 White Spar Road; tel. 445-2970. **Softball** fans have a good chance of seeing a game in season—Prescott bills itself the "Softball Capital of the World." Local newspapers *The Prescott Sun* and *The Prescott Courier* list what's going on in town.

### Events

Prescott's major annual events include: **May:** Zonta Home Tour visits about five outstanding Prescott homes, both historic and modern. Prescott Downs thoroughbred and quarter horse race season begins (held at the county fairgrounds most weekends and holidays from Memorial Day to Labor Day). George Phippen Memorial Western Art Show & Sale. Whiskey Row Marathon. **June:** Sharlot Hall Folk Art Fair celebrates pioneer skills; costumed participants demonstrate black-

smithing, horseshoeing, woodworking, spinning, weaving, churning, and cowboy cooking. Territorial Prescott Days features games, art shows, music, and dancing; on the same weekend as the Sharlot Hall Folk Art Fair. Local Yavapai Indians and other tribes put on the Indian Pow Wow and Art Show. The Square Dance Festival gets Prescott a-hoppin'. **July:** Frontier Days Rodeo and Parade, held over the Fourth of July holiday, draws spectators from all over Arizona and beyond for the "world's oldest rodeo" (since 1888), Western art show, entertainment, dances, and fireworks. Down-home musicians show their craft in the Bluegrass Festival. **August:** Antique Auto Show. Soroptimist Antique Show. Smoki Ceremonials (recreated Indian dances by white men). Mountain Artists Arts & Craft Show. **September:** Faire on the Square is a juried arts and crafts show, held Labor Day weekend on the Courthouse Plaza. Yavapai County Fair and Horse Show. **October:** Drivers of antique and classic cars dress in the time period of their vehicle for the Governor's Cup Rallye, a drive from Prescott to the Grand Canyon. The Air Festival brings vintage planes, stunt pilots, military flyovers, parachutists, and model plane exhibits to Prescott's airport. **December:** Courthouse Christmas Lighting and Christmas Parade.

### Shopping And Services

**Yavapai College Art Gallery's** monthly shows represent college, community, and state artists; open Tues.-Thurs. 11 a.m.-5 p.m. and Fri. and Sat. 11 a.m.-3 p.m.; located across from the campus entrance at 1100 E. Sheldon St.; tel. 776-2365. **The Basecamp** has a good stock of outdoor supplies, including hiking, backpacking, cross-country ski gear, and topo maps at 142 N. Cortez St.; tel. 445-8310.

The downtown **post office** is at the corner of Goodwin and Cortez sts., across from the Plaza. **Yavapai Regional Medical Center** provides hospital services at 1003 Willow Creek Road; tel. 445-2700. Go swimming at the **YMCA outdoor pool** in summer, 750 Whipple St.; tel. 445-7221. Or swim year-round at the indoor **Yavapai College pool** (turn north onto the campus from 1100 E. Sheldon St.; the swimming pool is in the first building on the left); tel. 776-2175 (schedule recording). Play **tennis** at Yavapai College, Prescott High School (on Ruth St.), or next to Ken Lindley Field (E. Gurley and Arizona sts.). **Arizona World Trail Rides, ALPH Stables** offers trail rides ($10/hour), cookouts, and haywagon rides year-round; located off Williamson Valley Road (go northwest on Grove Ave./Miller Valley Road/Iron Springs Road to Williamson Road, then turn right 5 miles to the sign); tel. 778-0559. Play **golf** on 18-hole courses at **Antelope Hills Golf Course** (next to the airport, 7 miles north of town on US 89; tel. 445-0583) or at **Prescott Country Club** (14 miles east on AZ 69; tel. 772-8984).

## Information

The **Prescott Chamber of Commerce** will help you find what you're looking for and tell you about upcoming events. Open Mon.-Sat. 9 a.m-5 p.m. (and sometimes Sun. in summer); tel. 445-2000 (or tel. 253-5988 in Phoenix). At other times call for a telephone recording of local sights and events. Office is at 117 W. Goodwin St. opposite the Plaza (write Box 1147, Prescott, AZ 86302). The **U.S. Forest Service** offices have maps and information about hiking, camping, and back roads in the Prescott National Forest. The **Supervisor's Office** has general information for the national forest and a bookstore at 344 S. Cortez St.; open Mon.-Fri. 8 a.m.-4:30 p.m.; tel. 445-1762. You'll get the best first-hand information for the Prescott area from rangers at the **Bradshaw Mountain District** office at 2230 E. Hwy. 69 (Prescott, AZ 86301), one mile east of town; open Mon.-Sat. 8 a.m.-4:30 p.m.; tel. 445-7253.

Prescott's excellent **public library** includes a Southwest collection; open daily except Sun. at 215 Goodwin St.; tel. 445-8110. **Yavapai College** also has a fine library, open daily during school terms; turn north onto the campus from 1100 E. Sheldon St.; tel. 776-2265. The **Worm** bookstore stocks topo maps and books about Arizona, as well a general reading, at 128 S. Montezuma St.; tel. 445-0361. The selection of regional and general reading at the **Satisfied Mind** is bound to please; 230 S. Montezuma St.; tel. 776-9766. **Prescott Newsstand** has a fine selection of periodicals and regional books at 123 N. Cortez St.; tel. 778-0072. The **Book Nook,** at 324 W. Gurley St., buys and sells used books; tel. 778-2130.

## Tours And Transport

On **Prescott Historical Tours,** Melissa Ruffner dresses in a turn-of-the-century costume to lead visitors around the original Prescott townsite or the old mining town of Jerome; tel. 445-4567. You may strike it rich on **Gold Prospecting Tours'** excursions to local mining sites; tel. 776-8170. **Prescott Tours and Limousine** can arrange almost any tour you'd like in Arizona or the Southwest; tel. 776-1993.

**Greyhound** has one bus daily south to Phoenix and north to Ash Fork with many onward connections; open weekdays 9 a.m.-5:30 p.m. and Sat. 1:30-5:30 p.m. at 820 E. Sheldon St.; tel. 445-5470. For a taxi, call **Ace** at 445-5510. Cars can be rented at the airport and in town; see the Yellow Pages.

# VICINITY OF PRESCOTT

## Granite Dells

With their giant boulders that have weathered into delicately balanced forms and fanciful shapes, the scenic Dells are a good place for a picnic or hike. Rock climbers like to tackle the challenging granite formations. Indians used to hide out here, and some ruins and artifacts have been discovered. From the 1920s to the '50s, Granite Dells Resort attracted crowds of vacationers; a large dance pavilion survives from that era. Watson Lake Park (camping and free day use) lies at the south edge of the Dells, 4 miles north of town on US 89.

## Thumb Butte Trail

This popular loop hike begins just west of town and climbs Thumb Butte Saddle (elev. 6,300 feet) for good views of Prescott and the surrounding countryside. The trail winds through a valley of dense ponderosa pines, then crosses windswept ridges where pinyon, juniper, oak, and prickly pear grow. Two short spur trails lead to vista points from which you can see the city, Granite Dells, Chino Valley, and seemingly countless mountains, including the distant San Francisco Peaks. Reaching the fractured granite summit of Thumb Butte takes some effort and skill; this last 200-foot ascent is best left to rock climbers. The trail itself is a moderately easy outing, 1.7 miles roundtrip with an elevation gain of 600 feet; allow 2½ hours. Signs identify many of the plants along the way. Local people like to come up for the sunset. Hiking season runs year-round, except after winter snowstorms. From downtown, head west 3.5 miles on Gurley St./Thumb Butte Road to Thumb Butte Park; the trailhead is on the left side of the road; picnic tables are nearby.

## Granite Mountain Wilderness
On a daytrip, hikers can explore the rugged Granite Mountain Wilderness and enjoy fine views from an overlook (elev. 7,125 feet). Rock climbers come to challenge the granite cliffs that offer a nearly complete range of difficulties. Five trails allow many hiking combinations, but only **Granite Mtn. Trail #261** climbs to the heights. This trail ascends gently 1.3 miles to a trail junction at Blair Pass, then turns right and switchbacks another 1.3 miles to a saddle on Granite Mountain; from here the trail turns southeast and climbs a bit more for another mile to a viewpoint. Ponderosa pines grow at the trailhead and on top of Granite Mountain, though much of the trail passes through manzanita, mountain mahogany, pinyon, agave, and other plants of the chaparral. Average hiking time for the 7.5-mile roundtrip hike is 6 hours. It's a moderately difficult trip with an elevation gain of 1,500 feet; carry water. Season lasts from about May to October. The Iron Springs and Jerome Canyon 7.5-minute topo maps cover this area. From W. Gurley St. in Prescott, turn northwest 4.3 miles on Grove Ave./Miller Valley Road/Iron Springs Road, then turn right 5 miles on Forest Route 374 past the campground and lake turnoffs.

## Other Hikes
Dozens of trails wind through the rugged Bradshaw and Mingus mountains near Prescott. See the Forest Service people for trail descriptions, maps, and back-road information; their Bradshaw District office is at 2230 E. Hwy. 69, one mile east of town; tel. 445-7253.

Probably the most unusual trail is the 1,200-foot **Groom Creek School Nature Trail,** built especially for blind people by the Sunrise Lions Club of Prescott. Trail pamphlets (obtain from the Bradshaw office) in both Braille and print explain natural features and processes. You'll find the trail just past the village of Groom Creek, 6 miles south of town on the Senator Highway.

## Crown King And Vicinity
Old mines, ghost towns, and wilderness surround this rustic village 55 miles southeast of Prescott. Prospectors discovered gold at the Crowned King Mine in the 1870s, but mine owners had to wait until the late 1880s before the ore could be processed profitably. A branch line of the Prescott and Eastern Railroad reached the site in 1904. Legal battles closed mine operations in the early 1900s, and today the mining camp attracts retired people and serves as an escape from summer heat. The Crown King Saloon goes way back to 1898, when it was built at Oro Belle camp, 5 miles southwest. Pack mules hauled it piece by piece to Crown King in 1910.

Rough roads discourage the average tourist, but the region can be explored with maps, determination, and preferably with a high-clearance vehicle. Easiest way in is from Cleator on Forest Route 259, which can be reached from the I-17 Bumble Bee or Cordes exits. You'll be following the twisting path of the old railroad on the drive up. Cautiously driven cars can make it OK. Rougher roads approach Crown King from Prescott and Mayer. The Prescott National Forest map, $2 from Forest Service offices, shows backroads and most trails.

In Crown King, you can have meals at the saloon or a restaurant, and there's a general store. No motels or RV parks here, but you can camp in the Forest Service campgrounds at **Horsethief Basin Recreation Site,** 7 miles to the southeast. Usual season for **Kentuck Springs** and **Hazlett Hollow** campgrounds (elev. 6,000 feet) is May 1 to Nov. 30; both are free. Hazlett Hollow and Turney Gulch (group reservation area) have drinking water. **Castle Creek Wilderness,** east of the campgrounds, has very steep and rocky terrain; vegetation ranges from chaparral to ponderosa pine. The staff at Crown King Work Center, up the hill from town, can tell you about trails and roads. They are mostly local people who know the area well. *Arizona's Best Ghost Towns* by Phillip Varney contains good information on this historic and very scenic part of Arizona.

*craft studio at Arcosanti*

## ARCOSANTI

The vision of Paolo Soleri, Italian laureate designer, can be seen under construction in the high-desert country between Flagstaff and Phoenix. The vision is a joining of architecture and ecology that Soleri has dubbed "arcology." The city, designed to make the best use of energy and land, will grow vertically, using pedestrian walkways and elevators instead of freeways. Arcosanti's strangely shaped buildings make efficient use of the sun's energy. Construction began in 1970, but it progresses slowly, as funds come in. When finished, the city will house 5,000 people.

The public is welcome to visit this project, the first of its kind, open daily 9 a.m.-5 p.m. all year. Tours, lasting about one hour, take visitors through some of the buildings and explain Soleri's goals; $4 adult, under 12 free. The Visitor Center (free admission) has a model of Arcosanti, architectural exhibits, books by Soleri, and crafts. The famous Cosanti bronze and clay windbells make attractive gifts and help finance the project. A cafe and bakery (open daily) serve good breakfasts and lunches. Arcosanti schedules festivals and frequently hosts concerts. Seminars and workshops allow interested people to participate in construction.

For information on seminars, workshops, music classes, and events, write Arcosanti, HC 74, Box 4136, Mayer, AZ 86333; or call 632-7135. Hotel accommodations cost $15 s, $20-25 d (reservation suggested). Arcosanti is easily reached from I-17 (34 miles southeast of Prescott and 65 miles north of Phoenix); take Cordes Junction Exit 262A, then follow signs 2.5 miles on a dirt road. You'll find a motel, cafes, RV park, and gas stations near the interchange.

# WESTERN ARIZONA

## INTRODUCTION

Few landlocked states can boast more than 1,000 miles of shoreline, but you'll find it in Arizona. The Colorado River, after its wild run through the Grand Canyon, begins a new life in the western part of the state. Tamed by massive dams and irrigation projects, the Colorado here flows placidly toward the Gulf of California. The deep blue waters of the river and the lakes it forms make up Arizona's west boundary, separating the state from California and Nevada. Boaters and fishermen have discovered this watery paradise, whether breezing along on water skis or seeking a quiet backwater for fishing. Once you step away from the life-giving waters, though, you're in desert country, the real desert, where legends have been made by those who lived here—the Indian tribes, hardy prospectors, determined pioneer families, and even a U.S. Army camel corps.

### THE LAND

Numerous small ranges of rocky hills break up the monotonous desert plains of western Arizona, much of which lies at elevations under 2,000 feet. The valley of the Colorado River, inhabited by most of western Arizona's population, drops from about 1,220 feet at the west boundary of the Grand Canyon to just 70 feet at the Mexican border. A few mountain ranges in the north rise high enough to support forests of manzanita, oak, pinyon and ponderosa pine, and even some fir and aspen. Highest and most notable of these "biological islands" are the Hualapai Mountains, easily reached by road from Kingman. Hualapai Peak (8,417 feet) crowns the range. Old mines and ghost towns dot the mineral-rich Cerbat and Black mountains, also in the

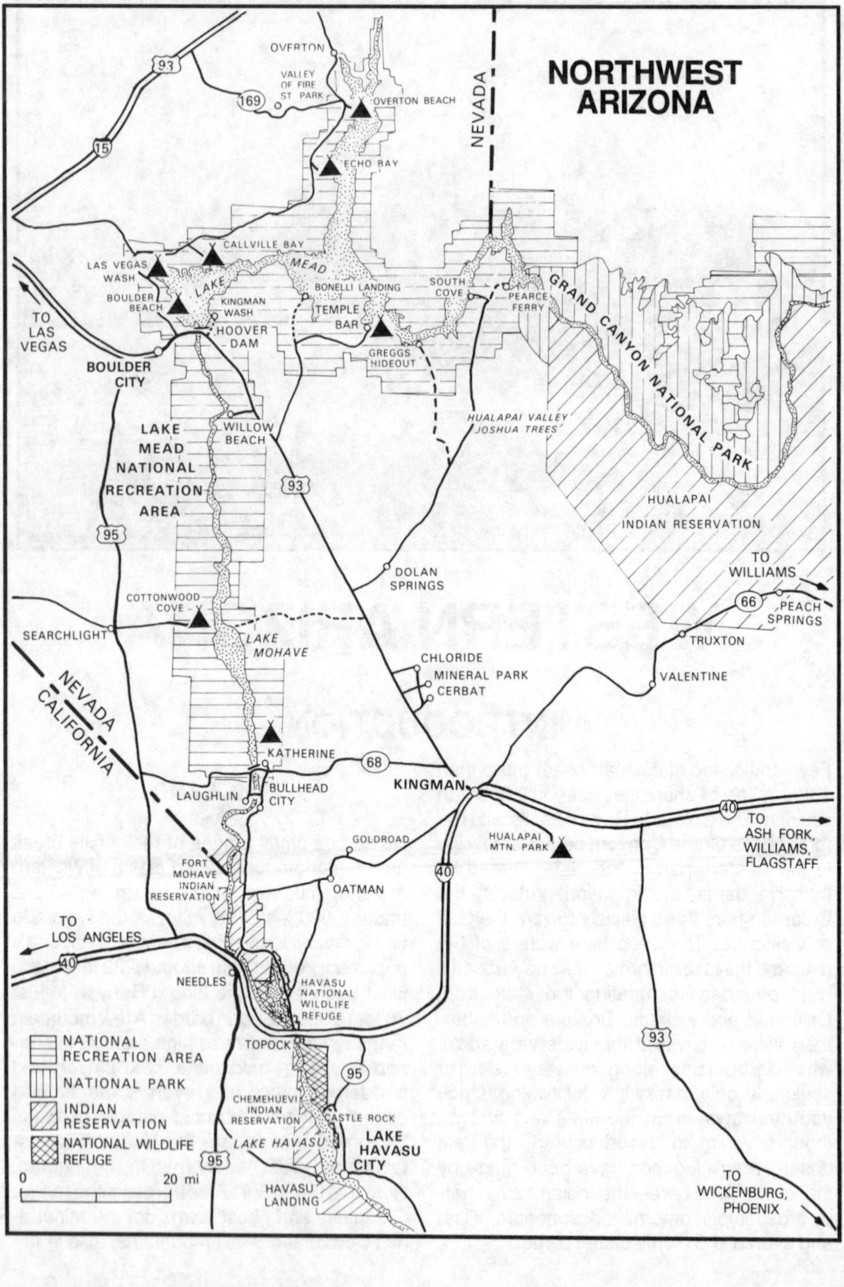

NORTHWEST
ARIZONA
OVERTON
VALLEY
OF FIRE
ST. PARK
169
OVERTON BEACH
93
15
NEVADA
ECHO BAY
CALLVILLE BAY
LAS VEGAS
WASH
LAKE
MEAD
BOULDER
BEACH
KINGMAN
WASH
BONELLI LANDING
TEMPLE
BAR
SOUTH
COVE
PEARCE
FERRY
GRAND CANYON NATIONAL PARK
TO
LAS
VEGAS
HOOVER
DAM
GREGGS
HIDEOUT
BOULDER
CITY
WILLOW
BEACH
HUALAPAI VALLEY
JOSHUA TREES
LAKE
MEAD
NATIONAL
RECREATION
AREA
93
HUALAPAI
INDIAN RESERVATION
95
DOLAN
SPRINGS
TO
WILLIAMS
66
PEACH
SPRINGS
COTTONWOOD
COVE
SEARCHLIGHT
Lake
Mohave
TRUXTON
CHLORIDE
MINERAL PARK
CERBAT
VALENTINE
NEVADA
CALIFORNIA
KATHERINE
68
KINGMAN
LAUGHLIN
BULLHEAD
CITY
40
TO
ASH FORK,
WILLIAMS,
FLAGSTAFF
GOLDROAD
HUALAPAI
MTN. PARK
FORT
MOHAVE
INDIAN
RESERVATION
OATMAN
40
TO
LOS ANGELES
40
NEEDLES
HAVASU
NATIONAL
WILDLIFE
REFUGE
NATIONAL
RECREATION AREA
NATIONAL PARK
INDIAN
RESERVATION
NATIONAL WILDLIFE
REFUGE
TOPOCK
95
93
CHEMEHUEVI
INDIAN
RESERVATION
CASTLE ROCK
Lake Havasu
LAKE
HAVASU
CITY
95
0
20 mi
HAVASU
LANDING
TO
WICKENBURG,
PHOENIX
© MOON PUBLICATIONS

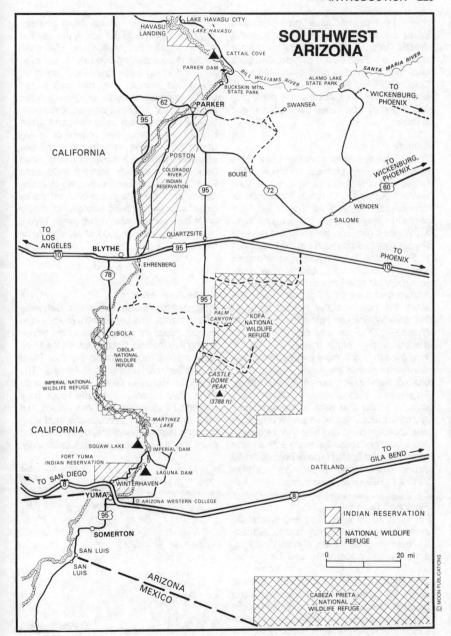

SOUTHWEST ARIZONA

north. The Kofa and Castle Dome mountains in the south make up the Kofa National Wildlife Refuge, a home for desert bighorn sheep, mule deer, desert tortoise, Gambel's quail, and rare native palm trees. Along the Colorado River, the three national wildlife refuges of Havasu, Cibola, and Imperial protect migratory and native birds, plants, and animals.

## Climate

The sun shines down from the azure skies nearly every day; perhaps no place in the United States receives more sunshine than western Arizona. In winter, thousands of "snowbirds" descend on the desert from northern climes to enjoy the sun and fresh air. Winter nights can be frosty, but daytime temperatures usually warm to the 60s or 70s F. Spring and autumn often have perfect weather—wildflowers, too, in the early spring. By May the snowbirds are gone, and Arizona towns along the Colorado River often make the news as the hottest spots in the country. Parker holds the record for Arizona—127° F on one day in 1905. Yet despite average highs that exceed 100° F from June to Sept., many visitors do come in summer to play in the water, cooling off by boating, water-skiing, swimming, and tubing. So western Arizona actually has two seasons...a winter that attracts many retirees and others who enjoy fishing, exploring ghost towns, prospecting, and hiking in the desert, and a summer season of more active water sports. Annual rainfall ranges from about 10 inches in the higher country to less than 3 inches in the south near Yuma.

## Flora And Fauna

For most of the year, plant and animal life in the desert appears very sparse. Actually it's there—a great variety of plants, reptiles, amphibians, mammals, and birds—but awaiting the right conditions to come out. With good winter or summer rains, dormant seeds will spring to life, quickly bloom, and produce new seeds; seemingly dead sticks sprout leaves and flowers. Cactus and other succulents rapidly absorb precious rain for the long dry spells ahead. Most animals, large and small, hide out during the daytime in caves, burrows, or bushes. The small pocket mice and kangaroo rats do not even require drinking water; they feed mainly on seeds and manufacture their own water! Larger animals include western spotted skunk, kit and gray fox, badger, ringtail cat, bobcat, mountain lion, mule deer, and desert bighorn sheep. Your best chance of seeing desert critters is in early morning and late afternoon; binoculars come in handy. Birds flock to the wetlands along the Colorado River in great numbers, especially in spring and autumn. Canada geese and many species of ducks winter here. Nesters include the great blue heron, great egret, green heron, least bittern, white-winged dove, and Yuma clapper rail.

# HISTORY

## Native Americans

Indians lived along the lower Colorado River's shores long before the first white men arrived. Frequent wars between the tribes, lasting into the mid-19th C., forced the Maricopa Indians to migrate up the Gila River to what is now southcentral Arizona. The victorious Mohave, Quechan, and Cocopa tribes were joined in the early 1800s by a nomadic Paiute group, the Chemehuevi, and they all lived simply in brush-and-mud shelters and farmed, hunted, and gathered wild plant foods from the desert. Surprisingly,

*kit fox*
(Vulpes macrotis)

*Mohave Indian chief, late 1800s*

some Hopi and Navajo from northeast Arizona also live on the Colorado River Reservation, established in 1865, in addition to Mohave and Chemehuevi. Their voluntary resettlement, begun in 1945, was possible because the reservation was intended to serve "Indians of said river and its tributaries" and because the Colorado River Tribal Council gave its permission.

## Spanish Explorations

Spanish explorers made their first tentative forays up the Colorado River in 1540, but they didn't stay. A tireless Jesuit priest, Eusebio Francisco Kino, explored the lower Colorado in 1700-02, collecting information for the map makers of the day. During the 1760s, fear of Russian expansion down the coast of California caused the Spanish to build coastal settlements there and to open a land route from Mexico. In 1780, Spanish troops and missionaries built two missions on the Colorado River, La Purisima Concepcion (opposite today's Yuma) and nearby San Pedro y San

Pablo de Bicuner. Abuses by the foreigners infuriated the local Quechan Indians, who revolted the following year. Father Francisco Garcés and most of the male Spaniards were killed, while women and children were taken captive. Spanish troops ransomed the captives but made no more attempts to settle along the Colorado River.

## Americans Arrive

Rugged mountain men like James Ohio Pattie, who later wrote an account of his travels (see "Booklist"), explored the Colorado River area in search of beaver skins and adventure during the early 1800s. The Army established Camp Yuma (later Fort Yuma) in 1851 at the river crossing of the Southern Overland Trail (Cooke's Road) to assist Americans headed west for California gold fields. Ten years later, troops built Fort Mohave upstream on the Colorado River to protect travelers taking the Beale Wagon Road across northern Arizona. Government surveyors explored much of the lower Colorado during the 1850s, but maps still showed the northwest corner of the territory as "unexplored." It wasn't until 1869 that John Wesley Powell filled the last big gap on his epic boat voyage down the Colorado from Green River, Wyoming, to Callville, Nevada (now under Lake Mead).

Although Spanish miners had worked gold deposits in western Arizona before Mexican independence in 1821, large-scale mining in the region didn't begin until the 1860s. Gold discovered in 1858 at Gila City, 20 miles upstream from Yuma, had attracted 1,200 miners by 1861. Yet 3 years later the gold played out; a traveler reported that "the promising metropolis of Arizona consisted of three chimneys and a coyote." Prospectors later found many other gold and silver deposits up and down western Arizona, hastening development of the region. Lead-zinc and copper mines opened too. Most of the old workings lie abandoned now, marked by piles of tailings, foundations, and decaying walls.

Steamboats plied the Colorado River after 1852, providing faster and safer transport than wagon trains. For more than 50 years they served the forts and mining camps along the shores. Some of the giant riverboats stood 3 decks high and were 140 feet long, yet drew only 2 feet of water. These giant sternwheelers took on their cargos from ocean ships at Port Isabel on the Gulf of California, then headed upstream as far as 600 miles. Boat traffic declined when the Southern Pacific Railroad went through Yuma in 1877, and it virtually ended in 1909 when the Laguna Dam was built.

Farmers in southern California had been eyeing Colorado River water, and in 1901 they began diverting it to their fields around the Salton Sink. Four years later, however, a flood destroyed controlling gates and the entire Colorado River roared down the canal, flooding the Imperial Valley. Frantic rockfilling by the railroad finally returned the river to its normal seaward course in 1907, but it left a new body of water behind—the 35-mile-long Salton Sea. More canals and dams have since been built on the Colorado, making it one of the most useful and used rivers in the world today.

# INDIAN TRIBES

Six tribes now live along the lower Colorado between the west end of the Grand Canyon and the Gulf of California. The three Yuman-speaking tribes, Mohave, Quechan, and Cocopa, have been here since prehistoric times. Later they were joined by Uto-Aztecan-speaking Chemehuevi, followed by some Hopi and Navajo of northeastern Arizona.

## Mohave
Northernmost of the Yuman tribes, the Mohave formerly lived in loosely organized bands, uniting only for warfare or defense. They farmed the bottom lands, hunted, and gathered wild foods. Crafts included finely made baskets, pottery, and beadwork. Ceremonial dances and long funeral wakes played an important role in their social life. Even today, the Mohave and Quechan cremate their dead—a rare practice among American Indian tribes. Mohave live on the Fort Mohave Reservation near Needles, Calif., and in a larger group on the Colorado River Reservation near Parker, Arizona. You can learn more about the tribe and see their crafts at the tribal museum just south of Parker.

## Chemehuevi
This group of Paiute Indians once roamed the eastern Mohave Desert as hunting and gathering nomads. They settled in the Chemehuevi Valley of the Colorado River in the early 1800s and took up the agricultural practices of their Mohave neighbors. The U.S. Government gave the Chemehuevi a reservation in 1907, but Lake Havasu inundated much of their farmland in 1938. The tribe now lives on the Chemehuevi Reservation opposite Lake Havasu City and on the Colorado River Reservation.

*Mohave squaws and children, 1880s*

*Quechan Indian family, 1884*

### Quechan
Formerly known as the "Yuma," the tribe now prefers to be called "Quechan." In the 19th C., their territory included much of the lower Colorado and about 25 miles of the Gila River valley. Federal government actions trimmed their land considerably during the late 19th and early 20th centuries. Today the tribe lives in California on the Fort Yuma Indian Reservation opposite Yuma, Arizona. They have a museum in a historic building that was once part of Camp Yuma.

### Cocopa
Before the coming of the white man, the Cocopa lived downstream from the Quechan in the Colorado River delta, once one of the most fertile areas in the Southwest. Like other Colorado River tribes, though, they suffered greatly from European-introduced diseases. Today they live on two tiny reservations south of Yuma and in the Mexican states of Sonora and Baja California.

## TRANSPORT

Regional airports in Yuma, Blythe (CA), Lake Havasu City, and Bullhead City have connections to Phoenix, southern California, and Las Vegas. Greyhound buses and Amtrak trains serve Kingman on their routes across northern Arizona and Yuma on their southern Arizona routes. Greyhound also stops at Needles (CA), Lake Havasu City, and Parker on its route between Las Vegas and Phoenix. LTR Bus connects Kingman with Las Vegas and Phoenix on a more direct route, bypassing the Colorado River towns. Boat cruises and raft trips show visitors some of the scenery in the Lake Mead National Recreation Area; other boat tours go through the scenic Topock Gorge between Lake Havasu City and Laughlin, Nevada. Cheapest trips of all are the free ferries across the river between Bullhead City and the gambling casinos at Laughlin. Your own car (or boat!) allows you to explore the quiet and scenic backcountry of western Arizona.

*Mohave camp, late 1800s*

*Kingman, ca. 1899*

# THE NORTHWEST CORNER

## KINGMAN

Kingman sits in high desert country (elev. 3,325 feet) surrounded by the Cerbat, Hualapai, and Black mountains. Lewis Kingman came through the area in 1880 while surveying a right-of-way for the Atlantic and Pacific Railroad between Albuquerque, New Mexico, and Needles, California. The railroad camp that later took his name grew into a major mining, ranching, and transportation center for northwestern Arizona. A county election in 1866 required the county seat to move from Mineral Park to Kingman, but residents of Mineral Park balked at turning over county records. Kingmanites, according to one story, then sneaked over to Mineral Park in the dead of night to snatch the records and bring them to Kingman, where they've stayed ever since. Mining has declined since WW II, and the last major operation (Duval's Mineral Park copper mine) shut down in 1981. Kingman (pop. 25,000) serves many motorists on their way across the country on I-40 or to Las Vegas or Phoenix. Kingman's boosters proclaim the town's 1,800 rooms and 50 restaurants as "fit for a king." Attractions in the vicinity that you might want to visit include Hoover Dam and the Lake Mead National Recreation Area, ghost towns and old town sites such as Oatman and Chloride, cool forests of Hualapai Mountain Park, London Bridge in Lake Havasu City, and glittering casinos in Laughlin and Las Vegas.

### Mohave Museum Of History And Arts

This museum's varied collection will give you a feeling for the history of northwestern Arizona. Dioramas, murals, and many artifacts show development from prehistoric times to the present. The Hualapai Indian Room contains a full-size "wickiup" (brush shelter), pottery, baskets, cradleboard, and other crafts. You can try your hand at grinding mesquite beans with the Indian *mano* and *metate*. Other things to see include paintings, sculpture, and crafts in the art gallery, photos showing construction of Hoover Dam, carved turquoise mined from the Kingman area, portraits of U.S. presidents with their first ladies, memorabilia of local-boy-turned-movie-star Andy Devine, and the outdoor mining exhibits. The museum even has a pipe organ, used in concerts here. History buffs can dig into the museum's library. A gift shop sells books on the region and Indian crafts. Open Mon.-Fri. 10 a.m.-5 p.m., Sat. and Sun. 1-5 p.m.; closed major holidays; donations accepted; tel. 753-3195. Located at 400 W. Beale St.; take I-40 Exit 48 and go east 0.3 mile on Beale Street.

### Wagon Tracks

Wagons creaking down the hill into Kingman from the 1870s to 1912 carved deep ruts into the soft volcanic bedrock here. Another road bypassed this spot in 1912, leaving the old road in its original condition. Evenly spaced holes beside the road have stirred up some debate. Some people think that wagon masters jammed long poles in them for braking; others say that the local board of supervisors

planned to dynamite the road for use by automobiles. The site lies near a pretty canyon just a short drive from town. From the museum, take Grandview Ave. north 0.4 mile from Beale St., then turn right 0.6 mile on Lead Street. Look for a wooden footbridge on the right and follow the path across it to the old wagon road.

### Bonelli House

This historic house of native tufa stone reflects the lifestyle and taste of a prominent Kingman family early in this century. The Bonellis built it in 1915 using both American and European designs to replace an earlier residence lost to fire. Thick walls insulate the interior from the temperature extremes of Kingman's desert climate. The Bonelli family lived here until 1973, when the city of Kingman purchased the house to restore as a bicentennial project. Open Thurs.-Mon. 1-5 p.m. except major holidays; donation; tel. 753-1413. Located at 430 E. Spring and N. Fifth streets (see map).

*wagon tracks*

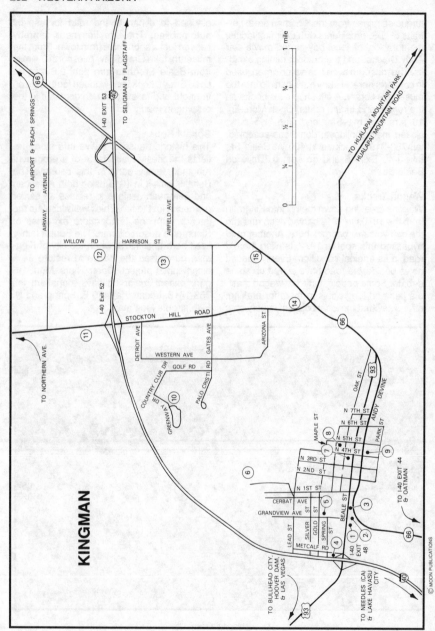

# KINGMAN

TO AIRPORT & PEACH SPRINGS

TO SELIGMAN & FLAGSTAFF

AIRWAY AVENUE

I-40 EXIT 53

66

40

TO NORTHERN AVE.

WILLOW RD    HARRISON ST

AIRFIELD AVE

12

13

15

I-40 Exit 52

STOCKTON HILL ROAD

14

66

11

DETROIT AVE

WESTERN AVE

GATES AVE

ARIZONA ST

ARIZONA ST

GOLF RD

COUNTRY CLUB DR

GREENWAY DR

PALO CRISTI RD

10

93

OAK ST

ANDY DEVINE

N 7TH ST

N 6TH ST

MAPLE ST

N 5TH ST

PARK ST

8

7

N 4TH ST

N 3RD ST

9

6

N 2ND ST

N 1ST ST

CERBAT AVE

GRANDVIEW AVE

LEAD ST

SILVER ST

GOLD ST

SPRING ST

METCALF RD

BEALE ST

5

3

1

2

4

I-40 EXIT 48

TO I-40 EXIT 44 & OATMAN

66

TO BULLHEAD CITY, HOOVER DAM, & LAS VEGAS

93

TO NEEDLES (CA) & LAKE HAVASU CITY

40

1 mile

3/4

1/2

1/4

0

TO HUALAPAI MOUNTAIN PARK

HUALAPAI MOUNTAIN ROAD

© MOON PUBLICATIONS

## Accommodations And Campgrounds

Most of Kingman's motels and restaurants line E. Andy Devine Ave. (AZ 66/US 93) between I-40 Exits 44 and 53 and also W. Beale St. (US 93) off I-40 Exit 48. Rooms often fill up on summer weekends, when reservations are a good idea.

The **Kingman KOA** is open year-round with a pool, showers, game room, store, and miniature golf; $13.96 tent or RV no hookups, $18.34 RV w/hookups; take I-40 Exit 53 (Andy Devine) and go northeast one mile on AZ 66, turn left on Airway one mile, then right on Roosevelt to the campground; tel. 757-4397. **Circle S Campground** has spaces year-round for tents ($10.95) and RVs ($15.33 w/hookups) with a pool, showers, and store at 2360 Airway; tel. 757-3235. RVers can also stay in **King's Rest RV Park** for $13.14 w/hookups; 3131 McDonald; tel. 753-2277. **Hualapai Mountain Park,** 14 miles southeast of town, offers tent and RV sites in cool pine forests, see "Vicinity of Kingman."

## Food

You'll find all the popular chain and fast-food places among the motels on Andy Devine. For local atmosphere, try **Nick's Coffee Mill** (2011 E. Andy Devine; tel. 753-3888); **City Cafe** (1929 E. Andy Devine; tel. 753-3550);

---

### KINGMAN

1. Mohave Museum of History and Arts
2. Kingman Chamber of Commerce
3. Locomotive Park
4. bus station
5. swimming pool
6. wagon tracks
7. library; post office branch
8. Bonelli House
9. Amtrak train
10. Kingman Municipal Golf Course
11. Kingman Regional Hospital
12. Centennial Park
13. Mohave County Fairgrounds
14. main post office
15. Lewis Kingman Park

---

**Route 66 Distillery** (Quality Inn, 1410 E. Andy Devine; tel. 753-5531); or **4th Street Social Club** (401 E. Andy Devine Ave.; tel. 753-7877). **Kingman 76 Auto-Truck Plaza** is open 24 hours at 946 W. Beale (I-40 Exit 48); tel. 753-7600. Get pizza and Italian food at **Buccilli's Pizza** (2775 Northern; tel. 757-7279) and **Pizza Hut** (3395 E. Andy Devine; tel. 757-3292). **La Poblanita** serves Mexican food at 1921 Club Ave., off Stockton Hill Road; tel. 753-5087. Dine Chinese at **House of Chan** (960 W. Beale; tel. 753-3232; closed Sun.); **Jade Restaurant** (3370 Stockton Hill; tel. 757-3207); and **Golden China Restaurant** (4135 Stockton Hill; tel. 757-5265).

## Entertainment And Events

For nightlife try the **Long Branch Saloon** with live or DJ country and Western music and dancing nightly, 2255 Airway Ave.; tel. 757-8756. Catch movies at **The Movies,** 4055 Stockton Hill; tel. 757-7985.

The Kingman Chamber of Commerce can fill you in on the following and other local happenings. Classic and antique cars get their kicks in the **Route 66 Fun Run Road Rally** in late April. Artists and craftsmen show their work in the **Festival of the Arts** the first weekend in May. Country music bands compete in the **Country Showdown** and chili chefs do their best in the **Chili Cookoff** on the same weekend in late May. Take in the exhibits and entertainment of the **Mohave County Fair** in September. Kingmanites and visitors celebrate **Andy Devine Days** with a parade, PRCA rodeo, and other festivities in late Sept. or early October. See handmade crafts in the **American Cancer Society Arts & Crafts Fair** the second weekend in November.

## Services

The main **post office** is at 1901 Johnson, though the downtown branch on N. Fourth St. (next to the library) can be more convenient. **Kingman Regional Medical Center** is at 3269 Stockton Hill Road (just north from I-40 Exit 52); tel. 757-2101. **Swimming pools** are located at the corner of Grandview Ave. and Gold St. (tel. 753-5636) and in Centennial Park at 3333 N. Harrison (tel. 757-7910).

**Centennial Park** also has tennis and racquetball courts, ballfields, and picnicking. **Kingman Municipal Golf Course** has nine holes at 1001 E. Gates (west off Stockton Hill Road); tel. 753-6593. **Valle Vista** offers an 18-hole course at 9686 Concho Dr. (14 miles northeast on AZ 66); tel. 757-8744.

## Information

The **Kingman Chamber of Commerce** can help you explore this corner of Arizona. Open daily 8 a.m.-9 p.m. from May to Sept., then daily 8 a.m.-6 p.m. the rest of the year; tel. 753-6106; downtown at 333 W. Andy Devine (Box 1150, Kingman, AZ 86402). Find out about recreation areas and the backcountry near Kingman from the **BLM's Kingman Resource Area** office; open Mon.-Fri. 7:30 a.m.-4:30 p.m. at 2475 Beverly Ave. (Kingman, AZ 86401); tel. 757-3161. The **public library** is in Kingman's original one-room schoolhouse, built in 1896, at 219 N. Fourth (north off Andy Devine and Beale); tel. 753-0707.

## Transport

**Greyhound** and **LTR** buses stop at the tiny station near Carl's Jr. Restaurant at 303 Metcalf Road, just east of I-40 Exit 48; open daily; tel. 753-2522. **Amtrak** has daily passenger train service west to Los Angeles and east to Flagstaff, Albuquerque, and beyond; tel. (800) 872-7245 for info and reservations; the terminal is downtown at the corner of Fourth St. and Andy Devine; tel. 753-6886. See the Yellow Pages for car rental agencies. For a taxi call **Kingman Cab**; tel. 753-3624.

# VICINITY OF KINGMAN

## Hualapai Mountain Park

The Hualapai Indians, whose name means "Pine-tree Folk," lived in these mountains until the military relocated the tribe northward in the 1870s. Now a county park, the mountains are easily reached by a 14-mile paved road that runs southeast from Kingman. The park offers dense forests, scenic views, hiking trails, picnicking, camping, and rustic cabins. Elevations range from 5,000 to 8,417

feet, attracting animals and birds rarely seen elsewhere in northwestern Arizona. The forested slopes support groves of manzanita, scrub and Gambel oak, pinyon and ponderosa pine, white fir, and aspen. Such animals as mule deer, elk, mountain lion, fox, and raccoon roam the forests. The park office has checklists of plants, animals, and birds found here. Hiking trails wind through the mountains, visiting overlooks and climbing Aspen and Hayden peaks.

Campsites have drinking water (except in winter) but no showers, $5/night. A small RV area offers hookups for $10/night. Cabins, built for a Civilian Conservation Corps camp in the 1930s, have cooking and bath facilities; $30-50. You can visit the park any time of year, though winter snows may call for chains or four-wheel drive. For information and reservations at the campground, RV park, or cabins, visit or call the Mohave County Parks Dept.; open Mon.-Fri. 8 a.m.-5 p.m.; 303 Oak St. (Box 390, Kingman, AZ 86402); tel. 753-0739. The Hualapai Ranger Station is near the park's entrance; tel. 757-3859.

The nearby **Hualapai Mountain Lodge** offers a motel, RV park, restaurant, and store. Some of the well-preserved buildings here also belonged to the Civilian Conservation Corps camp. The motel ($52.70 for 1-4 persons) and restaurant are open Tues.-Sun. year-round; the restaurant serves breakfast (except in winter), lunch, and dinner. Self-contained RVs can park overnight; no hookups. The grocery store is open summer only (May to mid-Sept.). From Kingman, drive to the county park, then turn left one mile at the fork just past the ranger station; tel. 757-3545.

The Bureau of Land Management's **Wild Cow Springs Campground** (free; no water) sits in a ponderosa pine and oak forest at an elevation of 6,200 feet; from Hualapai Mountain Park, continue south 5 miles on unpaved BLM Road 2123.

## Burro Creek Campground

A perennial stream flows through this scenic canyon area (elev. 3,000 feet). Visitors enjoy picnicking, birdwatching, swimming, hiking, jeeping, and rock hounding for agates. The

*Golden Gem Mill*

BLM campground has drinking water but no showers; $2 night. Head southeast 70 miles from Kingman on US 93 (or northwest 60 miles from Wickenburg).

## Cerbat

Gold and silver deposits in the Cerbat Mountains, north of present-day Kingman, attracted miners in the late 1860s. They founded the town of Cerbat and worked such mines as the Esmeralda, Golden Gem, and Vanderbilt. Cerbat became the Mohave County seat in 1871, but it lost the honor 2 years later to nearby Mineral Park. By 1912 Cerbat's post office had closed. The Golden Gem's mill and headframe still stand, structures that rarely survive in other ghost towns. You'll also see stone foundations and several buildings. The turnoff for Cerbat is 9 miles northwest of Kingman on US 93, near Milepost 62; head east 0.8 mile on a good dirt road, turn left 0.5 mile, then turn right 2 miles to the site. Keep left when passing a group of modern buildings just outside old Cerbat.

## Mineral Park

During most of the 1870s and 1880s, Mineral Park reigned as the county seat and most important town in the area, but it lost those distinctions in 1887 to Kingman. By 1912 Mineral Park had even lost its post office.

Very little remains to be seen today except the modern Duval copper mine, which shut down in 1981. The turnoff for Mineral Park is 14 miles northwest of Kingman on US 93, between Mileposts 58 and 59; turn east 5 miles on a paved road to the site.

## Chloride

After discovering silver chloride ore here in the early 1860s, prospectors founded this town—the oldest mining camp in northwestern Arizona. Hualapai Indians made life precarious during Chloride's first years until Army troops subdued the tribe. Several buildings survive from the town's long period of mining activity, which lasted into the 1940s. A few hundred people, including many retirees, now live here.

An old miner's shack and other buildings can be seen in the historical grounds. The Silver Bells, a group of women dedicated to preserving Chloride's history, run a playhouse and make and sell antique-style clothing at Sheps store.

Artist Roy Purcell painted giant, brightly colored murals in 1966 and 1975 on cliffs 2 miles southeast of town. He titled his work **"The Journey—Images from an Inward Search for Self."** Indian petroglyphs can also be found in the area. From Chloride, take Tennessee Ave. (the main road into town)

*detail from Roy Purcell's "The Journey"*

past the post office and Tennessee Mine, then follow signs; the road may be too rough for low-slung cars.

**Sheps Store** has apartment rentals (week or longer), RV park, cafe, and general store; on Second St. (1½ blocks south of the post office); tel. 565-3643. The **Tennessee Cafe and Bar** is at Tennessee and Second Street. **"Mellerdramas"** and a **swap meet** take place year-round on the first and third Saturdays. Townspeople dress up in old-fashioned clothing on **Old Miners' Day,** the last Sat. in June, for a parade, barbecue, games, and shootouts. Chloride is 20 miles northwest of Kingman on US 93, then east 3 miles on a paved road at Grasshopper Junction.

### Oatman

The weathered, old gold-mining town of Oatman sits on the western foothills of the Black Mountains, 28 miles southwest of Kingman. Elephant's Tooth, the gleaming white quartz pinnacle east of town, beckoned prospectors, who knew that gold and silver often occur with quartz. Gold mining began in 1904, attracting hordes of miners and business people. They named their community in memory of the Oatman family, victims of an Apache attack in 1851. Oatman prospered with many new businesses, seven hotels, 20 saloons, and even a stock exchange. Area mines produced nearly two million ounces of gold before declining in the 1930s. The town, which once had over 12,000 citizens, began to fade away. It might have disappeared altogether had it not become a travelers' stop on Route 66. Oatman lost the highway traffic in 1952, when engineers rerouted the road to the south. A few hundred citizens hang on today, relying largely on tourist business.

Many old buildings survive, some now in use as gift shops and cafes. The **Oatman Hotel,** a two-story adobe structure built in the 1920s, has exhibits upstairs of life in the boom days. Small rock shops and gift shops, cafes, and the post office lie along Main Street. Pick up a self-guiding tour sheet at one of the shops to learn more about Oatman's history. You're almost sure to meet the town's wild burros, which wander the streets looking for handouts from visitors; buy feed from one of the shops.

Oatman celebrates **Gold Camp Days** on Labor Day weekend with shootouts, a costume parade, and dancing. **Shootouts,** usually just in fun, also take place every Sat. and Sun. on Main Street.

*an Oatman burro*

The **Silvercreek Saloon and Steakhouse** serves Mexican and American food, or you could try the **Gold City Saloon** across the street for hamburgers, fried chicken, steaks, and other items. Both saloons feature live bands and dancing on Sat. and Sun. afternoons. RVs can stay at **Blackstone RV Park** (adults only) about 12 miles west of town; tel. 768-3303.

### Goldroad

This picturesque ghost town is about 3 miles northeast of Oatman on the way to Kingman. Goldroad thronged with life after the discovery of gold around 1901 but later faded away. By the early 1940s only weeds and desert critters inhabited the site. Foundations and crumbling adobe walls remain. Mine shafts and tailings cover surrounding hillsides. Take care when exploring Goldroad—walls and mine shafts are liable to collapse.

## BULLHEAD CITY

The growing community (pop. 25,000) lines AZ 95 and the Colorado River for about 11 miles. Gamblers, fishermen, and boaters enjoy their sports in this desert oasis. The site lay empty and remote in the 1940s, when construction workers arrived to build Davis Dam upstream. With completion of the dam in 1953, everyone thought the construction camp called Bullhead City would fold up. But instead it became a center for outdoor recreation. In addition to the Colorado River at the town's doorstep, 240 square miles of deep, blue water beckon 6 miles north in Lake Mohave. The "bullhead" rock formation that gave the place its name did disappear—under the waters of the lake. Bullhead City lies 35 miles west of Kingman via AZ 68, and 25 miles north of Needles (CA) on AZ 95. Bright lights of gambling casinos in Laughlin glitter from across the river in Nevada.

### It's Hot!

Even the chamber of commerce admits the town gets hot in summer. In 1984 Bullhead City "won" the distinction of being the hottest spot in the nation, with 71 days of national highs. Not everyone likes having the National Weather Service in town; in 1981, after being told Bullhead City was the nation's 1980 hot-spot, about 100 local merchants signed a petition protesting the nationwide coverage given to their hot weather. But life goes on. Air conditioning, low humidity, and the cool waters of the Colorado keep most residents and visitors happy. In winter, you'll appreciate the sunny, spring-like days characteristic of the region.

### Accommodations And Campgrounds

You have a choice of about 20 motels in Bullhead City, or you can stay across the river at the casinos in Laughlin. Try to have reservations for motels, casinos, and RV parks, especially if you're arriving on a weekend. You can save money at some places by visiting Sun.-Thursday. The casinos have weekday rates as low as $18 d!

Campgrounds and RV parks stay open year-round. Most RV parks prefer guests to stay a week or longer. **Happy Campers** accepts overnighters at Hwy. 95 and 2196 Merrill Ave., about one mile south of downtown; $14.85 tent, $16.50 RV w/hookups; facilities include pool, game room, store, and showers; tel. 763-2179. **Davis Camp Park,** maintained by Mohave County, offers beach sites for tents and RVs ($7 no hookups), RV sites ($13 w/hookups), picnic and boat ramp facilities ($2 day use), and showers (available to noncampers for $3); off AZ 95 just north of town; tel. 754-4606. Clark County, Nevada, runs **Sportsmens Park Campground** beside the river just below Davis Dam; sites cost $6; drinking water but no showers; located off Casino Dr. north of Laughlin; tel. (702) 298-3377. Many RVers just park for the night on the vast casino parking lots in Laughlin. You'll also find a motel, RV park, and campground 6 miles north at **Katherine Landing.**

### Food

For dining in Bullhead City, try **Branding Iron** for steak and seafood (3061 Hwy. 95; tel. 758-5445); **Captain's Table** for steak, prime rib, and seafood (River Queen Resort at

*Davis Camp, the original
Bullhead City*

Seventh and Long; tel. 754-3214); the **Rib Ranch's** ribs and other meat dishes (closed Sun., 135 Hwy. 95; tel. 754-3349); **Gerard's** at Silver Creek Inn for breakfast and lunch (1670 Hwy. 95; tel. 763-8400); **China Szechuan** for Mandarin and Szechuan styles (1490 Hwy. 95; tel. 763-2610); and **El Palacio** for Mexican dining (5230 Hwy. 95; tel. 768-1881). Some of your best eating deals will be on the Nevada side; most casinos have restaurants and buffets that will entice you with $1.99 breakfasts, $2.49 lunches, $3.69 dinners, and $4.95 seafood feasts.

### Events
Lake Mohave Resort sponsors the **U.S. Bass Fishing Team Tournament** in April. Also in April, find out which cook has the best recipe in the **Chili Cookoff** at Bullhead Community Park. In May, Nevadans celebrate **Laughlin River Days** with a parade, games, and food, and you can enjoy food and games, but no burro, at the **Burro Barbecue** at Bullhead Community Park. **Fireworks** light the skies on July Fourth. In Nov., take in the action at **Bullhead/Laughlin Rodeo.** Boats at Lake Mohave Resort (Katherine Landing) stage a **Parade of Lights** in December.

### Services And Recreation
**Bullhead Community Park,** just north of the chamber of commerce, is a pleasant spot for a picnic. The **post office** is downtown at 990 Hwy. 95. **Bullhead Community Hospital** is at 2735 Silver Creek Road; tel. 763-2273.

One of the best fishing areas along the Colorado River lies right in front of Bullhead City. The cold and swift waters from Davis Dam harbor large rainbow trout, channel catfish, and, during late spring and early summer, giant striped bass weighing in at 20 pounds and more. Golfers can play on the 9-hole **Chaparral Golf Course** (1260 E. Mohave Dr., 5 miles south of town; tel. 758-3939); the 9-hole **Riverview RV Resort Golf Course** (2000 E. Ramar, 3 miles south on AZ 95, then 1.5 miles east on Ramar; tel. 763-1818); or the 18-hole **Desert Lakes Golf Course** (10 miles south on AZ 95, then east on Joy Lane; tel. 768-1800).

### Information
The **Bullhead City Chamber of Commerce** staff will tell you about the area; open Mon.-Fri. 8 a.m.-5 p.m., Sat. 9 a.m.-3 p.m.; when the office is closed, you can pick up literature from the rack outside; located on the south side of Bullhead Community Park; write Box 66, Bullhead City, AZ 86430; tel. 754-3891. The **Laughlin Chamber of Commerce** will answer your questions about the casinos and events on the Nevada side; open Mon.-Fri. 8 a.m.-4:30 p.m. across from the Flamingo Hilton at 1725 Casino Dr., Laughlin, NV 89029; tel. (702) 298-2214 or (800) 227-5245. There's a **public library** in the south part of Bullhead City at 1130 E. Hancock Road; tel. 758-6867.

**Transport**
**Greyhound** has more than a dozen buses daily; the station is at 1010 Hwy. 95 between Sixth and Seventh streets; tel. 754-4625. **Stateswest Airlines** flies to destinations in California, Arizona, and Colorado; tel. (800) 759-3866. **Mesa Airlines** goes to cities in Arizona, New Mexico, Colorado, and Wyoming; tel. (800) MESA-AIR. The airport is just north of Bullhead City. See the Yellow Pages for auto rental agencies.

**Laughlin**
The casinos on the Nevada side of the river will happily accept your money in any of the usual gambling games of the state. Cheap bus tours from Arizona and southern California cities bring people by the thousands. Laughlin's casinos have a more casual, and some say more friendly, atmosphere than the

bigger gambling centers of Las Vegas and Reno. Besides the games of chance, you could check out the movies, live shows, hotel rooms, swimming pools, and dining bargains offered by many of the casinos.

Visit either the Bullhead City or Laughlin chambers of commerce to pick up information guides and pamphlets that list attractions and services offered by the casinos. **Laughlin River Tours** operates river cruises on the Colorado from the Edgewater Casino and Harrah's del Rio Casino docks; tel. (702) 298-1047 or (800) 228-9825 out of state. From Bullhead City you can drive across the Colorado River bridge just north of town or take the 8-mile route via Davis Dam farther north. Some casinos offer free passenger ferries that leave from the shore north of downtown Bullhead City. Shuttle buses connect the casinos.

# LAKE MEAD
# NATIONAL RECREATION AREA

The Colorado River forms two long lakes as it winds more than 177 miles through Lake Mead National Recreation Area. From Grand Canyon National Park, the blue waters flow around the extreme northwest corner of Arizona past black volcanic rocks, stark hillsides, and white, sandy beaches. Striking desert scenery and inviting waters make the area a paradise for boaters, fishermen, water-skiers, swimmers, and scuba divers. Visitors often sight bighorn sheep on the canyon cliffs and wild burros in the more level areas. Adventurous hikers can explore the hills and canyons of this wild country, knowing that it rarely sees human visitors. To get the most out of a visit to Lake Mohave and Lake Mead, you really need a boat; roads approach only at a few points. If you don't have your own, marinas offer rentals from humble fishing craft to luxurious houseboats. Boat tours take in some of the scenery of Lake Mead from Lake Mead Marina. You can also glide through Black Canyon below Hoover Dam on raft tours. The National Park

Service provides free boat ramps, campgrounds ($6/night; no showers or hookups), and ranger stations at most of the developed areas. Rangers patrol the recreation area and answer visitors' questions. Park Service people also staff the Alan Bible Visitor Center at the turnoff for Boulder Beach, 4 miles west of Hoover Dam.

The boating and camping season lasts all year at the lakes, but spring and autumn are ideal times to visit. Most people come in summer, and though it's hot, swimmers and water-skiers best appreciate the water then. In winter, you wouldn't want to hop in without a wetsuit, though topside temperatures are usually pleasant during the day.

**Fishing**
Both Lake Mohave and Lake Mead offer excellent fishing year-round. In either lake you'll find largemouth and striped bass, channel catfish, crappie, and bluegill. Lake Mohave's upper reaches have an especially good reputation for rainbow trout, while Lake Mead

has hot fishing for striped bass—some specimens top 50 pounds. Most marinas sell licenses and tackle. Marinas and ranger stations can advise on the current fishing regulations and the best spots to fish. Shore fishermen need a license only from the state they're in. If you fish from a boat, you'll need a license from one state and a special-use stamp from the other.

## LAKE MOHAVE

Heading upstream from Bullhead City, you'll first come to Lake Mohave. Squeezed between hills and canyon walls, the lake appears like a calmer Colorado River. Though 67 miles long, Mohave spreads only 4 miles at its widest. **Davis Dam,** which holds back the lake, is open daily 7:30 a.m.-3:30 p.m. MST for free self-guided tours. **Katherine Landing,** nicknamed "Katy's Gulch" by some people, is 6 miles north of Bullhead City. An **information center** near the entrance is open daily 8 a.m.-4 p.m. (irregular hours in

Katherine Landing

summer). Katherine Landing has a public swimming beach, boat ramp, campground ($6), marina with boat rentals (fishing, ski, patio, and houseboat), RV park ($15.75), motel ($60-83 d June 16-Sept. 15; $42-63 d the rest of the year), restaurant, and store. Showers and laundry are available too. For motel, RV park, and boat reservations, contact **Lake Mohave Resort,** Bullhead City, AZ 86430; tel. 754-3245 or (800) 752-9669.

**Cottonwood Cove** is about halfway upstream on the main body of water on the Nevada side. If driving there, turn off US 95 at Searchlight, and go east 14 miles on NV 164. You might enjoy a stop at Searchlight's small museum of river artifacts. Cottonwood Cove has a motel ($66.68 d April 1-Oct. 31; $42 the rest of the year), RV park ($12), campground ($6), restaurant, marina with rentals (including houseboats), and public swimming beach; contact **Forever Resorts,** Box 1000, Cottonwood Cove, NV 89046; tel. (702) 297-1464. Northward, the lake narrows at **Eldorado Canyon** and becomes a river again. Trout and trout fishermen hang out in the cold river currents upstream. A road (NV 165) approaches Eldorado Canyon from the Nevada side but there's no campground or resort.

About a dozen river miles before Hoover Dam you'll reach **Willow Beach** on the Arizona shore. It's only a 4-mile detour from US 93 if coming by car. No Park Service campground here, but Willow Beach has an RV park ($13.18-14.77), motel ($50.64 all year), restaurant, and marina with boat rentals (including houseboats) at **Willow Beach Resort,** Willow Beach Road, Willow Beach, AZ 86445; tel. (602) 767-3311. The "Wall of Fame" in the resort cafe and store has photos of fishermen and their trophy trout catches. **Willow Beach National Fish Hatchery,** 0.5 mile upstream by road, raises large numbers of rainbow trout for stocking the Colorado and lakes. Hatchery staff also study and propagate endangered native species—Colorado River squawfish, razorback suckers, and humpback chub. You're welcome to visit the raceways outside during daylight hours and the inside displays (open daily 8 a.m.-4:30

Hoover Dam under construction

p.m.); tel. (602) 767-3456. A popular **canoe trip** begins below Hoover Dam and follows the swift Colorado beneath sheer 1,500-foot cliffs of the Black Canyon to Willow Beach. Hot springs at the base of the cliffs make an enjoyable stop. Obtain permission to launch your canoe for this trip from the Bureau of Reclamation Warehouse, Box 299, Boulder City, NV 89005; tel. (702) 293-8356/8286. **Black Canyon Raft Tours** make this trip daily Feb. to Nov. for $60 adult and $35 children under 12, it includes 3 hours on the river, lunch, and transport from the Gold Strike Casino (between Boulder City and Hoover Dam); tel. (702) 293-3776 or (602) 767-3331.

### Arizona Hot Springs Hike

This 6-mile-roundtrip hike follows a canyon through layers of volcanic rock to hot springs near the Colorado River, downstream from Hoover Dam. The highly mineralized spring water surfaces in a side canyon at temperatures ranging from 113° to 142° F. Allow 5 hours for the hike down and back, plus more time to soak in the hot springs. You'll be descending 800 feet to the river. Hiking isn't recommended in summer, when temperatures can be hazardous. As for any desert hike of this length, bring water (one gallon per person) and wear a sun hat; also be alert for rattlesnakes and flash floods. Don't hike if thunderstorms threaten. Check trail conditions with a ranger beforehand—the way might be difficult to follow in spots. From Hoover Dam, drive 4.2 miles southeast on US 93 to a dirt parking area on the right at the head of White Rock Canyon. Follow the canyon on foot down to the Colorado River, then walk 0.25 mile downstream along the river to the side canyon with the hot springs. Climb a 20-foot ladder to reach the best springs.

### HOOVER DAM

When completed in 1935, this immense concrete structure stood as one of the world's greatest engineering feats. It remains almost as impressive today, especially when you consider the mind-numbing statistics: it contains 3,250,000 cubic yards of concrete, has a height of 726 feet above bedrock, and produces of 4 billion kilowatt-hours of energy each year. With all these numbers coming at you, it's easy to miss the beauty of the dam's form and decoration. Look for the graceful curves, sculptures of the Winged Figures

*Winged Figure of the Republic*

of the Republic, art deco embellishments, terrazzo floor designs, and other touches. Guided tours leave frequently every day 8 a.m.-6:45 p.m. from Memorial Day weekend through Labor Day and 9 a.m.-4:15 p.m. the rest of the year (Nevada time); $1 adult, $.50 seniors 62 and up, free for age 15 and under; tel. (702) 293-8367. There's also a free exhibit room with a relief map of the Colorado River, a model of a generating unit, and memorabilia from construction of the dam. A multimedia show, *How the Water Won the West,* is shown in the "blue bubble" nearby. Park at the lot on the south side of the highway one mile before the dam on the Nevada side and take a shuttle bus.

## LAKE MEAD

Lake Mead, held back by Hoover Dam, ranks as the largest artificial lake in the United States. The reservoir holds the equivalent of 2 years' flow of the Colorado River. In the shape of a rough "Y," one arm of Lake Mead reaches north up the Virgin River, while the longer east arm stretches up the Colorado River into the Grand Canyon. Boaters have lots of room on the lake's 110-mile length. Countless little beaches and coves provide hideaways for camping and swimming. Largemouth black bass, striped bass, channel catfish, bluegill, and crappie swim in the waters.

### Alan Bible Visitor Center
Park Service exhibits introduce Lake Mead National Recreation Area's fishing, boating, other water sports, wildlife, and desert travel. A 15-minute movie, *Some People Just Call It the Lake,* is shown every half-hour. A botanical garden outside helps identify local flora. Books on the history, geology, plants, and wildlife may be purchased. Nautical and topo maps are sold too. Rangers have handouts and can tell you about backcountry camping, roads, and trails. Drop in for evening programs on weekends from April to October. The Visitor Center is open daily 8:30 a.m.-4:30 p.m. (to 5:30 p.m. in summer); 601 Nevada Hwy., Boulder City, NV 89005-2426; tel. (702) 293-8906. Located on US 93 at the turnoff for Boulder Beach, 4 miles west of Hoover Dam.

### Boulder Basin
Above Hoover Dam, the lake opens into the broad Boulder Basin. Campgrounds and marinas are located at Boulder Beach, Las Vegas Wash, and Callville Bay. Boulder Beach, just a few miles by car from Hoover Dam, has good swimming. **Lake Mead Resort** at Boulder Beach has a motel ($49.35 all year) restaurant, and marina with boat rentals; 322 Lakeshore Road, Boulder City, NV 89005; tel. (702) 293-3484 or (800) 752-9669. Tour boats leave the marina for 75-minute cruises on the lake to Hoover Dam; $7.50 adult, $4 children 5-12; tel. (702) 293-6180 (702-384-1234 in Las Vegas). RVs can stay at Boulder Beach in **Lakeshore Trailer Village** ($10.50 w/hookups and showers), 268 Lakeshore Road, Boulder City, NV 89005; tel. (702) 293-2540. **Las Vegas Boat**

**Harbor,** at Las Vegas Wash, has a restaurant, store, and marina (fishing, ski, and patio boat rentals), Box 91150, Henderson, NV 89009; tel. (702) 565-9111. **Callville Bay Resort & Marina** offers an RV park ($15.23 w/hookups and showers), coffee shop, and boat rentals (including houseboats); write HCR 30, Box 100, Las Vegas, NV 89124-9410; tel. (702) 565-8958 or (800) 255-5561 (houseboat reservations). **Kingman Wash,** on the Arizona shore near Hoover Dam, has only primitive camping.

## Virgin Basin

Upstream from Boulder Basin you'll pass through 6-mile-long Boulder Canyon before emerging into Virgin Basin, the largest and most dramatic part of Lake Mead. Rock formations with such names as Napoleon's Tomb, the Haystacks, and Temple Bar are scenic landmarks. Many narrow coves snake far back into the mountains. Two resorts lie along the giant Overton Arm, which branches north into the Virgin River. **Echo Bay Resort** has a motel ($68.25-73.50 d all year), RV park ($15.75 w/hookups), restaurant, and boat rentals (including houseboats), Overton, NV 89040-0545; tel. (702) 394-4000 or (800) 752-9669. **Overton Beach Resort,** farther north, offers an RV park ($13 w/hookups), snack bar, store, and marina with fishing boat rentals, Overton, NV 89040; tel. (702) 394-4040). Both Echo Bay and Overton Beach

areas have Park Service campgrounds as well. **Valley of Fire State Park,** about 10 miles west of Overton Beach, is noted for its impressive rock formations of red Jurassic sandstone; the park is open all year with Visitor Center exhibits (open daily 8:30 a.m.-4:30 p.m.), two campgrounds ($2-4), picnic areas (free day use), and hiking trails; tel. (702) 397-2088. See Indian artifacts from Pueblo Grande de Nevada in the **Lost City Museum**; open daily 8:30 a.m.-4:30 p.m. at 721 S. Hwy. 69 in the town of Overton, 11 miles north of Overton Beach; tel. (702) 397-2193. The Indian villages, now mostly under Lake Mead, date from the 1st century A.D.

**Temple Bar Resort,** Arizona's only development on Lake Mead, has cabins ($37), motel ($58), kitchenettes ($73), RV park ($15.75), restaurant, and boat rentals; Temple Bar, AZ 86443; tel. 767-3211 or (800) 752-9669 for reservations. There's also a Park Service campground. From Hoover Dam, go southeast 19 miles on US 93, then turn left 28 miles on a paved road.

**Bonelli Landing,** a primitive campground on the Arizona shore, is reached by dirt road off the route to Temple Bar.

## South Cove

Upstream the lake narrows in Virgin Canyon before opening into South Cove, the uppermost large open-water area of Lake Mead.

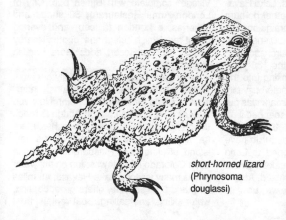

*short-horned lizard*
*(Phrynosoma*
*douglassi)*

There's a boat ramp on the Arizona side but no campground or resort. By car, South Cove is reached on a paved 45-mile road branching off US 93 between Hoover Dam and Kingman. You'll pass through Dolan Springs (small motel, RV parks, restaurants, and stores) and an area with Joshua trees as tall as 25 feet. They look like a strange cactus but really belong to the lily family. Primitive boat ramps and campsites are upstream at Pearce Ferry, reached by a dirt road.

*London Bridge*

# WESTCENTRAL ARIZONA

## LAKE HAVASU CITY

The late Robert McCulloch founded Lake Havasu City in 1964 to provide facilities for his new factories and a healthful environment for his employees. The planned city grew up on the east shore of Lake Havasu, 19 miles south of I-40 and 73 miles north of I-10, both major cross-country routes. Lake Havasu City might have become another ho-hum town had it not been for a brainstorm by McCulloch and his town planner, Disney man C.V. Wood. They decided to purchase London Bridge! Back in England, the 136-year-old bridge had been slowly sinking into the Thames. No longer able to handle busy city traffic, the famous London landmark was put up for sale in 1967. McCulloch snapped it up for the bargain price of $2,460,000, then spent more than twice that amount to have all 10,276 granite blocks shipped to Long Beach, California, trucked to Lake Havasu City, and painstakingly reassembled. After 3 years of construction, the bridge was up in its new home.

The Lord Mayor of London graciously came over in Oct. 1971 to preside at the bridge's dedication, much as King William IV and Queen Adelaide had done at the original dedication in 1831. London Bridge may be one of the stranger sights on the Arizona desert, but it put Lake Havasu City on the map!

More has been added since—an "English Village" complete with British pub, City of London Arms Restaurant, 50 shops and galleries, a London taxicab, and even a bright-red British telephone booth. Nearby London Bridge Resort adds more English atmosphere.

At first, the bridge spanned only dry land. Workers later dug a water channel underneath, cutting off Pittsburgh Point. Now you walk or drive across London Bridge to reach the campgrounds, RV parks, beaches, marina, airport, and other facilities on the new island, still known as Pittsburgh Point. As in other Colorado River towns, fun on the water draws many visitors. Lake Havasu, 45 miles long and 3 miles wide, offers great boating, water-skiing, and sailing. Boat rentals, boat tours, swimming beaches, tennis, and golf courses are readily available too. Present population of Lake Havasu City is more than 23,000.

## Accommodations

You have a choice of about 23 motels and resorts. Rates go up on Fri. and Sat. at many places. **Ramada London Bridge Resort,** close to London Bridge and the water, has a 9-hole golf course, tennis, swimming pools, and elegant decor; rooms run $71-104 d ($82-137 d overlooking the water). It's worth stepping inside the plush lobby to see the world's only replica of the ornate Gold State Coach. The original, built in 1762, has carried all the British monarchs since George III to their coronations at Westminster Abbey. Ramada London Bridge Resort is at 1477 Queen's Bay Road; tel. 855-0888 or (800)

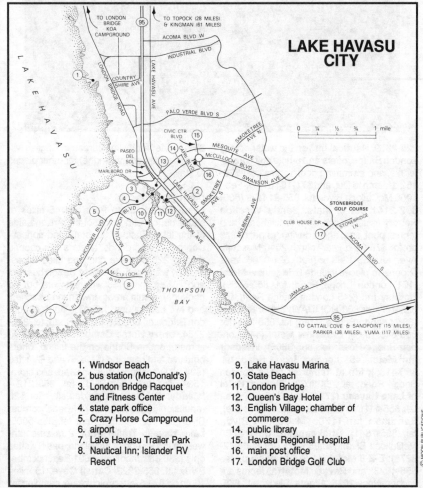

1. Windsor Beach
2. bus station (McDonald's)
3. London Bridge Racquet and Fitness Center
4. state park office
5. Crazy Horse Campground
6. airport
7. Lake Havasu Trailer Park
8. Nautical Inn; Islander RV Resort
9. Lake Havasu Marina
10. State Beach
11. London Bridge
12. Queen's Bay Hotel
13. English Village; chamber of commerce
14. public library
15. Havasu Regional Hospital
16. main post office
17. London Bridge Golf Club

© MOON PUBLICATIONS

THE CITY OF LONDON ARMS

BUILT BY THE CITY OF LONDON
ON THIS ACRE OF LAND GENEROUSLY PRESENTED BY
McCULLOCH PROPERTIES Inc.

OPENED BY
THE Rt. Hon. THE LORD MAYOR OF LONDON
ALDERMAN SIR PETER STUDD G.B.E., M.A., D.Sc.
9TH OCTOBER, 1971.

225-2879. **Nautical Inn,** on the water across London Bridge, offers an 18-hole golf course, tennis, and swimming pool; rooms cost $76-152 d March to Oct. and $71-104 d Nov.-Feb.; 1000 McCulloch Blvd.; tel. 855-2141 or (800) 892-2141 out of state. **Sands Vacation Resort** features suites (with kitchens) and tennis, pool, spa, and a driving range; rooms go for $76-98 d year-round; 2040 Mesquite Ave.; tel. 855-1388 or (800) 521-0306. Less expensive places include **Bridgeview Motel** (101 London Bridge Road; tel. 855-5559); **Holiday Inn** (245 London Bridge Road; tel. 855-4071 or 800-HOLIDAY); **Super 8 Motel** (305 London Bridge Road; tel. 855-8844 or 800-843-1991); **Lakeview Motel** (440 London Bridge Road; tel. 855-3605); **Windsor Inn Motel** (451 London Bridge Road; tel. 855-4135); **Inn at Tamarisk** (3101 London Bridge Road; tel. 764-3033); **Pioneer Hotel of Lake Havasu** (271 S. Lake Havasu Ave.; tel. 855-1111 or 800-528-5169 out of state); **Sandman Inn** (1700 McCulloch Blvd.; tel. 855-7841); **Shakespeare Inn** (2190 McCulloch Blvd.; tel. 855-4157 or 800-942-8278); **E-Z 8 Motel** (41 S. Acoma Blvd.; tel. 855-4023); and **Havasu Motel** (all rooms are kitchenettes, 2035 Acoma Blvd.; tel. 855-

2311). See the Visitor Bureau in English Village (beside London Bridge) for other places to stay.

## Campgrounds

**Lake Havasu State Park** has 45 miles of shoreline, covering most of the Arizona side of the lake. Besides the state and concession-run campgrounds, boaters can choose among 225 primitive camping sites accessible by water only. **Windsor Beach** has tent and RV camping ($6 with showers but no hookups), picnic areas, swimming beaches, and two boat ramps; 1.5 miles north of London Bridge off London Bridge Road; tel. 855-2784. **Crazy Horse Campground**, 0.5 mile across London Bridge on the island, offers primitive tent camping ($10.95) and RV sites ($24.09 w/hookups); has showers and store; 1534 Beachcomber Blvd.; tel. 855-2127. **Islander RV Resort** provides sites for $20 (adults only Nov. to April); 751 Beachcomber Blvd, just past Nautical Inn; tel. 855-5005. **Lake Havasu Trailer Park,** 2 miles southwest at the far end of the island, has RV sites only ($30.66 w/hookups); 601 Beachcomber Blvd.; tel. 855-2322. **Cattail Cove,** 15 miles south on AZ 95, offers picnicking, camping for

**1.** San Xavier Mission, near Tucson; **2.** Pima County Courthouse, Tucson; **3.** Desert View Watchtower, Grand Canyon National Park; **4.** Ned A. Hatathli Center at Navajo Community College, Tsaile; **5.** Tumacacori National Monument, south of Tucson (all photos by B. Weir)

**THE GRAND CANYON**
**1.** from Desert View on the South Rim; **2.** on the Bright Angel Trail; **3.** view from near Grandeur Point on the South Rim ; **4.** Angel's Window at Cape Royal on the North Rim; **5.** the Colorado River from Desert View (all photos by B. Weir)

tents and RVs ($8, all sites have hookups), showers, and a boat ramp; tel. 855-1223. Nearby **Sandpoint Marina** (take the Cattail Cove turnoff), offers RV sites ($14.77 w/hookups), store, and marina (fishing, patio, and houseboat rentals); tel. 855-0549. **London Bridge KOA**, 4.5 miles north of downtown, has spaces for tents ($12.60) and RVs ($17.33) and pool and showers; 3405 London Bridge Road; tel. 764-3500. **Havasu Landing Resort** has spots for both tents ($6) and RVs ($11); directly across the lake from Lake Havasu City (ferry service is available from English Village); tel. (619) 858-4595. **Park Moabi,** on the California side near the I-40 Colorado River bridge, offers spaces for tents ($9) and RVs ($14 w/hookups) with showers, boat ramp, marina with rentals, and store; tel. (619) 326-3831 (park office) or (619) 326-4777 (marina).

### Food

**King's Retreat Restaurant** in Ramada London Bridge Resort has a long list of continental, English, and American specialties at moderate prices; open daily for breakfast, lunch, and dinner; tel. 855-0888. Enjoy English food and atmosphere at **London Arms Pub & Restaurant** (English Village; tel. 453-3334) or **Lanies Shakespeare Inn & Pub** (2190 McCulloch Blvd.; tel. 855-1918). The **Versailles Restaurant** offers *cuisine française* and other continental fare; open Mon.-Sat. for dinner; 357 S. Lake Havasu Ave.; tel. 855-4800. For seafood and steaks try **Captain's Table** (open daily for breakfast, lunch, and dinner; Nautical Inn, 1000 McCulloch Blvd.; tel. 855-2141); **Jake's Place** (1530 El Camino Way; tel. 453-1001); or **Krystal's Fine Dining** (460 El Camino Way; tel. 453-2999). **Golden Horseshoe** offers steaks and other American favorites at 4501 London Bridge Road (5 miles north of town); tel. 764-3121. For pizza and other Italian dishes you have a choice of **Arturo's** (2122 McCulloch Blvd.; tel. 855-9995); **Petrossi's** (344 London Bridge Road; tel. 855-9468); **Pizza King** (2112 McCulloch Blvd.; tel. 855-2992); and **Pizza Hut** (1543 Marlboro Dr.; tel. 855-6071). Dine Chinese at **London Bridge**

*The City of London Arms (English Village)*

Chinese Restaurant (1971 McCulloch Blvd.; tel. 453-5002) or New Peking (2010 McCulloch Blvd.; tel. 855-4441). For Mexican food try Casa de Miguel (1550 S. Palo Verde; tel. 453-1550), or Taco Hacienda (2200 Mesquite Ave.; tel. 855-8932).

## Entertainment And Events

For movies, drop in at the Cinema Theatre (2130 McCulloch Blvd.; tel. 855-3111) or London Bridge Theater (English Village; tel. 453-5454).

Sailing or powerboat races are held on many weekends through the year. Major annual events take place on land and water. The Dixieland Jazz Festival enlivens the community in January. Lake Havasu City honors winter visitors with the Snowbird Jamboree, a day of entertainment under the bridge on the last Sat. in February. Blue Water Invitational Regatta takes place in March. Chili and live entertainment mark the Chili Cook Off in March. Corvette fanciers hit town for the Lake Havasu Corvette Stampede in late March. A Square Dance Jubilee is held under London Bridge in April. The Spring Art Festival in April features work of regional artists. Truckers show off their antique vehicles in the Trucking Western Nationals in April. Fishermen compete for the best catches in the Lake Havasu Striper Derby in May. Fireworks light up the sky on July Fourth. Blue Water Swingers Square Dance Festival livens the scene on the first weekend of October. London Bridge Days celebrates the dedication of the famous structure with a Grande Parade, triathlon, contests, games, live entertainment, and food; usually the second week in October. One of the country's largest gatherings of antique and classic autos converges for a parade and show in Relics and Rods Run to the Sun in mid-October. The IJSBA World Jet Ski Finals take place in late October. Artists show their work under London Bridge in the Fall Art Festival at the end of October. The Gem and Mineral Show is held in November. Radio-controlled model airplanes take off in the London Bridge Seaplane Classic on the first two weekends of November. Boaters compete in the Havasu Classic Outboard World Championships on Thanksgiving weekend in late November. A Christmas Boat Parade of Lights brightens early December. Check with the Visitor Bureau for dates and details.

## Recreation

For swimming, head 0.5 mile across London Bridge to State Beach; free. Windsor Beach, another park with beach areas, picnic areas, and boat ramps, is 1.5 miles north of London Bridge on the mainland; $3 day use, $6 camping; tel. 855-2784. London Bridge Racquet & Fitness Center has tennis and racquetball courts at 1425 McCulloch Blvd. (on the right just after crossing the bridge); tel. 855-6274. London Bridge Golf Club has two 18-hole courses, 2400 Club House Dr. (off S. Acoma Blvd.); tel. 855-2719. A third 18-hole course is at Nautical Inn, 1000 McCulloch Blvd. (one mile across London Bridge); tel. 855-2131.

Eleven places in town rent water sports equipment; ask the Visitor Bureau for their Recreation Guide. Fun Center, on the water next to English Village, rents canoes, pedal boats, jet skis, sailboats, and other craft; tel. 453-4386. The Nautical Inn, on the island, offers parasailing rides and jet ski rentals; tel. 855-2141. Lake Havasu Marina, 1100 McCulloch Blvd. (0.7 mile across London Bridge) rents fishing, pontoon, and ski boats; tel. 855-2159. You can rent houseboats across the lake at Havasu Landing Resort from Go Vacations; tel. (602) 855-3282 or (619) 858-4613. Sandpoint Marina, 14 miles south on the Arizona side (take the Cattail Cove turnoff), offers fishing, patio, and houseboat rentals; tel. 855-0549. Park Moabi, in California near the I-40 Colorado River bridge, also has a boat ramp and marina with rentals; tel. (619) 326-4777.

Fishermen discovered the lake well before any developer. Fishing was good (and still is!) for largemouth bass, crappie, and channel catfish. Saltwater striped bass, introduced in the early '60s as an experiment, have thrived. With weights up to 60 pounds, the landlocked fish is now the hottest thing in the lake. The stripers feed in spring and summer below Davis Dam, eating threadfin shad and other fish churned up by water flowing from the turbines. During fall and winter the bass return to the lake and are sought out by thousands of eager fishermen. Pick up a local fishing booklet for striper techniques.

## Services

The main **post office** is on the corner of 80 Civic Center and Mesquite. **Havasu Samaritan Regional Hospital** is at 101 Civic Center Lane; tel. 855-8185.

## Information

The **Lake Havasu Area Visitor & Convention Bureau** has two offices, both well stocked with literature. The one in the English Village is easier to find; it's open daily 9 a.m.-5 p.m.; tel. 855-5655. The main office is at 1930 Mesquite Ave., #3, Lake Havasu City, AZ 86403; open Mon.-Fri. 9 a.m.-5 p.m.; tel. 855-4115 or (800) 242-8278. **Lake Havasu State Park** rangers can tell you about their recreational areas, including boat camping; the office is just across London Bridge on the right; tel. 855-7851. The **BLM's Havasu Resource Area** office administers recreational areas along the Colorado River between Davis Dam and Quartzsite; open Mon.-Fri. 8 a.m.-4:30 p.m.; at the far south end of town on AZ 95 (3189 Sweetwater, Lake Havasu City, AZ 86403); tel. 855-8017. The **public library** is at 1787 McCulloch Blvd.; tel. 453-0718.

## Tours

A ferry and several boat tours leave from the shore at English Village. **Passenger ferries** cross the lake to Havasu Landing Resort on the Chemehuevi Indian Reservation, a 3.5-mile trip, one-way fares are $2 adult, $1 children 6-12; tel. (619) 858-4593. You can take a narrated 45-minute tour of the area with **Lake Havasu Boat Tours**; $7 adult, $3 children 5-12; tel. 855-7979. **Miner's Camp Excursions** offers daily 2-hour trips upstream into the spectacular Topock Gorge; $15 adult, $10 children 10-16; all-day cruises on Sat. and Sun. go upstream to Laughlin via Topock Gorge, spend about 4 hours at the

casinos, then return; $35 adult, $20 children under 16 roundtrip; the fare includes a buffet and "fun packages"; a passenger minimum applies on all the tours; office is in Island Fashion Mall, on the right after crossing London Bridge; tel. 855-5781. The gambling casinos in Laughlin offer free bus rides, free food, and other inducements to get you (and your money) there; look over their brochures at the Visitor Bureau.

## Transport

**Greyhound** buses go daily to Las Vegas via Needles (CA) and Searchlight (NV) and to Phoenix via Parker and Wickenburg; they leave from McDonald's, 100 Swanson Ave.; tel. 855-1039. **Stateswest Airlines** flies to destinations in California, Arizona, and Colorado; tel. (800) 759-3866. **Mesa Airlines** goes to cities in Arizona, New Mexico, Colorado, and Wyoming; tel. (800) MESA-AIR. The airport is located across London Bridge at the far end of the island.

Notice to Shippers!
———
THE COLORADO STEAM
NAVIGATION CO'S
STEAMERS

Newbern and Montana

*Leave San Francisco
for Mexican Ports and Mouth
of Colorado River,*

## VICINITY OF LAKE HAVASU CITY

### Topock Gorge by canoe

A perfect one-day outing on the cool waters of the Colorado River above Lake Havasu. The usual put-in point is Park Moabi (CA) or Topock (AZ) where I-40 crosses the river. Here swift currents speed canoeists on their way without rapids or serious turbulence. Take-out is at Castle Rock on the upper end of Lake Havasu, about 7 hours and 17 river miles later. Topock Gorge is in the Havasu National Wildlife Refuge, where hundreds of bird species have been spotted. Look for the mud nests of swallows clinging to the cliffs. Herons, ducks, geese, long-billed prospectors, and red-winged blackbirds are easily identified visitors to the canyon. If you're lucky, you may even spot a desert bighorn sheep on the steep slopes. Indian petroglyphs cover Picture Rock, a huge, dark mass about halfway between Devil's Elbow and Blankenship Bend. Sandy beaches make good stopping places for a walk or picnic, but no fires or camping are permitted.

Summer temperatures can get uncomfortable, but a hop in the river will always cool you off. Bring a hat and sunscreen to protect yourself from the Arizona sun. Other kinds of boats besides canoes can make the trip. Rafts need a little more time, and powerboat skippers need to watch for sandbars. Topo maps (1:24,000 scale) for the area are Topock, Ariz.-Calif. and Castle Rock, Calif.-Ariz.

**Bob's Canoe Trips** offers rentals and a shuttle service; tel. 855-4406. **Fun Center** has canoe rentals; tel. 453-4386. Many other canoe trips can be taken; for example, you can start at Needles for a 2-day trip or at Bullhead City for a 3- or 4-day canoe excursion.

### Havasu National Wildlife Refuge

The marshes, open water, and adjacent desert of the Refuge support many types of animals and birds. The main part of the Refuge includes Topock Marsh near Needles (CA) and extends southward to just north of Lake Havasu City. Another part protects the lower 12 miles of Bill Williams River south of Lake Havasu City. Most of the more than 40,000 acres lie on the Arizona side. In winter, the refuge is home for the snow goose, Canada goose, and other waterfowl. Boating, fishing, and other water sports are permitted except where signed. No camping is allowed in Mesquite Bay, Topock Gorge, or Topock Marsh (except at the concession). You may boat camp on the Arizona shore below the south entrance to Topock Gorge (except in Mesquite Bay). For a map, bird list, and regulations, visit the Havasu National Wildlife Refuge office at 1406 Bailey Ave., across from Needles Hospital, or write Box 3009, Needles, CA 92363; tel. (619) 326-3853.

**Five Mile Landing** is a private campground ($5.25 dry camping for tent or RV, $14.95 w/hookups) and marina (boat rentals, slips, and ramp) on the east side of Topock Marsh off AZ 95, 5 miles north of I-40 and 35 miles south of Bullhead City; tel. 768-2350.

## PARKER AND THE PARKER STRIP

From 1871 to 1908, Parker was just a post office on the Colorado River Indian Reservation. But when a railroad line came through, the town began to grow as a trading center for the reservation and nearby mining operations. Mining later declined, but agriculture and tourism thrived with the building of two dams upstream. The Headgate Rock Dam, finished in 1941, forms Lake Moovalya, whose waters irrigate farmlands of the reservation. In 1938 workers completed Parker Dam, which created Lake Havasu, to supply water and electrical power to southern California. Resorts and parks lining both shores of the river and Lake Moovalya draw visitors year-round. Better known as the "Parker Strip," this 11-mile stretch of scenic waterway begins several miles north of Parker and extends north to Parker Dam. Despite hot summer temperatures that rival the nation's highs, many people come to enjoy the excellent boating and water-skiing from around

Easter through Labor Day. In Sept. the scene calms and the temperature cools. Winter visitors, many of whom are retired, enjoy fishing, hunting, hiking, rockhounding, and exploring ghost towns.

## Accommodations

You have a choice of staying in town or upstream along the Parker Strip. The 8 or so motels in town are easy to find along Parker's two major streets, California Ave. and Agency Road/Riverside Drive. Heading north about 5 miles on AZ 95, you'll see a long line of RV parks, resorts, restaurants, bars, and marinas of the Parker Strip. Places to stay (with distances from the north edge of Parker): **Arizona Shores Resort Motel** (5.5 miles; tel. 667-2685); **Branson's Resort** (7.5 miles; tel. 667-3346); **Winners Circle Resort** (13 miles; tel. 667-3244); **Casa del Rio Resort** (15 miles; tel. 667-2727); and **Havasu Springs Resort** on Lake Havasu (16 miles; tel. 667-3361). You'll also find places on the California shore opposite the Parker Strip (distances from Parker): **River Shore Resort** (7 miles; tel. 619-665-2572); **Big River Inn** (8 miles; tel. 619-665-9440); **Big Bend Resort** (12 miles; tel. 619-663-3755); **River**

**Lodge** (14 miles; tel. 619-663-3891); and **Black Meadow Landing** on Lake Havasu (25 miles; tel. 619-663-4901).

## Campgrounds

RVs can stay in Parker at **Diekmann's Parker Trailer Park** (1509 Kofa Ave.; tel. 669-5487); **Lazy D Mobile Park** (15th and Reata; tel. 669-8797); **Parker Trailer Park** (1521 Kofa Ave.; tel. 669-5487); or **Park Place RV Park** (1501 Joshua; tel. 669-5216). More than three dozen trailer parks and campgrounds line the waters along the Parker Strip. The Parker Chamber of Commerce will give you a list and map.

**La Paz County Park** covers a long section of riverbank about 8 miles north of Parker; the park offers picnicking, tent and RV camping, hookups, showers, tennis, Emerald Canyon Golf Course (18 holes), swimming beach, and boat ramp; day-use fee $1/person age 12 and over, dry camping $6 car (2 persons), RV w/hookups $9 (2 persons); tel. 667-2069. **Buckskin Mountain State Park,** 11 miles north of Parker, sits on a secluded section of grassy shoreline backed by low cliffs; a concession runs a snack bar, marina, inner-tube rental, boat ramp, and store; tel. 667-3210. A

*Mohave Indians playing ring-toss game, 1850s*

short hiking trail begins opposite the highway turnoff; picnic sites and a campground (hookups and showers) are near the water; $3 day use, $6 camping no hookups, $8 camping w/hookups, $11 beach cabana site; tel. 667-3231. A second part of Buckskin Mountain State Park lies 2 miles farther upstream; this smaller **River Island Unit** offers picnicking, camping (showers but no hookups), swimming beach, and boat ramp; $3 day use, $6 camping; tel. 667-3386. **Empire Landing,** 8 miles from Parker on the California side, offers a beach, picnicking, and camping (no showers or hookups); free day use, camping costs $5/vehicle; tel. (602) 855-8017.

### Food
Look for American fare at **Coffee Ern's** (24 hours; 1707 California Ave.; tel. 669-8145); **Hole-in-the-Wall Coffee Shop** (daily for breakfast and lunch; 902 California Ave.; tel. 669-9755); **Grandma's Kitchen** (daily for breakfast, lunch, and dinner; 1000 Hope Ave.; tel. 669-9396); and **Juicy's Famous Foods** (daily for lunch and dinner; 1001 Eagle Ave.; tel. 669-8434). **Los Arcos** serves Mexican food; closed Sun. and Mon.; 1200 California Ave.; tel. 669-2375. **Canton Restaurant** offers Chinese lunches and dinners daily; 621 Riverside Dr.; tel. 669-2361. For pizza try **La Piazza** (closed Wed.; 801 11th St.; tel. 669-2441) or **Toby's Pizza Parlor** (closed Sun.; 1317 Joshua Ave.; tel. 669-9388). A variety of other restaurants lie along the Parker Strip north of town.

### Entertainment And Events
Catch movies at **Parker Theatre,** 1007 Arizona Ave.; tel. 669-2211. Annual events include **Parker Score 400** for off-road vehicles in late Jan. or early Feb.; **International Water Ski Race** in Feb.; **Lions Club Donkey Basketball** (teams battle for victory while riding donkeys) in Feb.; **La Paz County Fair** in March; **Parker Enduro Classic** races (9 hours of nonstop action) in March; **National Jet Boat Association** races March to May and Sept. to Nov.; **Southern California Speedboat Club** races in May; **Water Ski** shows on Wed. evenings in May, June, and July; **Inner-tube Race** in June; **Fireworks** on July Fourth; **Indian Day Celebration** in Sept.; **Parker Rodeo** in Oct.; **Southern California Sailing Regatta** in Nov.; **All Indian Rodeo** in Dec.; and **Christmas Lighted Boat Parade** in December.

### Recreation
The public **swimming pool** is at 1317 Ninth St.; tel. 669-5678. Play golf at **Emerald Canyon Golf Course's** 18 holes, across the road from La Paz County Park, 8 miles north of Parker (tel. 667-3366) or **Havasu Spring's** 9-hole course, 16 miles north of Parker (tel. 667-3361). No one offers boat tours in the area, but rentals are readily available from marinas along the Parker Strip. Fishermen head for the river below Headgate Rock Dam for largemouth and smallmouth bass, striped bass, catfish, crappie, and bluegill. Boaters and water-skiers discourage some fishermen from Lake Moovalya, but the fish are there. You'll need reservation fishing permits to fish in lower Lake Moovalya and the Colorado River downstream. Tubers enjoy leisurely trips downriver; a popular one is the 7-mile, 3-hour float from Parker to Big River Park on the California side.

### Services
The main **post office** is at the corner of Joshua Ave. and 14th Street. **Parker Community Hospital** is on Mohave Road in the south side of town; tel. 669-9201.

### Information
The **Parker Chamber of Commerce** staff will help you find the resort or other facilities you're looking for and tell you what's going on. The office is open Mon.-Fri. 9 a.m.-5 p.m. at 1217 California Ave. (Box 627, Parker, AZ 85344); tel. 669-2174. The **public library** is at the corner of 1001 Navajo Ave. and Agency Road; tel. 669-2622.

### Transport
**Greyhound** buses go daily to Phoenix and to Las Vegas from the stop at Parker Shell, 1100 California Ave.; tel. 669-6276. For a cab, call **Parker Taxi**; tel. 669-2811.

## VICINITY OF PARKER

### Colorado River Indian Reservation

President Lincoln signed the bill establishing this reservation in 1865. The 268,691 acres, most of which lie in Arizona, are the home of Mojave, Chemehuevi, Hopi, and Navajo Indians. Don't expect any picturesque Indian villages. The 6,000-plus inhabitants live in modern houses and work at their farms or jobs like anyone else along the Colorado River. To learn about the tribes and others who've passed this way, visit the **Colorado River Indian Tribes (CRIT) Museum** 2 miles south of Parker. You'll see artifacts from prehistoric Anasazi, Hohokam, and Patayan cultures, models showing traditional shelters of the modern tribes, and a large collection of baskets and other crafts. Old photos and artifacts show early reservation life. A library houses an extensive collection of books, manuscripts, photographs, and tapes relating to various tribes. Baskets, beadwork, and other Indian-made crafts are sold in the gift shop. The museum is open Mon.-Fri. 8 a.m.-noon and 1-5 p.m.; donations accepted; tel.

669-9211, ext. 335. From downtown Parker, head southwest 2 miles on either Agency or Mohave roads.

### Parker Dam

The world's deepest dam lies about 15 miles upriver from its namesake, the town of Parker. When building the dam, workers had to dig down 235 feet through sand and gravel of the riverbed before hitting bedrock needed to secure the foundation. Only the top third of the dam is visible. Lake Havasu, the reservoir behind the dam, has a storage capacity of about 211 billion gallons. Pumps transfer one billion gallons a day into the Colorado River Aqueduct for southern California destinations. You're welcome to take a free, self-guided tour of the dam and power plant, open daily.

### Quartzsite

Like swallows returning to Capistrano, thousands of "snowbirds" flock to this tiny desert town in winter. From an estimated 600-1,000 summer residents, the population jumps to about 6,000. Charles Tyson settled here in 1856, then built a fort to fend off Indian attacks. Tyson's Wells soon became an im-

*Hi Jolly monument in Quartzsite*

portant stage stop on the run from Ehrenburg to Prescott. Later the place was renamed "Quartzite," after the rock, but the post office added an "s" for "Quartzsite." Hadji Ali lies under a pyramid-shaped marker in the local cemetery. He was one of several camel drivers imported from the Middle East along with about 80 camels in 1856-57 by the U.S. Army. It was hoped that the large, hardy beasts would improve transportation and communication in the Southwest deserts. Although the camels showed promise, the Army abandoned the experiment during the Civil War. Most of the camels were turned loose on the desert, terrorizing stock and wild animals for many years; none have survived to the present. All the other camel drivers, homesick for their native lands, sailed home. Hadji Ali, whose name soldiers changed to "Hi Jolly," stayed in Arizona and took up prospecting.

Quartzsite is 35 miles south of Parker and 20 miles east of Blythe (CA) at the junction of I-10 and AZ 95. A couple of motels, some RV parks, and several restaurants serve passing motorists and the winter community. Most RVers, though, prefer the open freedom of the desert and head for **La Posa Long-term Visitor Area** just south of town. La Posa has four sections, vault toilets, and a dump station. Visitors pay a $25 fee for the Sept. 15 to April 15 season; the fee applies even for short visits. You can camp free (14-day limit) off-season at La Posa and year-round in undeveloped areas such as **Milemarkers 99 and 112** on US 95. The Bureau of Land Management's Yuma District office can advise on these recreation areas; tel. 726-6300.

The giant **Quartzsite Pow Wow Gem & Rock Show** hits Quartzsite in early February. More than 100,000 people attend the 10-day flea market to buy and sell rocks, minerals, gems, lapidary supplies, crafts, antiques, and other treasures.

### Alamo Lake State Park

This Alamo lies far from where Davy Crockett and his friends fought it out with the Mexicans. *Alamo* means "cottonwood tree" in Spanish. The lake, at an elevation of 1,200 feet, is the source for the Bill Williams River. When Alamo Lake began to fill in the mid-'60s, the cottonwood, mesquite, and palo verde trees were flooded and became the home of small fish. Hungry largemouth bass and channel catfish fed on the small bluegill, sunfish, and tilapia. Fishermen then moved in to feed on the bass and catfish.

A marina provides groceries, fishing supplies, and rental boats. The state park has picnic tables, campgrounds with showers and hookups, and boat ramp; $3 day use, $5 primitive camping, $6 developed sites, and $8 w/hookups; tel. 669-2088. Spring and autumn are the most popular times for a visit to this remote 2,600-acre desert lake. To get here, drive to Wenden (60 miles southeast of Parker or 108 miles northwest of Phoenix), then go 35 miles north on a paved road. An alternate route from Phoenix is the graded dirt road that takes off 23 miles northwest of Wickenburg; this sometimes bumpy back way is about 20 miles shorter than the paved route.

### Swansea

Of the ghost towns near Parker, Swansea is the best preserved. Ruins of a large brick smelter, mine, and over a dozen buildings remain. The Clara Consolidated Gold and Copper Mining Co. built the smelter in the early 1900s to process their ore locally, instead of sending it to faraway places like Swansea, Wales. Clara Consolidated closed the smelter in 1912, but mining was continued by other companies until 1924. A high-clearance vehicle should be used to navigate the dirt roads to the site. From Bouse, 27 miles southeast of Parker, take the road north across the railroad tracks and go 13 miles to the site of Midway, take the left fork (crossing under the power lines after about 0.3 mile) and go northwest 18.5 miles to a road junction, then turn right 6 miles to Swansea. Another approach is on roads east from Parker. Obtain local advice and good maps such as the Swansea 15-minute topo map.

# THE SOUTHWEST CORNER

## YUMA

Yuma's rich historical background and sunny, subtropical climate make it an attractive destination. In winter, an estimated 50,000 "snowbirds" double its normal population and fill the many trailer parks in town, along the river, and out on the desert. Boaters and fishermen can explore countless lakes and quiet backwaters on the Colorado River. Date palms, citrus trees, and vegetables grow on irrigated farmlands around Yuma. The Mexican city of San Luis offers shopping and another culture just 25 miles south.

### Yuma's Beginnings

The long recorded history of Yuma begins in 1540, nearly 70 years before the founding of Jamestown. Captain Hernando de Alarcón, the first white man to visit the area, led a Spanish naval expedition along the west coast of Mexico and then a short way up the Colorado River. He hoped to meet and resupply Francisco Vásquez de Coronado's expedition to the Seven Cities of Cibola farther east, but the two groups never met. First contacts between the Spanish and native Quechan Indians went well, but resentment and hostility flared in later years. While searching for a land route between Mexico and California, Spanish explorers discovered that the best crossing on the lower Colorado River was just below the mouth of the Gila River. Soldiers and missionaries built a fort and missions here, across from present-day Yuma, but angry Quechan destroyed the settlements during a violent uprising in 1781, ending Spanish domination of Yuma Crossing.

Although small bands of American mountain men started drifting through in the early

*Yuma Territorial Prison in its heyday*

YUMA

TO SAND DUNES (17 mi), SAN DIEGO, LOS ANGELES

WINTERHAVEN DR.

WINTERHAVEN

SAN PASQUAL RD.

S24

QUECHAN RD.

PICACHO RD.

IMPERIAL COUNTY ROAD S24 TO SOUTH MESA RECREATION SITE, SQUAW LAKE OF LAGUNA MARTINEZ RECREATION LANDS (20 mi)

1

INDIAN HILL RD.

4

COLORADO RIVER

CALIFORNIA
ARIZONA

FIRST ST.

2

STEAMBOAT LANDING

3

SECOND ST.

GISS

5    6    7

9    8    PKWY

10

PRISON HILL RD.

THIRD ST.

CARVER PARK

FIFTH ST.

ROOSEVELT ST.

MARCUS POOL

EIGHTH ST.

GISS PARKWAY

AVENUE B

AVENUE A

SECOND AVE.

FIRST AVE.

MADISON AVE.

MAIN ST.

GILA ST.

PACIFIC AVE.

TENTH ST.

BUS. 8

8

TO MARTINEZ LAKE (35 mi), QUARTZSITE (80 mi)

95

SIXTEENTH ST.

FOURTH AVE.

ARIZONA AVE.

11

12

TO GILA BEND (116 mi), PHOENIX (184 mi), TUCSON (240 mi)

TWENTY SECOND ST.

13

JOHN KENNEDY MEMORIAL PARK

TWENTY FOURTH ST.

TWENTY FOURTH ST.

YUMA REGIONAL MEDICAL CENTER

AVENUE B

AVENUE A

YUMA GOLF & COUNTRY CLUB

95

CLUBHOUSE

15

WINSOR AVE.

FORTUNA AVE.

TO I-8

TO SAN LUIS (25 mi), GULF OF CALIF. (95 mi)

THIRTY SECOND ST.

CLUBHOUSE

ARROYO DUNES GOLF COURSE

14

BUS. 8

0        0.5 mi

16

© MOON PUBLICATIONS

1800s, little attention was paid to the area until the Mexican War. Kit Carson, who had passed this way in 1829 with a group of trappers, returned in 1846 to guide Colonel Stephen Kearny and 100 soldiers in securing former Mexican lands between Santa Fe and San Diego. Colonel Philip Cooke followed with the Mormon Battalion and supply wagons, blazing the first transcontinental road across the Southwest. Crowds of '49ers, seeking gold in the Sierra Nevada of California, pushed westward along "Cooke's Road" a few years later. In 1851 the Army built Camp Yuma atop a hill on the California side to protect Yuma Crossing from Indian attacks. Nearby mining successes, the coming of steamboats, and road improvements encouraged the founding of Colorado City on the Arizona side in 1854. Residents changed the name to Arizona City in 1858, but they had to rebuild on higher ground after a disastrous flood 4 years later. The present name of Yuma was adopted in 1873. Yuma Territorial Prison, the town's first major construction project, boosted the economy in 1876. Laguna Dam ended the riverboat era in 1909, but it guaranteed water for the fertile desert valleys.

---

### YUMA

1. Quechan Indian Museum;
   St. Thomas Mission
2. Yuma Quartermaster Depot
3. Kofa National Wildlife Refuge office
   (U.S. Fish and Wildlife Service)
4. Yuma Territorial Prison
5. Century House Museum
6. Lute's Casino
7. Yuma Art Center; Amtrak train
8. Yuma County Chamber of Commerce
9. post office branch
10. public library
11. Yuma Mesa Shopping Center
12. bus station
13. main post office
14. Southgate Mall
15. Bureau of Land Management
16. airport

---

## Modern Yuma

Today Yuma is one of Arizona's most important cities and the center of a rich agricultural area. The military likes it here too. You'll probably see some hot aircraft speeding overhead from the Marine Corps Air Station on the southeast edge of town. The Army checks out combat vehicles, weapon systems, and other gear at the Yuma Proving Grounds, 26 miles north.

Downtown Yuma can be explored on foot. The Yuma County Chamber of Commerce makes a good starting point for a visit to shops and galleries on Main St.; follow the row of small shops signed "224 Main Street" west and across Madison Ave. to see the Century House Museum. Continue west and north several blocks to visit the Yuma Quartermaster Depot. You can see excellent artworks in the Yuma Art Center a few blocks east of the chamber.

## SIGHTS

### Yuma Territorial Prison

In 1875 the territorial Legislature was about to award $30,000 to Phoenix for construction of a major prison. But Yuma's representatives, Jose Maria Redondo and R.B. Kelly, did some fast talking and got the project for their hometown, and the "Hell-hole of Arizona" was born. Righteous citizens of the territory were fed up with murders, robberies, and other lawless acts of the frontier. They wanted bad characters behind bars. Niceties of reform and rehabilitation didn't concern them. Yuma, surrounded by hostile deserts and treacherous currents of the Colorado River, seemed the ideal spot for a prison. Prisoners endured searing 120° F summer temperatures, and if that wasn't enough, recalcitrant inmates faced the darkness of a dungeon rumored to be infested with scorpions. Actually, the prison provided benefits and services unknown at most others of the day—prisoners enjoyed a library, workshop, school, and hospital. Critics even accused it of being a "country club." Most of the stone and adobe walls had to be built by the prisoners themselves, as money and labor were scarce.

the prison today

Over the 33 years of prison operation, 29 women and about 3,000 men paced the floors and gazed between iron bars. The prison, after

a prison cell

withstanding the toughest outlaws of frontier Arizona's wildest years, outgrew its site and closed in 1909. The remaining 40 prisoners marched in shackles down Prison Hill to a train waiting to take them to a new prison in Florence. High school students in Yuma attended classes at the prison from 1910 to 1914 after their school burned. Even today the Yuma High School sports teams call themselves the "Criminals."

You can step inside the prison, now a state park, and imagine how it once was. Photos show faces of men and women imprisoned here. Read the stories about the inmates, guards, riots, and escape attempts. You'll learn about "Heartless" Pearl Hart and see her Colt 45 "Peacemaker." A Quechan Indian exhibit contains artifacts and old photos. Outside, you can explore the cellblocks, climb the main watchtower for views, and visit the prison graveyard. Picnic tables are on the grounds and in a small park off Prison Hill Road. **Yuma Crossing Park,** now under development, will have many historic exhibits along the river shore between the prison and Yuma Quartermaster Depot. Yuma Territorial Prison is open daily 8 a.m.-5 p.m.; $2 adult, 17 and under free (the receipt also allows admission to Yuma Quartermaster Depot); tel. 783-4771. Take Prison Hill Road off Giss Parkway.

## Yuma Quartermaster Depot

Another good place to get a feel for Yuma's history. The Army used the facilities from 1864 to 1883 to supply military posts in the Southwest during the Indian wars. Ships carried cargo to Port Isabel, near the mouth of the Colorado River, where dockworkers transferred it to river steamers for the trip to Yuma. Later the Customs Service took over the depot for an office and residence. The Signal Corps, Weather Bureau, and Bureau of Reclamation have all been based here too. Except for the stone-block reservoir, all the structures were built of adobe, because that was all the early builders had.

Stop first in the Quartermaster Depot (1871-72) to see museum exhibits and to begin a guided tour of the other buildings on the grounds. You can visit the commanding officer's quarters, built in the late 1850s and possibly the oldest Anglo house in Arizona, the cookhouse, reservoir, two surviving warehouses, and the spartan quarters of the corral house. Period rooms, old photos, guns, swords, steamboat relics, and letters tell the story of these historic buildings. They have been restored to their appearance in 1876 when the depot was at its peak, just before the railroad arrived and greatly reduced waterfront business. A steam locomotive and giant freight wagon sit outside. Open Thurs.-Mon. 8 a.m.-5 p.m.; $2 adult, free for age 17 and under (admission also includes the Territorial Prison); tel. 343-2500. Located at the north end of Second Ave. behind City Hall.

## Century House Museum

The influential businessman E.F. Sanguinetti once made his home in the Century House, now one of Yuma's oldest buildings. Exhibits inside relate the history and cultures of Yuma Crossing—those of the Indians, explorers, missionaries, soldiers, miners, riverboat captains, and early settlers. The garden out back harbors flaming bougainvillea and chattering parakeets, colorful parrots, and peacocks. Open Tues.-Sat. 10 a.m.-4 p.m. all year; free; tel. 782-1841. **Adobe Annex**, next to Century House, sells local crafts and an excellent selections of books on the region's history,

Indians, and gold mining. The **Garden Cafe** serves breakfast and lunch on a patio adjacent to the museum gardens. Century House is in the north part of town at 240 S. Madison Avenue.

## Quechan Indian Museum

Located on the hill just across the Colorado River from Yuma, the museum building dates from 1855, when it was part of Camp Yuma. Later, at the outbreak of the Civil War in 1861, the post's name changed to Fort Yuma. The site overlooks Yuma Crossing, the only ford in the area. Fort Yuma now belongs to the Quechan Indians, who have their museum and tribal offices here. Museum exhibits illustrate the arrival of the Spanish and missionary Father Francisco Garcés, the Quechan Revolt, history of Fort Yuma, and Quechan Indian life. Artifacts include clay figurines, flutes, gourd rattles, headdresses, bows and arrows, and war clubs. Open Mon.-Fri. 8 a.m.-noon and 1-5 p.m. from Nov. to June, then Mon.-Fri. 7:30 a.m.-noon and 1-4 p.m. from July to Oct. (Arizona times); $.50, free for children under 12; tel. 572-0661. The nearby St. Thomas Mission occupies the site of Concepcion Mission where Indians murdered Father Garcés in 1781. Take Indian Hill Road off Picacho Road (see map).

## Yuma Art Center

Inside the old Southern Pacific RR Depot you'll see contemporary work by many Arizonans. Anglo, Indian, and Hispanic artists interpret their cultures and feelings in the paintings, prints, sculptures, and crafts. Some works are for sale. Open Tues.-Sat. 10 a.m.-5 p.m. and Sun. 1-5 p.m.; may close in summer; $1 adult, $.50 children 12 and under; tel. 783-2314. Located at 281 Gila St. in the northeast corner of town.

## Arizona Western College

This community college has teamed up with Northern Arizona University to offer vocational, undergraduate, and graduate classes. Points of interest on the campus, 7 miles east of town, include **Gallery Milepost Nine** of changing art exhibits in the Fine Arts Center (open Mon.-Thurs. 8 a.m.-8 p.m.; tel. 344-7598) and the **library's special collection** of regional books (tel. 344-7660). The college's mailing address is Box 929, Yuma, AZ 85364; tel. 726-1000. From Yuma, take I-8 east to Exit 7, go north 0.4 mile, then right 1.7 miles.

# PRACTICALITIES

## Accommodations

Yuma, located midway between Phoenix and San Diego, makes a handy travelers' stop. Most of the 2 dozen or so motels in town lie along Business I-8 (old US 80) on 32nd St. and Fourth Avenue. Daily costs for some go up as much as $10 during the popular winter and spring seasons, but the less expensive places have little or no seasonal increase. The more deluxe motels include the **Airporter Stardust Inn** (711 E. 32nd St.; 726-4721); **Best Western Chilton Inn** (300 E. 32nd St.; tel. 344-1050); **Best Western Coronado** (233 S. Fourth Ave.; tel. 783-4453); **Days Inn Suite Hotel** (2600 S. Fourth Ave.; tel. 726-4830); **Desert Grove Motel** (3500 S. Fourth Ave.; tel. 726-1400); **El Rancho Motel** (2201 S. Fourth Ave.; tel. 783-4481); **Hacienda Motel** (2150 S. Fourth Ave.; tel. 782-4316); **Ramada Inn** (3181 S. Fourth Ave.; tel. 344-1420); **Regalodge Motel** (344 S. Fourth Ave.; tel. 782-4571); **Royal Motor Inn** (2941 S. Fourth Ave.; tel. 344-0550); **Shilo Inn Resort** (1550 Castle Dome Ave., off I-8 16th St. exit; tel. 782-9511); **Stardust Resort Hotel** (2350 S. Fourth Ave.; tel. 783-8861); **Travelodge Fourth Avenue** (2050 S. Fourth Ave.; tel. 782-3831); **Travelodge La Fuente** (1513 E. 16th St.; tel. 329-1814); and **Yuma Best Western Inn-Suites** (1460 S. Castle Dome Road, off I-8 16th St. exit; tel. 783-8341).

For lower budget accommodation ($20-30), try **Caravan Oasis Motel** (10574 S. Fortuna Road; tel. 342-1292); **El Cortez Motel** (124 S. First Ave.; tel. 783-4456); **Motel 6** (1640 S. Arizona Ave.; tel. 782-6561); **Motel 10 Inn** (2730 S. Fourth Ave.; tel. 344-3890); **Navajo Lodge** (2801 S. Fourth Ave.; tel. 344-1270); **Palms Inn** (2655 S. Fourth Ave.; tel. 344-4570); and **Sixpence Inn of Yuma** (1445 E. 16th St.; tel. 782-9521).

## Campgrounds

The more than 275 RV parks in and around Yuma cater mostly to retired people. Only a few parks welcome families with children, usually just in the slow season (summer and autumn). Ask the Yuma County Chamber of Commerce for their latest listing of RV parks. All of the following have showers. Families are welcome at **Lucky Park del Sur** (5790 W. Eighth St.; $9.50 tent or RV w/hookups; tel. 783-7201) and **Windhaven RV Park** (6620 E. Hwy. 80; $10 tent or RV w/hookups; tel. 726-0284). Those RV parks that prefer adults include **Blew-In** (1290 W. Third St.; $10 tent or RV w/hookups; tel. 343-1641); **Blue Sky** (10247 E. I-8 Frontage Road; $10.55 RV w/hookups; tel. 342-1444); **Bonita Mesa** (9400 N. Frontage Road, I-8 Exit 12; $17 RV w/hookups; tel. 342-2999); **Capri Mobile Park** (senior citizens; 3380 S. Fourth Ave.; $12.78 RV w/hookups; no pets; tel. 726-0959); **First Street Trailer Park** (1850 W. First St.; $10 RV w/hookups; tel. 782-0090); **Hidden Cove Trailer Park and Marina** (2450 W. Water St.; $12.50 RV w/hookups; tel. 783-3534); **Shangri-la** (10498 N. Frontage Road, I-8 Exit 12; $11.61 RV w/hookups; tel. 342-9123); and **Yuma Overnight Trailer Park** (201 W. 28th St.; $15.75 RV w/hookups; tel. 344-1012).

**Dateland Farm Plaza**, 65 miles east on i-8 (Exit 67), offers tent ($3/person) and RV ($8.50 w/hookups) camping (families welcome); cafe and a small motel; dates can be purchased too; tel. 454-2227.

Some of the best camping lies upstream on the Colorado River. **Laguna Martinez National Recreation Lands**, 20 miles north on the California side, are perfect for families and anyone wanting to enjoy desert walks, fishing, or boating. Cross the river to Winterhaven (CA) then turn north on Imperial County Road S-24 and follow signs. The **Imperial Dam Long-term Visitor Area** includes the sites of Quail Hill, Kripple Kreek, Skunk Hollow, Beehive Mesa, and Coyote Ridge for self-contained vehicles only (the sites lack improvements); a $25 season pass is needed for any stay within the Sept. 15 to April 15 season; at other times, camping is free but limited to stays of 14 days. **South Mesa Recreation Site,** also within the Imperial Dam LTVA, has water, restrooms, and outside showers; the same season and fee apply. **Squaw Lake Campground,** at the end of the road, offers water, restrooms, outside showers, paved parking, and a boat ramp; $5/night year-round. An easy 2-mile nature trail winds through river vegetation and desert hills from the north end of the parking lot. Contact the Bureau of Land Management's Yuma District Office for information on these and other recreation areas; tel. 726-6300. **Imperial Oasis** is nearby on the Arizona side, close to Imperial Dam; tent camping costs $8.40, RVs w/hookups cost $14.70; has showers (also available to visitors), store, and restaurant; tel. 783-4171.

**Martinez Lake** is reached on the Arizona side farther upstream, about 35 miles north of Yuma; go north 24 miles on US 95, then turn left 11 miles on Martinez Lake Road. **Fisher's Landing** has tent ($3/person) and RV ($12 w/hookups) camping, restaurant, store, and marina (but no boat rentals); tel. 783-6513. Nearby **Martinez Lake Resort** offers motel rooms (from $47.25), RV park ($21 w/hookups), restaurant, and marina with boat rentals; tel. 783-9589.

## Food

For American food, try **Bobby's Other Place** (2951 S. Fourth Ave.; tel. 344-0033); **Brownie's Restaurant** (1145 S. Fourth Ave.; tel. 783-7911); **Chester's Chuckwagon** (2256 S. Fourth Ave.; tel. 782-4125); **Golden Corral Family Steak House** (2401 S. Fourth Ave.; tel. 726-4428); or **Hungry Hunter Restaurant** (2355 S. Fourth Ave.; tel. 782-3637).

Good places for Mexican dining include **Beto's Mexican Food** (812 E. 21st St.; tel. 782-6551); **Chretin's** (485 S. 15th Ave.; tel. 782-1291); and **El Charro** (601 W. Eighth St.; tel. 783-9790).

Dine Chinese at **Gene's** (771 S. Fourth Ave.; tel. 783-0080); **Imperial China** (195 S. Fourth Ave.; tel. 783-4306); or **Mandarin Palace** (350 E. 32nd St.; tel. 344-2805).

Places for pizza include **Domino's** (741 S. Fourth Ave.; tel. 782-7561; and 710 E. 32nd St.; tel. 344-0555; and 1701 S. Avenue B; tel. 783-3030); **Rocky's New York Style Pizzeria** (2601 S. Fourth Ave.; tel. 344-4260); and **Village Inn Pizza Parlor** (2630 S. Fourth Ave.; tel. 344-3300; and 41 E. 16th St.; tel. 783-8353). You'll find supermarkets and many other restaurants along S. Fourth Ave. and E. 32nd St. (Business I-8).

Squaw Lake

### Entertainment

Catch movies at **Plaza 5 Theatres,** 1560 S. Fourth Ave.; tel. 782-9292. For local color visit **Lute's Casino** and play dominos, pinball, or pool; a snack bar serves burgers and tacos; 221 S. Main St.; tel. 782-2192. For the latest info on dining, night spots, concerts, plays, art exhibits, sports, and local goings-on, see "Sunsations," a magazine supplement to the Thursday *Yuma Daily Sun.*

### Events

You might want to catch some of the following annual events.

**January:** Gem and Mineral Show, All States Picnic (a big "snowbird" get-together), and a Fiddlers' Contest.

**February:** Yuma Crossing Day (pioneer craft demonstrations, Indian dances, and art exhibits), Quartzsite Pow Wow, Silver Spur Rodeo and Parade, and Kiwanis Gun Show.

**March:** San Diego Padres' spring training, Roadrunner Marathon, Senior Citizens Craft Show and Sale, and Square and Round Dance Festival.

**April:** Yuma County Fair.

**July:** Fourth of July Celebration.

**August:** World Championship Raft Race (8-mile course on the Colorado River).

**October:** Kiwanis Gun Show.

**November:** Arizona City Days (celebration of Yuma's pioneer days with music, art, and special museum exhibits), Military Appreciation Days (air show and static displays at the Marine base), horse racing (lasts through March), greyhound racing (lasts through March), and Gold Rock Ranch Roundup.

**December:** AKC All Breed Dog Show.

### Recreation

Jump in one of the public **swimming pools** (tel. 783-1271): **Carver,** corner Fifth St. and 13th Ave.; **Kennedy,** corner 24th St. and Kennedy Lane; and **Marcus,** corner Fifth St. and Fifth Avenue. Hit **tennis** balls at one of the nine **Desert Sun Courts** near the Convention Center, 35th St. and Ave. A; tel. 783-1271. Play **golf** on the 18-hole courses at **Arroyo Dunes** (32nd St. and Ave. A; tel. 726-8350); **Desert Hills Municipal** (1245 Desert Hills Dr.; tel. 344-4653); and **Mesa del Sol** (10583 Camino del Sol; tel. 342-1283).

Dogs head for the finish line at **Yuma Greyhound Park** from Nov. to March; 4000 S. Fourth Ave.; tel. 726-4655.

Fishermen on the Colorado River and lakes catch largemouth black bass, striped bass, channel catfish, tilapia, bluegill, crappie, and others. Check fishing regulations with **Arizona Game and Fish** on the Arizona side (tel. 344-3436) or the **Quechan Indian Fish and Game** on the California side (tel. 572-0544). The chamber of commerce has a fishing information sheet.

Go **rockhounding** in the hills for agate, jasper, petrified wood, fossils, and other treasures; a free rockhounding pamphlet from the chamber of commerce will get you started.

### Services

The main **post office** is at 2222 S. Fourth Ave.; a branch is downtown at 370 S. Main St. (across from the chamber of commerce). **Yuma Regional Medical Center** is at 2400 S. Ave. A; tel. 344-2000. **Sanborn's** has auto insurance and information for drives into Mexico at Schuman Insurance Agency;

670 E. 32nd St. #11; tel. 726-0300. **Broby's Backcountry** sells camping, backpacking, and climbing gear; rentals and guide services are available too; in Palm Plaza Shopping Center at 2241 S. Ave. A; tel. 783-2626.

## Information

The **Yuma County Chamber of Commerce** knows what's going on and where things are. They also have many useful handouts. Open Mon.-Thurs. 8:30 a.m.-5 p.m. and Fri. 9 a.m.-5 p.m.; a drive-in window is open on Sat. 10 a.m.-4 p.m. from Nov. to March; Box 10230, Yuma, AZ 85366-8230; tel. 782-2567. The office is downtown at the corner of Giss Parkway and Main St.; take I-8 Exit 1. The **Kofa National Wildlife Refuge** office of the U.S. Fish and Wildlife Service has information about the Kofa and can issue the permits required for entry to Cabeza Prieta; open Mon.-Fri. 8 a.m.-noon and 1-5 p.m.; downtown near the river at 356 W. First Street (Box 6290, Yuma, AZ 85366); tel. 783-7861. To enter Cabeza Prieta, you must have a permit (obtain here or in Ajo) and a suitable vehicle. Staff at the **Bureau of Land Management's** Yuma District office can advise on camping in the Imperial Dam area north of town and other areas of the region; open Mon.-Fri. 7:45 a.m.-4:30 p.m.; 3150 Winsor Ave., Yuma, AZ 85365; tel. 726-6300. The large and attractive **Yuma Library** is at 350 S. Third Ave.; open Mon.-Thurs. 9 a.m.-9 p.m., Fri. and Sat. 9 a.m.-5 p.m.; tel. 782-1871 or 782-5697 (reference services).

## Tours

Hop on the **Yuma Valley Railroad** for a short excursion along a levee beside the Colorado River. During the Oct. to July season, a 1941 diesel locomotive pulls a 1922 Pullman coach. Cocopah Indians meet passengers in a ramada at the end of the line with bead crafts and fry bread. The 4-hour trips cover about 12 miles of track and return; tickets cost $8 adult, $7 senior, $5 age 13-18, and $4 age 4-12; steak-dinner rides are sometimes offered on weekends; tel. 783-3456. To reach the starting point, head west 6 miles on Eighth St. from Fourth Avenue.

Skim across the Colorado River by jetboat with **Yuma River Tours** on narrated rides of 2 hours ($17.50), half day ($32), or all day ($49 including lunch), or take a sunset dinner cruise; children 12 and under go at half price. Trips go year-round; call for schedule and boarding point; tel. 783-4400. Office is in Durashield Bldg. at 1920 Arizona Ave. (between 18th and 19th streets).

The **Yuma County Chamber of Commerce** organizes tours to local points of interest during the winter months; participants provide their own transportation. Chamber staff can also advise on tour operators in the area; tel. 782-2567.

## Transport

For a taxi call **AAA Taxi** (tel. 782-0111); **DJ's Cab Co.** (tel. 782-1601); or **Yuma Cab Co.** (tel. 343-0544). Rent cars from **Avis** (airport; tel. 726-5737); **Budget** (airport; tel. 344-1822); **Hertz** (airport; tel. 726-5160); **National** (airport; tel. 726-0611); or **Ugly Duckling** (1201 S. Fourth Ave.; tel. 783-6501).

**Greyhound Bus** goes to Phoenix (4 daily; $34 one way), Tucson (4 daily; $37 one way), Los Angeles (5 daily; $36 one way), San Diego (5 daily; $30 one way), and other destinations. **Yuma Bus Co.** has service to the Mexican border near San Luis 2 or 3 times daily from the Greyhound terminal. Bus station is open Mon.-Fri. 7 a.m.-7:30 p.m., Sat. and Sun. 7 a.m.-1 p.m.; tel. 783-4403; it's at 170 E. 17th Pl. (off 16th St. behind Fed-Mart, and 2 blocks east of Fourth Ave.).

**Amtrak** trains run three times a week to Phoenix ($40 one way), Los Angeles ($56 one way), New Orleans ($196 one way), and other places; tel. (800) 872-7245. The depot is at 291 Gila St. next door to the Yuma Art Center, downtown.

**Yuma International Airport** is conveniently located on the south side of town, off 32nd Street. The airport has a travel agency, restaurant, and car rentals. **Sky West** (tel. 800-453-9417) and **America West** (tel. 800-247-5692) offer frequent service every day to Phoenix and Los Angeles with onward connections. Fares can vary widely depending on seat availability and competition.

## VICINITY OF YUMA

### San Luis (Mexico)

A different culture lies a mere 25 miles to the south. Shopping attracts many visitors, who simply park on the Arizona side and walk across the border. More than a dozen shops are within a few blocks of the crossing. Many local craftsmen work with leather; you'll probably see them turning out belts, bags, and saddles in the shops. Other crafts come from all over Mexico—including clothing, blankets, pottery, carved onyx chess sets, glassware, and musical instruments. San Luis Rio Colorado, the town's full name, was founded by farmers in 1906. The current population of about 150,000 makes it the largest city along the Arizona-Mexico border. A spacious park with welcome greenery and flowers marks the downtown area.

The nearby bus station, corner of Av. Juarez and Calle Quinta, has three bus lines to such places as Tijuana, Mexicali, Ensenada, San Felipe, Santa Rosalia, Hermosillo, Mazatlan, Guadalajara, and Mexico City. White sandy beaches, fishing, and swimming on the Gulf of California draw many sun lovers. El Golfo de Santa Clara, a small fishing village 70 miles south, and the larger town of San Felipe 125 miles southwest are both reached by paved roads.

U.S. citizens may visit San Luis, El Golfo, San Felipe, and Mexicali without formalities for as long as 72 hours. You'll need a tourist card for longer stays or more distant destinations; obtain cards at the border or from a Mexican consulate or Mexican tourist office. The cards are free, but you need to show proof of citizenship (passport, birth or naturalization certificate, voting registration card, or notarized affidavit of citizenship). Motorists also need a permit for their vehicles unless headed for border areas or Baja California; obtain at border by showing proof of ownership or a notarized affidavit by the owner authorizing the driver to take the car into Mexico. To avoid a stay in jail if there's an accident, purchase Mexican insurance beforehand. Farm Bureau Insurance sells insurance in Yuma at 1000 16th St.; tel. 782-1638.

Visitors from countries who need a U.S. visa can usually make a border-town visit without formalities, but check first with U.S. Immigration. For a longer visit, a multiple-entry or new visa will likely be needed to return to the United States. Hermosillo and other major Mexican cities have U.S. consulates.

### Sand Dunes

Though not typical of the Sonoran Desert, barren sand dunes lie about 17 miles west of Yuma on I-8. Movie producers have used the "Great American Sahara" for scenes in *Star*

*ceramic cowpoke factory in San Luis*

*Wars* and films of the *Beau Geste* type. Dune-buggie drivers like to play here too. A rest area off I-8 in the middle of the dunes provides a place to stop and park. From 1915 to 1926, motorists crossed the dunes on a road made from wooden planks strapped together. Remnants of this road can still be seen.

### Cabeza Prieta National Wildlife Refuge

The 860,000 acres of desert valleys and small rocky ranges remain as wild as ever. You won't find any paved roads, so 4WD vehicles are recommended. In the refuge, there's just the desert: very hot in summer, but beautiful with wildflowers in spring if some rain has fallen. Endangered Sonoran pronghorn, desert mule deer, and desert bighorn live here. Because the military sometimes uses the skies for gunnery and missile tests, be sure to get a permit before entering. Obtain permits from the U.S. Fish and Wildlife offices in Yuma or Ajo. The Refuge Visitor Center is in Ajo (see p. 434).

### Imperial National Wildlife Refuge

Plants and animals of the Colorado River receive protection within this long, narrow refuge. Birds are the most conspicuous wild-

*Gambel's quail* (Callipepla gambelii)

life, especially in spring and autumn when many water and land species visit. The refuge includes the river, backwater lakes, ponds, marshland, river-bottom land, and desert. Fishing, canoeing, and birding are popular activities, though some areas may be signed against entry. No camping is permitted in the refuge, but water-skiers may use two parts of it. Martinez Lake Resort and Fisher's Landing (see "Yuma Campgrounds," p. 261) offer camping, a motel, restaurants, and marinas just downstream from the refuge. For a bird list and more info on Imperial, visit the refuge headquarters on the north side of Martinez Lake or write Box 72217, Martinez Lake, AZ 85365; tel. 783-3371. The refuge is located about 40 miles north of Yuma; head north on US 95 and turn left 15 miles on Martinez Lake Road.

### Cibola National Wildlife Refuge

Cibola lies along the Colorado River just upstream from Imperial Refuge. Habitats and wildlife are similar to Imperial. Canada geese (up to 26,000) and sandhill cranes (up to 600) winter here. You're welcome to hike, boat, or fish, but camping is prohibited. For map and info, write Box AP, Blythe, CA 92226; tel. (602) 857-3253. Access to Cibola is best from the California side, off CA 78. Refuge Headquarters, in Arizona, is reached by taking the

*pronghorn* (Antilocapra americana)

I-10 Neighbours Blvd. Exit (2 miles west of Blythe, CA), then south 14 miles on Neighbours Blvd. to Farmers Bridge over the Colorado River, and 3.5 miles farther to the headquarters.

## Kofa National Wildlife Refuge

Desert critters such as coyote, cottontail, bobcat, fox, desert mule deer, and desert bighorn sheep live in the dry, rugged Castle Dome and Kofa mountain ranges. Gambel's quail scurry into the brush, while falcons and golden eagles soar above. Rare stands of native palm trees grow in Palm Canyon, reached by a short hike. Gold, discovered in 1896, led to development of the King of Arizona Mine, from which the Kofa Mountains got their name. Some mining claims remain today; they may be signed against trespassers. Several roads penetrate the scenic mountains and canyons, but these routes tend to be rough and best suited to 4WD vehicles. Hikers can explore this rugged country more extensively. The refuge covers 660,000 acres of wilderness, totally lacking in visitors' facilities—you must carry water and all supplies. A short hike up Palm Canyon reveals tall California fan palms *(Washingtonia filifera)* tucked into tiny side canyons. To reach the trailhead, go north 62 miles on US 95 from Yuma (or south 18 miles from Quartzsite) and turn east onto Palm Canyon Road between Mileposts 85 and 86. The road is dirt but OK for cars. At road's end, 9 miles farther, follow the trail into Palm Canyon for about 0.5 mile. You'll see the towering palms in clefts on the north side of the main canyon. Take care if climbing up to the palms because of sheer cliffs and loose rock. The trail pretty much ends here but it's possible to rock-scramble another 0.5 mile up the main canyon (watch for rattlesnakes) to a large natural amphitheater (no palm trees). Allow one hour from the trailhead to see the palms and return, or 3 hours to go all the way to the

*Palm Canyon*

amphitheater and back. Other areas of the Kofas are better for long hikes; ask a refuge employee for suggestions. For info on the Kofa Refuge, visit the Kofa National Wildlife Refuge office in Yuma at 356 First St. or write Box 6290, Yuma, AZ 85366; tel. 783-7861.

# SOUTHCENTRAL ARIZONA

## INTRODUCTION

Nowhere else in Arizona do you find such a contrast between city and wilderness as in the southcentral part. Over half the state's population lives in the urban sprawl centered on Phoenix in the Valley of the Sun. Yet just beyond its borders you'll find craggy mountains, vast woodlands, and seemingly endless desert. Man tends to keep close to the rivers, where he can find water to nourish his crops and cities. But a different kind of thirst—for gold and silver—lured many pioneers into the rugged mountains of southcentral Arizona. Most of the towns they founded have faded into memories; only those communities with copper, tourists, or other resources survive.

### The Land

None of the mountains in this region achieves great heights; most summit elevations range only from 3,000 to 8,000 feet. But what they lack in size is more than made up in their challenging terrain—off-trail travel can be very difficult. The major ranges, all with good hiking and a chance to experience wilderness, lie to the north and east of Phoenix. They include the Bradshaws, Mazatzals, Sierra Anchas, Superstitions, and Pinal mountains. South and west from Phoenix you'll find a very different sort of country—the often harsh desert most people associate with Arizona, plains of rock and sand with small craggy ranges breaking through here and there. Springs and streams are nearly nonexistent; only hardy desert plants and wildlife can make it here.

### Getting There And Around

Phoenix's Sky Harbor Airport has by far the best connections in Arizona. You also have a good choice of rental cars and long-distance bus connections from the city. Amtrak has train service across southern Arizona, stopping at Yuma, Phoenix, Casa Grande, Tucson, and Benson, but only three times a week in each direction.

# SOUTHCENTRAL ARIZONA

© MOON PUBLICATIONS

0   10   20   30 miles

## Climate

Because most of southcentral Arizona has elevations under 4,500 feet, temperatures stay on the warm side. This is great in the winter—you'll be enjoying spring-like weather while people in the north are digging out from snowstorms. Spring and autumn warm up to just where you like it. Higher country becomes very pleasant then, and it's a good time to be outdoors. In summer, though, the sun turns the desert valleys into a giant oven—highs over 100° F become commonplace. Drink plenty of liquids and wear a sun hat if out in this season's heat. Annual rainfall varies from about 5 inches in the lowest desert to over 20 inches in the highest mountains. Most moisture arrives in two seasons: between Dec. and March rains are gentle, but

during July and August there are violent thundershowers. These summer storms can kick up huge clouds of dust, cause flash floods, and start lightning-ignited brush fires.

## Flora And Fauna

The cacti feel right at home across most of this region—most common are prickly pear, cholla, barrel cactus, and the giant saguaro. Small plants and low trees also thrive. Good rainfalls prompt spectacular floral displays in early spring and a smaller show after the summer rains. Learn more about desert flora at the Desert Botanical Gardens in Phoenix and the Boyce Thompson Southwestern Arboretum near Superior. Most animals hole up during the day, though lizards seem to enjoy sitting on hot rocks. In the larger mountain ranges you might meet mountain lion, black bear, bighorn sheep, javelina, pronghorn, or deer. Always watch where you put hands and feet in the desert so you don't disturb rattlesnakes, Gila monsters, scorpions, or poisonous spiders.

# INDIANS

## Hohokam
Nomadic groups roamed across Arizona in seasonal cycles for thousands of years before learning to cultivate the land. Around 200-300 B.C., Indians we know as the Hohokam settled in the Gila and Salt river valleys, growing crops in fields irrigated by canals or runoff from storms. They also continued to gather many wild plants and hunt for game. For most of their history the Hohokam lived in pit houses built of brush and mud over shallow pits. Later some lived in square adobe houses. Larger towns had hundreds of houses and ball courts (large walled fields likely made to play a game with rubber balls). Hardy, drought-resistant corn was the main food, supplemented by beans, squash, and wild foods. The Hohokam made pottery, clay figurines, stone bowls, shell jewelry, paint palettes of slate, and cotton cloth. They were industrious agriculturalists, and the total length of their irrigation-canal network exceeded 300 miles in the Salt River Valley alone. The larger canals were more than 15 feet wide and 10 feet deep. Where the Hohokam came from and where they went remain mysteries, as they disappeared around A.D. 1450.

## Pima And Maricopa Appear
The Pima Indians followed the Hohokam, with whom they had much in common; the two groups may have been related. Living along the valleys of the Gila and Salt rivers, the Pima used the farming methods of their predecessors but suffered greatly when white men built dams upstream early in this century. Today the Pima farm, raise cattle, work in small industries, and do traditional handicrafts. Maricopa Indians, who originally

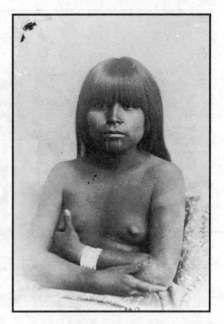

*Pima woman, late 1800s*

lived along the Colorado River, migrated up the Gila River to escape the more aggressive Mohave and Yuman tribes. Pima and Maricopa Indians now share reservations. The tribes maintain a museum, gift shop, and restaurant on the Gila River Reservation 30 miles southeast of Phoenix.

## Apache Resist
While the Pima and Maricopa got along peacefully with the white men, Apache groups strongly opposed the newcomers. Though nothing could stop men hungry for gold and land, the Apache certainly *discouraged* them. Apache resistance slowed the development of Arizona's towns and industries until late in the 19th century. Today the Apache live on the White Mountain and San Carlos reservations in eastern Arizona, several small reservations in northcentral Arizona, and with the Mohave Indians on Fort McDowell Reservation northeast of Phoenix.

# PHOENIX

Hub of the sprawling Valley of the Sun, Phoenix has a larger population, bigger businesses, and greater clout than any other city in Arizona. Here the state laws are made and the big corporate deals signed. The Phoenix area is also a cultural and sports center, often in keen competition with Tucson down the road. A Western sense of informality and leisure slows the pace of Phoenix a bit, and the relaxed style is quickly picked up by newcomers. And there have been a lot of them—Phoenix is now the 8th largest city in the country and one of the fastest growing. The city's population is nearly a million, more than twice that when the surrounding cities are added. Many retired people choose to live in the Valley of the Sun, and whole towns are planned just for them. You'll frequently hear people call the Phoenix area the "Valley of the Sun" but rarely see this name on a map. Still, it accurately reflects the Valley's pleasant winters and the 300 days of sunshine the area receives in an average year.

## The Mountains

Desert mountains form the skyline of the Valley everywhere you look. Some, like Squaw Peak, even poke up in the middle of Phoenix, rewarding hikers with a panorama of the city. Camelback Mountain provides another Phoenix landmark northeast of downtown. The bulky South Mountains offer nearly 15,000 acres for hiking, horseback riding, and picnicking—they're the world's largest city park. More remote are the Sierra Estrellas to the southwest and the White Tank Mountains to the west. The highest peaks of the area are northeast in the Mazatzals, crowned by 7,894-foot Mazatzal Peak. But the most famous range of all is the Superstitions to the east. Stories of Jacob Waltz's "lost" gold mine, which is supposed to exist somewhere in these jagged mountains, still excite the imagination.

## Climate

The city lies at an elevation of roughly 1,100

feet in the desert, where you can expect average summer highs to go *over* 100° F, dropping to the 70s or 80s at night. The Valley comes into its own from Oct. to May, when flocks of "snowbirds" migrate from the northern states and provinces. Even in midwinter, daytime temperatures range in the 60s or low 70s. You won't need a snow shovel. Average rainfall is only 7.45 inches a year.

## HISTORY

### Why Phoenix?

It's the water. Hohokam Indians tamed the Salt River in the Valley as early as 300 B.C., channeling its waters through intricate networks of canals to fields of beans, corn, squash, and cotton. At their peak, around A.D. 1100, the Hohokam settlements had grown to a population of 50,000 to 100,000.

Their culture may have been the most sophisticated ever developed north of Mexico in prehistoric times. Hohokam cities had multistory adobe buildings and ball courts. The Hohokam introduced cotton and weaving to the Southwest. For at least 1,700 years they tilled the soil until they mysteriously disappeared about A.D. 1450. You can see some of their ruins, canals, and artifacts at Pueblo Grande Museum. The Pima Indians, who later settled here, referred to their predecessors as "Hohokam," meaning "all used up" or "departed." American pioneers discovered the canal system in the 1860s and soon put it back to work for their farms.

### Americans Finally Arrive

Spanish and early American explorers overlooked the area. It wasn't until after the Civil War that stories of gold in Prescott and other

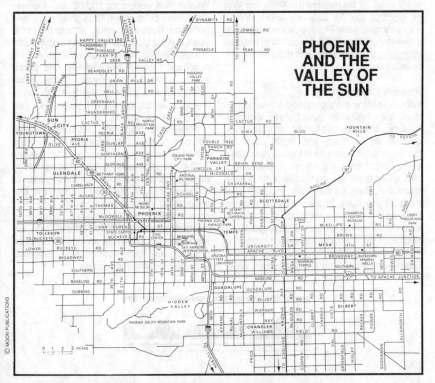

PHOENIX AND THE VALLEY OF THE SUN

© MOON PUBLICATIONS

0 1 2 3 miles

areas of central Arizona attracted streams of fortune hunters into this wild land. Pinal and Tonto Apache continued to discourage outsiders, but in Sept. 1865 the Army arrived to build Camp McDowell. Ranching and businesses soon followed as the region became safe. It was Jack Swilling, a former Confederate soldier-turned-prospector, who first took advantage of the Valley's farming potential. He formed a company in 1867 with $400, 8 mules, and 16 unemployed miners to dig out the Hohokam canals. By the summer of 1868 they had harvested the first crops of wheat and barley. Their success attracted 30 more farmers the following year, and soon there were the beginnings of a town. Darrel Duppa, one of the early settlers, predicted that a new city would rise from the ruins of the Hohokam civilization, just as the mythical phoenix bird arose from its own ashes. Surveyors laid out the new town in 1870, marking off lots that sold for $20-140 apiece. Wood was scarce in early Phoenix, so adobe buildings went up; they looked, according to some accounts, much like those in the ancient Hohokam villages.

### Phoenix Comes Of Age

With increasing prosperity and a nearby railroad line, residents built ornate Victorian houses, planted trees, put in sidewalks, opened an ice plant, and made other improvements; Phoenix soon looked like a town transplanted from the Midwest. By 1889 it had enough energy and political muscle to claim the state capital from Prescott. Not even 20 years old, Phoenix had established itself as the business, political, and agricultural center of the territory. Roosevelt Dam, dedicated by Theodore Roosevelt himself in 1911, assured water for continued growth. Easterners sought out the glamorous West,

now that it was safe, and flocked to dude ranches. Here they could dress like cowboys, ride the range, and eat mesquite-grilled steaks. World War II jerked Phoenix awake with urgent new industries and aviation training. Growth has been frantic since, helped by the availability of air conditioning that makes the summers bearable. Major manufacturing and service industries now dominate Phoenix's economic scene, but agriculture is still important. Farmers raise crops of citrus, cotton, melons, sugar beets, and vegetables.

## GETTING AROUND

Downtown Phoenix remains the heart of the Valley. You'll find the State Capitol, Phoenix Civic Center, Heritage Square, and many offices here. Streets are named for U.S. presidents—Van Buren, Monroe, Adams, Washington, Jefferson, and others. A newer downtown, or "midtown," has grown up a mile north on Central Avenue. Along this strip you'll find the Main Library, Art Museum, Little Theatre, Heard Museum, and still more office buildings. Central Ave., which runs north-south, connects and neatly divides both downtown and midtown. North-south roads west of Central are called "avenues," and those east are "streets."

**Phoenix Transit** (tel. 253-5000) will get you around the Valley with its extensive and low-cost bus service—if you're not in a hurry. A little planning and phoning before taking trips in this area will save a lot of time, as distances can be great and traffic slow. Despite some new freeways, traffic gets very thick during rush hour; there's certainly no "rush" to it. Smoke from industry and the many cars has created a serious air-pollution problem, something not normally associated with the blue skies of Arizona.

# SIGHTS

You'll find dozens of museums in the Valley: historical, archaeological, religious, art, and some unusual collections. Foreign visitors are amused to discover that Arizonans regard early 20th C. buildings as "very old." The Heard Museum (Southwest Indian) ranks as the most outstanding; it's a good choice if you have time to see only one museum in Phoenix. Because the Phoenix area is so large, you'll need a city map to find your way around (purchase from a convenience store or service station).

## DOWNTOWN PHOENIX

### Arizona State Capitol

The old state capitol, with its shiny copper dome, was completed in 1900, some 12 years before statehood. The Arizona Legislature outgrew this structure in 1960 and moved into new quarters just behind it. The old capitol became a museum, carefully restored to look as it did in 1912 when Arizona was a brand-new state. You'll see a lifelike statue of then-governor George W.P. Hunt sitting behind his desk, and you can hear a recording telling of Hunt's long career in public office. The Senate and House chambers and other rooms are full of Arizona history—photos, tales of frontier days, a bugle from the USS *Arizona,* Indian crafts, and other memorabilia. Guided tours leave at 10 a.m. and 2 p.m., or you can take a self-guided one; groups of 12 or more must schedule tours in advance. To dig deeper into the state's past, drop into the research library, Room 300. A gift shop is on the first floor. The Capitol is open Mon.-Fri. 8 a.m.-5 p.m.; free; tel. 542-4675. It's at 1700 W. Washington (free parking across the street in front; turn in from Adams St.).

### Arizona Hall Of Fame

Historic exhibits honor people who have made outstanding contributions to the state. The building has a classic/eclectic style. It

*Arizona State Capitol*

opened as Phoenix's Carnegie Public Library in 1908. Open Mon.-Sat. 8 a.m.-5 p.m.; free; tel. 255-2110. Located downtown at 1101 W. Washington.

### The Arizona Museum

Curators have packed the two rooms of this small museum with Indian crafts, pioneer memorabilia, and very odd oddities. Arizona's Indians are represented by baskets, pottery, Hopi kachina dolls, a war club, and other artifacts. You can see a large model of the battleship *Arizona* (launched in 1915 and sunk at Pearl Harbor on Dec. 7, 1941). Exhibits of early Phoenix include an ostrich egg from the old ostrich farm near Phoenix and tools used to build the State Capitol. There are also an 1883 steam engine that powered one of the first motorcycles (a high-wheeler!), a firearms collection, a portable spittoon, and much more! Two steam locomotives from early mining operations sit outside. The Arizona Museum is open Wed.-Sun. 11 a.m.-4 p.m.; free; tel. 253-2734. It's on the corner of Van Buren and 10th Avenue.

CENTRAL PHOENIX

### Galleria

The Security Pacific Bank Arizona has changing art exhibits at the 101 N. First Ave. and Adams St. office. Open Mon.-Fri. 9 a.m.-6 p.m. and Sat. 9 a.m.-1 p.m.; free; tel. 262-2209.

### Arizona History Room

First Interstate Bank has rotating exhibits of Arizona's history downstairs in their office at 100 W. Washington St. and First Avenue. Open Mon.-Fri. 10 a.m.-3 p.m.; free; tel. 229-4624.

### Arizona Museum Of
### Science And Technology

Kids especially will have lots of fun in this interactive museum. You get to operate computers, see your own thermal image, walk into an infinity chamber, generate electricity, step into a camera obscura, and experience many other science-related displays. The museum also has a small gift shop and an ice-cream parlor. Open Mon.-Sat 9 a.m.-5 p.m. and Sun. noon-5 p.m.; $3.50 adult, $2.50 children 4-12, and $2.50 seniors 65 and over; tel. 256-9388. Located at the corner of 80 N. Second and Adams sts. (across from Phoenix Civic Plaza).

### Rosson House And Heritage Square

The Victorian-style Rosson House, built in 1895, dominates this block of historic buildings. Meticulous restoration has given the Rosson House its original appearance at the turn of the century, when it was one of Phoenix's most elegant. You can tour the interior and learn about its construction and people who lived here; open Wed.-Sat. 10 a.m.-3:30 p.m. and Sun. noon-3:30 p.m.; $2 adult, $.50 children 3-12; tel. 262-5071. Tours start behind the house.

The Burgess Carriage House next door was built in a Colonial Williamsburg style of architecture rarely seen this far west. Originally at Second and Taylor, it's the only structure to have been moved to Heritage Square. Burgess Carriage House now contains an information center and a gift shop.

The other buildings on Heritage Square, all with free admission, are representative of early Phoenix. The Duplex (1923) is now used for offices; the Stevens House (1901) displays the Arizona Doll and Toy Museum; the Stevens-Haustgen House (1901) exhibits various products of the Craftsmen's Co-op Gallery; the Bouvier-Teeter House (1899) is now a dining room for the Heritage Cafe; the Silva House (1900) has Salt River Project exhibits; and a second Carriage House (about 1900) now houses the Heritage Cafe (offering sandwiches, soups, quiches, salads, and pastries daily). The Lath House Pavilion dates from only 1980 but is typical of early Phoenix architecture. Heritage Square is open Tues.-Sat. 10 a.m.-4 p.m. and Sun. noon-4 p.m. (call for summer hours); closed Aug.; at Sixth and Monroe sts., one block east of Civic Plaza.

---

## CENTRAL PHOENIX

1. Judaica Museum
2. Phoenix College Theatre
3. Encanto Park Bandshell
4. Arizona Mineral Museum
5. Arizona State Capitol
6. Arizona Museum
7. Heard Museum
8. Phoenix Art Museum; main public library; Phoenix Little Theatre
9. Ellis-Shackelford House
10. Phoenix Performing Arts Theatre
11. Visitors Bureau (Phoenix and Valley of the Sun)
12. YMCA
13. Galleria (Security Pacific Bank Arizona)
14. Arizona History Room (First Interstate Bank)
15. Amtrak
16. Phoenix Transit (local bus)
17. Arizona Museum of Science and Technology
18. Symphony Hall
19. Greyhound Bus
20. Rosson House and Heritage Square
21. youth hostel
22. Tonto National Forest (main office)
23. Sky Harbor Airport

## CENTRAL AVENUE CORRIDOR

### Ellis-Shackelford House

The Arizona Historical Society has restored this mansion to its original 1917 appearance at 1242 N. Central Avenue. Outside, you can ride Phoenix's last remaining street car from Central to Third avenues through Deck Park. (The house and street car are planned to open in autumn 1990.) Temporary exhibits on regional history can be seen in the Society's "Museum on Wheels" at 1120 N. Third Ave. (call for hours); tel. 255-4470. In the spring of 1991, a large, new museum in Papago Park will replace it.

### Phoenix Art Museum

A varied collection of more than 11,000 works of art spans the 15th through 20th centuries. Particularly strong are the 18th C. French painting exhibits and the Oriental, Contemporary, Mexican, and Western Art collections. Visiting exhibitions also occupy a large area. The museum schedules one-hour tours at 1:30 p.m. Kids will enjoy touching, exploring, and even creating their own art in the Junior Museum downstairs. The museum's reference library is also downstairs. You'll find art souvenirs just inside the entrance in the museum store. Open Tues.-Sat. 10 a.m.-5 p.m. ('til 9 p.m. on Wed.) and Sun. 1-5 p.m.; $3 adult, $1.50 student over 12, $2.50 senior 65 and up, free for children 12 and under; tel. 257-1222 (recorded information) or 257-1880. Located at 1625 N. Central Ave. at McDowell.

### Heard Museum

The Heard features the best exhibits on Southwest Indians you're likely to see *anywhere*. The collection is large enough to give a good overview of regional Indian cultures, but it's small enough that it won't overwhelm you. Indians talk about their culture in "Our Voices Our Land," an audio-visual program with beautiful photography and native music. See exhibits of the Southwest's land and people from prehistoric times to the present.

Clothing, tools, weapons, and even a Navajo hogan all demonstrate the resourcefulness of the tribes. Large displays show superb Indian jewelry, largely made by Navajo, Hopi, and Zuni craftsmen. A kachina collection from the Hopi and Zuni tribes fills an entire room. The Heard Museum also has large collections of Southwest pottery, weavings, basketry, and paintings.

Its Primitive Art Gallery exhibits work from the far corners of South America, Africa, the Pacific, and Asia. Two other galleries have visiting shows. For deeper research, you can visit the anthropology library. The museum's sizeable shop sells Indian art and crafts and books on Indian cultures. Open Mon.-Sat. 10 a.m.-5 p.m. and Sun. 1-5 p.m. but closed major holidays; $3 adult, $1 student, $2.50 senior 65 and up, and free for children 6 and under; tel. 252-8840. It's in a Spanish Colonial-style building at 22 E. Monte Vista Road (3 blocks north on Central Ave. from McDowell, then one-half block east on Monte Vista).

## NORTH PHOENIX

### Arizona Mineral Museum

Many of Arizona's pioneers came in search of the glitter of gold and silver or the brilliant colors signifying copper minerals. Here you'll see these and many others. Most eye-catching are the beautiful specimens of copper ore—azurite, malachite, chrysocolla, cuprite, chalcanthite, and turquoise. Old mining tools, lamps, assay kits, photos, and models show how miners did their work. A fluorescent room demonstrates the effect of two different wavelengths of ultraviolet light. Lapidary exhibits display the art of gem cutting and polishing. The museum staff can tell you of upcoming rock and mineral shows (most are held during the winter months) and put you in touch with local shops and clubs. A gift shop sells specimens, gold pans, and books. Open Mon.-Fri. 8 a.m.-5 p.m. and Sat. 1-5 p.m.; closed state holidays; free; tel. 255-3791. It's on the southwest corner of the State Fairgrounds at the corner of McDowell and 19th Ave.; enter the fairgrounds on 17th Ave. from McDowell.

## Judaica Museum

Learn about the Jewish ceremonies and religious holidays at Temple Beth Israel's museum. It displays many ancient artifacts from the Holy Land. Open Tues.-Thurs. 9 a.m.-2 p.m. and Sun. 9 a.m.-noon; closed in summer; free; tel. 264-4428. Located at 3310 N. 10th Ave. (approach from Osborn Road off either Seventh or 19th aves.).

## Cave Creek Museum

This history collection features prehistoric Indian artifacts and displays of mining and ranching of the area. The museum is open Thurs.-Sun. 1:30-4:30 (may be extended—call to check); closed June to Sept. and on major holidays; free; tel. 488-2764 or 488-3183. Cave Creek lies among foothills about 30 miles north of downtown Phoenix. Drive north on Cave Creek Road or head east from I-17 on AZ 74 (Exit 223). Turn south on Basin Road to Skyline Drive.

## Pioneer Arizona

The frontier comes back to life in this museum of living history. You'll see how residents of the territory lived from the mid-1800s to statehood in 1912. Walk around to see historic exhibits and craftsmen at work. Or hop on a wagon (weekends only) for a free tour of the village. Many of the 20 or so buildings are authentic, having been brought from other sites. The nearly complete little town has a school, church, sheriff's office, bank, blacksmith shop, carpenter shop, opera house, cabins, and houses (including the John Sears mansion, thought to be Phoenix's first frame house). Pioneer Arizona emphasizes historical accuracy, setting it apart from most other "western villages" based more on Hollywood fiction than fact. Mountain men, cavalry, gunfighters, and special exhibits enliven the community on the weekend nearest its birthday (Feb. 15th). You can usually catch a melodrama or other production in the opera house; call for times. Pioneer Arizona is open Wed.-Sun. 9 a.m.-5 p.m. from Oct. 1 to June 30; closed in summer; $4.50 adult, $4 student and senior (60+), $3 children 4-12; tel. 993-0212. It's set among rocky desert foothills about 30 miles north of downtown Phoenix. Take I-17 north to Pioneer Road (Exit 225) and follow signs. Pioneer Travel Trailer Park nearby (not connected with the museum) has RV sites for adults; $13.72 w/hookups; tel. 229-8000.

# WEST PHOENIX

## Wildlife World Zoo

This collection of exotic wildlife began as a breeding farm for rare and endangered

*miner's cabin (reconstruction) at Pioneer Arizona*

species in 1974, and it opened to the public 10 years later. You'll meet the patas monkey, fastest of all primates, which can run dog-like across the ground at 35 miles per hour. Larger animals include the scimitar-horned oryx, dama gazelle, addax (an antelope of the Sahara Desert), rhino, tapir, zebra, camel, and kangaroo. The zoo really shines in its bird collection—pheasants, toucans, cockatoos, macaws, curassows, ostriches (all five of the world's species), and some birds not displayed anywhere else in the country. A large, walk-in aviary contains Eyton's tree ducks of Australia, black-necked stilts of North America, and other unusual birds. Open daily 9 a.m.-5 p.m. (except mid-June to mid-Sept. when it's open Mon.-Fri. 9 a.m.-3 p.m. and Sat. and Sun. 9 a.m.-5 p.m.); $5.50 adult, $2.50 children 3-12; tel. 935-WILD. The zoo is about 18 miles west of I-17 on Northern Ave. (3 miles west of Litchfield Road), just past Luke Air Force Base.

*Mystery Castle*

## Sun Cities Art Museum
The gallery features both local and visiting exhibitions. Open Tues.-Sat. 10 a.m.-4 p.m. and Sun. 1-4 p.m.; closed in summer; free admission; tel. 972-0635. Located on the north side of Bell Road between Sun City and Sun City West at 17425 N. 115th Ave., northwest of Phoenix.

# SOUTH PHOENIX

## Mystery Castle
Boyce Luther Gulley dreamed of building his own castle, so one day in 1927 he left his wife and daughter and disappeared. His whereabouts and this castle remained unknown until after his death in 1945. The daughter, Mary Lou Gulley, now lives in the castle Boyce built and leads tours through the imaginative rooms. Everything from Stutz-Bearcat wheels to discarded bricks have gone into this strange mixture of American West and scrap yard. The tour is short (about 25 minutes), but anyone who has dreamed of castles should enjoy it. Open Tues.-Sun. 11 a.m.-5 p.m. from Oct. 1 to July 4; closed the rest of the year; $2.75 adult, $.75 children

5-14; tel. 268-1581. Mystery Castle is 7 miles south of downtown Phoenix near the entrance to South Mountain Park. Drive south on Seventh St. to its end at Mineral Road (1.75 miles south of Baseline Road) and turn left at the sign.

# EAST PHOENIX

## Pueblo Grande Museum
Exhibits show how archaeologists dig and analyze their finds. Scientists have been able to reconstruct the prehistoric Hohokam society and environment using pollen, plant and animal remains, artifacts, and burials. They know, for example, that the average Hohokam man stood 5 feet, 4 inches tall, weighed 130-140 pounds, and had a 40-year life span. You can see Hohokam crafts and stone tools and illustrations of their pithouses, pueblos, canals, and ball courts. After looking at the indoor exhibits, you'll better appreciate the ruin outside. The Hohokam began construction of the Platform Mound at Pueblo Grande about A.D. 1150 on a terrace overlooking the Salt River, and they occupied the site for about 300

**1.** Red Rock Crossing, near Sedona; **2.** Devil's Bridge, near Sedona; **3.** below Havasu Falls, Havasupai Indian Reservation; **4.** along the Echo Canyon Trail, Chiricahua National Monument; **5.** on Desert View Trail, Organ Pipe Cactus National Monument (all photos by B. Weir)

1. desert paintbrush; 2. teddy bear cholla cactus; 3. ocotillo blossoms; 4. prickly pear cactus;
5. saguaro cactus; 6. beavertail cactus (all photos by B. Weir)

Page 6
**PHOENIX GAZETTE**
Phoenix, Arizona
Thursday, December 28, 1944

## Wily Germans Elude Chase

The greatest man hunt in Arizona's history continued to baffle authorities Thursday as they pressed the search for the 19 escaped German prisoners of war.

Each tip received by authorities is being checked, but so far all have been without results.

Twenty - five Germans, many of them officers, escaped from the Papago Park camp last Sunday evening. Within a short time six had been captured or had surrendered. The remaining 19 have since remained at large.

The search is being concentrated in the desert area between Phoenix and the Mexican border, 191 miles to the south and extending to points near the Gulf of California.

Military personnel, agents of the Federal Bureau of Investigation, sheriff's deputies and other police officers, in addition to interested citizens, are taking part in the search.

Officials are authorized to pay up to $25 to the person or persons capturing a prisoner of war. They will pay $25 if the man is captured and returned to the camp. If the army is called to return a captured man, $15 will be paid.

Pictures of the 19 escaped Germans have been released to newspapers by the FBI in a hope that their publication will help lead to apprehension.

*Capt. Jurgen Wattenberg*

# $25 REWARD FOR EACH OF THESE MEN

| Kurt Mohrdieck | Capt. Jurgen Quaet Faslem | Reinhard Mark | Second Lt. Martin P. Reese | Johann Kremer | Heinrich Palmer |
| Walter Kozur | First Lt. F. Utzolino | Capt. Hans Werner Kraus | Capt. Wilhelm Gunther | First Officer Jurgen Schroder | Second Lt. Helmut Drescher |
| Capt. Fritz Guggenberger | Second Lt. Hans Zundorf | First Lt. Wolf Clarus | Friederich Sternberg | First Lt. Otto Hoferichter | Artur Karstens |

### National Income Booms To $159 Billion Peak
WASHINGTON, Dec. 28—(AP)— Wartime economic activity zoomed

### Inseparable Four Scattered By War

### Boston Judge Gets Tired Of Books Being Banned
BOSTON, Dec. 28—(AP)— Judge Elijah Adlow Thursday acquitted

*Military authorities thought the desert near Phoenix a perfect place to hold captured German submariners. These prisoners escaped by tunneling. All were recaptured, though two made it as far as Mexico.*

years. From the ruins you can see ancient canal banks and an oval-shaped depression thought to be a ball court. Earlier pithouse ruins nearby date from A.D. 500. A trail guide describes features of Pueblo Grande's construction. Open Mon.-Sat. 9 a.m.-4:45 p.m. and Sun. 1-4:45 p.m.; $.50; tel. 495-0901. The museum and ruins are 5 miles east of downtown at 4619 E. Washington Street.

### Arizona Military Museum
The museum tells the story of Arizona's military history from Spanish days to the present. Old maps, photos, weapons, uniforms, and other memorabilia illustrate each period. During WW II, the museum building served as part of the prison camp holding German submariners. Open Sat. and Sun. 1-4 p.m., Tues. and Thurs. 9 a.m.-2 p.m.; groups can schedule other times; free; tel. 267-2676. The museum is in the Arizona National Guard complex at 5636 E. McDowell Road, about 7 miles east of downtown; stop to check in at the entrance gate.

### Desert Botanical Gardens
If you've been curious about all those strange cacti and other desert plants of Arizona, this is the place to find out what they are. A 1.5-mile trail in the gardens winds past more than 2,000 species. Signs list their names and the trail guide tells more. The gardens display exotic plants from other regions too, representing more than half of all cactus

species in the world. If you're lucky enough to be here in the spring, you'll see many plants in bloom. A Wildflower Hotline operating during March and April tells you where wildflowers can be seen in Arizona; tel. 941-2867. The gift shop sells natural history books, souvenirs, and cactus specimens. Open daily from 9 a.m. (8 a.m. in June-Aug.) until sunset; $3.50 adult, $3 age 60 and over, and $1 children 6-12; tel. 941-1217 (recorded information) or 941-1225. The Desert Botanical Gardens are off Galvin Parkway in Papago Park (enter from either 6400 E. McDowell Road or 5800 E. Van Buren St.).

## Phoenix Zoo

Animals and birds from Arizona and all over the world inhabit 125 acres of rolling hills. The zoo uses moats and steep inclines, where possible, to give the animals an open and natural setting. Tropical rain forests, mountains, grasslands, temperate woodlands, and deserts recreate appropriate habitats for the more than 1,000 zoo residents. You'll see bighorn sheep from Arizona, oryx from the Arabian deserts, tigers from India, gorillas from Africa, wallabies from Papua New Guinea, and many others. Children will enjoy meeting the farm animals in the "Petting Zoo." If a lot of walking doesn't appeal, just hop on the "Safari Train" for a narrated tour of the grounds; $1. Picnic areas and snacks are available. The Phoenix Zoo is open daily 9 a.m.-5 p.m. (7 a.m.-4 p.m. from May 1 to Labor Day); $6 adult, $3 children 4-12 (with adult); tel. 273-7771 (recorded information) or 273-1341. It's off Galvin Parkway in Papago Park (enter from either 6400 E. McDowell Road or 5800 E. Van Buren St.).

## Hall Of Flame

Being a volunteer fireman in the old days carried great prestige. Men eagerly joined the local fire brigade, which also served as a social club. Firemen competed in drills and marched in parades with their glistening machines. The museum houses what may be the world's largest display of firefighting gear. Equipment in this amazing collection comes from all over the world. Many items are works of art in themselves.

The first gallery contains hand- and horse-drawn pumpers, hose carriers, and hook-and-ladder wagons from the 18th and 19th centuries. A second gallery displays antique motorized fire trucks. The third gallery features historic fire-alarm systems, including the world's first computerized dispatch system. The fourth gallery has a fire safety exhibit. Old prints show firefighters in action. Open Mon.-Sat. 9 a.m.-5 p.m.; $3 adult, $1 student 6-17, or $2 senior 62 and up; tel. "ASK-FIRE." The Hall of Flame is opposite Papago Park at 6101 E. Van Buren St. (turn south 0.2 mile on Project Dr.).

## Salt River Project History Center

The Salt River Project displays feature both the Hohokam and modern canal systems, Indian artifacts, construction of Theodore Roosevelt Dam, and the history of electric power. Open Mon.-Fri. 9 a.m.-4 p.m.; free; tel. 236-5422. The Center is at 1521 Project Dr., across from the Hall of Flame.

# SCOTTSDALE

Sometimes billing itself as "The West's Most Western Town," Scottsdale has porch-fronted shops that sell Western clothing, Western art, and Indian crafts. Chaplain Winfield Scott, the first resident, fell in love with the Valley and homesteaded here in the 1880s. During his frequent travels, he promoted the land as "unequaled in greater fertility or richer promise." A small, close-knit community soon formed at Brown Ave. and Main Street. But the little village has grown up—130,000 people live here now. Both residents and visitors enjoy the top-notch specialty shops, art galleries, cultural events, restaurants, resort hotels, and beautiful landscaping. Scottsdale, just east of Phoenix and just north of Tempe, makes an ideal base for a stay in the Valley, though it's a little more expensive than Phoenix.

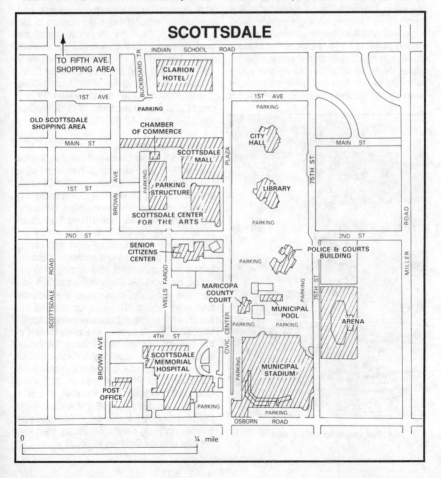

## SIGHTS

### The Little Red Schoolhouse

Scottsdale was so small in 1909, when this schoolhouse was built, that all the town's children could fit into the two classrooms. From the 1920s until the 1960s, Mexican agricultural workers used it as a schoolhouse and community center. The Mexican barrio and the cotton fields where they worked have disappeared, but the Little Red Schoolhouse has been preserved as a reminder of the town's past. Located near the center of the original Scottsdale, the schoolhouse makes a good place to begin a visit of the modern city. Scottsdale's chamber of commerce occupies the building today. They'll give you a pamphlet for a self-guided walking tour of Old Town Scottsdale and answer questions about

*frolicking in front of City Hall*

sights, shopping, restaurants, and places to stay. Ask for a Scottsdale Trolley schedule. The chamber is open Mon.-Fri. 8:30 a.m.-5 p.m.; 7333 E. Scottsdale Mall, Scottsdale, AZ 85251; tel. 945-8481. The schoolhouse is in the Civic Center Complex, just east of the intersection of Brown Ave. and Main Street.

### Scottsdale Center For The Arts

Scottsdale's residents have always had a keen interest in the arts. This facility contains a large gallery of contemporary art, an 800-seat performing arts theater, a cinema, and an outdoor amphitheater. Admission to the art gallery is free, but there's a charge for performances. Call 994-ARTS to find out what's coming up. The Center is open daily (call for hours). Part of the Civic Center Complex, it's located at Second St. and Civic Center Blvd. between the Little Red Schoolhouse and the library; write 7383 Scottsdale Mall, Scottsdale, AZ 85231.

### Cosanti Foundation

Italian-born Paolo Soleri first came to Scottsdale in 1947 to study architecture with Frank Lloyd Wright. In 1956 Soleri started Cosanti, his own foundation, with the goal of designing energy- and space-efficient cities. Still striving for those ideals, Soleri feels that urban sprawl, of which the Valley is a prime example, wastes agricultural land and harms society. He uses the word *arcology,* a combination of "architecture" and "ecology," to describe his work. At Cosanti Foundation you can see some of Soleri's unique structures and learn about his ideas for making the world better to live in. Books, drawings, sculpture, and Soleri's famous windbells for sale in the gallery/gift shop help finance the Foundation. To see arcology in action, visit Arcosanti—Soleri's city-in-the-making 65 miles north of Phoenix (see p. 222). The Cosanti Foundation is open daily 9 a.m.-5 p.m.; $1 donation; tel. 948-6145. It's at 6433 Doubletree Road; from central Scottsdale go 5 miles north on Scottsdale Road, then turn left one mile on Doubletree Road.

## Taliesin West

The renowned architect Frank Lloyd Wright didn't just design buildings according to a plan; he let them "grow" from the inside out. His idea for training student architects was similar. Apprentices had to grow and develop far beyond the learning of facts and formulas. Taliesin West began in 1937 as a winter home for Wright's Wisconsin school, opened 6 years earlier. Students at Taliesin West lived then in tents and simple shelters and now, more than 50 years later, still do! Most stay 3-5 years, living and working closely with one another, the faculty, and the surrounding desert. Wright died in 1959, but the Frank Lloyd Wright School of Architecture and Taliesin Associated Architects carry on his high standards. Docents or apprentices lead daily walking tours from Oct. 1 to May 30, beginning every hour on the hour 10 a.m.-4 p.m. and lasting about 45 minutes. In summer, tours depart on the hour 9-11 a.m. Besides touring some of the grounds, you'll see highlights of Wright's work in models, photos, and a slide presentation. Tours cost $6 ($2.50 children under 12); tel. 860-8810 (recorded information) or 860-2700. The Visitor Center has a good selection of related books and gift items. Taliesin West is set in the western foothills of the McDowell Mountains northeast of Scottsdale. From central Scottsdale, go north 10 miles on Scottsdale Road, turn right 4.3 miles on Cactus Road to 108th Street.

## Rawhide

A replica of an 1880s Old West town with about 25 buildings containing shops, Western exhibits, a museum, saloon, Golden Belle Restaurant (steaks, chicken, ribs), burro rides for the kids, and stagecoach rides. The museum displays such Western curiosities as Tom Mix's boots, Wyatt Earp's gun, and a pair of Geronimo's moccasins. Rawhide has free admission but there are plenty of places inside to spend your money. Open Mon.-Fri. 5-10 p.m. and Sat. and Sun. 11 a.m.-10 p.m. (daily 5-10 p.m. June 1 to Oct. 1); tel. 563-5111 (recording) or 563-

5600. From central Scottsdale, go north about 13 miles to 23023 N. Scottsdale Road (4 miles north of Bell Road).

## Fountain Hills

The world's highest fountain shoots 560 feet into the skies of this community 18 miles northeast of Scottsdale. A 15-minute display takes place daily on the hour from 10 a.m.-9 p.m. The surrounding park is a fine place for a picnic or stroll. From Scottsdale go north 6 miles on Scottsdale Road and turn right 12 miles on Shea Boulevard.

## Out Of Africa Wildlife Park

This unusual park features big cats from Africa, Asia, and North America. Shows demonstrate the relationship between them and humans. You can see the cats in their near-natural habitats and in shows, where cubs are often available for petting. A python and other scaled friends live in the reptile exhibit. Open daily except Mon. year-round (also open Mon. if a holiday) 10:30 a.m.-5 p.m., extended to 9 p.m. Fri. and Sat. from May 1 to Sept. 30. Continuous shows begin at 11 a.m.; tel. 837-7779/7677. A primitive playground, patio cafe, and gift shop are at the park. Admission costs $7.95 adult, $6.95 senior 65 and up, and $4.95 children 4-12. Out of Africa is east of Fountain Hills opposite the turnoff for the Fort McDowell Indian Reservation; take the Beeline Hwy. north 2 miles from the intersection with Shea Blvd. and follow signs.

## Hoo-hoogam Ki Museum

Pima and Maricopa Indians on the Salt River Indian Reservation exhibit their baskets, pottery, historic photos, and other artifacts just east of Scottsdale. The museum building incorporates adobe, desert plants, and stone in a traditional "sandwich" style of the tribes. Open Tues.-Fri. 10 a.m.-4 p.m. and Sat. 10 a.m.-2 p.m.; closed major holidays; $1 adult, $.50 children 6 to high school; tel. 941-7379. Take Thomas or McDowell roads east from Phoenix or Scottsdale to Longmore Road, then turn north to 10000 E. Osborn Road.

# TEMPE

An enterprising merchant—Charles Trumbull Hayden—arrived here in 1872 to set up a trading post. He chose this spot on the south bank of the Salt River because it was the safest place to cross with his freight wagons. Hayden also found it a good location for a flour mill and a ferry service. Darrel Duppa came over from Phoenix to visit Hayden's Ferry one day, and remarked that the Salt River Valley reminded him of the Vale of Tempe between Mt. Olympus and Mt. Ossa in Thessaly, Greece. Hayden liked the name and it stuck. Farmers settled in Tempe (pronounced "tem-PEE"), raising livestock, dairying, and growing a variety of crops. In 1885 the territorial Legislature established Arizona State Teachers College nearby, now Arizona State University; it has grown into one of the largest schools in the country.

Many of Tempe's original buildings have survived; you'll see Hayden's home, his flour mill (rebuilt in 1918 after a fire), and other old buildings along Mill Avenue. Sandwiched between Phoenix to the west and Mesa to the east, Tempe lies just south of Scottsdale.

### Niels Peterson House
Built in 1892, this Queen Anne/Victorian-style house uses a clever ventilation system to keep the interior livable in summer. You can tour the inside, restored to its 1930s appearance, Mon.-Sat. 10 a.m.-2 p.m.; free; tel. 350-5151. Staff can also tell you about the **Tempe Historical Museum,** scheduled to open at the Tempe Community Center in spring or summer of 1991. The house is on the northwest corner of 1414 W. Southern Ave. and Priest Drive.

*ASU campus*

*Grady Gammage Auditorium detail*

**Tempe Arts Center**

Contemporary artists display their dimensional art of fine crafts and sculpture. Exhibits, which change monthly, are free. Most work is for sale. The Sculpture Garden outside contains many modern pieces. Workshops take place occasionally at the Center. Open Tues.-Sun. noon-5 p.m.; tel. 968-0888. The Center is in Tempe Beach Park along the Salt River at the corner of Mill Ave. and First Street.

## ARIZONA STATE UNIVERSITY

Broad lawns, stately palms, and flowering subtropical trees grace the 600-acre campus of Arizona's largest university. After the Arizona Legislature founded the school in 1885, classes met in a four-room, red-brick structure set on 20 acres of cow pasture. Growth has been spectacular within the last 25 years, when most of the campus buildings have gone up.

The school now has more than 40,000 students and a teaching faculty of about 1,400. Undergraduates have 92 fields to choose from, while graduate students can earn a Master's in 68 areas of interest or a Doctorate in 42. Attractions on campus include the striking Gammage Auditorium, art galleries, and a variety of small museums. The well-landscaped campus is a pleasant place for stroll. Activity slows down in summer (it's hot!) but most of the galleries and museums stay open except as noted below.

**Getting Around**

Parking is tight, as you might expect with so many students (many of whom commute), but you can use the parking meters or several pay lots on campus or look for a spot on a side street off campus. See the map for campus parking areas. Most of the central campus is closed to motor traffic. Phoenix Transit (tel. 253-5000) connects the university with Tempe and the rest of the Valley. Metro Trolley (tel. 829-1226) has service in town. The open-air University Tram cruises the campus's outer areas.

**Grady Gammage Auditorium**

You'll see this circular structure, which commemorates one of the ASU presidents, on the southwest corner of the campus. Dedicated in 1964, it was the last major building designed by Frank Lloyd Wright. You can take a free half-hour tour inside, usually on Mon.-Sat. afternoons; call 965-4050 for tour times

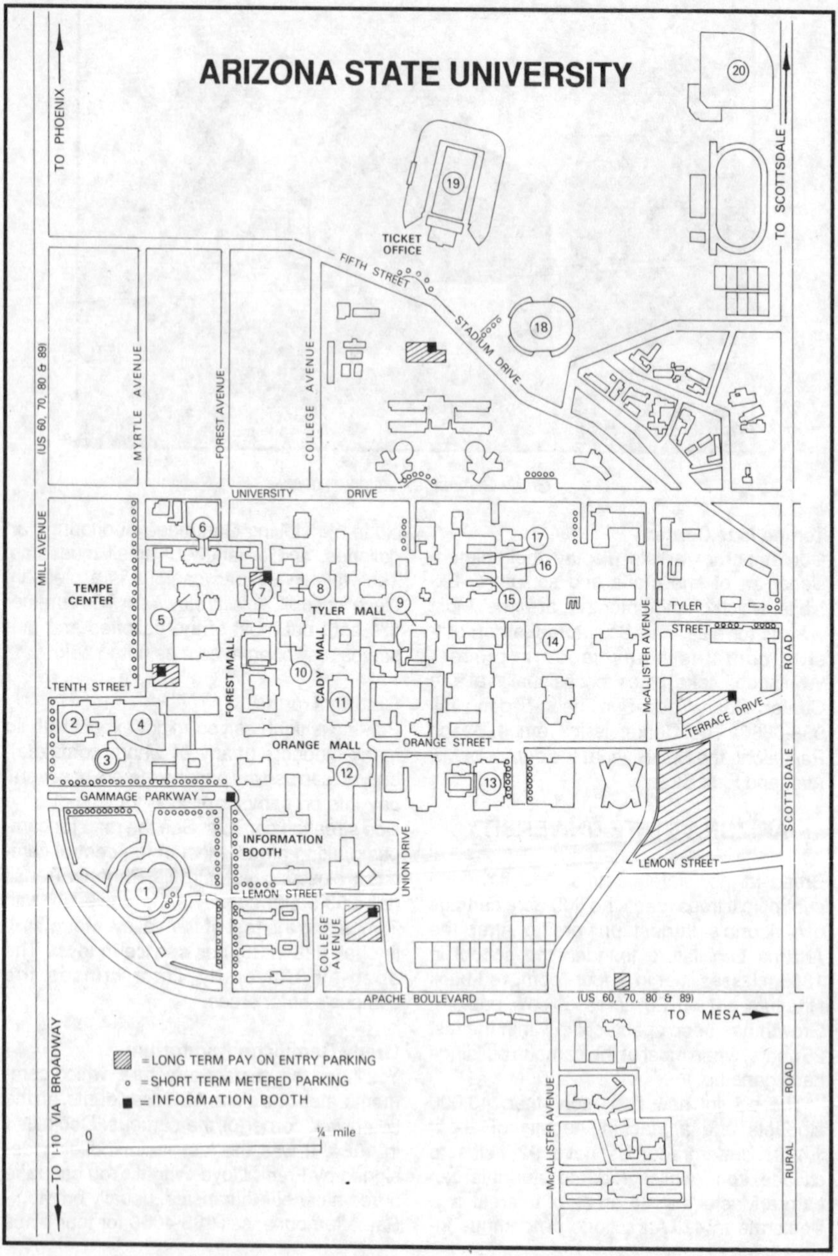

ARIZONA STATE UNIVERSITY

TO PHOENIX

TO SCOTTSDALE

(US 60, 70, 80 & 89)

TICKET OFFICE

FIFTH STREET

STADIUM DRIVE

MYRTLE AVENUE

FOREST AVENUE

COLLEGE AVENUE

UNIVERSITY DRIVE

MILL AVENUE

TEMPE CENTER

TYLER MALL

CADY MALL

FOREST MALL

TENTH STREET

ORANGE MALL

ORANGE STREET

GAMMAGE PARKWAY

INFORMATION BOOTH

LEMON STREET

UNION DRIVE

COLLEGE AVENUE

APACHE BOULEVARD

TO I-10 VIA BROADWAY

McALLISTER AVENUE

TYLER STREET

TERRACE DRIVE

SCOTTSDALE ROAD

LEMON STREET

(US 60, 70, 80 & 89)

TO MESA

McALLISTER AVENUE

RURAL ROAD

= LONG TERM PAY ON ENTRY PARKING

o  = SHORT TERM METERED PARKING

■ = INFORMATION BOOTH

0          ¼ mile

© MOON PUBLICATIONS

or 965-3434 for concert information. The Gammage Auditorium is easy to spot, set into a curve of the Phoenix-Mesa highway (US 60/70/80/89).

## University Art Museum
ASU's new **Nelson Fine Arts Center** houses galleries dedicated to American, contemporary, print, craft, and changing exhibits. Sculpture can be seen in the several outdoor terraces. The art museum is highly recommended for its quality, size, and diversity— and to see the highly unusual architecture of the building itself. The design, by architect Antoine Predock, called for a "village-like aggregation of buildings" to house the arts. Aspects of the existing campus and the Southwest can be seen in the choice of materials, forms, and colors of the building. Light coming in from skylights reflects off surfaces a total of 10 times before illuminating the artwork, a process intended to remove all harmful qualities of daylight.

---

### ARIZONA STATE UNIVERSITY

1. Grady Gammage Auditorium
2. Nelson Fine Arts Center (art museum)
3. Music Building
4. Galvin Playhouse
5. Harry Wood Art Gallery (Art Building)
6. Gallery of Design (College of Architecture)
7. Northlight Gallery (Matthews Hall)
8. Anthropology Museum
9. Zoology Display (Life Sciences Center)
10. University Art Museum (Matthews Center)
11. Hayden Library
12. Memorial Union
13. ASU Bookstore
14. Daniel E. Noble Science Library
15. Planetarium (Physical Sciences Center)
16. Geology Museum
17. Center for Meteorite Studies (Physical Sciences Center)
18. University Activity Center
19. Sun Devil Stadium
20. Packard Baseball Stadium

---

The Center includes the Galvin Playhouse and the University Dance Laboratory. Museum hours are Mon.-Fri. 8:30 a.m.- 4:30 p.m., Sat. 10 a.m.-4 p.m., and Sun. 1-5 p.m.; closed major holidays; free. tel. 965-2787. The gift shop sells a variety of crafts. ASU also has art collections in the Matthews Center and Matthews Hall (see below), though these will eventually move into the Nelson Fine Arts Center. The Fine Arts Center is on the southeast corner of Mill Ave. and 10th St. on the east side of campus; visitor parking is available in front and to the south.

### University Art Museum—Matthews Center
A varied display of paintings, prints, sculpture, and crafts by artists from the United States, Latin America, and other parts of the world. Visiting art exhibits appear too. Open Mon.-Thurs. 8:30 a.m.-4:30 p.m. and Sun. 1-5 p.m.; free; tel. 965-2787. The collection is on the second floor in Matthews Center.

### Northlight Gallery
Photographic exhibits, both historic and modern, are featured. Open Mon.-Thurs. 10:30 a.m.-4:30 p.m. and Sun. 12:30-4:30 p.m. (closed in summer); free; tel. 965-6517. Located in Matthews Hall (behind Matthews Center).

### Anthropology Museum
Displays illustrate prehistoric Hohokam and modern Indian cultures, archaeological techniques, and concepts of anthropology. Open Mon.-Fri. 8 a.m.-5 p.m.; free; tel. 965-6213. It's in the Anthropology Building, next to Matthews Center.

### Harry Wood Art Gallery
See student exhibitions of paintings, photography, or sculpture. Open Mon.-Fri. 8 a.m.-5 p.m. (may close in summer); free; tel. 965-3468. Located in the School of Arts building.

### Gallery Of Design
Learn the latest architectural techniques, illustrated by drawings and scale models. Open Mon.-Fri. 8 a.m.-5 p.m.; free; tel. 965-3216. The Gallery of Design, along with the

Howe Library of Architecture, is in the College of Architecture and Environmental Design.

## Hayden Library

The university's main library also has the Arizona, Chicano, East Asian, and Government Documents special collections. Open Mon.-Thurs. 7 a.m.-midnight, Fri. 7 a.m.-9 p.m., Sat. 10 a.m.-9 p.m., and Sun. 10 a.m.-midnight; tel. 965-5902/6164. Shorter hours during summer and breaks and for the special collections.

## Memorial Union

This social center of the university is a good place to visit. The Information Desk on the main floor can tell you about the latest concerts, movies, theater, art showings, and sporting events. It's open daily from early morning to late at night (shorter hours in summer and breaks); tel. 965-5728. Near the desk you'll find a bulletin board of apartments for rent and "for sales." Around the corner is a Ride Board; check it out if you're looking for a ride or someone going your way.

**Memorial Union Art Gallery,** at the north end of the building, often has visiting shows; open Mon.-Fri. 8 a.m.-8 p.m. But you might not make it that far, because you'll have to pass 14 tempting eateries on the way: a deli, pizza place, grill—everything from a Chicken Express to a Cafe Olé. Stop in "The Club" for regular cafeteria meals. Relax downstairs in a lounge or patio, go bowling, play a game of billiards, or see a movie.

## ASU Bookstore

A good selection of general-interest books as well as textbooks, supplies, and maps. You can pick out a Sun Devils T-shirt or other souvenirs. Open Mon.-Thurs. 8 a.m.-6 p.m. (Fri. 'til 5).

## Zoology Display

Meet the university's live rattlesnakes, Gila monster, and other reptiles in the hallway exhibits. Open Mon.-Fri. 8 a.m.-5 p.m.; free; tel. 965-3571. Located in the Life Sciences Building (east wing).

## Planetarium

Watch programs about the heavens during the main Sept. to May school terms; call 965-6891 for times. Located in Room B-350 of the Physical Sciences Center.

## Geology Museum

You can check the 6-story Foucault pendulum to see if the Earth is still spinning, or you can watch the seismograph to learn if it is shaking. Exhibits illustrate geologic processes and identify rocks, minerals, and fossils. Open Mon.-Fri. 9 a.m.-4 p.m. (closed summer); free; tel. 965-5081. Located in "F" Wing of the Physical Sciences Center.

## Center For Meteorite Studies

See visitors from outer space in Room C-139 and adjacent hallways of the Physical Sciences Center. The collection is thought to be the world's third largest. Open Mon.-Fri. 8 a.m.-4:30 p.m.; free; tel. 965-3576.

## Daniel E. Noble Science Library

Here you'll find the books used by the surrounding science and engineering departments. Hikers can plan their trips with the map collection and make needed photocopies. Hours for the main collection, during regular and summer terms, are Mon.-Thurs. 7 a.m.-midnight, Fri. 10 a.m.-9 p.m., Sat. 10 a.m.-9 p.m., and Sun. 10 a.m.-midnight. The map collection is open Mon.-Thurs. 8 a.m.-8 p.m., Fri. 8 a.m.-5 p.m., (closed Sat.), and Sun. 1-5 p.m.; tel. 965-2600 (circulation desk) or 965-3582 (map collection).

## Sports

ASU, as sports crazy as any large university, has fielded some top teams. You can see their trophies, clippings, and photos at the **Sports Hall of Fame,** located in the circular corridor of the Activity Center; open Mon.-Fri. 8 a.m.-5 p.m. Football takes place in the giant 70,000-seat Sun Devils Stadium; basketball in the 14,000-seat Activity Center, and baseball in the 8,000-seat Packard Stadium. Sun Devils Athletic Ticket Office sells tickets to the games; tel. 965-2381.

# MESA

Houses with neatly trimmed lawns line Mesa's broad streets. However, in March of 1877, when a group of 84 Mormon settlers arrived, this land was only desert with thin strips of vegetation along the Salt River. The eager families immediately began to rebuild the old Hohokam irrigation canals, hoping to turn the desert green and make a prosperous new life under the warm Arizona sun. Because the land reminded them of a table top, they named their settlement "Mesa." From the tiny adobe fort used by pioneers in the first years, Mesa has grown to be Arizona's third largest city, with a population of more than 270,000. More people arrive in winter to enjoy the sunny climate, the lakes, and the Superstition Mountains close at hand. Mesa, next door to Tempe and 15 miles east of Phoenix, is easily reached by the Superstition Freeway.

## SIGHTS

### Mesa Southwest Museum

Recreated cave and village displays will give you an idea of how prehistoric Indians lived. Pioneer exhibits show aspects of early Mesa life. Petroglyphs and a variety of Salado and Hohokam pottery can also be seen, as well as a stagecoach, an adobe schoolhouse, and a life-size, animated triceratops. Kids will enjoy visiting the authentic jail or trying to crack the big safe. Another project is deciphering the "secret" stone maps of the Lost Dutchman Mine. Outside you can grab a gold pan and try panning some gravel from the stream. A gift shop sells books and souvenirs. Open Tues.-Sat. 10 a.m.-5 p.m. and Sun 1-5 p.m.; $2.50 age 13-54, $1 age 5-12, $2 student and senior. In Dec. the museum has an animated Christmas display. Located downtown at 53 N. McDonald near the corner of W. First St.; tel. 644-2230 (recorded info) or 644-2169.

### Sirrine House

Joel Sirrine built this "Territorial Victorian" house in 1895 with an extra-wide porch for summer sleeping. Period furnishings inside include a 1906 washing machine. You can tour the house, one of the finest surviving from Mesa's early years; open Sat. 10 a.m.-5 p.m., Sun. 1-5 p.m., and on request; tel. 644-2760 (Sirrine House) or 644-2169 (Mesa Southwest Museum). It's located downtown at 160 N. Center, a couple of blocks from the Mesa Southwest Museum.

### Arizona Museum For Youth

Kids can participate in art programs and see art exhibits just for them. Open Tues.-Fri. 1-5 p.m., Sat. 10 a.m.-5 p.m., and Sun. 1-5 p.m.; call for exhibit schedule and for summer hours; tel. 644-2467. In downtown Mesa at 35 N. Robinson.

### Arizona Temple

Rising from beautifully landscaped gardens, the Mormon Church's Arizona Temple is Mesa's most notable landmark. The structure was completed in 1927 from a plan based on classical Greek architecture. Friezes at the top four corners of the exterior represent the gathering of the House of Israel from the four corners of the Earth. Marriages and other sacred ceremonies take place inside. The interior is closed to non-Mormons, but you're welcome to wander among the exotic plants in the gardens and see exhibits in the Visitor Center just north of the temple. Tours in the Visitor Center present the basic doctrines of the Church of Latter-day Saints, or Mormons, through a series of movies and animated dioramas. The presentation explains the importance of temples and shows slides of the Arizona Temple's interior. The one-hour tours begin on the hour and half-hour daily from 9 a.m.-9 p.m. (10 a.m.-10 p.m. in Dec.). Garden tours point out exterior architectural details and identify some of the trees and other vegetation; daily 7-9 p.m. Special events include the Easter Pageant in the week preceding Easter and the Christmas Lights display during December. If you'd like to know more about the Mormon religion, ask to see their

*Messerschmitt Bf-109E3 at Champlin Fighter Museum*

other movies and videotapes. The Arizona Temple is at 525 E. Main St., just east of downtown; tel. 964-7164.

## Champlin Fighter Museum

The excitement of viewing the world's hottest aircraft from WW I and WW II draws visitors to this unique collection. Here you'll also learn about the men who flew them. Autographed photos accompany stories of the fighter aces who fought in conflicts from WW I to Vietnam. Realistic paintings show aircraft in action. Then there are the planes, housed in two giant hangars. You'll see a replica of the Mercedes-powered Rumpler Taube—the world's first combat aircraft (1911), using only hand-thrown bombs; a Fokker Dr-I Triplane, the type flown by Manfred von Richthofen, the "Red Baron"; a British Sopwith Camel, one of which finally downed the Baron; the extremely rare German Messerschmitt 109 and Focke Wulf 190 so successful in WW II; the Supermarine Spitfire that helped win the Battle of Britain; the American P-51D Mustang, reputed to be the finest fighter of WW II; and dozens of other beautifully preserved planes. Famous aircraft engines include the 1941 rocket engine used in Messerschmitt 163 Komets and one of the eight engines used on Howard Hughes's "Spruce

Goose" on its first and only flight.

You can peek into the restoration area where mechanics keep these antique craft in flying condition. In a video presentation, you'll hear aces telling how they flew and fought and see actual combat footage taken during WW II and in Korea and Vietnam. A gift shop sells aircraft models, posters, and books. You can visit Champlin Fighter Museum's "Aircraft of the Aces" daily 10 a.m.-5 p.m.; $5 adult, $2.50 children 5-14; tel. 830-4540. It's at Falcon Field (off McKellips Road) on the northeast edge of Mesa about 7 miles from downtown.

## Arizona Farm And Heritage Museum

The people of Mesa have put together this remarkable collection of pioneer memorabilia and antique farm equipment. Each of the many rooms has a different character—done with a family or other theme. You'll see ornate saddles, harnesses, furniture, kitchens, a grist mill, and photos of the pioneers. Murals in the auditorium depict Southwestern history. Tours in the museum, itself a historic school building, operate Tues.-Sat. 9 a.m.-3 p.m.; $2 adult, $1 children 5-11; tel. 835-7358. Located in north Mesa at 2345 N. Horne (look for the impressive line-up of tractors outside).

On the way, you may want to stop at **Park of the Canals** to see remnants of the early Hohokam canal system, pioneer canals, and even a modern canal; the park also has picnic tables and a playground; 1710 N. Horne.

## Buckhorn Mineral Wells

One of the Valley's more unusual attractions. In 1939, hot underground water was discovered and developed into a health spa. You hop into your own tub (106° F) for $10 and get a rejuvenating massage for another $15. A sign lists the water's mineral content. You can also visit their museum of over 400 stuffed animals, most of which are native to Arizona. Birds hang from the rafters, javelinas glare from the walls, a coyote snarls from behind a couch, etc.; $2 adult, $1 children under 12. The museum and baths are open Tues.-Sat. 9 a.m.-5 p.m.; tel. 832-1111. You can also stay here; cottages start at $37.70 d ($27 d in summer). Buckhorn is 7 miles east of downtown Mesa at 5900 E. Main St. and Recker Road.

## Chandler Museum

Historic exhibits in the town of Chandler, just south of Mesa, show Indian artifacts, pioneer life, and agriculture. Open daily noon-4 p.m. from Oct. to June; tel. 786-2842. In downtown Chandler at 178 E. Commonwealth Ave., just east of A.J. Chandler Park. From Mesa, take the Superstition Fwy. to Country Club/AZ 87 Exit #8 and turn south. AZ 87 becomes Arizona Ave. and is the main street through Chandler. To reach the museum, go one block east on Buffalo St., one block south on Arizona Place, then one block east on Commonwealth Avenue.

## Arizona Railway Museum

Railroad enthusiasts have preserved a 1906 steam locomotive and a variety of other historic rolling stock in Chandler. Smaller exhibits can be seen in the museum building, which resembles an early Southwest railroad depot. Open Sat. and Sun. noon-4 p.m.; free; tel. 821-1108. From Arizona Ave., downtown, turn east on Erie St. to 399 N. Delaware Street.

## Gilbert Historical Center

Exhibits in six rooms tell the story of this small agricultural town from prehistory to the present. A lineup of antique farm machinery sits outside. Open Tues. and Thurs. 1-4 p.m.; free; tel. 926-1577. In central Gilbert, south of Mesa and east of Chandler, at 10 S. Gilbert Road.

*javelina at Buckhorn Mineral Wells*

# VALLEY OF THE SUN ACCOMMODATIONS

### Youth Hostel

Metcalf House AYH Hostel is probably the best choice for low-budget travelers. You can walk to many of Phoenix's sights from here or take a city bus. Facilities include kitchen, washer and drier, and info-packed bulletin boards. The hostel is rarely full, but you can make reservations (w/advance payment). Year-round cost is $9 members, $3 extra for nonmembers. The house parents sell YH passes. A 3-night stay limit may apply if the hostel is crowded. Check-in is 7-10 a.m. and 5-11 p.m. Located in a residential area, 1.5 miles northeast of downtown, at 1026 N. Ninth St. (between Portland and Roosevelt sts.), Phoenix, AZ 85006; tel. 254-9803. From the downtown Phoenix Transit terminal (near Greyhound Bus) at First St. and Washington, take Bus #10 and get off at the corner of Roosevelt and Ninth streets.

### Downtown YMCA

A central, inexpensive place for both men and women at 350 N. First Ave., Phoenix, AZ 85003; tel. 253-6181. Rooms cost $18 s, $34 d; weekly rates are $65 s, $80 d. Recreation facilities include racquetball and basketball courts, running track, weight room, sauna, and spa.

### Bed And Breakfasts

These are private houses open to travelers in the European tradition. The degree of luxury varies, but the hosts offer a personal touch not found in the usual motels. Advance reservations are requested.

**Bed and Breakfast in Arizona's** list includes many B&Bs in the Valley; Box 8628, Scottsdale, AZ 85252; tel. 995-2831. Prices range $35-120 d.

**Mi Casa Su Casa** is Spanish for "My house (is) your house." You'll find one of their more than 100 listings in almost any part of the Valley or state; Box 950, Tempe, AZ 85281;

tel. 990-0682 or (800) 456-0682. Prices range from $35 to $120 d.

## HOTELS AND MOTELS

Nowhere else in Arizona do you find such a wide selection and price range as in the Phoenix area. And you'll find almost any style imaginable, from super-cheap, elderly motels to posh, world-renowned luxury resorts. The most prominent resorts include the Arizona Biltmore, Marriott's Camelback Inn, and the Wigwam Resort and Country Club; all three received Five-Star ratings in the 1990 *Mobile Travel Guide*. The luxury hotels can be a bargain in summer—prices may plummet more than 50% as the mercury soars. Seasonal savings decrease with lower-priced accommodation, but competition helps keep prices reasonable. Most all the national chains are represented too—many in several locations. It's easy to find a place to stay, thanks to the local Visitors Bureau. You can use its numbers to make reservations for over 100 places in the Valley; tel. (800) 992-6005 in Arizona, or (800) 528-0483 out of state. At the airport you can pick up the free phones next to the hotel map near baggage claim areas. For the lowest-priced motels you're on your own, as they won't be listed by these services. Good places to look for them are along Grand Ave. between I-17 and Van Buren St. and along E. Van Buren St. between downtown and 40th Street. Grand and E. Van Buren was the old highway route and still has many motels, new and old, in the $10-30 range.

The Valley of the Sun has too many places to list in these pages. Check motel and resort listings in the free *Visitors Guide* put out by the Phoenix & Valley of the Sun Convention & Visitors Bureau and the telephone book's Yellow Pages.

## CAMPGROUNDS AND RV PARKS

Many of the Valley's trailer parks cater to retired people; children won't be welcome. The following accept families except as noted.

### Phoenix

**North Phoenix Campground** accepts both tenters and RVs at 2550 W. Louise Dr. (17 miles north of downtown, just off I-17 Deer Valley Road Exit 215); tel. 869-8189; $16.46 tent, $18.65 RV w/hookups. The nearby **Desert's Edge RV Park** accepts adults only, 22623 N. Black Canyon Hwy. (take I-17 Deer Valley Road Exit 215, then go 0.5 mile north on the frontage road); tel. 869-7021; $16.31 RV w/hookups. **Covered Wagon RV Park** offers sites for tents ($16.54) and RVs ($19.85) at 6540 N. Black Canyon Hwy. (Take I-17 Glendale Exit and go 0.5 mile south on the west frontage road); tel. 242-2500. Closer to downtown are the **Trailer Corral** (4040 W. Van Buren St.; go 2 miles west from I-17; tel. 278-6628; $12.14 RV w/hookups); **Green Acres RV Park** (2605 W. Van Buren St., just west of I-17; tel. 272-7863; $13.27 RV w/ hookups); and **Michigan Trailer Park** (3140 W. Osborn at Grand Ave.; tel. 269-0122; adults only; $15.60 RV w/hookups).

### Tempe

**Tempe Travel Trailer Villa** is an adult park one mile east of ASU campus at 1831 E. Apache Blvd.; tel. 968-1411; $14.18 RV w/hookups. **Green Acres II** accepts families nearby at 1836 E. Apache Blvd.; tel. 966-7399; $13.50 RV w/hookups. Or you can stay at **Green Acres III** at 1890 E. Apache Blvd.; tel. 829-0106; $13.50 RV w/hookups.

### Mesa

**Green Acres I** is near the Tri-City Mall at 2052 W. Main St.; tel. 964-5058; $13.50 RV w/hookups. **Goodlife RV Resort** (adults only) is 4 miles east of downtown at 3403 E. Main St.; tel. 832-4990; $20.23 RV w/hookups. Farther out is **Mesa Regal RV Resort** (adults only) at 4700 E. Main St.; tel. 830-2821; $15 RV w/hookups.

### Apache Junction

Both tenters and RVs can stay at **Apache Trail KOA** 1540 S. Tomahawk Road (1.5 miles southeast on US 60/89 from the junction with AZ 88); tel. 982-4015; $11.83 tent, $12.90 RV no hookups, $17.20 RV w/hookups. The **Lost Dutchman State Park** offers simpler facilities 6 miles northeast on AZ 88 from US 60/89 in the foothills of the Superstition Mountains; tel. 982-4485; $5 tent or RV (no hookups or showers). The **Lost Dutchman RV Resort** (adults only) is right in town at 400 N. Plaza Dr. (0.3 mile northeast on AZ 88); tel. 982-4173; $19.35 RV w/hookups. **Rock Shadows Travel Trailer Resort** (adults only) is at 600 S. Idaho Road; tel. 982-0450; $17.28 RV w/hookups. The **Pueblo RV Resort** (adults only) is at 201 E. Southern Ave.; tel. 983-3690; $19.38 RV w/hookups. RVers will find the largest selection of places to stay in the Valley in Apache Junction; the local chamber of commerce has a more complete list of RV parks.

### North Of Phoenix

**Ben Avery Shooting Range** offers sites ($5 primitive, $8 w/hookups; showers available) just west of I-17 at Exit 223 (26 miles north of Phoenix); tel. 582-8313. **Lake Pleasant County Park** has Dirty Shirt Campground (no hookups or showers); primitive camping can also be done by boaters along the lakeshore; $4/day (24 hours) park entrance fee per vehicle; take I-17 Exit 223 (26 miles north of Phoenix), go west 12 miles on AZ 74, and follow signs; tel. 566-0405. **Black Canyon City KOA** lies 46 miles north of downtown Phoenix in Black Canyon City; take I-17 Exit 242; tel. 374-5318; $13.60 tents or RV no hookups, $17.80 RV w/hookups.

**Seven Springs Campground** is in the Tonto National Forest just north of the Valley; large sycamore and ash trees provide shade; sites have picnic tables and pit toilets but no drinking water or fee. From the town of Cave Creek go 7 miles east on Cave Creek Road to a junction and keep left on Forest Route

24; the road becomes dirt after 2 miles, then it's another 11 miles to Seven Springs. **Cave Creek Campground,** which is a mile farther, is a group fee area and requires advance reservations.

**Bartlett Lake** is an irrigation reservoir on the Verde River with primitive camping (vault toilets but no drinking water), an unsurfaced boat ramp, and fishing for bass, crappie, catfish, and bluegill; the Mazatzal Mountains soar into the sky across the lake; from the town of Cave Creek go 7 miles east on Cave Creek Road, turn right 6 miles on Forest Route 205, then continue 8 miles on Forest Route 19 (dirt) to the lake. **Horseshoe Lake,** upstream from Bartlett, has primitive camping near the dam (vault toilets but no drinking water), primitive boat ramp, and fishing (var-

ies with the lake level); follow directions to Bartlett except turn left at the intersection of Forest Routes 19 and 205 and take Forest Route 205 all the way to the dam. Camping at both lakes is free. For more information, contact the **Cave Creek Ranger Station** at 7171 E. Cave Creek Road; open Mon.-Fri. 7:45 a.m.-4:30 p.m.; tel. 488-3441.

**Other Areas**
**Maricopa County parks** ring the Valley, offering camping in McDowell Mountain Regional Park to the northeast, Usery Mountain Park to the east, Estrella Mountain Park to the southwest, and White Tank Mountain Park to the west. Camping areas in some of these parks close in summer. See "Valley of the Sun Recreation," pp. 307-308.

# VALLEY OF THE SUN RESTAURANTS

The Valley has an amazing number of restaurants and range of cuisines—enough to fill a guidebook in themselves. And there *is* such a book, entitled *100 Best Restaurants in Arizona* by John and Joan Bogert, revised annually. Its detailed info would be handy for diners staying awhile in the Phoenix area. The *Visitors Guide,* put out free by the Visitors Bureau, also has a long restaurant listing. Another good source is the monthly *Phoenix Magazine.* Make reservations at the more expensive places; also check to see if coat and tie are required for the men. The following list has only a small selection of dining possibilities in the Valley.

Restaurants are marked: $=Bargain; $$=Moderate; $$$=Expensive.

## AMERICAN

**$$ The American Grill:** Offers a varied menu from grilled seafood and chowders to cheese grits casserole. In Scottsdale at Hilton Village, 6113 N. Scottsdale Road; tel. 948-9907. In Mesa at 1202 S. Alma School Road; tel. 844-1918. Open daily for lunch and dinner.

**$ Furr's:** Popular cafeteria chain with a wide choice of food. Open daily for lunch and dinner. In Phoenix at 3030 E. Thomas Road; tel. 956-8650; and 8114 N. Black Canyon Hwy.; tel. 995-1588. In Glendale at 4303 W. Peoria Ave.; tel. 931-2438. In Sun City at 10415 W. Grand Ave.; tel. 974-3639.

**$$ to $$$ Oscar Taylor:** Good food with Chicago Prohibition-era decor. Biltmore Fashion Park, 2420 E. Camelback Road, Phoenix; tel. 956-5705. Open daily for lunch and dinner.

**$$ to $$$ The Other Place:** Generous servings in attractive settings. In Scottsdale at 7101 E. Lincoln Dr.; tel. 948-7910. In Phoenix at 2600 E. Camelback Road; tel. 954-0488. In Mesa at 1644 S. Dobson Road; tel. 831-8877. Open daily for lunch and dinner and a Sunday brunch.

**$ Piccadilly:** Cafeteria with varied selections. In Phoenix at Chris-Town Shopping Center, 1501 W. Bethany Home Road; tel. 249-1172; at Westridge Mall, 7611 W. Thomas Road; tel. 849-6163; and at 620 W. Osborn Road; tel. 266-3795. In Scottsdale at 4571 E. Thomas Road; tel. 840-4670. In Tempe at 3300 S. Price Road; tel. 839-1537. Open daily for lunch and dinner.

**$ Sugar Bowl:** An old-fashioned ice cream parlor offering a myriad of temptations for sweet tooths. It also serves home-style meals daily for lunch and dinner. In Old Town Scottsdale at the corner of 4005 N. Scottsdale Road and First Ave.; tel. 946-0051.

## CHINESE

**$$ China Doll:** Very large selection of Cantonese specialties, including dim sum at lunch, 3336 N. Seventh Ave. at Osborn Road, Phoenix; tel. 264-0538. Open daily for lunch and dinner.

**$$ China Gate:** A Valley favorite with the best of Mandarin, Szechuan, and Hunan cuisines. In Phoenix at Colonnade Mall, 1815 E. Camelback Road; tel. 264-2600; and at Metrocenter, 3033 W. Peoria Ave.; tel. 944-1982. In Scottsdale at 7820 E. McDowell Road; tel. 946- 0720. And in Mesa at 2050 W. Guadalupe Road; 897-0607. Open Mon.-Sat. for lunch and daily for dinner.

*broad-tailed hummingbird*
(Selasphorus platycerus)

**$$ Golden Phoenix:** Mandarin cuisine in Phoenix at 6048 N. 16th St.; tel. 263-8049; and 1534 W. Camelback Road; tel. 279-4447. Open Sun.-Fri. for lunch and daily for dinner.

**$$ Sesame Inn:** Top Szechuan, Mandarin, and Hunan cuisine, 3912 W. Camelback Road, Phoenix; tel. 957-3993. In Scottsdale at 13610 N. Scottsdale Road; tel. 483-9696. Open daily for lunch and dinner.

**$$ Szechuan Inn:** Szechuan and Mandarin dining at 1617 E. Thomas Road, Phoenix; tel. 274-7051. Open Mon.-Fri. for lunch and dinner; Sat. and Sun. for dinner only.

## CONTINENTAL
## (RESERVATIONS REQUESTED)

**$$$ Avanti:** Italian cuisine dominates the varied menu, 2728 E. Thomas Road, Phoenix; tel. 956-0900. In Scottsdale at 3102 N. Scottsdale Road; tel. 949-8333. Open Mon.-Fri. for lunch and dinner; Sat. and Sun. for dinner only.

**$$$ The Compass:** Glide high above the city in the Hyatt Regency's revolving restaurant, 122 N. Second St. in downtown Phoenix; tel. 252-1234. Open Mon.-Fri. for lunch and dinner; Sat. for dinner only; Sun. for brunch and dinner.

**$$$ Gold Room:** The main dining room of the Arizona Biltmore Resort has the high standards you'd expect. Sunday brunch here ranks as one of Phoenix's great splurges, Missouri Ave. and 24th St., Phoenix; tel. 954-2504. Open daily for breakfast, lunch, and dinner (in summer, dinner is served Fri.-Mon.).

**$$$ La Champagne:** Sophisticated food and service. Registry Resort, 7171 N. Scottsdale Road, Scottsdale; tel. 991-3800. Open Tues.-Sat. for dinner only.

$$$ **Mancuso's:** Outstanding northern Italian and continental cuisine. The Borgata Shopping Center, 6166 N. Scottsdale Road, Scottsdale; tel. 948-9988. Open daily for dinner only.

$$$ **Orangerie:** Fine food and service at the Arizona Biltmore Resort, Missouri Ave. and 24th St.; tel. 954-2507. Open weekdays for lunch and Mon.-Sat. for dinner.

$$$ **Vincent Guerithault:** Imaginative French-classic cuisine with a Southwest touch and first-rate service. At 3930 E. Camelback Road, Phoenix; tel. 224-0225. Open weekdays for lunch and Mon.-Sat. for dinner.

## DELIS

$ **Gentle Strength Co-op & Deli:** Tasty and healthy vegetarian food in the deli, 234 W. University Dr., near ASU in Tempe; tel. 968-4831. Open daily for breakfast, lunch, and dinner.

$ **Katz:** 5144 N. Central Ave., Phoenix; tel. 277-8814. Open Sat.-Mon. for breakfast and lunch; Tues.-Fri. for breakfast, lunch, and dinner.

$ **Miracle Mile:** A kosher-style cafeteria with good portions of excellent food, 9 Park Central Mall, Phoenix; tel. 277-4783. In West Phoenix at Chris-Town Mall, 1733 W. Bethany Home Road; tel. 249-2904. Open Mon.-Fri. for breakfast, lunch, and dinner, Sat. for breakfast and lunch, and Sun. for lunch.

$ **Tamburino's:** Italian pizza, meats, and breads, 3255 E. Shea, Phoenix, tel. 996-6210. Open Mon.-Sat 9 a.m.-7 p.m. and Sun. 10 a.m.-3 p.m.

**Roman Carousel:** Another popular spot for Italian items, 7620 E. Indian School Road, Scottsdale; tel. 946-6656. Open Mon.-Fri. 9 a.m.-7 p.m. and Sat. 9 a.m.-6 p.m.

## FRENCH

$ **Cafe Casino:** An inexpensive French cafeteria and bakery. In Phoenix at 4824 N. 24th St. (at Camelback); tel. 955-3430. In Scottsdale at 1312 N. Scottsdale Road; tel. 947-1987. Open daily for breakfast, lunch, and dinner.

$$$ **Etienne's Different Pointe of View:** Perhaps the Valley's ultimate in sophisticated dining with a dazzling view of Phoenix. For a feast, check out the Sunday brunch. Pointe Resort at Tapatio Cliffs, 11111 N. Seventh St., Phoenix; tel. 866-7500. Open daily for dinner only; Sun. for brunch only.

$$ **French Corner:** Good food with informal service at 50 E. Camelback Road in Uptown Plaza, Phoenix; tel. 234-0245. Open daily for breakfast and lunch and Mon.-Sat. for dinner.

$$$ **La Chaumiere:** Excellent food in one of Scottsdale's older houses, 6910 Main St., Scottsdale; tel. 946-5115. Open Mon.-Sat. for dinner; closed in summer.

$$$ **Voltaire:** Superb food and friendly atmosphere, 8340 E. McDonald Dr., Scottsdale; tel. 948-1005. Open Tues.-Sat. for dinner only; closed in summer.

## GERMAN

$$ **Felsen Haus:** Authentic food and beer with lively polka music, 1008 E. Camelback Road, Phoenix; tel. 277-1119. Open daily for lunch and dinner.

## GREEK

$$ **Greekfest:** Tasty food at family prices, 1219 E. Glendale Ave., Phoenix; tel. 265-2990. Open Mon.-Sat. for lunch and dinner.

## INDIAN

**$$ Jewel of the Crown:** Both meat and vegetarian dishes are offered in *tandoori* and other styles, 5029 N. 44th St., Phoenix; tel. 840-2412. Open daily for lunch and dinner.

## INTERNATIONAL

**$$ to $$$ Trader Vic's:** Outstanding cuisines from the far corners of the world. Exotic South Seas decor, 7111 Fifth Ave., Scottsdale; tel. 945-6341. Open Mon.-Sat. for lunch and dinner; Sun. for dinner only.

## ITALIAN

**$$ Prego Ristorante:** Fine cuisine from both northern and southern Italy, 5816 N. 16th St., Phoenix; tel. 241-0288. Open Mon.-Fri. for lunch and dinner; Sat. and Sun. for dinner only.

**$$ Pronto Ristorante:** Features Italian-Swiss cuisine, 3950 E. Campbell Ave., Phoenix; tel. 956-4049. Open Mon.-Fri. for lunch and dinner; Sat. and Sun. for dinner only.

**$$ Tomaso's:** Northern Italian dining, 3225 E. Camelback Road, Phoenix; tel. 956-0836. Open Mon.-Fri. for lunch and dinner; Sat. and Sun. for dinner only.

**$$ Tony's New Yorker Club:** Great pasta in an informal, neighborhood restaurant, 107 E. Broadway, Tempe; tel. 967-3073. Open daily for dinner.

## JAPANESE

**$$ to $$$ Ayako of Tokyo:** Chefs offer teppanyaki table-top cooking, deep-fried tempura bar, and a sushi bar, Biltmore Fashion Park, 2564 E. Camelback Road, Phoenix; tel. 955-7007. Open Mon.-Fri. for lunch and dinner; Sat. and Sun. for dinner only.

**$$ Shogun:** You can choose from meat and seafood entrees or one of the many items in the sushi-sashimi bar, 12615 N. Tatum Road, Paradise Valley; tel. 953-3264. Open Mon.-Fri. for lunch and daily for dinner.

**$ Tokyo Express:** Inexpensive but good food. In Phoenix at 3517 E. Thomas Road; tel. 955-1051; at 5130 N. 19th Ave.; tel. 433-1311; and at 914 E. Camelback Road; tel. 277-4666. Open daily for lunch and dinner.

## KOREAN

**$$ Korean Hanil:** Flavorful *bulkogi* (barbecued beef) and other specialties; you can try the tangy kimchee (marinated vegetables) too. At 4214 W. Dunlap in Phoenix; tel. 842-0400. Open Mon.-Fri. for lunch and Mon.-Sat. for dinner.

## MEXICAN

**$$ Aunt Chilada's:** In a century-old, former general store. Pointe Resort at Squaw Peak, 7330 N. Dreamy Draw Dr., Phoenix; tel. 861-

*Gila woodpecker (Melanerpes uropygialis)*

5985; and at Pointe Resort South Mountain, 2021 W. Baseline Road, Phoenix; tel. 944-1286. Open daily for lunch and dinner.

**$ to $$ Garcia's:** This popular restaurant has grown into a chain across 11 states. In Phoenix at 2212 N. 35th Ave. (tel. 272-5584); 4420 E. Camelback Road (tel. 952-8031); and at 3301 W. Peoria Ave. (near Metrocenter; tel. 866-1850). Also in Scottsdale at 7633 E. Indian School Road; tel. 945-1647. In Tempe, Garcia's is at 1604 E. Southern Ave.; tel. 820-0400. All are open daily for lunch and dinner.

**$ Tee Pee:** Daily specials, 4144 E. Indian School Road, Phoenix; tel. 956-0178; open Mon.-Sat. for lunch and dinner.

## MIDDLE EASTERN

**$ Haji-Baba:** Excellent inexpensive meals. Also Middle Eastern groceries, magazines, records, and musical instruments; 1513 E. Apache Blvd., Tempe; tel. 894-1905. Open Mon.-Sat. for lunch and dinner (closes Sat. at 6 p.m.).

**$ Mediterranean House:** The cafe's owner has an Israeli and Yemeni background. 1588 E. Bethany Home Road, Phoenix; tel. 248-8460. Open Mon.-Fri. for lunch and Mon.-Sat. for dinner.

## PIZZA

**$ Pizzafarro's:** One of the Valley's best, 4730 E. Indian School Road, Phoenix; tel. 840-7990; and at 7120 E. Mercer Lane, Scottsdale; tel. 991-0331. Open daily except Mon. for dinner only.

**$ Tommy's Pizza:** In Phoenix at 518 E. Dunlap Ave. (tel. 997-7578); 5341 N. Seventh Ave. (tel. 274-8815); and 2301 W. Glendale Ave. (tel. 246-0050). Open daily for lunch and dinner.

## SEAFOOD

**$$ Famous Pacific Fish Company:** A good place to come for fresh seafood in a nautical setting. Many items are broiled over mesquite charcoal, 4321 N. Scottsdale Road, Scottsdale; tel. 941-0602. Open Mon.-Sat. for lunch and dinner; Sun. for dinner only.

**$$ to $$$ The Fish Market:** The upstairs "Top of the Market" features gourmet dining. Downstairs you can drop into the oyster bar or shop for fresh fish. Located at 1720 E. Camelback Road; tel. 277-3474. Open Mon.-Fri. for lunch and daily for dinner; fish market is open daily.

**$$$ Rusty Pelican:** Decor and food will convince you that you're beside the ocean. Near the Metrocenter at 9801-A N. Black Canyon Hwy., Phoenix; tel. 944-9646. Open Mon.-Fri. for lunch and dinner; Sat. and Sun. for dinner only.

## SOUL FOOD

**$ Golden Rule Cafe:** Good cookin' by Mrs. White, 808 E. Jefferson St., Phoenix; tel. 262-9256. Open Mon.-Fri. for breakfast, lunch, and dinner.

## THAI

**$ to $$ Char's:** Authentic and fiery cuisine in the restaurant that introduced Thai food to the Valley. In Phoenix at 7810 N. 12th St.; tel. 246-1077; open Tues.-Sat. for lunch and dinner; Sun. for dinner only. In Tempe at 927 E. University Dr.; tel. 967-6013; open daily for lunch and dinner.

**$ Daa's Thai Room:** Great food with pleasant surroundings. Don't ask for "hot" spices unless you can take it *very* hot! In Scottsdale at 7419 E. Indian Plaza (near the corner of Scottsdale and Camelback roads); tel. 941-9015. Open Mon.-Fri. for lunch and dinner; Sat. and Sun. for dinner only.

$ to $$ **Royal Barge:** Great selection of tasty Thai food. In Scottsdale at El Pueblo Shopping Plaza, 8220 N. Hayden Rd.; tel. 443-1953. Open Mon.-Sat. for lunch and daily for dinner.

$ **Thai Rama:** Inexpensive Thai food on a varied menu. In Phoenix at 1702 W. Camelback Road; tel. 246-8622. Open daily for lunch and dinner.

## VIETNAMESE

$ to $$ **To Do:** A chance to try another spicy Asian cuisine. In Phoenix at 7828 N. 19th Ave.; tel. 864-6759; and at 1702 W. Camelback Road; tel. 433-9440. Open daily for lunch and daily except Tues. for dinner.

## WESTERN

$$ **Don & Charlie's American Rib and Chop House:** Top-notch steaks and barbecue, 7501 E. Camelback Road, Scottsdale; tel. 990-0900. Open daily for dinner only.

$$ **Mining Camp:** Great Western grub, much of it all-you-can-eat, in a replica of an old mining camp's cook shanty. Great for the kids. Located 4 miles northeast of Apache Junction on AZ 88 at the easternmost end of the Valley; tel. 982-3181. Open daily for dinner only.

$$ **Pinnacle Peak Patio:** Country music every night, hayrides on weekends. Strictly cowboy-Western atmosphere—if you wear a tie inside, it'll be snipped off and added to the large collection on the rafters! Located in the foothills of the McDowell Mtns. about 20 miles northeast of Scottsdale, via Scottsdale and Pinnacle Peak roads at 10426 W. Jomax Road; tel. 967-8082. Open daily for dinner only.

$ **Real Texas Bar-B-Que:** The decor isn't much, but the ribs are great and you can't beat the prices, 2415 W. Bethany Home Road, Phoenix; tel. 249-9985. Open Tues.-Sat. for lunch and dinner.

$$ **Rustler's Rooste:** Country music every night and huge portions. Pointe Resort at South Mountain, 7777 S. Pointe Parkway, Phoenix; tel. 231-9111. Open daily for dinner.

$$ **Waterin' Hole Chuckwagon 'n' Saloon:** Cowgirls bring your steaks, ribs, chicken, or seafood in the rustic dining room. Located one-half mile south of Pointe Resort at Tapatio Cliffs, 11111 N. Seventh St. (enter on Clinton), Phoenix; tel. 944-4451. Open daily for lunch and dinner.

## SPECIALTY FOOD STORES

**Italian: DeFalco's Italian Grocery,** 2724 N. 68th St., Scottsdale; tel. 990-8660.

**Kosher: Norman's Kosher Star Market,** 4128 N. 19th Ave., Phoenix; tel. 265-3762.

**Mexican: Azteca Bakery & Tortilla Shop,** 1407 S. 16th St., Phoenix; tel. 252-5457. **El Molino Tamales,** 117 S. 22nd St., Phoenix; tel. 244-0364.

**Middle East: Ararat Foods,** 4119 N. 19th Ave., Phoenix; tel. 277-3517. **Middle Eastern Bakery and Deli, Inc.,** 3052 N. 16th St., Phoenix; tel. 277-4927.

**Natural: Gentle Strength Cooperative,** 234 W. University Dr., Tempe; tel. 968-4831. **Ceres Market & Eatery,** 1420 W. Southern Ave., Mesa; tel. 962-3839.

**Oriental: Win Fong,** 3838 N. 19th Ave., Phoenix; tel. 277-7717; and at 502 S. Dobson Rd., Mesa; tel. 461-3564. **Loi Phat,** 3637 N. 35th Ave., Phoenix; tel. 278-1408. **Lee Hing Oriental Food Center,** 1510 W. McDowell Road, Phoenix; tel. 254-9444.

# VALLEY OF THE SUN ENTERTAINMENT

## EVENTS

Concerts, festivals, shows, and other special events happen nearly every day in the Valley, and the Visitors Bureau can tell you what's going on. Pick up their *Calendar of Events* brochure or call the Visitors Hotline, tel. 252-5588. These are some of the best-known annual happenings:

**January:** The **Fiesta Bowl** kicks off on New Year's Day at Arizona State University's Sun Devil Stadium. Competitors put their best stock forward for the **Arizona National Livestock** Show. Top PGA golfers compete in the **Phoenix Open,** a 50-year-old tournament. **Parada del Sol** in Scottsdale features the world's longest horse-drawn parade and a big rodeo; events often continue into February.

**February:** The horsey set enjoys Scottsdale's **All-Arabian Horse Show and Sale.** Indians put on the **O'odham Tash Indian Pow Wow** near the city of Casa Grande, 45 miles south of Phoenix, with a parade, rodeo, dances, and crowning of the O'odham queen. Fountain Hills hosts the **Great Fair** featuring a hot-air balloon race, 5K and 10K runs, and the Southwest Arts and Crafts Show. Step back to the 16th century for **The Renaissance Festival;** the vast site southeast of Apache Junction turns into a medieval celebration with tournament jousting, theater, crafts, food, and costumed performers. **Lost Dutchman Days Rodeo and Parade** takes place in Apache Junction.

**March:** Renaissance Festival continues from February. **Phoenix Jaycees' Rodeo of Rodeos** hosts a parade, Western Hoe-Down Festival, and competition among top-ranked cowboys. The **Heard Museum Guild Indian Fair** presents Southwestern Indian food, dances, art, and crafts. **Maricopa County Fair** features entertainment, rides, and agricultural exhibits at the Arizona State Fairgrounds. **Old Town Tempe Spring Festival** exhibits work by some of the Southwest's best artists and craftsmen, along with food treats and live performances; action takes place along Mill Ave. at Fourth, Fifth, and Sixth sts.; often continues into April. Mesa celebrates **Mesa Day** with a miniature parade (everything's hand drawn) and arts and crafts displays.

**April: Yaqui Indian Easter Celebration** begins on Ash Wednesday and continues every Friday until Holy Week, then Wednesday to Easter Sunday. Dancers wear special masks and costumes in their re-enactment of the crucifixion. The ceremonies, said to be almost 300 years old, symbolize the battle between good and evil forces. Held by the Yaqui Indian community at the Church Plaza between Iglesia and San Angelo roads in Guadalupe, southeast of Phoenix. **Scottsdale All-Indian Days Annual Pow Wow** brings more than 50 tribes to town for competitions in art and crafts, music, dances, and other activities. **Phoenix Jazz Festival** attracts top-name performers to the city.

**May:** Mexican music, dancing, and food mark **Cinco de Mayo** (May 5th), the anniversary of Mexico's 1863 victory over France.

**June to September:** It's too hot! Valley residents head for the nearest swimming pool or drive to the high country. Those who stay can enjoy the **Summer Performing Arts** program of musicals, plays, and concerts held at the Herberger Theater Center and at Symphony Hall.

**October:** The **Arizona State Fair** in Phoenix features exhibits of the state's best in agriculture, livestock, and home crafts, along with concerts, rides, and games. Phoenix Art Museum puts on a **Cowboy Artists of America Exhibition.** Scottsdale's **Rodeo Showdown & Western Festival** pits some of the best Canadian riders and teams against the Americans; the festival has Western art, entertainment, food, and dances.

**November:** Bright colors fill the sky over northwest Phoenix as hot-air balloons take off for the **Hot Air Balloon Race and Thunderbird Balloon Classic,** a world-class event. Tempe's Old Town hosts the **Winter Festival of the Arts** to exhibit work of local and visiting artists; food, music, dance, and children's entertainment can be enjoyed too; may be held in December.

**December:** More than 100 Indian craftsmen exhibit and sell their work at Pueblo Grande Museum's **Indian Market**; tribes also perform native dances and serve traditional food. The Valley gets ready for the **Fiesta Bowl** with more than 40 events, including an impressive parade, marathon, bicycle races, and Pageant of Bands.

## THEATER AND CONCERTS

To find out what's happening in the Valley, call the Visitor Hotline; tel. 252-5588 (recording). Newspapers, especially the weekly *New Times* (free at newsstands), review the entertainment scene.

### Phoenix
**Arizona Theatre Company** performs classic and contemporary plays and some musicals from late Nov. to June at Herberger Theater Center, 222 E. Monroe St.; tel. 279-0534 (AZ Theatre Co. box office) or 252-8497 (Herberger Theater box office). The **Phoenix Symphony** offers a variety of concert series during their Sept. to May season at Symphony Hall in downtown Phoenix, the Gammage Center at ASU, Scottsdale Center for the Arts, and Pointe Resort at Tapatio Cliffs; tel. 264-4754. **Ballet Arizona** productions take place spring to autumn at Herberger Theater Center and at Symphony Hall; tel. 381-0184. **Arizona Opera** presents their productions Oct. to March at Symphony Hall; tel. 254-1664. (Symphony Hall is in downtown Phoenix's Civic Plaza at 225 E. Adams Street.) **Phoenix Little Theatre,** opened in 1920, stands as the theater with the longest continuous run in the country; it's in the Phoenix

Civic Center (behind the Phoenix Art Museum) near the corner of Central Ave. and McDowell Road; tel. 254-2151. (Note that the Civic Plaza and Civic Center are two different places.) The city of Phoenix presents free **evening concerts** April to Oct. in Encanto Park, featuring a variety of music; 15th Ave. and Holly St.; tel. 261-8991.

### Scottsdale
The **Scottsdale Center for the Arts** has diverse musical and theatrical offerings at 7383 Scottsdale Mall (one block south of Indian School Road and 2 blocks east of Scottsdale Road); tel. 994-ARTS. **Actors Lab Arizona** maintains regular productions (Oct. to May), touring shows, and acting classes at 7223 E. Second St.; tel. 990-1731 (box office), 990-7898 (administrative office).

### Tempe
The **Gammage Center for the Performing Arts,** on the ASU campus, offers a varied program of theater, concerts, and dance in its distinctive rotund structure. The Center can also tell you of other events on campus; tel. 965-3434 (box office).

### Mesa
**Mesa Little Theatre** offers productions from Oct. to April and more than 70 classes in the visual and performing arts at the Mesa Arts Center, 155 N. Center; tel. 834-9500.

### Sun City
The **Sundome Center for the Performing Arts** frequently hosts big-name performers at 19403 R.H. Johnson Blvd. in Sun City West; tel. 975-1900.

## SPORTING EVENTS

The **Phoenix Cardinals,** a professional football team, play their home games at Arizona State University's Sun Devil Stadium in Tempe; tel. 967-1402. The NBA **Phoenix Suns** professional basketball team's home games take place at Arizona Veterans Memorial Coliseum, 1826 W. McDowell Road; tel. 263-

SUNS. The **Phoenix Firebirds,** a minor-league baseball team, play ball at Phoenix Municipal Stadium, 5999 E. Van Buren St. (April to Aug.); tel. 275-0500. Several major league teams visit the Valley for spring training in March and April: the California Angels at Gene Autry Park in Mesa, the Chicago Cubs at Hohokam Park in Mesa, the Milwaukee Brewers at Compadre Stadium in Chandler, the Oakland A's at Phoenix Municipal Stadium, the San Francisco Giants at Scottsdale Stadium, and the Seattle Mariners at Tempe's Diablo Stadium.

**Arizona Condors** play soccer at Mesa Community College's Riggs Stadium in Mesa; season runs late April to late July; tel. 994-0299. Hockey is played by the **Phoenix Roadrunners** from Oct. to April at Veterans Memorial Coliseum; tel. 340-0001. The **Phoenix Open** attracts big-name professional golfers each Jan. to the Tournament Players Club in Scottsdale; tel. 870-0163.

The Arizona State University **Sun Devils** battle their opponents in an active program of football, baseball, basketball, swimming, gymnastics, archery, and other sports. To find out what's going on, call Sun Devil Sports; tel. 965-6592. The ASU Sun Devil football stadium hosts the annual **Fiesta Bowl,** one of the country's biggest NCAA bowl games, played on New Year's Day.

Engines roar as cars strain for the finish line Feb. to Nov. at **Manzanita Speedway,** 35th Ave. and West Broadway; tel. 276-9401 or 276-7575. **Phoenix International Raceway** holds four major events each year at S. 115th Ave. and Baseline Road; tel. 252-3833. **American Desert Racing** is for off-road vehicles all year at various locations (usually free admission); tel. 252-1900. Dogs hit the track at **Phoenix Greyhound Park** most nights year-round; you'll stay cool in the air-conditioned grandstands, E. Washington and 40th sts.; tel. 273-7181. **Apache Greyhound Park** offers race events in Apache Junction at 2551 W. Apache Trail; tel. 982-2371. Thoroughbred and quarter horses go for it at **Turf Paradise** from Oct. to May; 1501 W. Bell Road and 19th Ave.; tel. 942-1101.

*coyote* (Canis latrans)

*saguaro*
(Cereus gigantus)

# VALLEY OF THE SUN RECREATION

Valleyites take their sports seriously—the recreational facilities seem limitless. You can play golf, tennis or racquetball, go horseback riding, jump in the pool, tube the Salt River, and even go surfing! **Phoenix Parks and Recreation Dept.** has some excellent parks and a variety of educational and recreation programs for children, adults, and seniors; tel. 262-4994. Several large county parks ring the Valley, giving additional opportunities to escape city life; for info call the Maricopa County Parks and Recreation Dept.; tel. 262-3711. Two active outdoors groups, Central Arizona Hiking Club and Arizona Bicycle Club, can be reached through American Youth Hostels, 1026 N. Ninth St. Phoenix, AZ 85006. The book *Day Hikes and Trail Rides in and Around Phoenix* by Roger and Ethel Freeman has detailed trail descriptions for hikers and horseback riders.

## SPORTS

### Golf And Tennis
Both are extremely popular in the Valley and played year-round. Enthusiasts often spend their entire vacation at resorts offering top-notch facilities and professional instructors. Four Phoenix city parks have golf courses and 22 parks have tennis courts; tel. 262-4994. You'll find a list of both public and private golf courses and tennis courts in the Visitors Bureau's free *Visitors Guide*.

### Swimming
Phoenix alone has 24 public pools; see the Phoenix telephone book Yellow Pages under "swimming pools." If you're looking for waves and water slides, try Big Surf in Tempe or Oasis Family Water Park in Glendale.

**Big Surf:** It's all here—surf, sun, sand, and pretty girls! Artificial waves 3-5 feet high come crashing onto the broad, sandy beach. You can rent surfboards and rafts or bring your own. For added thrills try the 300-foot Surf Slide and whiz down at speeds up to 15 miles per hour. Small children have a shallow pool

*water slides at Oasis Family Waterpark*

to play in. The season runs from mid-March to the end of Sept. (call for hours), closed Monday. Big Surf is in northern Tempe at 1500 N. Hayden Road (south of McKellips Road); tel. 947-SURF or 947-2478.

**Oasis Family Waterpark:** Water slides and a wave pool provide the excitement. Bodysurfing and raft rental but no surfboarding. Small children have their own pools. Open from May to mid-Oct. (call for hours). From downtown Phoenix take I-17 north 17 miles to Pinnacle Peak Road (Exit 217), then go west 2 miles on Pinnacle Peak Road; tel. 266-5200.

### Tubing Down The Lower Salt River
Cool off in the summer on a leisurely float down the Salt River east of Mesa. Salt River Recreation rents inner tubes and provides

*tubing the Salt*

shuttle bus service back to the starting point for only $6.30/person or just a shuttle pass for $3.15; tel. 984-3305. Season runs from early May to the end of September. The shuttle bus serves five points along the river, giving a choice of floats from 1½ hours to all day.

An extra tube will carry your cooler of cold drinks (don't bring glass containers). Weekends often see large crowds, when the Salt becomes one big party. Beware of the sun—hats, long-sleeved shirts, pants, and sunblock lotion should be used. Wear tennis shoes to protect your feet when walking out into the river. Life jackets are a good idea and a necessity if you bring the kids along. Don't tie your tubes together; rather, lock your feet into each other's tubes. Below Granite Reef Dam the Salt is a river no more—the water is channeled into canals, leaving only a dry riverbed downstream most of the year. No camping is allowed on the lower Salt River (Stewart Mtn. Dam to Granite Reef Dam) from April 1 to October 31. From the east edge of Mesa, take Bush Hwy. north to the Salt River.

### Horseback Riding
The Phoenix area has miles of scenic trails suitable for horses. Many of the stables can arrange lessons, breakfast rides, steak cookouts, hayrides, overnight trips, and boarding. For rides into South Mountain Park, see **All Western Stables** (10220 S. Central Ave.; tel. 276-5862), **Ponderosa Stables** (10215 S. Central Ave.; tel. 268-1261), or **South Mountain Stables** (10005 S. Central Ave.; tel. 276-8131). One- or 2-hour guided trips into Phoenix Mountain Preserve leave from **Hole-in-the-Wall Stables** at the Pointe Resort, 7677 N. 16th St. in Phoenix; tel. 997-1466. Near Papago Park, you can ride from **Papago Riding Stable,** 400 N. Scottsdale Road in Tempe; tel. 966-9793. In Scottsdale, ride with **Old MacDonald's Farm,** 26540 N. Scottsdale Road; tel. 585-0239. **Rio Verde Ranch Riding Stable** offers trips of one hour to all day in the Tonto National Forest north of the Valley, about 25 miles north of Scottsdale; season is Nov. to April; tel. 471-7281. For guided all-day and overnight pack trips into the wild Superstition Mountains and other desert areas, see **Superstition/Peralta Stables** at 2151 N. Warner Road (off N. Meridian Road) in Apache Junction; tel. 982-6353; or **O.K. Corral Stables,** 2 miles northeast of Apache Junction on AZ 88, then left at the sign; tel. 982-4040. Riding season is Oct. to May.

### Ice Skating
Hit the ice at **Ice Palace** (3853 E. Thomas Road in Phoenix; tel. 267-0591); **Metro Ice Palace** (Metrocenter in Phoenix, I-17 and Peoria Ave.; tel. 997-6158); and **Oceanside Ice Arena** (next to Big Surf at 1520 N. Hayden Road in Tempe; tel. 947-2470).

### Roller Skating
Roll at **Rollero Family Roller Skating Center** (7318 W. Indian School Road, Phoenix; tel. 846-1510); **Skate World** (4451 E. Oak St., Phoenix; tel. 267-7116); and **The Great Skate** (10054 N. 43rd Ave., Glendale; tel. 842-1181).

# PARKS

### Encanto Park
A 222-acre oasis of lakes, picnic areas, two golf courses (9 and 18 holes), tennis courts, and swimming pool. You can check out sports equipment from the Recreation Building located south of the swimming pool. Park concerts often take place in the evenings from April to October. Encanto Park is just 2 miles north of downtown Phoenix at N. 15th Ave. and Encanto Boulevard.

### Papago Park
This large area on the east edge of Phoenix was once declared a national monument because of its desert flora and Indian history. Today it's a city park with numerous attractions, including the Phoenix Zoo, Desert Botanical Gardens, an 18-hole golf course, and Phoenix Municipal Stadium. The park also offers picnicking, hiking, a bike trail, and a small lake where children 15 and under may fish without a license. George W.P. Hunt, seven times governor of Arizona, now occupies the prominent pyramid tomb on a small hill. Enter Papago Park at 54th St. from McDowell Road.

### Squaw Peak Park
Squaw Peak crowns a group of desert hills 9 miles northeast of downtown Phoenix. It's a place for hiking, picnicking, and horseback riding in a natural setting. Saguaro cactus, palo verde, creosote bush, and barrel and cholla cactus are among the desert plants that thrive on the hillsides. The hike to the summit of 2,608-foot Squaw Peak makes a good half-day's outing. The trail climbs steeply in places, rising 1,200 feet in 1.25 miles, but it's easy to follow. On Sundays the peak hosts a remarkable crowd of teenagers, families, little old ladies, joggers wearing headsets, etc.—all puffing along. You can bring a dog with you if on a leash. Be sure to carry water and get an early start in the warmer months. For an easier hike, try the gentle trail from the end of the road.

### South Mountain Park
This is the world's largest city park, with 15,728 acres of desert mountain country. A paved road winds to the top for some great views of the Valley. On the way you'll pass several picnic areas and a children's playground. Forty miles of hiking and horseback trails lead through the backcountry. Stables, just outside the park's entrance, rent horses. Hikers will enjoy Hidden Valley, a half-day trip

*atop Squaw Peak*

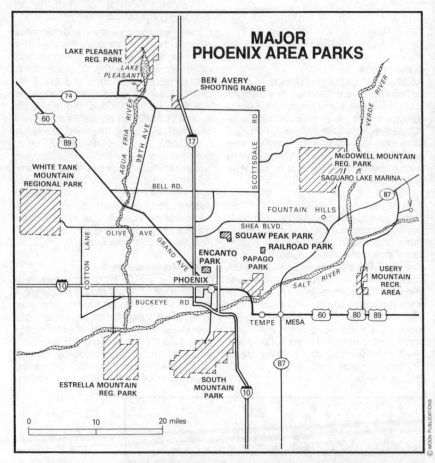

MAJOR
PHOENIX AREA PARKS

LAKE PLEASANT
REG. PARK

LAKE
PLEASANT

BEN AVERY
SHOOTING RANGE

McDOWELL MOUNTAIN
REG. PARK

SAGUARO LAKE MARINA

WHITE TANK
MOUNTAIN
REGIONAL PARK

BELL RD.

FOUNTAIN HILLS

SHEA BLVD.

SQUAW PEAK PARK

RAILROAD PARK

OLIVE AVE.

ENCANTO
PARK

PAPAGO
PARK

USERY
MOUNTAIN
RECR.
AREA

PHOENIX

BUCKEYE RD.

SALT RIVER

TEMPE MESA

ESTRELLA MOUNTAIN
REG. PARK

SOUTH
MOUNTAIN
PARK

AGUA FRIA RIVER

99TH AVE.

GRAND AVE.

COTTON LANE

SCOTTSDALE RD.

VERDE RIVER

0    10    20 miles

© MOON PUBLICATIONS

through a landscape of giant granite boulders
and stately saguaro. To reach the trailhead,
go 2 miles past the park entrance gate and
turn left onto the Summit Road, following it 4
miles; keep right past the turnoffs for two
lookout points, then stay left at the next fork
(don't go toward the TV towers). Follow signs
for "Buena Vista Lookout." At the road's end,
a sign "Hidden Valley 1.75 miles" marks the
trailhead. The first 0.25 mile follows a ridge
with good views before gently dropping into
a valley. After a mile or so, some large slick
rocks have to be negotiated before entering
wide, bowl-shaped Hidden Valley. Near the

lower end of the little valley, you'll pass
through a natural tunnel about 50 feet long.
This makes a good turn-around point, or you
can explore more of the valley and surrounding hills. In summer carry extra water and
avoid the heat of the day. South Mountain
Park is 7 miles south of downtown Phoenix
on Central Avenue.

### McCormick Railroad Park

Rail buffs of all ages will want to hop on the
5/12ths-scale trains for a ride around the
park's grassy acres. Two old railway stations
house shops with model-train supplies, rail-

road books, and souvenirs. Outside, a standard-gauge, Mogul-type Baldwin Steam Engine and some cars are on display. A Santa Fe caboose sells snacks. On Sunday afternoons you can visit several model-railroad clubs, each running a different scale train. McCormick Railroad Park, train rides, and a 1929 carousel are open daily. Rides operate 11 a.m.-5:30 p.m. in winter (extended to about 7:30 p.m. the rest of the year); $.50 fare. This unusual park is in Scottsdale at 7301 E. Indian Bend Road just east of Scottsdale Road; tel. 994-2312.

### Saguaro Lake

Scenery, fishing, and boating attract people year-round. The 10-mile-long lake (1,100 acres) within the Tonto National Forest is the last in the chain of lakes on the Salt River and the closest to Phoenix. Fishermen catch largemouth and yellow bass, channel catfish, bluegill, and walleye. **Saguaro Lake Marina** has a snack bar, boating supplies, and rentals of fishing and ski boats; tel. 986-0969. **Lakeshore Inn** serves breakfast, lunch, and dinner daily at moderate prices (closes 4:30 on Mon. and Tues.); tel. 984-5311. Boat tours make an 11-mile scenic loop from Oct. to April.

The Forest Service provides boat ramps and picnic areas near the marina at **Saguaro del Norte** day-use area. **Butcher Jones Recreation Area** has a picnic area on the north side of the lake; take the turnoff on the Bush Hwy. one mile north of the marina. Picnic and boating areas almost always fill up on Sun., and sometimes Sat., from mid-spring to mid-summer; try to arrive by early morning then. Boaters (only) can reach **Bagley Flat Campground** (tables, pit toilets, but no water; free) about 4 miles from the marina. Dispersed camping is also permitted, but again you'll need a boat.

Get to Saguaro Lake via the Bush Hwy., from either eastern Mesa or AZ 87. The **Mesa Ranger District** office of the Tonto National Forest has recreation information for the Saguaro Lake and lower Salt River areas at 26 N. MacDonald St. in Mesa; open Mon.-Fri. 7:45 a.m.-4:30 p.m.; tel. 835-1161.

### Ben Avery Shooting Range And Recreation Area

Shooters and archers can practice at this fine facility. Visitors also enjoy picnicking and camping ($8 w/hookups, $5 no hookups; showers available). The range operates Wed.-Sun. and the trap and skeet range is lighted for night use. It's located 26 miles north of downtown Phoenix, just west off I-17 Exit 223; tel. 582-8313 for rifle and pistol range; tel. 582-1901 for trap and skeet.

### Lake Pleasant Regional Park

The large lake has paved boat ramps, a marina, snack bar, and Dirty Shirt Campground (no hookups or showers). Primitive camping can also be done by boaters along the lakeshore. Small sailboats, windsurfs, and rowboats may be available for rent at the marina. The lake's open waters provide fine conditions for sailing; races are sponsored by the Arizona Yacht Club. Fishermen seek out largemouth bass, white bass, catfish, bluegill, and crappie. When completed in 1994, the new Waddell Dam will raise the lake level to about 1,700 feet in elevation during March and April; peak lake size will be about 10,000 acres. After drawdown for irrigation, the level will drop 100 feet or so by Sept.-Oct. of each year for a lake size of 3,500 acres. Park facilities will be relocated to accommodate the enlarged lake. Admission is $4/vehicle fee per day (24-hour period); tel. 566-0405. Lake Pleasant is about 30 miles northwest of Phoenix; take I-17 north to AZ 74 (Exit 223), go west 11.5 miles on AZ 74, turn north 2.2 miles on Castle Hot Springs Road, then turn right into the park. From Sun City you can go north 15 miles on 99th Ave. to AZ 74.

### McDowell Mountain Regional Park

You'll enjoy beautiful vistas from the eastern McDowells, 15 miles northeast of Scottsdale. A wide variety of desert plants grows at the 1,500- to 3,100-foot elevations. The park attracts nature lovers, artists, picnickers, hikers, and horseback riders. There's a campground ($8 w/hookups and showers; closed in summer); tel. 471-0173. Access is from Fountain Hills on the south side of the park via Fountain Hills Blvd. to McDowell Mountain Road.

## Usery Mountain Recreation Area

You'll have good views of the Salt River Valley and the Superstition Mountains from the pass between Pass Mountain and Usery Mountain Range, 12 miles northeast of Mesa. Picnicking, hiking, horseback riding, and an archery range are other attractions. There's a campground ($8 w/hookups and showers; closed in summer); tel. 986-2310. From Apache Blvd. (US 60/89) in Apache Junction, turn north on Ellsworth Road which turns into Usery Pass Road.

## Estrella Mountain Regional Park

Spanish explorers named the range Estrella ("star") after the pattern of deeply carved canyons radiating from the summit. **Sierra Estrella Mountain Golf Course,** in the northwest corner of the park, has 18 holes, pro shop, and a snack bar; tel. 932-3714. The recreation area offers picnicking, hiking, and horseback trails; tel. 932-3811. A rodeo arena has riding and rodeo events many evenings and weekends from Nov. to April; tel. 932-3277. From Phoenix, take I-10 about 20 miles west to the Estrella Parkway Exit, go south on Estrella Parkway to Vineyard, then turn left on Vineyard to the park entrance.

## White Tank Mountain Regional Park

Extensive trails for hikers and horseback riders twist through this range on the west side of the Valley. You might see petroglyphs and pottery shards left by Hohokam Indians. The park also offers picnic and camping areas. Campsites cost $5 with hookups and showers; tel. 935-2505. From Peoria, northwest of Phoenix, take Olive Ave. west for 15 miles.

# OTHER VALLEY OF THE SUN PRACTICALITIES

## SHOPPING

The Valley has thousands of shops eager to sell you something. Glittering department stores and boutiques display the latest in fashion. Or you can visit rustic, porch-fronted shops and be outfitted in Western duds from boots to bola ties. Western and Indian art make distinctive gifts. Anglo and Hispanic artists recall the frontier days in their paintings and sculpture, while Indian artists reveal their own heritage in artforms and crafts. Mexican import shops represent skilled craftsmen from south of the border.

### Old Town Scottsdale

Arts, crafts, clothing, and restaurants abound in the area centered around Brown St., just west of Scottsdale's Civic Center. More shops line Main St. west across Scottsdale Road to 69th Street.

### Fifth Avenue

Scottsdale's biggest shopping area lies along this curving street between Scottsdale Road and Indian School Road. Local businessmen promote the selection of over 350 shops here as "Arizona's ultimate shopping experience." Fifth Avenue is located 4 blocks north of Old Town Scottsdale.

### The Borgata

An elegant shopping center modeled after the Italian town of San Gimignano, north of Rome. It's complete with cobblestone paths, courtyards, and medieval towers and archways. Your credit cards will take a beating in most of the stores, but window shopping is fun; tel. 998-1822. The Borgata is at 6166 N. Scottsdale Road, 2 miles north of Old Town Scottsdale.

### Mercado

A Mexican marketplace with many specialty shops, restaurants, and a Hispanic cultural center. In Phoenix at the southwest corner of Van Buren and Seventh streets.

## El Tianguis
An Aztec word for "marketplace," this Mexican-style *mercado* houses inexpensive Mexican cafes and shops offering high-quality crafts from Mexico and other countries. It's operated by the Mexican-American and Yaqui Indian community of Guadalupe; tel. 838-4654. From I-10 near Tempe, exit east at Baseline Road then turn right on Avenida del Yaqui to Calle Guadalupe.

## Other Shopping Malls
**Biltmore Fashion Park,** Camelback Road and 24th St., Phoenix, has several restaurants and about 50 luxury shops including Saks Fifth Avenue, Polo/Ralph Lauren,

*The Borgata*

Gucci, and I. Magnin; tel. 955-8400. **Chris-Town Shopping Center,** 1703 W. Bethany Home Road, Phoenix, offers four large department stores, 27 places to eat, 11 movie theaters, a post office, and dozens of shops; tel. 242-9074. **Los Arcos Mall,** Scottsdale and McDowell roads, Scottsdale, contains two department stores, 14 restaurants, 66 shops, and two cinemas; tel. 945-6376. **Metrocenter** (exit west at Dunlap or Peoria aves. from I-17 in north Phoenix) is *big:* five department stores, 37 restaurants, 17 movie theaters, banks, hotels, miniature golf, ice-skating rink, etc.; tel. 996-3876 or 997-2641. **Park Central Mall,** at Central Ave. and Osborn Road, Phoenix, has a selection of 70 shops and 10 restaurants; a giant 1,600-pound statue of an Indian sun worshiper greets visitors at the entrance; tel. 264-5575. You'll find many more shopping centers listed in the Yellow Pages.

## Outdoor Supplies
**REI Co-op** has an excellent selection of gear for hiking, backpacking, bicycling, river running, downhill skiing, cross-country skiing, and other sports; rentals are available too. Optional lifetime memberships, available for a small fee, give dividends of about 10% of purchases at the end of each year. Located in Tempe at 1405 W. Southern Ave.; tel. 967-5494. **Arizona Hiking Shack** also has a fine array of outdoor gear and rentals at 11645 N. Cave Creek Road in north Phoenix; tel. 944-7723.

## Art Galleries
Scottsdale has most of the many galleries in the Valley. For a list of galleries and what's being shown, see the weekly newspaper *New Times*.

## Indian Music
**Canyon Records and Indian Arts** stocks hundreds of different Indian music titles from many American tribes, 4143 N. 16th St., Phoenix; tel. 266-4823.

## SERVICES

Phoenix's downtown **post office** is at 522 N. Central Ave.; tel. 253-4102. Other post offices include Scottsdale's at 7242 E. Osborn Road; Tempe's at 233 E. Southern Ave.; and Mesa's at 135 N. Center.

Exchange foreign currency at **First Interstate Bank,** 100 W. Washington St., Phoenix (or any branch office); tel. 271-6143; or at **Citibank Arizona,** 3300 N. Central Ave., Phoenix, International Div.; tel. 263-7227.

Need a doctor? **Maricopa County Medical Society** will refer you; open weekdays 8 a.m.-5 p.m.; tel. 252-2844.

Down and out? **Job Service** (Arizona Dept. of Economic Security), 438 W. Adams St., Phoenix, offers free services; tel. 252-7771.

## PHONE NUMBERS

Emergencies
   (police, fire, medical) . . . . . . . . . . . . . 911
Police (Phoenix) . . . . . . . . . . . . . 262-6151
Fire and Paramedics (Phoenix) . 253-1191
Maricopa County
   Sheriff . . . . 256-1011 or (800) 352-4553
Community Information & Referral
   Services . . . . . . . . . . . . . . . . . . 263-8856
Community Legal Service
   (Legal Aid) . . . . . . . . . . . . . . . . 258-3434
Lawyers' Referral
   (County Bar Assoc.) . . . . . . . . 257-4434
Doctors' Referral (Maricopa County
   Medical Society) . . . . . . . . . . . 252-2844
Phoenix Transit . . . . . . . . . . . . . . 253-5000
Visitor Hotline
   (Valley events) . . . . . . . . . . . . 252-5588
Phoenix & Valley of the Sun Convention
   & Visitors Bureau . . . . . . . . . . 254-6500
Valley Reservation System
   (in Arizona) . . . . . . . . . . . (800) 992-6005
   (outside Arizona) . . . . . . . (800) 528-0483
Arizona Office of Tourism
   (statewide) . . . . . . . . . . . . . . . 542-8687
Herberger Theater Box Office . . . 252-8497
ASU Gammage Center . . . . . . . . 965-3434
ASU Sun Devil Ticket Office . . . . 965-2381
Sportsline
   (latest sports scores) . . . . . . . . 258-1212
Civic Plaza Box Office . . . . . . . . . 262-7272
Forest Facts
   (U.S. Forest Service) . . . . . . . . 225-5296
Weather (state & local) . . . . . . . . 957-8700

## INFORMATION

**Tourist Offices**
**Phoenix & Valley of the Sun Convention & Visitors Bureau** has a free *Visitors Guide* and many brochures at 505 N. Second St., Suite 300, (Phoenix, AZ 85004); tel. 254-6500; open Mon.-Fri. 8 a.m.-5 p.m. The Visitors Bureau has branch offices downtown in the Hyatt Regency at the northwest corner of Adams and Second sts. (open Mon.-Fri. 8 a.m.-4:30 p.m.), and at Terminals 2 and 3 of Sky Harbor Airport (open Mon.-Fri. 9 a.m.-9 p.m. [to 5 p.m. in summer] and Sat. and Sun. 9 a.m.-5 p.m.).

Other helpful tourist offices in the Valley include **Scottsdale Chamber of Commerce** at 7333 E. Scottsdale Mall (Scottsdale, AZ 85251); open Mon.-Fri. 8:30 a.m.-5 p.m.; tel. 945-8481. **Tempe Chamber of Commerce** in the Tempe Mission Palms Hotel at 60 E. Fifth St., Suite 3 (Tempe, AZ 85281); open Mon.-Fri. 8 a.m.-5 p.m.; tel. 967-7891. **Mesa Convention & Visitors Bureau** at 120 N. Center (Mesa, AZ 85201); open Mon.-Fri. 8 a.m.-5 p.m.; tel. 969-1307. **Apache Junction Chamber of Commerce** in the City Hall complex at 1001 N. Idaho Road and Superstition Blvd./University Dr. (Box 1747, Apache Junction, AZ 85220); open Mon.-Fri. 8 a.m.-5 p.m.; tel. 982-3141.

The **Arizona Office of Tourism** has info about all regions of the state at 1100 W. Washington (Phoenix, AZ 85007); open Mon.-Fri. 8 a.m.-5 p.m.; tel. 542-8687.

**Tonto National Forest**
Find out about hiking and camping in the Tonto's 2,900,000 acres of forests and cactus located north and east of the Valley. The land includes the Superstition and Mazatzal

ranges and the lakes along the Verde and Salt rivers. Maps of the forest and some of Arizona's wilderness areas are sold ($2-4 each). Main office is at 2324 E. McDowell Road in Phoenix (Box 5348, Phoenix, AZ 85010); open Mon.-Fri. 7:45 a.m.-4:30 p.m.; tel. 225-5200 or 225-5296 (recorded info).

### Libraries

The main **Phoenix public library** is on the northeast corner of 12 E. McDowell Road and Central Ave.; open Mon.-Thurs. 9 a.m.-9 p.m., Fri. and Sat. 9 a.m.-6 p.m., and Sun. 1-5 p.m.; tel. 262-6451/4766. Call for information on the 10 branch libraries scattered around town. **Scottsdale's public library** is at 3839 Civic Center Plaza; open Mon.-Thurs. 10 a.m.-9 p.m. (9 a.m.-8 p.m. in summer), Fri. and Sat. 10 a.m.-6 p.m. (9 a.m.-5 p.m. in summer), and Sun. noon-5 p.m. (1-5 p.m. in summer); tel. 994-2476. Scottsdale has a branch library at 10101 N. 90th St.; tel. 391-6050. **Tempe's public library** is on the southwest corner of 3500 S. Rural Road and Southern Ave.; open Mon.-Thurs. 9 a.m.-9 a.m., Fri. and Sat. 9 a.m.- 5:30 p.m., and Sun. noon-5:30 p.m.; tel. 967-0890 (hours) or 731-8231. **Mesa's public library** is downtown at 64 E. First St.; open Mon.-Thurs. 9:30 a.m.-9 p.m., Fri. and Sat. 9:30 a.m.-5:30 p.m., and Sun. (Sept. to May) 1:30-5:30 p.m.; tel. 644-3100. **Apache Junction's public library** is in the City Hall complex, 1177 N. Idaho Road; open Mon., Wed., and Fri. 9 a.m.-5 p.m., Tues. and Thurs. 9 a.m.-8 p.m., and Sat. 9 a.m.-1 p.m.; tel. 983-0204.

The **State Capitol** has a research library on Arizona History in Room 300; other departments of the library have maps, state documents, federal documents, law, and genealogy; 1700 W. Washington; open Mon.-Fri. 8 a.m.-5 p.m.; tel. 542-4421/3701. You can also use the libraries on the ASU campus (see "Tempe").

### Newspapers And Magazines

*Arizona Republic* comes out every morning and has a big Sunday edition; its sister paper, *The Phoenix Gazette,* is published evenings Mon.-Saturday. For local news and happenings, also look for the weekly *New Times*, free at newsstands. *Scottsdale LIFE* reviews the art and entertainment scene there; published weekly by the *Scottsdale Progress* newspaper.

*Phoenix Magazine* comes out monthly with news and useful information about the Valley. Scottsdale has its own magazines too, the monthly *Scottsdale Scene* and the quarterly *Scottsdale Magazine.*

The U.S. Forest Service can tell you about recreation on the Salt River (pictured) and other areas of the Tonto National Forest

## Books And Maps

**The Book Store** has not only new and used books, but one of the best selections of magazines and out-of-town newspapers in the state, 4230 N. Seventh Ave.; tel. 279-3910. **Al's Family Book Store** claims to have over 500,000 books, new and used, paperback and hardback, at 1454 E. Van Buren St. in Phoenix; tel. 253-6922. **Bob and Faye's Paper Book Exchange** specializes in used books: in Phoenix at 1827 E. Indian School Road; tel. 264-6698; and in Tempe at 2043 E. University Dr.; tel. 966-2065. **Changing Hands** has a very large selection of new and used books at 414 S. Mill Ave. in Tempe; tel. 966-0203. Shopping malls have the popular book chains.

For maps of Arizona and the world, see **A Wide World of Maps** in Phoenix (2626 W. Indian School Road; tel. 279-2323); in Tempe (1526 N. Scottsdale Road; tel. 949-1012); and in Mesa (1440 S. Country Club Dr.; tel. 844-1134). Topo maps are also sold by **REI** (1405 W. Southern Ave. in Tempe; tel. 967-5494) and **Arizona Hiking Shack** (11645 N. Cave Creek Road in north Phoenix; tel. 944-7723).

# TRANSPORT

## Tours

The **Gray Line** has daily tours of the Phoenix area ($19) and longer day trips to the Superstitions and Apache Trail ($39), Tucson ($49), Sedona/Oak Creek Canyon ($40), and the Grand Canyon ($49); 2- and 3-day trips visit the Grand Canyon ($119-279), Lake Powell ($279-389), and other areas of the Southwest; 2929 Clarendon Ave., Phoenix, AZ 85017; tel. 266-0424 or (800) 766-3521 out of state.

To see some of Arizona's real backcountry, take a four-wheel-drive tour with **Big Red Desert Jeep Tours** (Box 34564, Phoenix, AZ 85067; tel. 263-5337) or **Arizona Awareness Jeep Tours** (2422 N. 72nd Place, Scottsdale, AZ 85257; tel. 947-7852). Guided dayhikes and overnights into the rugged desert and mountain country surrounding the Valley can be arranged by **Expeditions on Foot,** 2925 E. Villa Maria Dr., Phoenix, AZ

85032; tel. 482-3992. Raft the wild upper Salt River with **Desert Voyagers** (also Verde River whitewater in spring and year-round on the lower Verde and Salt; tel. 998-RAFT) or **Salt River Canyon Raft Trips** (tel. 968-1552 in state or 800-334-RAFT out of state).

Flights to the Grand Canyon and other highly scenic areas of the Southwest are offered by **Arizona Air** (tel. 991-8252) and **Sky Cab** (tel. 998-1778). Soar in a glider with **Turf Soaring School** (Pleasant Valley Airport; tel. 439-3621) or **Estrella Sailport Soaring School** (tel. 568-2318). Fly high over the Valley in a hot-air balloon during the cooler months with **Pegasus** (tel. 224-6111), **Unicorn Balloon** (tel. 991-3666), **Aeronautical Adventure** (tel. 992-2627), **Arizona Balloonport** (tel. 953-3924), or **Sky Climber** (tel. 483-8208). The Visitors Bureau's *Visitors Guide* lists many more tour operators. Sunday's *Arizona Republic* "Travel" section often advertises special travel deals. Las Vegas, anyone?

## Local Bus

**Phoenix Transit** will take you around the Valley, including the parks, shopping areas, most of the sights, and the airport for just $.75 to $1; transfers are free if asked for when boarding; tel. 253-5000. All-day passes cost only $2.50; purchase them at the downtown terminal at First and Washington, which also has timetables. Most buses head for home between 6 p.m. and 10 p.m., staying there completely on Sun. and major holidays. On those days you can use **Dial-A-Ride**; tel. 271-4545. They operate about 7 a.m.-7 p.m.; call at least 30 minutes before you want to be picked up; fares start at $1.50, depending on distance. Other useful services in the Valley include the **Molly Trolleys** in Scottsdale (tel. 941-2957) and **Metro Trolley** in Tempe (tel. 829-1226).

## Long-distance Bus

The **Greyhound Bus** terminal is downtown at 525 E. Washington St.; tel. 248-4050. You'll find other Greyhound stations in northwest Phoenix (2647 W. Glendale; tel. 246-4341), Tempe (502 S. College Ave.; tel. 967-4030);

Mesa (1423 S. Country Club Dr.; tel. 834-3360); and Sun City (10795 Grand Ave.; tel. 933-5716). Some destinations and one-way fares are Los Angeles (7 daily), $26; San Diego (4 daily), $26; El Paso (7 daily), $39; Tucson (11 daily), $18.45; Flagstaff (3 daily), $22.50; Globe (3 daily), $13; Wickenburg (6 daily), $11; Parker (1 daily), $16.10; Lake Havasu City (1 daily), $21.25; and Yuma (4 daily), $34. Roundtrip fares may have a small discount.

**LTR Bus** leaves the downtown Phoenix Greyhound terminal (tel. 248-4050) and northwest Phoenix (5540 W. Glendale Ave.; tel. 937-9487) daily for Kingman ($33), Laughlin ($25), Las Vegas ($35), and other destinations. **Nava-Hopi Express** connects Sky Harbor Airport and Phoenix with Sedona ($21.20 one way) and Flagstaff ($27 one way) twice daily; service to the Grand Canyon and tours of northern Arizona are offered too; tel. (800) 892-8687. **White Mountain Passenger Lines** leaves daily except Sun. from several locations in the Valley to Payson and Show Low; 321 S. 24th St., Phoenix; tel. 275-4245.

### Auto Rentals
The Valley moves on wheels; if you need some, check the Yellow Pages or the Visitors Bureau's *Visitors Guide.* Rental companies offer many different plans; most have offices at the airport or make free pick-ups. You can rent RVs too.

### Driveaways
These are autos that need delivering to another city. If it's a place you're headed, a driveaway can be like getting a free car rental. To do it you have to be at least 21 years old and make a deposit of $75-150. There will also be time and mileage limits. Ask for an economy car if you want the lowest costs. See the Yellow Pages under "Automobile Transporters & Driveaways."

### Taxis
**Ace Taxi** (tel. 254-1999) has lower than average rates. Other companies include **Arizona Taxi** (tel. 253-8294), **Checker Cab** (tel. 257-1818), and **Yellow Cab** (tel. 252-5252).

### Train
**Amtrak** has three eastbound and three westbound departures every week. Terminal is downtown at 401 W. Harrison St. and Fourth Avenue. For reservations and info, call (800) 872-7245. Westbound departs in the evening for Yuma and other points, arriving in Los Angeles the next morning (9 hours, $81 one way). Eastbound leaves in the morning for Tucson (2½ hours, $26 one way), and on to either New Orleans (1½ days, $196) or Chicago (2 days, $196). Amtrak gives generous discounts on roundtrip fares, making it more competitive with the bus and plane.

### Air
Commercial flights to the Valley land at Sky Harbor Airport, just 3 miles east of downtown Phoenix. See the Yellow Pages for the airlines, charters, and ticket agencies. Sky Harbor has three separate terminals, connected by a free 24-hour shuttle bus. The busy airport is well organized but you'll have to do some walking.

The **Visitors Bureau** staffs information desks in Terminals 2 and 3; open Mon.-Fri. 9 a.m.-9 p.m. (to 5 p.m. in summer) and Sat. and Sun. 9 a.m.-5 p.m. Free telephones near the baggage claims connect many Valley hotels and motels.

Taxis outside have widely varying fares—you might want to shop around. **Phoenix Transit** buses are the cheapest way into town; they leave the airport Mon.-Fri. every 30 min. about 6 a.m.-8:30 p.m. and Sat. about 8 a.m.-7 p.m.; tel. 253-5000.

# NORTHEAST OF PHOENIX

## PAYSON AND THE COUNTRY BELOW THE RIM

When the Valley bakes under the summer sun, many Phoenix-area residents drive northeast to the cool pine forests around Payson. This might be the reason why the road to Payson, AZ 87, has the nickname "Beeline Highway." From Mesa, the Beeline Hwy. crosses the two Indian reservations of Salt River and Fort McDowell, then climbs over a pass in the Mazatzal Range before turning north to Payson. In Payson, 78 miles from Mesa, you're at an elevation of 5,000 feet and in almost the exact center of Arizona. Sheer cliffs of the Mogollon Rim tower 2,000 feet higher in the north. Novelist Zane Grey fell in love with this country and built a lodge at the foot of the Rim. Here he wrote many of his books and set off on "hunting expeditions" to secure both ideas for stories and trophies for his walls. (See "Zane Grey's Lodge" below.) Today, sportsmen come in season to stalk elk, deer, turkey, and other game. Anglers are lured by trout-filled streams and stocked reservoirs. Hikers enjoy walks in the forest or more ambitious treks in the Mazatzal and Sierra Ancha Ranges. Although Payson (pop. 7,940) has no "sights" itself, the town makes a good base for exploring the surrounding countryside.

### History
It wasn't the cooler climate and pretty scenery that brought Payson's first settlers—it was the glitter of gold. Miners set up camp in 1881, but ranching and lumbering soon took over as more rewarding occupations. A fort provided protection against Apache raids in the precarious early years. The town's name honors Senator Louis Edwin Payson, who had nothing to do with the community and never came here! Frank C. Hise, the postmaster, assigned the name to repay a political favor.

### Accommodations
You have a choice of motels in town or secluded cabins in the surrounding forests, as well as campgrounds and RV parks. Make reservations for the weekend rush, especially in summer. In town, beginning from the south, you'll find **Super 8 Motel** (Beeline Hwy. and W. Phoenix; tel. 474-4526 or 800-843-1991); **Paysonglo Lodge** (1005 S. Beeline Hwy.; tel. 474-2382); **Trails End Motel** (811 S. Beeline Hwy.; tel. 474-2283); **Charleston Motor Inn** (302 S. Beeline Hwy.; tel. 474-2201); **Chelcie Inn Bed & Breakfast** (208 E. Bonita St.; tel. 474-6525); and **Swiss Village Lodge** (801 N. Beeline Hwy.; tel. 474-3241 or Phoenix toll-free tel. 255-0170).

Heading east from town on AZ 260 you'll find the **Pueblo Inn** (809 E. Hwy. 260; tel. 474-5241 or 800-888-9828); **Lazy D Ranch Motel and RV Resort** (4 miles east of Payson; tel. 474-2442, ext. 200); **Star Valley Resort** (4 miles east of Payson; tel. 474-5182); **Diamond Point Shadows** (6 miles east of Payson; tel. 474-4848); **Kohl's Ranch Resort** (motel, cabins, restaurant located 17 miles east of Payson; tel. 478-4211 or Phoenix toll-free tel. 271-9731); **Chris-**

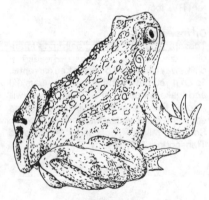

*spadefoot toad*
(Scaphiopus hammondi)

topher Creek Lodge (motel, cabins, restaurant, located 22 miles east of Payson in the resort village of Christopher Creek; tel. 478-4300); and Grey Hackle Lodge (Christopher Creek; tel. 478-4392).

## Campgrounds

The Forest Service (tel. 474-2269) maintains several campgrounds east of Payson on AZ 260, all open about mid-May to late Sept., with drinking water but no showers: Ponderosa (13 miles east; $5; also a group campground nearby); Lower Tonto Creek (17 miles east; $4); Upper Tonto Creek (17 miles east; $4; also a picnic area nearby); and Christopher Creek (22 miles east; $5).

For RV and trailer parks, try Cool Pines RV Park (0.5 mile east on AZ 260 from the Beeline Hwy.; tel. 474-2300); Houston Creek Adult RV Park (4 miles east on AZ 260; tel. 474-2636); C-Bar Diamond RV Park (4 miles east on AZ 260; tel. 474-2469); Lazy D Ranch Motel & RV Resort (4 miles east on AZ 260; tel. 474-2442); Ox Bow Estates RV Park (3 miles south on the Beeline Hwy.; tel. 474-2042); and Pine Trailer Park (19 miles north on the Beeline Hwy. in Pine; $12-15; tel. 476-3459).

## Food

Swiss Village Lodge at 807 N. Beeline Hwy. has a restaurant featuring both continental and American specialties; there's also a less expensive coffee shop; tel. 474-5800. The Swiss Village Bakery turns out great pastries, across from Swiss Village Lodge, 614 N. Beeline Hwy.; tel. 474-2307. Cactus Inn serves fine French-continental cuisine at 614 N. Beeline Hwy.; closed Mon.; tel. 474-0871. "Home cooking" is featured at Knotty Pine Cafe (1001 S. Beeline Hwy.; tel. 474-9927); Beeline Cafe (815 S. Beeline Hwy.; tel. 474-9960); 260 Cafe (803 E. Hwy. 260; tel. 474-1933); and Aunt Alice's Restaurant (512 N. Beeline Hwy.; tel. 474-4720).

Dine Mexican at El Rancho (200 S. Beeline Hwy.; tel. 474-3111) and La Casa Pequeña (911 S. Beeline Hwy.; tel. 474-6329). If you've always hankered after Mexican-Chinese food, head over to Pedro Wong's

Drive In (closed Wed.), 510 S. Beeline Hwy.; tel. 474-2305. The Mandarin House Restaurant serves good Chinese food at 1200 S. Beeline Hwy. (next to the Super 8 Motel); may close Mon.; tel. 474-1342. For Italian-American dining, try Mario's Villa, 600 E. Hwy. 260; tel. 474-5429. Pick up pizza at Mario's (above); Pizza Factory (238 E. Hwy. 260; tel. 474-1895); or Pizza Hut (113 S. Beeline Hwy.; tel. 474-1100). For groceries visit Basha's, Safeway, or Fairway in the shopping centers near the intersection of Hwy. 260 and Beeline Highway.

## Entertainment And Events

Payson Picture Show plays the current flicks in Payson Plaza, one block east on Bonita off Beeline Hwy.; tel. 474-3918. Nightspots for lively country and western, rock, or requests include the Oxbow Inn (607 W. Main St.; tel. 474-0875); Winchester Saloon (615 W. Main St.; tel. 474-9953); and Pete's Place (Star Valley, 4 miles east on Hwy. 260; tel. 474-9963). Major community events include the Old Timers Rodeo and an Arts & Crafts Show in May; High Country Car Show of classic and antique vehicles, Country Music Festival, and Junior Rodeo in June; Loggers/Sawdust Festival in July; the "world's oldest" Continuous Rodeo (since 1884) and Rodeo Parade in Aug.; the Fiddlers' Contest in September; and the October Art Festival in October.

## Services And Recreation

The post office is at 100 W. Frontier Street. Payson's hospital is at 807 S. Ponderosa St.; tel. 474-3222. You'll find a swimming pool, tennis courts, ball fields, and picnic grounds in Rumsey Park on N. McLane Road (from the junction of Beeline and Hwy. 260, go west on Overland and Longhorn roads then right 0.5 mile on McLane); tel. 474-5242 (park) or 474-2774 (pool). Play golf on the 18-hole Payson Golf Course, 1504 W. Country Club; tel. 474-2273. Rent horses for trail rides during the warmer months from Kohl's Ranch Stables (17 miles east on AZ 260; tel. 478-4226); OK Corral Stables (15 miles north on Beeline Hwy. in Pine; tel.

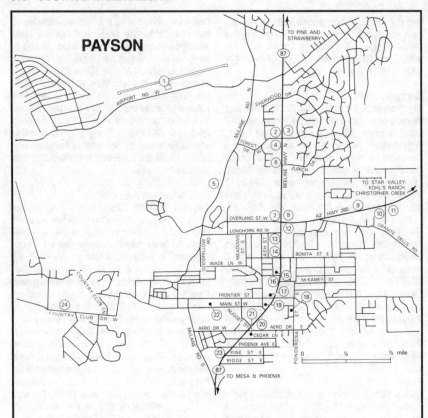

## PAYSON

1. Payson Municipal Airport
2. Swiss Village Bakery
3. Swiss Village Lodge and Restaurant
4. Cactus Restaurant
5. Rumsey Park; rodeo grounds
6. Aunt Alice's
7. Safeway
8. Payson Village (Basha's and Wal-Mart)
9. Mario's Villa
10. 260 Cafe
11. U.S. Forest Service (Payson Ranger District)
12. Fairway
13. Charleston Motor Inn
14. El Rancho Restaurant
15. Pedro Wong's Drive-in
16. Beeline Bus Agency
17. post office
18. Pyle Memorial Hospital
19. Payson Chamber of Commerce
20. Trails End Motel; Beeline Cafe; La Casa Pequeña
21. Paysonglo Motel; Knotty Pine Cafe
22. public library; Leaves of Autumn Books
23. Super 8 Motel; Mandarin House Restaurant
24. Payson Country Club

© MOON PUBLICATIONS

476-4303); and **Wilderness Journeys** (15 miles north on Beeline Hwy. in Pine; tel. 476-4382). **Frontier Outfitters** can arrange pack trips; Payson; tel. 474-3322. For camping, fishing, and hunting supplies and info, visit **Wal-Mart** (400 E. Hwy. 260; tel. 474-0029) or **Big Jeff's Sporting Goods** (512 S. Beeline Hwy.; tel. 474-4186).

### Information

The **Payson Chamber of Commerce** is on the corner of Beeline Hwy. and Main St. (Box 1380, Payson, AZ 85547); open Mon.-Fri. 8 a.m.-5 p.m. and Sat. and Sun. 10 a.m.-1 p.m.; tel. 474-4515. For camping, hiking, and backroad travel info, see the **Payson Ranger District** office of the U.S. Forest Service; open 7:45 a.m.-4:30 p.m. (daily May to Oct., Mon.-Sat. from Oct. to Jan., and Mon.-Fri. from Jan. to May); one mile east of town (1009 E. Hwy. 260, Payson, AZ 85541); tel. 474-2269. **Payson Public Library** is at 510 W. Main; tel. 747-2585. **Leaves of Autumn Books** carries a good selection of new and used books at 518 W. Main; tel. 474-3654.

### Transport

For a taxi, call **Pat's Payson Cab**; tel. 474-7123. **White Mountain Passenger Lines** buses headed southwest to Phoenix and northeast to Show Low stop at Beeline Bus Agency, 512 S. Beeline Hwy.; tel. 474-2550.

## VICINITY OF PAYSON

### Tonto Natural Bridge State Park

Deposits left by mineral springs have created the world's largest natural travertine bridge. The springs still flow as they have for about a million years, building the massive arch even larger and watering lush vegetation. You might not even realize you're standing on top when you arrive—the bridge measures 400 feet in width and spans a canyon 150 feet wide. Graceful travertine formations underneath look like those inside a limestone cave. A small waterfall cascades over the top of the arch, forming jewel-like droplets of water that sparkle in the sun and create pretty rainbows.

A precipitous but safe trail winds down to the canyon floor 183 feet below. To explore the underground tunnel you'll need shoes suitable for clambering over wet and muddy rocks. Visitors can also admire the bridge from viewpoints at the top overlooking each side of the arch. The park is open daily except Christmas; $3/vehicle admission. Lodge accommodations, campground, and restaurant were closed at press time; contact the park for opening dates. From Payson go 11 miles north on AZ 87, then turn left 3 miles on a gravel road at the sign; Box 1245, Payson, AZ 85547; tel. 476-4202.

### Strawberry

This tiny village sits just below the Mogollon Rim, 19 miles north of Payson. Wild strawberries grow here but they're hard to find nowadays. Turn west 1.5 miles at Strawberry Lodge to see Arizona's oldest **schoolhouse.** Pioneers built the one-room log structure in 1885. You can step in to see the restored interior during the summer; other times by appointment; ask at Strawberry Lodge. The road continues past Fossil Creek (good hiking) to Camp Verde, but it's hard going for cars. A better route to Camp Verde is to go north 8 miles on AZ 87 up onto the Rim, then turn left on the paved General Crook Trail (AZ 260).

Rooms in **Strawberry Lodge** cost $36.93-47.48, the more expensive having fireplaces and balconies; reservations for weekends should be made a couple of weeks in advance; tel. 476-3333. Dine at Strawberry Lodge, open daily for breakfast, lunch, and dinner.

### Payson Zoo

Many of the more than 60 residents have starred in motion pictures. Their training and close contact with humans seem to make the animals seem more at home here than at most zoos. You can meet such creatures as baboons, leopards, and tigers from distant lands and javelinas, black bears, coyotes, and ringtail cats from closer to home. The familiar pigs, chickens, and peacocks can be seen too. Open daily (weather permitting) 10 a.m.-4 p.m.; $3 adult, $1 children 12 and under; tel. 474-5435. From Payson, head east 6.5 miles on AZ 260 to Lion Springs Road, then turn right.

## Zane Grey's Lodge

The canyons, great forests, and expansive views of the Rim Country inspired author Zane Grey to build a hunting cabin here in about 1920. He made many stays over the next 9 years, enjoying the wilderness while working on novels about the American West. A major forest fire, however, burned the cabin in 1990. While it's being rebuilt, you can see photo exhibits in a small building nearby. Grey's books can be purchased too. Open daily 9 a.m.-5 p.m. from April 1 to Oct. 31, then 10 a.m.-4 p.m. from Nov. 1 to March 31. Call for winter road conditions; tel. 478-4243. From Payson head east on AZ 260 for 17 miles and turn left at the sign just past Kohl's Ranch, then go 5 miles in on a mostly paved road (the last mile isn't recommended for large rigs).

## Tonto Fish Hatchery

Rainbow, brook, and brown trout grow to eating size at this hatchery just east of Zane Grey's Lodge. You can take the interpretive walk, learn about the life history of trout in the visitor center, peer into the hatchery rooms, and see fingerlings and catchable trout in outdoor raceways; open daily 8 a.m.-4 p.m.; tel. 478-4200. Follow the same directions as to Zane Grey's Lodge, but keep straight on the paved road to its end.

## Mazatzal Wilderness

Indians knew this vast country of desert and mountains as Mazatzal, "Land of the Deer." The name still fits, because only scattered ruins remain of the Indians, pioneers, and miners who tried to live here. The wilderness, commonly pronounced "ma-ta-ZEL" but more correctly "MAH-zat-zall," covers over 250,500 acres in a block beginning 8 miles west of Payson that extends south for 30 miles and is as wide as 15 miles. The climate zones range from Lower Sonoran desert, with saguaro and palo verde (2,200-4,000 feet), up through dry grasslands, oaks, pinyons, and junipers of the Upper Sonoran desert (4,000-7,000 feet), to the Transition Zone, with ponderosa pines and a few pockets of firs on the upper slopes (7,000-7,900 feet). You might meet deer, javelina, black bear, or even a mountain lion. Hikers in this big country need to be self-sufficient with maps, compass, and water; springs and streams cannot be counted on during the summer.

Best times for a visit are spring and autumn; summer is OK if you're prepared for possible 100°-plus temperatures and late-season thunderstorms; winter is fine at the lower elevations, but severe snowstorms can hit the high country. You won't need any permits to hike or horseback in the wilderness. Of the 14 trailheads, the Barnhardt is the most popular: from just south of the Rye Creek bridge (14.5 miles south of Payson on AZ 87), go west 4.8 miles on Forest Route 419 to the end of the road. You have a choice of three trails here. A popular 19-mile, 2-day backpack loop encircles Mazatzal Peak via the **Barnhardt, Mazatzal Divide,** and **Y Bar Basin** (Shake Tree) trails. For detailed hiking

*collared peccary (javelina)*
(Tayassu tajacu)

info see the Forest Service people at Payson (tel. 474-2269), Phoenix (tel. 225-5200), or Carefree (tel. 488-3441). They'll give you free literature on hiking trails and sell you a Mazatzal Wilderness topo map for $2. *Arizona Trails* by David Mazel describes 10 hikes ranging from one to 6 days. Francois Leydet tells of his 6-day journey by horseback in the Mazatzals in the Feb. 1974 *National Geographic.*

## YOUNG

Remote and off the tourist track, Young has been called one of Arizona's last "cow towns." To get here you have to take largely unpaved roads: either south 25 miles on Forest Highway 12 from the Mogollon Rim (turn off AZ 260 at Milepost 284, about 33 miles east of Payson); or north 47 miles on AZ 288 (35 miles of dirt road) from near Roosevelt Lake (off AZ 88 between Roosevelt Dam and Globe). Roads to Young are best avoided in winter and just after heavy rains, though the north road is usually OK after rains.

In the late 1800s one of Arizona's bloodiest and most savage feuds took place in Pleasant Valley, between the Rim and Young. The trouble started when the Tewksbury clan gave protection to a band of sheep brought into the area in 1887. Cattlemen led by the Graham clan wouldn't stand for competition from the "woolies" and attacked, killing a Navajo sheepherder and destroying or driving away the animals. The Tewksburys retaliated and the war was on. The fighting didn't end until every Graham had been killed. All efforts by lawmen to restore order failed, and at least 30 people died during the 5 years of terror. History buffs can search out many of the battle sites near Young. The town's cemetery has marked graves belonging to five members of the Graham faction: Harry Middleton, Al Rose, Charles Blevin, William Graham, and John Graham. You'll find Young Cemetery behind Young Baptist Church on the main road, 0.5 mile east of Moon's Saloon.

Historians still debate details of the feud. Accounts of the tragedy are given in *A Little*

*one of Young's watering holes*

*War of Our Own* by Don Dedera, *Arizona's Dark and Bloody Ground* by Earle Forrest, and in *Globe, Arizona* by Clara Woody and Milton Schwartz. Zane Grey dramatized the events in his novel *To the Last Man.* Grey obtained his material during hunting trips in Pleasant Valley. Today, a very independent breed of people inhabit Young. These folks, many of whom are retired, don't like authority or development. Even the Forest Service (Young's biggest employer) represents too much government control for some residents.

### Practicalities

Young doesn't have any motels, but you'll find plenty of places to camp in the surrounding Tonto National Forest. Young's social life revolves around the **Antlers Bar and Cafe** (tel. 462-3511) and **Moon's Saloon Bar and Cafe** (no relation to Moon Publications!). Both places serve inexpensive breakfasts, lunches, and dinners daily. The Antler has a bonus of a free "museum"—everything from old saddles and mining gear to an Electrolux vacuum cleaner and a tuba; dusty bears and mountain lions also grace the walls. **Valley View Cabins** has rental units; tel. 462-3422. Other townspeople occasionally have cabins for rent; try asking around at the Antlers Cafe or Moon's Saloon. For fishing, hiking, and camping info, contact the Tonto National Forest's **Pleasant Valley Ranger District** office in Young; open Mon.-Fri. 7:45-11:45 a.m. and 12:30-4:30 p.m.; also open Sat. and Sun. from May 15 to Sept. 15; tel. 462-3311; turn off the main road 0.25 mile east of Moon's Saloon.

# VICINITY OF YOUNG

## North Of Young

The unfortunate Navajo sheepherder who fell as the first victim of the **Pleasant Valley War** lies in a lonely grave north of Young. A white cross, pile of stones, and sign mark the spot; from the main road, 4 miles north of Young and 20 miles south of AZ 260, turn west one mile on Forest Route 200.

**Valentine Ridge Campground** (no water or charge) is 18 miles north of Young and 6 miles south of AZ 260, then 1.5 miles east on Forest Route 188. **Colcord Campground** (no water or charge) is just east of the main road on Forest Route 33, about 3 miles south of AZ 260 and 21 miles north of Young. **Canyon Creek Campground** (no water or charge) and **Canyon Creek Fish Hatchery** lie just below the Rim at an elevation of 6,600 feet; follow Forest Route 33 in 5 miles. The fish hatchery has a self-guided tour, open daily 8 a.m.-5 p.m. Fishermen can try their luck in Canyon Creek for rainbow and some brown trout; use flies and artificial lures only; limits of two fish per day and a minimum length of 12 inches apply. **Colcord Lookout** (elev. 7,513 feet) has a sweeping panorama of the Young area and the Mogollon Rim; turn west off the main road onto Forest Route 291 (opposite the Forest Route 33 turnoff), and go in 3 miles.

## South Of Young

**Workman Creek Waterfalls** take a 200-foot plunge south of Young; to get there, go south on the main road from town for 21 miles and turn left 3.5 miles on Forest Route 487; park at the cattleguard, then walk 0.25 mile to the falls. This pretty valley supports dense stands of Douglas fir, white fir, and smaller numbers of Arizona sycamore and the relatively rare Arizona maple. You'll see several places to camp (no facilities) along the road to the falls. Swimmers can cool off in the **"Bathtubs,"** natural pools in Workman Creek; from the Workman Creek bridge (AZ 288), follow the trail downstream 250 yards. **Rose Creek Campground** (elev. 5,400 feet) is off the main road 23 miles south of Young; drinking water and pit toilets but no charge.

## Wilderness Areas Near Young

The **Sierra Ancha Wilderness** contains 20,850 acres lying 15 miles south of Young and 36 miles north of Globe. Lack of good roads and rugged terrain discourage most visitors—precipitous box canyons and sheer cliffs make travel difficult. Elevations range from 3,200 to 7,800 feet. Spring-fed creeks in the eastern part have carved several short but deep box canyons, including Pueblo, Cold Springs, and Devil's Chasm. Prehistoric Salado Indians built cliff dwellings in these canyons, then departed. Forest Route 203 (Cherry Creek Road) loops around the east side of the Sierra Anchas, providing views into these spectacular canyons. You'll need a high-clearance or 4WD vehicle for this trip; the northern part of the road is particularly rough. Allow 3½ hours for the drive. For hiking info and a wilderness map, contact the Forest Service in Young (tel. 462-3311) or Phoenix (tel. 225-5200). **Salome Wilderness,** 15 miles southwest of Young, protects the Salome and lower Workman Creek watersheds. **Hell's Gate Wilderness,** 13 miles northwest of Young, preserves parts of the drainages of Tonto, Haigler, Marsh, and Houston Creeks. Sheer cliffs rising above Tonto Creek form the "Hell's Gate"; good fishing here but only the most adventurous fishermen make it in (Forest Trail #37).

# EAST OF PHOENIX:
# THE APACHE TRAIL LOOP

Driving east through Phoenix, Tempe, Mesa, then Apache Junction, you might think the "city" will never end. But as soon as you turn onto AZ 88 in Apache Junction, the shopping centers, gas stations, and hamburger stands fade away...you're left with just the desert, lakes, and mountains. Here begins a 200-mile loop through some of the West's most rugged country. Allow 6 hours just for driving this circuit around the rugged Superstition Mountains, taking AZ 88 to Globe, then returning to Apache Junction via US 60/70. The big attractions, besides the wild scenery, are hiking and horseback riding in the Superstition Wilderness, boating on a chain of lakes within the Salt River Canyon, stepping inside prehistoric pueblo Indian dwellings in Tonto National Monument, seeing copper-mining operations near Globe, Miami, and Superior, and finally the Boyce Thompson Southwestern Arboretum—an amazing collection of plants from all over the world.

## SUPERSTITION WILDERNESS

The 159,700-acre wilderness lies south of the Salt River Canyon and Apache Trail, about 40 miles east of Phoenix. You'll find some of the Southwest's best desert hiking in the canyons and mountains of the Superstitions. Elevations range from about 2,000 feet along the west boundary to over 6,000 feet in the eastern uplands. Desert vegetation dominates, but a few pockets of ponderosa pine hang onto the highest slopes. Wildflowers put on colorful extravaganzas in early spring and following summer rains.

### Gold Fever
You can really believe the legends of a lost gold mine while gazing into these mysterious mountains. One set of stories tells how Don Miguel Peralta discovered fantastic amounts of gold somewhere among the Superstitions

*riding in the Superstitions*

*the "Narrows" of La Barge Creek
in the Superstitions*

in 1845, and how he and his miners later met their death at the hands of Apache Indians. The location of his "Sombrero Mine" remains a mystery. At least one of Peralta's party did survive the massacre and, 30 years later, revealed the mine's location to a German immigrant, Jacob Waltz. Locally known as the "Dutchman," Waltz worked the mine without ever revealing its location. Those who tried to follow him into the Superstitions were either lost in the maze of canyons or later found murdered. The power of the "Lost Dutchman's Mine" legends have intensified since the prospector's death in 1891. Although no rich gold deposits have ever been found—and geologists say the Superstitions are an unlikely location for gold—the legends persist.

### Climate
Spring and autumn bring the most pleasant weather for a visit to the Superstitions. Winter is often fine at lower elevations, though snow and cold can hit the higher areas. Summer,

which lasts from May to Oct., gets unbearably hot. Temperatures exceed 115° F in the shade at times, and there's precious little shade! You can venture into the Superstitions in the summer by making a crack-of-dawn departure and getting out by late morning when the heat hits. Carry plenty of water, especially in summer when springs and creeks are likely to dry up.

### Hiking
Twelve trailheads and 180 miles of trail provide all kinds of possibilities. Being so close to Phoenix, the Superstitions get unusually heavy traffic for a wilderness area. The western half receives the most use, especially near Peralta and First Water trailheads. You're more likely to see javelina, desert mule deer, mountain lion, black bear, and other wildlife in the eastern half of the range. You don't need a permit to hike or camp in the Superstitions; you're asked only to leave the area as you found it and limit groups to 15 people and stays to 14 days. Horses may be brought in too; bring feed, as grazing is prohibited. Laws protect the wilderness from any prospecting that involves surface disturbance, and no one can file new claims.

### Information
The U.S. Forest Service manages the Superstition Wilderness as part of the giant Tonto National Forest. Foresters can give advice on travel here in their offices in Phoenix (2324 E. McDowell Road or write Box 5348, Phoenix, AZ 85010; tel. 225-5200), Mesa (26 N. MacDonald St. or write Box 5800, Mesa, AZ 85201; tel. 261-6446), and Roosevelt (Box 649, Roosevelt, AZ 85545; tel. 467-2236). Offices sell a Superstition Wilderness topo map with background, trailhead, and trail information. *Arizona Trails* by David Mazel has the best trail descriptions and maps of any source; 23 hikes receive detailed coverage.

## FOUR PEAKS WILDERNESS

This wilderness covers 60,700 acres in the southern Mazatzal Mountains, lying north of Apache Lake opposite the Superstition Wilderness. Four Peaks are visible over a large section of central Arizona; they've been a major landmark since Indian times. From their deeply incised lower slopes along Canyon and Apache Lakes at an elevation of 1,600 feet, the mountains top off at Brown Peak, northernmost of the four, at 7,657 feet. Vegetation runs the whole range from saguaro cactus at the base to ponderosa pine, Douglas fir, and aspen near the top. Javelina, deer, black bear, mountain lion, and smaller animals inhabit the slopes. Black bear here are thought to make up one of the highest concentrations in Arizona; wise campers try to hang food out of reach at night. The Forest Service has a pamphlet describing trails in the Four Peaks area, available from the Phoenix, Mesa, and Roosevelt offices. Trailheads can be reached from AZ 87 to the west (northeast of Mesa) or from AZ 188 to the east (northwest of Roosevelt Dam).

## THE APACHE TRAIL: APACHE JUNCTION TO ROOSEVELT DAM

Once a raiding route for Apaches, the Apache Trail is now safe, but the surrounding country remains as primitive as ever. Jagged ridges, towering cliffs, and the desert itself remind man of his limitations and small scale. The road, designated a "National Scenic Byway," twists and climbs as it tries to find a way through the rugged land. Watch for narrow bridges and blind curves on some sections; the road isn't recommended for large trailers.

Weaver's Needle, the 4,535-foot landmark for gold seekers in the Superstition Wilderness, can be glimpsed to the south. Ten to one the stories about Jacob Waltz and his "Lost Dutchman's Gold Mine" are just tall tales. Despite the efforts of thousands of gold-crazed prospectors, no major finds have been confirmed. Geologists studying the mountains have found them to be remnants of volcanic calderas—an unlikely place for rich veins of the precious metal. Perhaps the crafty "Dutchman" worked as a fence for gold thieves employed in the Vulture Mine near Wickenburg: miners stealing nuggets wouldn't be able to sell their loot in Wickenburg, so Waltz may have run a "gold-laundering" operation by caching the Vulture gold in the Superstitions. If so, he still has a lot of people fooled about his "mine" even after 100 years!

**Mile 0.0: AZ 88** in Apache Junction.

**Mile 2.0: O.K. Corral Stables,** 2 miles left on Tomahawk Road at the sign. The stables offer a variety of guided and unguided horseback rides in the Superstition and Goldfield mountains; "legendary hayrides" and overnight pack trips can be arranged too; tel. 982-4040.

**Mile 3.5: Goldfield Ghost Town & Mine Tours.** Learn how miners did their work and see the equipment they used on tours within a recreated underground mine. Open Sat. and Sun. 10 a.m.-6 p.m.; $3 adult, $1.50 children 6-12; tel. 983-0333.

**Mile 4.2: Mining Camp Restaurant** on right has Western fare in a replica of an old mining camp's cook shanty. Open daily except Mon. for dinner; tel. 982-3181.

**Mile 4.8: Site of Goldfield** on the left. Goldfield boomed in the 1890s with the discovery of gold but became a ghost town when mining yields dwindled in 1915. People still mine gold in this area at times, and you'll see prominent "No Trespassing" signs when they do.

**Mile 5.4: Lost Dutchman State Park** on the right offers picnicking, day hiking, and camping at the base of the Superstition Mountains. A quarter-mile native plant trail near the park entrance identifies desert flora; the path is paved and handicapped-accessible. Longer trails loop into the adjacent Superstition Wilderness with fine views. Staff lead campfire programs and guided hikes from Oct. to April—the best time to visit. Entry costs $3/vehicle for day use or $5/vehicle for camping (water, but no hookups or showers); tel. 982-4485.

**Mile 5.7: First Water Trailhead** on right. Three bumpy miles takes you to this popular trailhead for hikes in the Superstition Wilderness. Many people camp along this road (no facilities) in the cooler months.

**Mile 7.3: Needle Vista Viewpoint** on right. Weaver's Needle, the striking high pinnacle rising among the Superstitions, has often figured in lost gold mine legends. The name honors frontier scout Pauline Weaver (a man). Local Indians had a different name—referring to a certain part of a stallion's anatomy! Climb a nearby hill for a better view.

**Mile 12.4:** Overlook on right for **Canyon Lake,** 950 surface acres. The series of lakes along the Salt River provides fishing and boating for visitors and precious water for Phoenix. Canyon Lake was created by Mormon Flat Dam, completed in 1925. Past the viewpoint, the road sweeps down from the heights to the lakeshore.

**Mile 14.5: Acacia Picnic Site** on left (swimming and fishing).

**Mile 14.8: Palo Verde Boating Site** on left (boat launch); **Boulder Picnic Site** on right (swimming and fishing).

**Mile 15.2: Canyon Lake Marina** on left; **Boulder Canyon Trailhead** on right. Facilities at the marina include boat rental and storage, fishing supplies, a snack bar, picnicking, and a campground; tel. 986-5546. Another camping area, **The Point,** can be reached only by boaters; it's on the left, 3 miles upstream from the marina. "Dolly's Steamboat" takes visitors on a scenic 90-minute narrated cruise and a 2-hour dinner cruise; tel. 827-9144 for times. Fishermen have hooked largemouth and yellow bass, trout, catfish, bluegill, carp, walleye, and crappie. During the busy mid-spring to midsummer season, Sunday crowds often fill all available parking places in the Canyon Lake area; try to arrive early.

Boulder Canyon Trail #103 begins across the highway, climbing up the ridge with spectacular views into the Superstitions and back over the Canyon Lake area. The trail continues on through La Barge and Boulder canyons, linking with several other trails in the Superstition Wilderness.

**Mile 15.6: Laguna Boating Site** on left.

**Mile 17.3: Tortilla Campground** on left; **Tortilla Flat** (cafe, hotel, curio shop) on right. The campground is open Nov. to April; water supply is questionable for drinking—it's better to bring your own; $6/night. Tortilla Flat, "pop. 6," the only town along this section of road, looks like it came straight from a movie set. The tiny community has been a popular traveler's stop ever since the road went through. A hungry pioneer, who saw the surrounding flat boulders as stacks of tortillas, gave the place its name, according to one story. The cafe serves inexpensive American and Mexican meals. Souvenirs and even a few hotel rooms are available; Box 34, Tortilla Flat, AZ 85290 (no telephone). Lots of old mining and farming relics lie around; look to see if the dummy "outlaw" is still strung up, swinging in the breeze.

**Mile 22.9:** Pavement ends. The next 22 miles to Roosevelt Dam is graded dirt road.

**Mile 24.0: Tortilla Trailhead** for the Superstition Wilderness is on the right.

**Mile 24.4:** Beginning of descent down **Fish Creek Hill** with spectacular views of the canyon below. Fish Creek Hill is the Apache Trail's most exciting part, especially for the driver, who must negotiate sharp bends as the road traverses a cliff face and drops 1,500 feet in 3 miles. Fish Creek, near the bottom, occasionally has a trickle of water but no fish. Hikers can head up Fish Creek Canyon.

**Mile 30.1:** Forest Route 212 on right to **Reavis Trailhead,** 3 bumpy miles. **Reavis Ranch Trail #109** crosses the eastern part of the Superstition Wilderness. Elisha Reavis lived a hermit's life on his ranch from 1872 until he died in 1896.

**Mile 30.2: Apache Lake Vista,** from which the lake can be seen in the canyon below. Held back by Horse Mesa Dam, Apache Lake with its 2,600 surface acres reaches nearly to Roosevelt Lake—a distance of 17 miles.

**Mile 32.1:** Turnoff on the left for **Apache Lake Recreation Area. Apache Lake Marina and Resort** has a boat ramp, fishing and ski boat rentals, boat storage, fishing and camping supplies, restaurant, tent area ($2 primitive camping), RV campground ($9.45 w/hookups and showers), and a motel w/kitchenettes ($29.68-57.24); Box 23, Tortilla Flat, AZ 85290; tel. 467-2511. Fishermen can catch smallmouth and largemouth bass, yellow bass, crappie, catfish, sunfish, and walleye. Officers man the **Maricopa County Sheriff Aid Station** at the lake on weekends and holidays; tel. 467-2619.

**Mile 39.0: Burnt Corral Campground** and boat ramp on left; the Forest Service has plans to add water and new roads to the campground in 1990-91.

**Mile 44.3: Theodore Roosevelt Dam** and end of the dirt road section. Workers built the dam with stone blocks between 1905 and 1911. An engineering feat of its day, the 280-foot-high structure is still the world's highest masonry dam. President Teddy Roosevelt motored over the Apache Trail in 1911 to dedicate the dam later named after him. Engineers have been worried that the original dam couldn't survive a moderate earthquake or a 200-year flood, so in 1990-94 a new concrete dam will be built over the old structure.

## ROOSEVELT LAKE

Roosevelt Lake, fed by Tonto Creek from the north and the Salt River from the east, stretches 23 miles and is as much as 2 miles wide. With approximately 17,335 surface acres, it's the largest of the four Salt River lakes. Summers at Roosevelt's 2,100-foot elevation are only slightly cooler than the Valley's, but water-skiing and boating attract many visitors. Fishermen enjoy the rest of the year, when it's not so hot. Known as a good bass and crappie lake, Roosevelt also contains catfish and sunfish. A flock of Great Basin Canada geese take up residence during the winter at Bermuda Flat on the north arm. Part of this area is closed to the public from Nov. 15 to Feb. 15, but you can view the geese from the highway. Bald eagles use the

*Theodore Roosevelt Dam (before new construction)*

middle third of the northern shore for nesting and foraging; no camping allowed here.

## Accommodations And Food

The Forest Service has many recreation sites both north and south of the dam. Visitors can use the camping areas (most are primitive with just outhouses), four paved boat ramps (one is for high water only), and one RV sewage-disposal site. **Cholla Campground** has developed sites with water and showers about 7 miles north of the dam. Boaters can use primitive sites in designated areas around the lake. **Roosevelt Marina,** 2 miles southeast of the dam, has a motel ($31.65-47.48), primitive campground (free), boat rentals (fishing and pontoon), wet and dry boat storage, a paved boat ramp, a snack bar, gasoline for boats and autos, and a store; tel. 467-2245. **Lakeview Trailer Park,** across the highway, has spaces with hookups ($12.50; no tents); tel. 467-2203. **Roosevelt Lake Resort** offers a motel ($32 s, $34 d), trailer park ($10 RV w/hookups), restaurant, boat storage, and service station 12 miles southeast of the dam (20 miles northwest of Globe), then east 0.6 mile; tel. 467-2276. **Spring Creek Store** and **Roosevelt Post Office** are 0.6 mile northwest of the resort turnoff; the store has groceries, camping and fishing supplies, and gasoline. **Rockhouse Store,** 6 miles north on the Young Highway (AZ 288), has groceries, gasoline, and a trailer park; tel. 467-2484. **Punkin Center,** a village 22 miles north of Roosevelt on AZ 188, has Punkin Center Lodge ($35.87 d, $47.48 d kitchenettes; tel. 479-2233/2229), Steak House (open daily except Mon. for lunch and dinner; live entertainment on weekends; tel. 479-2234), RV park ($10 w/hookups; tel. 479-2221), and store. Other RV parks are nearby.

## Information

Foresters at the **Roosevelt Ranger Station** will tell you about camping, fishing, hiking, and boating in the area; open Mon.-Fri. (and sometimes weekends in summer) 7:45-11:45 a.m. and 12:30-4:30 p.m.; Box 649, Roosevelt, AZ 85545; tel. 467-2236. The office is near the Roosevelt Lake Marina on AZ 88.

## TONTO NATIONAL MONUMENT

Two well-preserved cliff dwellings of the prehistoric Salado Indians overlook the blue waters of Roosevelt Lake. The Salado (Spanish for "salt") lived in this part of the Salt River Valley about A.D. 1150-1450. Skillful farmers, they dug irrigation canals to water their corn, squash, beans, grain amaranth, and cotton. They also roamed the desert hills for cactus fruits, mesquite beans, deer, pronghorn, and many other wild foods. Crafts included beautiful polychrome pottery and intricately woven cotton cloth. At first they built small, scattered pueblos along the river, but in about 1250 some of the Salado began living on more defensible ridgetops. Finally, from 1300 until their mysterious departure soon after 1400, part of the population moved into caves like those in the monument.

## Visitor Center And Ruins

Exhibits show how the Salado lived and what we know of their history. Stone tools, pottery, cotton cloth, and other artifacts demonstrate their artistry. A self-guided trail behind the Visitor Center climbs the hillside to the Lower Ruin, which you can enter. Originally the cave had 19 rooms, with another 12 in the annex outside, but the elements have worn away the exposed ones. Allow one hour for the trip; you'll be climbing 350 feet on a well-graded path. The Upper Ruin, reached by a different trail, is about twice the size of the Lower, but it's farther away and a visit takes advance planning—you must call or write at least 2 days ahead. Ranger-guided tours for the Upper Ruin leave at 10 a.m. (allow 3 hours for the 3-mile roundtrip hike); there's no extra charge. A nature trail near the Visitor Center identifies many desert plants. The monument is open daily 8 a.m.-5 p.m. (extended in summer), but the Lower Ruin Trail closes one hour earlier; Box 707, Roosevelt, AZ 85545; tel. 467-2241. The Visitor Center is one mile off AZ 88, 2 miles southeast of Roosevelt and 28 miles northwest of Globe; $3/vehicle admission. If you're driving the Apache Trail Loop, this is the halfway point in time; Apache

*Lower Ruin at
Tonto National
Monument*

Junction is 3 hours away by either the 80-mile Apache Trail or the 120-mile route via Globe.

## SALT RIVER CANYON WILDERNESS

About 60 miles of lively whitewater lies upstream on the Salt River from Roosevelt Lake. Boaters typically take 4 days to raft or kayak through the twisting canyons. Only experienced river runners should attempt this wild river, as several rapids can go to Class IV at certain water flows and one rapid, Quartzite Falls, is often unrunnable (can be portaged). Don't use large rafts (over 15 feet) or open canoes. The Forest Service requires that visitors keep group sizes to no more than 15, use suitable nonmotorized craft, observe safety precautions, and practice "no trace" camping. (The wilderness section extends between Gleason Flat and the mouth of Pinal Creek.) Trips beginning on the White Mountain Apache Indian Reservation need a tribal permit; see pages 364 and 366. The Forest Service has a detailed booklet on the Upper Salt River, available at the Globe (tel. 425-7189) and Phoenix (tel. 225-5200) offices.

Another option is to take a guided trip with one of several tour companies. Commercial trips on the Upper Salt are offered by **World Wide Explorations** (Box 686, Flagstaff, AZ 86002; tel. 774-6462); **Desert Voyagers** (Box 9053, Scottsdale, AZ 85252; tel. 998-RAFT); and **Far Flown Adventures** (Box 31, Terlingua, TX 79852; tel. 915-371-2489). **Salt River Canyon Raft Trips** (2242 W. Main St., Mesa, AZ 85201; tel. 968-1552 or 800-334-RAFT out of state) runs shorter trips above the wilderness boundary.

## GLOBE

Globe, tucked into a narrow valley between the Apache Mountains to the northeast and the Pinal Mountains to the south and west, is a handy stopping place for travelers. The town's 3,500-foot elevation gives it a pleasant climate most of the year. Though its years of glory as a big copper-mining center have passed, Globe still has a lot of character. On a drive down Broad St. you can visit the museum, see ruins of the Old Dominion Copper Mine, and look at the many buildings dating from the early 1900s. The chamber of commerce, also on Broad St., has a *Historic Globe/Miami Downtown Walking Tour* leaflet that gives you the history of these old structures. You can also pick up a *Drive Yourself Mine Tour* leaflet that describes six mines, historic and modern, visible from US 60 in the Globe and Miami areas; none of the mine sites are open to the public.

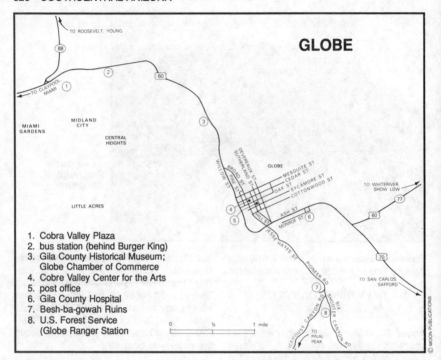

**GLOBE**

1. Cobra Valley Plaza
2. bus station (behind Burger King)
3. Gila County Historical Museum;
   Globe Chamber of Commerce
4. Cobre Valley Center for the Arts
5. post office
6. Gila County Hospital
7. Besh-ba-gowah Ruins
8. U.S. Forest Service
   (Globe Ranger Station

0      ½      1 mile

© MOON PUBLICATIONS

## History

In 1875, prospectors struck silver when they were scouring the hills of the western part of San Carlos Apache Indian Reservation. Their most remarkable find, a globe-shaped silver nugget, was said to have rough outlines of the continents scarred on its surface. Miners converged on the area, setting up camp on the east bank of Pinal Creek. The problem of this being Indian land was soon resolved by officially slicing it off the reservation. That didn't go over well with the Apache, who menaced the camp until Geronimo's surrender in 1886. Silver began to give out after only 4 years, but by then rich copper deposits had been discovered under the silver lodes. The Old Dominion Copper Company moved in and during the early 1900s grew to be one of the greatest copper mines in the world. Globe prospered too—its 50 restaurants and saloons never closed, and about 150 "working women" lived in neat little shacks along N.

Broad Street. George W.P. Hunt arrived in 1881 as a young man, and he worked his way up to become a leading merchant and banker of Globe before going on to serve as Arizona's first governor. Labor troubles and declining yields began to eat into mining profits, and the Depression shut down the Old Dominion completely in 1931. Copper mining shifted to nearby Miami, leaving Globe to doze on as a quiet county seat.

## SIGHTS

### Gila County Historical Museum

This small but varied collection represents the Indian, pioneer, and mining heritages of the area. Prehistoric Indian artifacts came from Besh-ba-gowah Pueblo right in town and from other sites near Globe. Displays also show crafts of present-day Indians. Period rooms—kitchen, bedroom, doctor's office, and mine superintendent's office—recreate pioneer days. Ore cars and large machinery sit outside. Open Mon.-Sat. 10 a.m.-4 p.m.; donation; tel. 425-7385. Located opposite the Old Dominion Copper Co. Mine at 1330 N. Broad Street. The museum building, which dates from 1914, served as the company's mine rescue station for many years.

### Cobre Valley Center For The Arts

Local artists have banded together and opened an art gallery in the old Gila County Courthouse, built 1906-07. Doing much of the restoration themselves, the artists have also added a theater used by the Community Players. You can see the art exhibits Mon.-Sat. 10 a.m.-4 p.m. and Sun. 1-4 p.m.; free. Located downtown at the corner of Broad and Oak sts.; tel. 425-0884.

### Besh-ba-gowah

Salado Indian villages lined both sides of Pinal Creek about 600 years ago. Besh-ba-gowah, exposed to the elements and man, is in poorer condition than the Tonto National Monument cliff dwellings, but its extensive foundations and few remaining walls testify to its original size. Archaeologists count 200 rooms at Besh-ba-gowah, built and inhabited between 1225 and 1450. An earlier village of houses in pits associated with the Hohokam sat on this site about 600-1150. The name comes from an Apache word meaning "metal camp." A self-guided trail winds through the ruins, some of which have been restored, some only stabilized, and some yet unexcavated. The restored rooms have baskets, pots, ladders, and other implements just as if the Salado were still living here. Archaeologists can often be seen working at the site. Pottery and other artifacts and exhibits of village life, trade, and archaeology can be seen in the adjacent museum. The ethno-botanical garden contains native and cultivated plants used by prehistoric Indians. Museum and ruins are open daily 9 a.m.-5 p.m. (except closed some holidays); $1 age 12 and up; tel. 425-0320. Besh-ba-gowah is 1.5 miles south of downtown Globe; follow S. Broad St. to its end, turn right across the bridge, curve left on Jesse Hayes St./Pioneer Road one mile, make a sharp right to "Globe Community Center," and follow signs around to the far side of the ruin. The surrounding park offers picnic tables and ballfields.

### Pinal Peak

A dirt road winds up the timber-clad slopes to the summit, elev. 7,812 feet. Weather permitting, you'll enjoy great views, hiking, picnicking, and two of the coolest campgrounds in the Tonto National Forest. For the 18-mile drive from Globe, follow S. Broad St. to its end, turn right across the bridge, curve left on Jesse Hayes St./Pioneer Road to the junction of Ice House Canyon and Six Shooter Canyon roads, turn right 2.5 miles on Ice House Canyon Road, turn right 3 miles on Forest Route 55 (pavement ends), then left 12.5 miles on Forest Route 651 to the summit.

## PRACTICALITIES

### Accommodations

You'll find Globe's motels either downtown on Broad St. or along US 60 (Willow and Ash sts.), which bypasses downtown. Coming in from the north or west, you'll pass **Best Western Copper Hills Inn** (US 60 between Miami and Globe; tel. 425-7151 or 800-528-1234); **Motel Villa** (US 60 and Manor Dr.; tel. 425-4425); **Willow Motel** (792 N. Willow St.; tel. 425-4573); **Belle-Aire Motel** (1600 N. Broad St.; tel. 425-4406); **Ember Motel** (1105 N. Broad St.; tel. 425-5736); **Apacheland Motel** (351 E. Ash St.; tel. 425-6608); **Copper Manor Motel** (637 E. Ash St.; tel 425-7124); **El Rey Motel** (1201 E. Ash St.; tel 425-4427); **El Rancho Motel** (1302 E. Ash St.; tel. 425-5757) and **Cloud Nine Motel** (1699 E. Ash St.; tel. 425-5741 or 800-432-6655).

### Campgrounds

RV's have overnight parking with hookups at **Casa de Monti** (east of Globe near the junction of US 60 and US 70; tel. 425-6574); **Alhambra Mobile Home Park** (109 Monterey Dr.; tel. 425-5192); and **Apache Trail Mobile Park** (6 miles north on AZ 88; tel.

425-1924). Tent campers and small RVs can head south into the Pinal Mountains. The Forest Service has free campgrounds open April to Dec. at **Pinal and Upper Pinal** (elev. 7,500 feet; water from May to Oct.; 18 miles south on Forest Route 651) and **Pioneer Pass** (elev. 6,000 feet; water from May to Oct.; 8 miles south on Forest Route 112; the upper site has horse facilities). **Jones Water Campground** (elev. 4,300 feet) offers sites in cottonwoods 15 miles north of town on US 60; no water or fee. See the Tonto Forest map or contact the Globe Ranger Station in Globe for camping information; tel. 425-7189.

### Food
Globe has some neat little cafes downtown. **Globe Cafe** serves American food daily at 396 N. Broad; tel. 425-0351. **El Rey Cafe** (999 N. Broad St.; tel. 425-6601) and **La Casita** (470 N. Broad St.; tel. 425-5029) serve Mexican food. **La Luz del Dia** is a Mexican bakery and coffee shop at 304 N. Broad St.; tel. 425-9875. **Peg's Kitchen** dishes up Mexican and American food at 247 S. Broad St.; tel. 425-4707. For steaks try the **Crestline Steak House**, about one mile east on US 60; tel. 425-6269. More restaurants, including the fast-food chains, are located on the outskirts at both ends of Globe on US 60.

### Entertainment And Events
**Globe Theatre** screens current movies at 141 N. Broad St.; tel. 425-5581. Some of Globe area's major events are the **Gila County Gem & Mineral Show** in Jan. or Feb.; **Historic Home/Building Tour & Antique Show** in Feb.; **Copper Dust Stampede Rodeo, Dance, and Parade** in April; **Spring Roundup Rodeo** (19 miles east in Peridot) in April; **Mining Country Boomtown Spree (arts and crafts fair in Miami)** in April; **Old Time Fiddlers Contest** in August; **Globe-Miami Latinos Fiesta & Parade** (Mexican Independence Day) in Sept.; **Gila County Fair** in Sept.; **horse races** in Oct.; **Apache Days** (dances, crafts, and food by

Apache and other Indian groups) in Oct.; and **Veterans Parade, Rodeo, and Pageant** (19 miles east in San Carlos) on Veterans Day weekend in November.

### Services
The main **post office** is downtown at Sycamore and Hill streets. **Gila County Hospital** is in eastern Globe at 1100 Monroe St.; tel. 425-5721. **Globe Community Center** has a swimming pool, picnic areas, and ball fields 1.5 miles south of downtown Globe; follow S. Broad St. to its end, turn right across the bridge, curve left on Jesse Hayes St./Pioneer Road one mile, then make a sharp right at the sign. **Cobre Valle Country Club** is open to the public with a 9-hole golf course and tennis and racquetball courts; located just north on AZ 88 between Globe and Miami; tel. 473-2542.

### Information
The **Globe-Miami Chamber of Commerce** is very helpful; open Mon.-Fri. 8 a.m.-5 p.m. (also open Oct.-April on Sat. 9 a.m.-5 p.m. and Sun. noon-5 p.m.); located next to the Gila County Historical Museum on N. Broad St.; Box 2539, Globe, AZ 85502; tel. 425-4495 or (800) 448-8983. The **Globe Ranger Station** of the U.S. Forest Service has maps and literature for the hiking trails (which tend to be steep) and camping of the area; the office is on Six-Shooter Canyon Road, 2 miles southeast of downtown; open Mon.-Fri. 7:45-11:45 a.m. and 12:30-4:30 p.m.; Rt. 1, Box 33, Globe, AZ 85501; tel. 425-7189. The **Globe Public Library** is at 339 S. Broad St.; tel. 425-6111. **Alicia's House of Po'pourri** has regional books, used paperbacks, and art supplies at 745 Broad St.; tel. 425-3944.

### Transport
**Greyhound Bus** stops at the station behind Burger King, on US 60 about 2 miles northwest of downtown. Greyhound has several westbound and eastbound departures daily; tel. 425-2301.

*Weaver's Needle from Fremont Saddle in the Superstitions*

## THE APACHE TRAIL: GLOBE TO APACHE JUNCTION

### Miami And Claypool

The strangeness of the manmade landscape is striking as you approach these two towns west of Globe. Many-tiered terraces of barren, buff-colored mine tailings from the crushers and dark slag dumps from the furnaces dominate the view. Miami and Claypool stretch along Bloody Tanks Wash, named for a massacre of Apache in 1864 by a band of whites and allied Maricopa Indians. Developers arrived in 1907 to lay out a townsite, calling it after the town of Miami, Ohio. Giant copper-ore reduction plants built by the Miami Copper and Inspiration Companies earned the title "Concentrator City" for the new town. Miami has had its ups and downs since, depending on copper prices. Currently prices are down, as you might guess from the appearance of downtown, but copper production continues. Miami has half a dozen historic buildings, described in a walking-tour leaflet available from Globe Chamber of Commerce, the **Copper City Motel** (tel. 473-2771), and several restaurants.

### Miami To Superior

Highway 60 climbs over the rugged Pinal Mountains with many fine views between these two towns. Six miles west of Miami you'll see the vast workings of the open-pit Pinto Valley copper mine. The road continues to climb to a pass, then descends into Devils Canyon. **Devils Canyon Picnic Site** is a pretty spot for lunch or overnight camping; turn 0.2 mile north from just west of Devils Canyon bridge, between Mileposts 232 and 233 (may not be signed). **Oak Flat Campground** (elev. 4,200 feet) lies in more open country nearby; turn 0.5 mile south on Magma Mine Road at the sign near Milepost 231 (4 miles east of Superior and 13 miles west of Miami). Both areas stay open all year; no water or fee. West of Oak Flat, the highway drops through steep-walled Queen Creek Canyon to Superior.

### Superior

Opening of the rich Silver King Mine in 1875, followed by development of the Silver Queen, brought streams of fortune hunters into this mineral-laden region. As in Globe, miners found rich deposits of copper when the surface silver began to play out. Superior lies just west of scenic Queen Creek Canyon in a valley surrounded by the rugged Pinal Mountains. North of town you'll see the high smokestack of a smelter (no longer in operation), machinery, and extensive tailings of the Magma Copper Mine, whose shafts plunge nearly 5,000 feet underground. Rockhounds may be able to collect "Apache tears" (a form of volcanic glass) for a fee at a site west of town; signs will indicate the turnoff and if the area is open.

El Portal Motel (tel. 689-2886) and several restaurants are in town. **Apache Tear Village RV Park and Motel** offers sites with showers for tents ($8) and RVs ($10 no hookups, $12.50 w/hookups) and motel cabins ($26.90 d) in a quieter spot just west of town; tel. 689-5800. **Apache Mobile Park** has RV sites and showers next door; $8; tel. 689-5331.

### Picket Post House

Copper-mining magnate William Boyce Thompson founded the Southwestern Arboretum in 1927 for botanical research and teaching. His 26-room mansion, Picket Post House, overlooks the grounds and can be visited on tours Mon.-Sat. 10 a.m.-5 p.m.; $3 (entry is separate from the Arboretum); tel. 689-5610. Entrance is 0.7 mile east of the Arboretum entrance.

### Boyce Thompson
### Southwestern Arboretum

You can see more than 1,500 different desert plants here. Short trails lead through yuccas and agaves, a cactus garden, native desert vegetation, riparian (stream bank) natives, exotic plants, palms, pines, and eucalyptus. More than 174 bird and 72 animal species have been spotted. Greenhouses contain cactus and succulents that wouldn't otherwise survive winter cold. Elevations range from 2,400 feet at the gardens to 4,400 feet atop nearby Picket Post Mountain. A heliograph station, which used mirrors to flash sun's rays, operated atop the peak during the Apache wars. The Visitor Center has some exhibits and a gift shop offering books, prints, posters, and seed packets. There's a large selection of cactus, other succulents, trees, shrubs, ground cover, and herbs for sale. The cooling tower exhibit at the Visitor Center creates a cool microclimate; its 30-foot tower is actually a giant evaporative cooler. Scheduled events include an Arid Land Plant Show on the first weekend in April and a Fall Landscaping Festival. A picnic area near the parking lot can be used by visitors. Today both the

University of Arizona and the State Parks Board have a part in running the Arboretum. Open daily (except Christmas) 8 a.m.-5 p.m.; $3 adult, $1.50 children 5-12; tel. 689-2811. The Arboretum, just off US 60, is located 3 miles west of Superior, 60 miles southeast of Phoenix, and 98 miles north of Tucson.

## FLORENCE JUNCTION TO APACHE JUNCTION

### Florence Junction

Not a town at all—just a junction. If you're interested in turquoise, drop into the **Hardy Turquoise** store just east of the junction; tel. 463-2371. The town of Florence, which has the excellent Pinal County Historical Museum, is 16 miles south on US 89 (see below).

### Peralta Trailhead

One of the most popular trailheads for the Superstition Wilderness is off US 60/89 about 9 miles northwest of Florence Junction (8 miles southeast of Apache Junction). Follow the graded, dirt Forest Route 77 in for 7 miles. You'll also see the Dons Camp on the left just before the trailhead. The **Dons Club,** an organization devoted to teaching the legends and beauty of the Southwest, hosts a big one-day event here, usually in March, when thousands of people descend on the Superstitions for hikes, demonstrations, and entertainment; tel. 258-6016.

There's good hiking here—three trails branch off into the wilderness. One of these, **Peralta Trail #102,** goes up Peralta Canyon to Fremont Saddle, where you get a great view of Weaver's Needle and beyond. (If you believe the stories about the Lost Dutchman's Gold Mine, you know that it lies in the shadow of Weaver's Needle.) It's 4 miles roundtrip and a 1,400-foot climb to the pass; carry water and avoid the heat of a summer day. Peralta Trail continues down the other side past the base of Weaver's Needle and connects with other trails in the Superstitions.

# SOUTH OF PHOENIX

On the drive between Phoenix and Tucson you'll be crossing desert plains with views of the Superstitions, Picacho Peak, Santa Catalina Mountains, and other rugged ranges. Desert flora along the roadside bloom in blazes of bright colors in spring. Several places are worth stopping for, whether you take the old Pinal Pioneer Parkway (US 89) or the speedier I-10.

## FLORENCE

Florence, one of the oldest white settlements in Arizona, dates back to the arrival of Levi Ruggles in 1866. Ruggles noted a safe fording place on the Gila River nearby and thought the valley suitable for farming. He laid out a townsite that soon became a trade center and stage stop for surrounding Army camps. Some people advocated Florence as the Arizona territorial capital, but the town had to settle for becoming the Pinal County seat. The first county courthouse went up in 1878, constructed of adobe blocks like most buildings of the time. It survives as McFarland State Historical Park. The second county courthouse was completed in 1891; its ornate cupola stands out as Florence's chief landmark. Not everybody comes to Florence by choice—the Arizona State Prison sits just outside town. Convicts completed the prison in 1909 to replace the territorial prison at Yuma. Inmates now make up nearly half of the town's 6,800 inhabitants! Florence has two museums and a number of historic buildings; you can pick up a visitor's guide at the tourist office or the Pinal County Historical Museum.

### Pinal County Historical Museum

You'll see a lot of history in this diverse collection. Indian pottery, baskets, and stone tools come from prehistoric and modern tribes of the area. An 1880 horse-drawn opera coach shows that the early pioneers did enjoy a bit of elegance. Also displayed are early settlers' tools, mining gear, household items, and clothing. News clippings describe the tragic death of silent-screen hero Tom Mix in a car accident nearby. Bullet aficionados will be thrilled to see hundreds of different types in a big display. The prison exhibits are sobering: hangman's nooses (the actual ones used) framing photos of their victims, a hanging board, gas-chamber chair, massive prison registers from Yuma and Florence, and the story of murderess Eva Dugan—hung (and at the same time accidentally decapitated) in 1930. The museum is open Wed.-Sun. 1-5 p.m. (closed July 15 to Aug. 31); donation; 715 S. Main St.; tel. 868-4382.

### McFarland Historical State Park

This adobe building served as Pinal County's first courthouse, sheriff's office, and jail from 1878 to 1891, then functioned for 50 years as the county hospital. In 1883 an angry mob took two murder suspects from the jail and strung them up in a corridor. Exhibits illustrate the history of Florence and the courthouse and its roles. You'll also learn about Ernest McFarland (1894-1984), who started his political career as Pinal county attorney in 1925, then rose to serve as a U.S. senator, Arizona governor, and chief justice of the State Supreme Court. Open Thurs.-Mon. 8 a.m.-5 p.m.; $1 (age 17 and under free with adult); tel. 868-5216; located near the north end of Main St. at Ruggles Street.

### Tom Mix Monument

October 12, 1940, was a sad day for fans of movie hero Tom Mix. Speeding north from Tucson in his big Cord, he lost control and rolled over in a ditch, now called Tom Mix Wash. A roadside monument, topped by a riderless horse, marks the spot, 17 miles south of Florence on US 89.

### Poston's Butte

Charles Poston explored and mined in what's now Arizona from 1853 to 1861, but his greatest achievement was successfully lobbying in Washington, D.C., for a territorial government. He went on to become the first superintendent of Indian affairs in Arizona and one of the first Arizona delegates to Congress. His congressional term finished, he traveled to India and became a "fire worshiper." Upon returning to Arizona in 1878, he built a continuous fire as a temple of the sun atop this hill, naming it "Parsee Hill." The flames died out several months later, ending a project that others called "Poston's Folly." He lies buried on the hill, renamed Poston's Butte, northwest from Florence across the Gila River.

### Practicalities

Stay at **Blue Mist Motel,** junction of US 89 and AZ 287; tel. 868-5875. RVs can park at **Chase's Shady Rest Trailer Villa** (850 S.

Main St.; tel. 868-4341) and **Caliente Casa de Sol** (4 miles north on US 89; tel. 868-5520). You'll find several restaurants on Main Street. For more information about the Florence area, go to the **Pinal County Visitor Center** at 912 Pinal St. (on Eighth St. 2 blocks east of Main); open Mon.-Fri. 9 a.m.-5 p.m. (10 a.m.-2 p.m. in summer); Box 967, Florence, AZ 85232; tel. 868-4331.

### CASA GRANDE RUINS NATIONAL MONUMENT

A short turn-off from AZ 87 just north of Coolidge leads to Arizona's biggest and most perplexing prehistoric building. The rectangular structure stands four stories high and contains 11 rooms above an earthen plat-

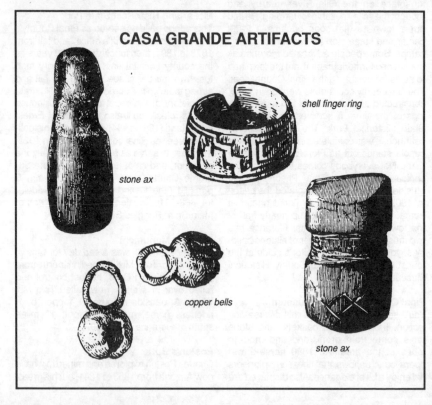

## CASA GRANDE ARTIFACTS

*stone ax*

*shell finger ring*

*copper bells*

*stone ax*

form. An estimated 2,800 tons of mud went into the project, whose walls range in thickness from 4.5 feet at the base to 1.8 feet near the top. Archaeologists don't know the purpose of Casa Grande, but some speculate that it was used for ceremonies or astronomical observations; certain holes in the walls appear to line up with the sun at the summer solstice and possibly with the moon during certain lunar events. Smaller structures and a wall, remnants of which still stand, surround the main building. Hohokam Indians, who had been farming the Gila Valley since about 200-300 B.C., built Casa Grande around A.D. 1350. It has little resemblance to other Hohokam pueblos; Mexican cultures may have influenced its construction. By about 1450, after just a few generations of use, the Hohokam abandoned it along with all their other villages. The Jesuit priest Eusebio Kino recorded the site in 1694, giving it the Spanish name for "big house."

### Visitor Center

Exhibits introduce you to the Hohokam—their irrigation canals, farming tools, jewelry, ball courts, and Mexican connections. Conjectures are raised as to the disappearance of the Hohokam culture. You can take a ranger-led tour of Casa Grande or the self-guided trail. Signs also identify cactus and other desert plants. Books on Arizona's Indians, settlers, and natural history are sold; open daily 7 a.m.-6 p.m.; $3/vehicle. The monument is located one mile north of Coolidge off AZ 87; these ruins shouldn't be confused with the modern town of Casa Grande, which is about 20 miles away.

## GILA RIVER ARTS AND CRAFTS CENTER

To learn about the Pima and Maricopa Indians, or just to take a break from freeway driving, stop at this cultural center on the Gila River Reservation. Museum exhibits display artifacts and interpret the history and of these two tribes. Crafts in the gift shop include pottery of Maricopa and New Mexican tribes,

Papago baskets, Hopi kachina dolls, and Navajo rugs. Jewelry, paintings, and prints come from many tribes. An inexpensive restaurant offers Indian fry bread and American foods. Outside, the Heritage Park contains traditional structures of the Hohokam, Pima, Maricopa, Papago, and Apache tribes; a booklet available at the gift shop describes the culture of each group. Gila River Arts and Crafts Center is open daily except some holidays 9 a.m.-5 p.m.; free admission; tel. 963-3981. Take I-10 Exit 175, 30 miles southeast of Phoenix (90 miles northwest of Tucson), and go west 0.5 mile on Casa Blanca Road.

**Casa Blanca RV Park,** next door to the cultural center, has sites year-round; $5.50 no hookups, $12.50 w/hookups; tel. 562-3205.

## PICACHO PEAK STATE PARK

Picacho Peak has been a landmark for Indians, Spanish explorers, American frontiersmen, and modern-day motorists. Park visitors can enjoy hiking, camping, and picnicking in this scenic area. Saguaro and other plants of the Sonoran Desert thrive on the rock hillsides. Monuments near the flagpole commemorate the Battle of Picacho Pass and the earlier building of the road by the Mormon Battalion.

The Battle of Picacho Pass, on April 15, 1862, was the westernmost conflict of the Civil War and the only one to take place in Arizona. Confederate forces killed Lt. James Barrett, leader of the Union detachment, and two privates, while losing two men themselves. Aware that Union reinforcements would soon arrive, the Confederates then retreated back down the Butterfield Road to Tucson. The battle site is thought to be just outside the state park boundary, toward the freeway.

### Practicalities

The park has several picnic areas and a campground with showers and hookups; $3/vehicle day use, $5 overnight parking, $6 tent camping, or $8 w/hookups; tel. 466-3183. Rangers often give programs at the amphitheater on Fri. and Sat. evenings from Nov. to April. Take I-10 Exit 219 (74 miles southeast of Phoenix and 46 miles northwest of Tucson) and follow signs in 0.5 mile.

### Hiking Trails

Inside the park, you can hike to the top of 3,374-foot Picacho Peak, a remnant of ancient lava flows, or try easier trails. **Hunter Trail** climbs 1,400 feet to the summit, a 4-mile roundtrip taking 4-5 hours. Be careful on the back side where the trail crosses some loose rock; posts and cables provide handholds in the rougher spots. An easier hike, also with expansive views, follows the Hunter Trail as far as the saddle, a 2-mile roundtrip hike taking 1½ hours. Easier still is the **Calloway Trail** to a low pass between Bugler's and Picacho peaks, 1.5 miles roundtrip, taking an hour. Both trails begin from the large parking area near Saguaro Ramada on the Barrett Loop Drive. Rangers have trail maps; bring water and sun protection. A **nature trail** loop introduces desert plants; you can begin across the road from the park office or from the campground; allow 30 minutes.

*petroglyphs at Painted Rocks State Park*

## GILA BEND

The town (pop. 2,000) sits near the Gila River 68 miles southwest of Phoenix. Father Kino, who came through in 1699, found a prosperous Maricopa Indian village here whose irrigated fields yielded two harvests annually. The Butterfield stagecoaches first rolled through in the early 1850s and a settlement later grew around one of their stations. Today the small town serves as an agricultural center and a travelers' stop. Surrounding farms raise cotton, wheat, barley, and other crops. San Lucy, a Tohono O'odham (Papago) Indian village, lies just north of town. On Business Loop I-8 you'll find seven motels, three RV parks, and a variety of restaurants. The **Tourist Center** has a small museum and information about the community and surrounding area; open Mon.-Fri. 8 a.m.-4:30 p.m. (also Sat. and Sun. 8 a.m.-4:30 p.m. in the cooler months); 644 W. Pima St. (Business Loop I-8) or write P.O. Drawer CC, Gila Bend, AZ 85337.

### Vicinity Of Gila Bend

Heading south on AZ 85 to Ajo and Organ Pipe Cactus National Monument, you'll pass through a small group of jagged volcanic mountains known as "Crater Range." **Painted Rocks State Park,** 25 miles northwest of Gila Bend, features a group of boulders covered with Indian petroglyphs and a primitive campground. Dark desert varnish (a natural manganese and iron-oxide stain) on the rocks provided an excellent working surface for prehistoric Indians, who pecked out symbols and figures of people and animals. You can picnic or camp here, but there's no water; free day use, $4 camping. The lake and a second campground below Painted Rock Dam, a 4-mile drive north, was closed at press time due to pesticide contamination in the water; tel. 683-2151. The park is used mostly in the cooler months—it gets too hot (over 100° F) in summer.

# NORTHWEST OF PHOENIX

## WICKENBURG

You still get a sense of the Old West in easygoing Wickenburg. Western-style buildings line the downtown streets, and horses are a common sight. Even a bit of gold fever lingers, still drawing prospectors to mine-scarred hills in search of the "mother lode." Cowboys continue to work the range, though now joined by guests from local dude ranches. The picturesque rocky hills around Wickenburg offer ideal horseback riding. Wickenburg's cool and sunny weather lasts from November to May. Summers at the town's 2,100-foot elevation often bring very hot weather. Located 58 miles northwest of Phoenix, you can get here from Phoenix via US 60/89 (Grand Ave.) or the longer but less congested route past Lake Pleasant via I-17 and AZ 74.

## History

Henry Wickenburg had been roaming the hills of Arizona for a year in search of gold before striking it rich at the Vulture Mine in 1863. According to some legends, he noticed the shiny nuggets when reaching down to pick up a vulture he'd just shot; others claim he noticed them when picking up a rock to throw at his burro. Either way, Wickenburg set off a frenzied gold rush. The Vulture Mine lacked water needed for processing, so miners hauled the ore 14 miles northeast to the Hassayampa River. The town that grew up around the mills became Arizona's third largest city in just a few years. It missed being the territorial capital in 1866 by only two votes. Prospectors located other gold deposits in the Wickenburg area until more than 80 mines operated at the height of the gold rush. Mining for gold and other minerals continues today but on a small scale—many people consider it just a hobby.

## SIGHTS

### Desert Caballeros Western Museum

This fine museum takes you back to Wickenburg's Wild West days. Dioramas illustrate the history of the Vulture Mine and the early mining community, the triumphs and tragedies. Period rooms and a street scene show how Wickenburg actually looked. An Indian Room displays a varied collection of prehistoric and modern crafts, including kachina dolls, pottery, baskets, and stone tools. Dazzling specimens can be seen in the Mineral Room. A large art gallery features outstanding Western paintings and sculpture by Remington, Russell, and other inspired artists. Walk over to a small park behind the museum to see *Thanks for the Rain,* a bronze sculpture by Joe Beeler. The museum and art gallery are open Mon.-Sat. 10 a.m.-4 p.m. and Sun. 1-4 p.m.; $2.50 adult, $2 senior 55 and over, $.50 children 6-16. Located at 21 N. Frontier St. (one block west of the downtown highway junction); tel. 684-2272/7075.

## Old Jail Tree

The town lacked a jail in the early days, so prisoners were shackled to this old mesquite tree. The tree stands behind the Circle-K store at the highway junction downtown.

## Hassayampa River

Normally you'll see just a dry streambed through town. The river's Apache name means "river that runs upside down," because its waters flow beneath the sandy surface. A wishing well and sign at the west end of the highway bridge tell the story that anyone drinking from the stream will never tell the truth again.

## Hassayampa River Preserve

The river pops out of the ground along a 4-mile section of riverbed below town and waters lush vegetation. The Goodding willow-Fremont cottonwood forest along the banks is one of the rarest forest types in North America. Spring-fed Palm Lake attracts many waterfowl not normally seen in the

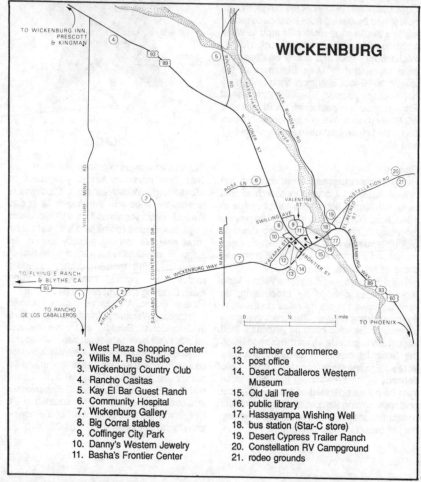

1. West Plaza Shopping Center
2. Willis M. Rue Studio
3. Wickenburg Country Club
4. Rancho Casitas
5. Kay El Bar Guest Ranch
6. Community Hospital
7. Wickenburg Gallery
8. Big Corral stables
9. Coffinger City Park
10. Danny's Western Jewelry
11. Basha's Frontier Center
12. chamber of commerce
13. post office
14. Desert Caballeros Western Museum
15. Old Jail Tree
16. public library
17. Hassayampa Wishing Well
18. bus station (Star-C store)
19. Desert Cypress Trailer Ranch
20. Constellation RV Campground
21. rodeo grounds

desert. Visitors have counted 230 species of birds, including the zone-tailed and black hawks that fly up from Mexico to nest. The preserve, managed by the Arizona chapter of the Nature Conservancy, provides a sanctuary for these hawks and several other endangered species of wildlife. Visitors have a chance to see them and to enjoy quiet walks through the natural settings. (Of Arizona's streamside habitats existing a century ago, only about 15% exists today.)

Check in at the Visitor Center for trail information and to see an aquarium of endanged fish; you can buy regional and natural history books and pick up literature on environmental concerns. The four-room adobe core of the Visitor Center, built in 1860, has served as ranch, stagecoach way station, and one of Arizona's first guest ranches. Borrow trail guides for the one-mile loop **Hassayampa River Nature Trail** and the half-mile **Palm Lake Nature Trail.** You can visit Wed.-Sun. (closed Mon. and Tues.) 8 a.m.-5 p.m. (Sept. 16-May 14) or 6 a.m.-noon (May 15-Sept. 15); a $3 donation by nonmembers is appreciated. The preserve schedules guided nature walks and bird walks, usually on weekends; call for schedule (reservations required); tel. 684-2772. Hassayampa River Preserve lies 3 miles southeast of Wickenburg on US 60/89 near Milepost 114.

## PRACTICALITIES

### Guest Ranches

Wickenburg prides itself as the "Guest Ranch Capital of the World." The degree of luxury varies, but all five guest ranches offer horseback riding and a swimming pool. The basic high-season rates listed here include service charge and tax. **Flying E Ranch** is open Nov. 15 to May 1; rates include meals: $105.50 s, $174 d.; 4 miles west on US 60, then one mile south; Box EEE, Wickenburg, AZ 85358; tel. 684-2690. **Kay El Bar Ranch** has been around so long that it's on the National Register of Historic Places; open Oct. 15 to May 1; rates include meals: $94.50 s, $173.25 d; go 3 miles north on US 89; Box 2480, Wickenburg, AZ 85358; tel. 684-7593. **Rancho**

**Casitas,** open year-round, is also 3 miles north off US 89; $927.50 one month (minimum stay); Box A-3, Wickenburg, AZ 85358; tel. 684-2628. **Wickenburg Inn** emphasizes tennis with 11 courts, pro shop, and lessons; located 7 miles north off US 89; open all year; rates include meals: $156 s, $240 d; Box P, Wickenburg, AZ 85358; tel. 684-7811. **Rancho de los Caballeros** is the most elegant of the group; open early Oct. to early May; guests have a pool, tennis courts, and an 18-hole golf course; rates include meals: $158 s, $253 d; go 3.5 miles west on US 60, then south 2 miles on Vulture Mine Road; Box 1148, Wickenburg, AZ 85358; tel. 684-5484.

### Motels

You'll find all the motels in town along US 60, named Wickenburg Way. From east to west are **Americinn** (850 E. Wickenburg Way; tel. 684-5461 or 800-634-3444); **La Siesta Motel** (510 E. Wickenburg Way; tel. 684-2826); **Best Western Rancho Grande** (293 E. Wickenburg Way; tel. 684-5445), **Mecca Motel** (162 E. Wickenburg Way; tel. 684-2753), **Wagon Wheel Motel** (573½ W. Wickenburg Way; tel. 684-2531), and **Westerner Motel** (680 W. Wickenburg Way; tel. 684-2493). For something different, check out the **Garden City Motel** on a hill 8 miles southeast of town; the quiet spot offers good views of surrounding mountains and a chance to see wildlife; no restaurant but some rooms have kitchenettes; Box 70, Wickenburg, AZ 85358; tel. 684-2334; look for the signs between Mileposts 118 and 119 on US 60/89.

### Camping

**The Desert Oasis,** 14 miles southeast on US 60/89, has the only full-service facilities for both tents ($6.33) and RVs ($10.55 w/hookups); tel. 388-2431. **North Ranch RV Park** is 10 miles northwest of town on US 89; $12.50 RV w/hookups and showers; tel. 427-6335. Closer in, RVs can stay at **Hospitality RV Park** (2 miles southeast on US 60/89; $12.65 RV w/hookups and showers; tel. 684-2519); **Aztec Trailer Park** (401 E. Wickenburg Way; $11.50 w/hookups and showers; tel. 684-2481); **Desert Cypress Trailer Ranch**

(adults only, behind McDonald's at 610 Jack Burden Road; $14.91 w/hookups and showers; tel. 684-2153); or **Constellation Park** (only $2 but no water or facilities, one mile northeast on Constellation Road). Another possibility for both tents and RVs is camping out in the desert; avoid washes and be sure you're on public land.

## Food
**Frontier Inn** (closed Mon.) has great Western-style barbecue, steaks, and seafood at 466 E. Wickenburg Way St.; tel. 684-2183. **La Casa Alegre** serves Mexican and American food at 540 E. Wickenburg Way; tel. 684-2152. For standard American fare, try **Willows Restaurant** (850 E. Wickenburg Way in Americinn; tel. 684-5461); **Country Kitchen** (545 E. Wickenburg Way; tel. 684-3882); **Kelly's Cafe** (530 E. Wickenburg Way; tel. 684-2583); **Gold Nugget Restaurant** (222 E. Wickenburg Way; 684-2858); **Horseshoe Cafe** (207 E. Wickenburg Way; tel. 684-7198); **Rancho Bar Seven Restaurant** (111 E. Wickenburg Way; tel. 684-2492); **Coffee Break Restaurant** (1605 W. Wickenburg Way in West Plaza Shopping Center; tel. 684-2294); **Cock 'N' Bull Restaurant** (445 N. Tegner St./US 89 N; tel. 684-2807), or **Charley's Steak House** (1101 W. Wickenburg Way; tel. 684-2413). Pick up pizza at **Sangini's** (107 E. Wickenburg Way; tel. 684-7828) or **Pizza Hut** (515 W. Wickenburg Way; tel. 684-2895). **Hungry Vulture Deli**, 683 W. Wickenburg Way, has sandwiches and a full menu; tel. 684-5236. **Sandwich Saloon** has a long list of offerings at 39 N. Tegner St.; tel. 684-2237. Buffets and à la carte offerings for lunch and dinner are offered at two of the guest ranches, **Rancho de los Caballeros** (tel. 684-5484) and **Wickenburg Inn** (tel. 684-7811); reservations needed at both. **El Tecalote** near Congress (16 miles northwest on US 89) has good Mexican-American food; tel. 427-6275. You'll find several fast-food places on the east side of town. **West Plaza Shopping Center** on the west edge of town and **Basha's Frontier Center** on N. Tegner St. have supermarkets and other stores.

## Entertainment
**Saguaro Movie Theater** screens the current films at 176 E. Wickenburg Way; tel. 684-7189. **Gold Rush Days** celebrates Wickenburg's Western heritage with a shootout, parade, rodeo, concerts, "mellerdramas," gold-panning contest, and other activities, usually the second weekend in February. The **Fourth of July** has fireworks and a watermelon feed. The **Wickenburg Bluegrass Festival** brings foot-tapping music and dancing to town in the fall, usually the second weekend in November.

## Shopping
View Western art at the **Wickenburg Gallery** on 662 W. Wickenburg Way and at **Willis M. Rue Studio** on W. Wickenburg Way at Aircleta Drive. **Danny's Western Jewelry,** 163 N. Tegner St., has Indian jewelry and other crafts.

## Services
**Post office** is at 55 E. Yavapai St. between N. Tegner and N. Frontier streets. The **Community Hospital** is at 111 Rose Lane, 0.8 mile north off Tegner St.; tel. 684-5421. **Coffinger City Park** offers picnicking, a swimming pool, tennis courts, and ball fields; off N. Tegner St., just across the Sols Wash bridge. Play golf year-round at the 9-hole **Wickenburg Country Club** course, go 2 miles west on US 60, then north on Country Club Road; tel. 684-2011. You might also be able to visit the 18-hole course at **Rancho de los Caballeros;** tel. 684-2704. **Big Corral** rents horses by the hour, half day, or full day; lessons, hayrides, and pack trips are available too; located off N. Tegner St., just before the bridge over Sols Wash; tel. 684-7679.

## Information
The very helpful **Wickenburg Chamber of Commerce** is in the old railroad depot on N. Frontier St. (one block west of N. Tegner St.); open Mon.-Fri. 9 a.m.-5 p.m.; Drawer CC, Wickenburg, AZ 85358; tel. 684-5479. The **public library** is at 164 Apache St. (one block north of Wickenburg Way and just west of the river); tel. 684-2665.

## Transport

**Greyhound** and **LTR** buses stop at the Star-C store, 444 E. Wickenburg Way; tel. 684-2601. Greyhound goes at least three times daily east to Phoenix, northwest to Las Vegas (one route is via Parker and Lake Havasu City), and west to California. LTR goes daily to Phoenix and Las Vegas (via Kingman).

## VICINITY OF WICKENBURG

It's fun to search out some of the old gold mines and ghost towns surrounding Wickenburg. Caution is needed on the dirt roads to the sites; get local advice on conditions and avoid traveling after heavy rains. The Vulture Mine would be worth seeing but it has been closed to visitors. Stanton, a ghost town northwest of Wickenburg, is open and may be visited.

### Stanton

Originally called Antelope Station, the settlement was begun in 1863 when prospectors found placer gold in Antelope Creek. Just 5 years later the population had reached 3,500. Three buildings remain from the old days: the stage stop, hotel, and opera house. A fourth building, the bathhouse, dates from only 1980. The gold began to play out by the early 1900s, and Stanton started fading away. Gold mining continues in Antelope Creek by members of the Lost Dutchman's Mining Association, though it's just for fun. Ask permission to look around the old site; no charge, though you could make a donation. From Wickenburg follow US 89 north for 18 miles (2 miles past Congress), then turn right on a graded dirt road signed for Stanton and Octave. You'll see old shacks, mine tailings, rusting machinery, and some new operations along this road. After entering Stanton, 6.5

*view of opera house from hotel porch, Stanton*

miles in, turn left through the Lost Dutchman's Mining Association gate. The main road continues another mile to the site of Octave (signed "No Trespassing"), then becomes too rough for cars. On Rich Hill, between Stanton and Octave, prospectors picked up gold nuggets the size of potatoes just lying on the ground. Another road turns off at Stanton and climbs the valley to Yarnell.

### Yarnell Hill Lookout

Southbound travelers can stop at the view tower for a sweeping scene of the desert and distant mountains below. The lookout is 25 miles north of Wickenburg and 0.5 mile south of Yarnell on US 89. (Northbound travelers don't have access to this stop.)

### Shrine Of St. Joseph

A short trail leads past statues depicting the stations of the cross. Giant granite boulders weathered out of the hillside add to the beauty of the spot. Free admission. Turn west at the sign in central Yarnell.

### Joshua Forest

Joshua trees *(Yucca brevifolia)* line US 93 for 16 miles. You'll see the first ones about 22 miles northwest of Wickenburg. Large clusters of pale-green flowers appear from early Feb. to early April.

# EASTERN ARIZONA

## INTRODUCTION

Eastern Arizona will surprise you. Instead of the arid desert country you might expect, you'll find 2,000 square miles of forested peaks, placid lakes, and sparkling streams of the White Mountains! The cool summer climate, abundant trout-filled waters, and winter sports are the big attractions for visitors. Mount Baldy, a peak sacred to the Apache Indians, crowns the range at 11,590 feet and is Arizona's second highest mountain. Sunrise Ski Resort, several miles north, has some of the Southwest's most challenging downhill runs. Cross-country skiers and summer hikers can find solitude almost anywhere in these mountains.

For a wildly scenic, high-country drive, try the Coronado Trail between Springerville and Clifton; slow and winding, the route offers almost unlimited picnicking, hiking, and camping possibilities. Over to the west, another highway offers a different surprise—you're driving along southwest of Show Low when suddenly the road begins to descend into a magnificent chasm. It's the Salt River Canyon, a smaller but equally colorful version of the Grand Canyon.

Traveling north from the White Mountains, you'll notice the scenery changing from mountain firs and pines to junipers and vast rangelands of lower, more arid country, and then to the multihued, barren hills of the Painted Desert. You can have a closer look at this striking desert country and its famous fossilized wood at Petrified Forest National Park.

Southward from the White Mountains, the drop in elevation is even greater—you'll be in cotton-growing country along the Gila River. "Islands" of high mountains, such as Mt. Graham (10,717 feet) near Safford, break up the often monotonous, low-desert country. A paved road runs nearly to the top of Mt. Graham, taking you from the Lower Sonoran Life Zone to the Hudsonian. The Galiuro Mountains to the west are a rugged wilderness with several peaks over 7,000 feet.

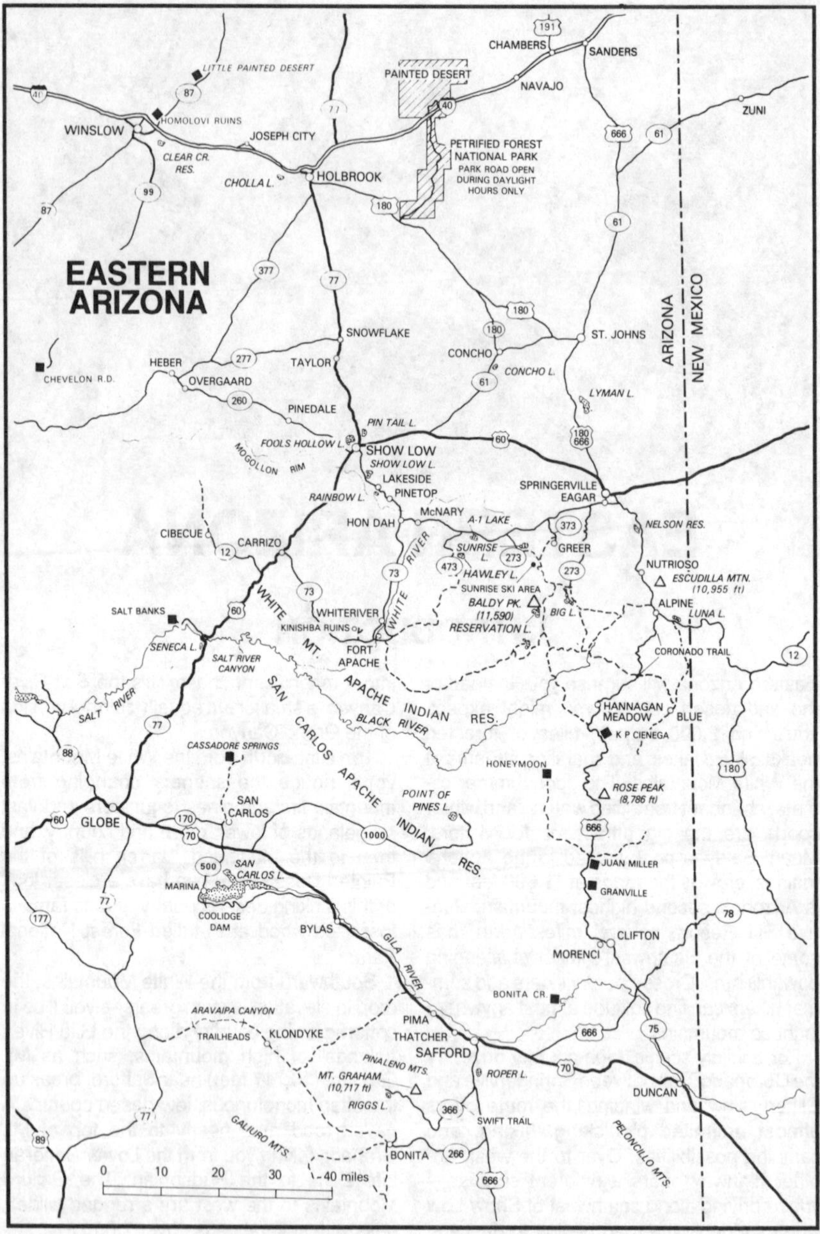

# EASTERN ARIZONA

CHAMBERS
SANDERS
191
NAVAJO
ZUNI
LITTLE PAINTED DESERT
PAINTED DESERT
87
WINSLOW
HOMOLOVI RUINS
JOSEPH CITY
PETRIFIED FOREST
NATIONAL PARK
Park road open
during daylight
hours only
41
77
40
666
61
CLEAR CR.
RES.
99
CHOLLA L.
HOLBROOK
180
87
180
61

ARIZONA
NEW MEXICO

377
77
SNOWFLAKE
180
ST. JOHNS
HEBER
277
TAYLOR
CONCHO
61
CONCHO L.
CHEVELON R.D.
OVERGAARD
260
PINEDALE
PIN TAIL L.
LYMAN L.
180
666
FOOLS HOLLOW L.
SHOW LOW
60
MOGOLLON RIM
SHOW LOW L.
LAKESIDE
SPRINGERVILLE
EAGAR
RAINBOW L.
PINETOP
McNARY
HON DAH
A-1 LAKE
NELSON RES.
CIBECUE
12
CARRIZO
73
SUNRISE
L.
473
GREER
373
273
NUTRIOSO
ESCUDILLA MTN.
(10,955 ft)
WHITERIVER
WHITE
73
HAWLEY L.
SUNRISE SKI AREA
273
BIG L.
ALPINE
LUNA L.
SALT BANKS
60
KINISHBA RUINS
WHITE
RIVER
BALDY PK.
(11,590 ft)
RESERVATION L.
CORONADO TRAIL
12
SENECA L.
SALT RIVER
CANYON
FORT
APACHE
MT.
SALT RIVER
88
77
SAN
CARLOS
APACHE
INDIAN
RES.
BLACK RIVER
HANNAGAN
MEADOW
BLUE
K P CIENEGA
CASSADORE SPRINGS
HONEYMOON
ROSE PEAK
(8,786 ft)
GLOBE
60
70
170
SAN
CARLOS
POINT OF
PINES L.
1000
180
666
500
SAN
CARLOS L.
MARINA
JUAN MILLER
177
77
COOLIDGE
DAM
BYLAS
GRANVILLE
GILA RIVER
CLIFTON
78
MORENCI
ARAVAIPA CANYON
TRAILHEADS
KLONDYKE
PIMA
THATCHER
SAFFORD
BONITA CR.
666
75
89
MT. GRAHAM
(10,717 ft)
PINALENO MTS.
ROPER L.
70
DUNCAN
77
RIGGS L.
366
SWIFT TRAIL
GALIURO MTS.
BONITA
266
PELONCILLO MTS.
666

0   10   20   30   40 miles

© MOON PUBLICATIONS

## Getting There And Around

Eastern Arizona almost requires private transportation. Only a few bus and train connections service the area. White Mountain Passenger Lines has the most extensive bus routes, connecting Show Low and Heber in eastern Arizona with Payson and the Phoenix area. Greyhound buses stop in Winslow and Holbrook on their runs across northern Arizona and at Globe and Safford on a southern route. Winslow is the only town served by Amtrak train. No scheduled commercial air service operated at press time.

## Climate

The high country provides welcome relief in summer from the searing heat of the deserts. Most eastern Arizona resort areas lie at elevations of 6,000 to 8,500 feet, where average summer temperatures run in the 60s and 70s F, and highs rarely exceed the mid-80s. Afternoon thunderstorms drench the forests almost daily from mid-July to early Sept., bringing about one-third of the area's 15 or so inches of annual precipitation. Early summer is the driest time of year.

Camping above 6,000 feet is difficult in winter, as heavy snowfalls and lows in the teens are common. Most winter days are bright and sunny, though, and highs often reach the mid-40s F. Skiers enjoy this weather, and even some fishermen will be out, chopping holes in the lake ice to get at the elusive trout. The high-desert country to the north, around Petrified Forest National Park, can be cold in winter and hot in summer but is usually free of snow. The low desert south of the White Mountains has mild winters and rarely gets snow. As in the rest of eastern Arizona, late summer is the rainiest time.

## THE APACHE

### Arrival

Close relatives of the Navajo, the Apache have similar language and customs. Groups of Apache are thought to have migrated from Canada, arriving in Texas and New Mexico in the 16th century. A few moved west, forming

*Alchesay, Apache chief and U.S. Army scout*

the tribes that now live on the White Mountain and San Carlos reservations in eastern Arizona and three small reservations in central Arizona. The early Apache lived a nomadic life—the men hunted game while the women searched out wild plant foods. They had few material possessions, and their homes were probably small conical huts covered with animal skins. Cultivation of corn, beans, and squash, learned from either the Pueblo or Navajo Indians, later supplemented hunting and gathering. Horses obtained from the Spanish gave the Apache great mobility, and by the mid-18th C. their raiding routes stretched from the Hopi mesas in the north to central Sonora in Mexico. Their predatory habits did not endear them to their neighbors—in fact, the name "Apache" may have come from a Zuni Indian word for "enemy."

### Troubles With The White Man

The Apache vigorously defended their lands from encroaching settlers, and they soon earned a reputation as the fiercest tribe in the

Southwest. Attempts over the years to exterminate them by the Spanish, the Mexicans, and finally the Americans caused the tribe to retaliate with a murderous vengeance. By 1870 the U.S. government finally realized that a military solution wasn't going to work.

## Reservation Life

The federal government then initiated a "Peace Policy," which placed all Indians on reservations and taught them to farm and raise livestock. The San Carlos Reservation, just south of the White Mountains, was created in 1871 as a home for various tribes—Mohave, Yavapai, Yuma, and several different Apache groups. Officials thought the Indians would be easier to control if centralized on one reservation, but the plan may actually have extended the Apache wars. Quarrels developed between the different groups, attempts at farming went poorly, and government agents frequently cheated the Indians. Geronimo and other war chiefs escaped at times to lead raids against settlements in southern Arizona and northern Mexico. By the time Geronimo surrendered in 1886, the federal government recognized that the San Carlos Reservation had failed and removed all tribes except the San Carlos Apache. Meanwhile, many of the White Mountain and Cibecue Apache had succeeded in holding onto part of their own territory to the north, which became a reservation in 1897.

In 1918, a ranching program issued five head of cattle to each of 80 Apache families. Although the program almost failed, the herds on the Fort Apache Reservation grew to 20,000 by 1931. Still, it wasn't until 1936 that the white men finally removed the last of their own cattle from the reservations. Recognizing the recreational value of their lands, in the 1950s the White Mountain Apache began to build access roads, reservoirs, campgrounds, marinas, motels, and restaurants. They also own and operate a large lumber industry. During this development, the tribe has taken care to preserve the great natural beauty of the reservation. San Carlos Apache have developed their lands for visitors as well, but on a smaller scale.

## Traditions

Driving through the Apache homeland, you might think that their culture is gone—you see members of the tribe living in modern houses, going to the shopping center, and working at regular jobs. But the Apache continue to use their own language and to preserve some old traditions. Boys still study under medicine men to learn the prayers, rituals, and medicinal plants used in healing ceremonies. Elaborate coming-of-age ceremonies still mark the passage into adulthood of young women. Known as "Sunrise Dances," these rites usually take place on weekends during summer; check local papers for dates or ask at the tribal offices in Whiteriver and San Carlos.

## Crafts

Frequently on the move in pre-reservation days, the Apache had only a few utilitarian crafts. Today, some of their products—baskets, cradleboards, and beadwork—are made and sold. Look for them at trading posts on the reservations. Buckskin dresses, worn by women before the introduction of calico, are occasionally seen at Sunrise Dances. Attractive designs in beadwork decorate necklaces, bolo ties, and other adornments. Woodcarvers have recently begun fashioning realistic dolls depicting dance movements of the Apache Spirit Dancers. Craftsmen on the San Carlos Reservation set peridot (a transparent yellow-green gemstone) in bolo ties, necklaces, earrings, and other jewelry.

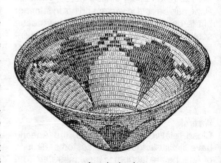

*Apache basket*

# THE HIGH DESERT

## WINSLOW AND VICINITY

Founded in 1882 as a railroad terminal, the town commemorates Gen. Edward Francis Winslow, president of the St. Louis and San Francisco Railroad, which was associated with the Atlantic and Pacific that ran through here. Ranchers turned the community into a major stock-raising center and shipping point. Trade and the railroad remain important to the community, though tourism, trucking, manufacturing, and a new state prison now boost the economy too. Winslow (pop. 8,795) sits in the Little Colorado River Valley at an elevation of 4,880 feet. Travelers find this a handy stopover: Meteor Crater is 25 miles west, the Hopi and Navajo reservations are just to the north, Petrified Forest National Park is 50 miles east, and the Mogollon Rim forest and lake country is 40 miles south.

### Brigham City
This Mormon settlement on the northeast edge of town predates Winslow by 5 years. The colonists' early optimism for the farming potential of bottom land along the Little Colorado soon faded as floods washed away dams and irrigation systems. Fear of Indian attacks caused the residents to protect their community with walls 200 feet long and 7 feet high. Although never attacked, Brigham City had to be abandoned in the 1880s due to continued irrigation difficulties. The city of Winslow plans to open the site as a historic park; check with the chamber of commerce.

### Homolovi Ruins State Park
Anasazi Indians lived in pithouses and later at six pueblo villages near present-day Winslow from about A.D. 600 to 1450, after which it's believed the inhabitants migrated north to the Hopi mesas. Legends passed through generations of Hopi relate how ancestors emerged from a world beneath the present

one and migrated in stages across the land to their present home. Clan elders guided the migrations through revelations from dreams and meditations. The Hopi hold these ruins sacred and still visit to leave *pahos* (prayer feathers) for the spirits. Serious archaeological studies have only recently begun. You're welcome to watch the archaeologists at work when they're here. The name Homolovi ("place of the low hills") applies to all the sites in the Winslow area; Homolovi II is the largest and forms the main area of the state park. Though badly weathered, the ruins show what a prehistoric site looks like before extensive excavation or reconstruction.

A visitor center and paved roads near the Homolovi I and II sites are scheduled for completion in the fall of 1990; a campground will open later. Park facilities will be designed for handicapped access. Take I-40 Exit 257 for AZ 87 (just east of Winslow), go 0.3 mile north, then turn left about 2 miles on a road past a gravel pit to the small site of **Homolovi I**. Nearby are the visitor center, a pithouse site, and **Sunset Cemetery**. The cemetery is all that remains of the first white settlement in the area; Lot Smith founded the Mormon community of Sunset in 1876, but drought and floods forced abandonment in 1887.

The trailhead for **Homolovi II** lies about 2.5 miles north of the visitor center on the park road. A three-quarter-mile trail follows an ancient path from the base of a box canyon up a mesa and along the top to the ruins. On the way, you'll see some petroglyphs pecked in boulders by the Anasazi. Signs interpret the rock art and describe the village. Homolovi II, occupied from 1250 to 1450, may have had a population as high as 3,000. The village comprised 700-1,200 rooms arranged around three plazas and probably stood two or three stories high. A group of rooms in the West Plaza has been excavated and stabilized to show their original floor plans. The village served as a major trade center and staging area on the northward migrations. Waters of the Little Colorado River below attracted game and nourished crops and wild plant foods.

The other sites in the park can be visited too; ask directions from park staff. **Homolovi III and IV** lie west across the Little Colorado River from Homolovi II and are reached by driving north from Winslow on North Park Drive, then turning east on dirt roads (may not be signed). Cottonwood Wash site is east of I-40 Exit 257 on a frontage road. **Chevelon Ruins** are the farthest out, about 15 miles southeast of Winslow, and will probably always be a backcountry area. Dirt roads in the

park become very slippery when wet and shouldn't be traveled then.

Visitors to any of the sites mustn't remove or disturb anything. Souvenir collecting has had a major impact in the past few years. Even the *tiniest* pottery shard must be left in place to preserve the sacred character of the sites. Federal and state laws prohibit removal of artifacts. Information about Homolovi Ruins State Park is available from the Winslow Chamber of Commerce or at the park office, 523 W. Second St. (Winslow, AZ 86047); tel. 289-4106; hearing-impaired people can call the TDD number, 289-4421).

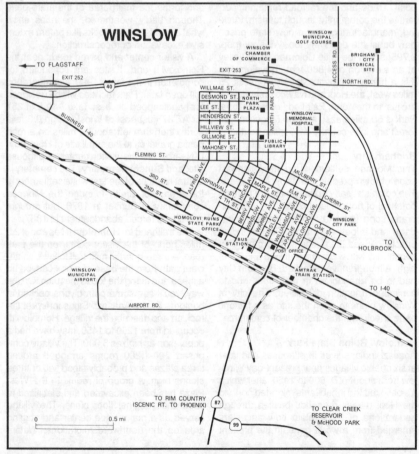

© MOON PUBLICATIONS

## Little Painted Desert County Park

Enjoy the views and beautiful sunsets from this park, located 13 miles northeast of Winslow on AZ 87 (I-40 Exit 257). Facilities include a 2-mile scenic rim drive overlooking colorful desert hills, a hiking trail, and picnic tables.

## McHood Park

On opposite banks of the Clear Creek Reservoir, McHood features swimming, boating, fishing, picnicking, and camping. Fishermen catch trout, bass, and catfish. Boaters may use the launch ramp and head 2.5 miles upstream into a scenic canyon with 200-foot cliffs (look for petroglyphs); this is also a good area for birdwatching. Park gates are open 8 a.m.-9 p.m. in summer and 8 a.m.-7 p.m. the rest of the year; day use costs $3 ($2 for city residents). The campground is open with drinking water and showers from mid-April to late Oct.; $6 ($7 w/water and electric hookups); tel. 289-3082 (ranger) or 289-2422 (city offices). From Winslow, head south 1.2 miles on AZ 87, then left 4.3 miles on AZ 99 to the park; turn left before the reservoir bridge to reach the campground, boat ramp, and swimming area or continue across the bridge and turn left to the picnic area and ranger residence.

## Accommodations And Food

Winslow has 24 motels and 28 restaurants, mostly along old Hwy. 66 (Bus. I-40) between I-40 Exits 252 and 257 and on North Park Dr. near I-40 Exit 253. The I-40 business route splits downtown into Third St. (westbound) and Second St. (eastbound).

## Campgrounds

**Sonoma Trailer Park** on W. Hwy. 66 (I-40 Exit 252) offers spaces for tents ($5) and RVs ($7 no hookups, $10 w/hookups); has showers; tel. 289-4312. Self-contained RVs can park at **Cox's North Park Service,** 2001 N. Park Dr. (just north of I-40 Exit 253); sites with electric hookups cost $6.42; tel. 289-4361.

## Events

Cowboys and cowgirls show their stuff in the **West Best Rodeo** in late September. The Christmas Parade starts off the holiday season on the third Sat. in November.

## Shopping And Services

For Indian crafts and jewelry, check **Bruchman's Curio Stores** at 113 W. Second St. and **Silver Nugget** at 106 E. Second Street. **Post office** is at 223 Williamson Ave. between Second and Third streets; tel. 289-2131. **Winslow Memorial Hospital** is on the north edge of town at 1501 Williamson Ave. (take I-40 Exit 253); tel. 289-4691. The **Winslow City Park,** at the corner of Colorado Ave. and Cherry St., has indoor and outdoor pools, tennis and racquetball courts, ball fields, weight rooms, and sports programs; tel. 289-2422 (city offices) or 289-4543 (indoor pool). Play golf at the nine-hole **Winslow Municipal Golf Course,** off North Park Dr.; tel. 289-4915.

## Information

Staff at the **Winslow Chamber of Commerce** have maps and info on sights and facilities in the area. An exhibit room introduces the land and people of northeast Arizona. The office is open daily 8 a.m.-5 p.m. in summer, then Mon.-Sat. 8 a.m.-5 p.m. the rest of the year. It's located just north of I-40 Exit 253 (look for the giant Indian totem); Box 460, Winslow, AZ 86047; tel. 289-2434.

Foresters at the **Chevelon Ranger District** of the Apache-Sitgreaves National Forest have maps and information about recreation in the Mogollon Rim country south of Winslow; open daily in summer 8 a.m.-4:30 p.m., then Mon.-Fri. 7:30 a.m.-4 p.m. the rest of the year; the office is 42 miles south of town on AZ 99 (HC 62, Box 600, Winslow, AZ 86047); tel. 289-2471. The **public library** has a good collection of books on Arizona and the Southwest at 420 W. Gillmore St.; tel. 289-4982.

## Transport

**Greyhound Bus** is downtown at 111 N. Warren Ave.; tel. 289-2171. **Amtrak** has rail service but there's no agent in town; call (800) 872-7245 for schedule and ticket information.

## Joseph City

Mormons established the farming community of Allen's Camp in 1876 under great difficulties. Attempts to dam the Little Colorado for irrigation failed repeatedly, leaving the crops to wither away. Although four other Mormon settlements along the Little Colorado were abandoned, this town, renamed Joseph City, persevered. It is the oldest community in Navajo County.

# HOLBROOK

The railroad reached this site in 1881 and named it for one of their engineers. Eastern investors recognized the surrounding rangelands as prime cattle country, and they wasted no time in seeking grazing rights. Within 2 years, the Aztec Land and Cattle Company, based near Joseph City, had 60,000 head of cattle on the land. The Aztec, better known as the "Hashknife" outfit for the shape of its brand, became the third largest cattle empire in the United States—its cowboys worked the longhorns across one million acres. On holidays, the cowpokes, looking for a good time, rode into Holbrook with guns blazing. Rustling and poor management troubled the Hashknife operation until it shut down about 1900, but Holbrook (pop. 5,960) remains a ranching center. Travelers often use Holbrook as a base for visiting the nearby Petrified Forest National Park and the Navajo and Hopi Indian reservations.

## Navajo County Museum

You can see some of the area's "Wild West" history in this fine collection. Period rooms and artifacts trace the changes from the prehistoric Indian era to the lawless frontier days to modern times. Don't miss seeing the dungeon-like jail downstairs. Exhibits are open in summer Mon.-Sat. 8 a.m.-8 p.m., then Mon.-Fri. 8 a.m.-5 p.m. the rest of the year. Located in the old (1898) county courthouse, downtown at the corner of 100 E. Arizona St. and Navajo Blvd.; tel. 524-6558. The Holbrook Chamber of Commerce office is here too and is open the same hours. A self-guided tour leaflet describes historic buildings in town, including the notorious Bucket of Blood Saloon.

## Accommodations And Food

Holbrook's 17 motels and 18 restaurants lie along Navajo Blvd. (north and south from I-40 Exit 286) and W. Hopi Dr. (east from I-40 Exit 285); the two streets meet downtown. The **International Youth Hostel,** in the historic Arizona Rancho Motel, is the choice of low-

Holbrook, Arizona *Dec 1st 1899*

Mr. *X. B. Berryhill*

You are hereby cordially invited to attend the hanging of one

### George Smiley, Murderer.

His soul will be swung into eternity on *Dec 8, 1899* at 2 o'clock, p. m., sharp.

Latest improved methods in the art of scientific strangulation will be employed and everything possible will be done to make the proceedings cheerful and the execution a success.  **F. J. WATTRON,**
Sheriff of Navajo County.

*Invitation to a hanging; this wording brought a letter of condemnation from President William McKinley to Territorial Governor Nathanial Oakes Murphy. Governor Murphy issued a one-month stay of execution and chastised Sheriff Wattron. The hanging took place Jan. 8, 1900.*

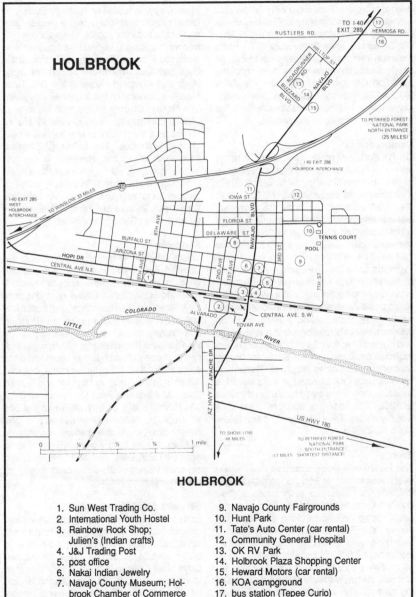

# HOLBROOK

1. Sun West Trading Co.
2. International Youth Hostel
3. Rainbow Rock Shop;
   Julien's (Indian crafts)
4. J&J Trading Post
5. post office
6. Nakai Indian Jewelry
7. Navajo County Museum; Holbrook Chamber of Commerce
8. public library
9. Navajo County Fairgrounds
10. Hunt Park
11. Tate's Auto Center (car rental)
12. Community General Hospital
13. OK RV Park
14. Holbrook Plaza Shopping Center
15. Heward Motors (car rental)
16. KOA campground
17. bus station (Tepee Curio)

budget travelers. Rates are only $6/person; a hostel card isn't required. The hostel sits just south of downtown, at the corner of Apache Dr. and 57 Tovar St.; tel. 524-6770. From the main intersection of Navajo and Hopi, go south across the train tracks, turn right one block on Central Ave. S.W., then left one block on Tovar to the hostel. The owner, Mrs. Lloyd Taylor, has been in Holbrook since the 1930s and can tell you many tales.

## Campgrounds

**OK RV Park,** just north of I-40 Exit 286 at the corner of Roadrunner and Buzzard, is open all year and has showers; $8 tent, $10.60 RV no hookups, $13 w/hookups; tel. 524-3226. The **KOA** campground is at 102 Hermosa, just off Navajo Blvd.; $16.37 tent, $19.66 RV w/hookups; has a store, pool, cabins, and showers; open all year; take I-40 Exit 286 or 289; tel. 524- 6689.

**Cholla Lake County Park,** 10 miles west of Holbrook near a power plant, offers picnicking, camping, fishing, water-skiing, windsurfing, and swimming. Fishermen pull largemouth bass, catfish, and sunfish from the 360-acre lake. The campground has showers and costs $6/night or $8 with water and electric hookups. Day-use fee is $3 ($2 for county residents); gates close at sunset. The park is open all year, though water and showers are available only from mid-March to late Oct.; tel. 288-3717 (park) or 524-6161, ext. 344 (county office). Take I-40 Exit 277 and follow signs for 2 miles.

## Events

The **Hashknife Pony Express** rides again every year in Jan. or Feb., when riders carry the mail from Holbrook to Scottsdale. (You can send your letter along too, by putting the usual stamp on and marking the lower left corner "Via Pony Express." Enclose it in a second envelope and send to Postmaster, Holbrook, AZ 86025.) Local firefighters show off on **Firemen's Fun and Games Day,** the first Sat. in May, with entertainment and training games. The Hispanic community celebrates **Cinco de Mayo** (May 5th) with a beauty pageant, dances, food, and games. **Old West Days,** in late May, features Bucket of Blood bicycle and foot races, a parade, arts and crafts exhibits, roping events, cowchip-throwing contest, horseshoe tournament, and a street dance. Fireworks and "the state's best barbecue" mark the **Fourth of July.** Hear foot-stomping music at the **Old Time Fiddlers Contest** on the first week in August. The **Navajo County Fair** is held the last full weekend in August. **Navajo County Horse Races** take place the first and second weekends in September. The **Arizona All-Indian Fair, Pow Wow, and Rodeo,** on the first weekend in Sept., presents a parade, championship finals rodeo, livestock judging, dances, and arts and crafts. A nighttime **Christmas Parade of Lights** brightens winter on the first Sat. in December.

## Shopping

You're forbidden to remove anything from the Petrified Forest National Park, but you can shop in Holbrook for the appealing wood-turned-to-stone. Small pieces cost just pennies; larger polished specimens run from a few dollars to thousands. Turquoise, geodes, and other natural treasures are available too. Try the **Rainbow Rock Shop** at 103 Navajo Blvd. or the shops just outside the south entrance of the national park. For Indian crafts, look into **Julien's** at the corner of Hopi Dr. and Navajo Blvd., **J&J Trading Post** (one block south at 104 Navajo Blvd.), **Sun West Trading** at 905 W. Hopi Dr., **Nakai Indian Jewelry** at 357 Navajo Blvd., and **Lewis Traders** (4 miles east of town, across from Holbrook Truck Plaza, near I-40 Exit 292). J&J and Sun West are old-style trading posts patronized mostly by Navajo and Hopi Indians.

## Services And Information

Holbrook's **Hunt Park** has a picnic area, playground, outdoor swimming pool, and tennis courts; turn east on Florida St. from Navajo Blvd.; tel. 524-3331. The nine-hole **Hidden Cove Golf Course** is about 3 miles west of town; take I-40 Exit 283 (Golf Course Road); tel. 524-3097. **Community General Hospital** is at 500 E. Iowa St.; tel. 524-3913. The helpful **Holbrook Chamber of Commerce** has both local and statewide literature in the old county courthouse, downtown at the corner of Navajo Blvd. and Arizona St. (100 E. Arizona St., Holbrook, AZ 86025); tel. 524-6558. The office and Navajo County Museum historical exhibits are open in summer Mon.-Sat. 8 a.m.-8 p.m., then Mon.-Fri. 8 a.m.-5 p.m. the rest of the year. The **public library** is at 451 First Ave.; tel. 524-3732.

## Transport
**Greyhound** buses stop at Tepee Curio near the corner of Hermosa and Navajo Blvd.; tel. 524-3832. (Closed Sat. afternoons and all day Sunday, but buses still stop.) You can rent cars from **Tate's Auto Center** (1001 Navajo Blvd.; tel. 524-6266) and **Heward Motors** (1500 Navajo Blvd.; tel. 524-2266).

# PETRIFIED FOREST NATIONAL PARK

The Petrified Forest National Park, like the Grand Canyon, presents an open book to the earth's past. The park's multicolored hills, part of a widespread geologic formation called the Chinle, provide a world-famous source of petrified wood and related fossils. The barren hills' delicately tinted bands of reds, grays, oranges, and whites have eroded to reveal remains of life, frozen in stone, from 225 million years ago. Rivers in that period carried fallen trees from distant mountains and buried them in low-lying plains. Before their fall, some of the giant trees had towered 200 feet high. Waterborne minerals transformed the logs to stone, replacing wood cells and filling spaces between them with brightly colored quartz and jasper crystals. This now-arid land would be unrecognizable today to its ancient inhabitants of primitive fish, massive amphibians, and fearsome reptiles.

Some of the strange animals that once crawled or swam here have been preserved; you'll see their fossilized remains in park exhibits. But it has been the trees that have traditionally attracted the most attention. In the late 1800s, much petrified wood was lost to collectors, who carted away some of the best logs for souvenirs or dynamited them for their crystals. The battle for preservation was won in 1906, when President Theodore Roosevelt signed a bill establishing the Petrified Forest National Monument. A 1958 act of Congress, followed by acquisition of new lands, changed the status to a national park in 1962.

## Flora And Fauna
A surprising amount of life exists in the park, despite the meager 9-inch annual rainfall and lack of permanent water. Prickly pear and cholla cacti are widespread. Evening primrose, Indian paintbrush, mariposa lily, sunflowers, and other plants bloom when they've received sufficient moisture. Also common are buckwheat (a shrub that turns orange-brown in the fall) and saltbush (named for the tiny salt crystals formed on its leaves to conserve moisture). The most frequently seen animals in the park are birds, small mammals, and lizards. Birds include the raven, rock wren, and horned lark. You're most likely to spot prairie dogs, black-tailed jack rabbits, and desert cottontails, but pronghorn, coyotes, and bobcats live here too.

## The Three Parts
The southern section—the original national monument—has some of the finest petrified wood specimens in the world. The central section contains the greatest number of prehistoric Indian sites. During their stay from about A.D. 300 to 1400, the Anasazi, Sinagua, and Mogollon tribes progressed from semi-nomadic hunters and gatherers to farmers who lived in permanent pueblos and had a complex ceremonial life. Scientists are trying to decode the numerous petroglyphs, and they have discovered that some were used as solar calendars. The northern section of the park encompasses part of the Painted Desert, famed for its landscape of ever-changing colors—the effect of the sun play-

ing on rocks stained by iron, manganese, and other minerals. Colors become most vivid near sunset and sunrise, fading toward midday. Added in 1932, this northern section is the largest in the park.

## Visiting The Park

Sightseeing in the park (average elevation 5,400 feet) can be good at any time of year; just protect yourself from the sun in the warmer months. You can begin the paved 28.6-mile scenic drive through the park at either end. Coming from the west, you'll find it more convenient to use the south entrance off US 180 from Holbrook. After visiting the park, continue on I-40 from the north entrance. Coming from the east, the north entrance is more practical. The drive is open daily in winter from 8 a.m.-5 p.m., extended in summer 6 a.m.-7 p.m.; winter snow or ice storms occasionally close the road. An early start is recommended; you can easily use a full day enjoying all the walks, views, and exhibits. Admission is $5/vehicle ($2/bus passenger, bicycle, or foot); free with a Golden Eagle, Golden Age, or Golden Access pass. For more information, contact the park staff at Petrified Forest National Park, AZ 86028; tel. 524-6228.

Visitor centers near both entrances offer exhibits of the park's geology, fossils, ecology, and human history. Books, postcards, posters, and maps are sold. You can also talk with a ranger and obtain backcountry permits. Don't remove any petrified wood or other objects from the park. Rangers estimate that people taking one "harmless little souvenir" could result in the loss of tons of wood every year!

## Services

No campgrounds or lodging are located within the park; you'll have to go west to Holbrook or east to the smaller communities of Navajo or Chambers. Picnic fixings come in handy, as there is just one restaurant (near the north entrance) and a snack bar (across from Rainbow Forest Museum, inside the south entrance). Only the developed areas have water; you'll probably want to carry something to drink. Shops sell souvenirs at three locations: outside the park near the south entrance, inside the park at the Rainbow Forest complex (near the south entrance), and next to the Visitor Center at the north entrance station.

## Backcountry Travel

Hikers may explore the two areas designated as wilderness. The backcountry remains relatively undiscovered; it's been estimated that only one out of a thousand park visitors

Petrified Forest
National Park

strays more than a short distance from his vehicle. Travel is usually cross-country, easy to do with plenty of landmarks and open terrain—you're free to roam. Water must be carried (no springs) and you'll need a hat for sun protection. Rangers can give advice and a hiking leaflet. They also issue the free permits required for overnight trips. Camping must be within the wilderness areas and more than one mile from the road. Even if planning a long dayhike, it's a good idea to tell your plans to rangers. Horseback riding and pack animals are permitted too; there's a limit of six animals per party and you'll need to carry feed and water. All backcountry users should note rules against campfires, pets (OK elsewhere in the park if on a leash), and firearms.

**Rainbow Forest Wilderness** (7,240 acres) has grasslands, badlands, abundant petrified wood, and traces of Indian inhabitants. It's in the southern half of the park; start from Flattops Trailhead.

**Painted Desert Wilderness** in the north is much larger (43,020 acres)—a colorful land of mesas, buttes, and badlands. Indian sites and their petroglyphs can be visited; ask a ranger for directions. Onyx Bridge, a 50-foot-long petrified tree in the Black Forest, also makes a good destination; it's about 4 miles roundtrip from the Kachina Point Trailhead. Pilot Rock (6,295 feet), about 7 miles northwest of the trailhead, is the highest point in the park.

## SCENIC DRIVE

Description runs from south to north, but the road can be driven in either direction. (Numbers in parentheses are distances from the north end of the drive.) Mileages are along the drive only and don't include side trips:

**Mile 0** (28.6): **Beginning of scenic drive from US 180.**

**Mile 0.1** (28.5): **Petrified Forest Museum and Trading Post** and **Crystal Forest Museum and Gift Shop** stand on opposite sides of the road just outside the park entrance.

Although neither place is connected with the park, they exhibit dazzling collections of polished petrified wood, including giant log cross-sections and carvings. Most pieces can be purchased, as can unpolished petrified wood and other minerals, rocks, and fossils. Petrified Forest Museum and Trading Post also has a gas station and a campground.

**Mile 0.2** (28.4): **Entering Petrified Forest National Park.** A ranger collects fees and gives out park brochures, which have a good map. If you've brought in unpolished wood or other objects, ask the ranger to mark or bag them to avoid any misunderstandings about their source, as it's against the law to take *anything* from the park.

**Mile 2.4** (26.2): **Rainbow Forest Museum and Visitor Center.** A ferocious phytosaur *(Nicrosaurus gregorii)* skeleton cast greets you on entering the museum. This large crocodile-like reptile roamed the forests and swamps here during the Triassic Period 225 million years ago. The phytosaur and other exhibits provide a look at the strange environment of cycads, ferns, fish, amphibians, reptiles, and other early life that existed then. Also see artifacts of the prehistoric Indians, now vanished, who lived here for more than 1,000 years. A "Conscience Wood" exhibit is full of stolen petrified wood, returned with apologetic and remorseful letters. The **Giant Logs Trail** begins behind the Visitor Center and winds in a half-mile loop past monster-sized logs—a rainbow of reds, yellows, grays, whites, blacks, pinks, and oranges. The base of one fallen tree stands higher than a man. **Fred Harvey's Curios and Fountain** offers souvenirs and a snack bar across the the road from the Visitor Center.

**Mile 2.5** (26.1): **Picnic area.**

**Mile 2.6** (26.0): **Long Logs Interpretive Trail** and **Agate House** turnoff (0.5 mile to parking). The self-guided nature trail is an easy half-mile walk, a good opportunity to have a close look at the ancient trees. The jumble of logs here is thought to have been a logjam, buried in mud, sand, and volcanic

*Agate House*

ash. Many logs measure over 100 feet long. Agate House, on a short side trail, is a pueblo occupied about 700 years ago. Indians built the unusual structure entirely with chunks of colorful petrified wood! Two of its seven rooms have been reconstructed to show their original size.

**Mile 5.2** (23.4): **The Flattops.** Hikers begin here for day and overnight backcountry trips to Puerco Ridge and other areas of the Rainbow Forest Wilderness.

**Mile 8.1** (20.5): **Crystal Forest Interpretive Trail.** Some of the prettiest and most concentrated petrified wood in the park lies along this paved three-quarter-mile trail.

**Mile 9.9** (18.7): **Jasper Forest** turnoff (0.5 mile to parking). There's a great view to the west and north from the overlook. Below you can see pieces of petrified wood eroded from the hillsides.

**Mile 10.1** (18.5): **Agate Bridge.** Erosion has carved out a gully beneath a large log, leaving it as a bridge. In years past, one of the Hashknife cowboys rode his horse across the log on a $10 bet. Rangers won't let you do this today, though! It's unsafe. Because of cracking, the log was braced with a concrete beam in 1917.

**Mile 12.9** (15.7): **Blue Mesa** turnoff (2.5 miles to parking). Blue Mesa has several panoramic overlooks and a one-mile-loop interpretive trail. The trail is a good introduction to the Chinle Formation and its badlands topography, showing how the hills formed and are now eroding.

**Mile 14.5** (14.1): **The Tepees.** Symmetrical cone-shaped hills can be seen from the overlook.

**Mile 16.5** (12.1): **Newspaper Rock** turnoff (0.3 mile to parking). An impressive collection of ancient petroglyphs covers a huge sandstone boulder below. The drawings have not yet been interpreted, but seem to represent animals, spiritual figures, and perhaps some doodling. Bring binoculars or use the pay telescopes to examine the artwork from the overlook.

**Mile 17.4** (11.2): **Puerco Indian Ruin.** Before A.D. 1100, local Indians lived in small scattered settlements. Their building of larger pueblos, such as Puerco, shows a change to an agricultural lifestyle requiring greater pooling of efforts. The broad, meandering Puerco River provided reliable water all year and its floodplain had rich soil for farming. The river also attracted birds, pronghorn, and other game. Indians built a one-story pueblo with about 76 rooms and at least two kivas (ceremonial rooms) around a rectangular plaza. You can see the foundations of these rooms and one of the kivas. Archaeologists think that this site was occupied between A.D. 1100 and 1200 and again from about 1300 to 1400. The last occupants appear to have packed up and left peaceably, perhaps over a period of years.

Please help protect the ruins by staying on the trail. Many fine petroglyphs cover the boulders below the village. Though more scattered, they are comparable to those at the better-known Newspaper Rock. One of the Puerco petroglyphs was found to mark the summer solstice, and rangers may have demonstration programs here from about June 10 to 30; ask at the visitor centers. About 14 sites with solar markings have been discovered in the park.

**Mile 17.7** (10.9): **Puerco River bridge.** The scene was probably far different when Indians occupied the pueblo. Records indicate that cottonwood trees grew along the flood-

*petroglyph at Puerco Indian Ruin*

plain as late as the 19th century. Ranchers took advantage of the abundant grasslands in the late 1880s by increasing their herds, but drought in 1891-94 dried up the grasses, and gross overstocking destroyed the range. Runoff carried high concentrations of salts into the river, killing less salt-resistant plants. Floods have worked their toll, scouring and widening the river and leaving loads of silt in their wake. Now the river is dry during much of the year.

**Mile 18.1** (10.5): **Bridge over the railroad tracks.** The Petrified Forest first gained national attention with the completion of the Atlantic and Pacific Railroad (later the Santa Fe) across northern Arizona. Train travelers disembarked at the nearby Adamana Station, now abandoned, to visit the "trees turned to stone."

**Mile 23.6** (5.0): **Lacey Point Overlook** of the Painted Desert.

**Mile 24.1** (4.5): **Whipple Point Overlook** of the Painted Desert. One of the first whites to visit the Petrified Forest, Lieutenant A.W. Whipple came in 1853.

**Mile 24.3** (4.3): **Nizhoni Point Overlook** of the Painted Desert. The hillside below appears to be covered with shards of glass shining in the sun. Actually these are natural pieces of selenite gypsum, a very soft mineral that can be scratched with your fingernail.

**Mile 25.4** (3.2): **Pintado Point Overlook** of the Painted Desert. You are now on a volcanic lava flow, which covers the entire rim and protects the underlying, softer Chinle Formation from erosion.

**Mile 26.0** (2.6): **Chinde Point Picnic Area** turnoff (0.3 mile). Water and restrooms are available in the warmer months.

**Mile 26.2** (2.4): **Painted Desert Inn** and **Kachina Point Overlook.** Herbert Lore built the original inn with Indian labor and local materials in 1924. Travelers bumping their way across Arizona on Route 66 stopped for meals and to shop for Indian crafts. The National Park Service purchased the inn and surrounding land in 1936 to add to the then national monument. Workers reconstructed and enlarged the inn as a park concession and information station, but its four sleeping rooms were not used after WW II. The inn closed when the Painted Desert Visitor Center opened in 1962. Plans were made for demolition of the old building, but enough people recognized its unique Southwestern architecture, a mixture of Spanish and Indian pueblo styles, that it was saved. Budget permitting, the inn will open in summers as a park museum; exhibits interpret man's history in the area from prehistoric to modern times. The trailhead for **Painted Desert Wilderness** (Onyx Bridge, Black Forest, etc.) begins near Kachina Point, behind the inn.

**Mile 26.7** (1.9): **Tawa Point Overlook** of the Painted Desert.

**Mile 27.5** (1.1): **Tiponi Point Overlook** of the Painted Desert.

**Mile 28.1** (0.5): **Painted Desert Visitor Center** and **North Entrance Station.** A 17-minute movie, shown on the hour and half hour, illustrates the park's features and formation of the petrified wood. Exhibits show plant and animal fossils, and you can see a "Conscience Wood" display. A ranger will answer your questions and issue backcountry permits. **Fred Harvey Painted Desert Oasis** offers a cafeteria, curio shop, and gas station.

**Mile 28.6** (0.0): **Junction with I-40.**

# NORTH OF THE WHITE MOUNTAIN APACHE INDIAN RESERVATION

## SHOW LOW

With so many recreation opportunities in the nearby Mogollon Rim country and White Mountains, Show Low has become an important summer resort. Attractions include excellent trout fishing, hiking, camping, horseback riding, golf, scenic drives, and big-game hunting. The town of 5,460 (more than 13,500 in summer!) sits on the pine-forested Mogollon Rim at an elevation of about 6,400 feet.

Show Low took its name from a winner-take-all poker game played in 1876. Corydon Cooley, a noted Indian scout, and his partner, Marion Clark, had established a 100,000-acre ranch here in 1870, but they found the place wasn't big enough for both of them. Agreeing to settle their differences with a game of cards, they sat down at the kitchen table in Cooley's house for a session of "seven-up." The two played through the night until finally Clark said, "Show low and you win." Cooley pulled out an unbeatable deuce of clubs and took the ranch. Several years later, the property was purchased and settled by the Mormons. The site where the game was played is now occupied by the town's Mormon church. Show Low's main street took its name "Deuce of Clubs" after the winning card.

### Sights
**Fool Hollow Lake** has 140 acres stocked with trout, smallmouth bass, catfish, and bluegill. It's just 3 miles northwest of Show Low (see the Apache-Sitgreaves Forest map). The free campgrounds on the west and east shores are open mid-April to mid-Oct.; no drinking water. A boat ramp is on the east shore. Plans are afoot to develop the lake as a multi-agency park.

You never know what kind of fish you're going to catch at **Show Low Lake:** rainbow or brown trout, largemouth bass, walleye, or catfish. A boat ramp, store, and boat rentals are available; boat motors are limited to eight horsepower. The Navajo County campground on the west side is open early May to sometime in Sept. and costs $6-7 (water but no showers); picnicking in the campground costs $2. The lake is about 5 miles south of Show Low; go south 4 miles on AZ 260 and turn east at the hospital 1.3 miles on Show Low Lake Road.

**Pin Tail Lake** is an unusual waterfowl area north of Show Low created between 1977 and 1979. Workers filled a natural volcanic depression with treated sewage effluent and built artificial islands for nesting sites. The marshland was an instant success with ducks and other wildlife. Go north 3.5 miles on AZ 77 and turn right 0.4 mile on Pintail Lake Road. A quarter-mile trail leads to an observation platform.

**Mogollon Rim Overlook and Nature Trail** is an easy 1.5-mile walk with signs describing the area's forests, medicinal plants, and history. You have good views of forested valleys and ridges below the overlooks. The trailhead is 7 miles south of Show Low on AZ 260, between Mileposts 347 and 348.

### Accommodations

Show Low's motels lie along Deuce of Clubs. From west to east are **Maxwell House Motel (Best Western)** (2437 W. Deuce of Clubs; tel. 537-4356); **Paint Pony Lodge (Best Western)** (581 W. Deuce of Clubs; tel. 537-5773); **KC Motel** (60 W. Deuce of Clubs; tel. 537-4433); **Kiva Motel** (261 E. Deuce of Clubs; tel. 537-4542); **Apache Pines Motel** (526 E. Deuce of Clubs; tel. 537-4328); **Thunderbird Motel** (1131 E. Deuce of Clubs; tel. 537-4391); **Downtown 6 Motel** (1457 E. Deuce of Clubs; tel. 537-4334); **Lone Pine Motel** (1640 E. Deuce of Clubs; tel. 537-2926); and **Whiting Bros. Motor Hotel** (1941 E. Deuce of Clubs; tel. 537-7694).

### Campgrounds

Both tenters and RVers can head to campgrounds at Fool's Hollow Lake and Show Low Lake, each described above, or to **Camp Town** (1221 W. McNeil; tel. 537-2578); **Country Lane Trailer Park** (Old Linden Road and N. Central; tel. 537-4783); **K-Bar RV Park** (300 N. 16th Ave.; tel. 537-2886); and **Rim Crest RV Park** (4.4 miles south on AZ 260; tel. 537-4660).

RVers can stay at **Juniper Ridge RV Resort** at White Mountain Lakes (7 miles north on AZ 77, then 5 miles east at sign; tel. 537-4805); **Pine Shadows Mobile Home Park** (3.7 miles south on AZ 260; tel. 537-

2895); **Ranchero RV Mobile Home Park** (2.9 miles south on AZ 260; tel. 537-4479); **Show Low Lake Trailer Park** (4 miles south on AZ 260; tel. 537-2426); **Timberline Adult RV Park** (one mile south on AZ 260; tel. 537-4857); **Venture In RV Resort** (1.3 miles west on AZ 260; tel. 537-4443); and **Waltner's RV Resort** (Waltner Way, 4 miles south near Navapache Hospital; tel. 537-4611).

### Food

Look for restaurants along Deuce of Clubs. You can find Western food at **Paint Pony Steakhouse** (581 W. Deuce of Clubs; tel. 537-5773) and **Branding Iron Steak House** (1261 E. Deuce of Clubs; tel. 537-5151). For Mexican dinners try **Guayos's** (350 E. Deuce of Clubs; tel. 537-9503); **La Casita** (4 miles south on AZ 260; tel. 537-5179); **Maxwell House** (2437 W. Deuce of Clubs; tel. 537-4356); or **White Mountain Restaurant** (1301 E. Deuce of Clubs; tel. 537-9880). Chinese food is served by **Asia Gardens** (49 W. Deuce of Clubs; tel. 537-4383) and **Hong Kong Cafe** (313 E. Deuce of Clubs; tel. 537-5407). Pick up pizza at **Little Sicily** (307 E. Deuce of Clubs; tel. 537-5261); **Pat's Place** (905 E. Deuce of Clubs; tel. 537-2337); or **Pizza Hut** (Pineway Center; tel. 537-5306). Other restaurants and the usual fast-food places are in town too.

### Events

The **Fourth of July** is celebrated with a big parade, a rodeo, and entertainment. You can loosen up at the **Square Dance Festival** on the second weekend in July. **Shootout in Show Low** in Aug. is a folklore festival with cavalry demonstrations, Indian dances, and arts and crafts. In Dec., the town dresses up in bright lights to celebrate the holidays. Softball tournaments and other events take place through the year too; see the Show Low Chamber of Commerce.

### Services And Recreation

The **post office** is at 191 W. Deuce of Clubs and McNeil; tel. 537-4588. **Navapache Hospital** is 4 miles south of Show Low on AZ 260, on the way to Lakeside; tel. 537-4375. The

**city park** offers picnic areas, playground, tennis, basketball, softball, racquetball, and volleyball courts; turn in on W. Owens opposite the chamber of commerce office; **Show Low Parks and Recreation** offers a year-round program of activities; tel. 537-2800. Play golf at **Show Low Golf and Country Club's** 18-hole course in town (860 N. 36th Dr.; tel. 537-4564) or **Silver Creek Golf Club's** 18-hole course at White Mountain Lakes (7 miles north on AZ 77, then 5 miles east at sign; tel. 537-2744).

### Information
The **Show Low Chamber of Commerce** can help you find accommodations and other services in town; open Mon.-Fri. 8 a.m.- 5 p.m. and Sat.-Sun. 10 a.m.-3 p.m.; W. Deuce of Clubs at S. Eighth Ave. (Box 1083, Show Low, AZ 85901); tel. 537-2326. The **public library** is at 20 N. Sixth St. and E. McNeil; tel. 537-2447.

### Transport
**White Mountain Passenger Lines** offers bus service from Show Low to the central Arizona communities of Payson, Mesa, Tempe, and Phoenix. Main office is at 1041 E. Hall St. (Box 460, Show Low, AZ 85901); tel. 537-4539.

## LAKESIDE AND PINETOP

Their names well describe the countryside of lakes and pine forests. The twin towns lie near the edge of the Mogollon Rim 8 miles southeast of Show Low. Lakeside was originally named "Fairview" at its founding in 1880 by Mormon pioneers, but it took on the present name when Rainbow Lake, the first of a series of reservoirs, was finished. Several smaller lakes have been added too, and the town seems to have almost as much water area as land. Soldiers making the long climb up the Mogollon Rim from Fort Apache in the 1870s stopped to rest at a place they called "Pinetop"; Mormon ranchers founded a settlement here in 1878. Today Lakeside (elev. 6,745 feet) and Pinetop (elev. 7,279 feet) are major recreational centers with countless

summer cabins and resorts. The area's year-round population of about 8,000 jumps to 25,000 in summer. Though starting as separate communities, the two towns have expanded along the highway and now appear as one.

### Sights
**Rainbow Lake** is an 80-acre reservoir in Lakeside just west of AZ 260. Rainbow trout are stocked along with brown trout and some smallmouth bass and catfish. You can fish from the shore (near the dam) or rent a boat. Lakeside Campground ($7), is open mid-May to late-September. Reservations can be made through MISTIX; tel. (800) 283-CAMP.

**Scott Reservoir** is a smaller fishing lake of 70 acres about 3 miles northeast of Lakeside on Forest Route 45; the turnoff from AZ 260 is near the Lakeside Ranger Station. The reservoir has a boat ramp and campground (no drinking water or charge). Only electric motors are permitted.

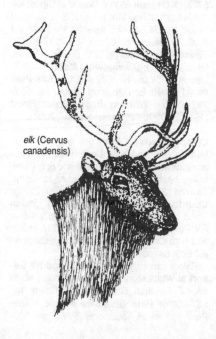

*elk (Cervus canadensis)*

**Woodland Reservoir** is an 18-acre, lure-only lake stocked with rainbow trout and some largemouth bass, catfish, and green sunfish. Fishing is best in spring and autumn. Electric boat motors only. There's picnicking but no camping. The lake is one mile west of Pinetop on Forest Route 316.

Lakeside Ranger Station (U.S. Forest Service), across the highway from Lakeside Campground, has two self-guided **auto tours** of the woodlands, wildlife, and history of the national forest; cassette tapes and players are loaned free. The **Porter Mountain Tour** is 33 miles long and takes about 2 hours. **Lake Mountain Tour** follows a 45-mile course; allow 4 hours.

**Blue Ridge Trail** (Forest Trail 107) is a popular 9-mile loop for hikers and horseback riders. Trailhead is near Lakeside off Forest Route 187, just past Springer Mountain Lookout. The Forest Service office has maps.

**Forest Route 300** follows the Mogollon Rim from Pinetop west nearly all the way to Camp Verde, with many panoramic views along the way. Most of the road is dirt—best suited for high-clearance vehicles, so check conditions first with the Forest Service. A 113-mile hiking and horseback trail also follows the rim for most of this distance on the old **General Crook Trail.** Army troops constructed the wagon road between 1872 and 1874 to move military supplies and troops between Camp Verde and Fort Apache. Ask at a forest service office about trail conditions and trailheads; also see *A Guide to the General Crook Trail* by Eldon Bowman, published by the Museum of Northern Arizona and the Boy Scouts of America in 1978.

### Accommodations And Campgrounds

In the largest resort area in the White Mountains, you have a choice of about two dozen motels and resorts, all nestled in cool pine forests. The Pinetop-Lakeside Chamber of Commerce has a list of places to stay and will help find what you're looking for. Two reservation services also offer assistance: **Central Lodging Reservations** (tel. 800-346-6280) and **White Mountain Central Reservations** (tel. 800-BEDTIME).

RVers can stop at **Blue Ridge Motel** (weekly and long term, in Pinetop; tel. 367-0758); **Elk Horn RV Park** (Lakeside; tel. 368-5343); **Hidden Pines RV Park** (Lakeside; tel. 368-6022); **Ponderosa Trailer Park** (Woodland Road in Lakeside; tel. 368-6989); and **Running Bear Mobile Resort** (Lakeside; tel. 368-6660). Tenters and RVers can stay at the **Lakeside Campground** in town or at **Show Low Lake** 4 miles north. Another possibility is just to head for the woods—you can camp free almost anywhere in the Apache-Sitgreaves National Forest. The Lakeside Ranger Station can suggest areas.

### Food

Restaurants are surprisingly good for such small communities. In Lakeside, try the **Lakewood Inn** (at Lake of the Woods; tel. 368-5153) or **Christmas Tree** (tel. 367-3107), both offering American cuisine. In Pinetop, choices include American at the **Chalet Restaurant** (tel. 367-1514) and **Roundhouse Resort** (tel. 369-4848), steaks at **Charlie Clark's Steak House** (tel. 367-4900) and **Moonridge Western Steak House** (tel. 367-1856), and Mexican at **La Casa Maya** (tel. 368-6444) and **El Rancho** (tel. 367-4557). Pinetop also has **G.J.'s Pizza** (tel. 367-3312) and a variety of fast-food places.

### Events

Sunrise Ski Area hosts a **Winterfest** with downhill and cross-country ski races and games in Jan., a family **Fun Festival** in Feb., and a **Spring Festival** in March. **Frontier Days** sets a Western theme for its large arts and crafts show, fiddlers' contest, chili cook-off, and other events in June. The **White Mountain Native American Arts Festival and Indian Market** in July attracts Indians from all over the Southwest for dances, music, art, crafts, demonstrations, and food. A colorful parade, arts and crafts show, and other presentations mark the end of summer during the **Fall Festival** in September.

### Services And Recreation

**Sports Village Athletic Club** in Pinetop has a swimming pool, tennis and racquetball courts, and other facilities open to the public; tel. 369-3333. You can go horseback riding from about May to Oct. with **The Outfitter** (Porter Mountain Road; tel. 368-5306) and **Wilderness Ranch Stables** (off Porter Mountain Road; tel. 368-5790). Play golf on the 18-hole course at **Pinetop Lakes Golf & Country Club**; tel. 369-4184.

### Information

Visit or write the **Pinetop-Lakeside Chamber of Commerce** to get the latest info about services and what's going on. Their office is centrally located in an A-frame cabin on the main highway (Box 266, Pinetop, AZ 85935); open Mon.-Fri. 8 a.m.-4:30 p.m. and often on Sat. and holidays in summer; tel. 367-4290. Staff at the **Lakeside Ranger Station** can inform you about camping, hiking, driving,

and cross-country skiing in the Apache-Sitgreaves National Forest; the office is across the highway from Lakeside Campground (or write Rt. 3, Box B-50, Lakeside, AZ 85929); open Mon.-Fri. 9 a.m.-5 p.m. and Sat. and Sun. about 9 a.m.-noon; tel. 368-5111. Get fishing and hunting licenses and info from **Arizona Game and Fish** on the south edge of Pinetop; tel. 367-4281. The **public library** and **senior center** are in Lakeside; tel. 368-6688.

### Transport

**White Mountain Passenger Lines** has bus connections in nearby Show Low with central Arizona (Phoenix, Tempe, Mesa, Globe, and Payson); tel. 537-4539. A **ski shuttle** makes the run to Sunrise Ski Area on Fri., Sat., and Sun. during the season; tel. 368-6834.

*Apache village, 1870s*

# WHITE MOUNTAIN APACHE INDIAN RESERVATION

You'll find some of Arizona's best outdoor recreation on the more than 1.6 million acres belonging to the White Mountain Apache. The only problem will be choosing among the many campsites, fishing streams, lakes, ski runs, and hiking possibilities. Farsighted planning and development by the tribe can be credited for the high-quality recreation available today. Though tribal permits are required for almost any activity, their costs are reasonable. You don't need state licenses for fishing, boating, or hunting—just the tribal permits. Some areas, such as the summit of sacred Baldy Peak, are closed or require a special-use permit. All Indian ruins, except for Kinishba, are closed areas. The best source of information is the **Game and Fish Dept.,** Box 220, Whiteriver, AZ 85941; tel. 338-4385/4386. The office is next to the White Mountain Apache Motel in Whiteriver. You can also get permits at Hon Dah, Hawley Lake, Horseshoe-Cienega Lake, A-1 Lake, Sunrise Lake, Reservation Lake, Carrizo, and Salt River Canyon Trading Post; off-reservation sources include White Mountain Sporting Goods in Pinetop and Tempe Marine in Tempe.

Use caution and keep an eye out for logging trucks on the reservation's many back roads. Some roads may be too rough for cars, especially after rains or snowmelt. The Game and Fish people can advise on current conditions. Most road junctions have signs, but it's a good idea to keep a map handy to find your way on the back roads.

The Apache and the federal government disagree on the name of the reservation; government officials tend to use the term "Fort Apache," while the Apache understandably prefer "White Mountain Apache." But either way, it's the same place.

## Events

The Apache enjoy participating in and attending rodeos, which take place on many weekends through the warmer months. Some major events are the **Headstart Rodeo** (Mother's Day weekend), **Cedar Creek Rodeo** (Memorial Day weekend), **Mountain Spirit Celebration** (July Fourth), and the **Labor Day Rodeo and Tribal Fair.** Rodeos, pow wows, and other area events are listed in the local paper, the *Fort Apache Scout.*

## Fishing

You have 400 miles of mountain streams and more than 25 lakes to cast your line in. The waters are stocked with fighting rainbow and brown trout from fish hatcheries at Williams Creek and Alchesay Springs. If you use a boat, you'll need a boat permit ($1/day or $10/year). Sunrise is the only lake where large motors are allowed; everywhere else you're limited to electrics. Fishermen can go out year-round; ice-fishing is popular where it's permitted (some lakes are closed in winter).

Fishing licenses cost $5/day; season fees are $50/summer (April 1-Oct. 31) or $70/calendar year. Children age 10-14 get a 50% discount (free under 10). An agreement with the San Carlos Apache Tribe honors the fishing permits from either tribe along both banks of the Black and Salt rivers where the reservations border, though a special-use permit will be needed.

## Hunting

Plentiful big and small game roam the reservation. The tribe holds regular seasons for elk, mountain lion, javelina, and pronghorn. You'll need a guide for hunting elk, lion, bear, and pronghorn—also lots of money! The guided hunts can cost $1000 a day, but they have a high success rate. Smaller animals and birds are more easily hunted; fees are $70 for either a javelina or small game license, and you aren't required to have a guide.

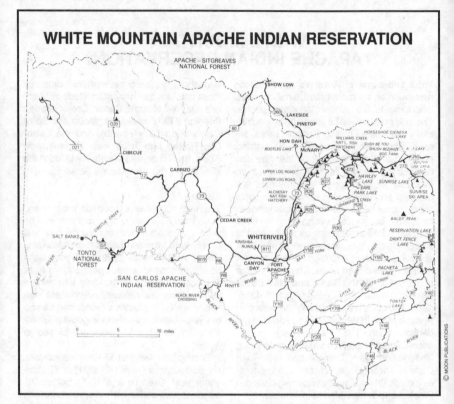

# WHITE MOUNTAIN APACHE INDIAN RESERVATION

APACHE – SITGREAVES
NATIONAL FOREST

© MOON PUBLICATIONS

## Others

You'll need a permit ($5 family) to have a picnic on the reservation unless you already have a current tribal permit for camping, fishing, or other activity. Camping facilities are basic, usually just picnic tables, fireplaces, and toilets; some campsites have drinking water. Backpacking is also permitted in certain areas, but be sure to have the proper special-use permit. Camping fees ($5/day) must be paid in advance at one of the places where permits are sold. Kayakers and rafters can enjoy a section of the Salt River Canyon on the reservation; best times are usually during the winter snow melt in April and May. A special-use permit is required. Sunrise Ski Area, with its many downhill runs, becomes a busy place in winter, and the tribe offers cross-country ski areas near Sunrise and McNary. Snowmobilers may operate near Sunrise. Cross-country ski and snowmobile passes must be purchased. The tribe prohibits ATVs, horseback riding (except with authorized concessions), and swimming everywhere on the reservation.

## SALT RIVER CANYON

Father Eusebio Francisco Kino visited this colorful canyon in 1698 and called it "Salado," for the salt springs in the area. You get great views of the canyon from US 60 as the highway swoops down to the bridge 48 miles southwest of Show Low. More of the area can be explored by driving on the dirt road that parallels the river. This route is highly scenic with towering cliffs above and the river below. Take the turnoff just north of the highway bridge until you come to a fork. At the fork, you have a choice of turning left and driving under the bridge 0.5 mile upriver to **Apache Falls,** or bearing right on the road downstream to Cibecue Creek (4 miles) and the Salt Banks (7.5 miles). You'll need a special-use permit, however, to drive past Cibecue Creek. The road is rough in spots but may be OK for a cautiously driven car. The desert country here at 3,000 feet contrasts sharply with the White Mountains, a short drive north. Saguaro cacti grow on the slopes to the right past the ford on Cibecue Creek. Don't cross if the water is fast-flowing and muddy.

To visit the **Salt Banks,** continue 3 miles past Cibecue Creek, turn left at the fork, and drive 0.5 mile to a parking area. Walk a little way downstream to the Salt Banks, a long series of salt springs that have deposited massive travertine formations. Minerals and

*Salt River Canyon*

algae color the springs with oranges, reds, and dark greens. This site has been sacred to the Apache who came to get salt and to perform religious ceremonies.

Past the Salt Banks turnoff, the road begins a steep climb and becomes too rough for cars. The White Mountain Apache have several primitive campsites (no drinking water) along the Salt River between the highway bridge and Cibecue Creek. Salt River Canyon Trading Post, near the highway bridge, has supplies and permits. Fishermen on the Salt River catch mostly channel catfish and some smallmouth bass and bluegill.

## CIBECUE

This small town in the western part of the reservation serves as the center for the Cibecue Apache, a group distinct from the White Mountain and San Carlos Apache. But for administration (and recreation permits), the Cibecue area is considered part of the White Mountain Reservation. Visitors can enjoy camping and good fishing for rainbow and brown trout in the upper 15 miles of Cibecue Creek nearby. The first fishing and camping spots are 5 miles north of town on the dirt road paralleling the creek. Elevations average about 6,000 feet. You'll need a special-use permit to go past the town. Apache Traders in Cibecue has gas and supplies. To reach Cibecue, turn northwest on Indian Route 12 from US 60, 8 miles south of Carrizo.

In the winter of 1880, a Cibecue medicine man named Noch-ay-del-klinne began teaching a new religion that predicted the expulsion of all white men. His enthusiastic following grew rapidly, worrying officers at Fort Apache. In the following August, officers dispatched troops and 23 Apache scouts to arrest the medicine man. Fighting broke out upon their arrival at Cibecue, and he was killed by the soldiers. The scouts then mutinied and joined the attack on the troops. Angry Apache pursued the survivors the entire 40 miles back to the fort. Captain Hentig and six other soldiers died in what is said to be the only revolt by Apache scouts in their 75 years with the Army.

## WHITERIVER

The administrative center of the White Mountain Apache lies in a valley at 5,000 feet, surrounded by high forested hills. It's easy to confuse the name of the town with that of the river flowing beside it, but the town is spelled as one word. Whiteriver has a trading post, motel, restaurants, shopping center, Indian Health Service Hospital, and tribal offices. The tribe owns and operates the giant Fort Apache Timber Company mill on the south edge of town.

### Practicalities

**White Mountain Apache Shopping Center,** just south of the town's center, has a supermarket, stores, movie theater, and post office. **White Mountain Apache Motel,** just beyond the shopping center, has modern rooms ($30 s or d), restaurant, and gift shop; tel. 338-4927. Get information and permits next door at the tribal **Game and Fish Department**; open Mon.-Fri. 8 a.m.-noon and 1-5 p.m., extended in summer Mon.-Thurs. 8 a.m.-5 p.m., Fri. 8 a.m.-7 p.m., and Sat. 7 a.m.-3 p.m.; Box 220, Whiteriver, AZ 85941; tel. 338-4385/4386.

## VICINITY OF WHITERIVER

### Fort Apache

In 1869, Major John Green selected this site near the confluence of the north and east forks of the White River as a supply base for troops in the field. Although the White Mountain Apache proved friendly, Army officers thought it wise to keep an eye on them and to prevent white settlers from encroaching on Indian land. Established as Fort Ord in 1870, the post's name was changed to Camp Mogollon, then to Camp Thomas, and finally to Camp Apache—all within one year! Troops and Apache scouts rode out to subdue rebellious Apache in the Tonto Basin (1872-73), and then to fight Victorio (1879) and Geronimo (1881-86). The last major action was the Mexican Campaign (1916-17). In 1922, the U.S. Indian Service converted the fort into a boarding school and named it in honor of President Theodore Roosevelt. Surprisingly, most of the first students were Navajo, but local Apache enrolled later. Plans call for the school to close in 1990, though the tribe may move its executive offices here.

Venerable buildings still standing include the commanding officer's quarters (built of

*"officers' row" at Fort Apache*

logs in 1871), adjutant's office (adobe, 1875), and officers' row (stone, 1890s). Drop into the **Apache Cultural Center** to see old photos, Apache crafts, and military artifacts and to learn about the history of the scouts and soldiers who manned the fort. One of the most prominent Apache scouts was Alchesay, whose name you see so often in the reservation. Known for his honesty and dedication to both the Army and his people, Alchesay helped put down rebellions of hostile tribes and assisted General Crook in making peace with Geronimo in 1886. The Apache Cultural Center is open Mon.-Fri. 8 a.m.-5 p.m. (7:30 a.m.-4:30 p.m. in summer) and sometimes on summer weekends (call first); free; tel. 338-4625. A few Apache crafts are sold. Go southwest 4 miles on the highway from Whiteriver and turn left across the river; the cultural center, a new building with a conical roof, is ahead on the left atop the hill.

### Kinishba Ruins
Kinishba is Apache for "brown house." Prehistoric Indians built two large pueblos and smaller buildings between A.D. 1232 and 1320 on both sides of a ravine. The mixed population came from areas of the Little Colorado, central Gila, and Salt rivers. Residents abandoned the village around 1350, possibly because of insufficient water. A University of Arizona team excavated the ruins from 1931 to 1939 and found 14 types of pottery and a great wealth of shell jewelry in more than 700 rooms. Only one of the large structures has survived. Because it has not been stabilized, entry is prohibited, but you can see the ruins by walking around outside. To reach the site from Whiteriver, go southwest 6 miles on the highway, then turn right on a dirt road; ruins are 2 miles in (keep left at the fork).

### Alchesay And Williams Creek National Fish Hatcheries
These hatcheries keep the streams and lakes of the reservation stocked with trout. Williams Creek receives eggs of four or five species of trout and raises the hatchlings to catchable size; large brood trout can also be seen in raceways. Alchesay specializes in raising

*Kinishba Ruins*

subcatchable rainbow and brown trout of 6 to 8 inches. Visitors are welcome to see exhibits and take a self-guided tour on weekdays 7 a.m.-3:30 p.m. at both facilities; closed holidays. Alchesay also has a picnic area. The turnoff for Alchesay Hatchery is between Mileposts 342 and 343, 4 miles north of Whiteriver; a paved road (signed) goes northeast 5 miles to the site. Roads to Williams Creek Hatchery turn off between Mileposts 351 and 352 (13 miles north of Whiteriver) and between Mileposts 353 and 354 (15 miles north of Whiteriver or 4 miles south of Hon Dah); follow signs 9 miles in on gravel roads.

## FISHING AND CAMPING SPOTS EAST OF WHITERIVER

### East Fork Of The White River
The stream has rainbow and some brown trout. Upper reaches are closed (signed) to fishing. From the turnoff east of Fort Apache, head east on Indian Route Y-55. Day use only.

*group of Apache*

### Upper And Lower Bonito Creek

Bonito is Spanish for "pretty." This stream has rainbow and brown trout, though you'll need a special-use permit for some sections. From the junction for Indian Route Y-70, 2 miles east of Fort Apache, turn in at the sign "Tonto Lake-Pacheta Lake-Maverick-Drift Fence Lake-Hurricane Lake-Reservation Lake." The road soon turns to gravel and offers fine views of the White River Valley while climbing Seven-Mile Hill. After 11.7 miles, turn left 3 miles on Y-70 for Upper Bonito (day use only) or continue straight 3 miles on Y-40 for Lower Bonito.

### Pacheta Lake

Best campsites are on the east side of this 68-acre lake (elev. 8,170 feet). Drinking water is available. Fishermen catch rainbow and brown trout. People say the name came from two cowboys playing cards around the turn of the century; both were caught cheating and called "pair-of-cheaters," a name that later became Pacheta. There are three ways to get here: follow the signs 40 miles east from Fort Apache on Indian Routes Y-70 and Y-20; take Y-55 east from Fort Apache; or take the better roads (AZ 273, Forest Route 116, and Y20) south from AZ 260 past Sunrise and Reservation lakes. Pacheta Lake is several miles east of the junction of Y-20 and Y-55.

### Drift Fence Lake

Cowboys gave the lake its name, because during cattle roundups, remaining stock drifted along the fence on the west side of the lake to lower pastures. The 16-acre lake lies close to the road between Pacheta and Reservation lakes; elevation is 8,900 feet. There are small campsites at each end of the lake, but large vehicles have more room at the north end.

### Reservation Lake

This 280-acre lake, the second largest on the reservation, offers good fishing for rainbow, brown, and brook trout. Cool forests of aspen, fir, and spruce grow at the 9,000-foot elevation. Rental boats, supplies, and permits are available from late May to early September. Several campgrounds surround the lake. The easiest way in is from the north: From Hon Dah, take AZ 260 east 20 miles to AZ 273 (road to Sunrise Lake); head southeast on AZ 273 for 14 miles, turn south 10 miles on Forest Route 116, then turn right 0.5 mile and cross a cattle guard to the lake. From Fort Apache, drive 46 miles east on Indian Routes Y-70 and Y-20 or take Y-55 and Y-20.

## FISHING AND CAMPING SPOTS NORTH OF WHITERIVER

### Diamond Creek

Rainbow and a few brown, brook, and native trout lurk in the creek. Special "quality fishing" regulations apply to a section of the creek; you'll need to obtain a Diamond Creek fishing permit for this area and obey additional fishing rules. Take the turnoff for Alchesay Fish National Hatchery, 4 miles north of Whiteriver, and turn right onto Indian Route R-25.

### North Fork Of The White River

Rainbow and brown trout are stocked, and you might catch a few brook and cutthroat. Fishing spots along this stream are reached via Upper Log Road, which parallels it. Take the Williams Creek Hatchery turnoff (Log Road), between Mileposts 351 and 352 (13 miles north of Whiteriver) or the turnoff between Mileposts 353 and 354 (15 miles north of Whiteriver and 4 miles south of Hon Dah).

### Bootleg Lake

At one time you could get illegal booze here, but now your best chance is for largemouth bass, rainbow trout, channel catfish, and sunfish. Special "quality fishing" regulations apply here, and you'll need a Bootleg Lake permit. Day use only. Elevation of the 10-acre lake is 6,800 feet. Turn west off AZ 73 at Milepost 355, 3 miles south of Hon Dah, and go in 2.2 miles.

## HON DAH

The Apache name for this travelers' stop means "be my guest." Stategically located 19 miles north of Whiteriver at the intersection of AZ Hwys. 260 and 73, the complex includes a motel ($25 s, $35 d), cabins with kitchens ($30 s, $45 d), restaurant (open daily for breakfast, lunch, and dinner), grocery store, and service station. Purchase reservation permits and fishing gear at the Hon Dah store. Motel address is Box 597, McNary, AZ 85930; tel. 369-4311.

## HISTORIC, FISHING, AND CAMPING SPOTS EAST OF HON DAH

### McNary

This old lumber town has an unusual history, though there's not much to see. Back in 1916, an energetic businessman in Flagstaff

*Apache warrior wearing owl-feather medicine hat*

*Na-ba-ka-la, a Cibecue Apache
armed with a 73 Winchester, ca. 1890*

named Tom Pollock chose the spot for a new lumber enterprise. He leased the land from the Apache, had a railroad line run in, and named the place "Cooley," after Corydon E. Cooley of the famous Show Low card game. Meanwhile, 1,000 miles east in McNary, Louisiana, the W.M. Cady Lumber Co. was running out of timbered land. To solve the problem, they bought out Pollock's Apache Lumber Co. and moved practically their whole town westward to Cooley in 1924. Renamed McNary, the town became known for its harmonious mixture of blacks, whites, Mexican-Americans, and Indians. When fire destroyed the sawmill in 1979, it was rebuilt 40 miles east near Eagar.

### Shush Be Zahze Lake

If you can't pronounce the Apache words, just call it "Little Bear." The 15-acre lake, at an elevation of 7,900 feet, has a small campground. You can try for rainbow, brown, and brook trout. Go 11 miles east of Hon Dah on AZ 260 and turn north 0.8 mile (keep left at the fork).

### Shush Be Tou Lake

The name is Apache for "Big Bear." The 18-acre lake has a campground and fishing similar to nearby Shush Be Zahze's. Directions are the same, except take the right fork.

### Hawley Lake

Trout swim in the waters of this 260-acre lake. In winter you can fish through the ice. Constructed in 1957, this was the first lake on the reservation designed for recreation. Facilities include a boat dock with rentals, service station/grocery store, campground ($5), trailer park ($15; has showers), cabins ($45-65 s or d), and kitchenettes ($45 s or d); tel. 335-7511. Dusty campers can use the trailer park's showers and laundromat for a small fee. Permits for fishing, camping, and other activities can be purchased in the store. Facilities are open from about mid-May to mid-October. From AZ 260, 11.3 miles east of Hon Dah, turn south 11 miles on AZ 473 (the first 9 miles are paved). Despite the 8,300-foot elevation, the road in is kept open year-round. **Earl Park Lake** (47 acres), 0.5 mile southeast of Hawley Lake, also offers fishing.

### Horseshoe-Cienega Lake

You can fish on this 121-acre lake (elev. 8,100 feet) for rainbow, brown, and brook trout. Information, camping and fishing supplies, boat rentals, and permits are available at the boat dock and store, open from about mid-May to mid-September. The road is cleared in winter for ice fishermen. Go 13.5 miles east of Hon Dah on AZ 260, turn south at the sign, and follow the road one mile across the dam to the south side of the lake.

### Little Bog Tank

This 12-acre lake (elev. 8,100 feet) is stocked with rainbow, brown, and brook trout. Day use only. Bog Tank is 14 miles east of Hon Dah on AZ 260, then 0.3 mile north. Nearby Horseshoe-Cienega Lake has groceries, fishing supplies, and permits.

## A-1 Lake

A 24-acre lake stocked with rainbow and brook trout. It's 18 miles east of Hon Dah on AZ 260 on the south side of the highway.

# SUNRISE RESORT AND SKI AREA

## Sunrise Lake

Fishermen know the 920-acre lake (elev. 9,200 feet) for its big rainbow trout. This is the only lake on the reservation where you can use gas motors (limit 10 horsepower). **Apache Sunrise Resort Lodge** offers a restaurant, indoor pool, sauna, jacuzzi, volleyball and other games, and seasonal horseback riding. Sky rides at the ski area are sometimes offered on holidays. The lodge closes for about 6 weeks at the end of the ski season in April, then reopens for summer visitors from Memorial Day to mid-Sept., then closes again until the ski season starts. Summer rates are $50 s or d; tel. tel. (800) 55-HOTEL in Arizona, or (602) 735-7676 outside Arizona. **Sunrise Marina** has fishing supplies and boat rentals near the lodge; tel. 735-7354. **Sunrise Station,** 0.5 mile south of the lodge, sells groceries, gas, supplies, and permits. From AZ 260, 20 miles east of Hon Dah or 18 miles west of Springerville, turn south 3.5 miles on AZ 273 to the lodge and marina. The campground is on the left just after turning onto the Sunrise Ski Area road, 0.7 mile past the lodge.

## Sunrise Ski Area

This cluster of three peaks—Sunrise, Apache, and Cyclone Circle—has 45 ski runs winding downward through pine and aspen forests of the White Mountains. The resort is largely geared to family skiing, with equal amounts of advanced, intermediate, and beginner terrain. A combination of three triple chairlifts, three double chairlifts, and four surface lifts helps keep lines short. Snow-making machines add to the natural snowpack for a season from Nov. to April. Lift rates run $24/full day ($12 for age 12 and under), $18/half day ($8 for age 12 and under). You can go night skiing on some weekends, $10. The resort offers a variety of group and private lessons. Shops rent equipment and have sales and repairs. Child-care services provide indoor and outdoor activities for kids age 3-6.

Sunrise Ski Area offers package deals including room, breakfasts, and lift tickets. Room-only rates start at $50/night s or d, but jump to $90 s or d during the holiday season (Dec. 20-Jan. 14) and on Fri. and Sat. during the peak ski season (Jan. 15-March 11). For the latest accommodation and skiing info, contact Sunrise Ski Area, Box 217, McNary, AZ 85930; tel. 735-7669 (office), 735-7518 (ski school). Recorded ski conditions: tel. (800) 772-SNOW in Arizona, or (800) 882-SNOW outside Arizona. Lodge reservations: tel. (800) 55-HOTEL in Arizona, or (602) 735-7676 outside Arizona. A shuttle bus connects Apache Sunrise Resort Lodge with the ski lifts and Sunrise Day Lodge about every 15 minutes. Accommodations get tight during the ski season and many skiers stay at Greer (15 miles east), Springerville (22 miles east), or Pinetop-Lakeside (30 miles west).

# EAST OF THE WHITE MOUNTAIN APACHE INDIAN RESERVATION

## GREER

This pretty valley is high in the White Mountains at 8,500 feet. The first settlers arrived in 1879, and later it was named for Americus Vespucius Greer, a prominent Mormon pioneer. The community comes to life in the summer, when visitors enjoy the fishing, forest walks, or just the cool mountain air. Winter is the next busiest season—snow worshipers flock to the slopes of nearby Sunrise Ski Area or they put on their "skinny skis" to glide along the miles of marked cross-country ski trails just outside Greer. The quietest times are mid-April to early May, when the first signs of spring appear, and autumn, a time of crisp days and aspens turning gold. You can fish the waters of the three Greer Lakes, just north of town, and the Little Colorado River—all stocked with trout. Greer lies 15 miles east of Sunrise Ski Area, 16 miles west of Springerville, and 225 miles northeast of Phoenix. From AZ 260, turn 5 miles south on AZ 373.

# GREER ACCOMMODATIONS

Greer, AZ 85927 (except for Bear Pond Inn)
(listed from north to south)

| RESORT | ADDRESS | RATES (+5.5%) | TEL. # | FEATURES |
|--------|---------|---------------|--------|----------|
| Bear Pond Inn | (3 miles north of town); Box 1525, Eagar, AZ 85925 | $38-48 d and up | 735-7576 (629-9739 in Tucson) | European cuisine; fishing pond; jacuzzi |
| Greer Mountain Resort | Box 145 (2.7 miles north of town) | $50 d kitchenette $65 d cabin $12.50 RV | 735-7560 | restaurant |
| White Mountain Lodge | Box 139 | $30-45 and up | 735-7568 | bed and breakfast in 1892 farmhouse |
| Molly Butler Lodge | Box 134 | $25-40 | 735-7226 | oldest guest lodge in Arizona (1910); open all year |
| The Aspens | Box 70 | $55-65 d | 735-7226 | cottages |
| Big Ten Resort | Box 124 | $60 d and up | 735-7578 | cabins; open all year |
| Greer Lodge Bed & Breakfast | Box 244 | $85 s, $130 d | 735-7515 | private trout pond; open all year |
| Four Seasons | Box 219 | $75-85 d | 735-7333 | cabins |
| Greer Point Trails End | Box 224 | $55-75 d | 735-7513 | cabins |
| Amberian Point Resort | Box 125 | lodge: $75 s, $95 d cabin: $90 d | 735-7475 | restaurant; open all year |

## Accommodations And Food

Greer's 15 or so resorts have rustic cabins, usually with a kitchen and cozy fireplace; see chart. **Pappy's Diner** in town serves American food and pizza; open daily for breakfast, lunch, and dinner; tel. 735-7483. The **Amberian Point Resort** offers American and continental cuisine; open daily for breakfast, lunch, and dinner; tel. 735-7475. **Greer Lodge** has generous family-style breakfasts and dinners daily; tel. 735-7515. **Molly Butler Lodge** offers dinners; tel. 735-7226. **Greer Mountain Resort** has breakfast and lunch daily; tel. 735-7560. **Bear Pond Inn** presents continental fare for dinner; tel. 735-7576 (reservations requested).

## Campgrounds

You'll pass the two national forest campgrounds of **Benny Creek** ($5) and **Rolfe C. Hoyer** ($7) on the way in to Greer. Both have water during the season of about mid-May to the end of September. Rolfe C. Hoyer Campground is larger and offers a nature trail, showers, and MISTIX reservations (tel. 800-282-CAMP).

## Services And Information

**Butler Canyon Trail** is a one-mile, self-guided nature trail just north of town; turn east off AZ 373 at the sign for Montlure Camp. **Greer Lakes** are three small reservoirs offering boating (electric motors OK), trout fishing, and picnicking; turn east off AZ 373 opposite Rolfe C. Hoyer Campground. **Greer Stables**, opposite Molly Butler Lodge, offers guided rides, hayrides, cookouts, and mountain bicycle rentals; tel. 735-7403. **Cross-country skiers** can enjoy a variety of loop trails in the woods northwest of town; local businesses and the chamber of commerce have trail maps. Obtain groceries, fishing gear, camping supplies, and cross-country ski rentals from The **Circle B Market**; tel. 735-7540. The **Greer Chamber of Commerce** will send you a business directory of resorts and services of the community; Box 54, Greer, AZ 85927; tel. 735-7230.

## MOUNT BALDY WILDERNESS

The pristine forests and alpine meadows of 11,403-foot Mount Baldy present a rare opportunity to visit a subalpine vegetation zone. You'll see magnificent forests untouched by commercial logging. Engelmann and blue spruce dominate, but quaking aspen, white fir, corkbark fir, Douglas fir, southwestern white pine, and ponderosa pine also cover the slopes. You might catch a glimpse of elk, mule or whitetailed deer, black bear, beaver, wild turkey, blue grouse, or other wildlife. Mount Baldy is an extinct volcano 8 or 9 million years old and worn down by three periods of glaciation.

**West Fork (#94)** and **East Fork (#95)** trails follow the respective branches of the Little Colorado River up the northeast slopes of Mount Baldy. Each trail is 6.5 miles long, and they meet on the grassy summit ridge. The summit is another mile away, but the last half mile of trail crosses White Mountain Apache land, which is closed to outsiders. The Apache enforce the closure—errant hikers have been arrested and had their gear confiscated—so it's not worth trying to sneak up. Apache Indians still make pilgrimages to their sacred peak. Hiking season lasts from June to Oct., but plan to be off the ridges by early afternoon in July and Aug. to avoid getting caught in a thunderstorm. The trailheads, about 4 miles apart by road, can easily be reached from Greer, Sunrise, or Big Lake via AZ 273. In fact, both trails also go north to Greer, about 5 miles away. The West Fork Trailhead (elev. 9,240 feet) lies just outside the wilderness boundary at the end of Forest Route 113J, 0.5 mile in from AZ 273. The East Fork Trailhead (elev. 9,400 feet) begins near Phelps Cabin, 0.2 mile in from AZ 273. An all-day or overnight loop hike can be done by using a 3.3-mile connecting trail that joins the lower ends of West Fork and East Fork trails; this trail may not be shown on maps, but it goes from the West Fork Trail (0.3 mile up from the trailhead) to the Phelps Cabin area.

Horseback riders are welcome on the trails and may use small corrals near Phelps Cabin. Fishermen catch brook, rainbow, and a few native cutthroat trout in the creeks. The Forest Service asks visitors to limit hiking and riding groups to 12 persons and camping groups to 6 persons. Forest Service offices sell a topo map of Mount Baldy Wilderness.

## BIG LAKE

Rolling mountain meadows and forested hills of spruce and fir surround this pretty lake. Top-rated for trout by many fishermen, Big Lake (575 acres) has a marina, camp-grounds, hiking trails, and a riding stable. The marina offers rental boats, motors, fishing supplies, gas pump, and groceries from late April/early May to late Nov.; a fish-cleaning station is across the parking lot and a public boat ramp is a short drive away. Nearby **Crescent Lake** (197 acres) has trout fishing and a smaller marina (boat rentals and snacks) but no campgrounds. Staff size per-mitting, the Forest Service operates a visitor center on the main road between the two lakes and offers naturalists' programs. You have a choice of four campgrounds at Big Lake—all with drinking water and a charge of $6-8/night: **Rainbow, Grayling, Brookchar,** and **Cutthroat**; both RVers and tenters can stay at Rainbow and Grayling, but only tent-ers at Brookchar and Cutthroat. Camping season with water lasts mid-May to mid-Sept.; Grayling, Brookchar, and Cutthroat stay open mid-April to Thanksgiving if wea-ther permits. Expect cool nights at the 9,200-foot elevation even in midsummer. Camp-sites can be reserved through MISTIX; tel. (800) 283-CAMP. Big Lake is on AZ 273 about 25 miles south from AZ 260; the turnoff from AZ 260 is 7 miles east of the Greer junction (or 4 miles west of Springerville). You might want to try your luck with rainbow trout on the way in at **Mexican Hay Lake** (bring your own boat; no facilities).

### Vicinity Of Big Lake
**Lee Valley Lake** (35-acres) has brook trout (best early and late in the season) and great scenery. The lake, near Mount Baldy Wilder-ness, is off AZ 273 between Big Lake and Sunrise. Elevation is 9,400 feet. **Winn Camp-ground** is at the end of Forest Route 554, 2 miles in from AZ 273. Greer, Lee Valley Lake, Sunrise Lake, Big Lake, and Crescent Lake are all within a 10-mile radius. Camping sea-son at the 8,800-foot elevation is from mid-May to the end of Sept.; sites, which can be reserved through MISTIX, have drinking water and $5 fee.

**East Fork of the Black River** offers fishing for rainbow trout. Stay at **Diamond Rock, Aspen,** or **Buffalo Crossing campgrounds** (no drinking water; free). Season runs from early May to the end of October. The area is 9 miles southeast of Big Lake and 10-14 miles southwest of Alpine.

**West Fork of the Black River** has fishing for rainbow and brown trout. **West Fork Campground** is beside the stream (no drink-ing water; free). You could do an 8-mile day or overnight hike downstream from the crossing of Forest Route 116 to West Fork Campground or vice versa. The Apache-Sitgreaves National Forest map shows the back roads in this area.

## SPRINGERVILLE AND EAGAR

Since Henry Springer's trading post opened in 1879, Springerville has grown to be an important trade, ranching, and lumbering center. Today the town makes a handy stop for travelers. Springerville and the adjacent town of Eagar lie in Round Valley beside the Little Colorado River at an elevation of 6,965 feet. Rolling grass-covered hills surround the valley. The *Madonna of the Trail,* an 18-foot statue in the middle of town, commemorates the hardy pioneer women of the covered wagon days.

### Renee Cushman Art Collection
This former resident willed her valuable col-lection of European art and furniture to the LDS Church in Springerville. Three display rooms house the items, which date from the Renaissance to the early 20th century. Open on request; telephone numbers are posted

on the front door of the museum and are available from the chamber of commerce. Located at the Springerville LDS Church at 150 N. Aldrice Burk, 1½ blocks off Main Street.

## Accommodations, Food, And Campgrounds
Six motels and a similar number of restaurants lie along Main St. (US 60) in downtown Springerville. **White Mountain KOA** campground is one mile northwest on US 60; open all year; $13.26 tent, $19.84 RV w/hookups; tel. 333-4632. Nearby Becker Lake offers trout fishing.

## Events
Cowboys and cowgirls, age 40 and up, show their skills at the **Old Timers' Rodeo** on Memorial Day weekend; other events include a parade, dances, chili cookoff, art show, and fishing derby. The community celebrates **July Fourth** with a parade, rodeo, barbecue, dance, hot-air balloons, and fireworks. **Eagar Daze,** the first weekend in Aug., features a talent show, games, barbecue, and a dance.

## Shopping And Services
**Round Valley Plaza,** just south of downtown on S. Mountain Ave., has a supermarket and other stores. Pick up fishing, hunting, and camping supplies at the **Sport Shack,** 329 E. Main St.; tel. 333-2222. **White Mountain Communities Hospital** is in downtown Springerville at 118 S. Mountain Ave.; tel. 333-4368. Eagar has the indoor **Round Valley Swimming Pool** at 116 N. Eagar St.; tel. 333-2238.

## Information
The **White Mountain Chamber of Commerce,** at Main and Apache in downtown Springerville, can tell you about the area and services; open Mon.-Fri. 8 a.m.-4 p.m. (and Sat. 1-4 p.m. in summer); Box 181, Springerville, AZ 85938; tel. 333-2123. For maps and the latest info on recreation and road conditions in the Apache-Sitgreaves National Forest, visit either of the two **U.S. Forest Service** offices on S. Mountain Ave.: the **Springer-**

**ville Ranger District Office** (just north of Round Valley Plaza) has specific information on Big Lake, Mt. Baldy, Greer, South Fork, and other areas of the district; open Mon.-Fri. 7:30 a.m.-4:30 p.m. (and Sat. 8 a.m.-4 p.m. in summer); tel. 333-4372; the **Supervisor's Office** (just south of Round Valley Plaza) has general information for all of the Apache-Sitgreaves National Forest; open Mon.-Fri. 7:30 a.m.-4:30 p.m.; tel. 333-4301; contact either office by mail at Box 640, Springerville, AZ 85938. Springerville's **public library** is downtown off Main St.; tel. 333-4694.

## VICINITY OF SPRINGERVILLE

### Lyman Lake State Park
Rain and snow melt from the White Mountains fill this 1,500-acre lake. Though it's cold here in winter due to the 6,000-foot elevation, fishermen will be out year-round. You're most likely to catch channel catfish, largemouth bass, walleye, crappie, and northern pike. Lyman Lake is large enough for sailing and water-skiing (no motor restrictions). Fishermen, however, have a section of the west end buoyed off as a no-wake area. The marina has a paved boat ramp and boat rentals. Excellent campground facilities include restrooms, showers, hookups, grocery store, and snack bar. Boaters can also use some campsites accessible only by water on the other side of the lake. Campers should be prepared for strong winds on the open terrain. Charges (per vehicle) are $3 day use, $6 camping, or $8 w/electric and water hookups. The park is 17 miles north of Springerville and 12 miles south of St. Johns on US 180/666; tel. 337-4441. Look for a herd of buffalo near the entrance.

### South Fork
Three resorts and a national forest campground are near the South Fork of the Little Colorado River (elev. 7,700 feet), 5 miles west of Springerville. **South Fork Campground,** 2.5 miles south of AZ 260 on Forest Route 560, is on both sides of the stream. Camping season is mid-May to the end of

Sept. (no water; free). A hiking trail follows the South Fork about 3 miles upstream. Resorts include **South Fork Guest Ranch** (tel. 333-4455), **Canyon Cove Resort** (rustic cabins; tel. 333-4602), and **White Mountain Resort** (modern condos; also tel. 333-4602).

## St. Johns

Spanish explorers named this spot on the Little Colorado River El Vadito ("Little River Crossing"). In 1871, Sol Barth founded a settlement along the river with his brothers and some Mexican families, then moved it 6 miles upstream to the present site the following year. Residents named the community "San Juan" after its first female resident, Senora Maria San Juan de Padilla de Baca. Supposedly, the postal authorities refused to accept a "foreign" name, so it was changed to Saint John, with an "s" added for phonetic effect. Mormon settlers arrived in 1879 from Utah. Today, St. Johns (pop. 3,740) serves as the Apache County seat; it's 29 miles north of Springerville and 44 miles southeast of Petrified Forest National Park.

You can learn more about the area's history and see pioneer and Indian artifacts in the **Apache County Museum.** It's on Cleveland (US 180/AZ 61); open Mon.-Fri. 8 a.m.-noon and 1-5 p.m. and sometimes on Sat. (closed holidays); donation; tel. 337-4737.

St. Johns has three motels and several restaurants. Events include **San Juan Day** in mid-June (parade, barbecue, dances, and games), **July Fourth** (barbecue, games, and fireworks), **Pioneer Day** on the weekend nearest July 24th (parade, rodeo, pageant, barbecue, and dances), **Classy Chassis Car Show and Two-Day Street Fair** in mid-Aug. (show, games, parade, barbecue, and dance), and **Apache County Fair** in Sept. (exhibits and horse races; a second set of horse races takes place one week later). The pleasant **city park** has covered picnic tables, playground, outdoor pool, and courts for tennis, volleyball, racquetball, and handball at Second West and Second South (from near the museum, turn south two blocks on Second West). The **St. Johns Chamber of Commerce** is at 120 Commercial St.; open Mon.-Fri. 8 a.m.-5 p.m.; Box 178, St. Johns, AZ 85936; tel. 337-2000. The **public library** is in the Apache County Annex at First North and First West.

## Kolhuwalawa

Arizona's 23rd Indian reservation was created in 1985 to give the Zuni (ZOO-nee) tribe back their "heaven." The 1,400 acres, located 14 miles north of St. Johns, is thought by the Zuni to be the place where the human spirit goes after death. Anthropologists think that

*Zuni dance mask of Sáyatäsha*

Zuni religious leaders have held sacred dances and ceremonies here since at least A.D. 900, when ancestors of the tribe began migrating from pueblos in Arizona to New Mexico. The Zuni people, like the Hopi, still live in pueblos and maintain many of their old traditions. You can visit Zuni Pueblo, one of the fabled Seven Cities of Cíbola sought by Coronado in 1540. Zuni is in New Mexico, 58 miles northeast of St. Johns.

## Concho Lake

Fish for rainbow and brook trout in this 60-acre lake, located about 16 miles west of St. Johns; no boat ramp or other facilities are available at present. The adjacent **Concho Valley Country Club** has a nine-hole golf course and a restaurant; tel. 337-4644. **Concho Valley Motel** and an **RV park** are nearby; contact the Concho Valley sales office at tel. 337-4695.

# THE CORONADO TRAIL

Seeking treasures of the legendary Seven Cities of Cíbola in 1540, Francisco Vásquez de Coronado and his men struggled through the rugged mountains of eastern Arizona. Though the Spaniard's quest failed, the name of this scenic highway honors his effort. You'll discover the *real* wealth on a drive over Coronado's old route—the scenery of rugged mountains, clad in majestic forests, rolling in blue waves towards the horizon. The blazing gold of aspen in the autumn is matched only by the dazzling display of summer wildflowers. The 123 miles of paved highway between Springerville and Clifton twist over country little changed from Coronado's time. Hikers, fishermen, and cross-country skiers will be far from the crowds when exploring this region.

A look at the Apache-Sitgreaves National Forest map shows many scenic loop possibilities in the backcountry. Allow enough time for the journey through this high country—even a nonstop drive on the highway will take 3½ hours. With some 460 curves between Alpine and Morenci, the route certainly isn't for the person in a hurry! But you'll probably want to stop many times to enjoy the views, do some walking, or perhaps have a picnic.

Drivers should stock up on groceries and gas before venturing on the 95 miles from Alpine to Morenci, as no towns are along this stretch. Winter snows can close the highway from Alpine to just north of Morenci between mid-Dec. and mid-March, but the section from Springerville to Alpine is kept open. Miles of good cross-country ski trails attract winter visitors to the forests surrounding Alpine.

### Nelson Reservoir

Rainbow, brown, and brook trout live in this 60-acre lake located 10 miles south of Springerville. Picnic tables, restrooms, and a boat ramp are provided, but there's no camping. Escudilla Mountain, the large rounded peak to the south, is Arizona's third highest.

### Escudilla Mountain And Wilderness

Coronado undoubtedly spotted the 10,912-foot summit of this ancient volcano in 1540. Perhaps a homesick member of his expedition named the mountain after an *escudilla*, a soup bowl used in his native Spain. In 1951 a disastrous fire burned the forests on the entire north face of Escudilla. Aspen trees then took over where mighty conifers once stood—the normal sequence after a moun-

*Terry Flat and Escudilla Mountain*

tain fire. Raspberries, snowberries, currants, elderberries, strawberries, and gooseberries flourished too. The forests of spruce, fir, and pine on top escaped the fire. Lower down you'll find surviving woodlands of aspen, Rocky Mountain maple, ponderosa pine, and Gambel oak. Elk, deer, black bear, and smaller animals roam the hillsides. Escudilla was once grizzly territory, but the last one was killed in the 1920s or '30s.

Now a wilderness area of 5,200 acres, Escudilla offers excellent hiking. Outstanding views from the fire lookout—the highest in Arizona—reward those who make the climb. The actual summit (10,912 feet) lies 0.5 mile to the north and 36 feet higher, but trees completely block the views there. **Escudilla National Recreation Trail,** a well-graded, 3.3-mile trail from Terry Flat (elev. 9,600 feet), ascends to Escudilla Lookout through aspen, meadows, and conifers. (The old Government Trail, though shown on some maps, is no longer maintained and isn't recommended; it originally began from Hulsey Lake.) From US 666 between Mileposts 420 and 421, about 21 miles south of Springerville and 6 miles north of Alpine, turn east 4.6 miles on Forest Route 56 to Terry Flat Loop, then take the left fork 0.4 mile to the trailhead. The **Terry Flat Loop** makes a worthwhile destination in itself; the 6-mile dirt road encircles Terry Flat Meadow with many fine views of Escudilla Mountain; cautiously driven cars can usually make the trip in dry weather.

# ALPINE

Mormon settlers founded this town in 1879 and named it Frisco, after the nearby San Francisco River. Later, thinking their mountains resembled the Alps, they renamed the community Alpine. The setting is pretty—a high mountain valley (elev. 8,046 feet) surrounded by extensive woodlands—but the Alps it's not! Alpine (pop. 525) makes an excellent base for hiking, fishing, hunting, horseback riding, golfing, scenic drives, and—in winter—cross-country skiing, sledding, and snowmobiling.

## Accommodations

**Sportsman's Lodge,** on US 666, has motel rooms at $30 s or d and kitchenettes at $37.50-45 s or d; tel. 339-4576. **Alpine Cabins,** in town next to the M&J Corral Restaurant, has a variety of kitchenettes at $26.38-36.93; tel. 339-4378. **Mountain Hi Lodge,** 0.5 mile east on Main St., has similar facilities at $23.21 s or d and kitchenettes at $30.60 s or d; tel. 339-4311. **Judd's Ranch,** 0.5 mile north of Alpine, has cabins (with kitchenettes), horseback rides, and a fishing lake; open from late April to late Oct., $26.50 s or d; tel. 339-4326. **Tal-Wi-Wi Lodge,** 3 miles north of Alpine, has motel rooms ($36.93 for up to 4 persons) and a restaurant serving breakfast and dinner daily; tel. 339-4319, (800) 323-3855 in Arizona, or (800) 533-3585 out of state. Tal-Wi-Wi Lodge also offers cross-country skiing (trails, instruction, rentals, and tours) and snowmobile tours in winter; tel. 339-4915.

## Campgrounds

**Alpine Divide Campground,** set in a forest of ponderosa pine and Gambel oak 4 miles north of Alpine, has great views. The sites, with drinking water, are maintained from mid-May to mid-Sept. and cost $5; the rest of the year camping is on a "pack-in/pack-out basis," free. **Luna Lake Campground,** 4 miles east of Alpine on US 180 near the New Mexico border, is in a ponderosa pine forest; open with drinking water from mid-May to mid-Sept.; $6; reservations can be made through MISTIX; tel. (800) 283-CAMP. Luna Lake (75 acres) has a boat launch, boat rentals, and a small store; open all year; tel. 339-4912 (recording of fishing news). Fishermen are after trout in all four seasons—even out on the ice in winter. RVers can also stay at **Alpine Village Trailer Park** (in town on US 180; tel. 339-4476), **Meadow View Trailer Park** (in town near the junction of US 666 and US 180; tel. 339-4533), and **Outpost RV & Trailer Park** (on US 180 near Luna Lake; tel. 339-4854).

## Food

For a variety of American and Mexican food, try the **Sundowner** (open daily all year for breakfast, lunch, and dinner; tel. 339-4451) and **M&J Corral** (open daily for breakfast, lunch, and dinner, then weekends in winter; tel. 339-4378). The **Alpine Country Club,** 5 miles out of town, serves lunch daily except Mon., and dinner Thurs.-Sat.; tel. 339-4944.

### Events

**Dog-Sled Races** liven up January. **Bush Valley Craft Fair, Fiddlers' Jam Session,** and **Luna Lake Trout Derby** take place in May. The **Alpine Rodeo** features a parade and rodeo excitement in June. Shop early in the **Bush Valley Christmas Bazaar** on Labor Day weekend.

### Services

**Alpine Hardware** and the **Tackle Shop** have outdoor supplies. **Judd's Ranch** (tel. 339-4326) has horseback riding. **Alpine Adventures** organizes trail rides, hayrides, pack trips, backcountry hiking, fishing trips, and hunting trips; Box 349, Alpine, AZ 85920; tel. 339-4434. For winter activities of snowmobile tours and cross-country skiing (trails, instruction, and rentals), contact Alpine Adventures at Box 626, Alpine, AZ 85920; tel. 339-4915. See how far you can hit a golf ball through the thin mountain air at **Alpine Country Club's** 18-hole course; has rental carts and clubs and a restaurant; open mid-May to mid-Oct.; head east 3 miles on US 180, then turn south 2 miles and follow signs; tel. 339-4944.

### Information

The **Alpine Chamber of Commerce** has a list of accommodations and services; write Box 410, Alpine, AZ 85920; tel. 339-4330. The **Alpine Ranger District** office of the Apache-Sitgreaves National Forest is very helpful with info on scenic drives, fishing, hiking, camping, and cross-country ski trails. The district covers the north half of the Coronado Trail, including Escudilla Mountain and most of the Blue Range Primitive Area; open Mon.-Fri. 8 a.m.-4:30 p.m. (and Sat. 9 a.m.-3 p.m. in summer); in town at the junction of US 666 and 180; Box 469, Alpine, AZ 85920; tel. 339-4633/4384. Alpine's **public library** is on US 180; tel. 339-4925.

## VICINITY OF ALPINE

### Blue River-Red Hill Scenic Loop

This backcountry drive visits the Blue River, remote ranches, and rugged hill country. The Forest Service has two small campgrounds along the way—Upper Blue (has spring water) and Blue Crossing; both lie near the Blue River at an elevation of 6,200 feet; no charge. From Alpine, head east 3 miles on US 180 and turn south on Forest Route 281 (Blue Road). After 10 miles you'll reach the Blue River; follow it downstream 9 miles to the junction with Forest Route 567 (Red Hill Road). A river ford here can be impassable during times of high water. The Red Hill Road twists and climbs out of the valley, often following ridges with good views, to US 666 (14 miles south of Alpine). If driving the other direction, you'll find the Red Hill Road turnoff between Mileposts 239 and 240 on US 666. The forest roads are gravel and should be OK in dry weather for cautiously driven cars. See the Alpine Ranger District office for more info on this and other scenic drives in the area.

Hikers may want to try **Red Hill Trail #56**; the 10-mile trail follows a jeep track to the Blue Range Primitive Area, descends along ridges via Red Hill (elev. 7,714 feet), drops into Bush Creek, and follows the creek to the Blue River. Upper trailhead (elev. 8,000 feet) is on Forest Route 567 one mile east of US 666; lower trailhead (5,790 feet) is on Forest Route 281 about 2 miles south of the junction with Forest Route 567.

## BLUE RANGE PRIMITIVE AREA

This rugged wilderness country lies south of Alpine along the Arizona-New Mexico border. The south-flowing Blue River, fed by several perennial streams, neatly divides the primitive area in two. The Mogollon Rim, whose high cliffs form the south boundary of the Colorado Plateau, crosses the area from west to east. Geologic uplifting and downcutting have created spectacular rock formations and rough, steep canyons. Elevations range from 9,100 feet near Hannagan Meadow to 4,500 feet in the lower Blue River. Hiking down from the rim, you'll find the spruce, fir, and ponderosa pine forests giving way to pinyon pine and juniper in the lower valleys. Wildlife you might run across include Rocky Mountain elk, Coues whitetailed deer, mule deer, black bear, mountain lion, javelina, and bobcat. You may also see such rare and endangered birds as the southern bald eagle, spotted owl, American peregrine falcon, aplomado falcon, Arizona woodpecker, black-eared bushtit, and olive warbler. The upper Blue River and some of its tributaries harbor small numbers of trout.

## Hiking

Hikers usually find the best weather from April to early July and from Sept. to late October. Violent thunderstorms lash the mountains in July and August. Snow covers much of the land from Nov. to March. Many dayhikes and backpacking trips are possible on Forest Service trails. You can hike from trailheads along the Coronado Trail (US 666), from Forest Route 281 (Blue Road), and from Forest Route 567 (Red Hill Road). Other trailheads are to the east in New Mexico and to the south off Forest Route 475. The Forest Service office in Alpine has maps and trail descriptions. The book *Arizona Trails* by David Mazel also has detailed info and maps.

## HANNAGAN MEADOW AND VICINITY

Splendid forests of aspen, spruce, and fir surround the tiny village of Hannagan Meadow (elev. 9,100 feet), 22 miles south of Alpine. A network of trails offers some great hiking in the area; several trails also lead into the adjacent Blue Range Primitive Area. You'll find some of the best cross-country skiing and snowmobiling in Arizona, though the area remains relatively unknown. The road from Alpine is normally kept open in winter, but storms occasionally close it for a few days.

## Hannagan Meadow Lodge

The rustic cabins in this remote region offer comfortable accommodations. Cabins, which start at $57.75/night, and the lodge dining room stay open all year. A small store, open June to Dec., sells groceries and gasoline. Cross-country skiers can glide along marked trails during the late Nov. to late March season. Contact Hannagan Meadow Lodge at Box 335, Alpine, AZ 85920; tel. 339-4370. If headed south, this is your very last chance to get gas or supplies until Clifton-Morenci, 70 miles away.

## Hannagan Meadow Campground

This national forest campground stays open from mid-May to mid-Sept.; no drinking water or fee; located 0.3 mile south of the lodge on the highway.

## Vicinity Of Hannagan Meadow

**K.P. Cienega Campground** overlooks a large meadow ("cienega" is Spanish for meadow) and a sparkling stream. Sites in this idyllic spot have spring water; free. Turn off the Coronado Trail 5 miles south of Hannagan Meadow and drive 1.5 miles on a dirt road to the meadow. **K.P. Trail #70** into the Blue Range Primitive Area begins here.

**Bear Wallow Wilderness** protects 11,000 acres west of the Coronado Trail, including what's thought to be the largest stand of virgin ponderosa pine in the Southwest. **Bear Wallow Trail #63** follows Bear Wallow Creek downstream through the wilderness west to the San Carlos Indian Reservation boundary, 7.6 miles one way; elevations range from 8,700 feet at the trailhead to 6,700 feet at the reservation boundary. Two shorter trails drop down to the trail and creek from the north. **Reno Trail #62** (1.9 miles one way) meets Bear Wallow Trail at Mile 2.6; **Gobbler Point Trail #59** (2.7 miles one way) meets Bear Wallow Trail at Mile 7.1. Upper trailheads are reached from Forest Route 25, which turns off US 666 opposite the road for K.P. Cienega Campground. Foresters at the Alpine Ranger District office have more detailed trail descriptions and can advise on current conditions.

**Blue Vista Overlook and Nature Trail** sit

view near K.P.
Cienega
Campground

on the very edge of the Mogollon Rim, 7 miles south of Hannagan Meadow. Turn 0.3 mile southwest to parking and picnic tables, but don't take this turnoff with a trailer or large vehicle! In clear weather you can see count-less ridges rolling away to the horizon from this 9,184-foot vantage point. Seventy miles to the south is Mt. Graham (elev. 10,717 feet), the highest peak of the Pinaleno Range. Learn more about the great variety of trees and plants on the one-third-mile nature trail to another viewpoint and picnic table.

## BELOW THE RIM

### Strayhorse Campground
The campground, at an elevation of 7,600 feet, has spring water; free. It's located 4 miles (and 1,600 feet!) below Blue Vista and 64 miles north of Clifton; turnoff is near Mile-post 221. **Raspberry Creek Trail #35** leads east to Blue River in the Blue Range Primitive Area, 10.5 miles and a drop of 2,500 feet. **Highline Trail #47** goes west 14.5 miles, linking with several other trails. This area, west of Strayhorse Campground, tends to be less used, and trails are harder to follow.

### Rose Peak
At an elevation of 8,786 feet, Rose Peak has great views. It's also a good place for bird-watching. The turnoff is near Milepost 207, about 17 miles south of Blue Vista and 51 miles north of Clifton. You can reach the forest lookout tower by a half-mile trail or by driving up a steep, narrow, one-mile road (unless the gate's locked).

### Juan Miller Campgrounds
Season runs from about April to Oct. at the upper (elev. 5,800 feet) and lower (5,700 feet) campgrounds; no drinking water or fee. Head east one mile from the Coronado Trail on Forest Route 475. The turnoff is near Mile-post 189, 35 miles south of Blue Vista and 33 miles north of Clifton. Forest Route 475 con-tinues east to Blue River, another 15 miles, passing many small canyons and ridges good for dayhiking.

### Honeymoon Campground
A secluded spot at the end of a 22-mile dirt road. You can fish for trout in Eagle Creek, stocked from May to September. No drinking water or fee; you're asked to carry out trash. Elevation is 5,400 feet. Turn west onto Forest Route 217 near Milepost 188 of the Coro-nado Trail. Many of the ranches on the way date back to the late 1800s.

### Granville Campground
This campground, and nearby Cherry Lodge Picnic Area, make a pleasant place to stop.

Sites at the 6,800-foot elevation have drinking water from May to Sept.; free. Campground and picnic area are on opposite sides of the road, about 20 miles north of Clifton between Mileposts 178 and 179.

## Morenci Open Pit Mine

From the overlook, 10 miles north of Clifton, you can gaze into one of the biggest manmade holes in the world! Giant 190-ton trucks appear like toys laboring to haul copper ore out of the ever-deepening pit. Most of old Morenci town lies deep under debris near the pit; when the town got in the way of the mining, Phelps Dodge built a new community and buried the old one. The move, completed in 1969, was easily made, because Phelps Dodge owned the town as well as the mine. From the mine overlook, the road drops to modern Morenci (elev. 4,080 feet), then switchbacks down to Clifton (elev. 3,502 feet). You'll pass a giant smelter (now closed), concentrators, and a solvent extraction/electrowinning plant on the way.

Contact Phelps Dodge if you'd like to see some of their operations; free tours lasting about 3½ hours take you inside the open pit mine and to the crushers, concentrators, and solvent extraction/electrowinning plant. Retired miners, who know the area and operations well, lead the tours. Visitors must sign a liability release and be at least 9 years old.

Tours start from the Phelps Dodge Employment Office Complex, across from the fire station, on US 666 in Morenci; tel. 865-4521, ext. 435.

## CLIFTON

Coronado's expedition marched through this area in 1540, unaware of gold deposits within the hills. Mexican miners discovered the gold in 1867 and began small-scale placer operations. As the gold played out, Eastern prospectors took note of the copper deposits. They registered claims and by 1872 had staked out the town of Clifton. The nearby mining towns of Joy's Camp (later renamed Morenci) and Metcalf were also founded at this time. Miners faced great difficulties at first—the nearest railhead was in Colorado, and Apache raids harassed operations. In 1878, Arizona's first railroad connected the smelter in Clifton with the Longfellow Mine at Metcalf, 9 miles north. Instead of a locomotive, mules pulled the empty ore cars uphill to the mine; on the way back down, the mules got a free ride. Three tiny locomotives, one on display in Clifton, later replaced the mules. Miners worked underground during the first 6 decades; in 1937, after a 5-year Depression-era hiatus, all mining shifted to the surface where it continues today.

*just one section of the concentrator works at Morenci*

*Chase Creek Street*

Both Metcalf and old Morenci are gone now—Metcalf abandoned and destroyed, and old Morenci deeply buried. The new Morenci has an attractive appearance, but lacks the character of an old mining town. Clifton, the Greenlee County Seat, still has its old buildings and the "Copper Head" locomotive (built in the 1880s). Booze joints and brothels, where desperados engaged in frequent shootings, once lined Chase Creek Street. Today Chase Creek St. is quiet and the old jail empty, but Clifton remains one of Arizona's more distinctive towns.

### Sights
Strolling along Chase Creek St., you can imagine how it once was—when the boisterous miners of old came looking for a good time. The street parallels US 666 on the Morenci side of town. Drop into the **Greenlee Historical Museum** at 317 Chase Creek St. to see exhibits and artifacts of the old days; open Tues., Thurs., and Sat. 2-4:30 p.m. or by appointment (call phone numbers on the door); tel. 865-3115. Clifton's old jail, beside the Valley National Bank, was built in 1881 by blasting and hacking a hole into the hillside. The jail's first occupant turned out to be the man who built it, Margarito Verala. After doing a fine job, Verala received his pay, got drunk on mescal, and proceeded to shoot up the

town until he was arrested. You're welcome to step inside the gloomy interior. If the gate's locked, check at the city hall or police station for the key. The "Copper Head" locomotive of the old Coronado Railroad sits next to the jail. Tours by the Phelps Dodge Company provide a close-up look at the copper mine operations in Morenci (see "Morenci Open Pit Mine" above).

A scenic drive on Forest Route 212 goes from Clifton up along the San Francisco River past ranches, old mines, and canyon scenery. Cars can go at least a few miles and high-clearance 4WD vehicles much farther. Frequent river fords limit most of this route to the dry season. Head up Frisco Ave. on the west side of the river, cross the river on a concrete bridge, and continue upstream. Staff at the Clifton Ranger District office and Greenlee County Chamber of Commerce can advise on this and other backcountry drives and hiking routes.

### Accommodations And Food
**Rode Inn Motel** is at 186 S. Coronado Blvd. in south Clifton; tel. 865-4536. **Morenci Motel,** 6 miles up the highway from Clifton, has the **Copperoom Restaurant**; tel. 865-4111. Another Morenci restaurant—the **Kopper Kettle Kafe**—is in the shopping center. In Clifton you have a choice of **Cole's Pizza**

**Parlor** (pizza, steaks, and seafood) on Ward's Canyon at the south edge of town, **PJ's Restaurant** at 307 Coronado Dr. (US 666), or several fast-food places along the highway.

## Events

**Horse races** take place during the spring. Drivers push their vehicles to the limit in the **Clifton Hill Climb,** a steep course in Ward's Canyon, on Labor Day weekend. The **Greenlee County Fair** is held during the first weekend of October.

## Shopping And Services

Stock up on groceries at the **Morenci Shopping Center,** especially if headed north, as no supplies or gas are available for the next 70 miles. Morenci has a **hospital** (tel. 865-4511) and an outdoor **swimming pool** (tel. 865-2003). Clifton has an outdoor **swimming pool** too, on Park Ave. (north Clifton); tel. 865-9934. Play golf at the **Greenlee Country Club's** nine-hole course in York Valley, 12 miles south of Clifton on AZ 75 (14 miles north of Duncan); tel. 687-1099.

## Information

The **Greenlee County Chamber of Commerce** has information about the history, sights, and facilities of the area. You can see old photos of Morenci, taken before it disappeared, and of Clifton in its busier days. Rockhounds can get directions to several agate digs. The office, at 251 Chase Creek St., is open weekdays 9 a.m.-noon and 1-5 p.m.; Box 1237, Clifton, AZ 85533; tel. 865-3313. For hiking and camping info on the southern half of the Coronado Trail, see the **Clifton Ranger District** office of the U.S. Forest Service on US 666 in the Chase Creek area; open weekdays 8 a.m.-4:30 p.m. and sometimes on summer weekends; Box 698, Clifton, AZ 85533; tel. 865-2432. Clifton's **public library** is across from the county courthouse at 102 School St.; tel. 865-2461; Morenci's **public library** is in the Morenci Shopping Center; tel. 865-2775.

*Copper Head locomotive*

*cotton harvesting in the low desert*

# THE LOW DESERT

## SAFFORD

Surrounded by the rugged Pinaleno, Gila, and Peloncillo mountain ranges, Safford (elev. 2,900 feet) lies in the broad Gila River Valley. Ancient Hohokam, Mogollon, and Anasazi sites in the valley date from about 300 B.C. to A.D. 1200. The Apache arrived about 1700 and managed to discourage European settlers until 1874. Then four Civil War veterans founded a town and named it after Anson P. Safford, territorial Arizona's third governor. Mormon settlers came to farm the valley beginning in 1879 and founded Smithville, later renamed Pima; they also settled at Thatcher, Central, Eden, Graham, and Bryce. The Jewish merchant Isadore Elkan Solomon arrived in the town later named for him, set up a store and other businesses, then helped start Gila Valley Bank, which later evolved into the Valley National Bank.

Though small, Safford (pop. 7,215) serves as Graham County Seat and as the main retail and service center for a large area of southeastern Arizona. Cotton, especially the long-staple Pima, is king in the valley, but the irrigated river-bottom land also supports sorghum, wheat, barley, alfalfa, and other crops. Highlights of the region for visitors include the scenic drive to the 10,000-foot level of Mt. Graham (hiking, fishing, and camping), Aravaipa and Bonita canyons (wildlife and scenery along perennial stream), the Galiuro Wilderness (for adventurous hikers), Graham County and Pima historical museums, and the Museum of Anthropology in Thatcher (archaeological exhibits).

### Graham County Historical Museum

Period rooms show different aspects of life in the pioneer days. Exhibits of Indian artifacts illustrate the area's long prehistoric history. Check with the chamber of commerce for hours; free; located at 808 Eighth Avenue.

## Cotton Gin Tours

All that cotton in Graham County fields comes to two cotton gins in the Safford area. Both offer tours of their operations during the ginning season, from about early Oct. through Dec. and sometimes into Jan.; call in advance to **Safford Valley Cotton Growers Co-op** (off US 666 in Safford; tel. 428-0714) or **Glenbar Gin** (just west of Pima; tel. 485-9255).

## Accommodations And Campgrounds

Safford's seven motels are along US 70, also signed as Fifth St. and Thatcher Boulevard. Each motel has air conditioning and the more expensive ones also have swimming pools—you may want both in summer when highs push 100 degrees. **Roper Lake State Park,** 6 miles south of downtown, has pleasant campsites on the shore of a small lake. It's open all year and has showers; $3 day use or $5 camping ($8 w/water and electric hookups); tel. 428-6760 (see "Vicinity of Safford," p. 388). The **Coronado National Forest** has several campgrounds ($5-6) in the cool forests atop Mt. Graham (see "Vicinity of Safford," pp. 388-389). RVers can stay at **Tower Mobile Court** (1.5 miles east on US 70; tel. 428- 6997); **Ivanho Mobile Home Park** (3 miles east on US 70; tel. 428- 3828); and **Lexington Pines Adult RV Resort** (1535 Thatcher Blvd.; tel. 428-7570).

## Food

The **Branding Iron** serves up Western-style dinners about 2.5 miles north of downtown; go north on Eighth Ave., then left on River Road; tel. 428-6252. **Golden Corral Family Steak House** is another popular place for Western food, in Gila Valley Plaza on W. US 70; tel. 428-4744. For Chinese cuisine, try the **Tiki** in the Desert Inn Motel at 1391 Thatcher Blvd.; tel. 428-0521. Dine Mexican at **Casa Manana** (corner US 70 and First Ave.; tel. 428-3170); **El Charro** (628 Main St.; tel. 428-4134); **El Coronado** (409 Main St.; tel. 428-7755); **Roberto's** (328 Main; tel. 428-1882); or **La Paloma** (5 miles east in Solomon; tel. 428-2094). Supermarkets and chain restaurants are in Mt. Graham and Gila Valley shopping centers on US 70 west of downtown.

## Events

The **Old-Time Fiddlers Convention** livens up the town in the third week of February. **Horse racing** takes place at the county fairgrounds on the last weekend of March and the first weekend of April. Take off for the **Graham County Air Show** in April. The **Gila Valley Rodeo** provides excitement in August. Bicycle racers strain for the finish line in the **Mt. Graham Hill Climb** in September. The **Graham County Fair** features entertainment, local agricultural accomplishments, and crafts in October. See the chamber of commerce for additional info; tel. 428-2511.

## Recreation

An outdoor public **swimming pool** (open from Memorial Day to Labor Day) is in Firth Park behind the chamber of commerce at 1111 Thatcher Blvd.; tel. 428-6666. **Tennis** players can use the lighted courts at Graham County Park, 2 miles south on US 666, or at the junior high school, 520 11th Street. **Graham County Park** also offers racquetball, basketball, ball fields, a jogging track, and picnicking; all but the track are lit for night use. Play golf year-round at the 18-hole **Mount Graham Golf Course,** 4 miles southwest of town (turn south on 20th Ave. and follow signs); tel. 428-1260.

## Services

The **post office** is on the corner of US 70 and Fifth Ave.; tel. 428-0220. **Mount Graham Community Hospital** is southwest of downtown at 1600 20th Ave.; tel. 428-1171. Hikers can purchase **topo maps** at Consolidated Title, 605 Main St.; tel. 428-0180. Feeling run-down with too many aches and pains? If so, you might want to "take the waters" at **Kachina Mineral Springs,** a hot springs spa 6 miles south of Safford; tel. 428-7212.

## Information

The **Safford-Graham County Chamber of Commerce** is very helpful and well stocked with literature and maps; open Mon.-Sat. 8 a.m.-5 p.m. and shorter hours on Sundays. The office is on the main highway just west of downtown at 1111 Thatcher Blvd., Safford,

AZ 85546; tel. 428-2511. **Safford Ranger Station** of the Coronado National Forest has travel and recreation info on the Mt. Graham Scenic Drive (Pinaleno Mountains) and Galiuro Wilderness and the lesser known ranges of Santa Teresa and Winchester; open weekdays 7:30 a.m.-4 p.m.; it's on the third floor of the post office downtown on the corner of US 70 and Fifth Ave.; or write Box 709, Safford, AZ 85548; tel. 428-4150. If you're going to visit Aravaipa Canyon, you'll need a permit from the **Bureau of Land Management** (BLM) office. Rockhounds can pick up brochures about the Black Hills (between Safford and Clifton) and Round Mountain (south of Duncan) areas, where fire agates and other gemstones can be collected. The BLM office is at 425 E. Fourth St., Safford, AZ 85546 (one block north of US 70, behind Bill McGlocklin Ford dealership). Open weekdays 7:45 a.m.-4:15 p.m.; tel. 428-4040. You can also get permits and info by mail. The **public library** is on 620 Seventh Ave. at Eighth St.; tel. 428-1531. The **Learning Resources Center** at Eastern Arizona College is a library and media center open to the public; it's on the northwest corner of Church St. and College Ave. in Thatcher; closed early July to mid-Aug.; tel. 428-1133, ext. 306.

### Transport
**Greyhound Bus** stops several times a day in each direction on its route between El Paso, Texas, and Phoenix. The station is at 1850 Thatcher Blvd. (W. US 70) next to McDonald's; tel. 428-2150.

# VICINITY OF SAFFORD

### Bonita Creek
This perennial stream flows through a pretty canyon in the Gila Mountains, about 25 miles northeast of Safford. Bonita is much like Aravaipa Creek (described below) but without the access restrictions. Drivers with high-clearance vehicles (4WD is best) can drive 15 miles up Bonita Creek from near its confluence with the Gila River to the San Carlos Indian Reservation boundary. Summer flash floods can take out the road, which has many stream crossings, so it's a good idea to first check conditions with the BLM office. Look for cliff dwellings and granaries in the canyon left by prehistoric Indians. Birding and hiking are best on weekdays, when few people come. You can camp almost anywhere—just keep well above the washes to avoid being surprised by a flash flood. Stop by the chamber of commerce or BLM offices in town for a map of the drive.

### Safford-Morenci Trail
Pioneer ranchers and farmers built this trail in about 1874 as a shortcut to haul their products to the booming mines in the Morenci area. The trail fell into disuse with the advent of the automobile during the early 1900s, but the Youth Conservation Corps, working with the BLM, has restored and marked the route. Hikers and horseback riders will enjoy the variety of desert and riparian environments along the way. The trail is 14 miles one way with an elevation range of 3,700-6,200 feet. Bonita Creek, crossed about midway, makes a good camping spot, though the BLM recommends carrying drinking water for the whole trip. Roads to both the west and east trailheads may require 4WD vehicles in wet weather. Contact the BLM office in Safford for maps and current hiking conditions.

### Museum Of Anthropology
Thatcher, just 3 miles northwest of Safford, is home for Eastern Arizona College, a 2-year school. Its museum has an excellent collection of old Indian pottery, axes, arrowheads, and jewelry. Visit the museum's library to learn more about archaeology and anthropology. Kids have special displays too: hands-on exhibits of fire-making, shell-jewelry crafting, and corn grinding. Hours are Mon.-Fri. 9 a.m.-4 p.m. during the school year (early Sept. to mid-May); free; tel. 428-1133, ext. 310. The museum is near the corner of Main St. (US 70) and College Avenue.

## Eastern Arizona Museum And Historical Society

Learn about the Indians and pioneers of the area. Open Wed.-Fri. 2-4 p.m. and Sat. 1-5 p.m.; visits can be arranged at other times too; free; tel. 485-2288. Exhibits are in an early Pima town hall on US 70, 9 miles northwest of Safford.

## Cluff Ranch Wildlife Area

The Arizona Game and Fish Department maintains the 1,300-acre Cluff Ranch as a wildlife sanctuary and recreation area. Streams from Mt. Graham fill four ponds totaling 23 acres and support lush riparian vegetation. Fishermen catch trout in winter and channel catfish, largemouth bass, crappie, and bluegill year-round. Boats (oar, sail, or electric) can be used. Visitors may camp at the ponds (no facilities). Birding is good and you're almost sure to see some free-roaming deer or javelina. Orphaned or injured animals are also brought here for eventual release into the wild. Strips of grain crops have been planted for wildlife.

Cluff Ranch is open all year; groups can arrange tours; tel. 485-9430. From US 70 in Pima (9 miles northwest of Safford), turn south 1.5 miles on Main St. at Pima Texaco; the road curves west and becomes Cottonwood Road; continue another 0.4 mile, then turn south 4.5 miles at the sign to the ranch.

## Roper Lake State Park

The shores of this pretty lake offer camping, picnicking, swimming, and fishing. Fishermen can launch their boats (electric motors OK) and try for catfish, bass, bluegill, and crappie (also trout in winter). Hedonists can step into the hot tub, fed by a natural spring. A short nature trail begins near the hot tub and identifies desert plants. Roper Lake is 6 miles south of Safford off US 666. **Dankworth Ponds** day-use area also has good picnicking and fishing; it's 3 miles farther south on US 666. Admission fees cover both areas: $3 day use or $5 camping ($8 w/water and electric hookups); group sites are available too. Open all year; tel. 428-6760.

## Mount Graham Drive

Mt. Graham (10,717 feet), in the Pinaleno Mountains, soars nearly 8,000 feet into the air above Safford—the greatest vertical rise of any mountain in Arizona. Visitors can enjoy the views, cool breezes, hiking, picnicking, camping, and fishing. A good road, called the Swift Trail, ascends the eastern slopes through a remarkable range of vegetation and animal life. Leaving the cactus, creosote bush, and mesquite of the lower Sonoran Desert at the start, you'll soon be among pygmy forests of juniper, oak, and pinyon pine. Higher on the twisting road, you'll enter dense forests of ponderosa pine, Douglas fir, aspen, and white fir. Thick stands of Engelmann spruce dominate the highest ridges. The Mt. Graham spruce squirrel, Mt. Graham pocket gopher, white-bellied vole, and Rusby's mountain fleabane (a wild daisy) exist only in the Pinaleno Mountains.

Fire-lookout towers on two peaks offer superb views. **Heliograph Peak** (elev. 10,028 feet) has one of the best panoramas in the region; on a clear day you'll see most of the ranges of southeastern Arizona, as well as the mines and tailings at Morenci; if the 2.2-mile road to the lookout is gated, you can walk up. The Army built a heliograph station here in 1886 to relay messages to troops by using mirrors and sunlight. **Webb Peak** (elev. 10,086 feet) has a better view of the Gila River Valley and surrounding mountains; it's reached by a 1.7-mile road that may also be gated.

The five developed campgrounds all have drinking water and are open from mid-May to mid-Oct.; fees are $5 ($6 at Riggs Lake). Campground elevations range from 6,700 feet at Arcadia to 9,300 feet at Soldier Creek. Anglers can camp and try for trout in Riggs Lake, near the end of the Swift Trail.

To drive the 34.5-mile-long **Swift Trail**, go 7 miles south from Safford on US 666 (or 26 miles north from I-10) and turn west at the sign. The first 27.5 miles are paved, followed by 7 of gravel. Winter snows close the higher parts of the road from about early Nov. to mid-May. The drive from Safford and back

*Mt. Graham and the Pinalenos, from Roper Lake State Park*

takes about 4½ hours, not including stops. Stock up on gas and supplies before leaving town. A road guide to the features of the Swift Trail and Coronado National Forest maps (Pinaleno Range) are available from the Safford Chamber of Commerce or U.S. Forest Service in Safford. Hikers have many trails but should be prepared for steep sections; pick up a leaflet of campground and trail descriptions in the Safford Forest Service office.

**Emerald Peak** is the proposed site of a series of large telescopes (Mt. Graham International Observatory). Protecting the habitat for the red squirrel has resulted in the closure of the side road to High Peak and some trails, so be sure to check with the Forest Service if planning a trip near the summit of Mt. Graham.

### Galiuro Wilderness

Rugged and brush-covered, the Galiuro Mountains rise in two parallel ranges above the desert. Prominent peaks along the east ridge are Bassett (7,671 feet), Kennedy (7,540 feet), and Sunset (7,094 feet); along the west ridge stand Rhodes (7,116 feet), Maverick (6,990 feet), and Kielburg (6,880 feet). The terrain is so rough and steep that you'll have to keep mostly to the network of trails. The 10 trails total 95 miles. You're not likely to see many other hikers in this little-known range. The Galiuros lie southwest of Safford, on the other side of the Pinalenos, and northwest of Willcox. The main trailheads are on the east slopes: Ash Creek, High Creek, and Deer Creek. Deer Creek Trailhead, at the end of Forest Route 253, is popular because it's usually passable by car and is near the start of several trails.

Vegetation changes with elevation and slope orientation: south and west slopes have dense growths of manzanita, live oak, and other brush, with juniper, pinyon, and oak trees higher up; the higher canyons and north-facing slopes are wooded with Arizona cypress, ponderosa pine, Chihuahua pine, Mexican white pine, Douglas fir, and some white fir. Sycamore, alder, aspen, and other deciduous trees grow along stream banks. Mule deer, whitetail deer, black bear, javelina, and mountain lion roam the rugged hillsides and canyons. The old Power's cabin (built 1910), mine shafts, and ore-milling machinery can be seen in Rattlesnake Canyon (Galiuro Corridor). Power's Garden cabin, also in Rattlesnake Canyon, may be open for use by hikers. Streams usually dry up during late spring and early summer. The more reliable springs (purify first) are Power's Garden, Mud, Corral, Holdout, Cedar, Jackson, Juniper, and South Field. The Muleshoe area, outside the wilderness at the south end of the Galiuros, has perennial streams; the Nature Conservancy operates its **Muleshoe Preserve** here. The 4WD Jackson Cabin Road (Forest Route 691) provides access from the south. See the Forest Service office in Safford for latest water, trail, and road conditions.

## Aravaipa Canyon Wilderness

A jewel in the desert, Aravaipa Canyon is renowned for its scenery and variety of wildlife. Waters of Aravaipa Creek flow all year, a rare occurrence in the desert, providing an oasis for birds and other animals. Giant ash, sycamore, and willow trees shade the canyon floor. Rocky hillsides, dotted with saguaro cactus and other desert plants, lie only a few steps from the lush vegetation along the creek. Birders have sighted more than 200 species in the canyon, including the bald eagle and peregrine falcon. Mule deer, javelina, and coyote frequent the area, and you might even see a mountain lion or bighorn sheep. Also keep an eye out for any of the several species of rattlesnakes.

Although there's no established trail, hiking is easy along the gravel creek bed. Tributary canyons invite side trips—Hell Hole Canyon is especially enchanting, despite its name. Tennis shoes work well, as you'll be wading across the creek frequently. Grassy terraces make inviting campsites. To visit the 11-mile canyon, *even for dayhikes,* you must get a permit from the BLM office in Safford (see "Safford Information"). Advance reservations are needed for weekends in spring and autumn, the best hiking seasons. Permits may also be available from rangers stationed near each end of the canyon, but call the Safford BLM office first to check. The BLM has a

2-night (3-day) stay limit. Horseback riders may visit on day trips only, and not more than five per group. Pets are prohibited.

Trailheads, though only 11 trail miles apart, require 160 miles of driving from one end to the other. The East Trailhead is reached by Klondyke Road (turn off US 70 about 15 miles northwest of Safford) or Fort Grant Road (turn off US 666 either 19 miles south of Safford or 17 miles north of I-10). Follow signs to Aravaipa Canyon Wilderness; don't go to the settlement called "Aravaipa." A ranger is stationed in Klondyke, 10 miles before the trailhead. **Fourmile Campground** (drinking water; free) is nearby; turn left just after Klondyke. You can also camp along Turkey Creek Canyon (no facilities), a pretty tributary of the Aravaipa Creek near the trailhead. The West Trailhead is much closer to Phoenix and Tucson but has no place to camp. From about midway between Winkelman and Mammoth on AZ 77, turn east 13 miles on Aravaipa Road to the ranger station and trailhead.

*saguaro cacti in Aravaipa Canyon*

## SAN CARLOS APACHE INDIAN RESERVATION

San Carlos Reservation has climates and scenery for everyone: cool pine forests in the northeast, grasslands and wooded ridges (pinyon and juniper) in the center, and cactus-studded desert surrounding San Carlos Lake in the southwest. The Black and Salt rivers form a natural boundary with the White Mountain Apache Indian Reservation to the north. Much of the land is fine cattle-grazing country and supports large tribal herds. You can reach San Carlos Lake and Seneca Lake by paved highways, but roads to other recreation areas may be too rough for cars, especially after rains or snow melt. You'll need a Recreation Access Permit ($5) to venture onto the reservation's back roads or trails unless you have a fishing, camping, or special-use permit.

### San Carlos

This small community is very much a government town in appearance. Neat rows of office buildings and apartments line the main street. Here you'll find most tribal offices, the post office, grocery store, San Carlos Cafe, and a service station. Check the store in San Carlos and trading posts for Apache crafts, such as baskets, beadwork, cradleboards, and peridot jewelry. Peridot is a deep yellow-green, transparent olivine mineral. The cut stones, sold mounted or loose, resemble emeralds.

### Events

Look for Apache dances, crafts, foods, and cowboys showing off their riding skills at the **San Carlos Rodeo** in late April and at the **Tribal Fair** in late Oct. or early November. **Traditional dances** are also held during the summer; call the tribal office for dates and places; tel. 475-2361. The Sunrise Ceremony occurs most frequently, usually on summer weekends. It marks the coming-of-age of young women with blessings and a strengthening of tribal ties.

*When the Warms Springs Apache were moved to San Carlos in 1877, Chief Victorio and a small band escaped. He led a savage campaign against Americans and Mexicans in 1879-80, killing nearly 1,000 people before being shot by a Mexican bounty hunter.*

### San Carlos Lake

The 19,500-acre lake measures 23 miles long by 2 miles wide when full, making it the largest lake completely within Arizona. All this water is held back by 880-foot-high Coolidge Dam, dedicated by President Coolidge himself in 1930. **San Carlos Lake Marina,** 2 miles north of the dam, has information, permits, fishing supplies, groceries, snacks, and gasoline; tel. 475-2756. A trailer park with hookups is next to the marina. **Soda Canyon Point Campground** is also nearby. Other campgrounds are on both the north and south sides of the lake. Though famed mostly for its prolific bass population, San Carlos Lake has produced state-record specimens of flathead catfish, crappie, and bluegill. The lake and marina, at an elevation of 2,425 feet, are 13 miles south from the town of San Carlos.

## Other Recreation Areas

**Talkalai Lake:** Chief Talkalai served as an Indian scout with the Army and helped capture Geronimo. Talkalai Lake has given up some sizeable largemouth bass, flathead and channel catfish, crappie, and bluegill. Gas motors up to 7½ horsepower are permitted. The lake and campground are about 3 miles north of the town of San Carlos.

**Cassadore Springs:** This small picnic area and campground has spring water; it's about 12 miles north of the town of San Carlos.

**Point of Pines:** The 35-acre trout lake and campground (no drinking water) are in the eastern part of the reservation; from US 70, 5 miles east of the San Carlos turnoff, head northeast 55 miles on Indian Route 1000 to the campground; all but the last 5 miles or so are paved.

**Seneca Park:** Fishermen catch trout, catfish, and largemouth bass in 27-acre Seneca Lake. The lake and campground are located in the northwest corner of the reservation just off US 60/AZ 77, 33 miles north of Globe and 5 miles south of the Salt River Canyon bridge.

## Camping And Picnicking

In winter you'll probably want to stick to the low country around San Carlos Lake, then head for the hills in summer. Campsites are usually open all year. You're also generally welcome to camp outside established sites if you have the appropriate camping or special-use permit. Camping and picnicking permits ($5/day) must be bought beforehand. Avoid camping near stock ponds. In summer, you may need to observe fire restrictions.

## Fishing, Boating, And Hunting

Fishing is the big attraction for most visitors—San Carlos Lake is known as Arizona's hottest bass spot. Farther north you can catch trout, catfish, or bass in the Black River, Point of Pines Lake, Seneca Lake, and over 100 stock ponds. Licenses cost $5/day or $50/year (free if under 12 and with a permit-holding adult). Boat permits are $1.50/day or $25/year. Gasoline motors can be used at San Carlos and Talkalai lakes; at other lakes you are restricted to a single electric motor. In some areas, such as the Black and Salt rivers, you'll need a special-use permit for fishing, hiking, camping, or river rafting ($10/person per day instead of the regular permits). You may fish on both sides of the Black and Salt rivers with either San Carlos or White Mountain permits, but permits of the two reservations are otherwise not interchangeable. Hunters can pursue big and small game; fees range from $50 to more than $1000, depending on what you're hunting and whether or not you're an Arizona resident. Certain areas of the reservation may be open only to tribal members.

## Permits And Information

Permits are needed for most activities on the reservation. For permits and the latest regulations, facilities, fees, and road conditions, contact the **San Carlos Recreation and Wildlife Department** office at the corner of Moon Base Road and US 70 (between Mileposts 272 and 273), 1.5 miles east of the AZ 170 junction for San Carlos; open Mon.-Fri. 8 a.m.-6 p.m. and Sat.-Sun. 8 a.m.-4:30 p.m.; Box 97, San Carlos, AZ 85550; tel. 475-2653/2343.

Other sources for permits include **Noline's Country Store** (nearby on US 70; tel. 475-2334), **San Carlos Lake Marina** (tel. 475-2756), **Pinky's Bait/Tackle** (Pima; tel. 428-5611), **Bob Keene's Store** (Ft. Thomas; tel. 485-2261), **Circle-K** (Globe; tel. 425-5942), **Tiger Mart** (Globe; tel. 425-2640), **Copper Hills Tackle Shop** (Miami; tel. 425-3331), **O'Leary's Market** (Miami; tel. 473-3640), and **Tempe Marine** (Mesa; tel. 844-0165).

# SOUTHERN ARIZONA

## INTRODUCTION

Southern Arizona is a sea of desert and grasslands from which mountains rise like islands. Giant saguaro and other hardy plants cover the Sonoran Desert from Tucson westward toward the Colorado River Valley, while desert grasslands fill most valleys to the east. Climate varies dramatically with elevation. Expect mild winters and very hot summers on the desert, slightly cooler and wetter weather on the grasslands. Four ranges have peaks over 9,000 feet where you could be up to your neck in snow during the winter—the Santa Catalinas, Santa Ritas, Huachucas, and Chiricahuas. Mount Lemmon, in the Santa Catalinas near Tucson, has downhill ski runs. Astonishing varieties of birds, animals, and plants find a niche in southern Arizona's varied topography. Some species, such as

the "whiskered" senita cactus and the colorful trogon bird, have come from Mexico and are rarely seen elsewhere in the United States.

When the Spanish entered this region about 1539, they found several groups of natives, most notably the warlike, nomadic Apache and the more settled and peaceful Tohono O'odham (Papago) and Pima. Most of the Spanish, Pima, and Apache have left southern Arizona, but their legacy in culture, place names, and legends remains strong. The Old West lives on as well—in the dozens of abandoned mining camps, on the ranches where cowboys still work vast ranges, and on the streets of Tombstone where the Earps and Doc Holliday shot it out with the Clanton gang. Allow time to explore southern Arizona. It's a big land with much to be discovered.

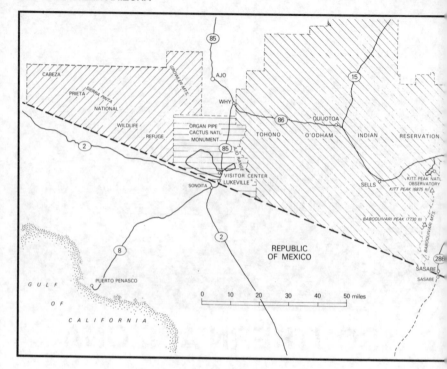

# TUCSON

Though the "Old Pueblo," as it's known locally, is modern and lively, its Old West heritage will surprise you. Tucson (pronounced "TOO-sawn") has some of the best cultural offerings in Arizona—a large university, historic sites, and a great variety of restaurants and nightlife. Yet it remains on a human scale—you can *walk* this city to see many of the sights. Set in a desert valley at an elevation of 2,400 feet, Tucson ranks as the state's second largest city, with a metro population of 700,000. Summers are warm but not as hot as those in Phoenix or Yuma. And Mt. Lemmon, at 9,157 feet, is just an hour's drive away. Temperatures peak in June and July with highs generally near 98° F and lows near 70°. Even in Dec. and Jan. it's spring-like with average highs in the mid-60s and lows in the

upper 30s. Of the 11 or so inches of annual rainfall, over half falls in the July to Sept. rainy season. Desert vegetation, with palo verde, cottonwood, and mesquite trees, is surprisingly lush. Many varieties of cacti display brilliant flowers from April to late May. The mountains ringing Tucson offer skiing in the winter and great hiking almost anytime. In just minutes, hikers can get out of town west to the Tucson Mountains, northeast to the Santa Catalinas, or east to the Rincons.

## HISTORY

Hohokam Indians farmed the valley floor at least as far back as A.D. 100. Pima and other Indian tribes had replaced the Hohokam long before the Spanish arrived in the 1500s. The

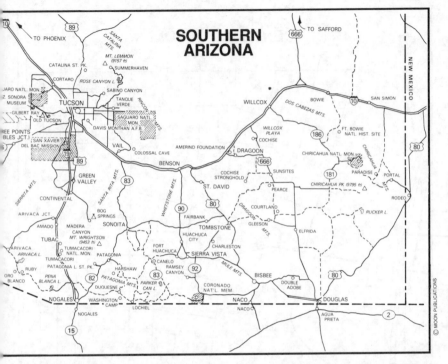

first Spanish visitors found a Pima Indian village, Stjuk-shon (*stjuk* means "dark mountain"; *shon* means "foot of"), at the foot of Sentinel Peak (the hill with the big "A" now painted on it). The Spanish changed the name to "Tucson" when they laid out the Presidio of San Augustín del Tucson in 1775. Attacks by roving Apaches made fortifications necessary, so adobe walls 12 feet high and 750 feet long went up to enclose the new settlement. Mexico inherited Tucson from Spain after the 1821 revolution, but little changed except the flag.

## Americans Take Hold

Tucson came under the wing of the United States with the Gadsden Purchase in June 1854, but 21 months of boundary-marking and bureaucratic delays passed before the arrival of American officialdom in the form of the Army's First Dragoons. Although Apache

continued to menace settlers and travelers in the area, Anglo-Americans began to arrive, and the Butterfield Overland Stagecoach opened service to Tucson. To cope with the desert climate, the Anglos adopted much of the food, building techniques, and other traditions that the Mexicans had developed. The results of these practices, as well as of Anglo-Mexican intermarriage, are seen today in Tucson's cultural mix.

## Wars And The Wild West

Confederate cavalry under the command of Captain Sherrod Hunter captured Tucson in Feb. 1862. Union troops led by Colonel James Carleton marched in from California two months later and clashed with the Confederates at Picacho Pass, on the Butterfield Road about 42 miles northwest of Tucson. After this battle, the most westerly of the Civil War, the outnumbered Confederates retreat-

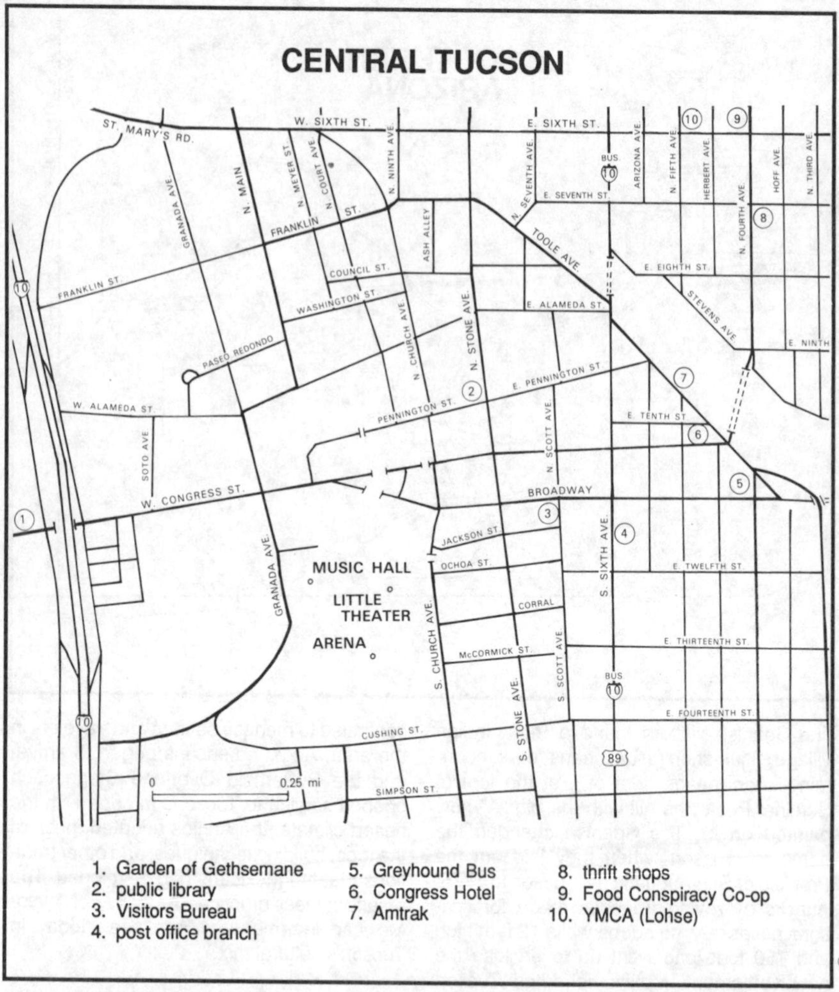

# CENTRAL TUCSON

1. Garden of Gethsemane
2. public library
3. Visitors Bureau
4. post office branch
5. Greyhound Bus
6. Congress Hotel
7. Amtrak
8. thrift shops
9. Food Conspiracy Co-op
10. YMCA (Lohse)

© MOON PUBLICATIONS

ed. The 1860s were Tucson's Wild West days. Shootouts took place frequently and men rarely ventured unarmed onto the dusty streets. Still, the town prospered after the war and served as the territorial capital from 1867 to 1877. By 1880, when the first train rolled in, the population had grown to over 7,000. The Arizona Territorial University opened its doors in 1891 on land donated by a saloon-keeper and a pair of gamblers. Davis-Monthan Field brought Tucson into the Air Age and became an important training base during WW II. Many of the airmen and others passing through the city during those hectic years returned to settle here. With its new postwar industries and growth of tourism, the "Old Pueblo" has been booming ever since.

## HISTORIC WALKING TOUR

### Northern Part

The historic walking tour provides a look at the Spanish, Mexican, and Anglo legacies of Tucson. The **Tucson Museum of Art** is a convenient place to start. Its permanent collection is noted for Spanish colonial paintings and furnishings and for pre-Columbian artifacts from Latin America. Special exhibitions frequently appear, too. Docent tours are available; call for times. The large gift shop sells books, cards, and local crafts. Open Tues.-Sat. 10 a.m.-4 p.m. and Sun. noon-4 p.m. (closed Mon.); admission is $2 adult, $1 students, $1 seniors 60 and over, free for children under 12; tel. 624-2333; at 140 N. Main.

Walk east across the courtyard to see the **Edward Nye Fish House,** built by a rich businessman in 1868 and now the **El Presidio Gallery.** It has 15-foot ceilings and solid adobe walls more than 2.5 feet thick; step inside to see the gallery's high-quality artwork, most of it from the Southwest. Next door to the Fish House on the north side is the **Stevens House,** part of which dates from 1856. Hiram Sanford Stevens was a good friend of Edward Fish, and much of Tucson's social life centered in their houses. The Stevens House is now the **Janos Restaurant.**

Of adobe construction, **La Casa Cordova** is one of the oldest houses in the area, dating from about 1848. Enter the courtyard from the back. Interior exhibits show life in the 1850s. It's maintained by the adjacent Tucson Museum of Art and is open the same hours; free. Next is **Old Town Artisans,** a shop displaying art and crafts by more than 150 artists representing Western, Indian, and Mexican styles. The sculptures, paintings, prints, and crafts are worth a look even if you're not buying. The front two rooms were built between 1862 and 1875 with adobe walls and saguaro-rib ceilings. Open Mon.-Sat. 9:30 a.m.-5 p.m. and Sun. noon-5 p.m. The Courtyard Cafe here serves soups, salads, and sandwiches. Lunch is also served in the Barrel Stave Room (closed Sun.).

Across the street is the **Romero House.** Built in the 1860s and modified many times, the house is now used by the Tucson Museum of Art School. It's located on the site of part of the original Presidio wall. A plaque marks the northwest corner of this wall at the corner of Washington St. and Main Ave., one block west of Romero House. Across Washington is the **Sam Hughes House,** now a series of garden apartments. Hughes came to Tucson for his health in 1858, joining the handful of Anglos here, and he became an important businessman and developer of early Tucson. He moved into this house with his bride in 1864, but he had to expand it considerably over the years for his 15 children. Hughes and his wife lived to celebrate their 50th wedding anniversary here. The **Steinfeld Mansion** is a Spanish mission-style brick and stucco house dating from the turn of the century. It's known for having one of Tucson's first bathtubs with piped-in water. The mansion has been restored for use as offices.

If you walk 2 blocks east to Court Ave., you'll find the house built by French stonemason Jules le Flein, now the **El Charro** Mexican restaurant. Le Flein came to Tucson in the late 1800s to remodel the St. Augustine Cathedral. In 1900 he built this house for his family with volcanic stone from Sentinel Peak. Next, if you're planning on exploring

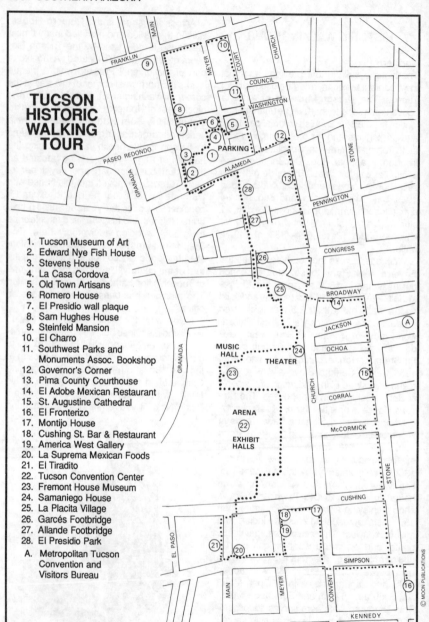

**TUCSON HISTORIC WALKING TOUR**

1. Tucson Museum of Art
2. Edward Nye Fish House
3. Stevens House
4. La Casa Cordova
5. Old Town Artisans
6. Romero House
7. El Presidio wall plaque
8. Sam Hughes House
9. Steinfeld Mansion
10. El Charro
11. Southwest Parks and Monuments Assoc. Bookshop
12. Governor's Corner
13. Pima County Courthouse
14. El Adobe Mexican Restaurant
15. St. Augustine Cathedral
16. El Fronterizo
17. Montijo House
18. Cushing St. Bar & Restaurant
19. America West Gallery
20. La Suprema Mexican Foods
21. El Tiradito
22. Tucson Convention Center
23. Fremont House Museum
24. Samaniego House
25. La Placita Village
26. Garcés Footbridge
27. Allande Footbridge
28. El Presidio Park

A. Metropolitan Tucson Convention and Visitors Bureau

© MOON PUBLICATIONS

more of Arizona, the **Southwest Parks and Monuments Association Bookshop** is a worthwhile stop. It has publications on the Southwest's history, Indians, wildlife, flora, hiking trails, and other topics. Open Tues.-Fri. 11 a.m.-5:30 p.m. and Sat. 10 a.m.-3 p.m.; tel. 792-0239. The Bookshop is at 223 N. Court in the old Stork's Nest building, built in 1883 and converted to a maternity center in 1922.

Turning left on Alameda, you'll come to **Governor's Corner.** Louis C. Hughes, territorial governor in 1893-96, had an adobe house on this site. The Valley National Bank building here now has a painting of this street corner as it appeared in 1893. Visitors are welcome to come in and see it during office hours. **Pima County Courthouse,** a colorful building constructed in 1928, replaced earlier structures of 1868 and 1881. The present courthouse is a mix of Southwest, Spanish, and Moorish architecture. Upstairs, a portion of the original Presidio wall is preserved in a glass case—find it in the south wing of the second floor, just before the Justice Courts.

### Southern Part

Go south 2½ blocks for **El Adobe Mexican Restaurant and Old Adobe Patio.** The restaurant and several small shops occupy the Charles O. Brown House. Brown owned the Congress Hall Saloon, a popular watering hole and gambling spot for politicians of the day. The oldest part of the house (on Jackson St.) dates from about 1858. Between 1868 and 1877 Brown built on Broadway (then Camp St.) and connected the two sections with an attractive patio and garden. Continuing 2 blocks down Stone, you'll come to **St. Augustine Cathedral,** constructed in 1896. Its impressive sandstone facade, fashioned after the Cathedral of Querétaro in Mexico, was added in the late 1920s, as were the stained-glass windows. A bronze statue of St. Augustine stands watch above the doorway with a saguaro, yucca, horned toad, and other symbols of the desert.

Four more blocks down Stone is the former office of **El Fronterizo** newspaper. Carlos Y. Velasco began publishing a Spanish-

*St. Augustine Cathedral*

language newspaper here about 1878. Around on Cushing St. is **Montijo House,** which has preserved the name of the well-known Mexican ranching family that once owned it. The house was completed during the Civil War and remodeled in the 1890s in an ornate Victorian style. The **Cushing Street Bar and Restaurant** has an attractive 1880s decor. Joseph Ferrin operated a general store and lived here about 100 years ago. Next door is **America West Gallery,** the home of rancher Francisco Carrillo in the 1860s. The well-preserved house contains exotic antiques and primitive art from many countries. The patio has a collection of Mexican millstones. Around the corner on Main is **La Suprema Mexican Foods;** pick up fresh tortillas or just watch them being made.

**El Tiradito,** or "Wishing Shrine," commemorates a tragic love triangle. The story has many versions, but one account tells of a love affair between young Juan Olivera and his mother-in-law. Juan was caught and killed

*El Tiradito*

by his father-in-law on this spot in 1880. Because he had sinned, the dead Juan could not be taken to the church cemetery, and he was buried where he fell. Pious people lit candles and prayed for his soul at the site. Later, parents prayed for their errant daughters at the shrine. The custom then developed that anyone could light a candle on the grave and make a wish. If the candle burned to its base, the wish would be granted. The shrine is said to be the only one in North America dedicated to a sinner.

Follow the sidewalk around the Exhibit Hall and Arena of the Tucson Convention Center to the **Fremont House Museum.** Its adobe building, constructed by the Soza family in about 1860 and subsequently owned by the Carrillo family, was saved in 1969 when surrounding houses were torn down. The old structure takes its name from the fifth territorial governor, John C. Fremont, who rented it in 1881. Inside you can imagine the life of a wealthy Tucson family in the 1880s. Tour guides point out and explain the architectural features of the house. Four different types of ceiling are used: saguaro rib, ocotillo, painted cloth, and redwood. Open Wed.-Sat. 10 a.m.-4 p.m.; free; 151 S. Granada Ave. in the Tucson Convention Center; tel. 622-0956. Staff at the Fremont House Museum lead guided tours of El Presidio Historic District on Sat. mornings, Nov. to April, lasting about 2 hours; $3. Call for reservations and time.

The building on the right as you leave the Fremont House is the **Tucson Community Center Music Hall.** Walk up the steps alongside it into an oasis of gardens, trees, and fountains. The small building ahead (to the east) is the **Leo Rich Theatre.** To the right is the giant **Arena** where sporting events are held. Just beyond the Theatre is **Samaniego House,** built in the 1840s. Mariano G. Samaniego, a stage-line owner, rancher, and local politician, purchased it about 1880. His well-preserved house, with adobe walls and saguaro-ribbed ceilings, is now a restaurant.

Follow the map around through **La Placita Village,** a group of modern offices and shops designed to resemble a Mexican marketplace. Continue on the **Garcés Footbridge** across Congress St., then the **Allande Footbridge** across Pennington St. to **El Presidio Park.** These modern bridges honor early Spaniards. Francisco Garcés, an explorer and Franciscan priest, was the first missionary to visit the Pima Indian village at the base of Sentinel Peak. Pedro Allande, first resident commander of the Tucson Presidio, once led a spirited defense against 600 warring Apache. Despite a severe leg wound, he continued to direct his 20 presidial soldiers and saved the settlement. El Presidio Park was Plaza de las Armas of the original Presidio. Soldiers drilled and held holiday fiestas on this spot 200 years ago. The soldiers have gone, but residents still have fiestas. The park is a quiet spot in which to rest and enjoy the sculptures and fountains. The **Tucson Museum of Art** is just a short walk away, returning you to your starting point.

## SIGHTS BETWEEN DOWNTOWN AND THE UNIVERSITY OF ARIZONA

### Tucson Children's Museum

Kids have fun with games and scientific experiments in this hands-on museum. They solve puzzles, use computers, learn how the human body works, and do many other projects. Exhibits change quarterly. A gift shop sells educational toys. Open Tues.-Sat. 10 a.m.-5 p.m. and Sun. 1-5 p.m.; ticket sales close one hour earlier. Closed Mon. and holidays. Admission is $1.50 children 3-18 and seniors, $3 adult; tel. 884-7511 (recording) or 792-9985. Located in the historic YWCA building at 300 E. University Blvd. between Fourth and Fifth avenues.

### Arizona Historical Society Museum

If you can visit only one of the dozens of historical museums in the state, make it this one! Beginning with prehistoric Indian displays, museum exhibits takes you through all the periods of Arizona's early history: Spanish, Mexican, Mountain Men, Territorial, and Early Statehood. Displays are well illustrated and full of artifacts. Visitors of all ages enjoy the early 1900s copper mine exhibit, where they walk through a realistic mine complete with sound effects and come out to a giant ore stamper and other processing machinery. Period rooms and special exhibits are also carefully prepared. A gift shop has a good selection of books and crafts. The headquarters of the Arizona Historical Society is here, with a research library open to the public. Open Mon.-Sat. 10 a.m.-4 p.m. and Sun. noon-4 p.m. (library closes at 1 p.m. on Sat. and all day Sun.); donation; tel. 628-5774. The museum is located at 929 E. Second St. and Park Avenue.

## UNIVERSITY OF ARIZONA

In 1885, the 13th territorial Legislature awarded Tucson $25,000 to establish Arizona's first university. Most townspeople didn't think much of the idea. They wanted to have the territorial capital (awarded to Prescott), or at least the territorial insane asylum (awarded to Phoenix and worth $100,000). It was left to a handful of determined citizens to get the school built. The walls started to go up after land was donated a mile from town by a saloonkeeper and two gamblers, but money ran out before the roof was finished. A federal loan put the roof on, and the university opened in 1891. Classrooms, library, offices, and dorms were all in one lone university building, today known as Old Main. The first year saw six faculty and 32 students, nearly all of whom were in the Preparatory School. (Like many other parts of the U.S. at the time, Arizona suffered from a lack of secondary as well as higher education.) The university has expanded to a present population of over 37,000 students and a faculty of about 2,100. Hundreds of programs are offered by 11 colleges and eight schools.

Visitors can enjoy theater and concert performances, the Flandrau Planetarium, sporting events, and several museums. For information, contact the **University Visitor Center** on the southeast corner of University and Cherry; open Mon.-Fri. 8 a.m.-5 p.m. and Sat. 9 a.m.-2 p.m.; tel. 621-5130 or 621-2211 (switchboard). The Visitor Center has literature, listings of U. of A. events, a videotape library for public viewing, rotating exhibits, and a route map of the free campus shuttle. Visitors can park behind the Visitor Center and use 15 free minutes on the meters to come in for assistance. Free **campus tours** of the University begin Mon.-Sat. at the Nugent Building; tel. 621-3641. The U. of A. campus is about a mile east of downtown.

### Arizona State Museum

A good place to learn about archaeology and Arizona's Indians, both prehistoric and modern. There's also a variety of natural history displays. The gift shop sells related books and Indian crafts. Open Mon.-Sat. 9 a.m.-5 p.m. and Sun. 2-5 p.m.; free; tel. 621-6302. Located on campus at the corner of E. University Blvd. and N. Park Avenue. The museum is in two buildings—exhibits are in the south one, library and offices in the north, across E. University Boulevard.

**UNIVERSITY OF ARIZONA**

▨ = VISITOR PARKING LOTS
○ = SHORT TERM METERED PARKING

1. UA Museum of Art
2. Drama Building (University Theater)
3. music (Crowder Hall)
4. Center for Creative Photography
5. Mineral Museum
6. Arizona Historical Society Museum
7. Arizona State Museum
8. Centennial Auditorium
9. Nugent Building
10. Student Union
11. science library
12. Bear Down Gym
13. main library
14. Flandrau Planetarium
15. Visitor Center
16. Arizona Stadium
17. McKale Mem. Center
18. pool

© MOON PUBLICATIONS

## UA Museum Of Art

The diverse collection spans the years from the Middle Ages through the Renaissance to the present. Changing exhibitions come from the University or other institutions. A gift shop sells books, magazines, posters, and cards. Open during the school year Mon.-Fri. 9 a.m.-5 p.m. and Sun. noon-4 p.m.; hours in summer (May 15-Sept. 1) are Mon.-Fri. 10 a.m.-3:30 p.m. and Sun. noon-4 p.m.; free; tel. 621-7567. You can park in the visitor section (metered) of the Park Avenue Garage, north of Speedway Blvd., and take the pedestrian underpass.

## Center For Creative Photography

Drop in to see rotating photographic exhibitions from the large collection of work by Richard Avedon, Ansel Adams, Paul Strand, Louise Dahl-Wolse, and other famous photographers. Traveling shows appear too. The Center also has an extensive library of books and periodicals on photography. Staff can tell you of other photographic exhibits in town. Open Mon.-Fri. 10 a.m.-5 p.m. and Sun. noon-5 p.m. during the main terms; call for summer hours; free; tel. 621-7968. It's in a new building on Olive, just southeast of the Museum of Art.

## Mineral Museum

See rare and wondrous minerals, some very delicate with unbelievable colors. Much of the collection comes from Arizona mines. There are fossils, too...giant mastodon skulls, dinosaur tracks, flying reptiles, fish, and birds. Open Mon.-Fri. 8 a.m.-3 p.m. (closed on school holidays); free; tel. 621-4227. Located in the Geology/Mineralogy Building on E. Second St. (northwest of the Student Union) on campus.

## Student Union

This building, in the center of the campus, is the best place to meet students and see what's going on. You'll find cafeterias, a variety of cafes, student services, and recreation areas here. In the basement, the Cellar is often jumping to live music during lunch hour. Sam's Place is busy with students playing pocket billiards, table tennis, and other games. Travelers might want to check the Ride Board to see if someone is going their way. Mail home a card at the post office, or pick up film at the Photo Shop. The first floor has several places at which to eat, an Information Desk (tel. 621-7755), and local art in Union Gallery. A cafeteria and the Cactus Lounge—a comfortable place to relax despite its name—are on the second floor. Union Club, on the third floor, has a fancier restaurant (lunch only) and sweeping views of the campus and mountains. Gallagher Theatre, on the east end of the building, shows popular movies nightly. On the west end is the ASUA Bookstore, well stocked with textbooks, general reading, school supplies, and U. of A. clothing.

## Flandrau Planetarium

Tucson has earned the title "Astronomy Capital of the World." With 45 telescopes operating in the city and surrounding peaks, astronomy is a major industry here—worth $40 million annually. Planetarium exhibit halls display astrolabes and early telescopes, meteorites, lunar specimens, excerpts from Apollo lunar videos, and photos of planets, the moon, stars, and nebula. A 16-inch telescope is available for stargazing on clear evenings. Dramatic planetarium or other shows are held most evenings and weekend afternoons. Call 621-STAR (recording) for program. The Astronomy Newsline lets you know what the planets and stars are doing in the heavens; tel. 621-4310. Open Mon. 1-4 p.m., Tues.-Thurs. 10 a.m.-4 p.m., Sat. and Sun. 1-5 p.m.; also open evenings Tues.-Sat. 7-9 p.m. Exhibits are free; shows cost $3.75 adult; $3 students, U. of A. staff, seniors 65 and over, and children 3-18 (no one under 3 allowed). A gift shop sells books, posters, and souvenirs related to astronomy. Located on campus at the corner of N. Cherry Ave. and E. University Blvd.; parking is available behind the Visitor Center across E. University Blvd. (Third St.); turn in from N. Campbell Avenue.

## Wildcat Heritage Gallery

See photos of Wildcat teams and players dating from 1897 to the present. Open Mon.-Fri. 8 a.m.-5 p.m.; located in the lower and second-floor levels of the west side of McKale Memorial Center. Purchase sports souvenirs at the Wildcatalog Store in the Center.

## Pharmacy Museum

Exhibits show the history of Arizona pharmacy through drugstore paraphernalia, old-time cure-alls, and antique medicine bottles. Look for the displays near the elevators on the first, second, and third floors and off the hallway between the third-floor elevator and the Dean's Office. Open Mon.-Fri. 8 a.m.-5 p.m.; free; tel. 626-1427. Located in the College of Pharmacy Building 4 blocks north of the main campus at Warren Ave. and Mabel Street.

# OTHER TUCSON SIGHTS

## WEST OF DOWNTOWN

### Garden Of Gethsemane
When Felix Lucero lay wounded on a WW I battlefield, he made a vow to create religious statues if he recovered. He did, and life-size sculptures of the Last Supper and other sub-

jects can be seen at the northeast corner of W. Congress St. and Bonita Ave. near I-10. Open 9 a.m.-4 p.m. daily; free.

### "A" Mountain
You can't miss this small peak just west of downtown. In earlier days it was a lookout point for hostile Indians, which explains its

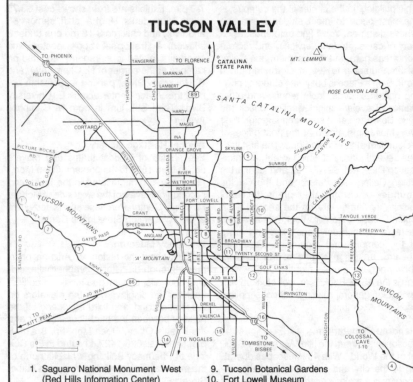

# TUCSON VALLEY

1. Saguaro National Monument West (Red Hills Information Center)
2. Arizona-Sonora Desert Museum
3. Old Tucson
4. R.W. Webb Winery
5. DeGrazia Gallery in the Sun
6. Sabino Canyon Visitor Center
7. downtown Tucson
8. University of Arizona
9. Tucson Botanical Gardens
10. Fort Lowell Museum
11. Reid Park and Zoo
12. Davis-Monthan A.F.B. (main gate)
13. Saguaro National Monument East (Visitor Center)
14. Mission San Xavier del Bac
15. Tucson International Airport
16. Pima Air Museum

© MOON PUBLICATIONS

original name—Sentinel Peak. The giant "A" dates from Oct. 23, 1915, when the local university football team beat Cal State Pomona in a 7-3 victory. Sports fans then headed over to paint on the "A." It became a tradition, and every year the freshman students whitewash the giant letter (and themselves) for all to see. To enjoy the panorama from the top, drive west on Congress St. and turn left at the sign to Sentinel Peak Road.

## Arizona-Sonora Desert Museum

This world-famous living museum contains animals and plants native to the Sonoran Desert of Arizona, the Mexican state of Sonora, and the Gulf of California region. Meet rattlesnakes, Gila monsters, scorpions, and other desert dwellers face to face (with glass separating you and them, of course). Watch frolicking otters and busy beavers through underwater panels. Try to spot the birds in the walk-in aviaries—not as easy as you'd expect—many desert birds blend well with their surroundings. Mountain lions, bighorn sheep, javelina, and over 200 other types of animals dwell in almost-natural surroundings. A Life Underground exhibit lets you step below the surface to observe wildlife in their burrows. A realistic limestone cave and earth science exhibits take you even deeper underground and far back in time. Desert flora are well represented and labeled in the gardens.

Bring a sun hat and good walking shoes—you'll need half a day to see all the exhibits. Animals are more active in the morning, making it a good time to visit. Special programs are scheduled daily to introduce you to some of the creatures living here. The setting is superb, with great views over the Avra Valley. Visible to the southwest are Baboquivari Peak (7,730 feet), sacred to the Papago Indians, and the nearer Kitt Peak (6,875 feet), site of important astronomical observatories. A gift shop and snack bar are near the entrance. Juan Santa Cruz Picnic Area is 0.25 mile away, back toward Tucson. The Desert Museum is open daily 8:30 a.m.-5 p.m. (7:30 a.m.-6 p.m. in summer); the ticket office closes one hour earlier; $6 adult, $1 ages 6-12; tel. 883-2702. No pets. The museum is lo-

*A desert bighorn sheep stands guard at Arizona-Sonora Desert Museum.*

*Old Tucson*

cated in Tucson Mountain Park, 14 miles west of Tucson. Take Speedway Blvd. west across Gates Pass. Large RVs and trailer-rigs must take Ajo and Kinney roads.

### Saguaro National Monument West
This half of the monument, the Tucson Mountains Unit, is smaller than the east part on the other side of Tucson, but it has denser and more vigorous stands of saguaro cactus (pronounced "sah-WAH-roe"). Stop at **Red Hills Information Center** (elev. 2,561 feet) to see a few exhibits and for books, maps, and hiking information; open daily 8 a.m.-5 p.m.; tel. 883-6366. Naturalist's talks or walks take place once or twice daily. Ask rangers for directions to the petroglyphs. There are five scenic picnic areas, too—four can be reached by road and one by trail. To reach the monument from Tucson, continue 2 miles past the Arizona-Sonora Desert Museum described above. If coming from Phoenix, take the I-10 Avra Valley Road Exit 242 and follow signs 13 miles.

A 100-yard, paved **Cactus Garden Trail** beside the Information Center introduces the unique saguaro and other plants of the Sonoran Desert. **Desert Discovery Nature Trail** makes a 0.5-mile loop; trailhead is 1.1 miles northwest of the Center.

The 6-mile **Bajada Loop Drive** takes in some of the scenic countryside; the graded, dirt road begins 1.6 miles northwest of the Information Center, which sells a guide booklet to the drive. **Valley View Overlook Trail** begins at the one-way section of the loop drive and climbs to a fine panorama; 1.5 miles roundtrip. Other trails wind through the scenic Sonoran Desert to Wasson Peak (4,687 feet) and other destinations. A trail map available a the Center shows trails, trailheads, and distances.

### Old Tucson
The West was won many times over at this famous movie studio. It began back in 1939 as the setting for the Columbia Pictures film *Arizona*. More than 200 features have been filmed here, including *Dirty Dingus McGee, Rio Lobo,* and *Death of a Gunfighter.* Such well-known TV shows as "Bonanza," "Gunsmoke," and "Little House on the Prairie," were shot here too. Old Tucson recreates Tucson in the 1860s with weathered adobe buildings, board sidewalks, and dusty streets. Stuntmen wear period clothing and stage blazing gunfights several times a day. Soundstage tours, the "Iron Door Mine," and stagecoach and train rides provide other excitement. A picnic area is available. Open daily 9 a.m.-9 p.m.; $9 adult,

$5 children age 4-11; admission includes all the activities; tel. 883-6457 (recording) or 883-0100. Located 12 miles west of Tucson in Tucson Mountain Park. Drive west on Speedway Blvd. (not suited for large rigs) or take Ajo and Kinney roads.

## International Wildlife Museum

Realistic dioramas show nearly 300 types of mounted mammals and birds. Hands-on exhibits and interactive videos in the McElroy Gallery help visitors to identify and learn about wildlife. The animals come from Arizona and the far corners of the world. Exhibits in the Taxidermy Studio demonstrate how the museum's specimens have been prepared. Visiting displays can be seen too. The museum has a gift shop and restaurant. Open Wed.-Sun. 9 a.m.-5:30 p.m. (Wed.-Sun. 8:30 a.m.-6 p.m. in summer); $4 adult; $3.50 student, military, and senior 62 and over; $1.50 children 6-12; tel. 624-4024 (recording) or 629-0100. Located at 4800 W. Gates Pass Road; from Tucson, head west 7 miles on Speedway Blvd. from I-10).

# NORTH OF DOWNTOWN

## Old Pueblo Museum

Permanent and changing exhibitions feature the Southwest's art, culture, science, and natural history. Open Mon.-Fri. 10 a.m.-9 p.m., Sat. 10 a.m.-6 p.m., and Sun. noon-5 p.m.; free; tel. 742-7191. In the Foothills Mall at 7401 N. La Cholla Blvd. at W. Ina Road.

## DeGrazia Gallery In The Sun

Designed to blend into the desert, the building is made of adobe and surrounded by desert plants. You enter through a gate patterned after the one at Yuma Territorial Prison, then pass through a short mine shaft. Ettore "Ted" DeGrazia, born in the Arizona mining district of Morenci, was fascinated from an early age by the desert colors and cultures of the Southwest. He became famous for his paintings, but he created ceramics, sculpture, and jewelry and wrote books as well. Although he died in 1982, the gallery continues as a museum. In a short movie,

DeGrazia tells of his life and work. Local artists also have exhibits in the gallery. From downtown go 4 miles east on E. Broadway to Swan Road, then north 6 miles to 6300 N. Swan Road (near Skyline Dr.); tel. 299-9191. Open daily 10 a.m.-4 p.m.; free; has a gift shop.

## Santa Catalina Mountains

The Santa Catalinas, crowned by 9,157-foot Mt. Lemmon, rise in ragged ridges from the north edge of Tucson. Lush woodlands grow on the higher slopes. Hikers can choose among trails totaling 150 miles in length that range from easy strolls to extremely difficult climbs. The **Pusch Ridge Wilderness** protects much of the range west of the Mt. Lemmon Highway. This paved mountain road and the Sabino Canyon Road offer easy access from Tucson for a visit to the mountains. The Santa Catalina topo map by the Southern Arizona Hiking Club shows all the main trails, distances, and trailheads. Purchase it at a U.S. Forest Service office or a hiking store. *Trail Guide to the Santa Catalina Mountains* by Eber Glending/Pete Cowgill and *Arizona Trails* by David Mazel have good descriptions of trails in the Catalinas.

In 1697, the tireless Jesuit Father Eusebio Francisco Kino visited a Tohono O'odham (Papago) village in what's now Tucson. He named it and the high ranges to the north and east "Santa Catarina." Spanish prospectors found gold in Cañada del Oro. They also reportedly mined gold in the Mine with the Iron Door and silver in La Esmeralda, both "lost" mines lying somewhere in the range. Raiding Apache discouraged mining until the late 1870s, when Anglo gold-seekers began placer operations in Cañada del Oro and tunneled into the hillsides. Most of the mines lie in the northeastern part of the mountains. Mount Lemmon honors botanist Sara Lemmon who, with her husband John, discovered many new species of plants on their 1881 expedition to the summit. As trails into the mountains improved, the citizens of Tucson headed to the hills more often for the cool air and scenery. The highway to the top was completed in 1949, built largely by federal prisoners.

**MT. LEMMON AND VICINITY**

CATALINA STATE PARK

TO TUCSON

EQUESTRIAN CENTER

CONTACT STATION

ROMERO CANYON TRAIL

SUTHERLAND TRAIL

MT. LEMMON TRAIL

ROMERO PASS

WEST FORK SABINO TRAIL

HUTCH'S POOL

WILDERNESS OF ROCKS TRAIL

Mount Lemmon (9,157 ft.)

SKI AREA Mt. Lemmon HWY

SKI LIFT

LEMMON ROCK LOOKOUT

MARSHALL GULCH

ASPEN TRAIL

MARSHALL SADDLE

SUMMERHAVEN

SPRUCE TRAIL

SOLDIER CAMP

Mount Bigelow (8,550 ft.)

BUTTERFLY TRAIL

PALISADE RANGER STATION

SAN PEDRO VISTA

GREEN MTN. TRAIL

ROSE CANYON

ROSE CANYON LAKE

GENERAL HITCHCOCK

BEAR CANYON

GEOLOGY VISTA

WINDY POINT

MOLINO BASIN

HWY

TO MT. LEMMON

TO TUCSON

BEAR CANYON TRAIL

SABINO CANYON TRAIL

PHONELINE TRAIL

SEVEN FALLS

BEAR CANYON TRAIL

LOWER BEAR PICNIC AREA

SABINO CANYON VISITOR CENTER

TO TUCSON

89

0    2 mi

© MOON PUBLICATIONS

## Catalina State Park

The 5,500-acre park in the western foothills of the Catalinas is popular for picnicking, camping, birding, hiking, and horseback riding. Hikers can follow a one-mile nature trail, a one-mile birding trail through a variety of bird habitats (pick up checklist at ranger station), a 2.3-mile **Canyon Loop Trail,** or climb all the way to the top of Mt. Lemmon (14 hard miles one way) via the **Sutherland** or **Romero canyon trails.** Natural swimming holes along the lower parts of the Sutherland and Romero Canyon trails make good dayhike destinations; both trails become very steep higher up. Admission is $3 for day use, $6 camping (showers but no hookups); tel. 628-5798. Your horse is welcome to stay too, in the equestrian center, and you can camp here. Catalina State Park is located 14 miles north of downtown Tucson on Oracle Road (US 89).

## Sabino Canyon

A desert oasis in the southern foothills of the Santa Catalina Mountains. Sabino Creek begins its journey on the slopes of Mt. Lemmon and bounces down through the canyon, supporting lush greenery and trees in which deer, javelina, coyotes, birds, and other animals find food and shelter. In the **Visitor Center,** at the entrance to the canyon, you'll see exhibits about the canyon and Santa Catalina Mountains and you can buy books and maps about the area. Naturalist-led walks might be scheduled, and there's a self-guiding nature trail behind the Center. The Visitor Center is open weekdays 8 a.m.-4:30 p.m. and weekends 8:30 a.m.-4:30 p.m., free; tel. 749-3223 (recorded announcements) or 749-8700 (Santa Catalina Ranger District office).

A road winds up through Sabino Canyon for 3.8 miles, crossing the creek many times. Private motor vehicles are prohibited beyond the Visitor Center to protect the beauty and peace of the area. You can explore the canyon by hiking, horseback riding, or hopping on the shuttle bus. Because Sabino and Bear canyons receive high usage, visitors must heed special closure notices that prohibit bicycle riding 9 a.m.-5 p.m. daily, glass containers, and dogs. The **shuttle** leaves the Visitor Center daily every 30 minutes from 9 a.m. to 4:30 p.m. from about mid-Dec. to early July; shuttles depart the rest of the year every 30 minutes on weekends and holidays and hourly on weekdays from 9 a.m. to 4 p.m. Fares are $5 adult, $2 ages 3-12; call 749-2861 (recording) to check schedules. You can get on and off as often as you choose at any of the nine stops. Hiking, birding, picnicking, and swimming are the big attractions. The Forest Service provides picnic areas and restrooms, though you'll find drinking water only at the Visitor Center and the first two stops. Camping isn't allowed in the canyon; to camp, backpackers must hike at least 0.25 mile in from trailheads.

Hikers have a choice of many destinations at the last stop: back to the Visitor Center via the **Phone Line Trail** high on the east slopes of Sabino Canyon (5.5 miles one way), to Lower Bear Canyon via Seven Falls (12 miles one way), up the West Fork of Sabino Canyon to Hutch's Pool (8 miles roundtrip), or to Mt. Lemmon's summit (13 hard miles one way).

Enjoy the special magic of Sabino Canyon on a **moonlight ride,** offered several evenings when the moon is full each month, March to December. Moonlight Shuttle fare is $5 adult, $2 children; reservations needed; tel. 749-2327.

Another shuttle bus leaves the Visitor Center for the 2.5-mile ride east to **Bear Canyon,** a picnic area and trailhead for the Catalinas. **Seven Falls,** a series of cascades 2.3 miles up Bear Canyon, is the most popular hiking destination. The good scenery doesn't begin until you leave the road, so there's no point in taking this shuttle unless you'll be hiking. Bear Canyon shuttle leaves hourly every day from 9 a.m. to 4 p.m.; fare is $3 adult, $1.25 ages 3-12. Sabino Canyon is 13 miles northeast of downtown Tucson. Take Tanqué Verde Road to Sabino Canyon Road and turn north 4.5 miles to the canyon entrance.

## Mount Lemmon Highway

In just an hour you can drive from the lower Sonoran Desert Zone to a Canadian Zone forest. Meadows bloom with wildflowers in spring and summer. Enjoy camping, picnicking, and hiking in the warmer months, skiing in winter. The 40-mile drive from Tucson leaves the saguaro, palo verde, and cholla behind, passes through juniper and pinyon, and enters pine forests at about 7,000 feet. Firs and aspen cling to the cool, north-facing slopes above 8,000 feet. *Be sure to fill up with gas before leaving Tucson, as none is available on the Mt. Lemmon Highway!*

**Molino Basin** (elev. 4,500 feet), 18 miles from Tucson, has the closest campground. It's open only from late Oct. to mid-April (in seasons when most of the higher campgrounds are closed); no water or fee. **General Hitchcock Campground,** 21 miles from Tucson, is at 6,000 feet and is usually open all year; no water or fee. In another 2 miles you'll come to **Windy Point,** whose sweeping panorama of the southern foothills and Tucson is pretty day and night. **Geology Vista,** one more mile, has a good view to the southeast and a sign describing the forces that created these mountains. **Rose Canyon Lake,** 33 miles from Tucson, has trout fishing and a nearby campground but no swimming or boating; sites are open mid-April to late Oct.; has drinking water and a $5/vehicle fee. You can see many mountain ranges to the east from **San Pedro Vista,** 0.5 mile beyond Rose Canyon turnoff. A sign identifies the ranges. **Green Mountain Trail** connects San Pedro Vista with General Hitchcock Campground. Allow 3 hours for the 4-mile (one way) hike.

At Palisades Ranger Station, 36 miles from Tucson, you can hike to the top of 8,550-foot **Mt. Bigelow,** a 1.5-mile roundtrip climb of 600 feet. The **Butterfly Trail** also begins at this trailhead and winds through ponderosa pine, Douglas fir, and juniper-oak woodlands to Soldier Camp, 5.8 miles to the northwest; allow 4-5 hours between trailheads. Primitive camping (no facilities) can be done along Bigelow Road and at Whitetail, across the highway and a bit farther up. **Spencer Can-**

**yon Campground,** 38 miles from Tucson, is open mid-April to late Oct. with drinking water and a $5/vehicle fee. **Soldier Camp** is 39 miles from Tucson and 0.25 mile north of the highway. Cavalry troops from Fort Lowell camped here in the 1870s while tracking rebellious Apache. Later the soldiers used the site as a summer resort.

You'll come to a fork in the highway about 41 miles from Tucson; keep left 0.5 mile for the tiny village of Summerhaven or keep right one mile to **Ski Valley.** The tiny village of Summerhaven has the **Alpine Inn** (bed and breakfast) with just six rooms ($69-96 d); reservations advised at Box 789, Mt. Lemmon, AZ 85619; tel. 576-1500. Its restaurant serves continental and American cuisine daily for breakfast, lunch, and dinner. The Hooter Saloon has live entertainment on Sat. nights (and Sun. afternoons in summer). The Inn sells some groceries but no gasoline (fill up before leaving Tucson). Alpine Inn may know of cabins for rent in Summerhaven.

**Aspen Loop Trail,** which begins its 3.8-mile loop near Summerhaven, is a good introduction to the high country. Start at Marshall Gulch Picnic Area, one mile south of Summerhaven; a sign, "Aspen Trail #93, Marshall Saddle 2.5," marks the start. A gate may block the road in winter, when you'll have to park and walk the last half mile. The trail climbs through aspen, fir, and ponderosa pine forests and has some good views. At Marshall Saddle turn right down Marshall Gulch 1.3 miles back to the picnic area.

At the Santa Catalina Ranger District office in the Sabino Canyon Visitor Center, foresters can tell you of backcountry areas to explore in other parts of the Santa Catalinas. **Peppersauce Campground** in the northeastern foothills lies among large sycamore trees at an elevation of 4,700 feet; open with water year-round; free. Take Forest Route 38 from Oracle or the rough Control Road (Forest Route 38) from the Mt. Lemmon Highway.

**Mount Lemmon Ski Valley** is the southernmost ski area in the United States. The double-chair lift takes summer visitors and winter skiers from 8,200 to 9,100 feet. Skiers have a choice of 16 runs, including a "bunny slope" for beginners. Rentals (skis, boots, and poles) cost $15; lessons are $16/hour for private or $10/2 hours for group lessons; lift tickets cost $22/day ($12 for children 12 and under). You can get a recording of current ski and road conditions by calling 576-1400 (call 576-1321 for the business office). In summer you can take the lift up to enjoy the views and cool forests; $4 ($2 children 3-12). A hiking trail also goes from the bottom of the ski lift through fir and aspen forests to the summit. It's unsigned, so ask someone to point out the start. Season is about May to Oct.; allow 2-3 hours for the 2.2 miles roundtrip. Several more hiking trails radiate from the summit, accessible by the trail noted above or the ski lift. The **Iron Door Restaurant** across the highway is open daily for lunch and on weekends for brunch. The highway continues past Ski Valley to an infrared observatory near the top of Mt. Lemmon, but both the road and observatory are likely to be closed to visitors.

# EAST OF DOWNTOWN

## Reid Park Zoo
A small but good collection of flamingos, lions, tigers, hippos, polar bears, and other exotic life. A walk-in aviary has birds from the far corners of the world. The zoo is active in breeding rare animals. It has a snack bar, gift shop, and, on the west side, a picnic area. Open daily 9:30 a.m.-5 p.m. from mid-Sept. to mid-March; summer hours are Mon.-Fri. 8:30 a.m.-4 p.m. (to 6 p.m. on Sat., Sun., and holidays); $2 adult, $1.50 seniors 62 and over, $.50 children 5-14; tel. 791-4022 (recording) or 791-3204. Reid Park is 3.5 miles east of downtown. Enter from 22nd St. just east of Country Club.

## Tucson Botanical Gardens
Plant lovers wanting to see a variety of flora, both native and exotic, will enjoy a visit. Garden exhibits include a xeriscape-solar demonstration, native crops, roses, herbs, irises, and a tropical greenhouse. You can attend classes, workshops, tours, and a variety of

special events; call for schedule; tel. 326-9255. Open daily 8 a.m.-4:30 p.m.; a gift shop is open daily, but shorter hours. Garden admission is $2 adult, $1.50 senior 62 and over, free for children under 12. The gardens are about 6 miles northeast of downtown at 2150 N. Alvernon Way, just south of Grant Road.

## Fort Lowell Museum
While the U.S. Army chased troublesome Apache in the 1860s, the troops needed a base. The Army established Camp Lowell on the outskirts of Tucson in 1866 and named it in honor of an officer killed in the Civil War. The camp was moved to its present site in 1873 and became a fort in 1879. It was a busy place during the Geronimo campaigns until the famous Apache chief surrendered in Sept. 1886. With the Indian wars finally over in Arizona, the Army no longer needed this fort and abandoned it in 1891.

The commanding officer's quarters have been reconstructed and furnished as they were in the 1880s. Exhibits of maps, documents, and photos show life of the frontier soldier. Ruins of the adobe hospital and other buildings are nearby. Open Wed.-Sat. 10 a.m.-4 p.m.; free; tel. 885-3832. The museum is in Fort Lowell Park at 2900 N. Craycroft Road, about 8 miles northeast of downtown.

## Davis-Monthan Air Force Base
Curious about what's going on at the local base? Tours are given by an informative Air Force guide twice weekly. Charles Lindburgh dedicated Davis-Monthan in 1927 as one of the country's first municipal airports. During WW II it became a training ground for crews of B-17 bombers and other aircraft. The base now has two distinct operations. One part trains pilots in combat aircraft while the other, known as AMARC (Aerospace Maintenance And Regeneration Center), stores a staggering number of surplus planes. The dry climate of Tucson is ideal for both activities. The WW II birds have all left for museums but a great variety of postwar fighters, transports, and bombers stretches for blocks. The rows of giant B-52 bombers are quite a sight. Bus

*F-104 Starfighter at Pima Air Museum*

tours (free) are given on Mon. and Wed. at 9 a.m., lasting 1 to 1½ hours. Call the Public Affairs Division as far in advance as possible to make reservations and to check on tour times; tel. 750-4570. Tours start near the main gate at Craycroft Road and Golf Links Road, 7 miles southeast of downtown. Ask where to park.

### Pima Air Museum
More than 150 historic aircraft display the dramatic advances in aviation technology. Many famous planes from WW II through the Vietnam era can be seen. A Norden bombsight, cut-away engines, uniforms, and other memorabilia are on exhibit too. A gift shop sells aircraft models, books, and posters. Open daily 9 a.m.-5 p.m. (entry closes at 4 p.m.); $4 adult, $3 seniors 62 and over and active military, $2 ages 10-17, under 10 free; tel. 574-0462. The museum is about 12 miles southeast of downtown. Take I-10 east, exit at Valencia Road, turn left, and go 2 miles.

### Saguaro National Monument East
This older and larger part of the monument has many huge saguaro. This giant cactus matures very slowly, taking about 25 years to grow just 2 feet. Youngsters need protective shade. Arms don't appear until saguaro are about 75 years old. The old-timers live over 200 years and reach 50 feet. Creamy white blossoms, the state flower, appear in early May. The fruit, which matures in midsummer, resembles a flower with shiny, black seeds surrounded by a bright red shell. Grazing cattle trampled the young saguaro for many years in this area. The cattle were removed beginning in 1958, but it will be a long time before the saguaro forest recovers. Today it has mostly very old and very young specimens. The **Visitor Center,** just inside the monument, contains exhibits of desert geology, ecology, flora, and fauna. A 10-minute slide program shown every half-hour illustrates the saguaro and its environment. Special programs and walks may be offered too.

Books, maps, and hiking information are available. Outside, the **Cactus Garden** has a variety of labeled desert plants.

The 8-mile **Cactus Forest Drive** winds through foothills of the Rincon Mountains and offers many fine views. After you've driven about 2.2 miles along this route, you'll find the **Mica View Picnic Area** to the north; it has picnic tables and outhouses but no water. At another 0.3 mile past the turnoff, look for the **Desert Ecology Trail** on the left. On this quarter-mile paved trail you can learn how plants and animals cope with the environment. **Freeman Homestead Nature Trail** begins on the right, 200 yards down the spur road to Javelina Picnic Area. The Freeman Trail is a one-mile loop that takes you through huge saguaro and into a wash filled with mesquite. **Javelina Picnic Area** has shaded picnic tables and outhouses but no water. More than half a dozen other trails wind through the desert hills near the Cactus Forest Drive. Many interconnect to allow a variety of loop hikes; ask for a trail brochure at the Visitor Center.

The **Tanque Verde Ridge Trail** begins near the Javelina Picnic Area and climbs into the rugged **Rincon Mountain Wilderness.** Mica Mountain, at 8,666 feet the highest peak, is 17.5 miles away by trail. **Douglas Spring Trail,** which begins at the east end of Speedway Blvd., crosses part of the northern monument to Douglas Springs (5.9 miles one way), then turns south to connect with Tanque Verde Ridge and other trails. *Arizona Trails* by David Mazel has detailed hiking info and maps for this and several other routes in the Rincons. Spring and autumn are the best hiking times. A free permit from the Visitor Center is needed for backcountry camping. Carry water (one gallon per day) and topo maps. The wilderness is especially dry and unforgiving in the heat of summer.

The Cactus Forest Drive is open daily 7 a.m.-7 p.m. from April 1 to Oct. 31, then daily 8 a.m. to 5 p.m. from Nov. 1 to May 31; the Visitor Center is open daily 8 a.m.-5 p.m. year-round; $3/vehicle admission ($1 bicyclist or foot traveler); tel. 296-8576. Saguaro National Monument East is just off Old Spanish Trail, about 16 miles east of downtown. Bicyclists enjoy riding the Drive, which can be reached from Tucson on a bike path that parallels the Old Spanish Trail.

**Colossal Cave**

A dry limestone cave with authentic outlaw history. The tour guide will point out the large, dusty formations and explain the geology, but he won't tell where the $60,000 in gold is hidden! More than 6 miles of passageway have been mapped. The tour covers only 0.75 mile, but many steps have to be climbed up and down. Tours leave every half-hour and last about 45 minutes. A snack bar and gift shop are outside the entrance; a free campground is nearby. Open daily Oct. to March 9 a.m.-5 p.m. (until 6 p.m. Sun. and holidays), then daily April to Sept. 8 a.m.-6 p.m. (until 7 p.m. Sun. and holidays). Admission is $4.75 adult, $3.50 children age 11-16, and $2 children age 6-10; tel. 791-7677. The cave is 22 miles east of downtown Tucson. Take I-10 east to Vail-Wentworth Exit 279, then go 7 miles north; or take the Old Spanish Trail to Saguaro National Monument East, then go 12 miles south.

**R.W. Webb Winery**

Arizona wine? Yes, and this commercial winery is the state's largest. You can learn about wine making on tours and tastings here that last 30-45 minutes; $1 charge. Open Mon.-Sat. 10 a.m.-5 p.m. and Sun. noon-5 p.m.; tel. 629-9911. Located 14 miles southeast of Tucson; take the I-10 Vail-Wentworth Exit 279, then turn east 1.5 miles on the north frontage road.

*Tucson and the Santa Catalina Mountains*

# TUCSON ACCOMMODATIONS

## HOTELS AND MOTELS

The **Congress Hotel,** opened in 1919, is the last of the good, old, downtown hotels. Rooms restored to their 1919 heyday cost $38.33 s, $42.71 d; standard rooms are $30.66 s, $35.04 d; its youth hostel accommodations are described below; all rooms have bath and a/c; tel. 622-8848. Located at 311 E. Congress St.; Greyhound and Amtrak stations are across the street.

Tucson has over 50 other hotels, motels, and resorts near the freeway, downtown, at the airport, near the university, and scattered around the valley. Good hunting grounds include the business route of old US 80 that

parallels I-10 south of downtown and old US 89 that runs north-south (especially the Miracle Mile and Oracle Road sections north of downtown). Look for listings in *The Official Visitors Guide to Metropolitan Tucson* and *Arizona Accommodations Directory,* both free at the Tucson Convention and Visitors Bureau. The Yellow Pages are another source.

## YOUTH HOSTEL AND YMCA

The **Congress Hotel,** noted above, has rooms for hostelers; $12.05 w/hostel card; guests without a card must be under 26 and pay $13.14; no reservations taken; a 3-day stay limit usually applies. The **L.A. Lohse**

**Memorial YMCA,** 516 N. Fifth Ave. (corner of Sixth St.), has single rooms for men only; $16/night or $75/week, bath down hall; tel. 623-7727. Rates are same for members and nonmembers. Conveniently located between the university and downtown. Guests receive a discount to use the swimming pool, racquetball courts, and gym.

## BED AND BREAKFASTS

These are private houses open to travelers in the European tradition. The degree of luxury varies, but the hosts offer a personal touch not found in the usual motels. Advance reservations are requested. Some B&Bs close for a month in summer. Ask the Visitors Bureau for brochures of local establishments or check listings in the *Tucson Visitors Guide.*

**Peppertrees Bed and Breakfast** is a turn-of-the-century house just 2 blocks from the university; $66.70 s, $72.18 d, $121.45 guest house; tel. 622-7167; 724 E. University Blvd. (look for the two pepper trees in front).

**La Posada Del Valle** is a 1929 house, also convenient to the university; $94-116 d; tel. 795-3840; 1640 N. Campbell Avenue.

**Bird in the Hand** is in the historic Barrio Libre area near downtown; rooms have Mexican antiques; $44.80 d with shared bath, $61.23 d w/bath; tel. 622-5428; 529 S. Meyer.

**Triangle L Ranch** sits in the northern foothills of the Catalinas 35 miles north of Tucson; it dates from the late 1800s and was a guest ranch in the 1920s; the area has good birding and hiking; cottages start at $42.40 s, $58.30 d; tel. 623-6732 (Tucson) or 896-2804 (Oracle); off AZ 77 near Oracle.

Three reservations services list some of the bed and breakfasts: **Old Pueblo Homestays** (Box 13603, Tucson, AZ 85732; tel. 790-2399) has a list of about 30 B&Bs in Tucson and the foothills and some in other parts of southeastern Arizona from $35-95 d. **Bed and Breakfast in Arizona** (Box 8628, Scottsdale, AZ 85252; tel. 1-995-2831) has a list of many Arizona B&Bs including some in Tucson; prices range $35-120 d. **Mi Casa Su Casa** (Box 950, Tempe, AZ 85281; tel. 1-990-0682 or 800-456-0682) is Spanish for "My house (is) your house"; the statewide listings include a variety in the Tucson area with rates ranging from $35 to $120 d.

## GUEST RANCHES

The Tucson area offers the world's largest choice of guest ranches. At all of them, you can enjoy Western hospitality and activities as well as high-quality accommodations and food. Horseback riding, hiking, birding, socializing, and relaxing are popular with guests. Many ranches have a heated pool and tennis courts; most are near a golf course. Meals are included with your stay and are often served family style. Advance reservations are usually required. Most guest ranches close during the hot summers, though a few remain open for hardy visitors. The following rates include service charges and tax.

**Hacienda del Sol Guest Ranch Resort** offers luxury in the desert just northeast of Tucson, 5601 N. Hacienda del Sol Road (off River Road), Tucson, AZ 85718; tel. 299-1501 or (800) 444-3999. Facilities include tennis courts, a pool, and riding stables; a 27-hole championship golf course is nearby. Daily rates are $80.88-256.60 d.

**Tanque Verde Guest Ranch** lies in the foothills of the Rincon Mountains 24 miles east of Tucson at 14301 E. Speedway, Tucson, AZ 85748; tel. 296-6275. The ranch dates from the 1880s. It now has two pools, a spa, an exercise room, tennis courts, horseback riding, bird banding, nature walks, and other activities. Daily rates during the peak season of Dec. 16 to April 30 are $232-287 s, $256-360 d; open the rest of the year at reduced rates.

**Lazy K Bar Guest Ranch** is an informal, family ranch 16 miles northwest of Tucson at the foot of the Tucson Mountains, 8401 N. Scenic Dr., Tucson, AZ 85743; tel. 744-3050. Guests can enjoy horseback riding, the swimming pool, tennis courts, other games, and hiking. Rates run $122-159 s, $195-244 d; a 3-day minimum stay is requested; closed July and August.

**White Stallion Ranch** sprawls over 3,000 acres 17 miles northwest of Tucson, at 9251 W. Twin Peaks Road, Tucson, AZ 85743; tel. 297-0252. The ranch has a pool, a spa, tennis courts, horseback riding, and varied ranch activities from early Oct. to the end of April; $135 s, $218-250 d.

**Rancho Santa Cruz Guest Ranch** is 49 miles south of Tucson near Tumacacori National Monument; Box 8, Tumacacori, AZ 85640; tel. 281-8383 or 798-3234. Activities include horseback riding, birdwatching, and swimming; $73.85-131.88 d from May to Sept. and $84.40-158.25 d Oct. to April; take I-19 Exit 29, then head south on the east frontage road or take Exit 25, then head north on the east frontage road.

**Rancho de la Osa Guest Ranch** dates back 250 years to when it was a Spanish land grant; it's located 66 miles southwest of Tucson near the Mexican border, Box 1, Sasabe, AZ 85633; tel. 823-4257. Guests have horseback riding, a pool, and lots of peace and quiet; open Sept. 1 to May 1; $115.43 s, $194.40 d (2-night minimum).

## RESORTS

**Canyon Ranch Spa** is a health-and-fitness vacation resort offering an active program of exercise classes, tennis, racquetball, swimming, hiking, biking, yoga, and meditation. Chefs prepare gourmet meals from natural ingredients. The 28-acre grounds are northeast of town near Sabino Canyon at 8600 E. Rockcliff Road, Tucson, AZ 85715; tel. 749-9000, or (800) 742-9000. A 4-night package starts at $1661 s or $2621 d. There's a 4-night minimum stay during the high season, but off-season you can stay at a daily rate of $369 s and $585 d. A "Spa Renewal Day" costs $195 without accommodations.

**Tucson National Resort & Spa** features extensive spa services, lakes, a 27-hole golf course, tennis, swimming, and fine dining on its 650 acres. Located at the base of the Catalinas on the northwest side of the city at 2727 W. Club Dr., Tucson, AZ 85741; tel. 297-2271 or (800) 528-4856. In high season, spa packages (2-night minimum) cost $307.72 s, $479.12 d per night; room-only rates are $143-191.

The **Westin La Paloma** has a 27-hole golf course, tennis, racquetball, a giant pool with waterfall, and a choice of restaurants. On the north edge of town next to the Catalinas at 3800 E. Sunrise Dr., Tucson, AZ 85718; tel. 742-6000 or (800) 222-1252. High-season rates are $261 s, $304 d.

**Sheraton Tucson El Conquistador Golf and Tennis Resort** and the nearby El Conquistador Country Club offer 45 holes of golf, 32 lighted tennis courts, 16 racquetball courts, athletic club, pools, spas, horseback riding, jeep tours, and a choice of Western, Mexican, or continental dining. On the northwest side of town below the Catalinas at 10000 N. Oracle Road, Tucson, AZ 85737; tel. 742-7000 or (800) 325-7832. High-season rates run $170-958.50 d.

**Loews Ventana Canyon Resort** nestles in the foothills of the Catalinas north of the city at 7000 North Resort Dr., Tucson, AZ 85715; tel. 299-2020 or (800) 234-5117. The 93-acre grounds enclose a natural waterfall, an 18-hole golf course, 10 lighted tennis courts, swimming pools, spa, health club, and a selection of restaurants. High-season rates start at $218 s, $240 d; suites are $426-1491.

## CAMPGROUNDS AND RV PARKS

**Catalina State Park,** 12 miles north of Tucson on Oracle Road (US 89), offers campsites in the foothills of the Catalinas; $6 (showers but no hookups); you and your horse can camp in the equestrian center; tel. 628-5798; see p. 409. The Coronado National Forest has several campgrounds on the **Mt. Lemmon Highway**; the closest to Tucson is **Molino Basin,** is 18 miles away; tel. 749-8700; see p. 410.

**Gilbert Ray Campground** is in Tucson Mountain Park, 8 miles west of town; $5 (or $7 w/hookups) for tents or RVs; no showers; tel. 883-4200. **Justin's RV Park** is an adult park (children OK in summer) 8 miles west of town near Tucson Mountain Park at 3551 San Joaquin Road; $9.95 w/hookups; the adjacent Justin's Water World is open in summer; tel. 883-8340. **Prince of Tucson RV Park** is at 3501 N. Freeway on the west side of I-10, 4 miles northwest of Tucson; take I-10 Exit 254 (Prince Road); it has a swimming pool, spa, and recreation room; RV spaces are $17.92 w/hookups; tel. 887-3501. **Tratel Tucson RV Park** is also 4 miles northwest of Tucson; take I-10 Exit 254 (Prince Road) then go south on the west frontage road of I-10 to 2070 W. Fort Lowell Road; has a pool and recreation room; charge for tents or RVs without hookups is $14.69, for RVs w/hookups it's $16.20; tel. 888-5401. **Rincon Country West RV Park** is 4 miles south of Tucson at 4555 S. Mission Road; take I-19 Exit 99 (Ajo Way), go 0.5 mile west on Ajo Way, then turn 0.5 mile south on Mission; adults only;

has spas and many organized hobby and social activities; $19.61 w/hookups (no tents); tel. 294-5608. **Crazy Horse RV Campground** is southeast of downtown at 6660 S. Craycroft Road (I-10 Exit 268, then 0.25 mile north on Craycroft); includes a heated pool, spa, recreation room, and RV repairs; $15.23 tent or RV w/hookups; tel. 574-0157. **Cactus Country RV Park** is 19 miles southeast of downtown off I-10, take Exit 275, then go 0.2 mile north to 10195 S. Houghton Road; has a pool, spa, and organized winter activities; $11.18 tent or RV no hookups, $15.44 RV w/hookups; tel. 574-3000.

You'll find listings of other RV parks and trailer parks in the *Tucson Visitors Guide* and in the Yellow Pages.

# TUCSON RESTAURANTS

The Mexican food in Tucson could hardly be beat in Mexico. Or a visitor can choose from Chinese, Middle Eastern, Greek, Italian, German, French, and more! Elegant service and food are presented by the seven or so continental restaurants. The more expensive places may require coat and tie for the men; ask when making reservations. And of course Tucson has cowboy food—the old standbys of steak, potatoes, beans, and biscuits. The following is only a small selection; see the Visitors Bureau for a longer listing.

Restaurants are marked **$=Inexpensive** (to $8); **$$=Moderate** ($8-15); and **$$$=Expensive** (over $15).

## AMERICAN

**$$ Cafe Sweetwater:** A variety—steaks, seafood, chicken, veal, and more in a casual atmosphere. Located just east of downtown at 340 E. Sixth St., at Fourth Ave.; tel. 622-6464, reservations requested. Open Mon.-Fri. for lunch and Mon.-Sat. for dinner.

**$ Egg Garden:** Eggs go in almost everything—omelets, quiches, seafood, hamburgers, salads. Just east of downtown, 509½ N.

Fourth Ave. at Sixth St.; tel. 622-0918. Open daily for breakfast and lunch and Tues.-Sat. for dinner.

**$ Furr's Cafeterias:** A huge selection of courses at three locations. Six miles east of downtown at 5910 E. Broadway; tel. 747-7881. Four miles north of downtown at 4329 N. Oracle Road; tel. 293-8550. Just north of downtown at I-10 and St. Mary's Road; tel. 624-1688. Open daily for lunch and dinner.

**$ Garland:** A good place for American, Mexican, Italian, and vegetarian food. Located 0.75 mile northeast of downtown, 119 E. Speedway Blvd. at Sixth Ave.; tel. 792-4221. Open daily for breakfast, lunch, and dinner.

**$$ to $$$ Jerome's:** Excellent American regional cuisine, including fresh seafood, Southwest, Cajun, and creole. About 8 miles east of downtown at 6958 E. Tanque Verde Road; tel. 721-0311. Open Tues.-Sun. for dinner and Sun. for brunch.

**$$ Pinnacle Peak:** Don't wear a tie to this informal family-style steakhouse—or else! Thousands of severed ties decorate the ceilings. Located in Trail Dust Town, 8 miles east of downtown at 6541 E. Tanque Verde Road; tel. 296-0911. Open daily for dinner.

$$ **Sizzler Steak Houses:** Good value on steak or seafood dinners, and there's a giant salad bar. Four locations in town. Just west of downtown at 470 W. Congress; tel. 623-2888. Four miles east of downtown at 4330 E. Broadway; tel. 326-5133. Five miles southeast of downtown at 2048 E. Irvington Road; tel. 889-5757. And in northwest Tucson at 3000 W. Ina Road; tel. 742-0989. Open daily for lunch and dinner.

$$ **CCC Chuckwagon Suppers:** Enjoy real cowboy beef, beans, and other trappings followed by Western music by the Sons of the Pioneers. Located near the Tucson Mountains about 12 miles from downtown at 8900 Bopp Road; tel. 883-2333 (reservations needed). Open Tues.-Sat. for dinner from late Dec. through April.

$$ to $$$ **The Tucson Cork:** One of the best steakhouses in Tucson; also a choice of chicken, seafood, and prime rib; there's an excellent salad bar. Eight miles east of downtown at 6320 E. Tanque Verde Road; tel. 296-1631. Open daily for dinner.

## CHINESE

$ **China Wall:** Enjoy a choice of Hunan, Szechuan, and Mandarin styles. Two miles east of downtown at 2547 E. Broadway; tel. 323-2024. Open daily for lunch and dinner.

$$ **Lotus Garden:** A long menu features Cantonese and Szechuan specialties. Six miles northeast of downtown at 5975 E. Speedway; tel. 298-3351. Open daily for lunch and dinner.

## CONTINENTAL
### (reservations requested)

$$ to $$$ **Arizona Inn:** The elegant dining room is open daily for breakfast, lunch, and dinner; 2200 E. Elm St. (between Campbell and Tucson Blvd.), 2 miles northeast of downtown; tel. 327-7646.

$$$ **Charles:** An old English manor sets the mood for elegant dining. Located 8 miles east of downtown at 6400 E. El Dorado Circle (from Speedway Blvd., go north 0.2 mile on Wilmot Road, then right on El Dorado Place and follow signs); tel. 296-7173. Open Mon.-Sat. for dinner, weekdays for lunch.

$$$ **Gold Room:** Noted for excellent food and service with a sweeping view of the city. Located at the Westward Look Resort, 9 miles north of downtown, 245 E. Ina Road; tel. 297-1151, ext. 413. Open daily for breakfast, lunch, and dinner.

$$ to $$$ **Iron Mask:** A suit of armor and Old English decor provide atmosphere. Four miles northeast of downtown, 2564 E. Grant Road (east of Tucson Blvd.); tel. 327-6649. Open Tues.-Fri. for lunch and Tues.-Sat. for dinner.

$$ to $$$ **Palomino:** Has one of the longest menus in town and some of the best continental, American, and Greek food as well. Eight miles northeast of downtown at 2959 N. Swan Road; tel. 795-5561. Open for dinner only; closed Sun., holidays, and month of August.

$$$ **Tack Room:** This highly rated restaurant is in an adobe hacienda. Ten miles northeast of downtown at 2800 N. Sabino Canyon Road; tel. 298-2351. Open daily for dinner only.

## FRENCH
### (reservations requested)

$$$ **Le Rendez-Vous:** Fine French food in a formal setting. Six miles northeast of downtown at 3844 E. Fort Lowell Road; tel. 323-7373. Open Tues.-Fri. for lunch and Tues.-Sun. for dinner.

$$$ **Penelope's:** Personal service and excellent food. Three miles east of downtown on 3619 E. Speedway Blvd.; tel. 325-5080. Open Tues.-Fri. for lunch and Tues.-Sun. for dinner.

## GREEK

$$ to $$$ **Olive Tree:** Generous portions and a choice of indoor or patio tables. Located 7 miles east of downtown at 7000 E. Tanque Verde Road; tel. 298-1845. Open Mon.-Sat. for lunch and daily for dinner.

## INDIAN

$$ **Cuisine of India (New Delhi Palace):** Seafood, meats, and vegetarian food prepared in tandoori and other styles. Located 6 miles east of downtown at 6751 E. Broadway Blvd.; tel. 296-8585. Open daily for lunch and dinner.

## ITALIAN

$ to $$ **Caruso's:** Southern Italian cooking in a Tucson institution dating back to the 1930s. Located just east of downtown at 434 N. Fourth Ave.; tel. 624-5765. Open daily for dinner.

$$$ **Scordato's:** One of the best Italian restaurants in town, with a wide selection and an extensive wine list. Six miles west of downtown at 4405 W. Speedway Blvd.; tel. 624-8946, reservations requested. Open daily for dinner only.

## MALAYSIAN

$$ **Selamat Makan:** Satay, rice curries, vegetarian dishes, and other flavorful food. About 4.5 miles northeast of downtown in Grant Road Plaza, 3502 E. Grant Road; tel. 325-6755. Open Tues.-Fri. for lunch and Tues.-Sun. for dinner.

## MEXICAN

$$ **Carlos Murphy's:** Tasty food downtown at 419 W. Congress; tel. 628-1956. Open daily for lunch and dinner.

$ to $$ **El Adobe:** Sonoran cuisine in one of Tucson's oldest buildings, 40 W. Broadway Blvd. (see historic walking tour map); tel. 791-7458. Open daily except Sun. for lunch and dinner. Ask for a table on the patio if the weather is fine.

$ to $$ **El Charro:** A longtime favorite (founded 1922), now in the historic Le Flein House downtown, 311 N. Court Ave. (see historic walking tour map); tel. 622-5465. Open daily for lunch and dinner.

$ to $$ **El Parador:** The dining room has a garden atmosphere and flamenco guitar music (several nights a week). Located 2 miles east of downtown at 2744 E. Broadway; tel. 881-2808. Open Mon.-Sat. for lunch and dinner, Sun. for brunch and dinner.

$ **El Torero:** Popular place with generous servings. Located in South Tucson at 231 E.

26th St. (near S. Fourth Ave.); tel. 622-9534. Open for lunch and dinner; closed Tuesdays. You'll find other Mexican restaurants in the neighborhood. South Tucson is a one-mile-square city-within-a-city just south of downtown Tucson.

**$ to $$ La Fuente Restaurant & Lounge:** Strolling mariachis serenade diners in the evenings. At 1749 N. Oracle Road; tel. 623-8659. Open daily for lunch and dinner, except closed Mon. from June to November.

**$ to $$ La Parilla Suiza:** Charcoal-grilled and other authentic Mexico City food. About 7 miles northeast of downtown at 5602 E. Speedway Blvd.; tel. 747-4838. Also 2 miles north of downtown at 2720 N. Oracle Road; tel. 624-4300. Open daily for lunch and dinner.

## SOUTHWESTERN

**$$$ Janos:** Exceptionally good and creative New Southwestern cuisine in the historic Stevens House. Downtown in the El Presidio district at 150 N. Main Ave. (see historic

walking tour map); tel. 884-9426. Open Mon.-Sat. (Tues.-Sat. in summer) for dinner.

**$$ to $$$ Painted Desert:** New Southwestern cuisine prepared with originality and attention to detail. Three miles north of downtown at 3055 N. Campbell Ave.; tel. 795-8503/8440. Open Mon.-Sat. for lunch and daily for dinner; call for summer hours.

## THAI

**$ to $$ Thai Thani:** Tasty curries, seafood, and vegetarian food. Three miles northeast of downtown at 4537 E. Speedway Blvd. and Orange Grove Road; tel. 795-1421. Open daily for lunch and dinner.

## VIETNAMESE

**$ to $$ Mekong:** Large selection of spicy cuisine. Seven miles north of downtown at 6462 N. Oracle Road; tel. 575-9402. Open daily for lunch and dinner.

# OTHER TUCSON PRACTICALITIES

## ENTERTAINMENT

You'll find listings of movies, performances, and social spots in the *Tucson Weekly,* free at newsstands, and in the entertainment sections of the *Arizona Daily Star* and *Tucson Citizen.*

### Movies

Newspapers list what's new, but to see something different try the **New Loft Theatre** for old classics and foreign films; it's at 504 N. Fremont Ave. (near Sixth St.), about 0.75 mile east of downtown; tel. 624-4981. **Gallagher Theatre** has inexpensive movies every evening when the university is in session; on campus at the east end of the Student Union; tel. 621-3102.

### Theater And Concerts

The **University of Arizona** offers many productions; tel. 621-1162 (Fine Arts Box Office; recorded announcement after hours). Performing groups include the **University Theatre** (Oct. to April in Main Street Theatre, Drama Bldg.), **Studio Theatre** (inexpensive student productions at Studio Y, Fifth and University; Oct. to April), and **University of Arizona Repertory Theatre** (summer productions). **University of Arizona Artist Series** brings prominent performers to Centennial Hall, just inside the main (east) gate on University Blvd. on campus; tel. 621-3341 (box office). **Arizona Friends of Chamber Music** gives concerts on campus at Crowder Hall from Oct. to April; tel. 298-5806.

Many performances take place at the **Tucson Convention Center's** Music Hall, Leo Rich Theatre, and Arena; tel. 791-4266 (ticket information; recording after hours) or 791-4836 (Charge Line). You can attend performances at the Tucson Convention Center ("TCC") by **Ballet Arizona** (Nov. to April; tel. 882-5022); by the **Tucson Symphony** (Thurs. and Fri. evenings Oct. to May.; tel.

882-8585); by the **Arizona Opera Company** (Oct. to March; tel. 293-4336); and by the **Southern Arizona Light Opera Company (SALOC)** (Sept. to May; tel. 323-7888). **Arizona Theatre Company** presents a series of plays from Oct. to May; tel. 622-2823. The experimental **Invisible Theatre** offers about seven performances from Sept. to June; one mile northeast of downtown at 1400 N. First Ave.; tel. 882-9721. For hilarious family entertainment, take in an old-fashioned melodrama at the **Gaslight Theatre,** Wed.-Sun. year-round, 7000 E. Tanque Verde Road (8 miles east of downtown); tel. 886-9428. **Tucson Jazz Society's** hotline lists upcoming jazz events; tel. 623-2463.

### Sporting Events

The University of Arizona **Wildcat** teams compete in football, basketball, baseball, tennis, swimming, track and field, and other sports during the school terms. For ticket info call the McKale Center; tel. 621-2411. Hi Corbett Field in Reid Park hosts two baseball teams, the **Tucson Toros** (tel. 791-4906) from April to Aug. and the **Cleveland Indians** (tel. 791-4266) in March and April (early spring training). Greyhounds hit the track at **Tucson Greyhound Park** in South Tucson (2 miles south of downtown Tucson) at 2601 S. Third Ave. at E. 36th St.; call for schedule; tel. 884-7576. Horses speed to the finish line at **Rillito Park** in the Catalina foothills, N. First Ave. at River Road; season runs from about Nov. to March; call for days and times; tel. 293-5011.

## EVENTS

Something's happening nearly every day, and the Visitors Bureau can tell you what it is. Ask for their *Calendar of Annual Events.* Some of best-known annual happenings...

**January:** The **Northern Telecom Tucson Open** draws more than 100 professional golfers. **Southern Arizona Square and Round**

*La Fiesta de los Vaqueros*

**Dance Festival** offers enthusiasts dances and workshops.

**February: Tucson Gem and Mineral Show** is considered the world's best. More than 100 hot-air balloons rise into the sky over the town of Marana in races and a mass ascension, 20 miles northwest of town, in the **Tucson Balloon Festival.** About 500 horses show their hunter-jumper skills in the **Tucson Winter Classic Horse Show.** Cowboys get together for a big 4-day rodeo and a colorful parade in **La Fiesta de los Vaqueros.**

**March:** The **Cleveland Indians** begin their spring training and exhibition baseball games at Hi Corbett Field in Reid Park. **Wa:k Pow Wow Conference** attracts Southwestern Indian groups for traditional and modern singing and dancing. **A Taste of Scotland** has a Scottish dinner followed by music and dance of the Seven Pipers Society of Tucson. Skiers celebrate their sport in the **Mt. Lemmon Ski Carnival** with competitions and games. Top women golfers compete in the **Circle-K LPGA Tucson Open.** Visit Davis-Monthan Air Force Base for **Aerospace and Arizona Days** open house and air show. **Tucson Festival** (Easter season) is a 6-week extravaganza of fiestas, concerts, theater, and music of the cultures and history of Tucson. Yaqui Indians of Pascua Village in Tucson stage the **Yaqui Easter Ceremonials,** a Passion play, during the Easter season; the ceremony is a mixture of Catholic and tribal beliefs about the forces of good overcoming evil. **San Xavier Pageant and Fiesta** (Easter season) celebrates the founding of the mission. **Simon Peter Passion Play** is a 3-hour Easter pageant performed at the Tucson Convention Center.

**April:** At the **Spring Fling,** university students put on a carnival with rides, games, and food. **Fourth Avenue Street Fair** features artists, crafts people, entertainers, and food outdoors on N. Fourth Ave. between University and Eighth St.; repeats in December. **Pima County Fair** has a carnival, entertainment, and livestock shows at the Pima County Fairgrounds. The **Tucson International Mariachi Conference** presents as stage extravaganza, workshops, and a fair.

**May:** The Hispanic community celebrates **Cinco de Mayo** (May 5th) with art, music, dances, and food. Local restaurants put their best food under one roof for the **Taste of Tucson** at the Tucson Convention Center. **Tucson Summer Arts Festival** begins mid-

May and runs to Labor Day with many art and cultural events.

**July:** Parades, picnics, and fireworks commemorate **Independence Day** on the fourth.

**August:** Youngsters aged 5-19 compete in riding and roping in the **Tucson Junior Rodeo,** held at Old Tucson. **Fiesta de San Agustín** honors the birthday of Tucson's patron saint with music, dancing, and food.

**September:** The **Mexican Independence Day Celebration** is a traditional Mexican fiesta with entertainment and food.

**October:** Experience Tucson's ethnic diversity in art, music, dance, and food sponsored by **Tucson Meet Yourself.** The **Tohono O'odham All-Indian Rodeo and Fair** features a parade, singing, dancing, crafts, and food—all put on by this Indian tribe on their reservation near Sells, 58 miles southwest of Tucson.

**November: Tucson Art Expo** showcases visual artists in exhibitions, galleries, and open studios. Students compete at the **University of Arizona Rodeo.** Thousands of bicyclists challenge each other and the clock in **El Tour de Tucson** races. **Holiday in Lights** begins the Christmas season in late Nov./early Dec. with lights, carriage rides, a Holiday Village, and other festivities.

**December: Fourth Avenue Street Fair** brings artists, crafts people, entertainers, and food outdoors to N. Fourth Ave. between University and Eighth Street. Football fans gather in Arizona Stadium at the end of the year for the NCAA **Copper Bowl.**

# RECREATION

## Tohono Chul Park

The name means "Desert Corner" in the Tohono O'odham language. Enjoy natural desert beauty within Tucson. Nature trails wind through the grounds, which have about 400 plants from northern Mexico and the Southwest arranged by genus. The Ethnobotanical Garden illustrates native crops and traditional cultivation methods. Javelinas, desert tortoises, collared lizards, chuckwallas, ground squirrels, desert cottontails, black-tailed jack-rabbits, and many species of wild birds inhabit the park. The Demonstration Garden has displays of landscaping, geology, and endangered fish. Other attractions include the Park Greenhouse (plants for sale), Exhibit House (visiting art or craft shows), tea room, and two gift shops. You can picnic at one of the shaded tables scattered through the park. Open daily 7 a.m.-sunset (shorter hours for the Exhibit House); a small donation is appreciated since the park is a nonprofit foundation; tel. 742-6455 (office) or 797-1711 (tea room). Located near the junction of Ina and Oracle roads in northwest Tucson; the main entrance is at 7366 N. Paseo del Norte.

## Reid Park

This spacious green park in the middle of Tucson has a small zoo, Hi Corbett baseball field, soccer field, rose garden, lakes, and picnic areas. The park is 3 miles east of downtown; enter from Country Club Road, 22nd St., or Camino Campestre. The **Tucson City Parks and Recreation** office, in the park at 900 S. Randolph Way, can tell you of facilities and programs offered at Reid and other parks; tel. 791-4873.

## Swimming

Tucson Parks and Recreation has 19 swimming pools (most open summer only). Addresses and phone numbers are in the telephone book under "Tucson City Government."

You can also swim at the L.A. Lohse Memorial YMCA (516 N. Fifth Ave.; tel. 623-7727) and in pools at University of Arizona's McKale Center (tel. 621-2599) and Student Union (tel. 621-7035).

## Tennis

With over 150 courts spread around Tucson, it's not hard to find one. See "Sports & Recreation" in the Visitors Bureau's *Visitors Guide.* The **Randolph Recreation Complex** has 24 tennis courts (11 lighted), instruction, and pro shop, as well as 10 racquetball courts; 3 miles east of downtown at 100 S. Alvernon Way (just south of E. Broadway); tel. 791-4896.

## Golf

Another sport enjoyed by many Tucsonans. About 17 courses are open to the public; see "Sports & Recreation" in the Visitors Bureau's *Visitors Guide*. **Randolph Park,** just east of Reid Park, has two 18-hole courses at 602 S. Alvernon Way; tel. 791-4336 (reservations) or 325-2811 (pro shop).

## Horseback Riding

Several stables let you see the scenery from atop a horse or haywagon; reservations should be made. **Desert-High Country Stables** has a choice of rides and cookouts in the foothills of the Tucson Mountains, about 15 miles northwest of downtown, at 6501 W. Ina Road (2 miles west of I-10); tel. 744-3789. **Pusch Ridge Stables** offers many trips in the Catalina foothills 14 miles north of downtown at 11220 N. Oracle Road; tel. 297-6908. **El Conquistador Stables** has rides and cookouts in the Catalina foothills 11 miles north of downtown in the Sheraton Tucson El Conquistador Resort, 10000 N. Oracle Road; tel. 742-4200.

*on the trail in the Sonoran Desert*

## Southern Arizona Hiking Club

Hikes organized by this active group range from easy to challenging. The club schedules dayhikes, backpacks, climbs, river trips, ski tours, and snowshoe trips. Members also promote conservation and build trails. Visitors are welcome on hikes. Contact the club at Box 12122, Tucson, AZ 85732.

## Skiing

At **Mount Lemmon Ski Valley** in the Santa Catalina Mountains you can enjoy downhill skiing during the late Dec. to late March season. See "Mt. Lemmon Highway," pp 410-411. One double chairlift and a beginner tow take skiers up the slopes. Longest run is 0.75 mile, dropping from 9150 to 8200 feet through fir and aspen forests; tel. 576-1321. To check on snow and road conditions, call 576-1400 for a recorded message.

# SERVICES

The **main post office** is 2.5 miles southeast of downtown at 1501 S. Cherrybell Stravanue; tel. 620-5142. The downtown branch is at 141 S. Sixth Avenue. Another branch is at 913 E. University Blvd., between Tyndall and Park aves., and there's one on the University of Arizona campus (in the basement of the Student Union). Exchange foreign currency at **Valley National Bank,** 2 E. Congress St. (downtown) or any branch; tel. 792-7317. **Pima County Medical Society,** will refer you to any type of doctor you might need; open Mon.-Fri. 8:30 a.m.-4:30 p.m.; tel. 795-7985. Down and out? **Temporary Employment** (Arizona Dept. of Economic Security), 22nd St., offers free services; tel. 628-5553.

# SHOPPING

## Fourth Avenue

The section of Fourth Ave. between Fourth and Seventh sts. has many unusual craft and antique shops and restaurants. Big street fairs take place here in late April and early December. Also, the **Salvation Army, Goodwill,** and **Tucson Thrift Shop** stores on Fourth Ave. (at Seventh St.) offer used clothing and other items. For health foods, visit the **Food Conspiracy Coop**; it has an herb room, whole-grain flours, etc.; open daily; nonmembers welcome; 412 N. Fourth Ave. (between Sixth and Seventh sts.); tel. 624-4821.

### Shopping Centers

Tucson has four giant malls open daily with department stores, specialty shops, and restaurants; all but Tucson Mall have movie theaters, though Tucson Galleria across the street from it has theaters and additional stores. The malls are enclosed and air-conditioned. **El Con Mall** has 130 stores, 3 miles east of downtown at 3601 E. Broadway; tel. 795-9958. **Park Mall** has 120 stores, 6 miles east of downtown at 5870 E. Broadway and Wilmot; tel. 748-1222. **Tucson Mall** has more than 170 stores, 4.5 miles north of downtown at 4500 N. Oracle and Wetmore; tel. 293-7330. **Foothills Center** has 55 stores and the Old Pueblo Museum, 10 miles north of downtown at 7401 N. La Cholla Blvd. and W. Ina Road; tel. 742-7191.

### Art Galleries

Be sure to see **DeGrazia's Gallery in the Sun,** described on p. 407. **Old Town Artisans,** in the middle of the downtown El Presidio District, is large and varied. Pottery, clothing, jewelry, woodcarvings, and other crafts are available by local, Indian, Mexican, and international artists. Open Mon.-Sat. 9:30 a.m.-5 p.m. and Sun. noon-5 p.m.; tel. 623-6024. It's on the corner of 186 N. Meyer Ave. and Telles St. (near Tucson Museum of Art). Tucson has dozens of other art galleries and craft shops. See the Yellow Pages or the Visitors Bureau for a list.

## PHONE NUMBERS

Emergencies
   (police, fire, medical) ............ 911
Police (Tucson) .............791-4452
Pima County Sheriff ...........622-3366
Crisis Counseling and
   Suicide Prevention ..........323-9373
Information and Referral
   Service (community services) ..881-1794
Road Conditions ..............294-3113
Weather recording ............623-4000
Tucson Parks and Recreation ...791-4873
Tucson Convention Center
   Box Office .................791-4266
   Charge Line ...............791-4836
University of Arizona Ticket Offices:
   Sports Events .............621-2411
   Centennial Hall Box Office ....621-3341
   Fine Arts Box Office ........621-1162
Sun Tran (city bus) ...........792-9222

## INFORMATION

### Tourist Office

The very helpful **Metropolitan Tucson Convention & Visitors Bureau** has an excellent *Visitors Guide* and many brochures of area

sights and services; downtown at 130 S. Scott Ave., Tucson, AZ 85701; tel. 624-1817. Open Mon.-Fri. 8:30 a.m.-5 p.m. (also Sat. and Sun. 10 a.m.-3 p.m. in winter); literature can be picked up outside when the office is closed.

### Coronado National Forest

The **Supervisor's Office** has general information for all the districts in the Coronado, which include many of the most scenic areas in southeastern Arizona; open Mon.-Fri. 7:45 a.m.-4:30 p.m.; downtown in room 6A of the Federal Bldg., 300 W. Congress St. (Tucson, AZ 85701); tel. 670-6483. For specific information on the campgrounds, trails, and backcountry of the Santa Catalinas, contact the **Santa Catalina Ranger District** office; open Mon.-Fri. 8 a.m.-4:30 p.m. and Sat. and Sun. 8:30 a.m.-4:30 p.m.; in the Sabino Canyon Visitor Center, 5700 N. Sabino Canyon Road (Tucson, AZ 85715); tel. 749-8700.

### Libraries

The main **city library** is downtown at 101 N. Stone between Pennington and Alameda; open Mon. noon-9 p.m., Tues.-Thurs. 10 a.m.-6 or 9 p.m., Fri. 10 a.m.-5 p.m., Sat. 9 a.m.-5 p.m., and Sun. 1-5 p.m.; tel. 791-4393/4010. The library has 19 branches.

**University of Arizona libraries** are open to the public and include some outstanding collections; pick up free information pamphlets in the main library lobby. The main library (see University map) is open Mon.-Thurs. 7 a.m.-2 a.m., Fri. 7 a.m.-9 p.m., Sat. 9 a.m.-9 p.m., and Sun. 10 a.m.-2 a.m.; shorter hours during summer and vacations; tel. 621-6441. Hikers and travelers can visit the map collection, where topographic maps of the entire country can be photocopied; open Mon.-Fri. 9 a.m.-5 p.m. and Sat. noon-4 p.m. during regular semesters; located on the first floor of the main library. Other collections include Arizona, Southwest, Government Documents, Music, and Oriental Studies.

### Newspapers

Tucson's major dailies are the *Arizona Daily Star* in the morning and the *Tucson Citizen* in the afternoon. The *Star's* Friday "Entertain-

ment" section reports nightlife, concerts, theater, and dancing. Sights and events are listed in its "Tucson Today" column (Mon.-Sat.). The "Art Calendar" in Sunday's entertainment section gives the art galleries and shows. The *Tucson Citizen* lists local happenings and movies in the "Living" section (Mon.-Fri.) and has more detailed reports in the Thurs. "Calendar" section. There's no Sun. edition. The *Tucson Weekly* calls itself "the city's news and arts journal"; you'll find 'most all the goings on in Tucson listed in its pages, along with feature articles and restaurant listings; free at newsstands.

### Bookstores

Shopping malls have the popular book chains. The **Southwest Parks and Monuments Association Bookshop,** downtown at Court and Council, offers excellent books on history, Indians, wildlife, and flora, as well as parks and monuments of the Southwest; tel. 792-0239. The **University of Arizona** sells Arizona and Southwest titles together with general reading and textbooks at the west end of the Student Union; closed on weekends; tel. 621-2426. **Bookman's Used Books** claims to be Arizona's largest used bookstore; it has new titles and a newsstand too; 1930 E. Grant Road at Campbell; open daily; tel. 325-5767. **Goodbooks** also has an excellent selection of new and used books; 431 N. Fourth Ave.; open daily; tel. 792-9551.

### Maps

For hiking, national forest, state, and Mexico maps visit the **Outdoor Adventure Center** (basement of the Bear Down Gym, U. of A. campus; tel. 621-8233); **Summit Hut** (4044 E. Speedway Blvd.; tel. 325-1554); or **Tucson Maps** (2590 N. First Ave.; tel. 623-1104).

## TRANSPORT

### Tours

**Tucson Tour Company** offers a city tour, shuttles out to Arizona-Sonora Desert Museum and Old Tucson, and longer trips to Nogales and other places; tel. 297-2911. **Gray Line Tours** has daytrips from Jan. to April to the Desert Museum ($25), Old Tucson ($25), and Nogales/Mexico ($32); they make longer trips of 2-3 days year-round to the Grand Canyon and other sights of northern Arizona ($119-219); Box 1991, Tucson, AZ 85702; tel. 622-8811. Other companies offering tours at similar prices to the sights around Tucson and southeastern Arizona include **Great Western Tours** (tel. 721-0980), **Sandpainter Guided Tours** (tel. 323-9290), **Old West Excursions** (tel. 885-0085), **Catalina Limousine and Transportation Services** (tel. 624-5466), **Off the Beaten Path Tours** (tel. 296-0909), and **Best of the West Detours** (tel. 749-5388). See the rugged backcountry on jeep tours by **Mountain View** (tel. 622-4488) and **Sunshine Jeep Tours** (tel. 742-1943). All these tour companies and more have brochures at the Visitors Bureau.

### Taxi And Auto Rentals
**Allstate Cab Company** is low cost; tel. 888-2999 (24 hours). Taxi fares differ greatly among the companies—you may want to shop around. Tucson has over two dozen car-rental agencies; several are at the airport; see the Yellow Pages.

### Auto Driveaways
These are cars to be delivered to another city. If it's a place you're headed, you have a "free" car rental. But the driveaway companies do place some restrictions on time and mileage, and you must make a deposit. Ask for an economy car if you want the lowest costs. See "Automobile Transporters & Driveaway Companies" in the Yellow Pages.

### Local Bus
**Sun Tran** takes you to the parks, sights, and shopping areas within the city and to the airport for only $.60, but *not* to the sights just outside Tucson. You must have exact change; transfers are free (ask driver when you pay your fare). Most buses go to bed about 7 p.m., although a few routes run until 10 p.m. on weekdays. The Visitors Bureau has free route maps. The Weekend Pass (purchase from driver, $1.20) allows unlimited travel from Fri. night thru Sun. night. Sun

Tran also operates the **Fourth Avenue Trolley** service between downtown areas and the University of Arizona Mon.-Sat. for only 25 cents. For Sun Tran info call 792-9222.

### Long-distance Bus
The **Greyhound** terminal is downtown at 2 S. Fourth Ave. at E. Broadway; tel. 792-0972 (fare and schedule) or 882-4386 (local terminal). Some destinations and one-way fares are Los Angeles (8 daily) $47; El Paso (7 daily) $42; Phoenix (11 daily) $15.90 local or $18.45 express; Flagstaff (2 daily) $35; Douglas (once daily on Bridgewater Transport via Fort Huachuca, Sierra Vista, and Bisbee) $17; and Nogales (9 daily on Citizen Auto Stage) $6.25. The station has lockers and a coffee shop.

### Train
**Amtrak** has three eastbound and three westbound departures every week. Terminal is downtown at 400 E. Toole Ave. (2 blocks north of the Greyhound station); for reservations and info call (800) 872-7245. Westbound departs in the evening for Phoenix (2¼ hours, $26 one way), Yuma, and other points, arriving in Los Angeles the next morning (11 hours, $97 one way). Eastbound leaves in the morning: one train goes to New Orleans (1½ days, $196), the other to Chicago (2 days, $196). Amtrak gives large discounts on roundtrip fares, making it more competitive with the bus and plane.

### Air
Tucson International Airport is 8.5 miles south of downtown. More than a dozen airlines and charters fly here. See the Yellow Pages for airline companies and ticket agencies. To reach the airport from downtown, you have a choice of taxis, airport shuttle, and Sun Tran Bus #25. **Arizona Stagecoach** provides 24-hour shuttle service outside the terminal to your destination. For pick-up to the airport, call 889-9681 at least 4 hours before the flight. **Arizona Shuttle Service** goes to Sky Harbor Airport in Phoenix from the El Con Mall, 3601 E. Broadway; tel. 795-6771 or (800) 8TUC-PHX.

# WEST TO ORGAN PIPE CACTUS
# NATIONAL MONUMENT

## TOHONO O'ODHAM
## INDIAN RESERVATION

Twenty-five miles west of Tucson on AZ 86 is the main Tohono O'odham (Papago) Reservation. The land appears inhospitable—dry sandy washes and plains, broken here and there by rocky hills or mountains. The first white men couldn't believe that people lived in such wild and parched desert, yet the Tohono O'odham Indians have thrived in it for centuries. Close relatives of the Pima, the Tohono O'odham once occupied a vast portion of the Sonoran Desert of southern Arizona and northern Mexico. Neighboring Indians called these desert dwellers "Papago," meaning "Bean People," but the tribe prefers the more dignified term—"Tohono O'odham," meaning "Desert People Who Have Emerged from the Earth." They believe that their tribe, like the plants and animals, belongs to the earth. Once the Tohono O'odham had both winter and summer villages, staying near reliable springs in the winter, then moving to fields watered by summer thunderstorms. They gathered mesquite beans, agave, cactus fruit, acorns, and other plant foods and hunted rodents, rabbits, deer, and pronghorn. Fields were planted with native tepary beans, corn, and squash.

After the 1854 Gadsden Treaty split their land between Mexico and the United States, the Mexican Tohono O'odham population gradually withered away as it was absorbed by Mexican culture. Some families migrated into Arizona. Today only about 200 Tohono O'odham remain south of the border. In 1874, the U.S. government began setting aside land for the tribe in the 71,095-acre San Xavier Reservation. Tohono O'odham land now totals about 2,800,000 acres (roughly the size of Connecticut). It's the second largest reservation in the country, stretching across much of southern Arizona, and is the home of more than 8,000 people. The old ways have largely disappeared upon contact with the white man's technology. Now most Tohono O'odham, like anyone else in Arizona, live in modern houses; they farm, ranch, or work for wages. Skilled basketmakers, their attractive wares are in much demand. You'll see Tohono O'odham crafts in trading posts and the Visitor Center at Kitt Peak. Early Spanish missionaries gained many converts—the Roman Catholic Church is the strongest on the reservation, though there are Protestant denominations as well. Almost all villages have a small chapel.

### Visiting The Reservation
Most Tohono O'odham are friendly, but the tribe has never shown much interest in tourism. Visitor facilities are sparse—gas stations are few and far between and campgrounds and motels nonexistent. Two attractions, in addition to the desert scenery, make a visit worthwhile: the Tohono O'odham All-Indian Rodeo and Fair and the world-famous Kitt Peak Observatory.

greater roadrunner
(Geococcyx californianus)

*McMath Solar Telescope*

### Tohono O'odham All-Indian Rodeo And Fair

Tohono O'odham cowboys show off their riding and roping skills in the tribe's big annual event, held in October. The Tohono O'odham put on a parade, exhibit crafts, serve Indian fry bread, and perform songs and dances. You can get the dates from the tribal office in Sells or the Visitors Bureau in Tucson.

## KITT PEAK

Planning a national observatory, astronomers took 3 years to study 150 peaks in the Southwest before choosing this one in 1958. Large, white domes, enclosing instruments that help to unravel the mysteries of the universe, cling to the 6,900-foot summit. The 19 telescopes come in many sizes and types, including one that uses radio waves. Some are owned by universities, foremost of which is the University of Arizona in Tucson. Nearly all the work is pure research, done by qualified astrono-

mers who apply a year or more in advance to a panel that makes the selections. Before Kitt Peak was operating, students and women found it almost impossible to get time at a major telescope, but here they have an equal chance. Astronomers use the equipment free of charge but no rain checks are issued! Workers learn to be philosophical after waiting many months and then getting clouded out. Computers control the instruments; the scientist can even operate his telescope from Tucson. It's rare for an observer actually to look through telescopes these days, and some instruments don't even have an eyepiece. Kitt Peak is funded by the National Science Foundation and managed by a consortium of 20 universities, the Association of Universities for Research in Astronomy.

### Visitor Center

You're welcome to drive up and see the observatory and astronomy exhibits. A short self-guiding tour leads around the grounds and to three of the most impressive telescopes, which you can step inside. These are the McMath Solar (which doesn't look like a telescope at all), the 2.1-meter (84-inch), and the Mayall 4-meter (158-inch) telescopes. Most telescopes at Kitt Peak are not designed for magnification as much as for light-gathering power (a distant star looks the same pinpoint size through even the biggest 'scopes). An exception is the McMath Solar Telescope, which produces a 30-inch image of the sun by using mirrors in a slanted 500-foot corridor. Three hundred feet of this length runs below ground. You can go inside to see the interior; a TV screen shows the sun's image. This telescope won an architectural award in 1962, rare for observatories! The 2.1-meter telescope nearby was the first large instrument on Kitt Peak for nighttime viewing. It's used to observe distant stars and galaxies in both the visible and infrared spectra. The Mayall 4-meter, one of the world's largest telescopes, is housed in a building 19 stories high. An elevator takes you to the 10th-floor observation deck offering panoramic views of southern Arizona and northern Sonora. Inside is a gallery where you can see the telescope and a short video about its construction.

Kitt Peak Observatory is open daily 10 a.m.-4 p.m., except New Year's Day, Thanksgiving Day, and Dec. 24 and 25; no charge. A shop in the Visitor Center sells Tohono O'odham basketry and astronomy-related posters, slides, and T-shirts. Films are shown daily at 10:30 a.m. and 1:30 p.m. Guided 1½ tours of the Observatory are given after the films on weekday afternoons and on weekend and holiday mornings and afternoons (except on days listed above); free.

On the drive up, you'll pass a picnic area on the left 1.5 miles before the Visitor Center. Bring your own picnic supplies, as Kitt Peak has no stores or restaurants. The air is cool up here (15-20° colder than Tucson), so a jacket or sweater will be useful most of the year. Kitt Peak is 50 miles southwest of Tucson via AZ 86. The last 12 miles are on a paved and well-graded mountain road. Winter storms can close the road for short periods; check by calling 620-5350.

## SELLS

Tribal headquarters and largest town on the Tohono O'odham Reservation. The dependable water here has made the place a popular stop for travelers since prehistoric times. Sells was originally known as Indian Oasis, but the name was changed in 1918 to honor Indian Commissioner Cato Sells. The town is 58 miles southwest of Tucson via AZ 86 (20 miles past the turnoff for Kitt Peak). Offices, schools, and shops are 1.5 miles south of the main highway. **Margaret Arts and Crafts** and **Melissa Shop** in Sells have Tohono O'odham baskets whose prices range from 10 to several hundred dollars. Groceries can be purchased at **Basha's.** Pick up a copy of the *Papago Runner* (in English) to learn about the tribe's current concerns. The **Papago Cafe** is on the main highway just west of the turnoff for Sells. You'll find another trading post with Tohono O'odham crafts 22 miles west at Quijotoa. Before camping or exploring the backcountry, check to see if you'll need a permit. Contact the **Tohono O'odham Tribe Administration,** Sells, AZ 85634; tel. 383-2221. Ask about road conditions if you plan to venture off the main highway; dirt roads can become impassable after rains.

*Tohono O'odham basket design*

## ORGAN PIPE CACTUS NATIONAL MONUMENT

The Sonoran Desert is at its finest in this remote area of Arizona. Some desert plants, such as the senita cactus and elephant tree, occur only here and in Mexico. The name of Arizona's largest national monument honors the giant organ pipe cactus, which grows well in this area. In appearance it's similar to the saguaro, but the organ pipe's many branches all radiate from the base. Animals adapt to the heat by hiding out during the hottest part of the day. They're most active at night or in the mornings and evenings. Wildlife you might see include lizards, birds, kangaroo rats, kit foxes, ringtail cats, bobcats, javelina, bighorn sheep, and pronghorn. The five species of rattlesnakes are nocturnal—a good reason to use a flashlight at night! About 40 species of birds stay year-round, and more than 230 others drop in on their migrations. Quitobaquito Oasis (described below) is a prime birding spot.

If you're lucky enough to be here in March or April after a wet winter, you'll see the desert ablaze with yellows, blues, reds, and violets. First to bloom are annual plants, which must quickly germinate and produce seeds before the summer heat, followed by the smaller cacti such as the chollas and prickly pears. Last to bloom are the big saguaros and organ pipes, whose blossoms peak in May or June. Scenic drives and hiking trails provide a chance to experience the Sonoran Desert.

### Visitor Center

For an introduction to the highly adaptable plants and wildlife that live here, start at the Visitor Center located 22 miles south of Why. A short slide program shows native animals and the effects of seasonal changes on the land. Another slide program shows desert wildflowers. Exhibits describe plants and animals of the region and illustrate man's effect on the desert. Just outside, a short nature trail identifies common plants and gives more info on the desert environment. Rangers can answer your questions and issue camping per-

*senita cactus (Lophocereus schottii)*

mits. Books, prints, and a topo map are sold. Naturalist programs take place during the cooler months at the Visitor Center, on trails, and at the campground. Summer is the quiet season at the monument, as daytime highs commonly range from 95° to 105° F. Thunderstorms appear in late summer, bringing about half of the annual 9.5 inches or so of rain. Winters run cool to warm with occasional gentle rains. The Visitor Center is open daily 8 a.m.-5 p.m.; tel. 387-6849. Monument admission is $3/vehicle.

### Puerto Blanco Scenic Drive

Varied desert environments, Quitobaquito Oasis, and rare desert plants of the Senita Basin are highlights of this 53-mile loop. A pamphlet explains features at numbered stops; pick it up at the Visitor Center or at the start of the drive, just west of the Visitor Center. Nearly all the route is graded dirt, designed for slow speeds—allow at least half a day. Note that a section of the drive is one way (counterclockwise) and that you can't turn back! **Quitobaquito,** one mile off the loop, has a large, manmade pond surrounded by large cottonwoods. The springs are 100 yards north up a trail. Ducks and other waterfowl, not what you'd expect in the desert, drop in during the spring and autumn. Coots stay here year-round. Father Kino and other early Spanish missionaries and explorers stopped here on their way to the Colorado River. The '49ers headed for the California gold fields came by too, taking a southern route to avoid hostile Indians farther north. Many gold seekers perished from thirst on the fearsome Camino del Diablo or "Devil's Highway" between Sonoita and the Colorado River. Quitobaquito was one of few sources of water on the route.

**Senita Basin,** 4 miles off the loop, is home of the senita cactus and elephant tree. Similar in appearance to organ pipe cactus, the senita is distinguished by its gray "whiskers" and far fewer ribs on each arm. The elephant tree looks like the root system of an upside-down tree! Perhaps you can see the resemblance to an elephant.

### Ajo Mountain Drive
Heading into the more rugged country of the eastern part of the Monument, this drive skirts the base of 4,808-foot Mount Ajo. Part of the 21-mile gravel loop road is one way; pick up a pamphlet describing the drive at the Visitor Center or at the start, just across the highway from the Visitor Center; allow at least 2 hours. You'll have good views from Diablo Canyon Picnic Area and from Bull Pasture Trail (starts at Estes Canyon).

### Hiking
Several trails begin at the campground, located 1.5 miles from the Visitor Center. On the **Desert View Nature Trail,** you'll travel up a wash, then climb onto a ridge with a good panorama. **Victoria Mine Trail,** 4.5 miles roundtrip, takes you to a historic mine that produced lead, silver, and gold. Also beginning at the campground are a one-mile trail encircling the camping area and a 1.3-mile trail to the Visitor Center. **Estes Canyon-Bull Pasture Trail,** off Ajo Mountain Drive, is the most spectacular established trail. The Estes Canyon part follows the canyon; the Bull Pasture part climbs a ridge. The trails meet and then continue to Bull Pasture, where ranchers once grazed cattle. The entire loop, including the spur trail to Bull Pasture, is 4.1 miles roundtrip; some sections are steep and have loose rock. Carry water. Countless other cross-country hiking trips are possible in the monument's open terrain. Rangers can help you to plan. You'll have to get a permit from them for any climbing or overnight hikes.

*cristate growth on an organ pipe cactus*

## Accommodations, Campgrounds, And Food

The 208-site campground near the Visitor Center is open all year; there's room for trailers to 35 feet. It has drinking water but no hookups or showers; sites cost $6/night. Tenters who want to leave the asphalt and flush toilets behind can camp at **Alamo Canyon Primitive Campground,** 14 miles away. This pretty spot is also a good base for day hikes. It's free but the only facilities are pit toilets; get the required permit and directions beforehand from a ranger. No trailers or RVs permitted here. For motels, stores, gas stations, and restaurants, you have to leave the monument; Lukeville (AZ), 5 miles south, and Sonoita (Mexico), 2 miles farther, are the nearest towns.

## VICINITY OF ORGAN PIPE CACTUS NATIONAL MONUMENT

### Lukeville

Just a wide spot on the road next to the Mexican border, Lukeville was named for WW I flying ace Frank Luke. Besides the immigration and customs offices, Lukeville has a gas station, small store, and the **Gringo Pass Motel and Trailer Park** (tel. 254-9284).

### Sonoita

Several restaurants, motels, curio shops, and an attractive little plaza lie 2 miles southwest of the Mexican border in Sonoita. Beaches, fishing, and seafood lure many visitors 63 more miles to Puerto Peñasco on the Sea of Cortez. Here you'll find seaside motels, restaurants, and trailer parks. A permit is required for travel beyond Sonoita. You can purchase auto insurance (strongly recommended) on both sides of the border.

### Why

Why Why? Why, because it used to be called "the Y" by motorists. Why is at the junction of AZ Hwys. 85 and 86 just north of Organ Pipe Cactus National Monument. Why has a small **motel, Coyote Howls Trailer Park** (tel. 387-9973), **Las Palmas RV Park** (tel. 387-6304),

**Belle Acres RV Park** (tel. 387-6962), grocery store, gas station, and a couple of bars.

## AJO

This pleasant small town appears lost in a sea of desert. It's 10 miles northwest of Why and 42 miles south of Gila Bend. The town's name (pronounced AH-ho) may have come from the Tohono O'odham word for paint, because the Indians collected copper minerals here to paint their bodies. Prospectors settled as early as 1854, but Ajo didn't really get going until early in this century when suitable ore-refining techniques became available. The New Cornelia Copper Company started in 1917 and was later purchased by Phelps Dodge. Squeezed between low copper prices and high costs, Phelps Dodge shut down the mine and smelter. Now in hard times, Ajo waits for higher copper prices. Graceful palms and flowering trees surround the Spanish colonial-style plaza and many public buildings downtown. Greenery and trees also decorate the miners' tiny houses.

### Sights

The **New Cornelia Open Pit Mine** just south of town is one of the world's largest, 1.5 miles across. To reach the mine lookout from downtown, turn southeast on La Mina Ave., then right on Indian Village Road, and follow signs to a ramada with exhibits overlooking the pit. The nearby **Ajo Historical Museum** houses pioneer and Indian exhibits in a former Catholic church. Open daily 1-4 p.m. but closed July 15 to August 15; from the mine overlook continue to the end of Indian Village Road and turn left; tel. 387-7105.

### Accommodations, Campgrounds, And Food

Stay at the **Manager's House Inn** bed and breakfast (1 Greenway Dr.; tel. 387-6505); **The Guest House Inn** bed and breakfast (Guest House Road; tel. 387-6133); **Marine Motel** (1966 N. Hwy. 85; tel. 387-7626); **La Siesta Motel** (2561 N. Hwy. 85; tel. 387-6569); or **Copper Sands Motel** (3711 N. Hwy. 85; tel. 387-7275). RVers can hook up at the **Marine Motel** (1966 N. Hwy. 85; tel. 387-7626) or **Del Sur RV Park** (2050 N. Hwy. 85; tel. 387-6907). **Copper Coffee Shop,** on the plaza, serves Mexican-American food. **The Depot,** also on the plaza, prepares sandwiches, salads, and baked goods. Other restaurants are north on the highway: **Pizza Hut** (627 N. Second Ave; tel. 387-6842); **Bamboo Village** (Chinese; 1810 N. Second Ave.; tel. 387-6332); **Dairy Queen** (1304 N. Second Ave.; tel. 387-7407); and **Palomino Restaurant** (Mexican-American; 3610 N. Hwy. 85; tel. 387-7525).

### Recreation And Information

The **Ajo Country Club** has a nine-hole golf course and a restaurant, 7 miles northeast of town via Well and Mead roads; tel. 387-5011. A public **swimming pool** (open in summer) and **tennis courts** are next to the high school on Well Road. Ajo's **public library** and **post office** are by the plaza. The helpful **Ajo District Chamber of Commerce** office is on the main highway near the plaza at 321 Taladro (Box 507, Ajo, AZ 85321); open Mon.-Fri. 8:30 a.m.-4:30 p.m. (also Sat. and Sun. 10 a.m.-3 p.m. in the cooler months if staffing permits); tel. 387-7742.

### CABEZA PRIETA NATIONAL WILDLIFE REFUGE

The 860,000 acres of desert wilderness west of Organ Pipe Cactus National Monument remains much as it has always been. Nobody lives here. There're no facilities, no paved roads, and no running water. Only jeep tracks and remnants of the old El Camino del Diablo ("Devil's Highway") cross the landscape. Twelve small mountain ranges rise above the desert floor. Wildlife and vegetation are similar to those in Organ Pipe Cactus National Monument, but the climate is harsher here. The Cabeza's annual rainfall averages about 9 inches in the east but tapers to only 3 inches in the west. Some areas go more than a year without rain!

You can visit this land with a permit, a suitable vehicle, and supplies for desert travel. Summer can be dangerous. Cabeza doubles as a gunnery range for Luke Air Force Base, so you'll want to time your visit carefully! Its schedules are made available at the first of each month and known by the refuge headquarters in Ajo and the U.S. Fish and Wildlife Service office in Yuma. Permits are required for entry and you'll have to sign a liability release for the military. Four-wheel-drive vehicles are recommended, though a dune buggy should be OK. Anything else is likely to get bogged in the loose sand. Vehicles must stay on designated roads and be licensed for highway use. Be aware that Cabeza Prieta's rough roads can be very hard on vehicles. The main administration office is in Ajo, where permits are available by mail or in person; you can also get information and permits (in person only) in Yuma. Contact the Cabeza Prieta Wildlife Refuge office of the U.S. Fish and Wildlife Service at 1611 N. Second Ave. (Ajo, AZ 85321), in a funny-looking building on the highway just north of town; tel. 387-6483; or at 356 W. First St. in Yuma; tel. 783-7861.

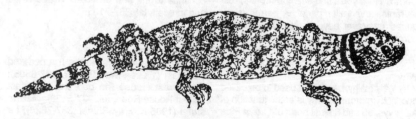

*Gila monster* (Heloderma suspectum)

*San Xavier del Bac*

# SOUTH FROM TUCSON TO MEXICO

Mexico lies at the end of a short drive south from Tucson via I-19, just 63 miles or 100 km—all of I-19 is signposted in metric. Except for the speed limits, that is—the Highway Patrol doesn't want you getting confused by the sight of a 100 km/h sign! You'll be following the Santa Cruz River Valley, one of the first areas in Arizona to be colonized by the Spanish. The Jesuit priest Eusebio Francisco Kino began mission work at Guévavi (near Nogales) and Tumacacori in 1691, then moved to San Xavier and other sites. Livestock, new crops, and the new religion introduced by Kino and later padres greatly changed the lives of the Indians here. You may want to stop for some of the many historic and scenic sights on the way.

## MISSION SAN XAVIER DEL BAC

This gleaming white church rises from the desert as a testimonial to the faith of early Spanish missionaries and the Tohono O'odham (Papago) Indians. One of the finest pieces of Spanish colonial architecture in the United States, its beauty has given rise to the name "White Dove of the Desert." Padre Kino founded the mission in 1700 and named it after his patron saint. The Indian village name of Bac means "where the waters gathered." The mission often lacked a resident priest and suffered many difficulties during its early years. Pima Indian revolts in 1734 and 1751 caused serious damage. Raiding Apache harassed residents and stole livestock. The mission's oldest surviving part dates from 1757-63, when the Jesuit Father Alonso Espinosa built a large, flat-roofed adobe church. This structure was later moved and butted up against the east bell tower of the present church and is now part of the south wing of the mission. Franciscan missionaries began construction of the present church about 1778. San Xavier is a marvelous example of Mexican folk baroque architecture. Shortage of materials and skilled artisans resulted in the "folk" character of the building—there was no marble, so the main altar was painted to look like marble; no glazed tiles *(majolica)* so

Grotto of Lourdes (replica) on Hill of the Cross

altar inside San Xavier del Bac

the dados were painted to look like tiles; and few chandeliers for lighting, so they were painted onto the walls! Some mystery surrounds the church. No one knows for sure who designed it and why the east bell tower and other parts were left unfinished. Records, however, indicate that the friars ran short of funds during construction.

You're welcome to step inside the church, where a recording tells of the history and identifies the many saints and symbols. Above the altar, a statue of St. Francis Xavier is the central figure; above him stands the Virgin of the Immaculate Conception; highest of all is a figure representing God. Flash photos are permitted unless a service is in progress. Indians should not be photographed during worship. The church is still a spiritual center for the Tohono O'odham. Masses are held Sun. at 8 a.m., 9:30 a.m.,

11 a.m., and 12:30 p.m.; weekdays at 8:30 a.m.; and Sat. at 5:30 p.m.

The small hill to the east has a replica of the Grotto of Lourdes. To the west stands a former mortuary chapel where two early Franciscan friars lie buried. Major celebrations are the San Xavier Pageant and Fiesta (first Friday after Easter), the Feast of St. Francis of Assisi (Oct.), and the Feast of St. Francis Xavier (Dec.). The mission has a gift shop on the east side. **San Xavier Plaza** across from the mission has shops selling Tohono O'odham, Zuni, Hopi, and Navajo crafts. Indians sometimes set up food stalls outside, especially on Sundays and religious holidays. Mission San Xavier del Bac is open daily 9 a.m.-6 p.m.; donations accepted; tel. 294-2624. It's 10 miles south of downtown Tucson. Take I-19 south to exit 95B (Valencia Road), go west 2 miles on Valencia Road, turn left (south) 2 miles on Mission Road, then left onto San Xavier Road; if coming from the south, take I-19 Exit 92 and follow signs 0.8 mile.

## TITAN II MISSILE MUSEUM

The U.S. Air Force maintained 18 Titan missile sites near Tucson, as well as 36 other sites in Kansas and Arkansas. While all have been deactivated, this one has been preserved as a memorial to the men and women who operated them. You can step inside the missile complex, operational from 1963 until 1982, to see the Titan II missile in its silo and the launch control center. You may feel that you're trespassing on a top secret installation—official Air Force vehicles, helicopter, giant antenna, and refueling equipment look ready for action. Tour guides show an introductory video and explain the operation of the missile site. You can see a rocket engine and other equipment on the surface, peer into the silo, then descend stairs 100 feet underground for a close look at the launch control center and the missile. One-hour tours depart daily (except Christmas) 9 a.m.-4 p.m. from Nov. 1 to April 30, then Wed.-Sun. 9 a.m.-4 p.m. the rest of the year. (The last tour of the day begins at 4 p.m.) Call first for reservations to be assured of a space; tel. 791-2929 (Tucson) or tel. 625-7736 (Green Valley).

Admission is $4 adult, $3 senior and military, $2 age 10-17. The museum is located about 20 miles southeast of Tucson near Green Valley; take I-10 to Duval Mine Road Exit 69, then turn west 0.75 mile to the entrance.

## SANTA RITA MOUNTAINS

Birdwatchers flock to Madera Canyon in the Santa Rita Mountains, 38 miles south of Tucson. The Santa Ritas, surrounded by a sea of desert, are the habitat of unusual wildlife, of which the coppery-tailed trogon bird *(Trogon elegans)* is the star attraction. During summer this colorful, parrot-like bird flies in from Mexico to nest in tall trees in the canyon bottoms. More than 200 other bird species have been spotted in Madera Canyon. April and May are best for birdwatching, though hummingbirds are most numerous in both spring and summer. Bear, deer, mountain lion, coatimundi, and javelina also share the spring-fed canyon. A 16-mile paved road from I-19 Exit 63 crosses the Santa Cruz Valley, then enters Madera Canyon. You'll leave the mesquite, ocotillo, and cacti of the desert behind as you drive through forests of juniper, oak, and pine. Obtain maps and trail information from the Forest Service at Tucson (tel. 629-6483) or Nogales (tel. 281-2296). The *Hiking Guide to the Santa Rita Mountains* by

*The Titan II missile: Crews had used this one for training; it was never fueled or armed. The nose-cone hole allows curious Soviet satelites to verify treaty compliance! A dummy worker stands on a service platform.*

Bob and Dotty Martin and *Arizona Trails* by David Mazel have detailed trail descriptions and maps.

## Hiking

The Santa Ritas have over 70 miles of hiking trails, many suitable for horseback riding. Most of the highest mountains lie within the **Mount Wrightson Wilderness.** Mount Wrightson, elevation 9,543 feet, crowns the range and makes a challenging 13-mile roundtrip hike. Two trails to the summit start near Madera Canyon's Roundup Picnic Area (elev. 5,400 feet): **Old Baldy Trail #94** and **Super Trail #134.** Super Trail is easier, as its name implies. Allow a full day (10 hours) or backpack. A popular dayhike is the 4.5-mile loop from Bog Springs Campground to Bog Springs and Kent Springs. The trail elevations range from 5,100 feet at the campground to 6,600 feet at Kent Springs. For topo maps see the 7.5-minute Mount Wrightson quadrangle or the Southern Arizona Hiking Club's 1:62,500-scale Santa Rita map. More leisurely hikes can be taken on the 4.2-mile trail through Madera Canyon between Proctor Parking Area at the mouth of the canyon and Roundup Picnic Area at the end of the road; maps here and at several access points along the way show the trail segments. The 0.6-mile lower section of trail and two short loops, between Proctor Parking and White House Picnic Area, have been paved and graded for wheelchair travel.

## Campground And Accommodation

**Bog Springs Campground** (elev. 5,600 feet) is open all year with water for $5/site; trailers to 22 feet OK. **Santa Rita Lodge** in Madera Canyon has 12 rental units with kitchenettes and a gift shop; HC 70, Box 5444, Sahuarita, AZ 85624; tel. 625-8746.

## Whipple Observatory

The Smithsonian Institution studies the heavens with the Multiple Mirror Telescope (one of the world's largest) on Mount Hopkins and a variety of other telescopes. Six-hour tours begin at the Observatory's Amado office, 35 miles south of Tucson, from March to November. After a short video presentation, you take a bus up a mountain road to the observatories. Be prepared for temperatures 15-20° cooler than in the valley, possible summer showers, and the thin air at Mount Hopkins' 8,550-foot summit. Call up to 4 weeks in advance for the schedule, directions, and required reservations; tel. 629-6741 (Tucson) or 398-2432 (Amado). Tours cost $5 adult, $2.50 children 6-12; children under 6 aren't permitted.

# GREEN VALLEY

Green Valley is a retirement village on rolling hills overlooking the Santa Cruz Valley. Visitors can enjoy the 18-hole golf course, tennis courts, pool, and other amenities by staying in Fairfield's **Desert Casitas,** Box 587, Green Valley, AZ 85622-0587; tel. 625-2010. Rates start at $63 s, $74 d from Jan. to March and $45 s, $54 d from April to December. Other motels and a good selection of restaurants are in town too. **Green Valley Chamber of Commerce** can tell you about the area and services; the office is in the Continental Shopping Plaza just west of I-19 Exit 63; Box 566, Green Valley, AZ 85622; tel. 625-7575. Green Valley is 25 miles south of Tucson; take I-19 Exits 69, 65, or 63.

## Sierrita Mine

This active copper mine lies west of Green Valley. You can see the massive terraces of waste rock from many miles away. The Sierrita pit measures 6,800 feet long, 6,000 feet wide, and 1,400 feet deep. Cyprus Minerals Company occasionally offers tours of the operation; tel. 648-8608.

# TUBAC

After the Pima Indian Revolt in 1751, the Spanish decided to protect their missions and settlers in this remote region. Tubac Presidio, the first European settlement in what's now Arizona, was founded the following year. Apache raids and political turmoil in following decades made life unbearable at times,

*U.S. Army troops
in hot pursuit of
Apache*

and Tubac's citizens fled on eight occasions. When the United States took over after the 1854 Gadsden Purchase, Tubac was only a pile of crumbling adobe ruins. Prospectors and adventure-seekers, fired by tales of old Spanish mines, soon poured in. Mines were found, and by 1860 Tubac had become a boom town with Arizona's first newspaper, the *Weekly Arizonan*. The Civil War brought the good times to an end when the troops guarding the town headed east to fight. Apache once again raided the settlement, and the inhabitants once again had to flee. Tubac came back to life after the Civil War, but the boom days were over.

Much later, when an art school opened in 1948, Tubac started on its way to becoming an artists' colony. Today, the village of Tubac has about 50 studios and galleries displaying modern jewelry, ceramics, woodcarvings, prints, batiks, paintings, and other works. You'll see the Tubac motto: "Where art and history meet." During the week-long Tubac Festival of the Arts in Feb., residents and visiting artists celebrate with exhibitions, demonstrations, and food. Life in Tubac slows down in summer and some shops close then. Tubac is 45 miles south of Tucson; take I-19 Exit 34.

**Tubac Center Of The Arts**
This gallery displays a variety of excellent work by local artists. It's open Tues.-Sat. 10 a.m.-4:30 p.m. and Sun. 1-4:30 p.m. from late Sept. to mid-May; free; tel. 398-2371. Located on Plaza Road near the entrance of Tubac.

**Tubac Presidio State Historic Park**
A museum just east of the artists' colony shows the ups and downs of Tubac's history since its founding in 1752. The printing press used for Arizona's first newspaper is here and you can buy a reproduction of the first issue, dated March 3, 1859. Other exhibits show how early residents made their own clothing, furniture, tools, and medicine. Models illustrate how the presidio appeared in the early years. Stairs lead underground to excavations of the original foundation and wall. Behind the museum is a schoolhouse built in 1885. (Tubac had Arizona's first school in 1789, but it no longer exists.) The historic park is open daily 8 a.m.-5 p.m.; admission is $1 age 18 and over. A mesquite-shaded picnic area is across the street; no camping.

**Practicalities**
**Tubac Valley Country Club,** one mile north, offers rooms ($50.40 s, $56.70 d and up from

Jan. 1 to April 30; lower prices off-season), the **Stables Restaurant** (breakfast, lunch, and dinner), an 18-hole golf course, tennis court, and pool; take I-19 Exit 40; tel. 398-2211. **Tubac Trailer Tether** has RV spaces on Burruel Street in town; $10.55-14.77 w/ hookups; tel. 398-2111. **Joanna's Café International** features German cuisine; open Sat. and Sun. for breakfast, Tues.-Sun. for lunch, and Thurs.-Sat. for dinner in Mercado de Baca off Tubac Road; tel. 398-9336. **The Hideout** has Mexican and American food for lunch and dinner near the entrance for Tubac; tel. 398-2158. **Sgt. Grijalva's Restaurant and Cantina** serves Mexican food at Otero and Burruel streets; tel. 398-2263. **Mom's Place** has sandwiches and pizza for lunch on Tubac Plaza; closed Sunday. The **post office, public library,** and **Tortuga Books** are along Tubac Road.

## TUMACACORI NATIONAL MONUMENT

This massive adobe ruin evokes visions of Spanish missionaries and devout Indian followers. Father Kino first visited the Pima village of Tumacacori in 1691 and said Mass under a brush shelter. Kino's successors continued the mission work of teaching religion and farming, but the present church was not begun until about 1800. Franciscan Father Narciso Gutierrez, determined to build a church as splendid as San Xavier del Bac, supervised the construction by Indian laborers. Work went slowly, and although never quite finished, the building was in use by 1822. Then the new Mexican government restricted funds for mission work and began to evict all foreign missionaries. Tumacacori's last resident priest, Father Ramon Liberos of Spain, was hauled off in 1828. Indians continued to care for the church and received occasional visits by missionaries from Mexico, but raiding Apache made life hard. The last devout Indians finally gave up in 1848, packed the church furnishings, and moved to San Xavier del Bac.

Tumacacori fell into ruins before it received protection as a national monument in 1908. A museum presents the history of the Indians and Spanish, shows architectural features, and displays some of the original wooden statues of the mission. A self-guided tour gives details about the circular mortuary chapel, graveyard, storeroom, and other ruined structures surrounding the church. Picnic tables are on the grounds but no camping is permitted. The Patio Garden has herbs, shade trees, and flowers planted in Spanish missions of northern Sonora; a booklet available at the Visitor Center explains their uses.

*Tumacacori Mission Ruin*

Books, slides, postcards, and videos are sold in the Visitor Center. **Tumacacori Fiesta** celebrates with Indian dances, crafts, and food on the first Sun. in December. The monument is open daily 8 a.m.-5 p.m.; admission is $1 age 17 and over or $3/car; tel. 398-2341. Located 48 miles south of Tucson near I-19 Exit 29, or just 3 miles south of Tubac on the east frontage road.

### Practicalities
**Tumacacori Restaurant** (across the street from the mission) and **Wisdom's Cafe** (0.3 mile north) have Mexican and American food. **Rancho Santa Cruz Guest Ranch** offers accommodations with horseback riding, swimming pool, and restaurant; $73.85-131.88 d from May to Sept. and $84.40-158.25 d Oct. to April; tel. 281-8383 or 798-3234; take I-19 Exit 29, then turn south on the east frontage road or take Exit 25, then turn north on the east frontage road.

# PENA BLANCA LAKE AND VICINITY

A scenic, 52-acre lake in the hills 16 miles northeast of Nogales. Pena Blanca (Spanish for "white rock") is named for light-colored bluffs overlooking the water. Fishermen come to catch bass, bluegill, crappie, catfish and, from Nov. to March, rainbow trout. At an elevation of 4,000 feet, the lake area is a bit cooler than Tucson. A trail leads around the lakeshore. Beside the water are a lodge with motel ($29.40-60.90 d), RV park ($5.25 tent, $7.35 RV w/hookups), restaurant, boat rentals, groceries, and fishing supplies. Reservations are recommended for lodging, especially on weekends; tel. 281-2800. To reach the lake and lodge, take I-19 Ruby Road Exit 12 and drive west 11 miles on AZ 289, a paved road.

**White Rock Campground** is in Pena Blanca Canyon upstream from the lake. There's drinking water year-round and room for trailers to 22 feet; $5. Turn left 0.1 mile onto Forest Route 39 at Milepost 10, one mile before the lodge.

### Atascosa Lookout Trail
Forest Trail #100 climbs steeply from 4,700 feet through desert vegetation, oaks, juniper, and pinyon pine to the summit at 6,255 feet. Allow half a day for the 6-mile roundtrip. Trailhead is 5 miles west of Pena Blanca Lake on Forest Route 39, a gravel road. Look for a parking area on the south side of the road; trailhead (unsigned) is on the north side. From the top, mountain ranges in Mexico can be seen to the south, Pena Blanca Lake and Nogales to the east, the Santa Ritas and Rincons to the northeast, the Santa Catalinas to the north, and the Baboquivaris to the west. The trail is shown on the 7.5-minute Ruby topo map. You can hike year-round except after snowstorms.

### Sycamore Canyon Trail
This trail is rough in spots but can be followed downstream all the way to the Mexican border, a distance of 6 miles one way. The scenic canyon contains plants and wildlife rarely found elsewhere in the United States. The trail crosses both the **Goodding Research Natural Area,** named for a prominent Arizona botanist, and the **Pajarita Wilderness.** The first 1.3 miles is easy walking, but then boulder-hopping and wading are necessary. Toward the end, the canyon opens up and you'll see saguaro on the slopes. A barbed-wire fence marks the Mexican border. The trailhead is about 10 miles west of Pena Blanca Lake on Forest Route 39; turn left 0.25 mile on Forest Route 218 to Hank and Yank Historical Site. These adobe ruins were part of a ranch started in the 1880s by two former Army scouts. Hiking in Sycamore Canyon is good all year. Elevation ranges from 4,000 feet at the trailhead to 3,500 feet at the border. Depending on how far you go, the hike can be an easy 2-hour stroll for the first mile or so or a long (10-hour) 12-mile roundtrip dayhike all the way to Mexico; see the Ruby topo map. No camping is allowed along the trail.

### Arivaca Lake
A beautiful 90-acre lake, 24 bumpy miles west on Forest Route 39 from Pena Blanca

Lake. Fishermen catch largemouth bass, bluegill, and catfish while enjoying the solitude of this remote spot. Facilities are minimal: just parking areas, a boat ramp, and outhouses. The best road in is from Amado (I-19 Exit 48, 37 miles south of Tucson) to the village of Arivaca, 20 miles (paved). From Arivaca go south 5 miles on Forest Route 39 (gravel), then left 2.5 miles to the lake. The other route is from Pena Blanca Lake on Forest Route 39; go 21 miles west from the lake, then turn right 2.5 miles. This route winds through the Atascosa Mountains past the ghost towns of Ruby (fenced off), and Oro Blanco.

# NOGALES

Nogales, astride the U.S. and Mexican border, is a truly international city. Most visitors to Mexico have shopping on their minds, and Nogales offers a huge selection of handicrafts. You'll also discover fine restaurants and serenading mariachi bands. Mexicans too, like to cross the border for shopping and sampling foreign culture—you'll see them trooping into Safeway and McDonald's.

## History

Indians have used Nogales Pass for at least 2,000 years for migration and trade. The Hohokam came through to reach the Gulf of California for shells prized as bracelet and necklace material. Pima, possibly descended from the Hohokam, settled and traveled in the Santa Cruz River Valley and Nogales area after A.D. 1500. During the Spanish era, missionaries, soldiers, ranchers, and prospectors also passed through. Apache used the pass on their raiding forays until well into the 19th century. Traders on the Guaymas-Tucson route knew the spot as Los Nogales (Spanish for "The Walnuts"). A survey team marked the international line here in 1855, one year after the Gadsden Purchase.

The town—or rather, the two towns (one in each country)—was started by two men in 1880. Juan José Vasquez established a roadhouse (refreshment and food for travelers) on the Mexican side, and some months later Jacob Isaacson set up a trading post on the American side. The first railroad line to cross the border between the USA and Mexico came through Nogales in Oct. 1882. Trade, silver mining, and ranching kept Nogales growing. In 1898 its population of 1,500 on the U.S. side made it the fifth largest city in Arizona. When Pancho Villa threatened Nogales in 1916, the worried U.S. Army established Camp Little on the edge of town. Relations between the two halves of Nogales remained good despite the political turmoil in Mexico, and Camp Little closed in 1933. Tourists "discovered" Nogales in the 1940s, and tourism, along with trade, keeps the border busy today.

## Sights

The **Pimeria Alta Historical Society Museum** gives a good introduction to Nogales. Artifacts and old photos illustrate the long and colorful history of southern Arizona and northern Sonora (Mexico). The building, put up in 1914 to house the Nogales (Arizona) City Hall and police and fire departments, is itself an attraction. You can see the old jail, horse-

*Pancho Villa (center) and associates, 1915*

*Nogales (Sonora) and border, ca. 1920*

drawn water pumper, law office, and other exhibits. The Society's research library has a wealth of books on regional history and is open to the public. Museum and library are open Mon.-Fri. 9 a.m.-5 p.m., Sat. 10 a.m.-4 p.m., and Sun. 1-4 p.m.; free; tel. 287-5402. The distinctive mission-style building is on the corner of Grand Ave. and Crawford St., 0.25 mile north of the border.

The square granite structure with a shiny aluminum dome, on the hillside to the northeast, is the former **Santa Cruz County Courthouse**, built in 1904. Local artists display their work in the **Hilltop Art Gallery**; open Wed.-Sun. 1-4:30 p.m. from Sept. to May; free; Hilltop Dr. (see map); tel. 287-5515.

### Accommodations
Places to stay in town, listed from north to south, include **Rio Rico Resort & Country Club** (has golf, tennis, a pool, and horseback riding, 12 miles north of town near I-19 Exit 17; $64.36 s, $74.91 d and up; tel. 281-1901); **Super 8 Motel** (I-19 and Mariposa Road; $34.75 s, $42.38; tel. 281-2242); **Motel 6** (1871 Grand Ave., just south of Mariposa

Road; $27.57 s, $34.20 d; tel. 281-2951); **Best Western Time Motel** (1200 Grand Ave.; $24 s, $37 d; tel. 287-4627); **La Hacienda Motor Hotel** (1118 Grand Ave., just north of the AZ 82 jct.; $24.53 s, $31.07 d.; tel. 287-2781); **El Dorado Motel** (1001 Grand Ave.; $39.78 s, $41 d; tel. 287-4611); **Best Western Siesta Motel** (910 Grand Ave.; $30.52 s, $37 d; tel. 287-4671); **Mission Motel** (863 Grand Ave.; $18.24 s, $22.10 d; tel. 287-2472); **Americana Motor Hotel** (850 Grand Ave.; $39.24-49 d; tel. 287-7211). About a dozen hotels are on the Mexican side, but they can be hard to find as streets aren't signed. Three are on Av. Juarez, 2 blocks west just south of the border crossing. Prices usually run US$10-30.

### Campgrounds
**Mi Casa RV Park** is 4.5 miles north of the border at 3420 Tucson-Nogales Hwy. (US 89); $8.48 tent, $15.37 RV w/hookups; tel. 281-1150. Campgrounds with and without hookups are also at **Pena Blanca Lake** (see p. 441) and **Patagonia Lake State Park** (see p. 448).

## Food

Grand Ave. is home for most of the restaurants on the Arizona side. Except for the Chinese, pizza, and fast-food places, nearly all offer both Mexican and American food. From north to south, you'll find **Mrs. C's**

**Supper Club** (live entertainment and dancing; 302 W. Mariposa Road; tel. 281-9000); **Grand China Restaurant** (Mandarin and Szechuan cuisine; 2049 N. Grand Ave. in Mariposa Shopping Center; tel. 281-2888); **Denny's** (1920 Grand Ave.; tel. 287-4572);

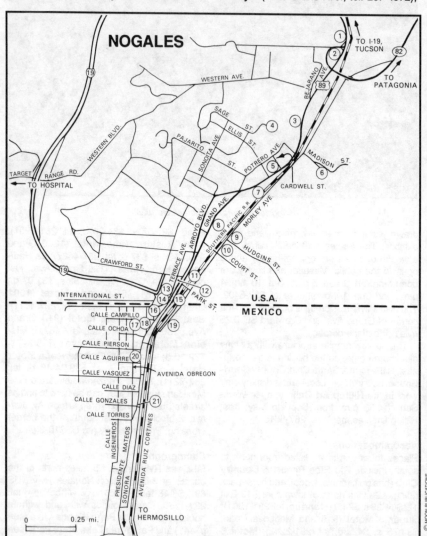

© MOON PUBLICATIONS

Zulas Papachoris' (1267 Grand Ave.; tel. 287-2892); **El Dorado** (1001 Grand Ave.; tel. 287-4611); **Americana** (live entertainment; 850 Grand Ave.; tel. 287-7211); **Pizza Hut** (624 Grand Ave.; tel. 287-9257); **Little Caesar's Pizza** (247 Grand Ave.; tel. 287-4144); and many others. **Molina's PK Outpost** has many historical artifacts on display and a long Mexican menu in the historic Pete Kitchen Ranch 3 miles north of Nogales on the I-19 east frontage road.

In Mexico, **La Roca** offers excellent Mexican food and nightly live music; 3 blocks east just south of the border crossing. **Pancho Villa Restaurant** in Hotel Olivia has mariachi music (corner of Av. Obregon and Aguirre). **Mi Wah Restaurant** serves Cantonese cuisine (Av. Obregon, 3 blocks west just south of the border crossing). Other restaurants are scattered around town; many have English menus and all accept US dollars.

### Events

The Mexican side celebrates **Cinco de Mayo** (late April to May 5th), **Independence Day** (Sept. 16), and **Revolution Day** (Nov. 20) with parades and other festivities. The U.S. side's biggest annual event is the **Santa Cruz County Fair** in Sept. or Oct.; see a cowchip chucking contest, fiddlers' competition, rooster-crowing contest, other entertainment, and agricultural exhibits. In Oct., many Arizonans take in the **Oktoberfest** with beer, German food, and entertainment. The Arizona side also has a **Christmas Parade** in late Nov. or early December. **Bullfighting** takes place on the Mexico side in the Guadalupe Plaza de Toros; ask the Nogales-Santa Cruz Chamber of Commerce for dates.

### Shopping

Most visitors to Ambos Nogales ("Both Nogales") park on the American side near the border ($3 all day) and set off on foot. This saves delays in crossing the border by car and finding parking spots in Mexico. When you cross into Mexico, all the shopkeepers know why you're there! Mexican craftsmen turn out an astonishing array of products, from Tiffany-style lampshades to saddles. Because a day's wages in Mexico come close to an hour's wages in the U.S., most crafts are real bargains. Be sure to shop around and haggle before laying out any cash! Even in the large fixed-price stores, it's worth asking for a discount. English is spoken by all the eager salespeople. There's no need to change money into Mexican pesos either; dollars and major credit cards are happily accepted. Crafts come from many corners of Mexico and merchants usually know their origin. Popular buys include chess sets of carved onyx (a soft stone with a layered pattern), clay reproductions of Mayan art, painted vases, embroidered clothing, glassware, hand-tooled leather pieces (bags, purses, and belts), wool blankets, and woodcarvings (including furniture). A few items are *very unpopular* with U.S. Customs and will be confiscated: guns and ammo, fireworks, illegal drugs, switchblades, meat, poultry, and sea-turtle oil. Adults can bring back other goods totaling US$400, including one quart of liquor—all duty-free—every 31 days. You can also shop for Mexican crafts on the Ari-

**NOGALES**

1. La Hacienda Motor Hotel
2. chamber of commerce
3. Denny's Restaurant
4. Hilltop Art Gallery
5. Pizza Hut
6. War Memorial Park
7. public library
8. Garrett Wray Curios
9. post office (Arizona)
10. old Santa Cruz County Courthouse
11. Pimeria Alta Historical Soc. Museum
12. Consulado de Mexico
13. bus station (Arizona)
14. Federal Building (U.S. Immigration and Customs)
15. border crossing
16. bus stations (Mexico)
17. Hotel Fray Marcos de Niza
18. post office (Mexico)
19. La Roca Restaurant
20. Hotel Olivia
21. Hotel Granada

*across the border
in Nogales,
Sonora*

zona side of the border; Garrett Wray Curios at 492 Grand Ave. offers a large and varied selection.

### Crossing The Border

No permit is needed to walk or drive across the border for visits in Nogales of 72 hours or less. To go beyond Nogales, U.S. citizens need proof of citizenship to get a tourist permit (good for 180 days) at the border. Visitors from other countries should check with a Mexican consulate for entry requirements; they should also see U.S. Immigration about re-entry before stepping across. In Nogales, Arizona, the Consulado de Mexico is at 137 Terrace Ave.; tel. 287-2521. A separate permit is needed for driving a car in Mexico beyond Nogales. Pick it up at the border by showing proof of car ownership. When an accident occurs in Mexico, all parties involved are considered guilty until proven innocent; having insurance can prevent a stay in jail. Most U.S. policies are worthless, so you'll need to purchase Mexican insurance. Numerous agencies along Grand Ave. in Nogales, AZ, advertise Mexican insurance; they have daily and longer rates. You don't need to change money within Nogales; dollars or pesos are welcomed on both sides of the border. For longer trips into Mexico, the local

currency is essential. You can save a little by purchasing pesos on the U.S. side. Safeway and other stores near the border almost always have a surplus of Mexican currency and will sell it at a better rate than banks.

### Services

The **post office** is just east of the border station (see map). **Holy Cross Hospital** is west of town at 1230 Target Range Road; tel. 287-2771. You'll find a public **swimming pool** and **tennis courts** near the War Memorial Park on Madison St. (see map). Golfers can tee off at **Meadow Hills** (9 holes; 3425 Country Club Road, northwest of town; tel.

281-2165); **Rio Rico Golf Course** (18 holes; 1410 Rio Rico Dr., 12 miles north near I-19 Exit 17; tel. 281-8567); and **Kino Springs Country Club** (18 holes; 5 miles northeast on AZ 82, Patagonia Road; tel. 287-8701).

## Information

The **Nogales-Santa Cruz Chamber of Commerce** is helpful with local events, facilities, and sights. Open Mon.-Fri. 8 a.m.-5 p.m. and Sat. 9 a.m.-1 p.m.; write Kino Park, Nogales, AZ 85621; tel. 287-3685. When entering Nogales from the north on Grand Ave. (US 89), turn right on the street just *past* the Patagonia Road interchange (AZ 82). The Mexicans also have a **tourist office** (to the west just south of the border crossing). The **Nogales Ranger Station** of the U.S. Forest Service has reference books about hiking, camping, history, and archaeology in the Nogales and other districts of the Coronado National Forest; open Mon.-Fri. 8 a.m.-4:30 p.m.; the office is at 2251 Grand Ave. (Nogales, AZ 85621), 3.3 miles north of the border on US 89; tel. 281-2296. Nogales, Arizona, has a **library** at 748 Grand Ave.; tel. 287-3343.

## Tours And Transport

**Desert Dimensions** can arrange tours to the

sights and shopping across the border; tel. 287-7411.

**Citizen Auto Stage** sends 10 buses daily to Tucson ($6.25 one way), five of which go on to Phoenix ($24.70 one way). The trip to Tucson takes 1¾ hours, and stops at Tumacacori, Tubac, and other places along the way. First departure is at 7 a.m., last at 8 p.m.; tel. 287-5628. Citizen Auto Stage is just 2 blocks from the border at 126 Terrace Ave. (next to Safeway). On the Mexican side, **Transportes Norte de Sonora (TNS)** and Autotransportes Tres Estellas de Oro, provide extensive bus services at low cost. Each has about 15 daily departures from about 7:30 a.m. to 9 p.m. The stations are on opposite sides of Pesqueira St., one block to the west just south of the border crossing.

An express **train** leaves every afternoon for Mexico City (42 hours) via Hermosillo (4 hours) and Guadalajara (28 hours). Sleeping cars are available. A ticket office is located in the Mexican Tourism Building near the border. The train station itself is about 4.5 miles south; take a taxi or the Av. Obregon bus.

The nearest major **airports** are at Tucson (64 miles north) and Hermosillo (174 miles south). Nogales has a small (but international!) airfield on Patagonia Road.

*Pimeria Alta Historical Society Museum*

# PATAGONIA AND VICINITY

The rolling hills of grass and woodlands surrounding Patagonia make up some of the state's choice cattle and horse lands. Patagonia, 19 miles northeast of Nogales, lies on the alternate route between it and Tucson. Many people like to make a loop between the two cities by driving through Sonoita and Patagonia in one direction (I-10, AZ Hwys. 83 and 82), and the Santa Cruz Valley (I-19) in the other.

## Patagonia Lake State Park

A pleasant place for picnicking, camping, boating, and fishing. The 265-acre reservoir offers largemouth bass, crappie, sunfish, bluegill, channel catfish, and, in winter, rainbow trout. The marina has a boat ramp, gas, boat and canoe rentals, and camping and fishing supplies; open daily 8 a.m.-6 p.m. in summer, then daily except Wed. the rest of the year; closed in December. The lake's west half is open for water-skiing and for jet-skis and similar watercraft on summer weekdays and daily off-season; the east half of the lake is a no-wake area. Swim at Boulder Beach (no lifeguard). **Sonoita Creek Trail** begins at the east end of the east camp-

ground and winds to the mouth of Sonoita Creek, 1.2 miles roundtrip. Petroglyphs on the far side of the lake can be reached by boat or on foot.

At an elevation of 3,750 feet, the park stays open all year; the favorite time is early spring through autumn. The campground, which has showers, normally fills by Fri. evening in summer. Boaters can also use primitive sites around the lake and on islands. Park fees are $6/vehicle ($8 w/hookups) for camping or $3/vehicle for day use; tel. 287-6965. From Nogales, go 12 miles northeast on AZ 82, then turn left at the sign and go 4 miles on a paved road. The park gate is closed about 10 p.m.-5 a.m.

## Museum Of The Horse

This amazing collection reflects Anne Stradling's life-long love of horses. Immaculate horse-drawn carriages, saddles, harnesses, Indian artifacts, Western art—even a 400-year-old Mexican ox cart—fill six large rooms. The museum also has an art gallery and gift shop. Open daily 9 a.m.-5 p.m.; $2 adult, $.50 under 12; tel. 394-2264. Located in Patagonia next to the Stage Stop Inn.

*adobe ruin near Harshaw*

## Patagonia-Sonoita Creek Sanctuary

The Nature Conservancy maintains 312 acres along Sonoita Creek as a wildlife preserve. Year-round water and a variety of habitats attract diverse birds; over 275 species have been identified. White-tailed deer, *chulo* (coati), javelina, bobcat, and other animals also live in the thickets and woods. The public is welcome to visit, but no picnicking, camping, or pets are allowed; open daily 6:30 a.m.-6:30 p.m. all year. Summer visitors should be sure to apply insect repellent to keep off chiggers. In Patagonia turn northwest off AZ 82 onto Fourth Ave., then turn left 0.9 mile on Pennsylvania Avenue. The pavement ends and you'll have to drive across a creek ford (don't cross if you can't see the bottom), and then you're in the sanctuary. Park near the main gate and start walking. An information board is just inside. To learn more, contact the **Nature Conservancy** at 300 E. University Blvd., suite 230, Tucson, AZ 85705; tel. 622-3861.

## Cave Of The Bells

A "wild" cave in the Santa Rita Mountains to the north. The variety of minerals and an underground lake attract experienced spelunkers. Obtain gate key and directions from the Forest Service office in Nogales or the supervisor's office in Tucson. **Onyx Cave,** nearby, can be visited with permission of the Escabrosa Grotto Inc., Box 3634, Tucson, AZ 85722.

## Ghost Towns

Decaying houses, piles of rubble, cemeteries, and old mine shafts mark deserted mining camps in the Patagonia Mountains to the south.

You'll need the topo or Forest Service maps to find the old sites. In a 45-mile loop drive, you can see the sites of Harshaw, Mowry, Washington Camp, and Duquesne. These ghost towns are described in *Arizona's Best Ghost Towns* by Philip Varney and in *Ghost Towns of Arizona* by Jim and Barbara Sherman. You can also drive east to the Huachuca Mountains, Parker Lake, or Coronado National Memorial on the back roads. Most are dirt and should be avoided if it's been raining or snowing.

## Practicalities

The **Stage Stop Inn** (Box 777, Patagonia, AZ 85624) sits in the middle of sleepy Patagonia; $43.35 s, $54.20 d, $65.05 d kitchenette, $86.80 d suite; tel. 394-2211. Tie up your horse on the hitching rings in the front. The restaurant next door has Mexican and American food and an all-you-can-eat Sunday buffet; open daily 6:30 a.m.-9 p.m. A couple of other restaurants, post office, and art galleries are in town too. **Richardson Park** has picnic tables and playground.

Participate in roundups and other cowboy chores or just nose along the trails at **Circle Z Ranch,** a working cattle ranch with guest accommodations. The ranch features horseback riding, swimming, hiking, birding, and tennis. Season runs Nov. 1 to May 15; per-person rates are $166 for a long weekend or $595-1036 weekly including lodging, food, and activities. Located 5 miles southwest of Patagonia; write for details at Box 194, Patagonia, AZ 85624; tel. 287-2091 (814-425-3768 in summer).

*coati* (Nasua narica)

# COCHISE TRAIL

Chief of the Chiricahua Apache, Cochise earned great respect from white man and Indian alike for his integrity and leadership skills. He never lost a battle. The southeast corner of Arizona was named Cochise County in his honor in 1881, despite his having waged war against troops and settlers from 1861 to 1872. Many historic sites of the Old West can be visited on a 206-mile loop through this varied country. Tourist offices call this drive the "Cochise Trail."

## TOMBSTONE

When prospector Ed Schieffelin headed out this way in March of 1877, friends told him that the only thing he would find among all the Apache and rattlesnakes would be his own tombstone. But he set out anyway, alone, and staked a silver claim, naming it Tombstone. When Ed struck it rich at an adjacent site, his brother Al said, "You're a lucky cuss." And the Lucky Cuss Mine became one of Arizona's richest. Other claims were equally descriptive: Contention, Tough Nut, and Goodenough. The town incorporated in 1879 and blossomed to a population

of as much as 15,000 just 5 years later. It was said that saloons and gambling halls made up two of every three buildings in the business district. The famous OK Corral gunfight took place in 1881; historians still debate its details (see below). Shootings and hangings in the 1880s made Boot Hill Graveyard a busy place. Tombstone's rough and wild times have fueled the imagination of countless novelists and scriptwriters. Fires nearly wiped out Tombstone on two occasions, but it was flooding in the mines in 1886-87 that sent the town into a swift decline. Tombstone, "the town too tough to die," managed to survive and now attracts visitors seeking out the Wild West.

### Allen Street

Guns still blaze and bodies hit the dust on Allen Street in staged gunfights and barroom brawls. The action, portrayed by the "Vigilantes," takes place on the second, fourth, and fifth Sundays of the month at 2 p.m. The show is free but you can make donations. On the first and third Sundays of the month the "Wild Bunch" puts on a demonstration at the OK Corral, culminating in the famous shootout; small admission fee.

## Boot Hill Graveyard
Lying here are "Dutch Annie" (a widely admired prostitute), the losers of the OK Corral shootout, hanging (or lynching) victims, and assorted gunslingers. Many of the estimated 276 graves are unmarked; those that are have much to say about life in old Tombstone. Boot Hill is just off US 80 on the north edge of town; enter through the Boot Hill Gift Shop; open daily 7:30 a.m.-6 p.m.; free.

## St. Paul's Episcopal Church
Built in 1881, this is the oldest standing Protestant church in Arizona. Located at corner of Third and Safford.

## Tombstone Courthouse
## State Historic Park
Dating from 1882, this red-brick building has witnessed many emotional trials. Some of the convicted were hanged in the courtyard to the northwest. Not everyone had the benefit of the courthouse gallows—John Heath, reportedly the brains behind a robbery and murder in Bisbee, was taken from jail and lynched by a mob in 1884. The six-man coroner's jury later declared that the unlucky fellow had died "...from emphysema of the lungs—a disease common to high altitudes—which might have been caused by strangulation, self-inflicted or otherwise." Officials abandoned Tombstone's courthouse in 1929 when the county seat

*the lynching of John Heath*

moved to Bisbee. The courthouse has been restored and now houses a museum of artifacts and photos of the old days. A gift shop offers books on Arizona history. Open daily 8 a.m.-5 p.m.; $1 adult 18 and over; tel. 457-3311; Third and Toughnut streets.

*the OK Corral*

## The OK Corral

The Earps and Doc Holliday shot it out with the Clanton cowboys on this site in Oct. 1881. Markers and life-size figures show how it all happened, or at least one version of the story. Other things to see are the studio and photos taken by Camilius S. Fly of early Tombstone, the old stables, carriages, a hearse that carried many a passenger to Boot Hill Graveyard, and even a red-light district shack. You can "walk where they fell" daily 8:30 a.m.-5 p.m. for $1 admission (children under 6 free). Located off Allen St. between Third and Fourth streets.

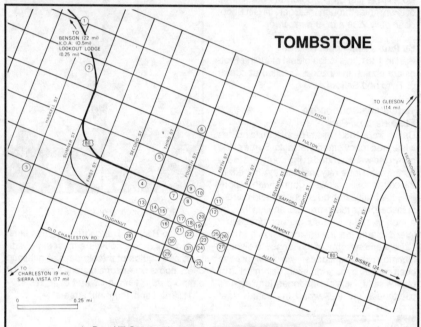

1. Boot Hill Graveyard
2. Top O' the Hill Restaurant
3. Roundup Trailer Ranch
4. Wells Fargo RV Park
5. St. Paul's Episcopal Church
6. Hacienda Huachuca Motel
7. Tombstone City Hall
8. Wagon Wheel Restaurant
9. Schieffelin Hall
10. Larian Motel
11. Tombstone Motel
12. Adobe Lodge Motel
13. Stage Stop Restaurant
14. city park (picnic tables)
15. OK Corral; Historama
16. Tombstone Chamber of Commerce
17. Market Spot Grocery
18. Lucky Cuss Restaurant
19. Crystal Palace Saloon
20. Tombstone *Epitaph*
21. Arizona Territorial Museum
22. Big Nose Kate's Saloon
23. Longhorn Restaurant
24. Pizza Magic
25. post office
26. Silver Nugget Museum
27. Bird Cage Theatre
28. Tombstone Courthouse State Historic Park
29. public library
30. Rose Tree Inn
31. Nellie Cashman Restaurant
32. Old Firehouse Art Gallery

© MOON PUBLICATIONS

### Historama

This 30-minute show recreates the major events of Tombstone with movies and animated figures. Presentations take place hourly 9 a.m.-4 p.m.; $1 (under 6 free). Located next door to the OK Corral entrance.

### Schieffelin Hall

Major theatrical companies of the day performed in this large adobe building dating from 1881. John Sullivan and a company of boxers gave exhibitions here. On the corner of Fremont and Fourth streets. Not currently open to the public.

### Rose Tree Inn

A rose slip sent as a wedding gift in the spring of 1885 from Scotland has grown to cover an amazing 7,000 square feet. The "tree," claimed to be the world's largest, is a Lady Banksia. Its sweet-scented white blossoms usually appear in early April. Rooms exhibit a collection of antique furnishings belonging to a pioneer who arrived by wagon train in 1880; open daily 8 a.m.-6 p.m.; $1 adult (under 14 free); Fourth and Toughnut streets.

*John P. Clum*

### Arizona Territorial Museum

Dioramas show scenes of life in early Tombstone; open daily 8:30 a.m.-4:30 p.m.; free; on Allen St. between Fourth and Fifth streets.

### Crystal Palace Saloon

Built in 1879, this watering hole and gambling house was the height of luxury in early Tombstone. As many as five bartenders stood on duty to serve the thirsty customers 'round the clock. The clientele has changed over the years, but the saloon still serves up drinks; Fifth and Allen streets.

### Tombstone *Epitaph*

As one story goes, the town's newspaper got its name when one of its founders, John P. Clum, took the stagecoach home from Tucson. Clum asked the passengers what they thought would be a good name. By coincidence, Ed Schieffelin was on board. He replied, "Well, I christened the district Tombstone; you should have no trouble furnishing the 'Epitaph.'" Clum founded the paper in 1880 and it's still being published. "Every Tombstone should have an Epitaph," residents say. You can visit the office to see the original press and other printing exhibits; open weekdays 9 a.m.-5 p.m. and weekends 10 a.m.-4 p.m.; free. Souvenir copies are sold—read your own *Epitaph*. Located on Fifth St. (between Fremont and Allen sts.).

### Bird Cage Theatre

This 1881 dance hall, gambling house, saloon, brothel, and theater was the favored hangout of local characters and desperados. During its first 3 years, the doors never closed. Birdcage-like stalls suspended from the ceiling gave the place its name. See if you can find some of the reported 140 bullet holes in the walls and ceiling. The well-preserved building is open daily 8 a.m.-6 p.m.; $2 adult, $1 children 13-18, and $.50 children 8-12; Allen and Sixth streets.

*Bird Cage Theatre*

### Silver Nugget Museum
See exhibits of outlaws, the law, Nellie Cashman—"Angel of Tombstone," photos, old documents, guns, and furnishings from pioneer homes. Open daily 9 a.m.-5 p.m.; $1, children under 12 free; Allen and Sixth streets.

## PRACTICALITIES

### Accommodations
**Adobe Lodge** ($26.75 s, $32.10 d) is on the corner of Fifth and Fremont sts.; tel. 457-2241. **Larian Motel** ($25.80 s, $30.10 d) is at 410 E. Fremont St.; tel. 457-2272. **Hacienda Huachuca Motel** ($18 s or d) is at 320 E. Bruce and Fourth St.; tel. 457-2201. **Tombstone Motel** is at 502 E. Fremont St. (US 80); tel. 457-3478. The Best Western **Lookout Lodge** starts at $37.63 s, $47.30 d; 0.7 mile

north on US 80, has a pool; tel. 457-2223 or (800) 528-1234.

### Campgrounds
**Wells Fargo RV Park** ($13.38 tent or RV no hookups, $15.52 RV w/hookups) is right in town at Third and Fremont sts.; has laundromat and showers; tel. 457-3966. **Round Up Trailer Ranch** ($8.56 tent, $12.31 RV w/hookups) is at 201 W. Allen St.; has laundromat and showers; tel. 457-3738. **Tombstone Hills KOA** is one mile north of downtown on US 80; $13.86 tent, $17.07 RV w/hookups, $23.49 Kamping Kabin; has a pool, laundromat, showers, and store; tel. 457-3829.

### Food
Not surprisingly, most restaurants feature Western decor and food. The **Nellie Cashman Restaurant and Pie Salon** is Tomb-

stone's oldest, established in 1882; open daily for breakfast, lunch, and dinner at Fifth and Toughnut sts.; tel. 457-3950. The **Longhorn Restaurant** offers Mexican, Italian, and American breakfasts, lunches, and dinners daily; Fifth and Allen sts.; tel. 457-3405. The **Lucky Cuss Restaurant** has lunch and dinners "1880s style" daily on Allen St. between Fourth and Fifth sts.; tel. 457-3561. The **Wagon Wheel** is open daily for breakfast, lunch, and dinner with steaks, chicken, and seafood; has live entertainment Fri.-Sun.; corner of Fourth and Fremont sts.; tel. 457-3656. Pull in at the **Stage Stop** for breakfast or lunch; open daily at the corner of Allen and Third sts.; tel. 457-3955. **Pizza Magic** features magic shows along with pizza, pasta, and sandwiches; 150 S. Fifth St.; tel. 457-3850. **Top O' the Hill Restaurant** serves Mexican and American meals; open daily for breakfast, lunch, and dinner; north on US 80 near Boot Hill; tel. 457-3641. Pick up groceries at the **Market Spot** on Allen St. between Fourth and Fifth streets.

### Events
**Shootouts** take place every Sun. afternoon (see "Allen Street," above). **Helldorado Days,** Tombstone's biggest celebration, features 3 days of shootouts, parades, and other lively entertainment beginning on the third Fri. of October. Smaller scale festivities are **Territorial Days** (first weekend in March), **Wyatt Earp Days** (Memorial Day weekend), **International Order of Old Bastards Parade** (third Sun. in June), **Nellie Cashman Day** (Aug. 15th), and the **Wild West Days** (Labor Day weekend).

### Shopping, Services, And Information
Many shops along Allen Street sell Old West souvenirs, rocks and minerals, books, clothing, jewelry, and crafts. Some also have small museums, usually free, that may be worth a look. Tombstone Association of the Arts supports the **Old Firehouse Art Gallery** in the original firehouse; open Wed.-Sun. 10 a.m.-4 p.m. at Fifth and Toughnut streets. **Post office** is on Allen St. between Fifth and Sixth streets. The **Tombstone Chamber of Commerce** is open many days (irregular hours) on the corner of Fourth and Allen sts.; Box 917, Tombstone, AZ 85638; tel. 457-2211 (Tombstone *Epitaph*). The public library's **Reading Station** is at Fourth and Toughnut streets.

## VICINITY OF TOMBSTONE

### Ghost Towns
Ghost-town enthusiasts may want to explore remnants of former mining towns. **Gleeson,** 15 miles east on a graded gravel road, flourished along with its copper mine from 1909 until the 1930s. Operations ended in 1953. A saloon on the old main street is still open and you can see ruins of the jail, cemetery, school, adobe hospital, and other buildings. Mine tailings and machinery rest on the hillside.

**Courtland,** now occupied solely by ghosts, is one mile east and 3 miles north of Gleeson on good gravel roads. A jail, several buildings, and numerous foundations remain. Watch out for open mine shafts in this area.

At the site of **Pearce,** 9 miles north of Courtland, Jimmie Pearce found gold in 1894. The Commonwealth Mine was a success, and the town's population reached 1,500 before the mine closed in the 1930s. Step into Pearce's old store to see a collection of antiques; many are for sale. Other reminders of the past include the cemetery (west on the road just north of the store), old post office (across from the store), Pearce Church (southwest of the store), abandoned houses, and the Commonwealth Mine ruins. Pearce can also be reached from I-10; take Exit 331 and head south 22 miles on US 666. Author Philip Varney devotes a whole chapter to these and other sites of the Tombstone area in his *Arizona's Best Ghost Towns.*

### San Pedro Riparian
### National Conservation Area
Residents of this choice wildlife habitat—one of the richest in the United States—are 350 bird species, 82 mammal species, and 45 reptile and amphibian species. The San Pedro River, though only a trickle at times,

nourishes willows, cottonwoods, and other streamside vegetation. From its beginning in Sonora, Mexico, the river flows north to join the Gila near Winkelman. The riparian area run by the Bureau of Land Management is 1-3 miles wide and stretches for 36 miles from the Mexican border to near St. David. Visitors enjoy birdwatching, nature walks, and horseback riding. You can camp with a permit from the San Pedro Project Office; $1.50/person per night but no facilities.

Archaeologists have unearthed bones of extinct mammoths, bison, and camels killed by ancient hunters at Murray Springs and Lehner Mammoth Kill Site. Spear tips and butchering tools left behind have identified these people as belonging to the "Clovis Man" culture about 11,000 years ago.

For information on visiting the area, contact the local San Pedro Project Office in Fairbank, beside the river off AZ 82 (Box 9853, RR 1, Huachuca City, AZ 85616; tel. 457-2265) or the Safford District Office (425 E. Fourth St., Safford, AZ 85546; tel. 428-4040). Both offices are open Mon.-Fri. 7:45 a.m.-4:15 p.m.

# FORT HUACHUCA

When raiding Apache threatened settlers and travelers in the San Pedro Valley in 1877, the Army set up a temporary camp near the Huachuca ("wa-CHOO-ka") Mountains. In 1886, Fort Huachuca became the advance headquarters for the campaign against Geronimo until the famous Apache leader surrendered in Sept. of that year. Although the Army later closed more than 50 forts and camps in the territory, it retained Huachuca to deal with outlaws and renegade Indians near the Mexican border. World Wars I and II and the Korean War saw new duties for the fort; finally, in 1954, it took on its current task of testing electronics and communications gear.

### Fort Huachuca Museum

The museum's large collection of photos, Indian artifacts, dioramas, and memorabilia date from Apache-fighting days to the present. One room honors the fort's black troops, known as Buffalo Soldiers. Barracks and ad-

*aerial view of Fort Huachuca, 1929*

FORT HUACHUCA

ministrative buildings from the 1880s line the parade ground outside. The museum is open weekdays 9 a.m.-4 p.m. and weekends 1-4 p.m.; free; tel. 533-5736. The collection is housed in two buildings on either side of Hungerford at Grierson. It's about 2.5 miles in from the main gate in Sierra Vista. Be sure to pick up a free visitor's pass at one of the gates (you may need to show a driver's license and vehicle registration).

## SIERRA VISTA

The town of Sierra Vista grew up outside the gates of Fort Huachuca as a service center. Many Army retirees have settled here; they like the climate and social and recreational opportunities, and they can continue to use base facilities. Sierra Vista (pop. 34,590) now includes Fort Huachuca and is the largest and fastest growing community in Cochise County.

### Accommodations And Food

When driving toward Sierra Vista, you have a choice of taking the bypass route or going downtown on Fry Blvd. and Garden Avenue. Fry Blvd. has a good selection of motels and restaurants, including a platoon of fast-food places. RV parks lie scattered around town.

### Events

In April, the nearby Coronado National Memorial hosts the **Coronado International Pageant** of music, dance, and crafts representing traditions of Indian, Mexican, and Western cultures. Runners test themselves in the **Mule Mountain Marathon** on the first weekend in May. Crafts are featured in the **Fort Huachuca Family Festival,** also on the first weekend in May. **Fireworks** light the sky in the July Fourth celebration. The **Ambassadors Airshow** takes place at Libby Army Airfield on the first weekend of October. **Art in the Park** attracts artists and crafts people from all over the West on the first weekend of October. Arizona's largest **Christmas Parade** starts off the holiday season on the first Sat. following Thanksgiving. The local chamber of commerce has a listing of sports events and other happenings in the area.

### Recreation And Services

The **city park** has an outdoor pool, picnic tables, playground, basketball court, and horseshoe pits at 3025 E. Fry Blvd.; tel. 458-6742. Play golf at the 18-hole **Pueblo del Sol Golf Course,** 2770 S. Saint Andrews Dr., off S. Hwy. 92; tel. 378-6444. **Apache Pointe Equestrian Center** offers trail rides of one hour to all day or overnight in the Huachucas or San Pedro Riparian Area; located off Ram-

*Geronimo (far right) with three braves; photo by C.S. Fly of Tombstone, ca. 1886*

sey Canyon Road, 7 miles south of town; tel. 378-0729. **Post office** is at 2300 E. Fry Blvd.; tel. 458-1853. **Sierra Vista Community Hospital** is at 300 El Camino Real, south off E. Fry Blvd.; tel. 458-4641.

### Information
**Sierra Vista Area Chamber of Commerce** can tell you about the sights and services of the region; open Mon.-Fri. 8 a.m.-5 p.m., south across Fry Blvd. from the city park (77 Calle Portal, Suite A 140, Sierra Vista, AZ 85635); tel. 458-6940. **Sierra Vista Ranger Station** has recreation information for national forest lands in the Huachuca, Dragoon, and Whetstone mountains; open Mon.-Fri. 8 a.m.-5 p.m. at 769 N. Hwy. 90 Bypass, Sierra Vista, AZ 85635 (just north of Wal-Mart); tel. 458-0530. **Sierra Vista Public Library** is at 2950 E. Tacoma in the northeastern part of town; tel. 458-4225. **Hastings Books, Music, and Video** has regional books in Plaza Vista (Hwy. 90 Bypass and Charleston Dr.).

### Transportation
**Bridgewater Transport** offers bus service to Tucson, Bisbee, and Douglas from the station at 28 Fab Ave. (south off W. Fry Blvd.); tel. 458-3471. **Stateswest Airlines** flies to Arizona and southern California destinations; tel. (800) 247-3866.

## HUACHUCA MOUNTAINS

The Huachucas, east of Sierra Vista, have many hiking possibilities and some scenic drives. **Miller Peak Wilderness** contains much of the higher country between Coronado National Memorial and Fort Huachuca. **Reef Campground** (at the site of a former mining camp) and **Ramsey Vista Campground** are in Carr Canyon on the eastern slopes. Contact the **Sierra Vista Ranger Station** of the Coronado National Forest for information on exploring the Huachucas.

The Army controls the northern part of the range—secret electronic installations cap some of the mountain tops. The road through the fort between Sierra Vista and the semighost town of Canelo passes over the northern foothills and has some fine views. Upon entering the fort, pick up a pass and drop it off at the other end when leaving.

### Ramsey Canyon
A year-round stream and an elevation range from 4,200 to 9,466 feet (Miller Peak's summit) provide habitats for many kinds of wildlife, including white-tailed deer, coati, and javelina. Up to 14 species of hummingbirds congregate here from spring to early autumn. Butterflies also appear in the warmer months.

The Nature Conservancy owns a 280-acre sanctuary for the hummers and other wildlife. The **Mile Hi/Ramsey Canyon Preserve's** bird observation area, **Nature Trail** loop, and the **Hamburg Trail** are open to the public 8 a.m.-5 p.m. daily; a $3 donation is appreciated from nonmembers. The Nature Trail makes a 0.7-mile loop through a pretty riparian area; pick up the trail guide at the Visitor Center. The Hamburg Trail goes through the preserve one mile, then continues a short way to an overlook (elev. 6,220 feet) in the Coronado National Forest. Visitors to the preserve should first register at the Visitor Center. A gift shop has hiking maps and an excellent selection of natural history and regional books. You must call to obtain a parking reservation for weekends or holidays; no reservations are needed for a weekday visit. Groups should always obtain advance permission. The small parking area cannot accommodate RVs or trailers. Don't bring pets. No picnicking or camping. Visitors can stay in rental cabins at The Mile Hi, $60 d ($360 d per week); write RR 1, Box 84, Hereford, AZ 85615; tel. 378-2785. **Ramsey Canyon Bed & Breakfast,** just outside the preserve, offers rooms starting at $57.75; tel. 378-3010. The preserve is 4 miles up Ramsey Canyon Road from AZ 92; the turnoff is 6 miles south of Sierra Vista.

### Coronado National Memorial

Francisco Vasquez Coronado marched through this area in 1540 in search of the Seven Cities of Cíbola. Although his backers judged the quest a failure, it was the first major European expedition into the American Southwest. Both this park in the Huachuca Mountains and the adjacent National Forest are named in honor of Coronado.

The Visitor Center, staffed by National Park Service rangers, has history, plant, and wildlife exhibits; open daily 8 a.m.-5 p.m.; tel. 458-9333. A nature walk outside introduces local flora. There's a picnic area nearby but no campground. In April the memorial hosts the **Coronado International Pageant**—a day of Apache, Pima, Mexican, and Western dancing with music and crafts. The turnoff for Coronado National Memorial is about midway between Sierra Vista and Bisbee on AZ 92. The Visitor Center is 4.5 miles in; Montezuma Pass is another 4 miles and 1,300 feet higher on a gravel road. You can also take the back roads (mostly dirt or gravel) from Patagonia or Nogales. Snowstorms occasionally close the pass in winter.

Outstanding views of Arizona and Mexico stretch to the horizon from the top of 6,864-foot Coronado Peak, reached by the 0.5-mile **Coronado Peak Trail** from Montezuma Pass; the path ascends 280 feet with many shaded benches for resting. Signs describe Coronado's expedition and natural features of the Huachuca Mountains. **Joe's Canyon Trail,** 3.1 miles one way, connects Montezuma Pass with the Visitor Center in the valley below; elevation change is 1,300 feet. You can reach Miller Peak (9,466 feet), the highest point in the Huachuca Mountains, on the **Miller Peak Trail,** a 12-mile roundtrip hike north from Montezuma Pass. This is the southernmost section of the **Arizona Trail,** which continues generally northward across the state. **Coronado Cave Trail** winds up the hillside behind the Visitor Center (check in here first) to a limestone cave with some formations; the first 0.25 mile is gentle, followed by a steep 0.5 mile to the cave entrance; elevation gain is 470 feet.

### Parker Canyon Lake

This 153-acre fishing lake east of the Huachucas is a rarity in a land of little surface water. Trout are stocked in the cooler months to join the year-round population of bass, bluegill, sunfish, and catfish. **Lakeview Campground** (elev. 5,400 feet) is open all year with drinking water but no showers or hookups; $3 day use, $5 camping. **Parker Canyon Lodge** nearby offers cabin rentals. A **marina** has groceries, fishing supplies, licenses, boat ramp, and boat rentals. You can rent a canoe, rowboat, or boat with electric motor. A 4.5-mile hiking trail goes around the lake. Parker Canyon Lake is 28 miles south of Sonoita on AZ 83, 23 miles southwest of Sierra Vista, and 15 miles northwest of Coronado National Memorial.

## BISBEE

Squeezed into Mule Pass Gulch, the old mining town of Bisbee is one of Arizona's most unusual towns. A tiny mining camp in 1877, Bisbee grew into a solid and wealthy town by 1910. The fine Victorian houses built in the boom years remain, so a visit to Bisbee is a step back in time. Brewery Gulch, a side canyon with more than 50 saloons in the early 1900s, earned a reputation for the best drinking and entertainment in the territory. Bisbee's riches, mostly copper ore, came from underground chambers and giant surface pits—tours now take visitors to both types. Bisbee is in the Mule Mountains, 24 miles south of Tombstone and 95 miles southeast of Tucson.

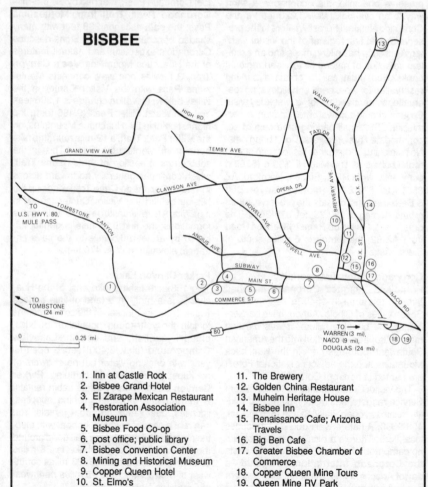

**BISBEE**

1. Inn at Castle Rock
2. Bisbee Grand Hotel
3. El Zarape Mexican Restaurant
4. Restoration Association Museum
5. Bisbee Food Co-op
6. post office; public library
7. Bisbee Convention Center
8. Mining and Historical Museum
9. Copper Queen Hotel
10. St. Elmo's
11. The Brewery
12. Golden China Restaurant
13. Muheim Heritage House
14. Bisbee Inn
15. Renaissance Cafe; Arizona Travels
16. Big Ben Cafe
17. Greater Bisbee Chamber of Commerce
18. Copper Queen Mine Tours
19. Queen Mine RV Park

© MOON PUBLICATIONS

## History

The story of Bisbee began over 100 million years ago, when a giant mass of molten rock deep in the earth's crust expelled great quantities of steam and hot water. These mineral-rich solutions slowly worked their way upward and replaced the overlying limestone rock with rich copper ores. While looking for silver in 1875, Hugh Jones became the first to discover minerals here, but annoyed to find only copper, he soon left. Two years later, Jack Dunn, an Army scout, also found ore. He couldn't leave his Army duties to go prospecting, so he and his partners made a deal with George Warren to establish a claim and share the profits. Warren, a tough old prospector and heavy drinker, "lost" Dunn's grubstake in a saloon while on the way the Mule Mountains. Warren quickly found new backers—Dunn and his partners not among them—and filed claims. Two years later he recklessly put his share on a wager that he could outrun a man on horseback, then lost everything. Warren died penniless, but the town south of Bisbee takes its name from him. The new electrical industries needed copper, and investors became interested in Warren's camp. Judge DeWitt Bisbee and a group of San Francisco businessmen bought the Copper Queen Mine in 1880, although the judge never did visit the mining community named for him. From the East, Dr. James Douglas of the Phelps Dodge Company came to Arizona and purchased property near the Copper Queen. After the two companies discovered that the richest ores lay on the property boundary, they merged rather than fight it out in court. A smelter filled the valley with smoke and the clatter of machinery. Streets were paved and substantial buildings went up. Labor troubles between newly formed unions and mine management culminated in the infamous Bisbee Deportation. In July 1917, more than 1,000 striking miners were herded at gunpoint into boxcars and shipped out of the state. Working conditions improved in the following years, but Bisbee's economic life rolled with copper prices. The giant Lavender Pit closed in 1974, when the rich ore bodies finally ran out, and underground mining ended the following year. The district had provided more than 8 billion pounds of copper! The town wasn't about to dry up and blow away, though. People liked it here—the climate (elev. 5,300 feet), the scenery, the character. Bisbee is

*Bisbee and the Mule Mountains*

*early Bisbee smelter*

now popular with visitors and retired people. Although mining has ended, a small leaching and precipitation operation continues to recover copper from waste ore.

## SIGHTS

You can learn the history of the many early 1900s buildings in town with the chamber of commerce's *Bisbee Walking Tour* pamphlet.

### Mining And Historical Museum

Mining dioramas, old photos, and artifacts illustrate life in Bisbee's early years. Open daily 10 a.m.-4 p.m.; $2 adult, free for age 18 and under; tel. 432-7071. The Shattuck Memorial Archival Library inside has extensive material on local history. The museum and library are housed in the former Phelps Dodge General Office Building (1897) in Queen Plaza downtown.

### Copper Queen Mine

Don a hard hat, lamp, and yellow slicker for a ride deep underground on a miner's tram. A guide, probably a miner himself, will issue the equipment and lead you through the mine. He'll explain about history, drilling tools, blasting methods, ore loading, and other mining features in the stope (work area) and tunnels. The mine, in use for over 60 years, shut down in 1943. Its four levels have 147 miles of passageways. The whole district has over 2,000 miles of them! The tour is highly recommended; bring a sweater or jacket as it's cold inside (47° F). There are some steps to the stope area but the rest of the walk is level. The 1- to 1½-hour tour leaves daily at 10:30 a.m., noon, 2 p.m., and 3:30 p.m.; $5 adult, $3 children 7-11, and $1.50 children 3-6; you'll get a discount if you take the tour with one of the others (see below); tel. 432-2071. Buy tickets at the Queen Mine Building, just south of downtown off US 80.

### Lavender Open Pit

A total of 380 million tons of ore and waste has been scooped out of this giant hole, which can be viewed from a parking area off US 80, one mile south of downtown. Press the button for a recorded description of the geology and mining of the Lavender Pit. A tour of the pit and still-operating leaching facilities is given daily at noon from the Queen Mine Building; 1½ hours; $4.

### Historic Bisbee Tour
See and learn about the historic districts of Bisbee and Warren. A guide tells the history and stories of the area; stops are made at viewpoints. Tours leave the Queen Mine Building daily at 10:30 a.m., 2 p.m., and 3:30 p.m.; 1½ hours; $4.

### Restoration Association Museum
You can see the old clothing, household items, and mining gear used by Bisbee's early settlers. Usually open Mon.-Sat. 10 a.m.-noon and 1-3 p.m.; closed Sun. and holidays; free. The museum is downtown at 37 Main Street.

### Muheim Heritage House
Tours lead visitors through this restored and furnished dwelling. Open Fri.-Mon. 1-4 p.m.; tours are by appointment; tel. 432-4461/7071; $1; at 207 Youngblood Hill (see map).

## PRACTICALITIES

### Accommodations And Campgrounds
The **Copper Queen Hotel** has been *the* place to stay since its construction in 1902 by the Copper Queen Mining Company. Rooms

differ in size and features, but all have been attractively restored and furnished in a 1940s style. John Wayne once stayed here, and his room has been the most popular since. The hotel has a saloon, gift shop, and swimming pool. Rooms cost $47-99 d; reservations: Box Drawer CQ, Bisbee, AZ 85603; tel. 432-2216 or (800) 247-5829 in state. This elegant four-story hotel is downtown on Howell Ave., behind the Mining and Historical Museum. The **Bisbee Inn** offers bed and breakfast in a restored hotel, formerly the LaMore, opened in 1917. Baths are shared; $31.76 s, $42.71 d; (no smoking, no pets). Make reservations at Box 1855, Bisbee, AZ 85603; tel. 432-5131; downtown at 45 OK Street, overlooking Brewery Gulch. The **Bisbee Grand Hotel** provides a "romantic getaway" in a 1909 building restored in a Victorian motif. Features include a Western saloon, ladies' parlor, and a small theater. Rooms, two with private bath, cost $49-87 d including a continental breakfast; reservations: Box 825, Bisbee, AZ 85603; tel. 432-5900; downtown at 61 Main Street. The **Inn at Castle Rock** has bed & breakfast in a former miners' boarding house. Rooms, all with private bath, start at $35 s, $45 d; reservations: Box 1161, Bisbee, AZ 85603; tel. 432-7195; 112 Tombstone Canyon Road. The **Oliver House,** built in 1906 as a hotel for mining executives, offers rooms with shared baths; $41.24 d; reservations:

*riding the "mule" into the Copper Queen Mine*

*a faro game running full blast at the Orient Saloon, Bisbee in 1903*

*Old-timers say, "Them damn good days have gone forever."*

Box 1897, Bisbee, AZ 85603; tel. 432-4286; located in Copper Queen Plaza. Several other small bed and breakfasts are in the area; see the chamber of commerce.

**El Rancho Hometel** offers kitchenettes (from $25.75 s, $30.65 d) and RV sites with showers ($10.75; tenters can stay too) at 1104 Hwy. 92, southwest of town; tel. 432-5969. **San Jose Lodge and RV Park** has motel rooms ($34.40 s, $37.63 d) with a swimming pool and 26 RV spaces ($12.93 w/hookups) situated 6 miles southwest of Bisbee at 1002 Naco Highway; tel. 432-5761. **Queen Mine RV Park** features great views and a central location; RVers and tenters can stay for $8 (no hookups) or $12 (w/hookups); has showers; take the road to Copper Queen Mine Tours and continue a short way up the hill; tel. 432-5006. **Shady Dell RV Park** has sites for tents and RVs ($8 no hookups, $11 w/hookups) and showers at 1 Douglas Road, behind the Chevron station near the traffic circle; tel. 432-7305. **Double Adobe Trailer Park** offers tent spaces ($3.50), RV sites ($8 w/hookups), and rental trailers ($12 d); has showers. Take US 80 east 4 miles toward Douglas, then turn left 4 miles on Double Adobe Road; tel. 364-9976.

### Food

The **Copper Queen Hotel's** restaurant has continental and American cuisine for breakfast, lunch, and dinner. **Renaissance Cafe,** next to the Lyric Theatre, offers sandwiches, pizza, and subs. The nearby **Big Ben Cafe** turns out meat pies, quiches, soups, sandwiches, and coffees. Dine Chinese at **Golden China,** 15 Brewery Gulch. **Café Maxi** serves American fare for breakfast, lunch, and dinner daily in the Bisbee Convention Center, across from the Mining and Historical Museum; tel. 432-7063. **Lillie's Cafe,** 4.5 miles south of town on AZ 92 (near turnoff for Naco), is a popular spot with locals. The **Outback** is north of Bisbee over Mule Pass, serving seafood, beef, and other dishes with a European touch; open Wed.-Sat. for dinner, and Sun. for brunch; tel. 432-2333 (reservations suggested). Buy natural foods at **Bisbee Food Co-op** downtown at 22 Main Street. **Safeway** supermarket is out of town at the turnoff for Naco.

### Shopping

Bisbee's mines have also yielded turquoise and other beautiful copper minerals. Several shops downtown sell stones set in silver as well as loose and rough stones. Another shop is at the Lavender Pit overlook. See paintings, ceramics, and other work of local artists in art shops downtown.

### Entertainment

Contact the chamber of commerce to find out what's playing in town. The **Bisbee Grand Theater** offers old and new melodramas and other pieces, usually Fri. and Sat. evenings and Sun. afternoons; tel. 432-5900. The

**Copper Queen Hotel's Saloon** has live easy-listening music Thurs.-Sat. evenings. For a variety of music, try the **Brewery** in Brewery Gulch Wed.-Saturday. **St. Elmo's**, also in Brewery Gulch, has country and rock music on some weekends.

## Events

**Vuelta de Bisbee** is a challenging multistage bicycle race held in April. Runners tackle the **Mule Mountain Marathon's** full 26-mile distance from Bisbee to Fort Huachuca or run shorter lengths in May. Rockhounds come to town for the **Bisbee Mineral Show** in October. The **Bisbee Home Tour** and **Holiday Market** mark the start of the holiday season on the weekend after Thanksgiving. Art festivals and other special events take place through the year; check with the chamber of commerce for dates.

## Recreation, Services, And Information

**Bisbee Golf Course** has nine holes and a restaurant off the Naco Hwy., 4.5 miles south of AZ 92; tel. 432-3091. **Copper Queen Community Hospital** is at Bisbee Road and Cole Ave., 3 miles south in Warren; tel. 432-5383. The **post office** and **city library** are at 6 Main St. in downtown Bisbee. The **Greater Bisbee Chamber of Commerce** is at 10 OK St. (Box BA, Bisbee, AZ 85603); open Mon.-Fri. 9 a.m.-5 p.m. and Sat. and Sun. 9 a.m.-2 p.m.; tel. 432-2141.

## Transport

**Bridgewater Transport** provides bus service to the Tucson airport and Greyhound station and to Sierra Vista and Douglas; purchase tickets from Arizona Travel next to the Lyric Theatre (see map); tel. 432-5359. For a taxi, call **Sun Arizona** at 432-5757.

## Vicinity Of Bisbee

**Naco** is a sleepy Mexican border town just 9 miles south of Bisbee. There's little to see or do here; the Mexican side is much like rural communities of interior Mexico. **Transportes Norte de Sonora (TNS)** buses will take you to Hermosillo, Juarez, Nogales, Casas Grandes, and other Mexican destinations.

# DOUGLAS AND AGUA PRIETA

The prettiest sight in Douglas, some residents used to say, was the billowing steam and smoke from the giant copper smelter just west of town. The busy ore-processing plant meant jobs. In 1900, the Phelps Dodge Company, finding Bisbee's smelter too small and inconvenient to handle ores from recently purchased mines in Mexico, began looking for a new smelter site in the Sulphur Springs Valley. They chose this spot and named the new town for Dr. James Douglas, president of the company. Douglas and its sister town in Mexico, Agua Prieta, boomed when prices of copper were high and suffered when they were low. Mexican government troops battled it out in Agua Prieta with revolutionaries—Captain "Red" Lopez in 1911 and Pancho Villa in 1915. Pancho Villa even made threats against the town of Douglas before retreat-

*Dr. James Douglas*

ing. An international airport—part of the runway was in the United States and part in Mexico—opened here in 1928.

Smokestacks of the Phelps Dodge smelter puffed their last in Jan. 1987, but the two cities have diversified into other industries. American companies operate manufacturing plants in Agua Prieta under the "twin plant" concept, using Mexico's inexpensive labor to assemble American products. With these new opportunities, Agua Prieta's population has tripled in the last 10 years to more than 75,000. Douglas (pop. 15,000) and Agua Prieta have few "sights," but many visitors and retired people choose Douglas as a base to explore the historic and scenic places nearby in Arizona and Mexico. The chamber of commerce has a self-guided driving-tour leaflet of historic sites in Douglas. Pioneer and Indian artifacts can be seen in a tiny **museum** in Room 3 of The Bakery Bldg., 1116 G Ave.; open Mon.-Fri. 10 a.m.-noon and 2-4 p.m.

## Accommodations

The massive five-story **Gadsden Hotel** dominates downtown Douglas and is a sight in itself. Built in 1907 and rebuilt in 1928, the hotel calls itself "the last of the grand hotels." The lobby has massive marble columns decorated with 14-kt gold leaf supporting a vault-ed ceiling with stained-glass panels. A Tiffany stained-glass mural 42 feet long decorates one wall of the mezzanine, reached by an Italian white marble staircase. Over 200 authentic cattle brands embellish the walls of the Saddle and Spur Lounge, just off the lobby. Rooms cost $27.38-93.08 s, $29.57-93.08 d; 1046 G Ave., Douglas, AZ 85607; tel. 364-4481. Douglas also has a Motel 6, a Travelodge, and several other motels.

**Price Canyon Ranch,** a working cattle ranch on the southeastern slopes of the Chiricahuas (elev. 5,600 feet), features horseback riding. Guests stay in bunkhouses ($80 s, $150 d including meals and riding) or the campground ($6 tent, $8 RV w/hookups); pack trips in the mountains can be arranged with at least one month's notice. Other activities include fishing, hiking, and birdwatching. Price Canyon Ranch is 42 miles northeast on US 80, then left 7 miles on Price Canyon Road (Box 1065, Douglas, AZ 85607); open year-round; tel. 558-2383.

## Campgrounds

RV parks on the north side of town include **Douglas Trailer Village** (1206 21st St.; tel. 364-4326); **Saddle Gap RV Park** (Hwy. 80 and Washington; tel. 364-5863); **Douglas Golf and Social Club** (Leslie Canyon Road; tel. 364-3722); and **Hidden Valley Mobile**

Gadsden Hotel lobby

**Rancho** (1900 N. G Ave.; tel. 364-9651); **Double Adobe Trailer Park** offers tent spaces, RV sites, and rental trailers 17.5 miles northwest (head west 8.5 miles on Double Adobe Road from US 666); tel. 364-9976.

## Food

The **Gadsden Hotel** has a Mexican-American restaurant, 1046 G Ave.; tel. 364-4481. **La Fiesta Cafe** is famed for its fine Mexican food, 524 Eighth St.; tel. 364-5854. Several other Mexican restaurants are scattered around town, and Agua Prieta has more. **Lee Garden** offers a variety of Chinese cuisines (closed Mon.), 1929 A Ave.; tel. 364-3583. You'll pass Burger King, McDonald's, and Pizza Hut on the west side of town on US 80.

## Events

**Two Flags International Festival of the Arts** on the third weekend in Jan. features a parade, art exhibits, entertainment, food, grand ball, 10-K run, and other events. The **July Fourth Celebration** has a parade, entertainment, car show, games, dance, and fireworks at Veteran Park. The **Labor Day Golf Tournament** in Sept. has been running longer than any other invitational golf tournament in the state. **Douglas Fiestas Celebration** in mid-Sept. honors Mexican independence with a ballet folklorico, mariachis, talent show, games, and food at Veteran Park. **Cochise County Fair** presents an intercollegiate rodeo, livestock exhibits, carnival, and other entertainment on the third weekend of Sept. at Cochise County Fairgrounds on Leslie Canyon Road.

## Shopping

Shops just across the border in Agua Prieta sell **Mexican crafts,** but on a much smaller scale than in Nogales. The Douglas Chamber of Commerce promotes this as "leisurely shopping," because nearly everything is fixed price. Arizona artists exhibit in the **Little Gallery** in Douglas, Pan American Ave. at 11th St., near the chamber of commerce; open Tues.-Sat. 1:30-4 p.m., closed July and Aug.; tel. 364-2633.

## Recreation And Services

**Veterans Park** has picnic tables, playground, outdoor pool, tennis, basketball, and ball fields at Dolores Ave. and Sixth St.; tel. 364-7038 (pool) or 364-4058 (Parks and Recreation Dept.). **Casey Park** is a smaller area with picnic tables and playground at 15th St. and Carmelita (near a pair of water towers). **Douglas Golf and Social Club** has nine holes northeast of town off Leslie Canyon Road; tel. 364-3722.

The **post office** is at the corner of 10th St. and F Avenue. **Southeast Arizona Medical Center** is 4 miles west of town on US 80, then north on County Road N.; tel. 364-7931.

No permits are needed to visit Agua Prieta. For longer trips into Mexico, obtain papers at the border station or in Douglas at the **Consulado de Mexico,** 515 10th St. at G Ave.; tel. 364-2275. Mexican auto insurance (highly recommended) is sold by **Sanborn's** (San Xavier Insurance Agency), 533 11th St.; tel. 364-2411 and by **Jones Associates,** 561 10th St. at F Ave.; tel. 364-8496.

## Information

The **Douglas Chamber of Commerce** is very helpful and has a good selection of maps and brochures. Office is located at 1125 Pan American Ave. at 12th St. (Douglas, AZ 85607); open Mon.-Fri. 9 a.m.-5 p.m.; tel. 364-2477. **Douglas Ranger Station** of the Coronado National Forest can tell you about camping, hiking, and back roads of the Chiricahua and Dragoon mountains; open Mon.-Fri. 7:30 a.m.-4:30 p.m.; Rt. 1, Box 228R, Leslie Canyon Road, Douglas, AZ 85607 (from US 80 just northeast of town, turn north on Leslie Canyon Road, then take the first right); tel. 364-3468. The **public library** is at 625 10th St. (between E and F aves.); tel. 364-3851.

## Transport

**Bridgewater Transport** buses go several times daily to Tucson's airport and Greyhound station with stops en route at Bisbee and Sierra Vista; 538 14th St. (between G and F aves.); tel. 364-2233. In Agua Prieta, **Transportes Norte de Sonora (TNS)** heads out to

Cananea, Nogales, Hermosillo, Ciudad Obregon, Tijuana, Guadalajara, and Mexico City. A train also goes to Nogales, but the bus is easier and faster. Rent cars from **Sun Valley**, 8 miles west on AZ 80; tel. 364-2485. For taxi service, call **Gadsden Taxi**; tel. 364-5555.

## VICINITY OF DOUGLAS

### Douglas Wildlife Park
Established for propagation of exotic animals and birds, the collection is now open to the public. Drop in to see parrots, peacocks, emus, deer, lemurs, apes, and other creatures of distant lands. Open daily 10 a.m.-5 p.m. except major holidays; $2.75 adult, $1.75 children 3-12; tel. 364-2515. From Douglas, head west 2.5 miles on US 80 to just past the Ford dealership, then turn north 1.7 miles on Plantation Road.

### Slaughter Ranch
John Slaughter, a former Texas Ranger, arrived in southeast Arizona in 1884. He purchased the 93,000-acre San Bernardino Ranch, then developed it over the next 30 years. His 1890s house, corral, and other structures have been restored to show what ranch life was like in territorial Arizona at the

turn of the century. Rooms have period furniture and photo exhibits of Slaughter's colorful career. Another section of the ranch has become the 2,330-acre San Bernardino National Wildlife Refuge (closed to public at press time). Ranch exhibits are open daily 10 a.m.-3 p.m.; $2 adult; tel. 558-2474. From Douglas, head east 16 miles on 15th St., which becomes the Geronimo Trail, to the ranch gateway.

## CHIRICAHUA MOUNTAINS

Rising from dry grasslands, the Chiricahua ("chee-ree-KAH-wah") Mountains are a wonderland of rock formations, spectacular views, diverse plant and animal life, and a variety of hiking trails. Volcanic rock, fractured by slow uplift of the region, has eroded into strangely shaped forms. Heavier weathering at the base of some columns leaves giant boulders balanced delicately on pedestals. The Chiricahuas harbor a unique mix of Mexican and Southwestern flora and fauna. Birders come to view coppery-tailed trogons, hummingbirds, and the many other species. Chiricahua Apache and other tribes once hid among the pinnacles and canyons while planning attacks on early European settlements on the plains below. Raids and

*Sugarloaf Mountain (on left) from Sara Deming Canyon Trail, Chiricahua National Monument*

*Cochise, from Cozzens' 1873*
*The Marvellous Country*

skirmishes with the white man lasted until 1886, when Geronimo surrendered.

Chiricahua National Monument has the most spectacular erosional features; a scenic drive and many trails provide easy access. Chiricahua Wilderness, to the south, protects the highest summits of the range, including 9,796-foot Chiricahua Peak. A narrow mountain road crosses the range from near the entrance of the national monument on the west side to Portal on the east side; it's not recommended for trailers and is usually closed by snow in winter. Fort Bowie National Historic Site lies just north of the Chiricahuas; take the gravel road south from Bowie or northeast from AZ 186.

## CHIRICAHUA NATIONAL MONUMENT

In 1924, President Calvin Coolidge signed a bill making the most scenic part of the mountains a national monument. The entrance is 70 miles north of Douglas, 36 miles southeast of Willcox, and 120 miles east of Tucson. *Be sure to fill up with gas before coming out, as no supplies are near the monument.*

### Visitor Center
A short slide show introduces the monument and its sightseeing possibilities. Exhibits illustrate the geology, ecology, wildlife, Chiricahua Apache, and early ranching in the area. Rangers can answer questions and advise on road and hiking conditions. Campfire programs are held mid-March to mid-Sept.; check for times. Other naturalist programs may be scheduled too. Books, prints, posters, videos, maps, and other items are sold. Open daily 8 a.m.-5 p.m.; tel. 824-3560. A $3/car entry fee is collected on the way in.

### Bonita Canyon Drive
This 6-mile paved mountain road from the Visitor Center climbs through Bonita Canyon to Massai Point (elev. 6,870 feet), where you'll see a geology exhibit and sweeping views. A short nature trail and longer day hikes start here. Look north to see the profile of Cochise Head. Winter storms can close the road, but snowplows come out as soon as a storm is over.

### Hiking
The Chiricahuas are best appreciated on foot, whether on a short nature trail or an extended hike. Pace yourself to allow for the altitude and rough terrain. Carry water on longer trips. Thunderstorms often build up in July and August; if caught, stay low and avoid exposed areas. Watch for rattlesnakes, too; this is their most active season, though they're also out in spring and autumn. You can hike any time of the year, but conditions are usually ideal from March to May and Oct. to November. Snow sometimes blocks trails from Dec. to February. Monument trails are for dayhikes only (no permit needed). Camping is restricted to the campground near the Visitor Center, but many backpack trips are possible in the nearby Coronado National Forest. Horseback riding is permitted in the monument, but rangers like to be told if horses are brought in. Maps sold at the Visitor Center include a Chiricahua recreation topo map with hiking trails, a geologic map, and a Coronado National Forest map. You can ride to the high country on the **hikers' shuttle,** then walk downhill back to the Visitor Center; the shuttle (supported by donations) operates daily March to Sept. and weekends in winter; check at the Visitor Center for times.

*"kissing rocks," Heart of Rocks Trail*

## Trails

The free monument brochure has a map showing all the trails. **Faraway Meadow Trail** is an easy 1.2-mile walk between Faraway Ranch and the Visitor Center. The path winds through lush vegetation watered by a small seasonal stream. It's a good place for bird-watching. A short side trail leads to the campground. The **Rhyolite Canyon Nature Trail,** beside the Visitor Center, is an easy 0.3-mile, self-guided trail that introduces local plant life; pick up a trail guide from the Visitor Center. Birdwatching is good here too. Learn about local geology and some of the higher elevation plants on the 0.5-mile **Massai Point Trail,** at the end of the drive.

The most impressive scenery awaits hikers on the Echo Canyon Loop and Heart of Rocks trails. **Echo Canyon Trail** winds through spectacular rock formations in a 3.5-mile loop; begin from Echo Park or Massai Point trailheads, both near the end of Massai Point Drive. **Heart of Rocks Trail** passes famous rock formations—Punch & Judy, Duck on a Rock, Big Balanced Rock, and others—on a 7-mile out-and-back trip from Massai Point. With half a day, you can make a 9-mile loop by returning on the **Sarah Deming** and **Echo Canyon** trails. **Inspiration Point** is a one-mile roundtrip excursion off Heart of Rocks Trail with views over the whole length of Rhyolite Canyon. You could also hike all the way down to the Visitor Center via **Rhyolite Canyon Trail. Sugarloaf Mountain** (elev. 7,307 feet) is the highest in the monument, with great views over Arizona, New Mexico, and the Chiricahuas. It's a 2-mile roundtrip hike to the summit from the Sugarloaf trailhead. **Natural Bridge Trail,** off Bonita Canyon Drive, offers pleasant but less spectacular hiking to a small rock bridge—actually a fallen rock column—2.5 miles from the road.

## Faraway Ranch

Members of the Erickson family lived on this ranch for 91 years before its purchase in 1979 by the National Park Service. Rangers lead tours through the old ranch house and other buildings daily in spring and summer, then some weekends off-season, and they tell you about the family, ranch life, and the surrounding region. You're welcome to visit the grounds during daylight hours any time of the year; signs relate stories about the ranch. Faraway Ranch is 1.5 miles west of the Visitor Center by road, then 0.25 mile in on foot, or you can take the 1.2-mile Faraway Meadow Trail from the Visitor Center or campground.

## Campgrounds And Services

**Bonita Campground,** 0.5 mile from the Visitor Center, costs $5 (no hookups or showers); trailers to 26 feet OK. Another possibility is to drive up Pinery Canyon Road into the Coronado National Forest. The turnoff for Pinery Canyon is on the right just outside the monument. Look for a likely spot after about 6 miles; no water or facilities; no charge. The nearest supplies and accommodations are 26 miles southeast in Sunizona, at the junction of AZ 181 and US 666, or farther west in Pearce and Sunsites. Willcox, 36 miles north of the monument, also has motels, restaurants, stores, and trailer parks.

## CHIRICAHUA WILDERNESS AND VICINITY

The national forest has many hiking and horseback trails. A scenic mountain road crosses the range through Pinery Canyon (on the west) to Onion Saddle (7,600 feet) and continues east to Cave Creek Canyon and Portal. The road is narrow and bumpy (mostly unpaved) but OK for cautiously driven cars. Snow and fallen trees may close the road from Dec. to March or April. A side road from Onion Saddle goes south along a ridge and climbs to Rustler Park (8,400 feet), usually closed in winter. From here, hikers can take the **Crest Trail** south to Chiricahua Peak (9,796 feet), a wilderness area and highest point in the range. Many other trails branch off in all directions. Forest trails in the Chiricahua Mountains total about 111 miles, but their conditions differ greatly. Trail locations and lengths are shown on the Chiricahua Mountains Trail and Recreation topo map (scale 1:62,500), available at Tucson hiking stores, some Forest Service offices, and Chiricahua National Monument. The Coronado National Forest (Douglas Ranger District) map shows trails but lacks contour lines and fine detail. *Arizona Trails* by David Mazel is a good source for trail descriptions of the Chiricahua Wilderness.

### Campgrounds
The Coronado National Forest has 15 campgrounds; see the national forest map for locations, seasons, and facilities. A $5-6 camp fee (half price for day use) is charged for sites with water; others are free. No permits are needed for backpacking or hiking.

## FORT BOWIE NATIONAL HISTORIC SITE

When the Butterfield Stagecoach line began to carry mail and passengers from Missouri to California in 1858, a station was built at a spring near Apache Pass. Although it was in the middle of Indian country, Cochise and his Chiricahua Apache allowed the station and stage to operate unhindered. All this changed 2½ years later when Second Lt. George Bascom falsely accused Cochise of kidnaping and theft. Troops attempted to capture Cochise by trickery, but the Indian chief escaped. Both sides executed hostages, and the war was on. Life became precarious for settlers and travelers. Cochise was determined to kill or drive all white men from the region. Unfortunately for the settlers, many Army troops left Arizona to fight the Civil War in the East.

On July 15, 1862, Brig. Gen. James Carleton and his California Column, on their way

*Fort Bowie, 1885*

Fort Bowie, 1985

to meet the threat posed by the Confederate invasion of New Mexico, were attacked by Indians at Apache Pass. Carleton fended them off, but he saw the need for a fort and had Fort Bowie constructed within the month. Indian raids continued until 1872, when Cochise made peace with the Army in exchange for reservation land. However, bad management by the Indian Bureau, followed by the government's taking back the reservation, was too much for some of the Apache. Cochise had died while at peace on the reservation, but Geronimo, the wily Apache leader, took bands of followers into Mexico in 1881 and started new raids. Army cavalry and scouts from Fort Bowie sought out the elusive Indians. Geronimo's small band was the last to surrender, 5 years later, ending Arizona's Indian wars. The fort was abandoned Oct. 17, 1894.

**Visiting The Fort**
Modern highways have bypassed the area. Only crumbling ruins and memories remain. The National Park Service maintains the historic site and a ranger station with a few exhibits; open daily 8 a.m.-5 p.m. Signs identify the fort buildings, the stage-station site, and battle and massacre locations. Old photos show how the fort appeared in its heyday.

To preserve the historic setting, visitors must approach the site by foot. From the main road, follow a 1.5-mile, one-way trail past the stage-station site, a cemetery, Battle of Apache Pass site, and Apache Spring to the extensive ruins of Fort Bowie. From the town of Bowie, on I-10, drive 12 miles south on a gravel road; parking is on the right, trailhead on the left. From Willcox (22 miles west) or Chiricahua National Monument (25 miles south), take AZ 186 to Apache Pass Road, drive over the pass, then look for the signed parking on the left. In bad weather, Apache Pass Road can become slippery and is not recommended. The fort site has water but no camping facilities. Picnic tables are at the trailhead and fort.

## WILLCOX

Started in 1880 as a construction camp for the Southern Pacific Railroad, Willcox became a supply and shipping point for local ranchers. Agriculture continues to be the most important industry. Apples, peaches, cherries, grapes, pecans, and pistachios now supplement the mainstays of cattle, cotton, and small grains. Willcox (pop. 3,825), just off I-10, is a convenient base for visiting the scenic and historic sights of the area.

The **Willcox Chamber of Commerce** and **Museum of the Southwest** in Cochise Visitor Center have history exhibits, information desk, gift shop, and art gallery. Open Mon.-Sat. 9 a.m.-5 p.m. and Sun. 1-5 p.m.; free; take I- 10 Exit 340 (AZ 186), then turn northeast 0.5 mile on Circle I Road; tel. 384-2272. **Stouts Cider Mill,** near the Visitor Center, has products from local apple orchards.

### Rex Allen Arizona Cowboy Museum

Growing up on a homestead near Willcox, Rex Allen sang and played the guitar. His musical skills led him into the recording industry, then into movies. *Arizona Cowboy,* released in 1950, was the first of his many films; he also starred in the TV series "Frontier Doctor." Inside the museum, you'll see photos, movie posters, guitars, saddles, sequined cowboy suits, and a buggy used in "Frontier Doctor." Open Mon.-Sat. 10 a.m.-4 p.m. and Sun. 1-4 p.m.; small admission; tel. 384-4583. The museum building, originally a turn-of-the-century saloon, is at 150 N. Railroad Ave.—Willcox's main street in the old days. You'll see other historic structures nearby. **Wildwood Gallery** next door has a variety of works by local artists in an old bank building. The **Willcox Commercial Store** (1881) on the corner is the oldest commercial building in Arizona that's still in use in its original location. Geronimo used to shop here!

### Practicalities

Willcox has a good selection of motels, RV parks, and restaurants along the I-10 business route and off I-10 Exit 340 (AZ 186). **Rex Allen Days** honors Arizona's "Mr. Cowboy" on the first weekend of Oct. with a PRCA rodeo, Western music and dances, golf tournament, and other activities. **Keillor Park** has picnic tables, playground, outdoor pool, and tennis courts; from I-10 Exit 340, take Rex Allen Dr. one block toward downtown, then turn right one block on Bisbee Avenue. **Twin Lakes Country Club** has a nine-hole golf course south of downtown off Willcox Dr.; tel. 384-2720. The **post office** is at the corner of 200 S. Curtis Ave. and Grant Street. **North-**

ern **Cochise Community Hospital** is at 901 Rex Allen Dr.; tel. 384-3541. The **public library** and adjacent **Willcox Art Center** are at the corner of 450 W. Maley St. and Tucson Ave.; tel. 384-4271.

## VICINITY OF WILLCOX

### Frontier Relics

Orville Mickens has packed this small museum with historical artifacts from Fort Bowie and other places of the Southwest. Open irregular hours, so it's best to call first; tel. 384-3481. Located in Dos Cabezas about 14 miles southeast of Willcox on AZ 186, on the way to Chiricahua National Monument.

### Willcox Playa

This giant lake bed south of Willcox is visible from I-10. It covers 50-60 square miles. The playa is usually dry, but after heavy rains it becomes a shallow lake. You may see mirages on the surface in summer. As many as 10,000 sandhill cranes and smaller numbers of ducks and geese winter here.

### Cochise Stronghold Canyon

The canyon is set in a beautiful wooded area of towering pinnacles in the heart of the Dragoon Mountains, 30 miles southwest of Willcox. During the 15 years that the great Apache chief Cochise and about 250 warriors hid out here, no white person was safe in the valleys below. Cochise was never defeated in battle; he agreed to peace in 1872 only when land was promised for his tribe. The Dragoon Mountains take their name from the Third U.S. Cavalry Dragoons.

Today the mountains offer picnicking, hiking trails, and a campground that has water from early April to mid-Sept.; the campground costs $2.50 for day use or $5 for an overnight stay. A self-guided nature trail, starting from the south end of the campground, explains the diverse plant life and other features of the area. **Cochise Stronghold Trail** continues up the valley past Cochise Spring and Half-moon Tank to Stronghold Divide, 6 miles roundtrip. It's also possible to continue down the other side of the range into West Stronghold Canyon. A rough but scenic drive crosses the range to the south at Middlemarch Pass, connecting the ghost town of Pearce with Tombstone to the west.

## Amerind Foundation

Amateur archaeologist William Fulton started the Foundation in 1937 to increase the world's knowledge of American Indian cultures. The name comes from a contraction of American and Indian. Especially active in research of Southwest and Mexican archaeology, the Foundation has amassed an outstanding artifact collection, some of which can be seen here. The museum features archaeological and ethnographic exhibits of the native peoples of the Americas. The Amerind's art gallery displays paintings and sculptures by Indian and Anglo-American artists of the 19th and 20th centuries. A museum store sells artworks, crafts, and books of native American cultures. A picnic area is nearby. Open daily 10 a.m.-4 p.m. (closed major holidays); it's a good idea to call for summer hours; $3 adult, $2 age 12-18 and senior 60 and over; tel. 586-3666. The Foundation is housed in Spanish-colonial revival buildings among rock formations of Texas Canyon, 64 miles east of Tucson between Willcox and Benson; take I-10 Triangle T-Dragoon Exit 318, go southeast one mile, and turn left 0.75 mile at the sign.

# BENSON

Benson is 36 miles west of Willcox and 45 miles east of Tucson. The Butterfield Stage crossed the San Pedro River nearby in the early 1860s, but the town didn't really get going until the railroad arrived in 1880, filling its saloons with cowboys, miners, Mexicans, and Chinese. The community is quiet now and has motels, restaurants, and camp-grounds for travelers. **Benson Chamber of Commerce** has information about the town and area; open Mon.-Fri. 9 a.m.-4 p.m. at Oasis Court, 363 W. Fourth St. (Box 2255, Benson, AZ 85602); tel. 586-2842.

## San Pedro Valley
## Arts And Historical Museum

Photos and artifacts show life in the early railroad, mining, and ranching days. Local handmade crafts are sold. Open Tues.-Fri. 10 a.m.-4 p.m. and Sat. 10 a.m.-2 p.m.; in summer hours are 9 a.m.-2 p.m., same days; free. From Fourth St., the main street through downtown, turn one block south on San Pedro to the museum; tel. 586-3070.

## Kartchner Caverns State Park

Beautiful limestone formations, delicately tinted in yellows and reds, decorate this pristine cave system. Magnificent columns (up to 50 feet high), delicate soda straws (one is a quarter of an inch in diameter and 20 feet long!), shields, stalactites, stalagmites, and nearly every other type of cave formation grow in this living cave. Kartchner Caverns became Arizona's 25th state park in 1988. Because exceptional care is being taken to preserve the interior formations and environment, the first sections of the 2.5-mile-long cave won't open until about 1993. It's located just off AZ 90 about 16 miles south of Benson. Check with the main state park office in Phoenix (tel. 542-4174), other state parks, or local chambers of commerce to find out if the caves are open to the public.

## Singing Wind Bookshop

This unique shop, on a ranch near Benson, has an excellent selection of regional books and other titles. Open daily; tel. 586-2425. Go north 2.3 miles on Ocotillo Road (I-10 Exit 304) from town, then turn right 0.5 mile at the sign (there's a gate halfway in).

RATTLESNAKES HAVE RIGHT OF WAY

# BOOKLIST

## DESCRIPTION AND TRAVEL

Aitchison, Stewart. *A Guide to Exploring Oak Creek and the Sedona Area*. RNM Press, 1989; 109 pages plus a color-photo section, $12.95. A series of natural history driving tours with brief mentions of hiking trails.

Babbitt, Bruce, ed. *Grand Canyon: An Anthology*. Northland Press, 1978; 258 pages, $15.95. Twenty-three authors from the Spanish days to the present relate their experiences with the Grand Canyon.

Bogert, John, and Joan Bogert. *100 Best Restaurants in the Valley of the Sun*. Arizona Desert Minerals Co., 1990 (revised annually); 200+ pages, $3.95. Handy guide to many of the best-value restaurants in the Phoenix area.

Brown, Bonnie, and Carol D. Bracken. *The Complete Family Guide to Navajo-Hopi Land*. Self-published, 1986; 112 pages, $8.95. Handy guide for visiting the home of these tribes in the Four Corners region. Full of practical advice on shopping, services, and where to stay and eat.

Butler, Ron. *The Best of the Old West, An Indispensable Guide to the Vanishing Legend of the American West*. Texas Monthly Press, 1983; 229 pages, $9.95. A lively guide to the places and institutions where the West lives on—towns and ghost towns, saloons, museums, dude ranches etc.; covers the western states.

Casey, Robert L. *A Journey to the High Southwest*. Pacific Search Press, 1983; 401 pages, $14.95. Introduction, history, and travel in southern Utah and adjacent Arizona, New Mexico, and Colorado.

Cook, James E. *Arizona 101*. Cocinero Press, Box 11583, Phoenix, AZ 85061; 1981; 70 pages, $3.95. Enroll in this humorous and factual short study of Arizona.

Dutton, Allen A., and Diane Tayor Bunting. *Arizona Then and Now: A comprehensive Rephotographic Project*. Ag2 Press, Phoenix, AZ; 162 pages, $59. A photo album comparing old photographs with present-day scenes; enjoyable to flip through.

Hammons, Lee. *Mineral and Gem Localities in Arizona*. Arizona Maps and Books, Box 1133, Sedona, AZ; 1977; 112 pages. An introduction and 30 color maps cover the entire state, showing locations of rocks, minerals, gems, and fossils. It's written for both rockhounds and prospectors.

Hirsch, Bob, and Stan Jones. *Fishin' Lake Powell*. Sun Country Publications; 96 pages, $8.50. Helpful advice on where and how to catch Lake Powell's game fish.

Hoefer, Hans (and others). *American Southwest*. APA Insight Guides, 1984; 305 pages, $16.95. Outstanding color photography illustrates this travel guide of Arizona, New Mexico, and adjacent areas. Many authors have contributed to the fine text.

Klinck, Richard E. *Land of Room Enough and Time Enough*. Peregrine Smith Books, 1958, 1984; 136 pages, $10.95. The geography, legends, and peoples of Monument Valley.

Leydet, Francois. *Time and the River Flowing: Grand Canyon*. Sierra Club-Ballantine Books, 1968; 160 pages. Essays and color photos of the Grand Canyon.

Lockard, Peggy Hamilton. *This is Tucson, Guidebook to the Old Pueblo*. Pepper Publishing, 433 N. Tucson Blvd., Tucson, AZ 85716-4744; 1988; 305 pages, $9.95. Excellent guide to the culture, sights, and restaurants of Tucson and vicinity.

Loving, Nancy J., and Tom Bean. *Along the Rim: A Road Guide to the South Rim of Grand Canyon.* Grand Canyon Natural History Assoc., 1981; 53 pages, $2.95. Beautifully done booklet about the viewpoints, history, and ecology along the Rim Drive.

*The Official Visitors Guide to Metropolitan Tucson.* Tucson Convention and Visitors Bureau, 130 S. Scott Ave., Tucson, AZ 85701; tel. (602) 624-1817; updated annually; free.

*Phoenix-Scottsdale and Valley of the Sun in Arizona.* Visitors guide published by Phoenix and Valley of the Sun Convention and Visitors Bureau, 502 N. Second St., Suite 300, Phoenix, AZ 85004; tel. (602) 254-6500; revised annually; free.

Sherman, James, and Barbara Sherman. *Ghost Towns of Arizona.* University of Oklahoma Press, 1969; 208 pages, $16.95. Brief histories of about 130 ghost communities. Well illustrated with b/w photos, but maps are poor.

Story Behind the Scenery series: *Grand Canyon. Canyon de Chelly. Petrified Forest. Lake Mead-Hoover Dam.* KC Publications, Las Vegas, NV; 32 to 64 pages, $4.50. Introductions and beautiful color photos.

Tegler, Dorothy. *Retiring in Arizona.* Fiesta Books, Inc., Box 30555, Phoenix, AZ 85046; 1987; 173 pages, $9.95. Full of facts for choosing your area, then settling in.

Thollander, Earl. *Back Roads of Arizona.* Northland Press, 1978; $12.95. Attractive sketches illustrate this road guide to the scenic but seldom-traveled roads of the state. Edward Abbey wrote the introduction.

Varney, Philip. *Arizona's Best Ghost Towns: A Practical Guide.* Northland Press, 1980;

142 pages, $12.95. Explore the ruins of Arizona's boom and bust towns with this easy-to-use guide.

Wallace, Robert. *The Grand Canyon.* The American Wilderness/Time-Life Books, New York; 184 pages, $8.95. A well-illustrated book covering many aspects of the Canyon. Ernst Haas did the excellent photography.

Writers' Program of the WPA. *Arizona: A State Guide.* Hastings House, 1940, 1956; 530 pages. Recently reprinted under the title *WPA Guide to 1930's Arizona.* This classic guidebook is still good reading.

# HIKING, BICYCLING, AND SKIING

Aitchison, Stewart. *A Naturalist's Guide to Hiking the Grand Canyon.* Prentice-Hall, 1985; 172 pages, $8.95. The author introduces you to the Canyon's climates, geology, "critters," and plants, then takes you on 30 hikes. Good maps make the descriptions easy to follow.

Aitchison, Stewart. *Oak Creek Canyon and the Red Rock Country of Arizona, A Natural History and Trail Guide.* Stillwater Canyon Press, 1978; 142 pages. (Out of print but worth looking up in libraries.) A well-illustrated guide to back roads and 24 hiking trails of the Sedona area. You also learn about Indians, early settlers, geology, plants, and wildlife of the region.

Aitchison, Stewart, and Bruce Grubbs. *The Hiker's Guide to Arizona.* Falcon Press Publishing, Co., 1987; 157 pages, $9.95. One of the best all-around hiking guides to the state; the 60 hikes include a wide variety of regions and terrain.

Annerino, John. *Hiking the Grand Canyon.* A Sierra Club Totebook, Sierra Club Books, 1986; 340 pages and a map, $10.95. Easily the most comprehensive guide to trails and routes within the canyon. A long introduction provides background on geology, natural history, Indians, and how to plan your hike. The large fold-out topo map clearly shows trails and routes. River runners will be pleased to find a section of trail descriptions beginning from the water's edge.

Bower, Peter L. *Bicyclist's Guide to Arizona*. Phoenix Books, 1980; 80 pages, $4.95. Short rides in the Phoenix and Tucson areas and longer rides throughout the state; has advice on riding and equipment.

Bowman, Eldon. *A Guide to the General Crook Trail*. Museum of Northern Arizona Press and the Boy Scouts of America, 1978; 31 pages, $2.50. Trail guide for Crook's historic military road. The route begins in Camp Verde (northcentral Arizona) and goes east along the Mogollon Rim for 113 miles. The Boy Scouts and other groups cleared and remarked the trail as a bicentennial project.

Bremner, Dugald. *Ski Touring Arizona*. Northland Press, 1987; 135 pages, $11.95. Introduction and tour descriptions lead the way into the beautiful snow country of eastern, northern, and even southern Arizona. Detailed topo maps show the routes.

Butchart, Harvey. *Grand Canyon Treks: A Guide to the Inner Canyon Routes*. La Siesta Press, 1976; 72 pages, $3.50. The classic hiking guide to the Canyon; this is the most useful of Butchart's three books.

Butchart, Harvey. *Grand Canyon Treks II: A Guide to the Extended Canyon Routes*. La Siesta Press, 1975; 48 pages, $1.95. Butchart describes rarely used trails and routes of Marble Canyon and western Grand Canyon.

Butchart, Harvey. *Grand Canyon Treks III: Inner Canyon Journals*. La Siesta Press, 1984; 72 pages, $3.95. Additional material adds to his earlier books.

Coello, Dennis. *The Mountain Bike Manual*. Dream Garden Press, 1985; 125 pages. Pedal away from the crowds and pavement with this book. Introduction explains how to choose and maintain a mountain bicycle. You'll also learn how to pack and plan for long-distance tours.

Fletcher, Colin. *The Man Who Walked Through Time*. Random House, 1967; 239 pages, $4.95. Well-written adventure tale of Colin's 2-month solo hike through the Grand Canyon. He was the first to travel the entire length of the Park on foot.

Freeman, Roger, and Ethel Freeman. *Day Hikes and Trail Rides In and Around Phoenix*. Gem Guides Book Co., 1988; 237 pages plus a color-photo section, $12.95. The rugged Sonoran Desert that surrounds Arizona's biggest city offers excellent hiking and horseback riding. Detailed trail descriptions introduce the parks and wilderness areas.

Ganci, Dave. *Hiking the Southwest: Arizona, New Mexico, and West Texas*. Sierra Club Books, 1983; 408 pages, $10.95. A handy guide with a good introduction, practical hints, and a variety of trails.

Glending, Eber, and Pete Cowgill. *Trail Guide to the Santa Catalina Mountains*. Rainbow Expeditions, 915 S. Sherwood Village, Tucson, AZ 85710; 1987; 128 pages, $7.95. Handy guide to trails and routes of this range north of Tucson.

Kaibab National Forest. *Recreation Opportunity Guide (North Kaibab Ranger District)*. Southwest Natural and Cultural Heritage Assoc., Drawer E, Albuquerque, NM 87103; 1989; 113 pages, $5. Trails, scenic drives, camp and picnic areas, history, and wildlife of the beautiful forest country north of the Grand Canyon.

Kals, W.S. *Land Navigation Handbook*. Sierra Club Books, 1983; 230 pages, $8.95. After reading this book you'll be able to confidently explore Arizona's vast backcountry. This handy pocket guide not only has details on using map and compass, but tells how to do altimeter navigation and use the sun and stars.

Kelsey, Michael R. *Canyon Hiking Guide to the Colorado Plateau.* Kelsey Publishing, 1986; 256 pages, $9.95. Perhaps the best guide to hiking in the canyon country. Geologic cross-sections show the formations you'll be walking through. The book has descriptions and maps for 38 hikes in Arizona, 64 trips in adjacent Utah, 13 in Colorado, and 2 in New Mexico. The author is ahead of his time in using just the metric system, but the book is otherwise easy to follow.

McMoran, Charles W. *Hiking Trails of the Huachuca Mountains.* Livingston's Books, Sierra Vista, AZ 85635; 1981; 36 pages, $4.95. Useful guide to the peaks and canyons of the Huachucas in southeast Arizona.

Martin, Bob, and Dotty Martin. *Hiking Guide to the Santa Rita Mountains of Arizona.* Pruett Publishing Co., 1986; 126 pages, $9.95. A guide to this group of mountains and canyons south of Tucson; topo maps, charts, and 52 hike descriptions guide your way.

Mazel, David. *Arizona Trails, 100 Hikes in Canyon and Sierra.* Wilderness Press, 1989; 312 pages, $13.95. An excellent hiking guide to many of the designated wilderness areas of the state: the Grand Canyon, Superstitions, Chiricahuas, Mazatzals, and others. The maps are so good you won't need to buy any others.

Morris, Larry A. *Hiking the Grand Canyon and Havasupai.* AZTEX Press, Tucson, 1981; 144 pages, $10.95. Background on the Grand Canyon and Havasupai Indians, hiking tips, and trail descriptions.

Nelson, Dick, and Sharon Nelson. *50 Hikes in Arizona.* Tecolote Press, 1981. A sampling of easy to difficult hikes with trail descriptions and maps.

Sheridan, Michael F. *Superstitions Wilderness Guidebook: An Introduction to the Geology and Trails including a Roadlog of the Apache Trail and Trails from First Water and Dons Camp.* Lebeau Printing Co., 1972; 52 pages.

Thybony, Scott. *A Guide to Hiking the Inner Canyon.* Grand Canyon Natural History Assoc., 1984; 43 pages, $2.50. Introduction and guide to the best-known trails of the Grand Canyon.

Waterman, Laura, and Guy Waterman. *Backwoods Ethics: Environmental Concerns for Hikers and Campers.* Stone Wall Press, 1979; 175 pages. Thoughtful commentaries on how the hiker can visit the wilderness with the least impact. Case histories dramatize need to protect the environment.

## RIVER RUNNING AND BOATING

Abbey, Edward. *Down the River.* E.P. Dutton, 1982; 242 pages, $7.95. Abbey expresses his joys of and concerns about the American West in thoughtful, witty, and wide-ranging essays.

Belknap, Buzz. *Grand Canyon River Guide.* Westwater Books; $6.95 ($10.95 waterproof). Covers the 288 miles of Colorado River through Marble and Grand canyons; begins at Lees Ferry and ends at Lake Mead.

Crumbo, Kim. *A River Runner's Guide to the History of the Grand Canyon.* Johnson Books, 1981; 55 pages and 26 maps, $4.95. Highly readable guide with a foreword by Edward Abbey.

Jones, Stan. *Boating and Exploring Map: Lake Powell and Its 96 Canyons.* Sun Country Publications, 1985; $3.50. Information-packed map showing natural features, marinas, Indian sites, hiking trails, and 4WD tracks. Map text describes points of interest, navigation, history, fishing, and wildlife.

Kelsey, Michael R. *Boater's Guide to Lake Powell.* Kelsey Publishing, 456 E. 100 North, Provo, UT 84606; 1989; 288 pages, $10.95. This comprehensive guide will help you explore the lake, whether traveling in a small inflatable raft, as the author did, or in a more luxurious craft. Includes many maps, photos, and hiking descriptions.

Simmons, George C., and David L. Gaskill. *River Runner's Guide to the Canyons of the Green and Colorado Rivers—With Emphasis on Geologic Features, Vol. III.* Northland Press, 1969; 132 pages, $5. This volume covers Marble Canyon and Grand Canyon.

Stephens, Hal G., and Eugene M. Shoemaker. *In the Footsteps of John Wesley Powell: An Album of Comparative Photographs of the Green and Colorado Rivers, 1871-72 and 1968.* Johnson Books and The Powell Society, 1987; 286 pages, $34.95. Fascinating photo album of identical river views taken nearly 100 years apart. Photos show how little—and how much—the forces of erosion, plants, and man have changed the Green and Colorado river canyons. The text describes geologic features for each of the 110 pairs of photos. Maps show locations of camera stations.

Stevens, Larry. *The Colorado River in Grand Canyon, A Guide.* Red Lake Books, 1984; 107 pages (waterproof), $11.25. Maps and concise guide to geology, Indian history, exploration, flora, and fauna.

Tejada-Flores, Lito. *Wildwater: the Sierra Club Guide to Kayaking and Whitewater Boating.* Sierra Club Books, 1978; 329 pages, $8.95. Comprehensive introduction to river running: choosing boats and equipment, river techniques, safety, practical advice on trip planning, overview of river possibilities in the U.S., and history of whitewater boating.

# HISTORY

Cline, Platt. *They Came to the Mountain: The Story of Flagstaff's Beginnings.* Northern Arizona University with Northland Press, 1976; 364 pages, $24.95. Highly readable account of Flagstaff's founding and early years.

Coolidge, Dane. *Arizona Cowboys.* University of Arizona Press, 1984; 160 pages, $7.95. Tales of working the range in the early 1900s.

Crampton, C. Gregory. *Land of Living Rock.* Alfred A. Knopf, Inc., 1972; 267 pages, $19.95. Story of the geology, early explorers, Indians, and settlers of the high plateaus in Arizona, Utah, and Nevada. Well illustrated with color and b/w photos, maps, and diagrams.

Crampton, C. Gregory. *Standing Up Country.* Alfred A. Knopf, Inc., 1964; 191 pages, $12.75. Illustrated historical account of the people who came to the canyon lands of Arizona and Utah—the Indians, explorers, outlaws, miners, settlers, and scientists.

Dellenbaugh, Frederick S. *A Canyon Voyage: A Narrative of the Second Powell Expedition Down the Green-Colorado River from Wyoming, and the Expeditions on Land, in the Years 1871 and 1872.* University of Arizona Press, reprinted 1984; 277 pages, $9.95. Dellenbaugh was an artist and assistant topographer of the expedition.

Faulk, Odie B. *Arizona: A Short History.* University of Oklahoma Press, 1979; 266 pages, $9.95. Popular account of Arizona from the first days of European exploration through the territorial years and statehood.

Forrest, Earle R. *Arizona's Dark and Bloody Ground.* University of Arizona, 1936, 1984; 385 pages, $12.95. An account of the ruthless Pleasant Valley War between cattlemen and sheepmen.

Hinton, Richard J. *The Handbook to Arizona, Its Resources, History, Towns, Mines, Ruins, and Scenery.* First published by Payot, Upham and Co. in 1878; reprinted by Arizona Silhouettes in 1954; 431 pages. This is what you might have been carrying 100 years ago! The volume gives a good insight into Arizona's early years.

Hilzinger, George. *Treasure Land, 1897, A Handbook to Tucson and Southern Arizona.* 160 pages. Another grand old book to look for in a library.

"The Heart of Ambos Nogales." *The Journal of Arizona History.* Vol. 17, #2. summer 1976: page 161. The story of Nogales.

Hughes, J. Donald. *In the House of Stone and Light.* Grand Canyon Natural History Assoc., 1978; 137 pages, $7.50. A well illustrated history of the Grand Canyon from the early Indians to the modern Park.

Johnson, G. Wesley, Jr. *Phoenix: Valley of the Sun.* Continental Heritage Press, 1982; 240 pages. Excellent text and photos trace the development of Phoenix from the ancient Hohokam to the modern metropolis.

Lummis, Charles F. *Some Strange Corners of Our Country.* University of Arizona Press, 1891, 1892 (reprinted in 1989); 270 pages, $12.95. Step back a century to visit the Southwest's Indian country, Grand Canyon, Petrified Forest, Montezuma Castle, and other sights.

Mitchell, John D. *Lost Mines of the Great Southwest.* Rio Grande Press, 1933, 1984; 174 pages, $10. Who isn't enthralled by legends of lost treasure? You'll be reaching for a pick and shovel after reading these!

Parker, Lowell. *Arizona Towns and Tales.* Phoenix Newspapers, Inc., Phoenix, AZ; 1975; 292 pages. Entertaining tales of personalities and places in the yesteryears.

Pattie, James Ohio. *The Personal Narrative of James O. Pattie.* University of Nebraska Press, 1984 (reprint of 1831 edition); 269 pages, $6.95. An early fur trapper tells of his experiences in the wild lands of the West during the 1820s. He claimed to be the first white American to see the Grand Canyon.

Powell, J.W. *The Exploration of the Colorado River and Its Canyons.* Dover Publications, reprinted 1961 (first pub. in 1895); 400 pages with great illustrations, $6.95. Powell's 1869 expedition—the first running of the Colorado River through the Grand Canyon; also a description of the 1870 Uinta Expedition.

Rusho, W.L., and C. Gregory Crampton. *Desert River Crossing: Historic Lee's Ferry on the Colorado River.* Peregrine Smith Books, 1981; 126 pages, $5.95.

Sikorsky, Robert. *Fools Gold: The Facts, Myths and Legends of the Lost Dutchman Mine and the Superstition Mountains.* Golden West, 1983; 143 pages, $5. History of the most famous lost mine of all.

Summerhayes, Martha. *Vanished Arizona.* University of Nebraska Press, 1979 (reprint of 1911 Salem Press second edition); 307 pages, $7.95. A young New England woman marries an Army officer in 1874, then sets out for some of the wildest corners of the West. Her accounts bring frontier Arizona life into sharp focus.

Trimble, Marshall. *Arizona Adventure: Action-Packed True Tales of Early Arizona.* Golden West, 1982; 160 pages, $5. Nineteen stories from Arizona's Old West.

Trimble, Marshall. *Roadside History of Arizona.* Mountain Press Publishing Co., 1986; 480 pages, $15.95. Fascinating tales to read as you travel; has many historic photos. Organized by region and highway for easy use.

Wagoner, Jay J. *Arizona Territory, 1863-1912: A Political History.* University of Arizona Press, 1970; 587 pages, $12.95. Excellent history of the territorial years.

Woody, Clara T., and Milton L. Schwartz. *Globe, Arizona.* The Arizona Historical Society, 1977; 262 pages. Stories of the early miners, pioneers, Indian battles, and the Graham-Tewksbury feud (Pleasant Valley War).

## ARCHAEOLOGY

Ambler, J. Richard. *The Anasazi: Prehistoric Peoples of the Four Corners Region.* Museum of Northern Arizona, 1977; 50 pages, $5.95. One of the best overviews.

Grant, Campbell. *Canyon de Chelly: Its People and Rock Art.* University of Arizona Press, 1978; 290 pages, $15.95. The geology, archaeology, and history of the canyons with many illustrations. Nearly half the text is devoted to the wealth of petroglyphs and pictographs left by the Anasazi, Hopi, and Navajo.

Gregonis, Linda, and Karl Reinhard. *Hohokam Indians of the Tucson Basin.* University of Arizona Press, 1979; 48 pages, $4.95. Introduction to the prehistoric Hohokam Indian archaeology and their life.

Lister, Robert, and Florence Lister. *Those Who Came Before: Southwestern Archaeology in the National Park System.* University of Arizona Press, 1983; 184 pages, $12.95. A well-illustrated guide to the history, artifacts, and ruins of prehistoric Indians in the Southwest. Describes parks and monuments containing their sites.

McGregor, John C. *Southwestern Archaeology.* University of Illinois Press, 1982; 511 pages, $16.95. Are you curious why archeologists like their work and how it's done? This book presents motivations and techniques of the scientists. It describes cultures and artifacts from the earliest known peoples to the present in a readable and useful form.

Noble, David Grant. *Ancient Ruins of the Southwest.* Northland Press, 1981; 156 pages, $10.95. Well-illustrated guide to prehistoric ruins of Arizona, New Mexico, Colorado, and Utah, with practical information on getting to sites, nearby campgrounds, and services.

Oppelt, Norman T. *Guide to Prehistoric Ruins of the Southwest.* Pruett Publishing Co., 1981; 208 pages, $8.95. Introduction to ancient cultures with descriptions of more than 200 sites in Arizona, New Mexico, Colorado, and Utah.

Viele, Catherine. *Voices in the Canyon.* Southwest Parks and Monuments Assoc., 1980; 76 pages, $5.95. Highly readable and well-illustrated book about the ancient Anasazi and their villages of Betatakin, Keet Seel, and Inscription House (now all in Navajo National Monument).

## ARIZONA INDIANS OF TODAY

Courlander, Harold. *Hopi Voices, Recollections, Traditions, and Narratives of the Hopi Indians.* University of New Mexico, 1982; 255 pages, $17.50. A selection of 74 Hopi narrations explaining their mythology, history, exploits, games, and animal stories. One of the best books on Hopi culture.

Dedera, Don. *Navajo Rugs: How to Find, Evaluate, Buy and Care for Them.* Northland Press; 114 pages, $8.95. Dedera gives the history of Navajo weaving, illustrates how it's done, shows regional styles, and gives practical advice on purchasing.

Dittert Jr., Alfred, and Fred Plog. *Generations in Clay: Pueblo Pottery of the American Southwest.* Northland Press, 1980; 149 pages, $17.95. An introduction to pottery of the pueblo Indians, both prehistoric and modern. Well-illustrated with b/w and color photos.

Dozier, Edward P. *Hano, A Tewa Indian Community in Arizona.* Holt, Rinehart and Wilson, 1966; 104 pages. A study of the Tewa's history, society, religion, and livelihood.

Dyk, Walter (recorded by). *Son of Old Man Hat, A Navajo Autobiography.* University of Nebraska Press, 1967 (original copyright 1938); 378 pages, $7.95. A Navajo relates the story of growing up in the late 1800s. He was born during his family's return from 4 years of internment at Fort Sumner.

Evers, Larry, ed. *The South Corner of Time.* University of Arizona Press, 1980; 240 pages, $17.50. Stories and poetry by contemporary Indians of the Hopi, Navajo, Tohono O'odham (Papago), and Yaqui tribes.

Fontana, Bernard. *Of Earth and Little Rain, The Papago Indians.* Northland Press, 1981; 140 pages, $27.50. Essays and photos on Tohono O'odham (Papago) life and their land.

Forrest, Earle. *The Snake Dance of the Hopi Indians.* Westernlore Press, 1961; 172 pages. Detailed look at Hopi mythology and ceremonies; illustrated with many old photos.

Gillmore, Frances, and Louisa Wetherill. *Traders to the Navajos.* University of New Mexico Press, 1934, 1983; 265 pages, $10.95. The Wetherills lived in and explored the Monument Valley region and traded with the Navajo. These are some of their stories about lost mines, early travelers, and the Navajo people.

Gilpin, Laura. *The Enduring Navajo.* University of Texas Press, 1968; 264 pages, $29.95. Excellent photo book about the Navajo, their homes, land, ceremonies, crafts, tribal government, and the trading posts.

James, Harry C. *Pages from Hopi History.* University of Arizona Press, 1974; 258 pages, $10.95. Beginning with the Hopi's mythological entrance into this world, their history is traced through early migrations, encounters with the Spanish, difficulties with Mexicans and Navajo, resistance to U.S. authority, and living today.

Kammer, Jack. *The Second Long Walk: The Navajo-Hopi Land Dispute.* University of New Mexico Press, 1980; 265 pages, $12.95. Background on both sides of the long-running land dispute between the Navajo and Hopi.

Locke, Raymond F. *The Book of the Navajo.* Mankind Publishing, 1976, 1989; 496 pages, $5.95. Navajo legends, art, culture, and history from early to modern times.

Luckert, Karl W. *Coyoteway: A Navajo Holyway Healing Ceremonial.* The University of Arizona Press and Museum of Northern Arizona Press, 1979; 243 pages, $13.95. A rare look at an important Navajo ceremony. The event requires 9 days and involves chanting, fire making, sand painting, and other rituals. Photos and translations of chants reveal some of the intricate Navajo beliefs.

Mooney, Ralph. "The Navajos." *National Geographic Magazine.* (Dec. 1972): page 740. The Navajo people and how they have balanced their traditions in 20th C. America.

Mullet, G.M. *Spider Women Stories.* University of Arizona, 1979; 142 pages, $9.50. Selected stories from Hopi mythology.

Page, Jake. "Inside the Sacred Hopi Homeland." *National Geographic Magazine.* (Nov. 1982): page 607. A rare look at the spiritual life of the Hopi.

Page, Susanne, and Jake Page. *Hopi.* Harry N. Abrams, Inc., 1982; 240 pages, $35. An unprecedented project recording the Hopi and their spiritual life. Everyday life, ceremonies, and sacred places rarely seen by outsiders are described and illustrated with large color photos.

Powell, Major J.W. *The Hopi Villages: The Ancient Province of Tusayan.* Filter Press, Palmer Lake, Colorado, 1972 (first pub. about 1891); 36 pages, $2.

Simmons, Leo, ed. *Sun Chief: The Autobiography of a Hopi Indian.* Yale University Press, 1942; 460 pages, $12.95. A Hopi tells of his experiences growing up in both the Hopi and white man's worlds, then returning to traditional ways.

Suntracks, Larry Evers. *Hopi Photographers/Hopi Images.* University of Arizona Press, 1983; 111 pages, $19.95. Photography of the Hopi, 1880-1980, with historic photos by Anglos and modern work by Hopi photographers; b/w and color.

Titiev, Mischa. *Old Oraibi: A Study of the Hopi Indians of Third Mesa.* Peabody Museum, vol. XXII—No. 1, 1944 (reprinted by Kraus Reprint Corp. 1968); 277 pages. Detailed account of Hopi society and ceremonies.

Webb, George. *A Pima Remembers.* University of Arizona Press, 1959 (reprinted 1982); 126 pages, $7.50. Traditional stories of the Pima Indians.

Wright, Barton. *Hopi Kachinas: The Complete Guide to Collecting Kachina Dolls.* Northland Press, 1977; 139 pages, $12.95. From clowns to ogres, a great many dolls are illustrated and their functions explained.

Wright, Margaret. *Hopi Silver.* Northland Press, 1989; 121 pages, $12.95. History and examples of Hopi silversmithing.

Yava, Albert. *Big Falling Snow.* University of New Mexico Press, 1978; 178 pages, $9.95. A Tewa-Hopi reports the history and traditions of the Tewa and Hopi, including the conflicts with missionaries and government officials who tried to Americanize the tribes.

Zolbrod, Paul G. *Diné bahanè: The Navajo Creation Story.* University of New Mexico Press, 1984; 431 pages, $22.50. Deities, people, and animals come to life in this translation of Navajo mythology.

## NATURAL SCIENCES

Arnberger, Leslie P., and Jeanne R. Janish. *Flowers of the Southwest Mountains.* Southwest Parks and Monuments Assoc., 1982; 139 pages, $9.95. You'll find descriptions and illustrations of flowers and common trees found at 7,000 feet and above.

Barnes, F.A. *Canyon Country Geology for the Layman and Rockhound.* Wasatch Publishers, Inc., 1978; 157 pages, $5. Geologic history and guide to rockhounding; emphasis is on southeast Utah and adjacent Arizona.

Chronic, Halka. *Roadside Geology of Arizona.* Mountain Press Publishing Co., 1983; 321 pages, $12.95. Well illustrated with photos, maps, and diagrams. Organized along major highway routes; also covers the national parks and some national monuments.

Dodge, Natt N. *100 Desert Wildflowers in Natural Color.* Southwest Parks and Monument Assoc., 1963; $4.95. Introduction and brief descriptions with a color photo for each flower.

Dodge, Natt N. *100 Roadside Wildflowers of Southwest Uplands in Natural Color.* Southwest Parks and Monuments Assoc., 1980; 64 pages, $4.95. Introduction, brief description, and color photos for 100 flowers found above 4,500 feet.

Dodge, Natt N. *Poisonous Dwellers of the Desert.* Southwest Parks and Monuments Assoc., 1981; 40 pages, $3.95. Creatures to watch out for—poisonous insects, snakes, and the Gila monster. Advice is given on insecticides and bite treatment. Some non-venomous animals often mistakenly thought poisonous are listed too.

Dodge, Natt N., and Jeanne R. Janish. *Flowers of the Southwest Deserts.* Southwest Parks and Monuments Assoc., 1985; 136 pages, $9.95. Desert plant and flower guide for elevations under 4,500 feet.

Doolittle, Jerome. *Canyons and Mesas.* Time-Life Books (American Wilderness Series), 1974; 184 pages, $12.95. Text and photos give a feel for the ruggedly beautiful country of northern Arizona and adjacent Utah and Colorado.

Earle, W. Hubert. *Cacti of the Southwest.* Phoenix: Desert Botanical Garden, 1980; 208 pages, $12.95. The 152 known species of cacti in the Southwest are listed with b/w and color photos, classification, and cultivation.

Elmore, Francis H., and Jeanne R. Janish. *Shrubs and Trees of the Southwest Uplands.* Southwest Parks and Monuments Assoc., 1976; 214 pages, $9.95. Color-coded pages help locate plants and trees above 4,500 feet (from the pinyon-juniper belt to tree line).

Halfpenny, James, and Elizabeth Biesiot. *A Field Guide: Mammal Tracking in Western America.* Johnson Books, 1986; 163 pages, $11.95. No need to guess what animal passed by. This well-illustrated guide shows how to read trails of large and small wildlife. More determined detectives can study the scatology chapter.

McKee, Edwin D. *Ancient Landscapes of the Grand Canyon Region.* Northland Press, 1982; 52 pages, $3. Brief account of how the Grand Canyon area came to be.

Manning, Reg. *What Kinda Cactus Izzat?* Reganson Cartoon Books, 1969; 108 pages, $3.95. A fun-to-read book on "who's who in the desert"—the cacti and other desert plants in the Southwest.

Nelson, Dick, and Sharon Nelson. *Easy Field Guide Series of Arizona: Snakes, Insects, Birds, Mammals, Cactus, or Trees.* Primer Publishers (various dates); about 32 pages, $1 each. Easy-to-carry mini-guides.

Olin, George. *House in the Sun.* Southwest Parks and Monuments Assoc., 1977; 236 pages, $4.95. A guide to the Sonoran Desert, why it exists, and how life has adapted to it. Also tells how *you* can adapt to the sometimes harsh conditions and enjoy the desert in safety; many color photos.

Olin, George, and Dale Thompson. *Mammals of the Southwest Deserts.* Southwest Parks and Monuments Assoc., 1982; 97 pages, $6.95. Well illustrated with b/w and color drawings.

Powell, Lawrence Clark, and Michael Collier. *Where Water Flows: The Rivers of Arizona.* Northland Press, 1980; 64 pages, $25. Es-

says and beautiful color photos about seven of Arizona's rivers.

Smith, Robert L. *Venomous Animals of Arizona.* University of Arizona, 1982; 134 pages, $12.95. Ever wonder about a scorpion's love life? Good descriptions of poisonous insects and animals; with medical notes.

Stokes, William L. *Scenes of the Plateau Lands and How They Came to Be.* Starstone Publishing Co., 1969; 66 pages, $7.95. How mesas, canyons, volcanos, and other geologic features were formed.

Sweet, Muriel. *Common Edible and Useful Plants of the West.* Naturegraph Publishers, 1976; 64 pages, $3.95. Nontechnical descriptions of plants and trees that have food, medicinal, and other uses. Most of these were first discovered by Indians and used by pioneer settlers.

Whitney, Steve. *A Field Guide to the Grand Canyon.* William Morrow, 1982; 320 pages, $14.95. Excellent, well-illustrated guide to the Canyon's geology, early Indians, flowers, trees, birds, and animals. Most of the information also applies to other canyons on the Colorado Plateau. Practical advice for visiting and hiking in the Grand Canyon is included.

## ONWARD TRAVEL

Barnes, F.A. *Utah Canyon Country.* Utah Geographic Series, Inc., no. 1, 1986; 120 pages, $15.95. Stunning color photos illustrate this book about the land, people, and natural history of southern Utah. The text also describes parks, monuments, and practicalities of travel in this fascinating region.

Cahill, Rick. *Border Towns of the Southwest: Shopping, Dining, Fun & Adventure from Tijuana to Juarez.* Pruett Publishing Co., 1987; 200 pages, $9.95. An introduction tells of the pleasures and practicalities. Detailed border town descriptions have many maps and photos. Includes a short Spanish vocabulary.

Castleman, Deke. *Nevada Handbook.* Moon Publications, 1989; 301 pages, $10.95. Only someone with Deke's sense of humor could capture the soul of Nevada's glittering cities and mix it in with healthy doses of wilderness, history, and small backcountry towns! This book will give you hundreds of insider's tips.

Franz, Carl. *The People's Guide to Mexico.* John Muir Publications, 1989; 608 pages, $14.95. This hefty guide is about experiencing Mexico. It's crammed with useful advice on driving, public transport, accommodation, cantinas, markets, and staying healthy.

Harris, Richard. *22 Days in the American Southwest.* John Muir Publications, 1988; 130 pages, $7.95. Itineraries and suggested schedules can help you cover the highlights in a short time. Not for leisurely or serendipitous touring!

Metzger, Stephen. *New Mexico Handbook.* Moon Publications, 1989; 350 pages, $11.95. Experience the landscapes, ancient pueblos, Spanish sites, wilderness areas, art, and cities with this informative guidebook.

Noble, John, Daniel Spitzer, and Scott Wayne. *Mexico, A Travel Survival Kit.* Lonely Planet Publications, 1989; approx. 800 pages, $17.95. The guide offers an introduction, the sights and cities, where to stay, and how to get around.

Weir, Bill. *Utah Handbook.* Moon Publications, 1988; 450 pages, $11.95. Explore the magical canyon country north of Arizona with this handy and comprehensive guide! Also learn about Utah's unique history, city sights, mountains, and deserts.

## REFERENCE

Comeaux, Malcolm L. *Arizona: A Geography.* Westview Press, 1981. Geographies of the United States series. A 336-page volume full of info on Arizona's physical geography, settlement, population, resources, and agriculture.

*Arizona Statistical Review.* Valley National Bank, Box 71, Phoenix, AZ 85001; revised annually; 80 pages, free at any bank office. Maps and tables summarize population, finances, education, climate, and mining in Arizona.

Walker, Henry P., and Don Bufkin. *Historical Atlas of Arizona.* University of Oklahoma Press, 1986; 130 pages, $13.95. Clear maps and concise text illustrate the geography, Indian tribes, exploration, and development of Arizona.

## MISCELLANEOUS

Fischer, Al, and Mildred Fischer. *Arizona Cook Book.* Golden West, 1974; 142 pages, $3.50. A culinary guide to the state—Indian, Western, barbecue, and backpacking. Prepare your own cactus jelly and other delicacies.

Kavena, Juanita Tiger. *Hopi Cookery.* University of Arizona Press, 1980; 115 pages, $9.95. Learn how to make *piki* bread, bake a prairie dog, fix a squash and fresh corn casserole, make a yucca pie, and more!

# INDEX

Bold-faced page numbers offer the primary reference.
*Italicized* page numbers indicate an illustration or caption.
See the front matter for lists of MAPS and CHARTS.

# ABOUT THE AUTHOR

Back in school, Bill Weir always figured that he'd settle down to a career job and live happily ever after. Then he "discovered" traveling. After graduating with a B.A. degree in physics from Berea College in 1972, Bill wound up as an electronic technician in Columbus, Ohio. But the very short vacation times just weren't enough for the trips he dreamed of. So in 1976 he took off with his trusty bicycle "Bessie" and rode across the United States from Virginia to Oregon with Bikecentennial '76. The following year he did an even longer bicycle trip—from Alaska to Baja California. Then the ultimate journey—a bicycle cruise around the world! That lasted from 1980 to 1984, with most of the time spent in the South Pacific and Asia. Naturally Bill used Moon's excellent *South Pacific Handbook* and *Indonesia Handbook*. Correspondence with the authors led to some text and photo contributions for their books and the idea of doing a guidebook of his own.

From New Delhi in India, Bill returned to his home base of Flagstaff, Arizona, and set to work researching and writing the *Arizona Traveler's Handbook*. The immense project took 1½ years of writing and nearly another year of production.

As soon as the writing of the Arizona book came to an end, Bill headed north across the Grand Canyon to the Beehive State. The *Utah Handbook* turned out to be a big challenge, too, though the rewards of travel there matched his efforts. With Utah "out the door" to the printer, Bill did a 40-day trek in the Mount Everest area of Nepal, before hurrying back to rewrite this major new edition of Arizona. How he's off to do a new edition of Utah, then he's....

Still free and single, Bill's major interests continue to be writing, 35-mm and video photography, and travel. The diverse worlds of the American West and Asia remain his favorites.

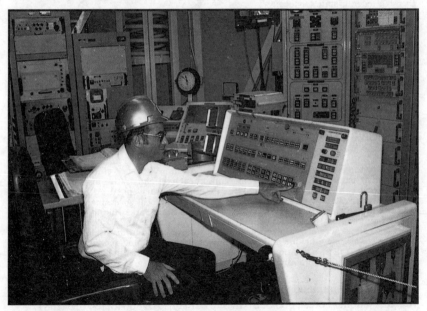

*Bill loves to push buttons! Here he's at the controls, deep underground, of a Titan II missile. All circuits seem to check OK. Titan II Missile Museum, south of Tucson near Green Valley.*

# ARIZONA TRAIL

The Arizona Trail will be a continuous and unpaved trail (over 700 miles long) that traverses the state from the Arizona-Mexican border to the Arizona-Utah border. The primary users will be hikers and equestrians. "Mountain" bicyclists are anticipated users where permissible, although bicycles are prohibited in wilderness areas and parts of Grand Canyon National Park. The Arizona Trail will not seek to change that management policy. When and where possible, parts of the Arizona Trail will be used by cross-country skiers.

In order to provide a functional, cross-state trail within a desirable amount of time, low-volume "back roads" will be used to connect existing trail systems. The trail will not be promoted for motorized vehicle use. Unless desired by the managing agency, an effort to close roads to motorized vehicles will not be made. However, priorities and plans will be sought for re-routing the trail away from or parallel to roads. The ultimate objective is an Arizona Trail that is a non-motorized, unpaved pathway across the state.

Recreational rights-of-way through private lands will be sought. However, over ninety per cent of the identified route will pass through federal, state, or locally-administered lands. Control of each of the segments will remain with the managing agency. The Kaibab National Forest and Arizona State Parks are presently coordinating the Arizona Trail project. It is anticipated that a non-profit, Arizona Trail Association-Foundation will emerge to assist in the coordination of volunteers and other trail concerns.

Maintenance and operation of the Arizona Trail will be through a partnership between government agencies, volunteers, and the private sector. For example, Kaibab Forest Products Company has sponsored the construction of over 50 miles of new trail on the Kaibab National Forest. The Sierra Club has pledged to maintain the Kaibab Plateau segment of the Arizona Trail.

Integral to the project will be a network of volunteers. A central volunteer, or steward, will be matched with agency recreation staff on each administrative district - U.S. Forest Service, National Park Service, Bureau of Land Management, Arizona State Parks, Arizona State Land Department,          and local governments. Recruitment and training of stewards will be assisted by Arizona State Parks Hiking And Equestrian Trails Committee (AHETC) sub-committee on long distance trails. These stewards will then develop a cadre of volunteers who will help establish and maintain each section of trail. This work may include additional route definition, signing according to agency and Arizona Trail specifications, litter collection, treadway maintenance, interpretive site development, and information distribution.

For the latest information to help or hike, contact the Arizona Trail Coordinator, Kaibab National Forest, 800 S. Sixth St., Williams AZ 86046; tel. 635-2681.

map courtesy of Dawson Henderson

## Moon Handbooks—The Ideal Traveling Companions

**Open a Moon Handbook and you're opening your eyes and heart to the world. Thoughtful, sensitive, and provocative, Moon Handbooks encourage an intimate understanding of a region, from its culture and history to essential practicalities. Fun to read and packed with valuable information on accommodations, dining, recreation, plus indispensable travel tips, detailed maps, charts, illustrations, photos, glossaries, and indexes, Moon Handbooks are ideal traveling companions: informative, entertaining, and highly practical.**

**TO ORDER BY PHONE: (800) 345-5473 • Monday-Friday • 9 a.m.-5 p.m. PST**

# The Pacific/Asia Series

**BALI HANDBOOK** by Bill Dalton
Detailed travel information on the most famous island in the world. 12 color pages, 29 b/w photos, 68 illustrations, 42 maps, 7 charts, glossary, booklist, index. 428 pages.  **$12.95**

**INDONESIA HANDBOOK** by Bill Dalton
This one-volume encyclopedia explores island by island the many facets of this sprawling, kaleidoscopic island nation. 30 b/w photos, 143 illustrations, 250 maps, 17 charts, booklist, extensive Indonesian vocabulary, index. 1,050 pages.  **$17.95**

**SOUTH KOREA HANDBOOK** by Robert Nilsen
Whether you're visiting on business or searching for adventure, *South Korea Handbook* is an invaluable companion. 8 color pages, 78 b/w photos, 93 illustrations, 109 maps, 10 charts, Korean glossary with useful notes on speaking and reading the language, booklist, index. 548 pages.  **$14.95**

**SOUTHEAST ASIA HANDBOOK** by Carl Parkes
Helps the enlightened traveler discover the real Southeast Asia. 16 color pages, 75 b/w photos, 11 illustrations, 169 maps, 140 charts, vocabularies and suggested reading, index. 873 pages. **$16.95**

**PHILIPPINES HANDBOOK**  by Peter Harper and Evelyn Peplow
Crammed with detailed information, Philippines Handbook equips the escapist, hedonist or business traveler with a thorough introduction to the Philippines' colorful history, landscapes and culture. Color and b/w photos, illustrations, maps, charts, booklist, index. 400 pages. **$12.95**

**HAWAII HANDBOOK**  by J.D. Bisignani
Winner of the 1989 Hawaii Visitors Bureau's Best Guide Book Award and the Grand Award for Excellence in Travel Journalism, this guide takes you beyond the glitz and high-priced hype and leads you to a genuine Hawaiian experience. 12 color pages, 86 b/w photos, 132 illustrations, 86 maps, 44 graphs and charts, Hawaiian and pidgin glossaries, appendix, booklist, index. 879 pages.  **$15.95**

**KAUAI HANDBOOK**  by J.D. Bisignani
*Kauai Handbook* is the perfect antidote to the workaday world. 8 color pages, 36 b/w photos, 48 illustrations, 19 maps, 10 tables and charts, Hawaiian and pidgin glossaries, booklist, index. 236 pages.  **$9.95**

**MAUI HANDBOOK: Including Molokai and Lanai**  by J.D. Bisignani
"No fool-'round" advice on accommodations, eateries, and recreation, plus a comprehensive introduction to island ways, geography, and history. 8 color pages, 60 b/w photos, 72 illustrations, 34 maps, 19 charts, booklist, glossary, index. 350 pages.  **$10.95**

**OAHU HANDBOOK**  by J.D. Bisignani
A handy guide to Honolulu, renowned surfing beaches, and Oahu's countless other diversions. Color and b/w photos, illustrations, 18 maps, charts, booklist, glossary, index. 354 pages. **$11.95**

**BIG ISLAND OF HAWAII HANDBOOK**  by J.D. Bisignani
An entertaining yet informative text packed with insider tips on accommodations, dining, sports and outdoor activities, natural attractions, and must-see sights. Color and b/w photos, illustrations, 20 maps, charts, booklist, glossary, index. 347 pages.  **$11.95**

**SOUTH PACIFIC HANDBOOK**  by David Stanley
The original comprehensive guide to the 16 territories in the South Pacific. 20 color pages, 195 b/w photos, 121 illustrations, 35 charts, 138 maps, booklist, glossary, index. 740 pages. **$15.95**

**MICRONESIA HANDBOOK:**
**Guide to the Caroline, Gilbert, Mariana, and Marshall Islands**  by David Stanley
*Micronesia Handbook* guides you on a real Pacific adventure all your own. 8 color pages, 77 b/w photos, 68 illustrations, 69 maps, 18 tables and charts, index. 287 pages.  **$9.95**

**FIJI ISLANDS HANDBOOK**  by David Stanley
The first and still the best source of information on travel around this 322-island archipelago. 8 color pages, 35 b/w photos, 78 illustrations, 26 maps, 3 charts, Fijian glossary, booklist, index. 198 pages.  **$8.95**

**TAHITI-POLYNESIA HANDBOOK**  by David Stanley
All five French-Polynesian archipelagoes are covered in this comprehensive guide by Oceania's best-known travel writer. 12 color pages, 45 b/w photos, 64 illustrations, 33 maps, 7 charts, booklist, glossary, index. 225 pages.  **$9.95**

**NEW ZEALAND HANDBOOK** by Jane King
Introduces you to the people, places, history, and culture of this extraordinary land. 8 color pages, 99 b/w photos, 146 illustrations, 82 maps, booklist, index. 546 pages. **$14.95**

**BLUEPRINT FOR PARADISE: How to Live on a Tropic Island** by Ross Norgrove
This one-of-a-kind guide has everything you need to know about moving to and living comfortably on a tropical island. 8 color pages, 40 b/w photos, 3 maps, 14 charts, appendices, index. 212 pages. **$14.95**

# The Americas Series

**NORTHERN CALIFORNIA HANDBOOK** by Kim Weir
An outstanding companion for imaginative travel in the territory north of the Tehachapis. 12 color pages, b/w photos, 69 maps, illustrations, booklist, index. 759 pages. **$16.95**

**NEVADA HANDBOOK** by Deke Castleman
*Nevada Handbook* puts the Silver State into perspective and makes it manageable and affordable. 34 b/w photos, 43 illustrations, 37 maps, 17 charts, booklist, index. Approx. 400 pages. **$12.95**

**NEW MEXICO HANDBOOK** by Stephen Metzger
A close-up and complete look at every aspect of this wondrous state. 8 color pages, 85 b/w photos, 63 illustrations, 50 maps, 10 charts, booklist, index. 350 pages. **$11.95**

**TEXAS HANDBOOK** by Joe Cummings
Seasoned travel writer Joe Cummings brings an insider's perspective to his home state. 12 color pages, b/w photos, maps, illustrations, charts, booklist, index. 483 pages. **$11.95**

**ARIZONA TRAVELER'S HANDBOOK** by Bill Weir
This meticulously researched guide contains everything necessary to make Arizona accessible and enjoyable. 8 color pages, 194 b/w photos, 74 illustrations, 53 maps, 6 charts, booklist, index. 505 pages. **$13.95**

**UTAH HANDBOOK** by Bill Weir
Weir gives you all the carefully researched facts and background to make your visit a success. 8 color pages, 102 b/w photos, 61 illustrations, 30 maps, 9 charts, booklist, index. 452 pages. **$12.95**

**ALASKA-YUKON HANDBOOK** by Deke Castleman, Don Pitcher, and David Stanley
Get the inside story, with plenty of well-seasoned advice to help you cover more miles on less money. 8 color pages, 26 b/w photos, 92 illustrations, 90 maps, 6 charts, booklist, glossary, index. 384 pages. **$11.95**

**WASHINGTON HANDBOOK** by Dianne J. Boulerice Lyons
Covers sights, shopping, services, transportation, and outdoor recreation, with complete listings for restaurants and accommodations. 8 color pages, 92 b/w photos, 24 illustrations, 81 maps, 8 charts, booklist, index. 400 pages. **$12.95**

**OREGON HANDBOOK** by Stuart Warren and Ted Long Ishikawa
Brimming with travel practicalities and insider views on Oregon's history, culture, arts, and activities. Color and b/w photos, illustrations, 28 maps, charts, booklist, index. Approx. 400 pages. **$12.95**

**WYOMING HANDBOOK** by Don Pitcher
All you need to know to open the doors to this wide and wild state. Color and b/w photos, illustrations, over 70 maps, charts, booklist, index. Approx. 500 pages. **$12.95**

**BRITISH COLUMBIA HANDBOOK** by Jane King
With an emphasis on outdoor adventures, this guide covers mainland British Columbia, Vancouver Island, the Queen Charlotte Islands, and the Canadian Rockies. 8 color pages, 56 b/w photos, 45 illustrations, 66 maps, 4 charts, booklist, index. 381 pages. **$11.95**

**GUIDE TO CATALINA and California's Channel Islands** by Chicki Mallan
A complete guide to these remarkable islands, from the windy solitude of the Channel Islands National Marine Sanctuary to bustling Avalon. 8 color pages, 105 b/w photos, 65 illustrations, 40 maps, 32 charts, booklist, index. 262 pages. **$9.95**

**YUCATAN HANDBOOK** by Chicki Mallan
All the information you'll need to guide you into every corner of this exotic land. 8 color pages, 154 b/w photos, 55 illustrations, 57 maps, 70 charts, appendix, booklist, Mayan and Spanish glossaries, index. 391 pages. **$12.95**

**CANCUN HANDBOOK and Mexico's Caribbean Coast** by Chicki Mallan
Covers the city's luxury scene as well as more modest attractions, plus many side trips to unspoiled beaches and Mayan ruins. Color and b/w photos, illustrations, over 30 maps, Spanish glossary, booklist, index. 257 pages. **$9.95**

**BELIZE HANDBOOK** by Chicki Mallan
Complete with detailed maps, practical information, and an overview of the area's flamboyant history, culture, and geographical features, *Belize Handbook* is the only comprehensive guide of its kind to this spectacular region. Color and b/w photos, illustrations, maps, booklist, index. 212 pages. **$11.95**

# The International Series

**EGYPT HANDBOOK** by Kathy Hansen
An invaluable resource for intelligent travel in Egypt. 8 color pages, 20 b/w photos, 150 illustrations, 80 detailed maps and plans to museums and archaeological sites, Arabic glossary, booklist, index. 510 pages. **$14.95**

**PAKISTAN HANDBOOK** by Isobel Shaw
For armchair travelers and trekkers alike, the most detailed and authoritative guide to Pakistan ever published. 28 color pages, 86 maps, appendices, Urdu glossary, booklist, index. 478 pages. **$15.95**

**MOSCOW-LENINGRAD HANDBOOK** by Masha Nordbye
Provides the visitor with an extensive introduction to the history, culture and people of these two great cities, as well as practical information on where to stay, eat, and shop. Color and b/w photos, illustrations, maps, charts, booklist, index. Approx. 250 pages. **$12.95**

# IMPORTANT ORDERING INFORMATION

**TO ORDER BY PHONE:** (800) 345-5473 · **Monday-Friday** · **9 a.m.-5 p.m. PST**

**PRICES:** All prices are subject to change. We always ship the most current edition. We will let you know if there is a price increase on the book you ordered.

**SHIPPING & HANDLING OPTIONS:**
   1) Domestic UPS or USPS 1st class (allow 10 working days for delivery): $3.50 for the 1st item, 50 cents for each additional item.

**Exceptions:**
   · **Moonbelt** shipping is $1.50 for one, 50 cents for each additional belt.
   · Add $2.00 for same-day handling.
   2) UPS 2nd Day Air or Printed Airmail requires a special quote.
   3) International Surface Bookrate (8-12 weeks delivery): $3.00 for the 1st item, $1.00 for each additional item.

**FOREIGN ORDERS:** All orders which originate outside the U.S.A. must be paid for with either an International Money Order or a check in U.S. currency drawn on a major U.S. bank based in the U.S.A.

**TELEPHONE ORDERS:** We accept Visa or MasterCard payments. Minimum order is US$15.00. Call in your order: 1 (800) 345-5473. 9 a.m.-5 p.m. Pacific Standard Time.

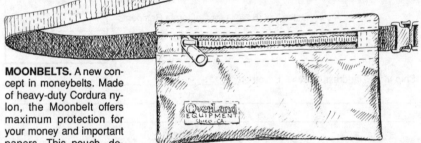

**MOONBELTS.** A new concept in moneybelts. Made of heavy-duty Cordura nylon, the Moonbelt offers maximum protection for your money and important papers. This pouch, designed for all-weather comfort, slips under your shirt or waistband, rendering it virtually undetectable and inaccessible to pickpockets. Many thoughtful features: 1-inch-wide nylon webbing, heavy-duty zipper, and a 1-inch high-test quick-release buckle. No more fumbling around for the strap or repeated adjustments, this handy plastic buckle opens and closes with a touch, but won't come undone until you want it to. Accommodates traveler's checks, passport, cash, photos. Size 5 x 9 inches. Available in black only.    **$8.95**

# ORDER FORM

**FOR FASTER SERVICE ORDER BY PHONE: (800) 345-5473 · 9 a.m.-5 p.m. PST**
**(See important ordering information on preceding page)**

Name:_____ Date:_____

Street:_____

City:_____

State or Country:_____ Zip Code:_____

Daytime Phone:_____

| Quantity | Title | Price |
|----------|-------|-------|
|          |       |       |
|          |       |       |
|          |       |       |
|          |       |       |
|          |       |       |
|          |       |       |
|          |       |       |

|  | Taxable Total | |
|--|---------------|--|
| | Sales Tax (6.25%) for California Residents | |
| | Shipping & Handling | |
| | **TOTAL** | |

Ship to: ☐ address above   ☐ other_____

_____

_____

Make checks payable to:
**Moon Publications, Inc., 722 Wall Street, Chico, California 95928, U.S.A.**
We Accept Visa and MasterCard
To Order: Call in your Visa or MasterCard number, or send a written order with your Visa or
MasterCard number and expiration date clearly written.

**Card Number:**   ☐ **Visa**   ☐ **MasterCard**

☐☐☐☐   ☐☐☐☐   ☐☐☐☐   ☐☐☐☐

expiration date:_____

**Exact Name on Card:** ☐ same as above

☐ other_____

Signature_____

# WHERE TO BUY THIS BOOK

**Bookstores and Libraries:**
Moon Publications Handbooks are sold worldwide. Please write our Sales Manager for a list of wholesalers and distributors in your area that stock our travel handbooks.

**Travelers:**
We would like to have Moon Publications handbooks available throughout the world. Please ask your bookstore to write or call us for ordering information. If your bookstore will not order our guides for you, please write or call for a free catalog.

**MOON PUBLICATIONS INC.**
**722 WALL STREET**
**CHICO, CA 95928 U.S.A.**
**tel: (800) 345-5473**
**fax: (916) 345-6751**